SWEDEN

Baltic Sea

SWEDISH POMERANIA

PRUSSIAN POMERANIA

POLISH PRUSSIA

PRUSSIA

BRANDENBURG

POLAND

Brunswick
4 July

Brandenburg
Berlin
17 July

elmstadt
(Helmstedt)

Magdeburg
12 July

Potsdam

LUSATIA

SAXONY

Grossen Havn
(Grossenhain)

Leignitz (Liegnitz)
4 Sept.

Breslau
30 Aug.

Ohlau

Dresden
21 July

Schweidnitz

Grotkau (Grottkau)

Neisse

Aussig

Landshut
(Lanshut)

SILESIA

27 July

Konigingratz
(Königgrätz)

Glaatz
8 Sept.

Jagerndorf

Troppau
29 Aug.

Prague
10 Sept.

Nimburg

Pilsen

Rokitzan

BOHEMIA

Olmütz

MORAVIA

ICONIA

Iglau
29 July

Brunn
(Brünn)

mberg
Sept.

Amberg

Retz

Danube

Cremnitz
16 Aug.

Kreutz

Schemnitz

Tirnau

Leopoldstadt

31 July

Vienna
26 Aug.

Pressburg
14 Aug.

BAVARIA

Comorn
(Komorn)

Buda
19 Aug.

Pesth
(Pest)

AUSTRIA

Danube

HUNGARY

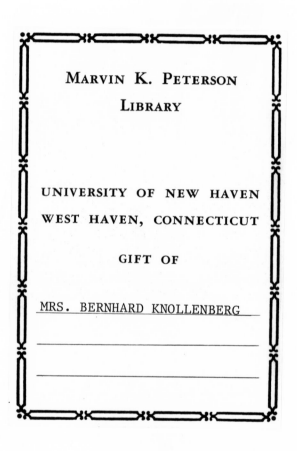

THE YALE EDITION

OF

HORACE WALPOLE'S

CORRESPONDENCE

EDITED BY W. S. LEWIS

VOLUME THIRTY-NINE

HORACE WALPOLE'S CORRESPONDENCE

WITH

HENRY SEYMOUR CONWAY
LADY AILESBURY
LORD AND LADY HERTFORD
LORD BEAUCHAMP
HENRIETTA SEYMOUR CONWAY
LORD HENRY AND
LORD HUGH SEYMOUR

III

EDITED BY W. S. LEWIS
LARS E. TROIDE
EDWINE M. MARTZ
AND
ROBERT A. SMITH

NEW HAVEN
YALE UNIVERSITY PRESS
LONDON · OXFORD UNIVERSITY PRESS

1974

TABLE OF CONTENTS

VOLUME III

LIST OF ILLUSTRATIONS

VOLUME III

ford being Lord Chamberlain) had never invited Mr Fox to their parties till he came into office, when Lord Hertford *Ratted*—Their whole family were remarkably tall [HW underlined 'little' in the caption].'

From HERTFORD, Monday 1 July 1765

Printed for the first time from a photostat of BM Add. MSS 23218, ff. 214–15.

Paris, July 1st 1765.

Dear Horry,

I AM unwilling to send a messenger[1] to England and not tell you your friends at Paris are well. We have expected for some time to hear every day that our ministers were changed,[2] but I have yet received no letter in form signed either with the name of Grafton or William Pitt, though the private correspondences acquaint me I am to expect my orders or my recall from one of those persons.[3]

Indeed my not having received a letter for some time from the office[4] would make me suspect everything was not sound and secure there, if the English gentlemen who frequent this house did not so positively assert it. I have not yet received Mr Hume's appointment,[5] though it has been so long promised; perhaps by this time Sir C. Bunbury, who I am told did all he could to conceal his own promotion in order to have both doors open, is by this time trying the new

1. Presumably James Bullock (*ante* 13 Feb. 1764, n. 1), by whom Hertford sent his dispatch to Halifax of 1 July (S.P. 78/267, ff. 13–15).

2. On 12 June the Duke of Bedford had gone to the King and complained of the latter's uncivil treatment of his ministers and his countenancing of their enemies; the Duke 'prescribed' a month for the King to decide whether to change his ministers or start acting favourably towards them (HW to Mann, 26 June 1765, MANN vi. 307 and n. 3; *Bedford Corr.* iii. 286–8; Geo. III's *Corr.*, ed. Fortescue, i. 116–19; *Grenville Papers* iii. 194; D. of Newcastle's *Narrative of the Changes in the Ministry 1765–1767*, ed. Mary Bateson, 1898, p. 21). Upon this, the King resolved once again to rid himself of them, and a meeting at Claremont, the Duke of Newcastle's seat, 30 June the Opposition leaders voted 12–6 to accept office (Lord Albemarle, *Memoirs of Rockingham*, 1852, i. 218–20). The chief ministers of the new administration (Rockingham, Grafton, Conway) kissed hands 10 July (*Grenville Papers* iii. 217; *Bedford Corr.* iii.

310; Grafton, *Autobiography*, ed. Anson, 1898, p. 54; P. Langford, *The First Rockingham Administration 1765–1766*, Oxford, 1973, pp. 4–16).

3. Grafton was secretary of state for the northern department in the new ministry, while Pitt refused office, ostensibly because Lord Temple would not come in with him (MANN vi. 309–10 and n. 3). Mr John Brooke suggests (Namier and Brooke iii. 297) that the real reason for Pitt's refusing office was that he was unwilling to form an administration with the Duke of Cumberland's followers.

4. Halifax's last dispatch to Hertford is dated 11 June, his next, 2 July (S.P. 78/266, f. 204; 267, f. 1).

5. He received word of it shortly after this letter was written. 'It is with great pleasure I acquaint your Excellency that his Majesty has been graciously pleased to comply with your request in appointing Mr Hume secretary to your Embassy, and that the usual instruments are preparing at my office' (Halifax to Hertford 2 July, S.P. 78/267, f. 9). See *ante* 20 June 1765 and n. 13.

ministers, to be reinstated in what he gave up. But it is now too late; the appointment is made public here, and I shall expect it to be done by those who think me worth employing here for some time longer. Knowing the first part of what I have said to be a fact in the opinion of those who saw him in London, I suspect he may try the Duke of Grafton, who is a Suffolk friend of his.[6] I expect to hear my brother will have that justice and honour done him which he so well deserves[7] and that will give me real satisfaction.

The Bénédictins at St Germain's, which is one of the largest and most considerable establishments of that order in France, have lately petitioned the assembly of the clergy now sitting at Paris[8] to throw off the habit and embrace the secular one, to be no longer under the obligation of attending the choir, nor under the restraint of eating fish oftener than is incumbent upon all Roman Catholics, for which reasonable indulgences they plead the disrepute into which the monastic orders are fallen.[9] The other Bénédictin convents it is said proposed likewise petitioning, but were prevented by timely notice being given and proper means used to prevent it.[10] The Cordeliers are said also to be in a flame and with reluctance continue to wear a habit which now carries with it so little respect.[11]

Adieu, my dear Horry,

Yours ever most sincerely,

HERTFORD

6. Bunbury was M.P. for Suffolk, where Grafton had great influence.

7. He kissed hands as secretary of state for the southern department 10 July (*Grenville Papers* iii. 217; *Bedford Corr.* iii. 310; Langford, op. cit. 25–6).

8. The *Gazette de Leyde* 19 July, *sub* 'Paris, le 12 juillet,' mentions 'l'assemblée générale du clergé' meeting twice a day at Paris.

9. '*1 juillet*. Il se répand une *Requête des Bénédictins au Roi*, imprimée, et qui a été présentée à S. M. par M. le duc d'Orléans. C'est une feuille de 4 pages, signée par un grand nombre de religieux de St Germain des Prez et autres. . . . Ils se plaignent sommairement d'être astreints à des pratiques minutieuses, à des formules puériles, à une règle gênante et qui n'est d'aucune utilité à l'État. Ils demandent à n'être plus tondus, à faire gras, à porter l'habit court, à ne plus aller à matines, à minuit, etc.; en un mot, à être comme séculiers' (Louis Petit de Bachaumont, *Mémoires secrets*, 1780–9, ii. 206). '*13 juillet* . . . On n'a vu dans cet ouvrage qu'un désir effréné de secouer le joug, et sans un examen bien réfléchi. M. de St Florentin en a témoigné le mécontentement du Roi aux Supérieurs dans une lettre. . . . Dom Pernetti, Dom Lemaire, qui avaient la plus grande part à cet ouvrage très bien fait, sont exilés' (ibid. ii. 210). See also Grimm, *Correspondance*, ed. Tourneux, 1877–82, vi. 345–7.

10. However, the Benedictines of the convent of the Blancs Manteaux at Paris printed a reclamation against the *Requête* of the Benedictines at Saint Germain, vindicating 'leur froc, leur tunique, toutes les cérémonies . . . dont on voulait les défaire' (Bachaumont, op. cit. ii. 212–13, *sub* 22 July; Grimm, op. cit. vi. 346).

11. Hertford wrote essentially the same paragraph in his dispatch to Halifax of 1 July (S.P. 78/267, ff. 13–14).

To Conway, Wednesday 3 July 1765

Printed from *Works* v. 115–16.

Wednesday noon, July 3, 1765.

THE footing part of my dance with my shocking partner the gout is almost over.[1] I had little pain there this last night, and got, at twice, about three hours sleep; but whenever I waked found my head very bad, which Mr Graham[2] thinks gouty too. The fever is still very high: but the same sage is of opinion, with my Lady Londonderry,[3] that if it was a fever from death, I should die; but as it is only a fever from the gout, I shall live. I think so too, and hope that, like the Duke and Duchess of Marlborough, they are so inseparable, that when one goes, t'other will.

Tell Lady A., I fear it will be long before I shall be able to compass all your terraces again.

The weather is very hot, and I have the comfort of a window open all day. I have got a bushel of roses too, and a new scarlet nightingale, which does *not* sing 'Nancy Dawson'[4] from morning to night. Perhaps you think all these poor pleasures; but you are ignorant what a provocative the gout is, and what charms it can bestow on a moment's amusement! Oh! it beats all the refinements of a Roman sensualist. It has made even my watch a darling plaything; I strike it as often as a child does. Then the disorder of my sleep diverts me when I am awake. I dreamt that I went to see Madame de Bentheim[5] at Paris,

---

1. HW had been confined to his room with the gout since 29 June (Montagu ii. 159). This attack, his fourth and the most severe so far, did not begin to abate until August (see *post* 27 July 1765; More 41; Mann vi. 322–3).

2. Presumably Daniel Graham, apothecary (*ante* 27 May 1745, n. 13).

3. Lady Frances Ridgeway (ca 1702–72), m. 1 (1717) Thomas Pitt (d. 1729), cr. (1719) Bn and (1726) E. of Londonderry; m. 2 (1732) Robert Graham (d. 1749).

4. An extremely popular air of the time. The words, attributed to George Alexander Stevens (1710–84), were set to the tune of a hornpipe danced in the *Beggar's Opera* (this tune is still familiar as that of the nursery rhyme, 'Here we go round the mulberry bush'). Beginning 'Of all the girls in our town,/ The black, the fair, the red, the brown,/ Who dance and prance it up and down,/ There's none like Nancy Dawson,' the song commemorates Nancy Dawson (?1730–67), a fashionable dancer at Covent Garden and Drury Lane, who made her fame dancing the aforesaid hornpipe. Complete texts of the song can be found in the *Vocal Magazine*, 1778, p. 67, and *Notes and Queries*, 1860, 2d ser. x. 110–11. See also DNB *sub* 'Nancy Dawson' and 'George Alexander Stevens'; and *Enciclopedia dello spettacolo*, Rome, 1954–62, iv. 254–5.

5. Marie-Lydie de Bournonville (1720–91), m. (1746) Friedrich Karl Philipp, Graf von Bentheim (du Deffand ii. 11, n. 5).

and that she had the prettiest palace in the world, built like a pavilion, of yellow laced with blue; that I made love to her daughter,[6] whom I called Mademoiselle Bleue et Jaune, and thought it very clever.

My next reverie was very serious, and lasted half an hour after I was awake; which you will perhaps think a little light-headed, and so do I. I thought Mr Pitt had had a conference with Madame de Bentheim, and granted all her demands. I rung for Louis at six in the morning, and wanted to get up and inform myself of what had been kept so secret from me. You must know, that all these visions of Madame de Bentheim flowed from George Selwyn telling me last night, that she had carried most of her points,[7] and was returning. What stuff I tell you!—But, alas! I have nothing better to do, sitting on my bed, and wishing to forget how brightly the sun shines, when I cannot be at Strawberry.

From HERTFORD, Thursday 4 July 1765

Printed for the first time from a photostat of BM Add. MSS 23218, f. 216.

Paris, July 4th 1765.

Dear Horry,

I HAVE just heard that Lord Granard is dead, so the young man I wrote to you about is now Lord Forbes.[1]

I have just asked the King's leave to return to England for a few days in order to settle some private affairs, either this summer or autumn, as it may best suit me and be least inconvenient to his Majesty's business;[2] but you will not allow this to make the least alteration in your motions. I wish to have it in my power to go when it may be convenient, but I mean to stay but a very few days whenever I undertake it, and I have not precisely fixed any time.[3]

HW did visit her later in the year at Paris; see post 2 Oct. 1765.

6. Mme de Bentheim apparently had only 'un fils né en 1748, et mort en bas âge' (La Chenaye-Desbois ii. 908; see also F.-A. Gruyer, Chantilly. Les Portraits de Carmontelle, 1902, p. 17).

7. These points have eluded us. For Selwyn and Mme de Bentheim, see DU DEFFAND ii. 11; SELWYN 213, 251; and

J. H. Jesse, George Selwyn and his Contemporaries, 1882, i. 395.

---

1. See ante 20 June 1765.

2. Hertford made his request in a letter to Halifax, 4 July, alluding to a 'loss' he suffered by his absence, presumably a business loss (S.P. 78/267, f. 29).

3. Hertford subsequently received from the new ministry an offer of the post of

I propose going to Compiègne on Monday next,[4] where the Court is fixed till the middle of August.[5]

I am curious to hear how your political negotiations will end.[6]

Do not suppose, because I talk so coolly of France[7] and because I am so well received here, that I propose passing all my life here. My children make me think of England, and his Majesty may settle me there honourably as soon as he pleases upon that account.

I remain, dear Horry,

Ever yours,

HERTFORD

From HERTFORD, Saturday 27 July 1765

Printed for the first time from a photostat of BM Add. MSS 23218, f. 219.

London,[1] July 27th 1765.

Dear Horry,

I AM very impatient to see you on every account, and am much concerned you are still troubled with the gout.[2] Allow me to ask you if you can come to town;[3] if not, I will take the first occasion, though I am much hurried, of coming to you.[4]

Yours ever,

HERTFORD

lord lieutenant of Ireland, which determined his trip to London towards the end of the month. See *post* 27 July 1765, n. 1, 12 Aug. 1765, n. 4.

4. 8 July. He wrote to Halifax from Compiègne 10 July (S.P. 78/267, f. 43).

5. 'Le Roi est parti avant-hier [2 July] de la Meute pour Compiègne. . . . La Reine en a pris la route hier' (*Gazette de Leyde* 12 July, *sub* 'Versailles, le 4 juillet'). The King was still at Compiègne 25 August (ibid. 3 Sept., 'Supplément,' *sub* 'Paris . . . 26 août'), but returned shortly after.

6. See *ante* 1 July 1765, n. 2.

7. Presumably a slip for 'England.'

1. Hertford arrived in London 26 July

in the morning (*Daily Adv.* 27 July) 'to make his option between Ireland and Paris' (HW to Mann, 30 July 1765, MANN vi. 315). See *post* 12 Aug. 1765, n. 4.

2. HW had been convalescing since 20 July at SH, where 'I had not only the disappointment of not getting better, but a bad return in one of my feet' (HW to Montagu 28 July 1765, MONTAGU ii. 162; HW to Mann 30 July 1765, MANN vi. 315).

3. 'Though so little fit to be moved,' HW came to town 30 July (ibid.).

4. HW wrote to Montagu 28 July 1765 that he proposed going to town because Hertford's visit to him at SH would be too brief (MONTAGU ii. 163).

To HERTFORD, ca Sunday 11 August 1765

Missing; answered *post* 12 Aug. 1765.

From HERTFORD, Monday 12 August 1765

Printed for the first time from a photostat of BM Add. MSS 23218, f. 220.
Address: To the Honourable Horatio Walpole at Strawberry Hill.

Monday, August 12th 1765.

My dear Horry,

I AM much obliged to you for your kind note.[1] I could have wished to have attended my brother today to Strawberry,[2] but I am prevented by a person[3] who comes to me on Irish business.[4] If you do not come soon to town, I will endeavour to see you in the country.

Yours ever most faithfully,

HERTFORD

To CONWAY, Tuesday 27 August 1765

Missing. 'This morning, reading that Sir Charles Howard was dead, I immediately wrote a note to Mr Conway to advertise him of another ribband vacant, and to put in a caveat (as he is going to dine at Claremont) against the Duke of Newcastle promising it to some head of a college at Cambridge' (HW to Mann 27 Aug. 1765, MANN vi. 332). See *post* 28 Oct. 1765.

1. Missing.
2. Conway and the Duke of Richmond dined 12 Aug. at SH, whence HW had returned by 9 Aug. (MANN vi. 322; MORE 40).
3. Not identified.
4. Hertford had been appointed Weymouth's successor as lord lieutenant of Ireland 1 Aug. (*Daily Adv.* 2 Aug.). The offer of the post had been sent to him 10 July '*from his brother's office*' (HW to Montagu 11 July 1765, MONTAGU ii. 161); he received it by 15 July (Lady Hertford to Dr William Hunter 15 July, BM Add. MSS 23218, f. 217). HW wrote to Mann, 30 July 1765, that Hertford chose Ireland over Paris 'not very gladly, but to accommodate his brother and his nephew Grafton [Lady Hertford was Grafton's aunt]' (MANN vi. 315–16). For Hertford's instructions from the King, dated 9 Aug., see J. A. Froude, *The English in Ireland in the Eighteenth Century*, 1887, ii. 44–7, and *Calendar of Home Office Papers, 1760–1765*, ed. J. Redington, 1878, pp. 559–60, 592.

By September HW felt sufficiently recovered from the gout to undertake at last his journey to France, where he hoped the change of air might prove beneficial (HW to Strafford 3 Sept. 1765, Chute 316–17; to Grosvenor Bedford 5 Sept. 1765; Cole i. 95). He was also escaping from the new administration, for he was deeply wounded by Conway's failure to offer him a post upon coming into power. Conway's neglect HW attributed to 'insensibility' rather than ingratitude; he preserved a friendly veneer towards Conway, and eventually recovered their earlier association. See Appendix 7.

To Conway, Wednesday 11 September 1765

Printed from *Works* v. 116–18.

Amiens,[1] Wednesday, Sept. 11, 1765.

Biau[2] Cousin,

I HAVE had a very prosperous journey till just at entering this city. I escaped a Prince of Nassau[3] at Dover, and sickness at sea, though the voyage lasted seven hours and a half.[4] I have recovered my strength surprisingly in the time; though almost famished for want of clean victuals, and comfortable tea and bread and butter. Half a mile from hence I met a coach and four with an equipage of French, and a lady in pea-green and silver, a smart hat and feather, and two *suivantes*. My reason told me it was the Archbishop's concubine; but luckily my heart whispered that it was Lady Mary Coke.[5] I jumped out of my chaise—yes, jumped, as Mrs Nugent[6] said of herself, fell on my knees, and said my first *ave maria, gratia plena!* We just shot a few politics flying—heard that Madame de Mirepoix had toasted me t'other day in tea—shook hands, forgot to weep, and

1. HW left London 9 Sept., landed at Boulogne 10 Sept., and arrived at Amiens 11 Sept. at 6:30 in the evening ('Paris Journals,' du Deffand v. 258–9).

2. A late Old French variant of 'beau' (OED).

3. Not identified.

4. '*10* [*Sept.*] Embarked at 7 o'clock at Dover, but being becalmed, and wind not fair, could not make Calais, nor land at Boulogne till half an hour after two' ('Paris Journals,' du Deffand v. 258).

5. '*11* [*Sept.*]. Met Lady Mary Coke coming out of Amiens, on her way to England' (ibid. v. 259).

6. Anna Craggs (ca 1697–1756), m. Robert Nugent. She was very fat, and this remark of hers was a standing joke between HW, Conway, and Lady Ailesbury. See *ante* 8 Nov. 1752, *post* 29 Dec. 1772.

parted; she to the Hereditary Princess,[7] I to this inn, where is actually resident the Duchess of Douglas.[8] We are not likely to have any intercourse, or I would declare myself a Hamilton.[9]

I find this country wonderfully enriched since I saw it four-and-twenty years ago. Boulogne is grown quite a plump smug town, with a number of new houses. The worst villages are tight, and wooden shoes have disappeared. Mr Pitt and the City of London may fancy what they will, but France will not come a-begging to the Mansion House[10] this year or two. In truth, I impute this air of opulence a little to ourselves. The crumbs that fall from the chaises of the swarms of English that visit Paris, must have contributed to fatten this province. It is plain I must have little to do when I turn my hand to calculating: but here is my observation. From Boulogne to Paris it will cost me near ten guineas; but then consider, I travel alone, and carry Louis most part of the way in the chaise with me. *Nos autres milords anglais* are not often so frugal. Your brother,[11] last year, had ninety-nine English to dinner on the King's Birthday.[12] How many of them do you think dropped so little as ten guineas on this road? In short, there are the seeds of a calculation for you; and if you will water them with a torrent of words, they will produce such a dissertation, that you will be able to vie with George Grenville next session in plans of national economy[13]—only be sure not to tax travelling till I come back, loaded with purchases; nor, till then, propagate my ideas. It will be time enough for me to be thrifty of the nation's money, when I have spent all my own.

Clermont, 12th.

While they are getting my dinner, I continue my journal. The Duchess of Douglas (for English are generally the most extraor-

7. Princess Augusta (1737–1813) of England, m. Karl Wilhelm Ferdinand, Hereditary Prince of Brunswick-Wolfenbüttel. The Hereditary Prince and Princess were paying a visit to England, and had arrived in London 9 Sept. (*Daily Adv.* 9, 11 Sept.).

8. Margaret Douglas (d. 1774), m. (1758) Archibald Douglas, 3d M. of Douglas 1700, cr. (1703) D. of Douglas.

9. The memorable cause between the houses of Douglas and Hamilton was then pending (HW); see 'Paris Journals' loc. cit.

and *ante* 12 April 1764, n. 11. HW is alluding to his aversion to meeting any English abroad; see MORE 48.

10. Of the lord mayor of London.

11. Francis Earl of Hertford, then ambassador at Paris (HW).

12. See *ante* 6 June 1764.

13. Grenville 'valued himself on his knowledge of finance, and . . . wanted not redundancy of words' (*Mem. Geo. III* ii. 62). As first lord of the Treasury he had of course been responsible for the budget.

dinary persons that we meet with even out of England) left Amiens before me, on her way home. You will not guess what she carries with her—Oh! nothing that will hurt our manufactures; nor what George Grenville himself would seize. One of her servants died at Paris; she had him embalmed, and the body is tied before her chaise:—a droll way of being chief mourner!

For a French absurdity, I have observed that along the great roads they plant walnut trees, but strip them up for firing. It is like the owl that bit off the feet of mice, that they might lie still and fatten.

At the foot of this hill is an old-fashioned château belonging to the Duke of Fitz-James, with a *parc en quincunx*[14] and clipped hedges. We saw him walking in his waistcoat and ribband, very well powdered; a figure like Guerchy. I cannot say his seat rivals Goodwood or Euston.[15] I shall lie at Chantilly tonight,[16] for I did not set out till ten this morning—not because I could not, as you will suspect, get up sooner—but because all the horses in the country have attended the Queen to Nancy.[17] Besides, I have a little underplot of seeing Chantilly and St-Denis in my way;[18] which you know one could not do in the dark tonight, nor in winter, if I return then.

Hôtel de feue Madame l'Ambassadrice d'Angleterre,[19]

Sept. 13, 7 o'clock.

I am just arrived.[20] My Lady Hertford is not at home, and Lady Anne[21] will not come out of her burrow: so I have just time to finish this before Madame returns; and Brian[22] sets out tonight and will carry it. I find I shall have a great deal to say: formerly I observed

14. *Parc en quinconce,* planting arranged in groupings of five (four at the corners, and one in the middle).

15. Seats of the Dukes of Richmond and Grafton, descendants of Charles II through his mistresses Louise de Penancoët de Kéroualle, Duchess of Portsmouth, and Barbara Villiers, Duchess of Cleveland; Fitzjames was descended from a mistress of James II.

16. HW arrived at Chantilly at 9:30 ('Paris Journals,' DU DEFFAND v. 260).

17. Stanislaus King of Poland, father to the Queen of Louis XV, lived at Nancy (HW). See ibid. v. 259; *post* 10 March 1766.

18. For HW's impressions of Chantilly and St-Denis, which he saw 13 Sept., see 'Paris Journals,' DU DEFFAND v. 260.

19. Lord Hertford was at this time recalled, and the Duke of Richmond appointed to succeed him in the embassy at Paris (HW).

20. HW reached Paris at six o'clock (DU DEFFAND loc. cit.).

21. Lady Anne Seymour Conway, afterwards married to the Earl of Drogheda (HW). She was apparently quite shy (*ante* 11 March 1764; *Leinster Corr.* i. 435).

22. Presumably one of the Hertfords' servants.

nothing, and now remark everything minutely. I have already fallen in love with twenty things, and in hate with forty. Adieu!

Yours ever,

Hor. Walpole

To Hertford, ca Saturday 14 September 1765

Missing; listed in 'Paris Journals' (du Deffand v. 376).

To Conway, ca Wednesday 18 September 1765

Missing; listed in 'Paris Journals' (du Deffand v. 376).

To Lady Ailesbury, ca Friday 20 September 1765

Missing; listed in 'Paris Journals' (du Deffand v. 376).

To Conway, ca Sunday 22 September 1765

Missing; listed in 'Paris Journals' (du Deffand v. 376) with the jotting 'note 18.'

To Hertford, ca Monday 30 September 1765

Missing; listed in 'Paris Journals' (du Deffand v. 376), as sent 'by Lord Beauchamp.'

To Conway, Wednesday 2 October 1765

Printed from *Works* v. 119–22. Sent by Joly, 3 Oct. ('Paris Journals,' DU DEFFAND v. 376). Wrongly dated 6 Oct. in *Works* and all subsequent editions. HW writes that he supped at Mme du Deffand's 'last night,' which is dated 1 Oct. in 'Paris Journals' (DU DEFFAND v. 266); he mentions the arrival of Wilkes 'two days ago,' dated 30 Sept. in 'Paris Journals' (ibid.); and says that he is to sup with the d'Ussons 'on Sunday,' which was 6 Oct. (ibid. v. 267). HW's remark that he was robbed 'the night before last' suggests that he completed this letter 3 Oct., as the theft apparently took place the night of 1–2 Oct. (see 'Paris Journals,' ibid. v. 266, 268, *sub* 2, 29 Oct.).

Paris, October 6 [2], 1765.

I AM glad to find you grow just, and that you do conceive at last, that I could do better than stay in England for politics.[1] *Tenez, mon enfant,* as the Duchesse de la Ferté[2] said to Madame Staal;[3] *comme il n'y a que moi au monde qui aie toujours raison,*[4] I will be very reasonable; and as you have made this concession to me, who knew I was in the right, I will not expect you to answer all my *reasonable* letters. If you send a bullying letter to the King of Spain,[5] or to *chose,* my neighbour here,[6] I will consider them as written to myself, and subtract so much from your bill[7]—nay, I will accept a

1. 'He [Conway] no sooner discovered that my intention was to remain in France much longer than he expected, than he broke out into complaints, entreaties, and reproaches . . . and . . . tried with angry words to divert me from my purpose; urged the occasion he should have for my advice, and called my retreat desertion of my friends. . . . I reminded him of the declaration I had often made of quitting the party as soon as they should be successful . . . and . . . said I knew the obligations the party had had to me; I knew none I had to them' (*Mem. Geo. III* ii. 151, cited Appendix 7). It is noteworthy that HW was able to write as usual to Conway despite his understandable resentment of Conway's neglect of him.

2. Madeleine d'Angennes (1629–1714), m. (1655) Henri de Saint-Nectaire, Maréchal-Duc de la Ferté (DU DEFFAND i. 169, n. 6).

3. Marguerite-Jeanne Cordier de Launay (1684–1750), m. (1735) Baron de Staal (ibid. i. 78, n. 27).

4. 'Tiens, mon enfant, je ne vois que moi qui aie toujours raison' (Mme de Staal, *Mémoires,* 1755, i. 269; HW's copy is Hazen, *Cat. of HW's Lib.,* No. 1286). Mme de Staal goes on to add that 'cette parole a servi, plus qu'aucun précepte, à m'apprendre la défiance de soi-même, et je me la rappelle toutes les fois que je suis tenté de croire que j'ai raison' (loc. cit.).

5. Mr Conway was now secretary of state for the foreign department (HW).

6. The King of France, Louis XV (HW). *Chose* here is equivalent to 'what's-his-name.'

7. HW favoured the new administration's adopting a firm policy towards Spain and France in the negotiations over payment of the Manila ransom and the Canada bills, and the demolition of the harbour at Dunkirk (*ante* 18 Oct. 1763, 27 Aug. 1764, nn. 27, 29): 'It would be glorious for them to extort what the peacemakers had not dared to insist on; or, baffled, the shame would lie at the door of their predecessors' (*Mem. Geo. III* ii. 161). France he felt especially ripe for

line from Lady A. now and then in part of payment. I shall continue to write as the wind sets in my pen; and do own my babble does not demand much reply.

For so reasonable a person as I am, I have changed my mind very often about this country. The first five days I was in violent spirits—then came a dismal cloud of whisk and literature, and I could not bear it. At present I begin, very *Englishly* indeed, to establish a right to my own way. I laugh, and talk nonsense, and make them hear me. There are two or three houses where I go quite at my ease, am never asked to touch a card, nor hold dissertations.[8] Nay, I don't pay homage to their authors. Every woman has one or two planted in her house, and God knows how they water them. The old Président Hénault[9] is the pagod at Madame du Deffand's,[10] an old blind *débauchée* of wit, where I supped last night.[11] The President is very near deaf, and much nearer superannuated. He sits by the table: the mistress of the house, who formerly was his,[12] inquires after every dish on the table, is told who has eaten of which, and then bawls the bill of fare of every individual into the President's ears. In short, every mouthful is proclaimed, and so is every blunder I make against grammar. Some that I make on purpose, succeed; and one of them is to be reported to the Queen today by Hénault, who is her great favourite.[13] I had been at Versailles;[14] and having been much taken notice of by Her Majesty, I said, alluding to Madame de Sévigné,

being coerced, as 'the desperate situation' of French finances and the spirit of parliamentary opposition aflame in the country made France 'less in a situation than we were to recommence war' (ibid. ii. 162). About this time he wrote to Conway advising the administration to authorize the Duke of Richmond, the new ambassador, to 'talk big to the French Court,' advice which Conway heartily approved (ibid.). Conway had already in Aug. instructed Rochford at Madrid to press the matter of the Manila ransom at the Spanish Court (Conway to Rochford 20 Aug., MS now WSL).

8. For the visits which HW had made up to this time, see 'Paris Journals,' DU DEFFAND v. 260–6. Just which houses he means is not clear.

9. Charles-Jean-François Hénault (1685–1770), président de la première chambre des enquêtes; author of the *Nouvel*

Abrégé chronologique de l'histoire de France (HW's copy is Hazen, op. cit. No. 964); 'cavalier servant' of Mme du Deffand since 1730 (DU DEFFAND i. 3, n. 3).

10. Marie de Vichy-Champrond (1696–1780), m. (1718) Jean-Baptiste-Jacques-Charles du Deffand de la Lande, Marquis de Chastres, called Marquis du Deffand; HW's intimate friend and correspondent.

11. 1 Oct.; he first visited Mme du Deffand 17 Sept. ('Paris Journals,' ibid. v. 261, 266).

12. Theirs was a somewhat mysterious relationship, lacking in affection, and referred to by 'Lucien' (C.-A.-L. Herpin) as a 'liaison semi-conjugale' (*Le Président Hénault et Madame du Deffand*, 1893, p. 189).

13. He was superintendant of the Queen's household (DU DEFFAND ii. 442).

14. 1 Oct. in the morning; see below.

La reine est le plus grand roi du monde.[15] You may judge if I am in possession by a scene that passed after supper. Sir James Macdonald[16] had been mimicking Hume: I told the women, who, besides the mistress, were the Duchesse de la Valière,[17] Madame de Forcalquier,[18] and a demoiselle,[19] that to be sure they would be glad to have a specimen of Mr Pitt's manner of speaking; and that nobody mimicked him so well as Elliot.[20] They firmly believed it, teased him for an hour, and at last said he was the rudest man in the world not to oblige them. It appeared the more strange, because here everybody sings, reads their own works in public, or attempts any one thing without hesitation or capacity. Elliot speaks miserable French; which added to the diversion.

I had had my share of distress in the morning, by going through the operation of being presented to the whole royal family, down to the little Madame's[21] pap-dinner,[22] and had behaved as sillily as you

15. HW quotes this bon mot also to Lady Hervey, 3 Oct. 1765 (MORE 52). According to Mary Berry's note to this letter in *Works* v. 529, 'Madame de Sévigné thus expresses herself of Louis XIV after his having taken much notice of her at Versailles. See her letters.' However, the quotation has not been found in Mme de Sévigné's letters, though it does appear in several letters *to* her, from her cousin, the Comte de Bussy (those of 20 Aug. 1677 and 17 Jan. 1681; see his *Correspondance*, ed. L. Lalanne, 1858-9, iii. 329, v. 218). Bussy, in his *Histoire amoureuse des Gaules* (HW's copy Hazen, op. cit., No. 1235), attributes to her a similar sentiment expressed under the conditions described by Mary Berry: 'Un soir que le Roi venait de la faire danser, et s'étant remise à la place, qui était auprès de moi: "Il faut avouer, me dit-elle, que le Roi a de grandes qualités, je crois qu'il obscurcira la gloire de tous ses prédécesseurs"' (ed. P. Boiteau and C. L. Livet, 1856-76, i. 309-10).

16. An elder brother of Sir A[rchibald] Macdonald [1747-1826], the present lord chief baron of the Exchequer [1793-1813]. He died at Rome the year following, leaving behind him a distinguished character for every mental accomplishment (HW). Sir James Macdonald (1742-66), 8th Bt, 1746 (DU DEFFAND i. 110, n. 19; Namier and Brooke iii. 80).

17. Anne-Julie-Françoise de Crussol (1713-93), m. (1732) Louis-César de la Baume le Blanc, Duc de la Vallière (DU DEFFAND i. 17, n. 38).

18. Marie-Françoise-Renée de Carbonnel de Canisy (1725 – ca 1796), m. 1 (1737) Antoine-Françoise de Pardaillan de Gondrin, Marquis d'Antin; m. 2 (1742) Louis-Bufile de Brancas, Comte de Forcalquier (d. 1753); HW's correspondent (ibid. vi. 280).

19. Not mentioned in 'Paris Journals.'

20. Sir Gilbert Elliot of Minto (HW). a *bête noir* of HW's (MONTAGU ii. 94; ante 15 Feb. 1764, n. 86).

21. Marie - Adélaïde - Clotilde - Xavière (1759-1802), daughter of Louis, Dauphin, m. (1775) Charles Emmanuel, P. of Piedmont, later (1796) Charles Emmanuel IV of Sardinia (La Chenaye-Desbois viii. 594; Isenburg, *Stammtafeln* ii. taf. 18, 114). The Dauphin also had an infant daughter, Élisabeth-Philippine-Marie-Hélène (3 May 1764 – 1794) (La Chenaye-Desbois loc. cit.; Isenburg, op. cit. ii. taf. 18).

22. HW told Chute, 3 Oct. 1765, that 'the whole [ceremony] concludes with seeing the Dauphin's little girl dine.' He was introduced by Hans Stanley to the governess of the *Enfants de France*, Mme de Marsan ('Paris Journals,' DU DEFFAND v. 266).

will easily believe; hiding myself behind every mortal. The Queen called me up to her dressing-table, and seemed mightily disposed to gossip with me; but instead of enjoying my glory like Madame de Sévigné,[23] I slunk back into the crowd after a few questions. She told Monsieur de Guerchy of it afterwards, and that I had run away from her, but said she would have her revenge at Fontainebleau[24]—so I must go thither, which I did not intend.[25] The King, Dauphin, Dauphiness, Mesdames, and the wild beast, did not say a word to me. Yes, the wild beast, he of the Gévaudan.[26] He is killed,[27] and actually in the Queen's *anti-chambre,* where he was exhibited to us with as much parade as if it was Mr Pitt. It is an exceedingly large wolf, and, the connoisseurs say, has twelve teeth more than any wolf ever had since the days of Romulus's wet-nurse. The critics deny it to be the true beast; and I find most people think the beast's name is *legion, for there are many.*[28] He was covered with a sheet, which two chasseurs lifted up for the foreign ministers and strangers. I dined at the Duke of Praslin's with five-and-twenty tomes of the *corps diplomatique;* and after dinner was presented, by Monsieur de Guerchy, to the Duc de Choiseul. The Duc de Praslin is as like his own letters in D'Éon's book[29] as he can stare; that is, I believe, a very silly fellow.[30] His wisdom is of the grave kind. His cousin, the first minister,[31] is a little volatile being, whose countenance and manner had nothing to frighten me for my country. I saw him but for three seconds, which is as much as he allows to any one body or thing.[32]

23. Bussy, in his *Histoire amoureuse des Gaules* (n. 15 above), writes of Mme de Sévigné: 'Pour avoir de l'esprit et de la qualité, elle se laisse un peu trop éblouir aux grandeurs de la Cour. Le jour que la Reine lui aura parlé, et peut-être demandé seulement avec qui elle sera venue, elle sera transportée de joie,' etc. (i. 309).

24. Where the Court took up residence 5 Oct. (Léon Deroy, *Les Chroniques du château de Fontainebleau,* [1909], p. 170), remaining there until after the Dauphin's death on 20 Dec.

25. 'I don't love courts' (HW to Anne Pitt 8 Oct. 1765, MORE 56). His subsequent attack of the gout (see *post* 28 Oct. 1765) furnished him with the necessary excuse for not going; see MONTAGU ii. 180.

26. See *ante* 26 March 1765 and n. 31.

27. 20 Sept., by Jean-François Antoine (b. 1724), Chevalier de St-Louis and Porte Arquebuse; it was presented to the King the day HW saw it (MANN vi. 289, n. 12).

28. 'My name is legion, for we are many' (the response to Christ of the man possessed by unclean spirits, Mark 5.9).

29. *Lettres, mémoires et négociations particulières du Chevalier d'Éon,* 1764 (*ante* 27 March 1764, n. 12).

30. In his letter to Mann of 9 April 1764, HW ridicules Praslin's plan 'to make the French language universal, by publishing a monthly [actually a weekly] review,' discussed in a letter to d'Éon of 17 May 1763 (MANN vi. 218 and n. 16).

31. Choiseul.

32. See HW's portrait of Choiseul in *Mem. Geo. III* ii. 172–4.

Monsieur de Guerchy,[33] whose goodness to me is inexpressible, took the trouble of walking everywhere with me, and carried me particularly to see the new office for state papers[34]—I wish I could send it you. It is a large building, disposed like an hospital, with the most admirable order and method. Lodgings for every officer; his name and business written over his door. In the body is a perspective[35] of seven or eight large chambers: each is painted with emblems, and wainscoted with presses with wired doors and crimson curtains. Over each press, in golden letters, the country to which the pieces relate, as *Angleterre, Allemagne,* etc. Each room has a large funnel of bronze with *or moulu,*[36] like a column, to air the papers and preserve them. In short, it is as magnificent as useful.[37]

From thence I went to see the reservoir of pictures at Monsieur de Marigny's.[38] They are what are not disposed of in the palaces, though sometimes changed with others. This *refuse,* which fills many rooms from top to bottom, is composed of the most glorious works of Raphael, L. da Vinci, Giorgione, Titian, Guido, Correggio, etc. Many pictures, which I knew by their prints, without an idea where they existed, I found there.

The Duc de Nivernois is extremely obliging to me.[39] I have supped

33. He had been ambassador in England (HW). He had returned to Paris the beginning of Aug. on leave of absence, doubtless glad to escape temporarily the scandal caused by the indictment brought against him by d'Éon (see *ante* 26 March 1765; GM 1765, xxxv. 391; J. B. Telfer, *The Strange Career of the Chevalier D'Éon de Beaumont,* 1885, pp. 170–87). Presumably the ostensible reason for his going was the same as the summer before, i.e. to review the regiment of which he was colonel (*ante* 17 May 1764; GM 1764, xxxiv. 347).

34. The new *Dépôt des Archives des Affaires Étrangères* at Versailles, designed by Jean-Baptiste Berthier (1721–1804) and opened in 1763; it had formerly been 'dans le donjon du vieux Louvre' (*Dictionnaire de biographie française,* 1933– , vi. 215–16; A. Baschet, *Le Duc de Saint-Simon son cabinet et l'historique de ses manuscrits,* 1874, pp. 226–30, 234, 248–9). Emmanuel, Duc de Croÿ, called it 'réellement superbe' and 'le plus beau morceau

du monde, en ce genre' (*Journal inédit,* ed. Grouchy and Cottin, 1906, ii. 90, 121, *sub* 1 July, 25 Sept. 1763).

35. 'La plus riche enfilade que j'aie vue' (ibid. ii. 90).

36. Originally 'ground gold' used for gilding metals; later, an imitation alloy of copper, zinc, and sometimes tin was used instead. This is the earliest use of the term in OED; the English form is 'ormolu.' See MANN vii. 211–12 and nn. 19, 20.

37. For a more detailed description of the *Dépôt,* see Charles Hirschauer, 'Jean-Baptiste Berthier,' *Revue de l'histoire de Versailles,* 1930, pp. 152–4.

38. Mme de Pompadour's brother; director-general of the buildings, gardens, arts and manufactures of the King (*ante* 23 Jan. 1764, n. 10). See Barbara Scott, 'The Marquis de Marigny: A Dispenser of Royal Patronage,' *Apollo,* Jan. 1973, Vol. XCVII, No. 131 (n.s.), pp. 25–35.

39. HW mentions being in Nivernais's company on 30 Sept. and 2 Oct. ('Paris Journals,' DU DEFFAND v. 265–6).

at Madame de Bentheim's,[40] who has a very fine house, and a woeful husband.[41] She is much livelier than any Frenchwoman.[42] The liveliest man I have seen is the Duc de Duras:[43] he is shorter and plumper than Lord Halifax, but very like him in the face. I am to sup with the Dussons on Sunday.[44] In short, all that have been in England are exceedingly disposed to repay any civilities they received there.[45] Monsieur de Caraman wrote from the country[46] to excuse his not coming to see me,[47] as his wife is on the point of being brought to bed,[48] but begged I would come to them—so I would, if I was a man-midwife: but though they are easy on such heads, I am not used to it, and cannot make a party of pleasure of a labour.

Wilkes arrived here two days ago,[49] and announced that he was going minister to Constantinople. Today I hear he has lowered his credentials, and talks of going to England, if he can make his peace.[50] I thought, by the manner in which this was mentioned to me, that the person meant to sound me: but I made no answer; for, having given up politics in England, I certainly did not come to transact

40. 29 Sept. (ibid. v. 265).

41. Friedrich Karl Philipp (1725–1803), Graf von Bentheim (ibid. vi. 248).

42. She was originally from Flanders (La Chenaye-Desbois ii. 908).

43. Whom he saw at Mme de Bentheim's 29 Sept. ('Paris Journals,' DU DEFFAND V. 265).

44. 6 Oct., which he did; the invitation was presumably made at Mme de Bentheim's 29 Sept. (ibid. v. 265, 267).

45. Nivernais was ambassador to England 1762–3 and visited SH in April 1763 (MANN vi. 136); Mme de Bentheim visited England and presumably SH the past summer (ante 3 July 1765); and the d'Ussons visited England the spring of 1763, Mme d'Usson breakfasting at SH 17 May (ante 21 May 1763, n. 2; MONTAGU ii. 70).

46. From his country seat at Roissy (DU DEFFAND passim).

47. Caraman had come to England the preceding March and been entertained at SH 10 June (ante 26 March 1765; MONTAGU ii. 156).

48. She gave birth to their second son 7 Oct.; this was Maurice-Gabriel-Joseph de Riquet de Caraman (1765–1835), later Comte de Caraman (La Chenaye-Desboiç xvii. 130; DU DEFFAND iv. 86, n. 1).

49. 30 Sept.; so recorded in 'Paris Journals' (DU DEFFAND V. 266). Actually he arrived the day before, 29 Sept. (Wilkes to Mary Wilkes, 30 Sept., to Humphrey Cotes, 30 Sept. in Wilkes, Correspondence, ed. Almon, 1805, ii. 185, 206). He had been at Geneva the past two months (ibid. ii. 179–85, 203–6; Horace Bleackley, Life of John Wilkes, 1917, pp. 172–3).

50. After his outlawry (HW). The change of administration in July had prompted Wilkes to come to Paris and open negotiations with Rockingham to obtain the reversal of the sentence of outlawry against him (see ante 25 Nov. 1764); in addition to this he wanted to be named ambassador to Constantinople. His efforts, however, resulted only in the Ministers' offer of £1000 a year to be paid from their own salaries (Bleackley, op. cit. 173–5); as Edmund Burke wrote, ante 14 Jan. 1766, 'Lord R[ockingham] is extremely averse from asking any thing for him from the K[ing] at the same time that he is willing to do almost any thing for him from his private pocket' (Burke, Correspondence, Vol. I, ed. T. W. Copeland, Cambridge, 1958, p. 231).

them here. He has not been to make me the first visit, which, as the last arrived, depends on him: so, never having spoken to him in my life, I have no call to seek him.[51] I avoid all politics so much, that I had not heard one word here about Spain. I suppose my silence passes for very artful mystery, and puzzles the ministers, who keep spies on the most insignificant foreigner. It would have been lucky if I had been as watchful. At Chantilli I lost my portmanteau with half my linen;[52] and the night before last[53] I was robbed of a new frock, waistcoat and breeches, laced with gold, a white and silver waistcoat, black velvet breeches, a knife and a book.[54] These are expenses I did not expect, and by no means entering into my system of extravagance.[55]

I am very sorry for the death of Lord Ophaly,[56] and for his family. I knew the poor young man himself but little, but he seemed extremely good-natured.[57] What the Duke of Richmond will do for a hotel, I cannot conceive.[58] Adieu!

Yours ever,

Hor. Walpole

To Conway, ca Thursday 3 October 1765

A 'note,' missing; listed in 'Paris Journals' (du Deffand v. 376) as sent 'by Mr Stanley.'

51. Wilkes visited HW twice between 10 and 16 Oct., during HW's confinement with the gout, and HW in return called on Wilkes 31 Oct. ('Paris Journals,' du Deffand v. 267, 269; Montagu ii. 180). Apparently the calls were purely social.
52. 'From before my chaise at noon while I went to see Chantilly [13 Sept.]' (Cole i. 98; 'Paris Journals,' du Deffand v. 260).
53. See headnote above.
54. For HW's frustrating efforts to get the Paris police to look into the theft, see 'Paris Journals,' du Deffand v. 267, 268–9.
55. See ante 11 Sept. 1765.
56. George Fitzgerald (1748 – 26 Sept.

1765), styled Lord Offaly and (after 1761) E. of Offaly; heir apparent to the Marquess of Kildare.
57. HW saw him act in a play at Holland House in 1761 (Montagu i. 335).
58. Richmond had been named to succeed Hertford as ambassador to Paris; his credentials and instructions are dated 24 Oct. (D. B. Horn, British Diplomatic Representatives 1689–1789, 1932, p. 22). He and the Duchess arrived at Paris 6 Nov. ('Paris Journals,' du Deffand v. 270), and took up residence in the Hôtel de Brancas, Hertford's old residence (Almanach royal, 1766, p. 134).

From HERTFORD and LADY HERTFORD,
Thursday 10 October 1765

Printed for the first time from a photostat of BM Add. MSS 23218, ff. 222–4. The postscript is by Lady Hertford.

Hollywell,[1] October 10th 1765.

Dear Horry,

ROYALTY[2] has its inconveniences. We broke our chaise and were overturned *en famille* the first day's journey. I hope it is not a bad omen for the administration I am going to undertake, as we escaped so well. The rest of the journey to this place has been favourable, though I would not wish it to be a picture of my situation in Dublin. We have had storms and bad weather. At Chester I received great honours from the Town and Corporation. The most distinguished mark of their attention was a very singular one. It happened to be their fair day[3] when we arrived, which made it the more striking. In the middle of one of the great streets my coach was stopped by two beadles. I looked out at the window and beheld upon a sort of stage prepared for that purpose the Mayor[4] and Corporation of the Town in their habits of form. The Recorder[5] immediately began to make me a speech prepared for the occasion, which I was to answer out of the coach before thousands of people, and we then drove off amidst loud acclamations. After dinner we were entertained in the Town Hall by the Corporation with a great dessert and wines to drink his Majesty's health, and it concluded with a ball where Lady Grosvenor appeared with her turban on her head.[6] You would have been entertained with the whole scene, if your journey to France has had the same effect upon you that a two

1. About 17 miles northwest of Chester. Hertford and Lady Hertford set out for Dublin from London 8 Oct. (*Gazetteer and New Daily Advertiser* 9 Oct.). Lady Hertford had left Paris 22 Sept., reaching London on the 27th ('Paris Journals,' DU DEFFAND v. 263; *Daily Adv.* 28 Sept.). The Hertfords were accompanied to Ireland by Lord Beauchamp and their three eldest daughters (see below).

2. As lord lieutenant of Ireland, Hertford was now 'viceroy.'

3. 10 Oct. (*Rider's British Merlin*, 1765).

4. Richard Ollerhead (G. L. Fenwick, *A History of . . . Chester*, Chester, 1896, p. 540).

5. Robert Townshend (ca 1708–91), recorder of the city of Chester 1754–87 (ibid. 547; GM 1791, lxi pt i. 491).

6. See *ante* 12 Feb. 1765. Lord Grosvenor's seat was at Eaton, 4 miles south of Chester.

HON. FRANCIS INGRAM-SEYMOUR-CONWAY, LORD
BEAUCHAMP, BY TILLY KETTLE

years' residence at Paris has had on me. Everything here is so different I cannot at once reconcile myself to it.

I still think of the place I have left with pleasure and some regret; however it is a consolation to have some prospect of serving a friend. Trail[7] you know is a bishop.[8] A few such opportunities will satisfy me. I am not ambitious of power for its own sake; I find it is not my taste. My desires will be bounded by doing the King's business with reputation, and serving a few whom I love and esteem, without adding either to the establishment or pension list.[9]

I did not go to Wooburn, though you will see it in the papers;[10] both my time and courage failed me. You know I love the Duke of Bedford,[11] but I did not know whom I might have met there,[12] and I conceived it possible that the scene might be an unpleasant one to others, though I might have felt easy enough under it myself.

My son Beauchamp and my three eldest daughters[13] are with me here. Con[14] arrived just in time to set out for Dublin.[15]

7. James Trail, Hertford's chaplain.

8. 'The King has been pleased to order letters patent to be passed under the Great Seal of . . . Ireland . . . for the promotion of Dr James Trail, to the united bishoprics of Down and Connor, void by the translation of . . . Dr Arthur Smyth' (*London Gazette* No. 10561, 28 Sept. – 1 Oct., *sub* St James's, 1 Oct.; see Henry Cotton, *Fasti Ecclesiæ Hibernicæ*, Dublin, 1848–51, iii. 211).

9. 'It is reported, that a great personage has declared that no more places or pensions shall be granted on the Irish Establishment, either for life or years' (*St James's Chronicle* 10–12 Oct., *sub* 12 Oct., postscript). As to existing pensions Hertford's instructions (*ante* 12 Aug. 1765, n. 4) declared that 'should the revenue fall short of the cost of the establishment, you will take care that the same is not applied to the payment of pensions, till the rest is first paid. If there be not enough, you will abate the pensions' (J. A. Froude, *The English in Ireland in the Eighteenth Century*, 1887, ii. 46).

10. Rumour may have had it that Hertford visited the Duke of Bedford, who had been lord lieutenant of Ireland 1756–61, to ask for last-minute advice on how to govern that kingdom.

11. Rigby wrote from Dublin to the Duke, 23 Nov., that 'Lord and Lady Hertford . . . forever sound your praises' (*Bedford Corr.* iii. 322).

12. Hertford was perhaps thinking of Lord Halifax, who while secretary of state for the south had expressed his dissatisfaction with Hertford and tried to get Hertford recalled as ambassador at Paris (see *ante* 3 Dec. 1764, n. 32). Of course, he may have been hesitant to visit the Duke simply because the Duke was now in Opposition.

13. Lady Anne Seymour Conway (1744–84), Lady Sarah Frances Seymour Conway (1747–70), m. (1766) Robert Stewart, cr. (1789) Bn Londonderry, and Lady Gertrude Seymour Conway (1750–93), m. (1772) George Mason Villiers, styled Vct Villiers, 1st E. Grandison, 1782.

14. Beauchamp.

15. Hertford had chosen Beauchamp to be his secretary in Ireland; he had originally intended to have Hume share the secretaryship with his son, but this scheme fell through (J. Y. T. Greig, *David Hume*, New York, 1931, pp. 322–4; Hume, *Letters*, ed. Greig, 1932, i. 516–17, 519; idem, *New Letters*, ed. Klibansky and Mossner, Oxford, 1954, p. 130). Beauchamp's appointment was reported in the *Daily Adv.* 5 Aug. Beauchamp left Florence, where he had been tarrying waiting for orders, ap-

Pray tell me all the news of Paris; I am much interested in it. I desire likewise that you will pay the proper compliments from me to all who have not forgot me. I hear the Irish do not wish that either I, my family or any of my servants should wear a French thing (it is extremely reasonable),[16] but I will tell you more of them before I will allow you to pronounce. I am told they are disposed to think and act well by me; a little time will make this matter clear. I shall endeavour to deserve well, and feel a great deal of philosophy upon such occasions.

I remain, with perfect truth and regard, my dear Horry,

Most faithfully and sincerely yours,

HERTFORD

[Postscript by Lady Hertford]

Dear Sir,

My Lord leaves me very little room[17] to tell you how much I long to hear from you; and I am sure you are too good to me to refuse me such a satisfaction. I am anxious to the greatest degree about you; therefore tell me how you are, and give me a journal of all you have done and are doing, and likewise what is become of my friends at Paris, for I have lived so long with them, and so agreeably, that I feel quite interested about them. Don't think me affected when I say that English beauties and English manners have lost all charms for me. My sister[18] says I am much altered, because I receive visitors in

parently on 14 Sept., passing through Paris 30 Sept., and arriving back in London 7 Oct. (MANN vi. 336, 338, 344; *post* 1 Nov. 1765; *Gazetteer and New Daily Advertiser* 8 Oct.).

16. 'Dublin, Oct. 19 . . . The Earl of Hertford has given directions, that the clothes for his pages and domestics be made of Irish manufacture; and we hear that his Excellency and his Lady have repeatedly declared their resolution, to give every encouragement to the manufactures of this kingdom' (*Daily Adv.* 26 Oct.). In his speech to the Irish parliament, 22 Oct. (*post* 1 Nov. 1765), Hertford mentions the 'linen manufacture in its several

branches' as being 'the principal object of industry, as the staple of commerce' in Ireland, and emphasizes the importance of safeguarding and developing this manufacture (*London Gazette* No. 10569, 26–9 Oct., *sub* Dublin Castle, 22 Oct.), and the *London Chronicle* 2–5 Nov., xviii. 436 *sub* Dublin, 29 Oct., reports that on 25 Oct. 'there was a grand and brilliant drawing room at the Castle, at which the Countess of Hertford, and the young ladies her daughters, appeared in Irish silk.'

17. She continued her postscript on an additional scrap of paper.

18. Lady Harrington.

a morning and have a French maid; but I believe she will find herself much disappointed, as I believe she wishes I was changed.[19]

We beg you will send us *Sara*[20] and anything else that is published that is worth having; they may [be] directed to us to the care of Mr Larpent[21] in General Conway's office. Pray tell Mr Hume I have been so much hurried it has not been in my power to write to him. How does Madame de Mirepoix do?[22] I tremble for our voyage, the wind is got into such a violent way.[23]

To HERTFORD, ca Friday 11 October 1765

Missing; listed in 'Paris Journals' (DU DEFFAND v. 376) as sent 'by Mr Elliot.' Presumably answered by Hertford's letter *post* 1 Nov. 1765.

To LADY AILESBURY, ca Sunday 13 October 1765

Missing; listed in 'Paris Journals' (DU DEFFAND v. 376); sent 'by Mr Ramsay.'

To CONWAY, ca Thursday 24 October 1765

Missing; listed in 'Paris Journals' (DU DEFFAND v. 377); sent 'by M. de Guerchy.'

19. That is, more like the unconventional Lady Harrington.

20. *Sara Th . . . Nouvelle traduite de l'anglais,* by Jean-François de Saint-Lambert (1716–1803) (Grimm, *Correspondance,* ed. Tourneux, 1877–82, vi. 357; NBG). It was an original *nouvelle,* not a translation, and before being printed separately had appeared in the *Gazette littéraire de l'Europe* for 15 Aug. The story of a woman of quality who gives up family and fortune to marry her servant and live a peasant's life with him, it was perhaps inspired by the marriage the year before of Lady Henrietta Watson Wentworth to her footman, William Sturgeon (see *ante* 1 Nov. 1764). The story was dismissed as 'mediocre' by Grimm (loc. cit.).

21. John Larpent (1710–97), first clerk in the southern department of the secretary of state's office (MANN vi. 449, n. 7; *Court and City Register,* 1765, p. 107).

22. HW had visited her 6 Oct. ('Paris Journals,' DU DEFFAND v. 267); see HW to Anne Pitt, 8 Oct. 1765 (MORE 55).

23. See *post* 1 Nov. 1765.

To Lady Hertford, ca Saturday 26 October 1765

Missing; listed in 'Paris Journals' (DU DEFFAND v. 377); sent 'by Mr [William] Burrell' (1732–96), LL.D.; 2d Bt, 1788; antiquary.

To Conway, Monday 28 October 1765

Printed from *Works* v. 122–4. Dated 29 Oct. in 'Paris Journals' (DU DEFFAND v. 377); sent 31 Oct. 'by Comte Lauraguais's English coachman' (ibid.).

Paris, October 28, 1765.

MR Hume[1] sends me word from Fontainebleau,[2] that your brother, some time in the spring of 1764, transmitted to the English ministry *a pretty exact and very authentic account of the French finances;* these are his words: *and that it will be easily found among his Lordship's dispatches of that period.*[3] To the other question[4] I have received no answer; I suppose he has not yet been able to inform himself.

This goes by an English coachman of Count Lauragais, sent over to buy more horses: therefore I shall write a little ministerially, and, perhaps, surprise you, if you are not already apprised of things in the light I see them.

The Dauphin will probably hold out very few days. His death, that is, the near prospect of it, fills *the philosophers* with the greatest joy, as it was feared he would endeavour the restoration of the Jesuits.[5] You will think the sentiments of *the philosophers* very odd *state news*—but do you know who *the philosophers* are, or what the term means here? In the first place, it comprehends almost everybody; and in the next, means men, who avowing war against popery, aim, many of them, at a subversion of all religion, and still many more, at the destruction of regal power. How do you know this? you will say; you, who have been but six weeks in France, three of which you have

1. The celebrated David Hume was secretary of embassy to the Earl of Hertford during his residence at Paris (HW).

2. The letter is missing.

3. The account is not among Hertford's dispatches for that period in S.P. 78/260–2.

4. Not ascertained.

5. HW claims that the Dauphin's piety was just a veneer (*Mem. Geo. III* ii. 170–1).

been confined to your chamber.[6] True: but in the first period I went everywhere, and heard nothing else; in the latter, I have been extremely visited,[7] and have had long and explicit conversations with many, who think as I tell you, and with a few of the other side, who are no less persuaded that there are such intentions. In particular, I had two officers here t'other night,[8] neither of them young, whom I had difficulty to keep from a serious quarrel, and who, in the heat of the dispute, informed me of much more than I could have learnt with great pains.

As a proof that my ideas are not quite visions, I send you a most curious paper;[9] such as I believe no *magistrate* would have pronounced in the time of Charles I.[10] I should not like to have it known to come from me, nor any part of the intelligence I send you; with regard to which, if you think it necessary to communicate it to particular persons, I desire my name may be suppressed. I tell it you for *your* satisfaction and information, but would not have anybody else think that I do anything here but amuse myself: my amusements indeed are *triste* enough, and consist wholly in trying to get well; but my recovery moves very slowly. I have not yet had anything but cloth shoes on, live sometimes a whole day on warm water, and am never tolerably well till twelve or one o'clock.

I have had another letter from Sir Horace Mann,[11] who has much at heart his ribband[12] and increase of character.[13] Consequently you know, as I love him so much, I must have them at heart too.[14] Count

6. With the gout; HW's attack began 7 Oct. ('Paris Journals,' du DEFFAND v. 267). He resumed visiting the evening of 30 Oct. (ibid. v. 269).

7. See HW's list of his visitors, ibid. v. 267–8.

8. Not in HW's list.

9. Missing; not identified.

10. Presumably the paper was by a particularly outspoken member of one of the French parliaments, advocating the overthrow of the King; see *Mem. Geo. III* ii. 174–6.

11. That of 12 Oct. 1765 (MANN vi. 344–7), his second directed to HW at Paris (ibid. vi. 338, 344, 349).

12. For Knight of the Bath.

13. Which would enable him to meet the added expense of his ministry en-

tailed by the establishment of the new grand ducal Court at Florence, and which would put him on at least an equal footing with the other ministers at the Court; see ibid. vi. 318–22, 329, *et passim.* Mann, at this time Resident, received his credentials as envoy extraordinary ca 30 Dec. (ibid. vi. 371, nn. 1, 2). He did not get his ribbon until 1768 (ibid. vii. 63).

14. Though HW had been soliciting Conway for Mann's ribbon since July (see *ante* 27 Aug. 1765, MANN vi. 309), this was his first appeal for an increase of character, which he had originally opposed making, partly for fear it might interfere with the obtaining of the ribbon (ibid. vi. 341, 352, 358). He presumably made a second appeal in his missing letter of ca 6 Nov.

Lorenzi[15] is recalled, because here they think it necessary to send a Frenchman[16] of higher rank to the new Grand Ducal court.[17] I wish Sir Horace could be raised on this occasion. For his ribband, his promise is so old and so positive,[18] that it is quite a hardship.

Pray put the colonies[19] in good humour; I see they are violently disposed to the new administration.[20]

I have not time to say more, nor more to say if I had time; so good night. Let me know if you receive this, and how soon: it goes the day after tomorrow. Various reports say, the Duke of Richmond comes this week.[21] I sent you a letter by Monsieur de Guerchy.[22]

Dusson, I hear, goes ambassador to Poland.[23] Tell Lady A. that I have five or six little parcels, though not above one for her,[24] of laces and ribbands, which Lady Cecilia[25] left with me; but how to convey them the Lord knows.

Yours ever,

Hor. Walpole

15. Luigi Roland (d. 1766), Conte Lorenzi; France's representative in Tuscany 1735–65 (ibid. i. 62, n. 32).

16. Lorenzi was a Florentine (ibid.). Mann wrote to HW 12 Oct. 1765 that the Duc de Choiseul had notified Lorenzi that the 'King's service . . . requires that a subject should attend to for the future' (ibid. vi. 346).

17. The Archduke Leopold, second son of the Emperor Francis I, had succeeded his father as Grand Duke of Tuscany upon the latter's death, 18 Aug. 1765 (ibid. vi. 328–9; Isenburg, Stammtafeln i. taf. 19), and was in the process of establishing his Court at Florence. Lorenzi was succeeded by the Marquis de Barbantane (MANN vi. 434, n. 20).

18. Mann had been promised the ribbon upon 'the first proper occasion' in a letter from Stuart Mackenzie of 6 July 1762 (ibid. vi. 235, 317).

19. Of America.

20. A letter from Boston, 11 Sept., extracted in the London Chronicle (17–19

Oct., xviii. 380–1), reports that the news of the change of administration in July, received 10 Sept., was greeted with joy, in apparent anticipation of the new administration's reversal of the Stamp Act, which had by no means yet been decided upon; see Mem. Geo. III ii. 153–6.

21. He and the Duchess arrived 6 Nov. ('Paris Journals,' DU DEFFAND v. 270).

22. The missing letter of ca 24 Oct.

23. He did not; the Marquis de Conflans was sent the following spring to compliment Stanislas Poniatowski upon his accession to the throne (Recueil des instructions données aux ambassadeurs et ministres de France . . . Pologne, ed. L. Farges, 1888, ii. 256).

24. Perhaps the parcel sent along with HW's letter to Conway post 29 Nov. 1765; HW also sent Lady Ailesbury a lappet along with his letter to her post ca 23 Nov. 1765.

25. Lady Cecilia Johnston, who had visited HW with her husband 22 Oct. ('Paris Journals,' DU DEFFAND v. 268).

From HERTFORD, Friday 1 November 1765

Printed for the first time from a photostat of BM Add. MSS 23218, ff. 225–7.

Dublin Castle,[1] November 1st 1765.

Dear Horry,

I AM concerned to hear of all your misfortunes,[2] but I would rather you was robbed[3] than ill;[4] as Paris does not seem to please nor agree particularly well with you, I hope when you have surveyed all the curiosities of it you will return to Strawberry and your friends.

You require of me that I should talk about myself; you will therefore not think it vanity if I do it in compliance with a friend's commands.[5] Lady Hertford stayed as long at Paris as she could, waiting her son's arrival, and as you know came away at last without him.[6] He arrived however in London four and twenty hours before I was obliged to leave it.[7] On this account and from the multiplicity of affairs I had to settle both public and private,[8] I deferred setting out as long as I could. It however so far answered my wishes that I left London *en famille,*[9] and was overturned with my wife and children[10] on the first day's journey by travelling too late at night. I was detained at Hollyhead[11] till I was frightened extremely lest I should not get to Dublin before the meeting of Parliament;[12] however by bringing Lady Hertford away in rough weather with a contrary wind and

1. The Hertfords reached Dublin 18 Oct. (*London Gazette* No. 10568, 22–6 Oct., *sub* Dublin Castle, 18 Oct.).

2. Presumably in HW's missing letter to Hertford of ca 11 Oct.

3. See *ante* 2 Oct. 1765.

4. See *ante* 28 Oct. 1765, n. 6.

5. The information in this paragraph is mostly repeated from Hertford's letter to HW *ante* 10 Oct. 1765.

6. 22 Sept.; she had had her audience of leave at Versailles 2 Sept. Lord Beauchamp passed through Paris 30 Sept. on his return from Florence (ibid., nn. 1, 15; David Hume, *New Letters,* ed. Klibansky and Mossner, Oxford, 1954, p. 110; *Mercure historique,* 1765, clix. 309–10).

7. Beauchamp arrived in London 7 Oct. (*ante* 10 Oct. 1765, n. 15).

8. Hertford had so much business to attend to after his return from France in July that he was not able to go back to take official leave of the French Court; this was done for him by Lady Hertford (see *Mercure historique* loc. cit.).

9. 8 Oct. (*ante* 10 Oct. 1765, n. 1).

10. Lord Beauchamp, and Ladies Anne, Sarah Frances and Gertrude Seymour Conway.

11. From which they embarked ca 17 Oct. (*Daily Adv.* 26 Oct.).

12. Which was scheduled for 22 Oct.; Conway, informed of the delay, wrote the lords justices of Ireland 17 Oct. authorizing 'a further prorogation of the Parliament in case the Earl of Hertford does not arrive in time' (*Calendar of Home Office Papers, 1760–1765,* ed. J. Redington, 1878, p. 609).

an high sea, we got here in time, to the infinite satisfaction of my mind.

I was received as all new governors are with loud acclamations.[13] I have made my speech to Parliament,[14] in which you will not condemn me for taking notice of the peculiar connection I had with this country.[15] I have received addresses from the two Houses in answer,[16] wherein that circumstance is mentioned with great confidence.[17] I have likewise received compliments and addresses from the College, the Dissenters, the Quakers, the French Protestants, etc. These are the usual forms. Their expressions indeed are more confidential towards me on account of my property in this kingdom,[18] and the conduct I have always held in what related to their interests; but what is particular to myself and what will give you satisfaction, is to hear that the public voice and the popular opinion are in my favour and for

13. 'Dublin Castle, Oct. 18 . . . The Earl of Hertford . . . was received at landing by the Lord Mayor, aldermen, sheriffs and commons of the city of Dublin. The foot forces in garrison lined the streets, through which his Excellency (attended by a squadron of Horse) proceeded, amidst the acclamations of the people, with the usual ceremony, to the Castle, where in Council his Excellency took the oaths appointed to be taken . . . and received the sword from . . . the lords justices: After which the great guns in his Majesty's park the Phoenix were fired, and answered by volleys from the regiments on duty, which were drawn out upon College Green: And his Excellency repairing to the Presence Chamber received there the compliments of the nobility and other persons of distinction' (London Gazette loc. cit.).

14. 22 Oct., opening the new session (Journals of the House of Commons . . . Ireland xiv. 9).

15. 'Long and personal experience have raised in my mind the most honourable sentiments of your zeal and affection for his Majesty's service' (ibid.). Hertford is referring to his large Irish estates and Irish title; he was the first lord lieutenant appointed since 1688 who had such an extensive Irish connection.

16. 24 Oct., preceded by the customary addresses to the King (London Gazette No. 10570, 29 Oct. – 2 Nov.).

17. The Lords observed that 'the long experience we have had of your knowledge in what relates to the real interests of this kingdom, with your powerful and ready assistance in support of them, gives us an enlarged prospect of enjoying the utmost benefit which can result from a well-informed benevolent administration,' while the Commons characterized Hertford as 'eminently distinguished . . . for his affectionate regard for our welfare,' mentioning their 'satisfaction' at his appointment. The Lords' address to the King mentions Hertford's 'long and experienced attention to the particular interests of this kingdom,' while the Commons' address mentions his 'peculiar and well-founded affection for this country' (ibid.).

18. Lord Charlemont, in his Memoirs, wrote that 'the designation . . . of Lord Hertford was, in all appearance free from objection. His birth and station were in the highest degree illustrious. His property was immense, and as a great portion of it lay in this country, it might well be supposed that even his avarice, the vice most objected to him, would operate in our favour, and that he would be a friend to the soil from which he drew his beloved wealth' (Hist. MSS Comm., 12th Report, App. pt x, Charlemont MSS, Vol. I, 1891, p. 23).

the support of my administration. There is a general confidence expressed in me, and it goes so far that the chief leaders of opposition,[19] who have been strangers in their wishes to the measures of government, and my predecessors, have acquainted me that they have refused all opposition to me; that they are persuaded I shall do all my situation will allow to promote the interest of Ireland, and under that opinion will support me without any private views.

Lord Kildare is to be in opposition if he can persuade anybody to join him; hitherto he has done nothing.[20] He has acquainted me that he wishes well to Lord Hertford, but cannot see him[21] as Lord Lieutenant, since the usage to him[22] has been so bad for some years past that he will not attend the King in person.[23] His friends have remonstrated against his conduct, told him it was considered as disappointment, as peevish and against the inclination of the country, but his Lordship is firm and received the remonstrances with passion and ill temper. Mr Ponsonby behaves well and I dare say will not deceive me.[24] Upon the whole it requires great prudence, management and attention to conduct the affairs of this country, circumstanced as they are, and some few unavoidable difficulties may now and then occur; but I am persuaded upon the whole it will go well and that I have reason to expect some credit from my present employment.[25]

Gaieties and diversions I have left behind me. You may be in possession of them at Paris. I am immersed in business, with my thoughts and time fully employed upon the King['s] service and the good of this country.

19. Except Lord Kildare, the most influential of all (see below); next in importance to him were Lord Shannon (*ante* 17 Nov. 1763) and John Ponsonby, speaker of the Irish House of Commons and Shannon's father-in-law (J. A. Froude, *The English in Ireland in the Eighteenth Century*, 1887, ii. 50–2).

20. Hertford mentions an 'opposition of nine' in a letter acknowledged by Conway 7 Nov. (MS now wsl), while Hunt Walsh wrote to Lord Townshend from Dublin, 5 June 1766, that 'the patriots began the sessions with a minority of about ten' (Hist. MSS Comm., 11th Report, App. pt iv, *Townshend MSS*, 1887, p. 402).

21. Hertford.

22. Kildare.

23. In 1762 Kildare, Master-General of the Irish Ordnance, had been exasperated by the slowness of the government in reaching a decision on his plan to reorganize the Irish Ordnance along the lines of the English Ordnance, and in 1763 the government had rebuffed his application for a regiment; see Brian Fitzgerald, *Emily, Duchess of Leinster 1731–1814*, 1950, pp. 94, 99, 114. Kildare's rancour was soothed next year upon his being created Duke of Leinster.

24. However, see *post* 10, 21 May 1766.

25. However, as might be expected from the chronic unrest in Ireland, Hertford's hopes proved too sanguine; see subsequent letters and especially *post* 21 May 1766.

In May next I hope to see you in London in a state of more freedom.

Lady Hertford is extremely well and often speaks of Paris with
regret. Can you believe that she could ever be so much inclined to
France?[26] I remain, dear Horry,

Ever most truly yours,

HERTFORD

When the Irish Members of Parliament will permit me, I will
recommend Mr Fitzgerald[27] for a commission.

To LADY HERTFORD, ca Tuesday 5 November 1765

Missing; listed in 'Paris Journals' (DU DEFFAND v. 377), as sent 'by Mr Grafts
and Mr Rhadel, two merchants.'

To CONWAY, ca Wednesday 6 November 1765

Missing; listed in 'Paris Journals' (DU DEFFAND v. 377) as sent 'by the post.' In
this letter HW presumably made another appeal for Mann's ribbon and
increase of character; see MANN vi. 363, *ante* 28 Oct. 1765.

To LADY AILESBURY, ca Monday 11 November 1765

Missing; listed in 'Paris Journals' (DU DEFFAND v. 377) as sent 'by Comte Lauraguais's tailor.'

26. Where at first she was shy and ill-
at-ease (see *ante* 28 Oct., 11 Nov. 1763,
and 28 Dec. 1763, n. 6), but by the time
of her departure she had so warmed to
that society that the ladies of Paris could
claim 'that France has given [her] the *ton*
of the world' (Gilbert Elliot to Charles
Jenkinson, 26 Aug. 1765, *Jenkinson Pa-*

pers 1760–1766, ed. N. S. Jucker, 1949, p.
383; *post* 20 Jan. 1766).

27. George Robert Fitzgerald (ca 1748–
86), of Turlough, co. Mayo; adventurer;
grandson of Lady Hervey, HW's correspondent; commissioned lieutenant in
the 69th Foot, Ireland, 5 Nov. 1766 (MORE
113 and n. 4; *Army Lists*, 1767, p. 124).
See *post* 4 Feb., 10 March 1766.

From CONWAY, ca Wednesday 20 November 1765

Missing; a 'short' letter mentioned by HW *post* 29 Nov. 1765, presumably answered *post* ca 29 Nov. 1765. Conjecturally dated a few days anterior to Conway's missing letter of ca 22 Nov. 1765.

From CONWAY, ca Friday 22 November 1765

Missing; a 'long' letter answered by HW *post* 29 Nov. 1765. Conjecturally dated by the approximate time it would take for a letter to reach Paris from London after it had been sent first to Fontainebleau (see *post* 29 Nov. 1765).

To HERTFORD, ca Saturday 23 November 1765

Missing; listed in 'Paris Journals' (DU DEFFAND v. 377) as sent 'by Col. [Edward] Ligonier.'

To CONWAY, ca Saturday 23 November 1765

Missing; listed in 'Paris Journals' (DU DEFFAND v. 377) as sent 'by Col. Ligonier.'

To LADY AILESBURY, ca Saturday 23 November 1765

Missing; listed in 'Paris Journals' (DU DEFFAND v. 377) as sent 'by Colonel Ligonier' with a 'lappet' (a streamer for a lady's head-dress).

To CONWAY, ca Friday 29 November 1765

Missing; listed in 'Paris Journals' (DU DEFFAND v. 378) as sent 'on business,' 'by Louis's cousin.' Presumably the 'very long' letter in answer to Conway's missing 'short letter,' mentioned *post* 29 Nov. 1765.

To Conway, Friday 29 November 1765

Printed from *Works* v. 124–6. Sent 1 Dec. by Andrew Staley (ca 1733–1813), King's messenger ca 1762–95, with a parcel for Lady Ailesbury (DU DEFFAND v. 378; MANN viii. 1, n. 2; *Court and City Register* 1762–95 *passim*).

Paris, November 29, 1765.

AS I answered your short letter[1] with a very long one,[2] I shall be shorter in answer to your long,[3] which I received late last night from Fontainebleau: it is not very necessary; but as Lord William Gordon[4] sets out for England on Monday,[5] I take that opportunity.[6]

The Duke of Richmond[7] tells me that Choiseul has promised everything.[8] I wish it may be performed, and *speedily,* as it will give you an opportunity of opening the Parliament[9] with great *éclat.* My opinion you know is, that this is the moment for pushing them and obtaining.[10]

Thank you for all you say about my gout. We have had a week of very hard frost, that has done me great good, and rebraced me. The swelling of my legs is quite gone. What has done me more good, is having entirely left off tea, to which I believe the weakness of my stomach was owing, having had no sickness since. In short, I think I am cured of everything but my fears. You talk coolly of going as far as Naples, and propose my going with you.[11] I would not go so far, if Naples was the direct road to the new Jerusalem. I have no thought or wish, but to get home, and be quiet for the rest of my

1. Missing.
2. Presumably HW's missing letter *ante* ca 29 Nov. 1765.
3. Also missing.
4. (1744–1823), M.P. Elginshire 1779–84, Inverness-shire 1784–90, Horsham 1792–6.
5. 2 Dec.
6. However, Lord William apparently did not leave until 4 Dec., and HW's letter went by Staley 1 Dec. (see headnote; DU DEFFAND v. 378).
7. Who had arrived in Paris 6 Nov. (ibid. v. 270).
8. I.e., the payment of the Canada bills (see *ante* 27 Aug. 1764, n. 27). However, Choiseul continued to prevaricate; this 'promise' was apparently one of the flippancies and 'evasions' of the Duc mentioned by HW in *Mem. Geo. III* ii. 161.

Conway, in a letter to Richmond of 10 Dec., complains of the French minister's levity, and threatens to bring the affair before Parliament if satisfaction is not forthcoming (MS now WSL). In Jan. Choiseul agreed to almost total compensation, and the agreement was signed in London 29 March 1766 by Conway and the Comte de Guerchy. See MORE 97 and n. 11; SELWYN 213 and n. 2; *Mem. Geo. III* ii. 162–3.
9. Which had been prorogued until 17 Dec. (*Journals of the House of Commons* xxx. 435–7).
10. See *ante* 2 Oct. 1765, n. 7.
11. Conway was already chafing over the burden of being secretary of state; see below.

HON. HENRY SEYMOUR CONWAY, BY J. BERWICK

days, which I shall most certainly do the first moment the season will let me; and if I once get to London again, shall be scarce tempted ever to lie in an inn more. I have refused to go to Aubigné,[12] though I should lie but one night on the road. You may guess what I have suffered, when I am grown so timorous about my health.—However, I am again reverted to my system of water, and trying to recover my hardiness—but nothing has at all softened me towards physicians.

You see I have given you a serious answer, though I am rather disposed to smile at your proposal. Go to Italy! for what?—Oh! to quit —do you know, I think that as idle a thought as the other. Pray stay where you are, and do some good to your country, or retire when you cannot—but don't put your finger in your eye and cry after the holidays and sugar-plums of Park Place. You have engaged and must go through, or be hindered. Could you tell the world the reason?[13] Would not all men say you had found yourself incapable of what you had undertaken? I have no patience with your thinking so idly. It would be a reflection on your understanding and character, and a want of resolution unworthy of you.

My advice is, to ask for the first great government that falls, if you will not take your regiment again; to continue acting vigorously and honestly where you are. Things are never stable enough in our country to give you a prospect of a long slavery. Your defect is irresolution. When you have taken your post, act up to it; and if you are driven from it, your retirement will then be as honourable (and more satisfactory) than your administration. I speak frankly, as my friendship for you directs. My way of acting (though a private instance) is agreeable to my doctrine. I determined, whenever our opposition should be over, to have done with politics;[14] and you see I have adhered to my resolution by coming hither; and therefore you may be convinced that I speak my thoughts. I don't ask your pardon, because I should be forced to ask my own if I did not tell you what I think the best for you. You have life and Park Place enough to come, and *you* have not had five months of gout. Make yourself independent honourably, which you may do by a government; but if you will take my advice, don't accept a ministerial place when you

12. Richmond's dukedom in France.
13. Probably Conway had pleaded his philosophical indifference to politics, a favourite theme with him; see *ante* 18 April 1765, n. 18.

14. That is, with internal politics; HW was quite busy now advising both Conway and Richmond on how to deal with the Court of France (see above and *Mem. Geo. III* loc. cit.).

cease to be a minister. The former is a reward due your profession and services, the latter is a degradation. You know the haughtiness of my spirit; I give you no advice but what I would follow.

I sent Lady A. *The Orpheline léguée;*[15] a poor performance; but the subject made me think she would like to see it.[16] I am over head and ears at Count Caylus's[17] auction, and have bought half of it for a song[18]—but I am still in greater felicity and luck, having discovered, by mere accident, a portrait of Count Grammont,[19] after having been in search of one these fifteen years, and assured there was no such thing.[20] Apropos, I promised you my own: but besides that there is nobody here that excels in painting skeletons; seriously, their painters are bitter bad, and as much inferior to Reynolds and Ramsay, as Hudson[21] to Vandyck. I had rather stay till my return. Adieu!

Yours ever,

Hor. Walpole

15. A three-act comedy in *vers libre* by Bernard-Joseph Saurin (1706–81), first performed 5 Nov. before the King and Queen at Fontainebleau, and introduced the next day at the Comédie-Française. HW had seen the Dumesnil in it on 13 Nov., and sent a copy of it also to Lady Hervey (More 77 and nn. 7, 8). For the play's reception and critical comments, see Martin Mühle, *Bernard-Joseph Saurin: Sein Leben und seine Werke,* Dresden, 1913, pp. 176–84.

16. The real subject of the play is *l'anglomanie,* 'notre admiration excessive pour les anglais et pour tout ce qui vient d'eux' (Louis Petit de Bachaumont, *Mémoires secrets,* 1780–9, ii. 257). HW wrote to Lady Hervey 28 Nov. 1765 that the play's 'intended name was the *Anglomanie;* my only reason for sending it' (More 77; see also Petit de Bachaumont, op. cit. ii. 256).

17. Anne-Claude-Philippe de Tubières (1692 – 5 Sept. 1765), Comte de Caylus; patron of artists, and author of the seven-volume *Recueil d'antiquités égyptiennes, étrusques, grecques et romaines,* published 1752–67 (*Dictionnaire de biographie française,* 1933– , vii. 1518–22). HW attended the auction 14 and 26 Nov., according to 'Paris Journals' (du Deffand

v. 271, 275). See also William Cole, *Journal of My Journey to Paris in the Year 1765,* ed. Stokes, 1931, pp. 243–4.

18. Miniatures of the Duc de Vendôme, the Princesse Palatine, and the Duchesse de Montpensier, by Petitot; 'Michael Angelo's Bacchus, made in the china of the Comte de Lauragais'; 'a bottle of purple glass,' 'clouded ewer of polished earth,' 'German pitcher and cover,' etc.; and a bronze inkstand, are listed as 'from the collection of the Comte de Caylus' in HW's 'Des. of SH' (*Works* ii. 408, 422, 499–501, 510). According to Cole, op. cit. 244, HW had intended also to bid for miniatures of the Duke d'Épernon, M. Barbesieux, Madame la Connêtable Colonna, and the Duchesse de la Vallière, and for 'an ancient writing box or écritoire.'

19. Philibert (1621–1707), Comte de Gramont.

20. HW discovered the portrait 28 Nov. at the convent of the Grands-Augustins (More 77–8 and n. 11). He had been searching for a portrait of Gramont for the edition of Anthony Hamilton's *Mémoires du Comte de Grammont* that was finally printed at SH in 1772 with this portrait as frontispiece (ibid. n. 10).

21. Thomas Hudson (1701–79), portrait painter.

From Lady Ailesbury, ca December 1765

Missing; acknowledged by HW *post* 5 Dec. 1765, *sub* 9 Dec.

To Conway, Thursday 5 December 1765

Printed from *Works* v. 126–8. Sent, 17 Dec., by Andrew Stuart (see postscript below).

Paris, December 5, 1765.

I HAVE not above a note's worth to say; but as Lord Ossory sets out tomorrow,[1] I just send you a line.

The Dauphin, if he is still alive, which some folks doubt, is kept so only by cordials;[2] though the Bishop of Glandève[3] has assured the Queen that he had God's own word for his recovery, which she still believes, whether her son is dead or not.

The remonstrance of the parliament of Paris, on the dissolution of that of Bretagne, is very decent; they are to have an audience next week.[4] They do not touch on Chalotais,[5] because the accusation against him is for treason. What do you think that treason is? A correspondence with Mr Pitt, to whom he is made to say, *that Rennes is nearer to London than Paris.*[6] It is now believed that the anonymous letters, supposed to be written by Chalotais, were forged by a Jesuit[7] —those to Mr Pitt could not have even so good an author.

1. See below, *sub* 9 Dec.
2. He died 20 Dec.
3. Gaspard de Tressemanes de Brunet (1721–84), Bp of Glandèves 1755–72. HW reported this anecdote also to Lady Suffolk 5 Dec. 1765 (More 79), and recorded it in 'Paris Journals' 12 Dec. 1765 (du Deffand v. 284–5).
4. See *ante* 9 Feb., 22 March 1765. As a result of continued resistance to the central administration, in mid-November six members of the parliament of Rennes were arrested, others exiled, and a commission appointed by the King substituted for the parliament itself (Selwyn 206, n. 19). The parliament of Paris subsequently drew up a remonstrance protesting the substitution of the commission; this was presented 8 Dec. (ibid. n. 21).

5. Louis-René de Caradeuc de la Chalotais (1701–85), procureur-général of the parliament of Rennes; champion of the Breton parliament against the central administration. He had been arrested 11 Nov. (ibid. n. 20).
6. 'Les amis de M. de la Chalotais . . . répandaient le bruit . . . qu'on n'avait trouvé autre chose à lui reprocher que d'avoir correspondu sans permission avec M. Pitt' (Marcel Marion, *La Bretagne et le duc d'Aiguillon 1753–1770*, 1898, p. 366). However, this rumoured correspondence was not brought up at the trial; see ibid. n. 2.
7. La Chalotais had been one of the first magistrates in France to contribute to the abolition of the Jesuits, by his *Comptes rendus des Constitutions des*

The Duke of Richmond is still at Aubigné; I wonder he stays, for it is the hardest frost alive. Mr Hume does not go to Ireland, where your brother finds he would by no means be welcome.[8]—I have a notion he will stay here till your brother's return.[9]

The Duc de Praslin, it is said, will retire at Christmas.[10] As La Borde,[11] the great banker of the Court, is trying to retire too,[12] my cousin,[13] who is much connected with La Borde, suspects that Choiseul is not very firm himself.[14]

I have supped with Monsieur de Maurepas,[15] and another night with Marshal Richelieu: the first is extremely agreeable and *sensible;* and, I am glad, not *minister.*[16] The other is an old piece of tawdry,

Jésuites au parlement de Bretagne, 1761, 1762 (NBG). However, these anonymous letters were a central issue in the trial. Two in number, they had been posted in June from Rennes to the Comte de Saint-Florentin, one of the King's secretaries of state, and were alleged by the King's handwriting experts to be by La Chalotais: (1) 'dis a ton Maitre que Malgre Lui nous chasserons ses 12 j[uges] [who had remained after a walk-out by the parliament of Rennes in May] et Toy ausi'; (2) 'Tu est j[ean] f[outre] auttunt que Les 12 j f Magistras qui ont echapé a La deroutte generalle raporte cecy a Louis pour quils conunce [connaisse] donc nos affaire et puis ecris en son non [nom] mais sans son su belle epitres au 12 j f Magistra' (Barthélemy Pocquet, *Le Duc d'Aiguillon et La Chalotais,* 1900, ii. facsimile opp. p. 224; Marion, op. cit. 337–41). La Chalotais vigorously denied their authorship, and the whole process eventually bogged down in counter-accusations. Finally the King in 1769 cleared him of any crime, but confirmed his suspension from his functions (SELWYN loc. cit.). See *post* 30 July 1771.

8. 'I have in my possession the letter which Lady Hertford wrote to Hume to induce him not to go to Ireland; the chief topic is the prejudice against him as both a sectarian and a free-thinker' (Croker MS cited by Cunningham iv. 450, n. 2). Hume had written to Adam Smith 5 Sept. that he intended to visit Ireland after the arrival of Richmond in Paris, but wrote to the Rev. Hugh Blair, 1 Jan. 1766, that he had decided 'not to go to Ireland. . . .

Lord Hertford has been so good as to excuse me,' giving as his reason, however, not the antipathy of the Irish to him but the late arrival of Richmond and his engagement with Rousseau, whom he had agreed to settle in England (Hume, *Letters,* ed. J. Y. T. Greig, Oxford, 1932, i. 521, 532).

9. He left for England 4 Jan. 1766 with Rousseau (J. Y. T. Greig, *David Hume,* New York, 1931, p. 331; *post* ca 4 Jan. 1766).

10. Currently minister of foreign affairs, Praslin on 8 April 1766 became minister of the marine and colonies, and was named *chef du conseil des finances.* See *post* 8 April 1766.

11. Jean-Joseph (1724–94), Marquis de La Borde; financier.

12. HW may have heard this from La Borde himself, whom he called on 4 Dec. (MORE 80; DU DEFFAND v. 280).

13. Thomas Walpole, English banker in Paris.

14. For the time being, Choiseul's position was safe; he was disgraced in 1770, at which time La Borde, whom Choiseul had made marquis and Court banker in return for financial services, also retired (NBG; *post* 29 Dec. 1770).

15. Jean-Frédéric Phélypeaux (1701–81), Comte de Maurepas.

16. Maurepas, formerly minister of the marine, had been disgraced in 1749, 'a very favourable event . . . for us,' as he was 'one of our bitterest enemies, and the greatest promoter of their marine' (HW to Mann 3 May 1749 OS, MANN iv. 51). He came into office again upon the ac-

worn out, but endeavouring to brush itself up; and put me in mind of Lord Chesterfield, for they laugh before they know what he has said—and are in the right, for I think they would not laugh afterwards.

I send Lady A. the words and music of the prettiest *opéra comique* in the world[17]—I wish I could send her the actors too. Adieu!

Yours ever,

Hor. Walpole

December 9th.

Lord Ossory put off his journey; which stopped this letter, and it will now go by Mr Andr[ew] Stuart.[18]

The face of things is changed here, which I am impatient to tell you, that you may see it is truth, not system, which I pique myself on sending you. The vigour of the Court has frightened the parliaments. That of Pau has submitted.[19] The procureurs, etc. of Rennes, who,

cession of Louis XVI in 1774; see *post* 28 Sept. 1774.

17. Presumably *La Fée Urgèle, ou ce qui plaît aux dames, comédie en 4 actes, meslée d'ariettes, représentée devant Leurs Majestés, par les Comédiens italiens ordinaires du Roi, à Fontainebleau, le 26 octobre, et à Paris, le 4 décembre suivant* (Bibl. Nat. Cat.); the play was by Charles-Simon Favart (1710–92) and Claude-Henri Fusée (1708–75), Abbé de Voisenon, and the ariettes by Egidio Romualdo Duni (1709–75) (*Enciclopedia dello spettacolo*, Rome, 1954–62, iv. 1134–6, v. 90–4, ix. 1758–9; Auguste Font, *Essai sur Favart et les origines de la comédie mêlée de chant*, Toulouse, 1894, p. 350). HW first saw the play 7 Dec. (DU DEFFAND v. 282), which suggests that this paragraph was written on that date or after. He may have sent Lady Ailesbury either the above edition, or an earlier edition published between the play's performance at Fontainebleau and its début in Paris (see Bibl. Nat. Cat.).

18. (1725–1801), lawyer for the Hamiltons in the famous Douglas-Hamilton case (see *ante* 11 Sept. 1765); M.P. Lanarkshire 1774–84, Weymouth and Melcombe Regis 1790–1801. He went with the letter 17 Dec. (DU DEFFAND v. 378).

19. 'Paris, Dec 14 . . . They write from Pau that the Parliament made their re-entry there the 12th of last month' (*London Chronicle* 21–4 Dec., xviii. 606, *sub* 24 Dec., postscript). The parliament of Pau, in defiance of the central government, had stopped meeting after 17 May 1765, and a large number of its members had handed in their *démissions*, because of differences with the *premier président* and other grievances. The central government sent a royal commission to Pau to take over the government of the province and embarked on severe punitive measures, viz. the imprisonment and exiling of members of the parliament and the reduction of the parliament to two-thirds its former number. This harsh treatment, like the treatment of Rennes, evoked strong remonstrances from other provincial parliaments and the parliament of Paris. See *Mercure historique* June–Dec. 1765, Jan.–Feb. 1766, clviii. 661, clix. 67–70, 176–87 *et passim*; clx. 76–7, 197; A. Le Moy, *Le Parlement de Bretagne et le pouvoir royal au xviiie siècle*, 1909, pp. 335–7; É. Glasson, *Le Parlement de Paris*, 1901, ii. 295–6.

it was said, would not plead before the new commission,[20] were told, that if they did not plead the next day they should be hanged without a trial—no bribe ever operated faster![21]

I heard t'other day, that some Spanish minister, I forget his name, being dead,[22] Squillace[23] would take his department, and Grimaldi[24] have that of the West Indies.[25]—He is the worst that could have it, as we have no greater enemy.

The Dauphin is certainly alive, but in the most shocking way possible: his bones worn through his skin, a great swelling behind, and so relaxed, that his intestines appear from that part; and yesterday the mortification was suspected.

I have received a long letter from Lady A.,[26] for which I give her a thousand thanks; and would answer it directly, if I had not told you every earthly thing I know.

The Duke and Duchess[27] are, I hear, at Fontainebleau: the moment they return, I will give the Duchess Lady A.'s commission.[28]

From Lady Hertford, Monday 16 December 1765

Printed for the first time from a photostat of BM Add. MSS 23218, ff. 228–9.

Dublin Castle, December the 16th 1765.

Dear Mr Walpole,

YOU must think me the most ungrateful creature in the world. I have received two of the most kind and the most entertaining letters that ever were wrote,[1] and have been here many weeks with-

20. See above, n. 4.

21. See *post* 10 March 1766.

22. Perhaps HW had heard a premature report of the death of Luis D'Ibarra y Larrea (ca 1686 – 18 Dec. 1765), member of the King's council and the council of finances, and minister of the royal chamber of commerce and of the exchequer (*Gazette de Leyde* 21 Jan. 1766, *sub* Madrid 24 Dec.; *Mercure historique* 1766, clx. 68).

23. Leopoldo de Gregorio (d. 1785), Marchese di Vallesantoro e di Squillace, a Sicilian of humble origin who became in 1746 Charles III's financier and by 1754 one of his chief ministers at Naples, and followed him to Spain (1759) where he

was minister of finance and war (Mann v. 330, n. 6).

24. Pablo Jeronimo Grimaldi Palavicini y Spinola (1720–86), Spanish minister of foreign affairs 1763–76 (ibid. v. 560, n. 20).

25. No such changeover seems to have taken place. Ibarra y Larrea was succeeded by Rosendo Sáez de Parayuelo (*Gazette de Leyde* 28 Jan. 1766, *sub* Madrid 7 Jan.). See *post* 6, 8 April 1766.

26. Missing.

27. Of Richmond (HW).

28. Not ascertained.

───

1. Presumably HW's missing letters *ante* ca 26 Oct., ca 5 Nov. 1765.

out thanking you for either. Before I have finished this letter I shall convince you how little encouragement one has to write from Dublin. The little news the place affords, is not worth repeating to a stranger; the ceremonies we go through are as little worth mentioning, as they have not varied since the Duke of Ormond's[2] time, and of course everybody has heard them described; and the manner of passing our time is much the same as in London, with only this difference, that we are allowed here very few hours of the four and twenty to be out of company.

Consider then, my dear Mr Walpole, upon what an inequality I I write when I address myself to you, who are the most agreeable correspondent in all respects, that I ever met with, and are now writing from a part of the world that produces all sort of entertainments. I was quite happy to hear that you was recovered, for it grieved me to think of you suffering pain in an *hôtel garni,* at a time when I was at such a distance that I could not offer my best services to you. You had my best wishes for your speedy recovery, but those could have no effect; nor had they any merit, as you command them from everybody that has the happiness of knowing you.

I hope my old acquaintance Demange[3] was not accessory to your being robbed,[4] but the other part of the account of him I can easily believe, for we always supposed him to be our spy; but as we were to have one, it was the same to us whether it was him or anybody else. I long to ask after a thousand people that you do not name, but I am fearful of tiring you; however, pray tell me how the Duchesse de Praslin and the Maréchale de Mirepoix do, and assure them of my gratitude for all their goodness to me. I gave orders for some paper Madame de Mirepoix wanted for a room, while I was in London, and desired Doctor Hunter to take care to send it to her as soon as it was made, and I should be glad to know if she has got it.

I fancy you very seldom frequent the assembly at the Hôtel de Beaupréau,[5] for I know the lady[6] is not a particular favourite of yours, and there is nothing so vulgar as an English assembly at Paris. Mr and Mrs Fitzroy[7] passed a month here and are just returned to

---

2. James Butler (1610–88), 12th Earl of Ormond, cr. (1661) Duke of Ormonde; lord lieutenant of Ireland 1643–7, 1649–50, 1662–9, 1677–85.

3. Not identified; presumably a servant in the Hôtel de Brancas.

4. See *ante* 2 Oct. 1765.

5. In the Rue de l'Université (DU DEF-

FAND v. 267, n. 74; Marquis de Rochegude and M. Dumolin, *Guide pratique à travers le vieux Paris*, 1923, p. 504).

6. Probably Lady Berkeley (MORE 93 and n. 2; 'Paris Journals,' *passim;* OSSORY i. 24).

7. Charles Fitzroy, later Bn Southampton, and his wife. He had been appointed to

England. I never saw her seem to enjoy a place so much as she did Dublin, and both Mr Fitzroy and her were vastly liked here. Loo was in great perfection while Mrs Fitzroy stayed, for they played it with forces[8] and unlimited,[9] which made it very lively, and the parties sometimes did not break up till six o'clock in the morning. Mr Rigby stayed here a very short time,[10] but behaved so handsomely to my Lord, and desired so much that his friends would support my Lord in the strongest manner, that I beg it may with you, as well as it has done with me, wipe off past omissions.[11] . . . son justice in . . . here begged that he would . . .

[12]Pray tell me what is become of our friend Lord Ossory,[13] and make my best compliments to him.

To LADY AILESBURY, ca Tuesday 17 December 1765

Missing; listed in 'Paris Journals' (DU DEFFAND v. 378) as sent 'by Mr Stuart.'

To CONWAY, ca Friday 20 December 1765

Missing; listed in 'Paris Journals' (DU DEFFAND v. 378) as 'on Mr Pitt,' and sent 'by courier.'

colonel of the 14th Dragoons, stationed in Ireland, on 11 Sept. (*Army Lists*, 1766, p. 42).

8. I.e., forcing another player's hand.

9. I.e., a player losing a hand had to pay the whole amount of the pool. See OED *sub* 'loo.'

10. See his letter to the Duke of Bedford, Dublin, 23 Nov., *Bedford Corr.* iii. 322–3. The *London Chronicle* 14–17 Dec., xviii. 582, *sub* 17 Dec., postscript, announced his return with Fitzroy.

11. At this point, most of a page has been torn off; the last four words are at the top of the remaining scrap, and the two phrases following are beneath these four words and on the verso of the scrap, respectively.

12. This postscript is written at the front of the letter, presumably for lack of space at the end.

13. He presumably left Paris for England sometime after 13 Dec., the last time he is mentioned in 'Paris Journals' (DU DEFFAND v. 285).

From HERTFORD, Friday 20 December 1765

Printed for the first time from a photostat of BM Add. MSS 23218, ff. 230–1.
Charade (in HW's hand):

> Pour aller jusqu'à moi il faut plus que sept pieds,
> Et souvent en chemin on dit son patenôtre;
> Mon Tout est séparé d'une de mes moitiés;
> L'une de ces moitiés sert à mesurer l'autre.

The editors suggest 'cimetière' as the solution. In going to the cemetery the eight feet of the pallbearers are necessary, and of course the Lord's prayer would be often recited; a cemetery would never be found on a peak ('cime'), and peaks can be measured in meters ('metière' = 'mètre').

Dublin Castle, December 20th 1765.

Dear Horry,

DO not condemn me if I am a bad private correspondent. I am got into a scene of business that employs me fully. I now and then get an hour for shooting and a little exercise, and those minutes are stolen from the solicitors of Government. What would you take to be thus employed? Nothing; you would despise the laurels I am endeavouring to acquire at such a price. However, my son is getting praise and reputation very fast,[1] and if I leave my daughters behind me in this country[2] you will not pity the private loss I shall sustain. I must endeavour to comfort myself; I have a large family and it is my duty to labour for it even at my own expense.[3]

Do not inquire how I pass my time here; there are few idle hours as you see. I go sometimes in an evening to assemblies, but they do not entertain me after Paris; I confess I left the pleasure of society at that place. I likewise go once in a week to the play,[4] with guards and all the attendants of a King, but I am not flattered by such ap-

1. The praise was not universal, for Lady Holland, replying to Lady Kildare 26 Feb. 1766, wrote: 'I can't believe what is said of Lord Beauchamp; he is a favourite of mine' (*Leinster Corr.* i. 435–6). HW alludes to Beauchamp's avarice as secretary in his MS 'foul copy' of *Mem. Geo. III*, p. 272, and Beauchamp's vanity did not make him popular (see *Leinster Corr.* i. 398, 436).

2. As married women; see subsequent letters.

3. Before he left Ireland, Hertford's 'economic temper . . . and too great propensity to heap emoluments on his children,' along with Beauchamp's avarice, were seized upon by the Opposition to occasion to him 'several mortifications' (MS 'foul copy,' *Mem. Geo. III*, loc. cit.; see also *Leinster Corr.* i. 436–7 and *post* 21 May 1766).

4. There were two rival theatres in Dublin, the Smock Alley and the Crow Street. See La Tourette Stockwell, *Dublin Theatres and Theatre Customs (1637–1820)*, Kingsport, Tenn., 1938, pp. 120–35.

pearances. I would rather go in private to a better performance; pride is not my folly. Lady Hertford is now playing at faro, which she does every Tuesday and Friday; Mr Ohara[5] deals; I do not tell you it is very entertaining.

I have retired without being able to convey a compliment to you about it; after having paid my court to the Members of Parliament and their wives, I feel at liberty to tell you how happy I shall be to meet you again somewhere. What are you doing? Are you settled in France, or do you return to England? Perhaps the American stamps frighten you and you mean to give the politics of your country time to settle before you venture. If you come here, which you never mean to do, you shall be well received and served in Sève china to put you in mind of Paris.

I hear little that is very certain or very interesting by the last letters from London. The Ministry seems in a good way; some alterations will I suppose be made. Mr Pitt seems more likely to support their measures than to disapprove;[6] Lord G. Sackville will I hear be with them.[7] C. Townshend is still the same, uncertain and irresolute.[8] America is a very serious matter, and sufficient to employ all the parties in England.[9]

5. Presumably Charles O'Hara (ca 1705–76), of Annaghmore, co. Sligo; M.P. Irish House of Commons, Ballinakill Borough 1761–8, Armagh Borough 1769–76 (see HW to O'Hara 17 Sept. 1757, n. 1; Edmund Burke, *Correspondence*, Vol. I, ed. T. W. Copeland, Cambridge, 1958, p. 137).

6. George Onslow wrote to Newcastle, 15 Dec., that 'Beckford declares, he [Pitt] is thoroughly and unalterably averse to the late people, and that he talked of coming up the first day [of Parliament, 17 Dec.; see n. 9 below], if he thought it possible for them to think of carrying a question against us. In short, he is as friendly as we could possibly expect' (BM Add. MSS 32972, f. 251). In early January Pitt declared his 'readiness to come into the King's service and act with Lord Rockingham, the Duke of Grafton, and Mr Conway,' but demurred at the time because of his antipathy to Newcastle, with whom he had resolved 'never to be in confidence' (Pitt to George Cooke 7 Dec., *Chatham Corr.* ii. 342–3; Rockingham to Newcastle 2 Jan., Newcastle to

Page 7 Jan. 1766, BM Add. MSS 32973, ff. 13, 55).

7. Rockingham, in a list of arrangements for the opening of Parliament, dated 27 Nov., included Sackville among those who were to manage for administration 'in case of attack,' and wrote to Newcastle on 1 Dec.: 'Sir Jeffrey [Amherst] told me that he was sure Lord George was determined to be a supporter, and was ready to take part if anything offered' (Rockingham MSS, cited Namier and Brooke iii. 393; BM Add. MSS 32972, f. 94). Sackville was subsequently offered and accepted the post of joint vice-treasurer of Ireland, and was re-appointed to the Privy Council of Great Britain 20 Dec. (Namier and Brooke iii. 390).

8. Rockingham wrote to Newcastle, 1 Dec.: 'Charles Townshend continues professing the most favourable intentions, but does not seem to choose to be now called to the Cabinet' (BM Add. MSS 32972, f. 93).

9. See the King's speech opening the new session of Parliament 17 Dec., *Journals of the House of Commons* xxx. 437.

I remain, with the best compliments of the family, dear Horry,

Ever yours,

HERTFORD

To HERTFORD, ca Thursday 26 December 1765

Missing; listed in 'Paris Journals' (DU DEFFAND v. 378) as sent 'by courier.'
Presumably answered *post* 13 Jan. 1766.

From CONWAY, ca January 1766

Two letters, missing; acknowledged by HW *post* 12 Jan. 1766.

To LADY HERTFORD, ca Saturday 4 January 1766

Missing; listed in 'Paris Journals' (DU DEFFAND v. 378) as sent 'by Mr Hume.'
See *post* 20 Jan. 1766.

To CONWAY, before Sunday 12 January 1766

Missing; written in answer to one of the above missing letters. See *post* 12
Jan. 1766 and n. 3.

To Conway, Sunday 12 January 1766

Printed from *Works* v. 128–30. Sent 'by the post' ('Paris Journals,' DU DEFFAND v. 379).

Paris, January 12, 1766.

I HAVE received your letter by General Vernon,[1] and another, to which I have writ an answer,[2] but was disappointed of a conveyance I expected. You shall have it with additions, by the first messenger that goes; but I cannot send it by the post,[3] as I have spoken very freely of some persons you name, in which we agree thoroughly. These few lines are only to tell you I am not idle in writing to you.

I almost repent having come hither; for I like the way of life and many of the people so well, that I doubt I shall feel more regret at leaving Paris than I expected. It would sound vain to tell you the honours and distinctions I receive, and how much I am in fashion; yet when they come from the handsomest women in France, and the most respectable in point of character, can one help being a little proud? If I was twenty years younger, I should wish they were not quite so respectable. Madame de Brionne,[4] whom I have never seen, and who was to have met me at supper last night at the charming Madame d'Egmont's,[5] sent me an invitation by the latter for Wednesday next.[6] I was engaged, and hesitated. I was told, 'Comment! savez-vous que c'est qu'elle ne ferait pas pour toute la France?' However, lest you should dread my returning a perfect old swain, I study my wrinkles, compare myself and my limbs to every plate of larks I see, and treat my understanding with at least as little mercy. Yet, do you know, my present fame is owing to a very trifling composition, but which has made incredible noise. I was one evening[7] at Madame

1. Gen. Charles Vernon (*ante* 24 Jan. 1756, n. 15), who arrived in Paris 11 Jan., and presumably delivered Conway's letter to HW the same day (MORE 95 and n. 1).
2. All three letters are missing.
3. It apparently went 'by Rochester postillion' 18 Jan., while the present letter went 'by the post' 12 Jan. ('Paris Journals,' DU DEFFAND v. 379).
4. One of the great beauties of the day (*ante* 5 May 1753, n. 12).
5. Jeanne - Sophie - Élisabeth - Louise-

Armande-Septimanie Vignerot du Plessis-Richelieu (1740–73), daughter of the Maréchal-Duc de Richelieu, m. (1756) Casimir Pignatelli d'Egmont, Comte d'Egmont (DU DEFFAND i. 42, n. 9). See 'Paris Journals,' ibid. v. 294. Mme de Brionne apparently did not attend because of ill health (see MORE 95).
6. 15 Jan.; see 'Paris Journals,' DU DEFFAND v. 295.
7. 23 Dec. (*Works* iv. 250; DU DEFFAND v. 289).

Geoffrin's,[8] joking on Rousseau's affectations and contradictions, and said some things that diverted them. When I came home I put them into a letter, and showed it next day to Helvétius and the Duc de Nivernois;[9] who were so pleased with it, that, after telling me some faults in the language, which you may be sure there were, they encouraged me to let it be seen.[10] As you know I willingly laugh at mountebanks *political* or literary, let their talents be ever so great, I was not averse. The copies have spread like wildfire; *et me voici à la mode!* I expect the end of my reign at the end of the week with great composure. Here is the letter:[11]

Le Roi de PRUSSE à Monsieur ROUSSEAU.

Mon cher Jean Jacques,

Vous avez renoncé à Genève votre patrie; vous vous êtes fait chasser de la Suisse, pays tant vanté dans vos écrits; la France vous a décrété. Venez donc chez moi: j'admire vos talents; je m'amuse de vos rêveries, qui (soit dit en passant) vous occupent trop, et trop longtemps. Il faut à la fin être sage et heureux. Vous avez fait assez parler de vous par des singularités peu convenables à un véritable grand homme. Démontrez à vos ennemis, que vous pouvez avoir quelquefois le sens commun: cela les fâchera, sans vous faire tort. Mes états vous offrent une retraite paisible: je vous veux du bien, et je vous en ferai, si vous le trouvez bon. Mais si vous vous obstiniez à rejeter mon secours, attendez-vous que je ne le dirai à personne. Si vous persistez à vous creuser l'esprit pour trouver de nouveaux malheurs, choisissez les tels que vous voudrez. Je suis roi, je puis vous en procurer au gré de vos souhaits: et ce qui sûrement ne vous arrivera pas vis-à-vis de vos ennemis, je cesserai de vous persécuter quand vous cesserez de mettre votre gloire à l'être.

Votre bon ami,

FRÉDÉRIC

8. Marie-Thérèse Rodet (1699–1777), m. (1713) François Geoffrin (ibid. *passim*).

9. According to HW in *Works* loc. cit., 'Paris Journals' (DU DEFFAND v. 290), and his letter to Anne Pitt 25 Dec. 1765 (MORE 90), he showed the letter to Nivernais at Mme de Rochefort's 25 Dec.

10. According to HW in *Works* loc. cit., Président Hénault also had a hand in correcting the letter. It began circulating 28 Dec. (GRAY i. 41, n. 277), and ultimately became the cause of the famous Hume-Rousseau quarrel (see F. A. Pottle, 'The Part played by Horace Walpole and James Boswell in the quarrel between Rousseau and Hume: A Reconsideration,' in *Horace Walpole: Writer, Politician, and Connoisseur*, ed. W. H. Smith, New Haven, 1967, pp. 255–91).

11. HW also sent copies to Selwyn 12 Jan. 1766 (SELWYN 212), to Anne Pitt 19 Jan. 1766 (MORE 100–11), to Chute 15 Jan. 1766 (CHUTE 117), and to Cole 25 Feb. 1766 (COLE i. 110–11).

The Princesse de Ligne,[12] whose mother[13] was an Englishwoman, made a good observation to me last night.[14] She said, *Je suis roi, je puis vous procurer de malheurs,* was plainly the stroke of an English pen. I said, then I had certainly not well imitated the character in which I wrote. You will say, I am a bold man to attack both Voltaire and Rousseau. It is true; but I shoot at their heel, at their vulnerable part.[15]

I beg your pardon for taking up your time with these trifles. The day after tomorrow we go in cavalcade with the Duchess[16] to her audience;[17] I have got my cravat and shammy shoes.[18] Adieu!

Yours ever,

HOR. WALPOLE

From HERTFORD, Monday 13 January 1766

Printed for the first time from a photostat of BM Add. MSS 23219, ff. 1–2.

Dublin Castle, January 13th 1766.

Dear Horry,

I THANK you a thousand times for your last letter from Paris.[1] I am always glad to hear from you, and you are not mistaken in thinking I have not forgot that place. I feel interested in all the little events of it by remembering the people so well, and I will confess

12. Henriette-Eugénie de Béthisy de Mézières (1710–87), m. (1729) Claude-Lamoral-Hyacinthe-Ferdinand, Prince de Ligne (La Chenaye-Desbois xii. 106; *Répertoire . . . de la Gazette de France,* ed. de Granges de Surgères, 1902–6, iii. 404).

13. Eleanor Oglethorpe, daughter of Sir Theophilus Oglethorpe of Yorkshire, m. (1707) Eugène-Marie de Béthisy, Marquis de Mézières (*ante* 5 May 1753, n. 9).

14. See 'Paris Journals,' DU DEFFAND v. 294.

15. I.e., at their thirst for fame. In a world-weary letter to Montagu of 21 Nov. 1765 HW branded 'the hypocrite Rousseau' and 'the scoffer Voltaire,' along

with the 'Jesuits, Methodists, philosophers, politicians . . . the Encyclopedists, the Humes, the Lytteltons, the Grenvilles,' Frederick II of Prussia and Pitt, as 'impostors' whose objects were 'fame or interest' (MONTAGU ii. 184).

16. Of Richmond (HW).

17. At Versailles as ambassadress (HW); see 'Paris Journals,' DU DEFFAND v. 295.

18. Soft, pliable shoes made of chamois or imitation chamois leather (see OED), worn by HW to soothe his gouty feet, as the cravat was worn to protect his neck against the cold.

———

1. Presumably the missing letter ca 26 Dec. 1765.

to you that I have still a tenderness for it. There is more pleasure in society than in power, even in its most easy state, and there is always a Dr Lucas,[2] some malevolent or ungrateful spirit, working to do mischief. Surely it is an enchantment that makes us connect with politicians when we can with ease avoid them. However my station here is likely to be attended with advantage to my children, and for their sakes I would be solicited for all that is to be given in Europe. My son grows daily in reputation, and my daughters are much in fashion. You will not therefore be surprised if I should leave two of them in Ireland.[3]

Our business has gone on easily and we have a most powerful majority.[4] I complain only of the evils that must attend power, and yet perhaps I feel less of them than any of my predecessors; in short I am unreasonable and spoiled by Paris.

What do you mean to do, stay there and be spoiled likewise, or return to your friends in England? I am glad you are in love with Madame d'Egmont; it is a necessary ingredient to French happiness, and she is an agreeable woman, though she can never rival Madame de Monaco.[5]

I do not quite admire your set at Paris; I think there is more agreeable company than those you have named, and if you stay at Paris you may be acquainted with them.

I have been shooting these holidays in the country and killed hundreds of woodcocks.

My brother writes me word that he is overloaded with business before that of Parliament is added to it.[6] I do not hear of any

---

2. Charles Lucas (1713–71), M.D.; Irish patriot. For his stormy opposition in the Irish parliament to a bill to prevent temporarily the exportation of grain, see DNB; *Journals of the House of Commons . . . Ireland*, xiv. 123, 142–4, 159–65; *London Chronicle* 18–21 Jan., 25–8 Jan., xix. 70, 94, *sub* Dublin, 14, 21 Jan.

3. See *post* 4 Feb. 1766.

4. The Opposition in the Commons had lost a total of five divisions in opposing the grain exportation bill, by votes of 69-34, 62-34, 60-17, 31-8, and 39-15, while the dissentient opinion on the bill in the Lords was signed by only five (*Journals of the House of Commons . . . Ireland*,

xiv. 159, 162–3; *London Chronicle* 21–3 Jan., xix. 73–4). However, before the session was over the Opposition did manage to carry a question against the Castle; see *post* 10, 21 May 1766.

5. Marie-Catherine de Brignole (1739–1813), m. 1 (1757) Honoré-Camille-Léonor Goyon-de-Matignon de Grimaldi, P. of Monaco; m. 2 (1808) Louis-Joseph de Bourbon, Prince de Condé (DU DEFFAND i. 61, n. 4); she was much admired by Hertford (HW to Thomas Brand 19 Oct. 1765, and to Mme du Deffand 10 June 1766, DU DEFFAND i. 72).

6. The Parliament, which had adjourned for the Christmas holidays, was

plans either of opposition or defence; everything seems uncertain[7] except as to numbers, which are generally allowed to be with Government. Charles Townshend's last letter to a friend here was the language of dissatisfaction. On the day of the Address he spoke for Administration,[8] and perhaps by this time he is doing as much.[9] I hear he is more than ever under the influence of his brother.[10]

Lady Hertford passes her time very well in Dublin, better I believe for having been at Paris, as she loves company and suppers much better.

I am in business and relapsed into good hours. I desire my compliments to all those who remember me at Paris, and am, dear Horry,

Most truly and affectionately yours,

HERTFORD

The best compliments of all the family attend you.

---

to meet again 14 Jan. (*Journals of the House of Commons* xxx. 445; *Journals of the House of Lords* xxxi. 232).

7. Conway had written to Hertford 27 Dec. 1765 that 'as to our affairs here I can tell you nothing new; at least with any certainty' (MS now WSL).

8. In the Commons debate 17 Dec. on the address to be returned to the King on his speech delivered that day, George Grenville moved an amendment to the address declaring the American colonies to be in a state of rebellion. That night Conway wrote to the King that 'Mr Charles Townshend . . . spoke exceeding well, and in the fullest, handsomest, and strongest manner against the amendment' (Geo. III's *Corr.*, ed. Fortescue, i. 202). However, other reports of the debate show Townshend's speech to have been more equivocal vis-à-vis the administra-

tion than Conway suggests, though he did vote with the government; see Sir Lewis Namier and John Brooke, *Charles Townshend*, 1964, p. 138.

9. For Townshend's political activities in January, see ibid. 138–40.

10. George, Vct Townshend. Conway mentions to Hertford in his letter of 27 Dec. a rumour that the two brothers were forming 'a band apart,' while the King included them both in a plan outlined 16 Jan. of an administration to be composed of men unconnected with any party (Namier and Brooke, op. cit. 139). Lord Townshend had the previous July influenced Charles not to accept effective office in the new Rockingham administration because of his hostility to the Duke of Cumberland, under whose auspices the new administration was formed (ibid. 135–7).

From LADY HERTFORD, Monday 20 January 1766

Printed for the first time from a photostat of BM Add. MSS 23219, ff. 3–6.

Dublin Castle, January the 20th.

My dear Mr Walpole,

THE last time I wrote to you[1] I thought it necessary to make excuses for being so long silent, and at present I find I have so little to say that I think it as necessary, for thanking you for a very kind letter today that I received from you so lately as yesterday;[2] but there is a part of it that requires an immediate answer, which is in regard to the china. The old china at Paris is so different from what I imagined, and also the difficulty of getting it to England, that I shall beg to retract my proposal[3] and to desire you not to buy any for me. I thought it might be entered as faience, and that it was chiefly in great jars and beakers, which if they had been remarkably cheap, would have been noble ornaments for our great rooms at Ragley and would then have been very well worth buying for that purpose.

I can easily imagine you have near ruined yourself in the Rue St-Honoré,[4] and fancy you found very little temptation at the Palais Marchand[5] to complete your undoing. We supposed the Duke and Duchess of Richmond in London, till you mentioned the party you had with her on Christmas Eve.[6] I hope the Duchess likes Paris, and I dare say she does better than I did at first, as she has had the advantage of knowing a great deal of the manners. I am sure at the end she cannot like it better, for I met with so much goodness and attention, and felt so much at my ease, that I cannot help thinking

1. *Ante* 16 Dec. 1765.
2. Presumably HW's missing letter *ante* ca 4 Jan. 1766.
3. Presumably made in the missing part of her letter to HW *ante* 16 Dec. 1765.
4. HW shopped at Poirier's, Du Lac's, and Said's shops for porcelain; all were in (or near) the Rue St-Honoré (F. J. B. Watson, 'Walpole and the Taste for French Porcelain,' *Horace Walpole: Writer, Politician and Connoisseur*, ed. W. H. Smith, New Haven, 1967, p. 189; see also Gustave Pessard, *Nouveau dic-*

tionnaire historique de Paris, 1904, p. 1344, for the shops there).
5. The shops in the galleries of the Palais de Justice; see ibid. 793; A. R., *The Curiosities of Paris*, 1757, pp. 47–8; [— Le Sage], *Le Géographe parisien*, 1769, i. 100. HW had visited them with the Duchess of Richmond on New Year's Eve, where they 'were trampled to death to no purpose' (HW to Duchess of Grafton 31 Jan. 1766, OSSORY i. 26; see also MORE 93; DU DEFFAND v. 291).
6. A slip for New Year's Eve (n. 5 above).

with regret that the time is over; but I hope it will not be a great while before I see it again, which will give me double pleasure, as I shall then have an opportunity of repeating the gratitude I feel, and shall always retain, for their goodness to me.

I grieve for the Dauphin, and feel quite anxious how the Queen and the Dauphiness have bore the shock of losing him.[7] I like the society you are in excessively; my Lord thinks you might have chose still better. For beauty, you might certainly, but not for conversation. The Duchesse d'Aiguillon is one of my first favourites, and I am glad you like her as much as I do. You don't mention the Prince of Conti, who I think you must like, as he is so very agreeable when he has a mind to gain anybody; and I am sure he must agree with the rest of the world in thinking you a most valuable acquisition.[8]

Lord Charlemount sailed for England last night. He is a great loss here, where there are so few men that have lived much in the world.[9] Mrs Vesey[10] is here, and inquires constantly after you. She is one of my constant morning visitors, and I like her very much. I am grown so affected as to like a woman's company much better because she has been abroad.

The holidays have been so long here that I am quite tired of them. For three weeks my Lord and the Beau Richard[11] were upon a shooting-party out of town, during which time even the beggars forsook the Castle, and there was such a gloomy stillness in it, that if I had not had an aversion to living with anybody I should have taken refuge in some of the villas near Dublin.

7. The *Gazette de Leyde* 10 Jan., *sub* Paris, 3 Jan., reported that 'Madame la Dauphine a demandé de ne voir du monde, qu'au bout de six semaines.' The death of the Dauphin also weighed heavily on the Queen, whose sorrow was aggravated by the death of her father in February; see *post* 10 March 1766.

8. HW had supped with the Prince at Mme de Luxembourg's 17 Dec., and been to his levee 3 Jan. (DU DEFFAND v. 286, 292; MORE 91; HW to Chute 7 Jan. 1766). However, any possibility of HW's becoming a member of the Prince's circle was ended after the Prince and Mme de Boufflers rebuked him 14 Jan. for his pretended letter to Rousseau from the King of Prussia (MORE 101; DU DEFFAND v. 295; GRAY ii. 156–7); HW wrote to Conway *post* 26 Dec. 1774 that the Prince 'is one

of the least to my taste; we quarrelled about Rousseau, and I never went near him after my first journey.' See also Mme de Boufflers to HW 4 May 1766; MANN vi. 434; and MORE 136.

9. Burke wrote Sir Charles Bingham 30 Oct. 1773 of Charlemont's 'cultivated taste' and 'natural elegance of mind' and commented, 'that he adorns his present residence in Ireland much the more for having resided a long time out of it' (*Correspondence*, Vol. II, ed. L. S. Sutherland, Cambridge, 1960, p. 479).

10. Elizabeth Vesey (ca 1715–91), m. 1 William Handcock; m. 2 (before 1746) Agmondesham Vesey; bluestocking; HW's occasional correspondent.

11. Fitzherbert Richards (*ante* 9 Feb. 1765, n. 12). See postscript below.

The Parliament meets next Thursday,[12] and the Tuesday after,[13] my drawing-rooms, which are not very agreeable. The deep mourning[14] puts a stop to the balls at the Castle, which is a great loss to the young people. I hear poor Lady Kildare is much better than she was, both in her health and spirits. Her eyes are better than they have been for many years, which has been a great relief to her.[15] I fear I shall have no opportunity of seeing her when she comes to settle in Dublin, as Lord Kildare does not come to the Castle.[16]

Doctor Lucas has been as troublesome to Government as it was in his power to be;[17] but I won't attempt telling you the particulars, as they are tedious, and I know I should not explain them well.

I hope Madame de Mirepoix will receive her ten pieces of paper soon;[18] I have wrote to Doctor Hunter to send it directly, and I know he has had it a great while. She insisted upon my letting her know what it cost; therefore if she asks, you will be so good as to tell her twelve pounds English, which is I believe about eleven louis and nine livres.[19] I am surprised Lady Harvey did not acknowledge the receipt of the book,[20] as I sent it to her the morning after I arrived in London. At the same time I sent the knives to Lord Rockingham,[21] and carried the parcel[22] myself to Lady Townshend, but did not find her at home.

I pity Mr Jephson[23] very much, who is a person I believe you know, at least from character. He has just lost his pension,[24] has not a hundred a year in the world, and is gone to England to marry a

12. 23 Jan. (*Journals of the House of Commons . . . Ireland*, xiv. 165–6).

13. 28 Jan.

14. For Prince Frederick William, who died 29 Dec.; see *London Gazette* Nos 10587, 10611, 28–31 Dec. 1765, 22–5 March 1766, *sub* 'Lord Chamberlain's Office,' 31 Dec., 24 March.

15. Besides suffering from chronically poor eyesight, Lady Kildare had so far gone through the rigours of bearing thirteen children and was currently pregnant with her fourteenth child, Lord Gerald, born 15 March; the previous year she had lost two of her children, Lady Louisa, aged five, and Lord Offaly, aged 17, who died 26 Sept. (see *ante* 2 Oct. 1765; Brian Fitzgerald, *Emily Duchess of Leinster 1731–1814*, 1950, pp. 115–16; *Leinster Corr.* i. 450–1).

16. See *ante* 1 Nov. 1765. However, the Hertfords did see her at Carton in May,

while Lord Kildare was in England; see *post* 25 May 1766.

17. See *ante* 13 Jan. 1766 and n. 2.

18. See *ante* 16 Dec. 1765.

19. This is just the equivalency given in *The Gentleman's Guide . . . through France*, 1788, pp. 7–8.

20. Not identified; 'I sent your Ladyship two little French pieces that I hope you received' (HW to Lady Hervey 13 Oct. 1765, MORE 60).

21. A knife purchased at Clermont for 20 livres (DU DEFFAND v. 376, 399).

22. Two knives purchased for 48 livres (ibid.).

23. Robert Jephson (1736–1803), poet and dramatist; later HW's occasional correspondent and author of *The Count of Narbonne*, a dramatic adaptation of HW's *Castle of Otranto* (see *post* 18 Nov. 1781).

24. A pension of £300 per annum on the Irish establishment procured for Ed-

Miss Barry,[25] who is ten or twelve years older than him, and who has no fortune.

We have a very fair prospect of settling our two eldest daughters very greatly here, which makes us very happy.[26] I don't dare mention more about it at present, but in about a week I fancy we shall know absolutely, and my Lord I am sure will acquaint you immediately, as you are one of our best friends; and in the meantime pray don't even give a hint of what I have said.

I would have you preserve your taste for Paris till May, but not longer, as Strawberry Hill and this family cannot dispense with your absence longer. Has Madame de Bussy[27] produced an heir to her riches? I am sure you will have the goodness to continue to express our gratitude to our friends in France. I am, with the truest regard,

Most faithfully yours,

I. HE.

[28]. . . Mr Richards[29] begs before you leave Paris that you will buy him a suit of black Vellourras[30] and have it made up for him at

mund Burke by his patron William Gerard Hamilton in 1763, the proceeds of which were assigned to Jephson in 1765. 'On the 16th December, 1765, it ceased, pursuant to his Majesty's letter of that date, and lord lieutenant's warrant thereon, dated 13th January, 1766' (statement from the vice-treasurer's office, Dublin, dated 25 Aug. 1824, quoted in James Prior, *Life of . . . Edmund Burke,* 1854, [reprint, 1968], i. 142). However, a new pension for the same amount was later secured for Jephson with, according to Charles O'Hara, 'the arrears paid up from the time of its [i.e., the former pension's] being recalled' (letter to Burke 22 Oct. 1767, quoted in Burke's *Correspondence,* Vol. I, ed. T. W. Copeland, Cambridge, 1958, p. 226, n. 3); this new pension Jephson enjoyed until his death (Martin S. Peterson, *Robert Jephson,* Lincoln, Nebraska, 1930, p. 10). The original pension had been terminated because of a quarrel between Burke and Hamilton; see ibid. 10–11; Prior, op. cit. i. 139–42; Burke, op. cit. 163–226 *passim;* T. W. Copeland, 'Burke's First Patron,' *History Today* 1952, ii. 394–9.

25. Jane Barry (?ca 1724–6 – ?after 1777),

daughter of Sir Edward Barry, an eminent Dublin physician who had left Ireland to practise in London; m. (1767) Robert Jephson (DNB; Peterson, op. cit. 14: Garrick, *Private Correspondence,* ed. Boaden, 1831–2, ii. 272).

26. See *post* 4 Feb. 1766.

27. Marie-Charlotte-Justine, Comtesse de Messey (after 1735 – ?after 1773), Chanoinesse de Mons, m. (by contract of 2 June 1765, as his second wife) Charles-Joseph Patissier de Bussy (1720–85), a commander of French forces in India who had made a fortune there and purchased the marquisate of Castelnau. They had no children (*Dictionnare de biographie française,* 1933– , vii. 721–2; La Chenaye-Desbois iv. 525, xii. 138, xiii. 786; *Répertoire . . . de la Gazette de France,* ed. de Granges de Surgères, 1902–6, i. 598; DU DEFFAND iii. 362).

28. The following fragment is apparently part of an otherwise missing continuation of the present letter; the MS is the bottom of a page, the top of which has been cut off.

29. See above, n. 11.

30. *Sic* in MS; presumably 'velours.'

DeLage the tailor's, Rue St-Marguerite. My Lord admires his[31] good nature as much as we do.[32] Col. Keene[33] has recommended himself very much, by being in great part the means of getting Lady Anne settled. I may venture to say to you it is Lord Drogheda,[34] who we are . . .[35]

To LADY AILESBURY, ca Friday 31 January 1766

Missing; listed in 'Paris Journals' (DU DEFFAND v. 379) as sent by 'Mrs Shirley' (?Mary Sturt [d. 1800], m. [1749] Hon. George Shirley, of Twickenham; see DU DEFFAND *passim*).

From HERTFORD, Tuesday 4 February 1766

Printed for the first time from a photostat of BM Add. MSS 23219, ff. 7–8. Received ca 24 Feb. (MORE 113).

Dublin Castle, February 4th 1766.

Dear Horry,

YOU are a friend to my family and will be satisfied to know anything that interests it. My two eldest daughters are going to be married: Lady Ann to Lord Drogheda,[1] who is a very unexceptionable man and I think the best match in this kingdom; the second[2] to Mr Moore,[3] who is the eldest son[4] and heir to Lord Mountcashell,[5]

---

31. Richards'.

32. George Selwyn calls him 'bien sauvage' but a 'fort honnête garçon' in a letter to Lord Carlisle 11 Oct. 1775 (Hist. MSS Comm., 15th Report, App. pt vi, *Carlisle MSS*, 1897, p. 294).

33. Whitshed Keene (ca 1731–1822), 'an Irish officer of no fortune' who had served as a colonel in the Portuguese army. 'He then went to Paris, and . . . soon became acquainted with Lord Hertford, then ambassador,' and became 'by degrees his intimate dependant' (*Last Journals* i. 382). He was made secretary to the lord chamberlain by Hertford in 1772, and was M.P. Wareham 1768–74, Ludgershall 1774, and Montgomery 1774–1818 (ibid.; Namier and Brooke iii. 3). He was a friend of

Richards (see *Carlisle MSS*, pp. 294, 483, 537).

34. See *post* 4 Feb. 1766.

35. The remainder of this sentence apparently ran on to a new page, which is missing.

1. Lady Anne Seymour Conway married Charles Moore, 6th E. of Drogheda, 15 Feb. 1766. According to Lady Elizabeth Laura Waldegrave to Anne Clement, 22 June 1794, Lord Hertford gave his married daughters dowries of £6000 each (MS now WSL).

2. Lady Sarah Frances Seymour Conway.

3. Stephen Moore (1730–90), who became 2d Vct Mountcashell upon the death

an old infirm man with a very considerable estate. This young gentleman has the advantage of a very good character and great connection; indeed I know of no defect except his having been bred up too much with his family and not having that advantage in his behaviour which a more public education would have given him. It is a circumstance one would wish to change, but it is not essential if his wife does not think it so, and his figure is good enough to satisfy any woman.

The eldest may possibly be married next week; the other is not so far advanced and the settlements are to undergo a father's approbation, but he has sent me word he would do everything that was right to merit the connection.

Lady Hertford has been seriously ill of a disorder in her bowels, but is now quite recovered and only looks thin. My son[6] has likewise been confined with the mumps. I have just got a vacant ensigncy in the 26th Regiment of Foot upon this establishment, for which I will recommend Mr Fitzgerald.[7] The business of this country goes on as I can wish it. The opponents to Government have tried by little arts to disturb it, but they have not succeeded, and I believe will find it very difficult. Tell me all the news of Paris and when you will come home. I remain, with the best compliments of the family, dear Horry,

Ever yours,

HERTFORD

To HERTFORD, ca Wednesday 5 February 1766

Missing; listed in 'Paris Journals' (DU DEFFAND v. 379) as sent by 'Colonel Gordon' (probably Hon. William Gordon [1736–1816], Lt-Col. 105th Ft 1762; half-pay 1763; see MORE 103; Namier and Brooke ii. 518–19).

of Lord Mountcashell 26 Feb.; cr. (1781) E. Mountcashell. The marriage did not take place, Lady Sarah later in the year marrying Robert Stewart, afterwards Bn Londonderry; see *post* 21, 25 May 1766.
  4. An elder brother, Richard, had died in 1761.
  5. Stephen Moore (1695 – 26 Feb. 1766), cr. (1764) Bn Kilworth of Moore Park

and (22 Jan. 1766) Vct Mountcashell.
  6. Lord Beauchamp.
  7. George Robert Fitzgerald (*ante* 1 Nov. 1765, n. 27). Two vacant ensigncies in the 26th were filled by George Cuppaidge and Edw. Pearce Willington 18 April and 16 May; Fitzgerald was given a lieutenancy in the 69th Foot 5 Nov. (*Army Lists* 1767, pp. 80, 124).

To Conway, ca Friday 14 February 1766

Missing; listed in 'Paris Journals' (DU DEFFAND v. 379) as sent 'by messenger. long letter.'

To Conway, ca Monday 17 February 1766

Missing; listed in 'Paris Journals' (DU DEFFAND v. 379) as sent 'by Duke of Richmond,' who went on leave and did not return (see D. B. Horn, *British Diplomatic Representatives 1689–1789*, 1932, p. 22).

To Lady Ailesbury, ca Monday 17 February 1766

Missing; listed in 'Paris Journals' (DU DEFFAND v. 379) as sent 'by Duke of Richmond.'

To Hertford, ca Monday 24 February 1766

Missing; listed in 'Paris Journals' (DU DEFFAND v. 380) as sent by 'young Elliots' (Gilbert and Hugh Elliot; see *ante* 28 July 1764, n. 6). Apparently written in reply to Hertford's letter *ante* 4 Feb. 1766 (MORE 113).

To Conway, ca Monday 24 February 1766

Missing; listed in 'Paris Journals' (DU DEFFAND v. 380) as sent by 'young Elliots.'

To Conway, ca Thursday 6 March 1766

Missing; listed in 'Paris Journals' (DU DEFFAND v. 380) as sent 'by M. de Lillebonne' (*ante* 9 March 1765).

To Hertford, Monday 10 March 1766

Sent 13 March 'by Mr Jennings'; received 2 April (DU DEFFAND v. 380; *post* 2 April 1766). Printed from the MS, now WSL. First printed in Toynbee, *Supp.* i. 126–9. The MS was sold Sotheby 2 Dec. 1910 (Autograph Letters and Historical Documents Sale), Lot 101 (with ten other HW letters), to B. F. Stevens. It belonged ca 1918 to Messrs Dodd and Livingston, N.Y.C. (Toynbee *Supp.* i. 126, n.), and was bought ca 1922 by Alfred C. Meyer of Chicago. It was sold AAAA 13 Jan. 1938 to Retz and Storm, N.Y.C.; resold April 1940 to Mrs Frank F. Dodge, Stonington, Conn., who bequeathed it to WSL 1964.

Paris, March 10th 1766.

IF ever there was a beast, and a brute and an ungrateful monster, I am one; I am all these, and deserve as many names as a sentimental woman calls a lover that quits her. What can you think of me, when I literally *forgot* to thank you for your kindness to Mr Fitzgerald?[1] I don't haggle about it, nor pretend to excuse myself. It rushed into my head last night, and I have blushed ever since. I might pretend that the marriages of your daughters, and the Parliament of England,[2] and my dissipation here, put it out of my head— perhaps they did; but would that be an excuse? No, there is none for ingratitude; and I think, to punish me you should make *me* an ensign, instead of Mr Fitzgerald; I should not forget it again in haste. If *he* forgets your goodness, I shall not wonder: he receives benefit by it—but I that only received an obligation! There is no precedent for *such* ingratitude. Well, as most people thank and forget, I hope that I who have not thanked, shall remember.

The weather is at last fine, and just now I am confined again. It is called an inflammation in my eyes,[3] but I say of the gout; as Lady Dorchester[4] said to Ratcliffe,[5] 'Doctor, whatever illness I have, always

1. Apparently in his missing letter *ante* ca 24 Feb. 1766 answering Hertford's letter *ante* 4 Feb. 1766. HW mentions his distress at this omission also to Lady Hervey (Fitzgerald's grandmother) 10 March 1766; see MORE 113.

2. Parliament was debating the repeal of the Stamp Act and related matters; the repeal bill had passed the Commons 4 March, was passed by the Lords 17 March, and enacted 18 March as 6 Geo. III c. 11 (*Journals of the House of Commons* xxx.

627, 667; *Journals of the House of Lords* xxxi. 313–14; Owen Ruffhead, *Statutes at Large*, 1763–1800, x. 152).

3. Which he had contracted 7 March; he was visiting again the 11th ('Paris Journals,' DU DEFFAND v. 306–7).

4. Catherine Sedley (1657–1717), mistress of James II, who made her Cts of Dorchester in 1686; m. (1696) Sir David Colyear, 2d Bt, cr. (1699) Bn Portmore and (1703) E. of Portmore.

5. John Radcliffe (1650–1714), physician.

have an eye to the pox.'[6] The gout is such a harlequin, that it wears any dress, and skips from one place to another. It is not quite prudent to write with this disorder, but it is going off, and I am impatient to show you that my ingratitude is gone off too.

There has been a violent clap of thunder here. T'other morning[7] the King, with all his lightnings about him, appeared suddenly in the parliament, ordered four privy councillors, not peers,[8] to follow him into the chamber and sit at his feet,[9] where he bid them read a *Discours*,[10] in which he informed the giants, that they are nothing but magistrates and rebels, and that he alone is Jupiter Omnipotent and Omniscient.[11] He forbids union with the Titans of other parliaments,[12] and prohibits their forging and printing any more remonstrances in Ætna. They may whisper in his divine ear, but no more murmurs.[13] He then dispatched a courier to Roan,[14] for three presidents, whom he sent back again still more haughtily, only referring them to his *Discours*.[15] As he crossed the Pont Neuf, he met his neighbour the Bon Dieu, lighted from his eagle, kneeled down in the

6. For other anecdotes of Lady Dorchester, see Ossory ii. 528–9 and n. 25, and *Works* iv. 315–16 and n. 1.

7. 3 March.

8. Jean-Baptiste Paulin d'Aguesseau, Pierre Gilbert de Voisins, Louis-Jean Bertier de Sauvigny, and Jean-François Joly de Fleury, conseillers d'état, along with the Comte de St Florentin, ministre et secrétaire d'état (*Mercure historique*, 1766, clx. 295–6, 303; *Almanach royal*, 1766, pp. 142–64 *et passim*).

9. 'In a place where they had no right' (*Mem. Geo. III* ii. 177); see *Mercure*, clx. 297.

10. Printed in *Remontrances du Parlement de Paris au XVIIIe siècle*, ed. Jules Flammermont and Maurice Tourneux, 1888–98, ii. 556–9. It was read by Joly de Fleury (ibid. 556), and was in response to a series of remonstrances of the parliament of Paris against the King's treatment of the parliaments of Rennes and Pau; see ibid. 485–530, 534–54.

11. 'C'est en ma personne seule que réside la puissance souveraine . . . C'est de moi seul que mes cours tiennent leur existence et leur autorité . . . la plénitude de cette autorité, qu'elles n'exercent qu'en mon nom, demeure toujours en moi,' etc.

(ibid. 557). The *séance* of this day became famous as the 'séance de la flagellation' (É. Glasson, *Le Parlement de Paris*, 1901, ii. 315).

12. 'Je ne souffrirai pas qu'il se forme dans mon royaume une association qui ferait dégénérer en une confédération de résistance le lien naturel des . . . devoirs et des obligations communes' (Flammermont and Tourneux, op. cit. ii. 556).

13. 'Les remontrances seront toujours reçues favorablement quand elles ne respireront que cette modération qui fait le caractère du magistrat et de la vérité, quand le secret en conservera la décence et l'utilité, et quand cette voie si sagement établie ne se trouvera pas travestie en libelles' (ibid. 558).

14. *Sic* in MS; presumably 'Rouen.' See next note.

15. On 4 March the King received a deputation of 13 members of the parliament of Rouen, rebuked them for their remonstrances of 22 Aug. 1765 and 15 Feb. 1766, and referred them to 'les vrais principes' contained in 'la réponse que j'ai faite à mon parlement de Paris. Qu'elle vous serve de règle' (*Mercure*, clx. 304–5; A. Floquet, *Histoire du parlement de Normandie*, 1840–2, vi. 529–31).

dirt, and as Trincalo says in *The Tempest*,[16] acknowledged the vice-roy over him.[17] The new god's back was no sooner turned, than Messieurs the Titans appointed a committee to consider what was to be done. They sat several days and nights—and what do you think was the first thing they determined—to send three of their body, now shrunk like Milton's devils to pygmies,[18] to condole on the death of King Stanislas.[19] A voice from a cloud said, 'Je n'ai que faire de vos condoléances.'[20] Well, they sent again to beg to know when the god might be approached? 'What have you to say?' 'We don't know.' 'Return and bring me word.' They went, came, and said, 'Our soul is humbled to the dust, hear us, good Lord, hear us!' Jupiter named seven o'clock last night;[21] forty-two commissioners went with a collect of repentance, to which, it is said, they have tacked a remonstrance ten times stronger than their former; and thus have stolen a march upon omniscience.[22] The supreme power can play the jockey too: the *avocats* at Rennes refused to plead before the *soi-disant parlement*.[23] They have been ordered to ballot for the militia.[24]

I tell you all this, my dear King, that you may make the compari-

16. HW is referring loosely to the following passage: '*Stephano* [to Caliban]. Monster, I will kill this man [Prospero]: his daughter and I will be king and queen, save our Graces: and Trinculo and thyself shall be viceroys: Dost thou like the plot, Trinculo? *Trinculo*. Excellent' (*Tempest* III. ii. 112–16).

17. This happened on 3 March. 'A son retour du palais, le Roi rencontra, au bout du Pont Neuf, le St Sacrement qu'un prêtre de la paroisse de St Germain l'Auxerrois portait à un malade; S. M. descendit précipitamment de son carosse et se jetta à genoux sur le pavé, qui, dans cet endroit, était couvert de boue: ce qui fit redoubler les cris de *Vive le Roi*' (*Mercure*, clx. 304; see also Flammermont and Tourneux, op. cit. ii. 555, 560, nn.).

18. *Paradise Lost* I. 777–81.

19. Stanislas I (Leszczýnski) (1677–23 Feb. 1766), K. of Poland 1704–9, 1733; D. of Lorraine and Bar 1737–66; father-in-law of Louis XV. He died of burns suffered when he fell into the fire 5 Feb.; see HW to Mann 1 March 1766, MANN vi. 402–4 and nn. 15–16.

20. 'Dans l'assemblée du 6 mars, on lut une lettre par laquelle le Comte de St-Florentin marquait au parlement que le Roi le dispensait de le complimenter sur la mort du Roi de Pologne' (*Mercure*, clx. 438).

21. 9 March.

22. See ibid. clx. 427–8. In their remonstrance, printed Flammermont and Tourneux, op. cit. ii. 561, they protested against the severity of the King's response of the 3d and against the publicity given to it; for this, they were again rebuked (ibid. 561–2).

23. Under pressure from the parliament of Paris the King, who had substituted a royal commission for the parliament of Rennes (see *ante* 5 Dec. 1765 and n. 4), had restored that parliament; however, his ministers had arranged it so that it was now fewer in number and composed of members 'plus soumis à la Cour' (Emmanuel, Duc de Croÿ, *Journal inédit*, ed. Grouchy and Cottin, 1906–7, ii. 226; see also *Mercure*, clx. 197, 445; A. Le Moy, *Le Parlement de Bretagne et le pouvoir royal au XVIIIe siècle*, 1909, pp. 352–7).

24. Under this threat they resumed service 8 April; see ibid. 358; *Mercure*, clx. 446.

son of how much pleasanter it is to govern by gaining the hearts of subjects.

The Prince of Montauban[25] is dead and Madame de Lambert.[26] The Queen has been in great danger with an inflammation in her lungs, but is said to be out of danger; but one never knows the truth about gods till they are dead.[27]

That odious horse-race,[28] which I mentioned to you in my last,[29] has created, or brought out, most disagreeable animosities between the two nations. Lauragais's horse was taken ill on the very morning, ran, but could not complete the course and died that evening. It was affirmed that a jury of farriers swore it was poisoned, but they only said that a drink which had been given to it, had occasioned its death. As Lauragais is a bit of a chemist and a good deal of a quack,[30] he probably killed his horse by some invigorating measures; the more moderate accuse an English groom of patriot jealousy, but most of the French tax Lord Forbes himself. In short, they have been very impertinent.[31] Lauragais disappeared in two days, for which different reasons are assigned. He is certainly in England, as he told Lord George,[32] on information that a *lettre de cachet* was issued against him, at his father's[33] request. There are many more circumstances re-

25. Charles de Rohan (1693 – 25 Feb. 1766), Prince de Rohan-Montauban (La Chenaye-Desbois xvii. 515).

26. Louise-Thérèse de Menou (1714 – 28 Feb. 1766), m. (1740) Henri-François de Lambert (DU DEFFAND *passim*). HW described her to John Craufurd 6 March 1766 as 'one of the worst' of the hypocrites who abused Mme du Deffand behind her back while pretending to be her friend.

27. She was suffering from a cold and fever, and had a relapse in April, but recovered again and did not die until 1768. Her illness, aggravated by the deaths of her son, the Dauphin, and her father, King Stanislas, had been so serious at the beginning of March that she was given last rites. See SELWYN 218–19 and n. 20; *post* 8 April 1766; and DU DEFFAND i. 5.

28. Run 25 Feb. between the Comte de Lauraguais and Lord Forbes on the *plaine de Sablon* near the Bois de Boulogne ('Paris Journals,' ibid. v. 304; COLE i. 109–10).

29. HW's missing letter *ante* ca 24 Feb. 1766; evidently HW wrote of his intention of seeing the race, since the race took place after that letter was written. Lauraguais was Hertford's former landlord at Paris (see *ante* 22 March 1764), while Forbes was the young man who had courted his daughter, Lady Anne, the year before (see *ante* 20 June 1765).

30. See *ante* 22 March 1764, n. 8.

31. For further details of the race and its aftermath, see COLE loc. cit.; MORE 107; and HW to John Craufurd 6 March 1766.

32. Lord George Henry Lennox (1737–1805), brother of the Duke of Richmond; army officer; M.P. He was currently secretary to his brother at Paris, had stayed behind as chargé d'affaires after the Duke's departure for England 17 Feb., and was named minister plenipotentiary 1 July, which post he held until October (*ante* ca 17 Feb. 1766; D. B. Horn, *British Diplomatic Representatives 1689–1789*, 1932, p. 23).

33. Louis de Brancas (1714–93), Duc de Villars-Brancas (DU DEFFAND iii. 61, n. 23). Lauraguais was on bad terms with both his father and his wife: see *ante* 22 March 1764 and n. 7.

lating to this whole affair which I will tell you when we meet—at present, my eyes beg to be excused.

Your ungrateful cousin,

H. Walpole

To Conway, ca Friday 14 March 1766

Missing; listed in 'Paris Journals' (du Deffand v. 380) as sent by 'Mr Sackville,' possibly John Frederick Sackville (1745–99), 3d Duke of Dorset, 1769.

To Conway, ca Friday 21 March 1766

Missing; listed in 'Paris Journals' (du Deffand v. 380) as sent 'by messenger.'

To Lady Ailesbury, ca Friday 28 March 1766

Missing; listed in 'Paris Journals' (du Deffand v. 381) as sent 'by a Swiss.'

To Lady Ailesbury, ca Monday 31 March 1766

Missing; listed in 'Paris Journals' (du Deffand v. 381) as sent 'by the post.'

From Lady Hertford, Wednesday 2 April 1766

Printed for the first time from a photostat of BM Add. MSS 23219, ff. 9–10. *Address:* To the Honourable Horatio Walpole in Arlington Street, London. *Postmark:* 2 AP FREE. DUBLIN.

Dear Mr Walpole,

MY Lord won't write to you, because he is doubtful whether you are at Paris or in London;[1] I write on purpose to tell you it grieves me that you have forsaken me; for I had flattered myself I

1. HW was at Paris till 17 April (*post* 8 April 1766, n. 39).

had possessed a great share of your esteem, and you could not have bestowed it on one who would have valued it more. Perhaps it will not occur to you that I have cause of accusation; but I am so anxious about my friends that I am easily alarmed. It is three months since I wrote to you,[2] since which time you have not taken any notice of me; and even in a letter my Lord got from you today,[3] you did not say one kind word to me. I am heartily sorry to hear the gout still plagues you, but I hope soon to hear you are perfectly well in London. The recess begins tomorrow, and the Houses are adjourned to the 28th of April;[4] we shall all be glad to get to England, but don't expect it till the end of May. My Lord and my son desire to be remembered kindly to you; their reign goes on gloriously, and they are quite happy and in perfect health.

You would be pleased to see how much my daughter[5] is already settled in a family way,[6] and is vastly happy and satisfied. She and Lord Drogheda are gone out of town today for the holidays, to his sisters.[7] Excuse my writing in such a hurry, as the packet-boat is going to sail; adieu, dear Sir, repent of your ingratitude, and believe me at all times

Your most faithful and affectionate

I. HE.

We go to Lisburn on Monday[8] for a fortnight or three weeks.

2. Lady Hertford had last written to HW *ante* 20 Jan. 1766.

3. HW's letter *ante* 10 March 1766.

4. The Commons had adjourned 27 March; see *Journals of the House of Commons . . . Ireland* xiv. 248.

5. Lady Anne, now Countess of Drogheda.

6. Her first child, Lady Isabella, was born 22 Nov. (Mervyn Archdall and John Lodge, *Peerage of Ireland*, 1789, ii. 115).

7. Lady Sarah Moore (d. 1778), m. (1748) William Pole of Ballyfin, Queen's County; and his half-sister Lady Lucy Moore (b. 1739). Another half-sister, Lady Alice, b. 1740, died young (ibid. ii. 114, iii. 69).

8. 7 April.

To Conway, Sunday 6 April 1766

Sent 7 April 'by the post' ('Paris Journals,' DU DEFFAND v. 381; *post* 8 April 1766); printed from *Works* v. 130–2.

Paris, April 6, 1766.

IN a certain city of Europe[1] it is the custom to wear slouched hats, long cloaks and high capes. Scandal and the government called this dress, *going in mask,* and pretended that it contributed to assassination.[2] An *ordonnance* was published,[3] commanding free-born hats to be cocked, cloaks to be shortened, and capes laid aside. All the world obeyed for the first day;[4] but the next everything returned into its old channel. In the evening[5] a tumult arose, and cries of 'God bless the King! God bless the kingdom! but confusion to the Prime Minister.'[6]—The word was no sooner given, but his house was beset, the windows broken, and the gates attempted. The guards came and fired on the *weavers*[7] of cloaks. The weavers returned the fire, and many fell on each side.[8] As the hour of supper approached and the mob grew hungry, they recollected a tax upon bread,[9] and demanded

1. Madrid.
2. The Marchese di Squillace (see below, n. 6) made this claim in a letter to Roda, the Spanish minister of justice, 21 Feb. 1766 (Archives of Simancas, Gracia y Justicia 790, cited in Ludwig, Freiherr von Pastor, *History of the Popes,* Vol. XXXVII, trans. E. F. Peeler, 1950, p. 49 and n. 2).
3. 10 March 1766 (ibid. 48, 49 and n. 1).
4. Actually for 13 days, though there were minor insubordinations; see ibid. 49–50.
5. Actually the afternoon, of 23 March (ibid. 50).
6. Squillace, an Italian, whom the King was obliged to banish (HW). The cry was 'Viva el Rey! Viva España! Muera Esquilache!' (Antonio Ferrer del Rio, *Historia del reinado de Carlos III en España,* Madrid, 1856, ii. 14–15). The Marchese di Squillace was Charles III's minister of finance and war (*ante* 5 Dec. 1765, n. 23). Aside from the unpopularity of certain of his measures, he was hated as a foreigner, and suspected of enriching himself at the

expense of the people (Pastor, op. cit. 49 and nn. 4, 5).
7. Alluding to the mobs of silk-weavers which had taken place this year in London (HW). The weavers had rioted in May when a bill for their relief was thrown out of the House of Lords; they had besieged the house of the Duke of Bedford, who had been responsible for the bill's rejection. See *ante* 20 May 1765.
8. Actually, the tumult began when two men dressed in defiance of the edict resisted attempts by the hated Walloon Guards to arrest them. The Guards were overpowered by a mob which came to the support of the two men, and this mob then moved on to Squillace's house, intending to murder him. Squillace, however, had escaped in disguise to the royal palace (Pastor, op. cit. 50; cf. *Annual Register,* 1766, pp. 15–16).
9. An increase in the prices of bread, oil and wine, caused by a series of summer droughts, but blamed upon the machinations of Squillace (Grimaldi to Choiseul, 2 April 1766, Archives of Sim-

the *repeal*.[10] The King yielded to both requests, and hats and loaves were set at liberty.[11] The people were not contented, and still insisted on the permission of murdering the first minister;[12] though his Majesty assured his faithful commons that the minister was never consulted on acts of government, and was only his private friend, who sometimes called upon him in an evening to drink a glass of wine and talk botany.[13] The people were incredulous, and continued in mutiny when the last letters came away.[14]

If you should happen to suppose, as I did, that this *history* arrived in London, do not be alarmed; for it was at Madrid; and a nation who has borne the Inquisition cannot support a cocked hat!— So necessary it is for governors to know when lead or a feather will turn the balance of human understandings, or will not.

I should not have entrenched on Lord George's[15] province of sending you news of revolutions, but he is at Aubigné;[16] and I thought it right to advertise you in time, in case you should have a mind to send a bale of slouched hats to the support of the mutineers. As I have worn a flapped hat all my life, when I have worn any at all, I think myself qualified, and would offer my service to command them; but being persuaded that you are a faithful observer of treaties, though a friend to repeals,[17] I shall come and receive your commands in person. In the meantime I cannot help figuring what a pompous protest my Lord Lyttelton might draw up in the character of an old grandee against the revocation of the act for cocked hats.[18]

Lady A. forgot to send me word of your recovery, as she promised;

---

ancas, Estado 4557, cited Pastor, op. cit. 49 and n. 3; cf. *Annual Register*, p. 15).

10. An allusion to the Stamp Act, whose repeal had been ordered by Act of Parliament 18 March (*ante* 10 March 1766, n. 2).

11. The demands of the mob, including a demand for the banishment of Squillace, were made and granted 24 March; see *post* 8 April 1766.

12. Actually, as the note above indicates, the mob's lust for Squillace's blood had abated by the time they presented their demands to the King.

13. This last, pure fiction with respect to Charles III and Squillace, is meant as an allusion to George III and Lord Bute, who was fond of botany; after Bute left office King George continually denied be-

ing influenced by him, but was generally disbelieved.

14. For subsequent developments, see *post* 8 April 1766.

15. Lord George Lenox, only brother to the Duke of Richmond (HW).

16. The Duke of Richmond's country seat in France (HW).

17. Conway had moved the question for the repeal of the Stamp Act 21 Feb., and brought in the bill 26 Feb. (MANN vi. 404, nn. 35–6).

18. Lyttelton had drawn up one or both of the two protests lodged against the repeal of the Stamp Act in the House of Lords; see ibid. vi. 410 and *Mem. Geo. III* ii. 218. These protests are printed *Journals of the House of Lords* xxxi. 303–5, 311–13.

but I was so lucky as to hear it from other hands.[19] Pray take care of yourself, and do not imagine that you are as weak as I am, and can escape the scythe, as I do by being low:[19a] your life is of more consequence. If you don't believe me, step into the street and ask the first man you meet.

This is Sunday, and Thursday[20] is fixed for my departure; unless the Clairon should return to the stage on Tuesday sennight,[21] as is said;[22] and I do not know whether I should not be tempted to borrow two or three days more, having never seen her:[23] yet my lilacs[24] pull hard, and I have not a farthing left in the world.[25] Be sure you do not leave a cranny open for George Grenville to wriggle in, till I have got all my things out of the custom-house. Adieu!

Yours ever,

HOR. WALPOLE

19. Conway had been ill since the latter part of March from a 'scorbutic eruption' which turned to a cold and fever; characteristically careless during his convalescence, he did not recover fully until the latter part of April. See MANN vi. 413, 416, and Ross J. S. Hoffman, *Edmund Burke, New York Agent*, Philadelphia, 1956, p. 343.

19a. 'Grass, that escapes the scythe by being low,' a poetic quotation that appears also in CHUTE 218.

20. 10 April; he did not leave until the 17th (*post* 8 April 1766, n. 39).

21. 15 April.

22. See *ante* 29 April 1765. 'Mlle Clairon . . . s'était engagée à remonter sur le théâtre, supposé qu'on accordât aux comédiens l'état de citoyen, que moins la loi qu'un reste de préjugé et d'opinion gothique leur refuse. Lorsque cette af-

faire a été proposé au conseil du roi [5 April], avec le projet d'ériger la Comédie-Française en académie royale, quelques-uns de conseil ont observé que les privilèges accordés aux comédiens par Louis XIII n'ayant pas été révoqués, il ne tenait qu'à eux de les faire valoir dans l'occasion. Sur quoi le roi a décidé qu'il n'y avait rien à innover à cet égard.' Upon which 'Mlle Clairon . . . [a redemandé] de nouveau sa retraite,' which was granted her (Grimm, *Correspondance*, ed. Tourneux, 1877–82, vii. 10; see also ibid. vi. 356, 492, and Louis Petit de Bachaumont, *Mémoires secrets*, 1780–9, iii. 8, 11, 15, 17, 19, 24).

23. HW first saw her act at Mme du Deffand's in Aug. 1767 ('Paris Journals,' DU DEFFAND v. 316).

24. At Strawberry Hill.

25. Because of his extravagant purchases.

To Conway, Tuesday 8 April 1766

Sent 10 April 'by Lord Tavistock' ('Paris Journals,' DU DEFFAND v. 381); printed from *Works* v. 132–4.

Paris, April 8, 1766.

I SENT you a few lines[1] by the post yesterday, with the first accounts of the insurrection at Madrid. I have since seen Stahremberg, the Imperial minister, who has had a courier from thence; and if Lord Rochford[2] has not sent one, you will not be sorry to know more particulars. The mob disarmed the invalids;[3] stopped all coaches, to prevent Squillace's flight; and meeting the Duke de Medina Celi,[4] forced him and the Duke d'Arcos[5] to carry their demands to the King.[6] His most frightened Majesty granted them directly; on which his Highness the people dispatched a monk[7] with their demands in writing, couched in four[8] articles: the diminution of the gabel on bread and oil; the revocation of the *ordonnance* on hats and cloaks; the banishment of Squillace; and the abolition of some other tax, I don't know what.[9] The King signed all; yet was still forced to appear in a balcony, and promise to observe what he had granted.[10] Squillace was sent with an escort to Carthagena, to

1. *Ante* 6 April 1766.
2. The English minister at Madrid.
3. According to the *Annual Register*, 1766, p. 16, and the Conde de Fernan-Núñez (*Vida de Carlos III*, ed. Morel-Fatio and Paz y Mélia, Madrid, 1898, i. 202), this happened 25 March, after the flight of the King to Aranjuez (see below); HW implies that it happened 24 March, before the flight.
4. Luis Antonio Fernández de Córdova-Figueroa de la Cerda (1703–68), Duque de Medinaceli (*Enciclopedia universal ilustrada*, Barcelona, [1905–33], xxxiv. 139; *Genealog. hist. Nachrichten*, 1768–9, 3d ser. viii. 487–8).
5. Antonio Ponce de Léon y Spinola (1726–80), Duque de Arcos; general (*Enciclopedia universal ilustrada*, xlvi. 252).
6. 24 March. The Dukes had been sent by the King to pacify the mob (Ludwig, Freiherr von Pastor, *History of the Popes*, Vol. XXXVII, trans. E. F. Peeler, 1950, pp. 50–1).

7. Yecla, Prior of San Juan in La Mancha (ibid. 51–2).
8. Eight.
9. There were five other articles: (1) The formation of a ministry of Spaniards; (2) the dissolution of the food commission; (3) the withdrawal of the Walloon Guards; (4) general pardon for all that had occurred; and (5) the King's assent to this petition to be given in the Plaza Mayor ('Capitulaciones del pueblo de Madrid con el Rey el dia 24 de Marzo de 1766,' MS in the Archives of the Province of Toledo in Madrid, Chamartin, P, cited in Pastor, op. cit. 51 and n. 4).
10. This public appearance was one of the eight original demands, not a later one (n. 9 above). The King had at first hesitated to appear for fear of his life, simply instructing Yecla to assure the people of his good will, but agreed to it after conferring with his entourage, and at this time gave his assent to the petition (Pastor, op. cit. 52).

embark for Naples,[11] and the first *commis* of the Treasury[12] appointed to succeed him;[13] which does not look much like observation of the conditions.[14] Some say Ensenada[15] is recalled, and that Grimaldi[16] is in no good odour with the people.[17] If the latter and Squillace are dismissed, we get rid of two enemies.

The tumult ceased on the grant of the demands; but the King retiring that night[18] to Aranjuez, the insurrection was renewed the next morning, on pretence that this flight was a breach of the capitulation.[19] The people seized the gates of the capital, and permitted nobody to go out.[20] In this state were things when the courier came away.[21] The *ordonnance* against going in disguise looks as if some suspicions had been conceived; and yet their confidence was so great as not to have 2,000 guards in the town. The pitiful behaviour of the

11. He fled with the King to Aranjuez (see below), whence he departed 27 March for Cartagena. He embarked for Naples 24 April, arriving there 5 or 6 May (Pastor, op. cit. 54; MANN vi. 414, n. 10).

12. Miguel de Muzquiz (b. 1719), later Conde de Gausa (Fernan-Núñez, op. cit. i. 203; Antonio Ferrer del Rio, *Historia del reinado de Carlos III en España*, Madrid, 1856, ii. 52 and n. 1).

13. As minister of finance; he was succeeded as minister of war by Juan Gregorio Muniain (b. ca 1700), commanding general of Estremadura (ibid.; Fernan-Núñez, loc. cit.). The real prime minister after Squillace's downfall was the Conde de Aranda, named President of the Council of Castile (Pastor, loc. cit.).

14. HW is apparently assuming that the 'first *commis*' would be Squillace's man; however, Muzquiz was a native-born Spaniard, and is described by Fernan-Núñez, loc. cit., as an 'hombre honrado.'

15. Zénon de Somodevilla y Bengoechea (1702–81), Marqués de la Ensenada. An able minister of finance under Ferdinand VI, he had, due to a palace intrigue, been disgraced in 1754. His banishment was lifted by Charles III in 1760, but he was not restored to power. Cheered by the rioters in the present revolt, he was represented to the King as an ambitious person who was taking advantage of the opportunity to regain power; Tanucci, the King's former tutor and most trusted confidant, called him

'il più gran fomentatore' of the revolt in a letter to Cattolica of 24 June 1766 (MS in Archives of Simancas, Estado 5997). As a result, instead of being restored to power, he was banished again 19 April (*Enciclopedia universal ilustrada*, lvii. 348–9; Pastor, op. cit. 61 and n. 3).

16. The minister of foreign affairs (*ante* 5 Dec. 1765, n. 24).

17. An Italian like Squillace, his house was attacked after Squillace's the first night of the revolt (Pastor, op. cit. 50–1). However, though one of the demands of the people was for a 'ministry of Spaniards,' which would exclude Grimaldi, he remained in his post.

18. The night of 24–5 March (ibid. 52; *Annual Register*, p. 16).

19. The people were offended by the King's doubting their fidelity, and feared that troops would close in on Madrid, that the concessions would be withdrawn, and that the rioters would be punished (Pastor, op. cit. 52; *Annual Register*, pp. 16–17).

20. 'A large body of the populace, consisting of 10,000 men, . . . surrounded the city, and suffered neither carriage, mule, or man to go out' (ibid. 16).

21. The same day a messenger was dispatched to Aranjuez, who brought back assurances from the King that he would keep the promises he had made the day before; this satisfied the populace, and the revolt came to an end. See Pastor op. cit. 52–3; *Annual Register*, p. 17.

Court makes one think that the Italians[22] were frightened, and that the Spanish part of the ministry were not sorry it took that turn. As I suppose there is no great city in Spain which has not at least a bigger bundle of grievances than the capital, one shall not wonder if the pusillanimous behaviour of the King encourages them to redress themselves too.[23]

There is what is called a change of the ministry here; but it is only a crossing over and figuring in. The Duc de Praslin has wished to retire for some time; and for this last fortnight there has been much talk of his being replaced by the Duc d'Aiguillon, the Duc de Nivernois, etc.; but it is plain, though not believed till *now,* that the Duc de Choiseul is all-powerful.[24] To purchase the stay of his cousin Praslin, on whom he can depend, and to leave no cranny open, he has ceded the marine and colonies to the Duc de Praslin, and taken the foreign and military department himself.[25] His cousin is besides named *chef du conseil des finances;*[26] a very honourable, very dignified and very idle place, and never filled since the Duc de Béthune[27] had it. Praslin's hopeful cub the Viscount,[28] whom you saw in England last year,[29] goes to Naples,[30] and the Marquis de Durfort,[31] to Vienna[32]—a cold, dry, proud man, with the figure and manner of Lord Cornbury.[33]

Great matters are expected today from the parliament, which reassembles. A *mousquetaire,* his piece loaded with a *lettre de cachet,* went about a fortnight ago to the notary who keeps the parliamentary

22. Squillace and Grimaldi.

23. Riots broke out also in Saragossa, Barcelona, Salamanca, Murcia, Corunna, and Ascoitia. In every case the major grievance was the increased cost of food (Pastor, op. cit. 53).

24. He remained in power until 1770; see *post* 29 Dec. 1770.

25. See *Almanach royal,* 1766, pp. 144–5; 1767, p. 144. Choiseul already had the military department.

26. See ibid. 1766, p. 143; 1767, p. 143.

27. Paul-François de Béthune (1682–1759), Duc de Béthune-Charost; chef du conseil royal des finances 1746–59 (La Chenaye-Desbois iii. 123–4; *Almanach royal* 1746–59 *passim*).

28. De Choiseul, Praslin's son (*ante* 10 April 1765).

29. See *ante* 10, 18 April 1765.

30. In the place of the Marquis de Durfort, ambassador there since 1760. His instructions are dated 1 Nov. 1766; he was ambassador at Naples until 1771 (*Recueil des instructions données aux ambassadeurs . . . Naples et Parme,* ed. Joseph Reinach, 1893, pp. 85, 104–5).

31. Émeric-Joseph de Durfort-Civrac (1716–87), Marquis de Durfort, later Duc de Civrac (DU DEFFAND *passim; Répertoire . . . de la Gazette de France,* ed. de Granges de Surgères, 1902–6, ii. 340).

32. His instructions are dated 21 Sept. 1766; he was ambassador there until 1770 (*Recueil des instructions données aux ambassadeurs . . . Autriche,* ed. Albert Sorel, 1884, pp. 411, 439). For all the foregoing changes, see *Mercure historique,* 1766, clx. 448–9.

33. Henry Hyde (1710–53), styled Vct Cornbury (*ante* 16 Feb. 1741 OS).

registers, and demanded them. They were refused—but given up, on the *lettre de cachet* being produced.[34] The parliament intends to try the notary for breach of trust,[35] which I suppose will make his fortune; though he has not the merit of perjury like Carteret Webb.[36]

There have been insurrections at Bourdeaux and Toulouse, on the militia,[37] and 27 persons were killed at the latter: but both are appeased. These things are so much in vogue, that I wonder the French do not dress *à la revolte.*

The Queen is in a very dangerous way.[38]

This will be my last letter; but I am not sure I shall set out before the middle of next week.[39]

Yours ever,

Hor. Walpole

34. 'Le . . . 27 mars, lendemain du jour où le parlement était entré en vacance, un huissier de la Chaine fut trouver M. le Breton, greffier du criminel du parlement, pour lui signifier un arrêt du conseil, qui ordonnait, que toutes les procédures criminelles faites au parlement de Paris concernant les affaires de Bretagne seraient remises à cet huissier. Le greffier ayant répondu, que le parlement ne reconnaissait point les arrêts du conseil, non revêtus de lettres patentes, l'huissier lui montra une lettre de cachet, qui enjoignait de remettre sur le champ les procédures sous peine de désobéissance. Le greffier lui dit alors, qu'elles étaient entre les mains de M. Goeslard de Mount-Saber, rapporteur du procès, dont les pièces faisaient partie . . . l'on croit, que c'est un mousquetaire, qui a été envoyé chez M. de Goeslard; et que les pièces ont été remises suivant l'ordre du roi' (*Mercure historique,* 1766, clx. 438-9). The documents were seized 28 March; M. Goislard de Montsabert reported the seizure to the Parliament 8 April (*Remontrances du parlement de Paris au XVIIIe siècle,* ed. Jules Flammermont and Maurice Tourneux, 1888-98, ii. 565; see also *Almanach royal,* 1766, p. 209; É. Glasson, *Le Parlement de Paris,* 1901, ii. 317-18; A. Le Moy, *Le Parlement de Bretagne et le pouvoir*

royal au XVIIIe siècle, 1909, pp. 333-72).

35. No such trial seems to have taken place; instead, 'le parlement . . . [arrêta] de faire des représentations au roi, sur la remise de pièces . . . le roi reçut ces représentations le 13 avril, et y répondit, ainsi qu'il suit: "Il n'y a rien, dans ce qui vient de se passer, qui puisse mettre en danger l'état, la fortune et l'honneur de mes sujets" ' (*Mercure historique,* clx. 553; see also Flammermont and Tourneux, op. cit. ii. 565-6). Not content with this response, the parliament drew up a remonstrance which it presented to the King 1 June (printed ibid. ii. 566-86).

36. Deleted in *Works;* restored by Wright. For his indictment for perjury, see *ante* 23 Jan. 1764.

37. The *Mercure historique* for Feb. 1766 announced that 'on va lever 74,500 hommes de milice' (clx. 185). The ordinance regulating this *levée,* dated 27 Nov. 1765, is summarized in the *Gazette de Leyde* 25 Feb. 1766, supplement, *sub* 'suite des nouvelles de Paris du 17 février.'

38. She recovered, and lived until 1768. See *ante* 10 March 1766 and n. 27.

39. HW left Paris 17 April, reaching London 22 April ('Paris Journals,' du Deffand v. 314).

To LADY HERTFORD, ca Thursday 10 April 1766

Missing; listed in 'Paris Journals' (DU DEFFAND v. 381) as sent 'by Lord Tavistock.'

From HERTFORD, Saturday 10 May 1766

Printed for the first time from a photostat of BM Add. MSS 23219, f. 11.

Dublin Castle, May 10th 1766.

Dear Horry,

I HAVE not written to you for some time,[1] imagining you was upon your journey to England and that my letter might travel to Paris when you was upon your journey to London; but not hearing of you or from you and seeing in the public papers that you was arrived in Arlington Street,[2] I must endeavour to remove all doubts.

I was in hopes to have set out upon my return about this time, but the public bills sent to England and not yet returned from thence keep the Parliament setting,[3] so I suppose it may be doubtful whether I shall get to London by the Birthday.[4] The business here, except the formal part of it in passing such as England shall think proper to return us, is I believe now over. It has not however ended without furnishing an event for conversation. The Speaker,[5] upon a very improper Address to the Crown, chose to quit the service of Government and by dint of application to carry the point against it.[6]

1. Not since 4 Feb.
2. 'Yesterday [23, actually 22 April; see *ante* 8 April 1766, n. 39] the Hon. Horatio Walpole, Esq., arrived at his house in Arlington Street, St James's, from France' (*London Chronicle* 22–4 April, xix. 390, *sub* 24 April).
3. Until 7 June (*post* 11 June 1766, n. 1). Four public and five road bills returned from England were read for the first time to the Commons 21 May, three public and two road bills 23 May, and three public bills 3 June (*Journals of the House of Commons . . . Ireland*, xiv. 264–5, 269–70, 281). A total of seven public

and four private bills were not returned (ibid., index).
4. 4 June; see *post* 11 June 1766, n. 4.
5. Of the Commons, John Ponsonby.
6. On 5 May, 'a motion was made and the question . . . put, that a committee be appointed to draw up an humble address to his Majesty . . . imploring his Majesty that he will suffer the universal prayers of his loyal people of Ireland to assist the representations and endeavours of his chief governor of this kingdom, towards inducing the best of princes to return . . . the bill [the so-called Septennial Bill], transmitted to Great Britain,

He has since been at the Castle to express his contrition and his resolution of acting otherways for the future, which as it agrees with the sentiments and representations of all his friends I take it for granted he will have steadiness enough to adhere to for the remaining few days we are to set.[7]

The Opposition tried a question yesterday in hopes the weak fit might still be upon him, but they were beat with disgrace and contempt.[8] I remain, dear Horry,

Ever yours,

HERTFORD

for limiting the duration of Parliament, this session.' Upon the House dividing, the motion carried 90-88. The address was presented to Hertford 7 May, and he immediately transmitted it to the King (*Journals of the House of Commons . . . Ireland*, xiv. 257; *Calendar of Home Office Papers . . . 1766-1769*, ed. Joseph Redington, 1879, p. 42). The House had already (2 May) presented an address to Hertford asking him to urge the King to return the bill; Hertford had answered that, though he was sympathetic to the bill, 'I have received information of the most authentic nature, that the bill . . . will not be returned during this session' (*Journals*, xiv. 253-5). The King, in his answer to the address made to him (read to the House 5 June), rebuked the House for having made it: 'The sentiments of his faithful Commons were already known to his Majesty, by their passing the heads of that bill; nor can any solicitation add weight to that ancient and constitutional way of signifying their desires on the like occasions' (ibid. 283).

7. Lord George Sackville wrote to Gen. Irwin, 27 June, that 'the Speaker is not in good humour, he played the old game upon the Lord Lieutenant of dropping in questions where popularity might be lost. As soon as he had done it he apolo-gized for his conduct, and then the Opposition, who thought themselves sure of him, were more angry with him than even Lord Hertford was, so that, finding all sides had abused him, he thinks the best way is to be out of humour with government, but in the meantime he does not object to being one of the lords justices and of holding the employment of Commissioner of the Revenue' (Hist. MSS Comm., *Stopford-Sackville MSS*, Vol. I, 1904, p. 113).

8. Two questions were tried 9 May, the first 'that the Deputy Clerk of the Council shall by the Speaker be required to make true answer to the House, whether the oath taken by a privy councillor, and the oath taken by the deputy clerk or deputy clerks of the Council . . . be the only oath of office administered,' and the second 'that the Deputy Clerk . . . shall be required . . . to make true answer . . . whether anything was secretly transacted in the Council with respect to the privileges of this house, and to the bill for better securing the freedom of Parliament, by ascertaining the qualifications of knights, citizens and burgesses of Parliament.' Both questions were defeated, by votes of 99-43 and 106-35 (*Journals of the House of Commons . . . Ireland*, xiv. 262).

From HENRIETTA SEYMOUR CONWAY, Friday 16 May 1766

Printed for the first time from a photostat of BM Add. MSS 23219, f. 12.

Chichester, May the 16th 1766.

Good Sir,

I HAD the satisfaction to hear by my sister Harris, that you was safe arrived and have brought over with you good health and *French* spirits, which I hope is needless to assure you the pleasure it gives me, as no person can have your welfare more sincerely at heart than I have.

I doubt you found my poor brother[1] but in a bad state of health, which is not to be wondered at considering the fatigue and busyness he has gone through this winter. It is true he has got great glory and honour by it, but, alas, what recompense can that *make* for the loss of health. Nothing could make me so happy as to hear he had taken his leave of a court life. I know I shall be laughed at for this by the *fine* and gay part of the world, but what care I for that, I am a free-spoken Briton. I suppose you will soon pay a visit to sweet Strawberry Hill. You will soon have my brother Hertford and family in town. I give you joy of our relation Lady Drogheda being so happily settled in Ireland; now the knot is broke, I hope the rest will follow in order.[2] When you see my sister Harris I beg you will make my compliments to her and tell her I received her letter of the 10th and am glad to hear she is got so much better to venture out to private parties, is all from good Mr Walpole's

Most obliged friend and humble servant,

H. SEYMOUR CONWAY

1. Conway.
2. I.e., now that the eldest daughter is married, she hopes the remaining daughters will follow suit.

From HERTFORD, Wednesday 21 May 1766

Printed for the first time from a photostat of BM Add. MSS 23219, ff. 13–14.

Dublin Castle, May 21st 1766.

Dear Horry,

WHEN I shall see you I do not know; the business we have now here we can finish by Tuesday next,[1] but there are still some few bills to be returned from England,[2] and the great Lords in that kingdom do not dispatch business in holiday-time.[3]

We have not been able to finish the session without a difficulty; my brother I suppose has told you that a question has been carried against the Castle by the Speaker's means.[4] I really flattered myself I should have done wonders and carried him uniformly through the session against his nature; but it was too strong not to show itself, and upon a very popular question he declared himself against the Crown, and the motion was carried by two voices. The proposal was made in the House to strike out my name by unanimous consent[5] and to throw the difficulty upon the Crown; but my friends very properly thought it became me not to be excluded upon such dishonourable terms, but to be beat with credit and to leave the disgrace upon the weakness and irresolution of those who were the cause of it.[6] Thus we yielded to one defeat, and if you will allow me under such circumstances to have any vanity, it is a proof of my strength in this country, since we were surprised and scarce beat with all the means that could be used against us upon a very popular occasion.

The Speaker now repents of having betrayed me, and vows the most absolute allegiance for the future. We carried a question today by 119 to 12 or some such number,[7] and so we should have gone

1. 27 May; the Commons adjourned from 24 to 30 May (*Journals of the House of Commons . . . Ireland*, xiv. 276).

2. Six public and two road bills; see *ante* 10 May 1766, n. 3.

3. The Ministers, specifically the Privy Council, dealt with Irish legislation, not the English House of Lords, which had adjourned from 14 to 26 May (*Journals of the House of Lords* xxxi. 396–400).

4. See *ante* 10 May 1766.

5. This would have been a compliment to Hertford.

6. On 6 May, 'a motion was made, that an amendment be made to the said address, by expunging the words "in assistance of the representations and endeavours of the chief governor of this kingdom" '; the motion was defeated 72-71 (*Journals of the House of Commons . . . Ireland*, xiv. 259).

7. 123 to 19, defeating the motion 'that

through the session if the Speaker had acted uniformly. I will only add that the dissatisfied are so much afraid of my influence in this kingdom that they want to make me sick of it and to prevent my return by setting a sugar-boiler to pelt me in print with lies and abusive language.[8] Such is the state of this country, I can carry on business from my connection with it, but I do not know upon the present footing whether it can be done by a man who may be quite unconnected with it. The people are poor and ignorant, and they are encouraged by faction to be mad.[9]

My daughter Sarah is going to be married to Mr Stewart,[10] a gentleman of the county of Downe, who is heir to a great property[11] and already in possession of many amiable and good qualities.

I remain, dear Horry, with the truest regard,

Ever yours,

HERTFORD

the Deputy Clerk of the Hanaper may by the Speaker be required to make true answer upon oath to the House, whether he did not engross the bill for better securing the freedom of Parliament, by ascertaining the qualifications of knights, citizens and burgesses of Parliament' (ibid. xiv. 266).

8. Lord George Sackville wrote to Gen. Irwin, 27 June, that 'the latter part of the session was very satisfactory to . . . [Hertford], but he underwent for some months every abuse that could be offered to a chief governor' (Hist. MSS Comm., Stopford-Sackville MSS, Vol. I, 1904, pp. 112–13). Hertford's principal weak points were his 'economic temper . . . and too great propensity to heap emoluments on his children' (Mem. Geo. III ii. 220; see also Charles O'Hara to William Burke, 14 Aug., in Ross J. S. Hoffman, Edmund Burke, New York

Agent, Philadelphia, 1956, p. 356). Another weak point was Lord Beauchamp, who was disliked for his avarice and vanity (see ante 20 Dec. 1765, n. 1; Leinster Corr. i. 447; Hist. MSS Comm., 12th Report, App. pt x, Charlemont MSS, Vol. I, 1891, p. 23).

9. 'Our present gov[ernor] becomes every day more and more obnoxious to the mob' (Leland to Charlemont, 11 March 1766, ibid. 278).

10. Robert Stewart (1739–1821), cr. (1789) Bn, (1796) E. and (1816) M. of Londonderry; m. 1 (3 June 1766) Lady Sarah Frances Seymour Conway (d. 1770); m. 2 (1775) Frances Pratt. Lady Sarah, like her sister Lady Anne, received a dowry of £6000 (see ante 4 Feb. 1766, n. 1).

11. He was son and heir of Alexander Stewart (d. 1781) of Ballylawn Castle, county Donegal, and of Mount Stewart, county Down.

From LADY HERTFORD, Sunday 25 May 1766

Printed for the first time from a photostat of BM Add. MSS 23219, ff. 15–16.

Dublin Castle, May the 25th.

Dear Mr Walpole,

I FLATTERED myself I should before this time have had it in my power to have thanked you in person for your last kind letter from Paris;[1] but the pleasure of seeing you is deferred, and I must take this method of telling you how much I am obliged to you for it. The bills have been so long delayed in England that we are still kept here; they are expected this week,[2] and my Lord imagines he shall be able to get away about this day fortnight.[3] You will of course have heard how much abuse has been thrown out here; but it can have no effect upon you, as you know my Lord has not a fault, and that it is only the produce of Opposition and faction. When our day is fixed for setting out I shall let you know, as we must beg that you will be in London when we arrive; both my Lord and myself are very impatient to see you. We are much hurried with the preparations for our journey, and at the same time for the King's Birthday, which we are to keep here;[4] and it makes it extremely inconvenient, as we are obliged to send away all our baggage before that day.

My Lord told me that he had acquainted you[5] that Sarah was going to be married to Mr Stewart; the writings are almost finished, and I believe they are to be married next Monday or Tuesday.[6] My Lord and I breakfasted with Lady Kildare three or four days ago at Carton.[7] She is still very beautiful and more agreeable than anybody. She and Lady Louisa Conolly[8] both inquired very much after you. I have passed my evening very disagreeably; I have been making

1. Presumably HW's missing letter *ante* ca 10 April 1766.

2. Three public bills subsequently arrived and were read to the Commons for the first time 3 June (*ante* 10 May 1766, n. 3).

3. See *post* 11 June 1766.

4. For a description of the festivities 4 June, see *London Gazette* No. 10632, 10–14 June, *sub* Dublin, 5 June.

5. *Ante* 21 May 1766.

6. They were married Tuesday, 3 June.

7. Lord Kildare's country seat. This visit was possible because Lord Kildare, who had vowed never to see Hertford, was in England (*Leinster Corr.* i. 447, 450). See *ante* 1 Nov. 1765, 20 Jan. 1766.

8. Lady Kildare's sister. Her husband's seat, Castletown, was about five miles from Carton (Brian Fitzgerald, *Emily Duchess of Leinster*, 1950, p. 63).

my visits of *congé* to peeresses and privy councillors' wives. It is quite a solemn procession. The horses go as slow as they can walk; I am attended by battle-axes and such a mob the whole time, that I am now almost distracted with the noise I have been in for near three hours together.

I am sure you have been very much frightened about Mr Conway while he was ill.[9] My Lord was quite miserable about him, and now fears he does not take enough care of himself.[10]

Dublin is exceedingly disagreeable at this time of year, and more so to me than to anybody, as I hate the trouble of going out of town, either to dinner or breakfast, and the parties in town are hot and unpleasant. I hear General Mountague[11] is here, but I have not seen him yet. Mrs Harris writes me word she is to leave London on the 2d of June, which leaves me no hopes of seeing her till next winter. It would be a kindness in Mr Harris to have a slight fit of the gout; it would be of use to his health, and very agreeable to her friends.

I am ashamed to send you so dull a letter, but Dublin is a sad spot for news, and produces nothing but scandal and abuse. My Lord etc. desire to be remembered kindly to you. I am with the greatest truth

Your most faithful and affectionate friend,

I. HE.

Dublin Castle, Monday the 26th.

I have just found out I have dated my letter twice, but it must go so, as I have not time to alter it. My Lord bids me tell you he never hears from you now,[12] though he does not know he has any right to complain.[13] He fears you are not politician enough for him since you have lived at Paris, and he is become more so than ever.

---

9. See *ante* 6 April 1766 and n. 19.

10. See ibid.

11. Charles Montagu (*ante* 24 Oct. 1754, n. 4), who had been appointed colonel of the second (or Queen's royal) regiment of foot, Ireland, in 1760, and made lieuten-

ant-general in the army in 1761 (*Army Lists*, 1766, p. 56).

12. Not since HW's letter *ante* 10 March 1766.

13. Before Hertford's letter *ante* 10 May 1766, he had not written to HW for over three months.

From LADY HERTFORD, Wednesday 11 June 1766

Printed for the first time from a photostat of BM Add. MSS 23219, f. 17.
Address: To the Honourable Horatio Walpole in Arlington Street.
Postmark: 16 IV CHESTER FREE.

Chester,[1] Wednesday the 11.

Dear Mr Walpole,

WE landed at twelve today,[2] and intend setting out tomorrow for Ragley, where we shall stay two or three days.[3] We shall be in town Tuesday or Wednesday,[4] and will let you know by next post with more exactness, as we insist upon seeing you as soon as possible. I am so tired I can only assure you that I am, with great truth,

Most faithfully yours,

I. HE.

From HON. HENRY SEYMOUR-CONWAY (LATER LORD HENRY SEYMOUR) Tuesday ?June 1766

Printed for the first time from a photostat of BM Add. MSS 23219, f. 179. Dated after Mrs Crewe's wedding 4 April, and after HW's return to England 22 April 1766, but this and the two subsequent letters could have been written later.

Tuesday, Lincoln's Inn.

Dear Sir,

WILL you allow Mrs Bouverie, Mrs Crewe,[1] and four or five men to breakfast with you at Strawberry Hill some day this

1. The Irish Parliament had been prorogued 7 June, and the Hertfords embarked from Ireland 10 June (*Journals of the House of Commons . . . Ireland,* xiv. 292; *Calendar of Home Office Papers . . . 1766–1769,* ed. Joseph Redington, 1879, p. 51). Hertford did not return to Ireland as lord lieutenant, but was named Master of the Horse in September, and lord chamberlain of the King's household in November, a position which he held (with one small break) till 1783.

2. At Parkgate (ibid.; *London Chronicle* 12–14 June, xix. 566, *sub* 14 June).

3. 'On Friday [13 June] . . . the Earl of Hertford arrived at his seat at Rugley [*sic*] in Warwickshire' (*Daily Adv.* 16 June).

4. 17 or 18 June. 'Yesterday [17 June] . . . arrived at his house in Grosvenor Street . . . the Earl of Hertford, and Lord Beauchamp, from the Earl's seat at Rugley. . . . The Countess is expected in town tomorrow [19 June]' (ibid. 18 June).

1. Frances Anne Greville (d. 1818), m. (1766) John Crewe, cr. (1806) Bn Crewe.

week? They are very desirous of seeing the place, and as you were so good as to tell me I might bring a party there, I take the liberty of proposing it to you. Pray tell me if it is not quite convenient to you.

I am, dear Sir, yours etc.

H. S. Conway

To Hon. Henry Seymour-Conway (later Lord Henry Seymour) ?June 1766

Missing; a reply to the preceding letter, implied in the following.

From Hon. Henry Seymour-Conway (later Lord Henry Seymour) Wednesday ?June 1766

Printed for the first time from a photostat of BM Add. MSS 23219, f. 180.

Almacks, Wednesday.

Dear Sir,

WE are very much obliged to you for your civility about Strawberry. If you have no objection to Sunday, it will be the most convenient for us. We are to dine afterwards at Hampton Court; it was part of our original plan, and it would be encroaching too much upon you to fasten upon you for the whole day.

Yours ever,

H. S. Conway

In May 1766 she was at Crewe Hall, Cheshire, and made a visit to Southampton, where Mrs Bouverie was (*Leinster Corr.* i. 450, 452).

To Conway, Thursday 2 October 1766

Printed from *Works* v. 134–5.

Bath, October 2, 1766.

I ARRIVED yesterday at noon, and bore my journey perfectly well, except that I had the headache all yesterday; but it is gone today, or at least made way for a little giddiness which the water gave me this morning at first.[1] If it does not do me good very soon, I shall leave it; for I dislike the place exceedingly, and am disappointed in it. Their new buildings that are so admired, look like a collection of little hospitals; the rest is detestable; and all crammed together, and surrounded with perpendicular hills that have no beauty. The river[2] is paltry enough to be the Seine or Tyber. Oh! how unlike my lovely Thames!

I met my Lord Chatham's[3] coach yesterday full of such Grenville-looking children,[4] that I shall not go to see him this day or two;[5] and today I spoke to Lady Rockingham in the street. My Lords Chancellor and President[6] are here, and Lord and Lady Powis. Lady Malpas arrived yesterday. I shall visit Miss Rich[7] tomorrow. In the next apartment to mine lodges —— ——.[8] I have not seen him some years; and he is grown either mad or superannuated, and talks without cessation or coherence: you would think all the articles of a dictionary were prating together at once. The Bedfords are expected this week.[9] There are forty thousand others that I neither know

1. HW had been suffering since the beginning of August 'with pains in my stomach and limbs' which turned to 'an attack on my stomach, bowels, and back' (HW to Mann, 9, 25 Sept. 1766, MANN vi. 450, 454). He apparently set out for Bath 29 Sept. (see Coke, *Journals*, i. 62; COLE i. 119, n. 2).

2. The Avon.

3. William Pitt, made lord privy seal and virtual prime minister in July, when he formed a new administration replacing Rockingham's, had been created Earl of Chatham 4 Aug.

4. George Grenville was Chatham's brother-in-law. Chatham had at this time five children, aged five to ten, and Grenville seven, aged five to thirteen (Collins, *Peerage*, 1812, ii. 418, v. 73). 'Mr Walpole

in general disliked being in company with children, to whom he was little accustomed' (Mary Berry). HW is, of course, alluding primarily to his antipathy to Grenville.

5. Chatham had come to Bath for the gout, and visited HW later in the month (see *post* 18 Oct. 1766, n. 4).

6. Camden and Northington.

7. Mary Rich (*ante* ca 25 March 1753).

8. Possibly 'Sir Robert,' i.e. Field Marshal Sir Robert Rich, Mary Rich's father. He was 81, had apparently been near death the year before (see *ante* 11 June 1765, n. 8), and died in Feb. 1768 (GEC, *Baronetage* iv. 73). HW last mentions him in his letter to Hertford *ante* 22 Jan. 1764.

9. They arrived 9 Oct. (*London Chronicle* 9–11 Oct., xx. 358, *sub* 11 Oct.).

nor intend to know. In short, it is living in a fair, and I am heartily sick of it already. Adieu!

Yours ever,

Hor. Walpole

From Lady Hertford, Wednesday 8 October 1766

Printed for the first time from a photostat of BM Add. MSS 23219, ff. 19–20.

London, October the 8th 1766.

Dear Mr Walpole,

THIS family is so anxious to hear that the Bath waters have done you good, that I am employed by them (as they are in a great hurry) to request that you will let us know. My Lord intends to set out tomorrow for Paris,[1] and your account of yourself is to follow him there, if you favour me with it soon. He is luckily so confined in time that he cannot stay above a fortnight there,[2] so that you see I shall not have opportunities of writing many letters to him during his stay there.

I must acquaint you with one family anecdote that I think you will approve of. Lord Beauchamp has given up today the place he was to have had of constable of the Castle of Dublin, as his mind was so delicate he could not reconcile himself to accept that with an additional salary of a thousand pounds a year, after having often declared in Ireland that he thought augmentations wrong. After this step I think the world have no right to look upon this family as jobbers; and Lord Beauchamp is the first Secretary that ever quitted that situation without having been rewarded.[3]

1. See *London Chronicle* 9–11 Oct., xx. 354, *sub* 10 Oct.

2. He stayed apparently until 4 Nov., arriving back in London 8 Nov. (ibid. 4–6, 8–11 Nov., xx. 442, 458, *sub* 5, 10 Nov.). See his letter to Conway from Paris, 20 Oct., on his conversation with Choiseul, in *Chatham Corr.* iii. 117–20.

3. Rigby had written to Bedford, 25 Sept., that 'Lord Beauchamp is made constable of Dublin Castle for life, in the room of an old Mr Hatton. Lord Hertford gives Mr Hatton a thousand pounds to quit his employment, which was five hundred a year; a thousand more is added' (*Bedford Corr.* iii. 345; see also Wedderburn to Grenville, 25 Sept., *Grenville Papers* iii. 325). Hertford while in Ireland had been criticized for his 'too great propensity to heap emoluments on his children, in which his son and secretary . . . did not discourage him' (HW's MS 'foul copy,' *Mem. Geo. III*, p. 272); however, though Beauchamp gave

There is no news in this part of the world, and I have no time to add a word more as I have a thousand things to prepare for my Lord and my son, one for Paris and the other for Warwick. I wish you to stay at Bath if it has a chance of doing you good; and yet I wish you here, as nobody is more happy than I am when I am in your company. I am, dear Mr Walpole,

Your most faithful and affectionate etc.

I. He.

To Conway, Saturday 18 October 1766

Printed from *Works* v. 135–6.

Bath, October 18, 1766.

YOU have made me laugh, and somebody else[1] makes me stare. How can one wonder at anything he does, when he knows so little of the world? I suppose the next step will be to propose me for groom of the Bedchamber to the new Duke of Cumberland.[2] But why me? Here is that hopeful young fellow Sir John Rushout, the oldest member of the House,[3] and, as extremes meet, very proper to begin again; why overlook him? However, as the secret is kept from me myself, I am perfectly easy about it. I shall call today or tomorrow to ask his commands, but certainly shall not obey those you mention.[4]

The waters certainly are not so beneficial to me as at first: I

up the post of constable, it was given instead to his younger brother Henry (*Calendar of Home Office Papers . . . 1766–1769*, ed. Joseph Redington, 1879, p. 146; Robert Beatson, *Political Index*, 1806, iii. 342).

———

1. Lord Chatham.
2. Prince Henry Frederick, the King's youngest surviving brother, was created Duke of Cumberland 22 Oct. Lord Chatham had proposed that HW move the Address at the opening of Parliament 11 Nov.; Grafton wrote to Chatham, 17 Oct.: 'Mr Conway would be as glad as your

Lordship to have the motion by Mr Walpole; but he knows that there is not a member in the House whom he could not induce to undertake it sooner than him' (*Chatham Corr.* iii. 112). The Address was moved by Augustus Hervey (Geo. III's *Corr.*, ed. Fortescue, i. 416; L. B. Namier, *Additions and Corrections to Sir John Fortescue's Edition of the Correspondence of King George the Third, Vol. I*, Manchester, 1937, p. 66).
3. He was 81.
4. Chatham visited HW; his visit is described *Mem. Geo. III* ii. 261–2.

have almost every morning my pain in my stomach. I do not pretend this to be the cause of my leaving Bath.⁵ The truth is, I cannot bear it any longer. You laugh at my regularity; but the contrary habit is so strong in me, that I cannot continue such sobriety. The public rooms, and the loo, where we play in a circle, like the hazard on Twelfth-Night,⁶ are insupportable. This coming into the world again, when I am so weary of it, is as bad and ridiculous as moving an address would be. I have no affectation, for affectation is a monster at nine-and-forty; but if I cannot live quietly, privately, and comfortably, I am perfectly indifferent about living at all. I would not kill myself, for that is a philosopher's affectation, and I will come hither again, if I must; but I shall always drive very near, before I submit to do anything I do not like. In short, I must be as foolish as I please, as long as I can keep without the limits of absurdity. What has an old man to do but to preserve himself from parade on one hand, and ridicule on the other?⁷ Charming youth may indulge itself in either, may be censured, will be envied, and has time to correct. Adieu!

Yours ever,

Hor. Walpole

Monday evening.

You are a delightful manager of the House of Commons, to reckon 540, instead of 565!⁸ Sandwich was more accurate in lists, and would not have miscounted 25, which are something in a division.

---

5. HW left 22 Oct. (Coke, *Journals*, i. 82).

6. The *Annual Register . . . for 1764*, 1765, p. 45, mentions 'the ancient custom of public hazard playing at Court on twelfth night,' which 'now seems to be entirely laid aside'; see CHUTE 204 and n. 25.

7. HW had written to Mme du Deffand 10 Oct. 1766: 'Dès le moment que je cessais d'être jeune, j'ai eu une peur horrible de devenir un vieillard ridicule' (DU DEFFAND i. 151).

8. That is, the number of members, but between 1754 and 1790 there were only 558 members (Namier and Brooke i. 2).

From HENRIETTA SEYMOUR CONWAY, Tuesday 3 February 1767

Printed for the first time from a photostat of BM Add. MSS 23219, f. 20.

Chichester, 3d February 1767.

Good Mr Walpole,

I TAKE the liberty of writing a few lines to congratulate you on your recovery,[1] which I very sincerely do; I am glad you made trial of the Bath waters, especially as I am informed they have had the desired effect.[2] I hope you were very careful of yourself in the severe weather we have had.[3] We have now a great change for the better.[4] I walked yesterday and it was mild and pleasant as in the spring. Thank God, I have enjoyed my health this winter better than I have done for a long time, even in the extreme cold weather, so that I have been a partaker of the assemblies, and what little gaieties Chichester affords; as possibly you may hear of by some of our Goodwood[5] friends, I had like to have been drawn into a terrible scrape at General Capel's[6] election ball. I think 'twas the greatest crowd I ever was in and most of the gentlemen drunk, so could expect no protection from them, though never wanted it more, as I am not qualified at all to bustle through a crowd. I think I never was more happy than when I got into the sedan chair and was at home by eight o'clock. Nothing made me amends for the fatigue and danger I went through but the appearance of our beautiful Duchess,[7] who looked handsomer than ever; she was quite a Diana. I won't trespass

1. This refers to HW's illness the preceding autumn, from which he had largely recovered by late Oct., after his return from Bath (see MANN vi. 461); Henrietta Seymour Conway's news about HW was usually several months in arrears.

2. 'The Bath waters were serviceable to me' (HW to Mann 26 Oct. 1766, ibid.).

3. 'We have a most dreadful winter, the coldest I ever remember' (idem to idem 21 Jan. 1767, ibid. 479).

4. The frost broke on 21 Jan. (ibid. n. 6).

5. Seat of the Duke of Richmond, 3 miles NE of Chichester.

6. Hon. William Keppel (1727–82), Maj.-Gen. 1762; Col. 14th Ft 1765; M.P. Chi-

chester 26 Jan. 1767–1782. Keppel had been returned for Chichester in the room of Lord George Henry Lennox, who vacated his seat; he sat for the borough on the interest of Richmond, his cousin (Namier and Brooke i. 390, iii. 11). Perhaps the 'scrape' Henrietta Conway refers to arose from some overzealous supporter of Richmond, who was in Opposition, baiting her on her relationship to Conway (see below), who was secretary of state for the north until Jan. 1768; also, Hertford's being lord chamberlain of the Household (which he became the preceding Nov., to the envy and dismay of many) may have been a source of discord.

7. Of Richmond.

any further on your time, but sincerely wish you the compliments of the season and many returns.

Believe me, good Sir, your affectionate humble servant

H. SEYMOUR CONWAY

PS. If there be any such person in being as Mr Secretary Conway, be so good to tell him that no mortal is more his than I am.

From BEAUCHAMP, Saturday ? 7 March 1767

Printed for the first time from a photostat of BM Add. MSS 23219, f. 177. Dated conjecturally by the contents.

Saturday night.

My dear Sir,

I AM amazed that you should suspect me of taking ill what you said to me in friendship. I should be unworthy the place I flatter myself I hold in your esteem if I did not feel infinitely obliged to you for your plainness and sincerity to me when you think me in the wrong. I wish I was as free from other imputations as I am from the aspersion of being a stock-jobber.[1] I can scarcely talk on such a subject without laughing; if to attend a few India courts at a moment when all mankind are thinking of what passes there,[2] to buy a thousand pounds' stock as a claim to get in there,[2a] be such a sin, God help the Chancellor of the Exchequer.[3] For my part I have done nothing that with all your delicacy you can really think wrong,

1. In the East India Company. See below.

2. The government in late 1766 began an inquiry into the affairs of the East India Company, with a view to determining what portion of the Company's revenues should revert to them; hitherto the Company had been in effect completely independent and kept all revenues for itself. See Lucy S. Sutherland, 'The First Parliamentary Intervention, 1766–7,' in *The East India Company in Eighteenth-Century Politics*, Oxford, 1952, pp. 138–76.

2a. A holding of £500 was necessary to qualify for a vote in the General Court of Proprietors.

3. Charles Townshend, whose speculations in East India stock by April 1767 earned him over £7000 (Sir Lewis Namier and John Brooke, *Charles Townshend*, 1964, p. 167). HW wrote to Mann, 19 March 1767, that Townshend 'had dealt largely in India stock, cried up the Company's *right* to raise that stock, has sold out most advantageously, and now cries [it] down' (MANN vi. 498).

but as we live in factious and censorious times you may depend on it that I will neither attend general courts, nor will I undertake either in private or in public the defence of my brother proprietors.[4] I am happy in the idea of being honoured with your esteem, for it is an higher honour in my opinion to be esteemed by one virtuous man than to be hallooed and applauded for such ingenious buffoonery as we heard last night by an unanimous House of Commons.[5] I remain ever, my dear Sir,

Your most faithful servant,

NO RISCOUNTER[6] PROPRIETOR

To CONWAY, ca Saturday 2 May 1767

Missing. In early 1767 illness forced Lord Chatham's withdrawal from politics, though he did not formally resign. On 30 April, Conway, prompted by Chatham's withdrawal, asked HW to negotiate a new administration with the Duke of Richmond. HW refused, and 'a few days after I gave him my reasons in writing' (*Mem. Geo. III* iii. 9–10).

4. Nevertheless, Beauchamp voted 26 May against the bill to regulate the Company's dividends (Namier and Brooke iii. 424).

5. On 6 March the House resolved *nem. con.* 'that an humble address be presented to his Majesty . . . that he . . . order . . . laid before this House all proposals that have been made within six months . . . past, to . . . his Majesty's ministers, by the directors of the East India Company, relative to the affairs of the said company' (*Journals of the House of Commons* xxxi. 207). During the debate 'the two Oppositions [Grenville's and Rockingham's] could not agree on a single point, and so did not dare to divide' (HW to Mann 8 March 1767, MANN vi. 494), and 'the military and naval chiefs . . . Lord Granby and Sir Edward Hawke blabbed out the secret which the ministers were veiling' that there had been a split in the Cabinet over the Company's proposals (*Mem. Geo. III* ii. 305); throughout Charles Townshend 'acted in his usual, wild, romancing, indiscreet manner' (HW to Mann 8 March 1767, loc. cit.).

6. Presumably from 'rescounter,' 'the balancing of contra-accounts; settlement or payment of differences on accounts, in later use specifically on the Stock Exchange' (OED).

HON. HENRY SEYMOUR CONWAY,
BY THOMAS GAINSBOROUGH

From HERTFORD, ca ? July 1767

Printed for the first time from a photostat of BM Add. MSS 23218, f. 60. Conjecturally dated; during July 1767 Conway and other members of the Grafton administration were negotiating with Rockingham, Grenville, and the Bedfords in an attempt to resettle the government on a stronger basis; see *Mem. Geo. III* iii. 43–71.

Address: To the Honourable Horatio Walpole in Arlington Street.

Monday night.

My dear Horry,

YOU must not say a word of my brother's scheme; he will not allow it to be spoke of a[s] his, and probably did not show it in the Closet, as Lord Shelburne was there with him.[1]

Yours ever most affectionately,

HERTFORD

From CONWAY, Sunday 9 August 1767

Printed for the first time from the MS now WSL. The MS was apparently among those sold ca 1843 by the 5th D. of Grafton, as executor of the 6th Earl Waldegrave's estate, to Richard Bentley, the publisher; bought by WSL, 1937, from the estate of Richard Bentley the younger (MANN x. 40–3).

Park Place, Sunday.

I WANTED to tell you, but hurried out of town the moment Court was over,[1] that the King told me the affair of the Ord-nance was settled with Lord T[ownshend] and that he intended it for me.[2]—I then spoke to Lord T[ownshend] myself who said, what

1. Presumably Conway's scheme of government excluded Shelburne, who was currently secretary of state for the south and remained so until Oct. 1768. Shelburne, Chatham's protégé, was disliked by the King and the other ministers, with whom he consistently disagreed on matters of policy (John Brooke, *King George III*, 1972, pp. 135, 143).

1. 'Yesterday [7 Aug.] the Right Hon. Henry Seymour Conway set out for Park Place' (*Daily Adv.* 8 Aug.).
2. 'We hear that on Friday [7 Aug.] Mr Secretary Conway was appointed lieu-tenant-general of the Ordnance'; he apparently kissed hands for the post 12 Aug. (ibid. 10, 12 Aug.). At a meeting to fix the administration 28 July, Hertford,

I dare say was true, that the King said something about wanting to make an *arrangement about the Ordnance;* but so that he did not clearly understand what he meant; that however his intention was to declare to his M[ajesty] his entire acquiescence in whatever was for his M[ajesty]'s service, and indeed spoke to me in the openest and handsomest way in the world about it.—So that as I told Lady Ailesbury I went away full of unpleasant feels in the thought of taking a thing from him which he had such good pleas to keep, and the more as he gave it up so handsomely to me.

And I do confess I should have felt much pleasanter if it had anyhow been refused me.—So that now the idea of adding it to my secretaryship grows heavier and heavier to me.[3]—If therefore the Duke of Grafton could now see a practicability in my acting *jointly* with Ch[arles] T[ownshend] in the House and promising to take the direct and absolute lead if he *failed*[4] and even to take *any* civil place again, if it proved necessary, it would make me prodigious happy.—and I must own my foolish head is so framed that I shall not be so without it.—

We have an haunch of venison at your service for Wednesday. Let us know if you want it.—That is, send to Lantun[5] for it in town.—

Yours most sincerely,

H. S. C.

Conway, HW and Grafton had 'settled that Conway should be either Cabinet-counsellor and lieutenant-general of the Ordnance, or third secretary of state for America' (*Mem. Geo. III* iii. 71). Townshend had been lieutenant-general of the Ordnance since 1763, and on 12 Aug. kissed hands as lord lieutenant of Ireland, replacing Lord Bristol (*Daily Adv.* 13 Aug.).

3. Conway, weary of the ministry, was anxious to resign as secretary, but had so far been prevailed upon to remain. After becoming lieutenant-general of the Ordnance (which he remained until Oct. 1772), he continued as secretary of state

for the north until Jan. 1768, though scrupulously refusing to continue to draw the salary for that office (MANN vi. 559 and n. 2). See Namier and Brooke ii. 244–5.

4. Conway was temperamentally unsuited to lead the Commons; 'could not be induced to traffic with members,' 'allowed too much to his scruples,' and 'thought nothing a virtue but his own moderation' (ibid. 244; *Mem. Geo. III* ii. 297–8, 321, iii. 91). Upon resigning as secretary of state in January, he gave up the lead in the Commons to Lord North.

5. Presumably Conway's butler; not further identified.

From HERTFORD, ca Thursday 20 August 1767

Printed for the first time from a photostat of BM Add. MSS 23218, ff. 62–3. Dated by the references to HW's departure for Paris (20 Aug. 1767) and to Charles Townshend's wife being made Baroness of Greenwich (19 Aug.) (see below, nn. 6, 8).

My dear Horry,

I AM just returned from passing three days and great part of three nights with Lady Hertford's good friends at Coventry.[1] Upon my return home I have found this evening at Ragley the Comte de Sarsfield,[2] Messrs Croftes[3] and Richards,[4] and Barry the player.[5]

I am unhappy with such frequent and repeated proofs of my brother's irresolution, and when you are gone[6] I shall have lost my great support.[7] I will return to town as soon as I can, but that cannot be before next month except some particular occasion required it. Must you go? I hate and lament the thoughts of your absence. When I return to town I will do the best I can in pursuance of your advice.

C. Townshend is not to be trusted a moment. I think of him as all the world does, and yet should be at a loss to advise the conduct to be pursued with him; perhaps giving the peerage so soon was an error;[8] I should have been cautious if my opinion alone had weighed to set such principles at liberty.[9] Excuse me, my dear Horry, if I do not add more at present than my best wishes for your health and

1. Possibly Lord and Lady Craven, whose seat was Combe Abbey outside of Coventry. Their nephew and heir had just married Lady Elizabeth Berkeley.

2. Guy-Claude (1718–89), Comte de Sarsfield (SELWYN 179, n. 4; DU DEFFAND i. 286, n. 10); probably the M. de Sarsfield HW met several times in Paris 1765–6, and who possibly dined with him at SH in April 1765 ('Paris Journals,' ibid. v. 270, 292, 307, 311; SELWYN 179).

3. Perhaps Richard Croft (d. 1793), the banker (MANN vi. 278, n. 1).

4. Presumably Fitzherbert Richards (ante 9 Feb. 1765, n. 12).

5. Spranger Barry (1719–77), actor.

6. HW left for Paris 20 Aug., arriving there 23 Aug. ('Paris Journals,' DU DEFFAND v. 315–16).

7. Their primary concern at this time was to persuade Conway to remain in office.

8. Townshend's wife, Lady Dalkeith, was created Baroness of Greenwich 19 Aug.

9. For Townshend's duplicity and ingratitude, see post 17 Sept. 1767.

safe and quick return. The family desire their best compliments and I am, dear Horry,

Always most truly and affectionately yours,

HERTFORD

My children improve, thank God, and make me happy here and everywhere.

To CONWAY, Friday 21 August 1767

Missing; listed in 'Paris Journals' (DU DEFFAND v. 385). Presumably written at Calais to inform Conway of his safe passage (see ibid. v. 315; *post* 14 Sept. 1767).

To CONWAY, ca Sunday 23 August 1767

Missing; mentioned *post* 9 Sept. 1767 as sent by 'Mr Fletcher.' Tentatively dated just after HW's arrival at Paris 23 Aug.

To HERTFORD, ca Sunday 23 August 1767

Missing; mentioned *post* 14, 17 Sept. 1762 as sent by 'Mr Fletcher.' Tentatively dated as the above.

From CONWAY, ca September 1767

Two letters, missing (see *post* 14 Sept. 1767); one was answered *post* 9 Sept. 1767.

To HERTFORD, Sunday 6 September 1767

Missing; listed in 'Paris Journals' (DU DEFFAND v. 385) as sent 'by Mr Lee.'

To Conway, Sunday 6 September 1767

Missing; listed in 'Paris Journals' (DU DEFFAND v. 385) as sent 'by Mr Lee.'

To Hertford, Wednesday 9 September 1767

Missing; listed in 'Paris Journals' (DU DEFFAND v. 385) and acknowledged *post* 14 Sept. 1767. Sent 'by Lady Mary Coke.'

To Conway, Wednesday 9 September 1767

Delivered by Lady Mary Coke; printed from the MS now WSL. First printed in part Wright v. 181–3 and in full Toynbee vii. 129–31. For the history of the MS, see *ante* 29 June 1744 OS.
Endorsed: Mr H. W. 9 Sep. 67 Paris.

Paris, Wednesday, Sept. 9, 1767.

I RECEIVED your long, kind and melancholy letter[1] a few hours after the post was gone out, or I had told you sooner how infinitely I pity you and the Duke of Grafton;[2] I know what both must feel; though abstractedly from good nature, you are not more concerned in the unfortunate accident, than in one that happens in any part of the globe. You could not prevent what you neither knew nor could foresee. One is not to blame for building a house, that may be neglected,[3] fall and crush a family an hundred years hence.

1. Missing; received 7 Sept. ('Paris Journals,' DU DEFFAND v. 318; Coke, *Journals*, ii. 121).
2. 'Mr Conway . . . wrote him [HW] word of the dreadful accident the poor Duke of Grafton had had, of one of the horses of his chaise, as he was driving, treading upon a man, of which hurt he was since dead' (ibid.). As Grafton 'was driving General Conway in the evening to town from the Lord Chancellor's . . . near Deptford an unhappy old man, extremely drunk, reeled against the shoulder of one of the horses, who by being stopped instantly wounded the calf of his leg so much, that joined to a bad habit of body, he is since dead, notwithstanding all the relief that the most ready and able assistance could give him' (Grafton to George III, 1 Sept., Geo. III's *Corr.*, ed. Fortescue, i. 502).
3. 'Lieutenant-General Conway who mentioned this affair on Friday [28 Aug.], thought the accident could not be attended with any bad consequences, this is a proof that the poor man's state of body was the cause of his death' (George III to Grafton 1 Sept., ibid. i. 503). See also GM 1767, xxxvii. 474.

Last night by Lord Rochford's courier[4] we heard of Charles Townshend's death,[5] for which indeed your letter had prepared me.[6] As a man of incomparable parts, and most entertaining to a spectator, I regret his death. His good humour prevented one from hating him, and his levity from loving him—but in a political light, I own I cannot look upon it as a misfortune. His treachery alarmed me, and I apprehended everything from it. It was not advisable to throw him into the arms of the Opposition—his death avoids both kinds of mischief. I take for granted you will have Lord North for chancellor of the Exchequer.[7] He is very inferior to Charles in parts—but what he wants in those, will be supplied by firmness and spirit.

With regard to my brother,[8] I should apprehend nothing, were he like other men: but I shall not be astonished, if he throws his life away:[9] and I have seen so much of the precariousness of it lately, that I am prepared for the event, if it shall happen.[10]

I will say nothing, about Mr Harris; he is an old man, and his death will be natural.[11]

For Lord Chatham, he is really or intentionally mad—but I still doubt which of the two.[12] T[homas] Walpole has writ to his brother[13]

4. Lord Rochford was ambassador at Paris 1766–8 (D. B. Horn, *British Diplomatic Representatives 1689–1789*, 1932, p. 23).

5. HW heard the news from Robert Walpole ('Paris Journals,' DU DEFFAND v. 319). Townshend died 4 Sept. at Sudbrook (*Daily Adv.* 5 Sept.).

6. Thomas Whately wrote to Grenville 24 Aug. of Townshend's 'having been not well of a long time' and looking 'still worse' (*Grenville Papers* iv. 158). See *post* 14 Sept. 1767.

7. See *post* 17 Sept. 1767.

8. Sir Edward Walpole.

9. Sir Edward was near death (*Mem. Geo. III* iii. 58). Conway wrote to Grafton, 29 Aug.: 'Sir E. Walpole who has been for some time in a very doubtful state and has frequent relapses is now I doubt worse than ever' (Grafton Papers, Grafton ETI/3/107. No. 300, in W. Suffolk County Record Office at Bury St Edmunds, copy kindly supplied by the Hon. David Erskine). However, Sir Edward recovered and lived until 1784.

10. HW stood by Sir Edward's death to

lose his share of one of his employments, the Collectorship of Customs, amounting to about £1400 a year, or 'half my income' (MANN x. 52–4; *Mem. Geo. III* loc. cit.). Conway wrote to Grafton (n. 9 above) to ask about the possibility of securing this share for HW; his query, however, was unsolicited by HW, who scorned to make an appeal (*Mem. Geo. III* loc. cit.).

11. John Harris, Conway's brother-in-law, died 5 Oct., aged 77 (Namier and Brooke ii. 590).

12. Though suspected of feigning illness for political reasons (see *post* 17 Sept. 1767), he apparently was suffering from an attack of manic-depressive psychosis, and did not return to politics until the autumn of 1769 (Namier and Brooke iii. 298).

13. The Hon. Robert Walpole (1736–1810), HW's cousin, who was presumably on his way to Madrid, where he had been named secretary of the Embassy (see Horn, op. cit. 136; OSSORY ii. 400, n. 3; n. 5 above).

here, that the day before Lord Chatham set out for Pynsent, he executed a letter of attorney with full powers to his wife, and the moment it was signed, he began singing—this comes from Nuthall.[14]

You may depend upon it I shall only stay here to the end of the month;[15] but if you should want me sooner, I will set out at a moment's warning, on your sending me a line by Lord Rochford's courier. This goes by Lady Mary Coke, who sets out tomorrow morning early, on the notice of Mr Townshend's death, or she would have stayed ten days longer.[16] I sent you a letter[17] by a Mr Fletcher,[18] but I fear he did not go away till the day before yesterday.

I am just come from dining *en famille* with the Duc de Choiseul;[19] he was very civil—but much more civil to Mr *Wood*[20] who dined there too. I forgive this gratitude to the *peacemakers*.

I must finish, for I am going to Lady Mary,[21] and then return to sup with the Duchess de Choiseul,[22] who is not civiller to anybody than to me. Adieu!

Yours ever,

H. W.

To Lady Ailesbury, Sunday 13 September 1767

Missing; listed in 'Paris Journals' (du Deffand v. 385).

14. Thomas Nuthall (d. 1775), solicitor to the Treasury; Chatham's intimate friend and legal adviser (DNB; this corrects earlier identifying notes in Gray and Mann). On 17 Aug. Lady Chatham wrote to Nuthall that 'the great state of weakness which my Lord feels from the continuance of his illness makes the transacting of any business so uneasy to him, that he is extremely desirous of giving to me a *general* letter of attorney, empowering me to transact all business for him. He . . . wishes you would . . . prepare one . . . and bring it with you . . . in the course of this day' (printed *Chatham Corr.* iii. 282).

15. HW left Paris 8 Oct. after delaying a few days because of illness ('Paris Journals,' du Deffand v. 323–4).

16. See ibid. v. 319 and Coke, op. cit. ii. 121–2. She was a sister of Townshend's widow, Lady Greenwich.

17. Missing.

18. Not identified. HW also sent a letter by Fletcher to Hertford, which Hertford had some difficulty in recovering; see *post* 14, 17 Sept. 1767.

19. See 'Paris Journals,' loc. cit.

20. Robert Wood, who as under-secretary of state had been involved in preparing the preliminaries of the Peace of Paris (see *ante* 9 Dec. 1763, n. 41; Namier and Brooke iii. 655–6). HW mentions Choiseul's preference for Wood also to Conway *post* 31 Dec. 1774.

21. See Coke, op. cit. ii. 122 and 'Paris Journals,' loc. cit.

22. See ibid.

From HERTFORD, Monday 14 September 1767

Printed for the first time from a photostat of BM Add. MSS 23219, ff. 21–2.

London, September 14th 1767.

Dear Horry,

I CAME here on Wednesday last,[1] having been kept something longer in Warwickshire than I expected. This morning I received your letter[2] of the 9th by Lady Mary Coke, and it is the first account we have had of you since you left Calais.[3] I have already sent into the City to make inquiry after Mr Fletcher, but I have as yet heard nothing of him nor of the letter I should have received from his hands.[4] It gives me some pain, as you tell me it was a particular one, but I dare say I shall be able at last to preserve it from falling into other hands.

My brother tells [me] he has wrote to you twice.[5] C. Townshend's death will make no sort of alteration except in filling up his place by someone who will certainly not speak so ingeniously in the House of Commons. Lord Rochford sets out for Paris on Friday,[6] and I will write to you more particularly by him;[7] as this subject may be a matter of curiosity at the post offices, I will satisfy no such inquirer by anything I can say, and I am sure you will approve it.

Lord Townshend goes to Ireland[8] and sets out about the 25th.[9]

Lady Grenwich[10] remains at Sudbrook.[11] The world blame her for not having attended earlier than she did to Mr Townshend's case. He was not thought to be in any danger, and it was treated as a nervous complaint till the disorder was too deeply rooted.[12] He has

1. 9 Sept.
2. Missing.
3. Presumably a reference to HW's missing letter to Conway *ante* 21 Aug. 1767.
4. See *post* 17 Sept. 1767.
5. Both letters are missing.
6. 18 Sept. 'Yesterday [18 Sept.] . . . the Earl of Rochford . . . set out from his house in Dover Street, on his embassy to the Court of France' (*Daily Adv.* 19 Sept.).
7. See Hertford to HW *post* 17 Sept. 1767.
8. As lord lieutenant; see *ante* 9 Aug. 1767, n. 2.

9. He took leave of the King on the 25th, but did not set out until Oct. (*Daily Adv.* 26 Sept. *et seq.*). He continued as lord lieutenant until 1772.
10. Townshend's widow.
11. Where Townshend had died (*ante* 9 Sept. 1767, n. 5).
12. Lady Greenwich 'at first said that Mr Townshend's disorder was only lowness of spirits; but at last called in Sir William Duncan' (Thomas Whately to Grenville, 24 Aug., *Grenville Papers* iv. 158).

been opened, and they talk of an adhesion to the side, but I believe the cause of his death was an inflammation in his bowels.[13] It is said that Lady Townshend[14] has offered to settle twenty thousand pounds upon the children if Lady Grenwich will do as much.[15] Some say Mr Townshend is dead in very moderate circumstances, and others, worth eighty thousand pounds.

I shall be very happy to see you in London and hope nothing will tempt you to defer your return; at the same time I cannot say that this event, received as it has been, makes it immediately necessary, but the sooner you come, believe me, the better, and the Court and all its gaieties will be gone to Fontainebleau.[16]

Pray speak properly for me to all who remember me at Paris. Lady Hertford and the family are much yours. I remain, dear Horry, most sincerely and affectionately

Your friend and servant,

HERTFORD

To CONWAY, Wednesday 16 September 1767

Missing; listed in 'Paris Journals' (DU DEFFAND v. 385).

13. 'Sir William Duncan . . . pronounced it to be a slow fever of the putrid kind' (idem to idem, 24 Aug., loc. cit.).

14. I.e., the Dowager Lady Townshend, mother of Lord Townshend and Charles Townshend.

15. According to an account in the *London Chronicle* 22–4 Sept., xxii. 294, *sub* 24 Sept., 'Lord Townshend . . . advised Lady Townshend (his mother) to alter her will in favour of his late brother's children, and insisted upon their being left sole legatees to her fortune and effects, he alleging, his brother did not die in such good circumstances as the world may imagine, and that his own children will be amply provided for without her Ladyship's favour and assistance.' Townshend died intestate, with his affairs in great confusion (Sir Lewis Namier and John Brooke, *Charles Townshend,* 1964, p. 184 and n. 2). Lady Mary Coke wrote on 15 Sept.: 'By all I can find out, he trusted so many different people with his money, that I fear there will be losses, as it was very frequent with him to order his money to be placed out in other people's names' (*Journals,* ii. 126; see also ibid. ii. 130–1).

16. The King and Queen left for Fontainebleau 22, and the Dauphin 23 Sept. (*Gazette de Leyde* 2 Oct., *sub* Versailles, 23 Sept.).

From HERTFORD, Thursday 17 September 1767

Printed for the first time from a photostat of BM Add. MSS 23219, ff. 23–7.

London, September 17th 1767.

My dear Horry,

I HAVE at last recovered the letter[1] you sent by Mr Fletcher. I have with some difficulty found out the gentleman and he has delivered it; but neither you nor I have any reason to be satisfied with his behaviour about it. Mr Townshend's death I told you in my last letter by the post[2] made no alteration. I will explain myself now more particularly. The Duke of Grafton, who was concerned with him in the same office and more immediately exposed to difficulties from the daily inconstancy and vanity of his nature, from the moment of his death I believe felt himself relieved. My brother is fully sensible of all his weaknesses, and upon the whole thinks it may be an advantage to Government. He is still sensible that the load lies heavier upon him in the House of Commons, as he now remains the only man to be attacked and does not know that he has any able advocate who will be willing and able always to assist. He is however not at all shaken by this event. The Seal of the Exchequer was immediately offered to Lord North,[3] who declined it[4] but with the strongest assurances of attachment to the present system, saying he was diffident of his own abilities and was unwilling to engage in anything which would separate him from his father,[5] who was in a very low-spirited and declining state,[6] but that he should be equally ready upon all occasions to take the most active part in their service.

1. Missing.
2. *Ante* 14 Sept. 1767.
3. By Grafton, at the King's command, in a letter of ca 5 Sept. (see Grafton, *Autobiography*, ed. Anson, 1898, p. 166).
4. At Court 9 Sept. (MANN vi. 552, n. 11); however, see below, n. 6.
5. Francis North (1704–90), 3d Bn Guilford, 1729, cr. (1752) E. of Guilford.
6. He suffered from the stone (see Alan Valentine, *Lord North*, Norman, Oklahoma, 1967, i. 153); Charles Lloyd wrote to Temple, 10 Sept., that 'Lord Guilford is said to be in a dangerous way, so as not to be likely to live even a few weeks' (*Grenville Papers* iv. 162). However, upon North's return to Wroxton after his Court appearance 9 Sept., he found his father 'astonishingly recovered' and declared himself ready to assume the chancellorship in a letter to Grafton, 10 Sept. (printed Grafton, op. cit. 167). His appointment was approved by the King in a letter to Grafton of 12 Sept. (printed in Geo. III's *Corr.*, ed. Fortescue, i. 505) and the seals were delivered 7 Oct. (*London Chronicle* 6–8 Oct., xxii. 342).

I came to town just at this time and went with my brother to the Duke of Grafton, who told us upon thinking of this subject with all the consideration he could give it, and weighing the merits of all such as could be competitors for it, he could think of no methods so likely to answer the purposes of Government as the two which he should submit to our consideration: the one, to appoint Barrington chancellor of the Exchequer, who had executed the office part of the business extremely well in difficult times,[7] and to appoint for his successor[8] Lord Clare,[9] Mr Ellis[10] or any other person of that rank in the House of Commons who might be thought more proper;[11] the other, to put the seal[12] as a less laborious office, if he could reconcile himself to it, into my brother's hands, and thereby to open the seals[13] for Lord Hillsbro'[14] and to give the Post Office to Lord Edgecombe[15] or whomever he should think more useful. My brother did not object to this proposal as a thing to which he might not have yielded, but said that he chose to decline it because the finances of this country have not been his particular study, and therefore he might be found deficient in them; that at present he could in debate take up such parts as he understood and decline the rest without reflection, but that if he was called upon in office he could not without exposing himself avoid answering every objection; and upon his asking my opinion I could not differ with him, especially as the office in the Ordnance which he has lately accepted[16]

7. 'In a hurrying moment, I offered . . . [the seals] with the King's leave to Lord Barrington [in a letter of 12 Sept., in Shute Barrington, Bp of Durham, *Political Life of . . . Viscount Barrington*, 1815, pp. 112–15]. His Lordship accepted the offer [his letter of acceptance is printed ibid. 115–18] . . . and expressed his hopes, that it would be only a temporary appointment, until his Majesty could consider where to better place them' (Grafton, loc. cit.). Barrington had been chancellor of the Exchequer from March 1761 to May 1762, while the Seven Years' War was still in progress; in his letter of acceptance he wrote that 'the office part of the business I have done when it was much more laborious, comprehensive, and difficult,' but that he felt that 'to the Parliamentary part (now much more important and nice . . .) I am not equal' (Barrington, op. cit. 116).

8. As secretary at war.

9. Robert Nugent (*ante* 24 May 1753, n. 8) had been created Vct Clare (in Ireland) 19 Jan. 1767. He was currently first lord of Trade.

10. Welbore Ellis.

11. Hans Stanley was rumoured as a candidate (Charles Lloyd to Temple, 10 Sept., loc. cit.; Thomas Bradshaw to Barrington, 11 Sept., Barrington MSS, quoted Namier and Brooke iii. 471).

12. Of the Exchequer.

13. Of secretary of state.

14. Currently joint paymaster general.

15. George Edgcumbe (1721–95), 3d Bn Edgcumbe, 1761; cr. (1781) Vct Mount Edgcumbe and (1789) E. of Mount Edgcumbe; brother and heir of HW's friend 'Dick' Edgcumbe.

16. See *ante* 9 Aug. 1767.

is, from its being an office of account and in some measure mixed or dependent upon the Treasury, perhaps incompatible with it. It stands therefore at present as most likely to go into the hands of Lord Barrington, and if it should, I suggested to the Duke of Grafton that it might be prudent to consult Lord Granby[17] before another secretary at war was appointed,[18] as every temper might not submit to the present method of doing that business, to gratify his Lordship. The Duke of Grafton is now out of town.[19] My brother tells me he has heard today, but is not certain of his intelligence, that Lord North repents and wishes to have it.

C. Townshend is, I think, as little lamented as you can suppose him. Lady Grenwich is not thought to be in absolute despair; Lady Mary Coke, who loves grief, has flown to her retirement at Sudbrook;[20] the Dowager Lady Townshend is much afflicted. Lord Townshend feels his loss in his present situation, but was at Court today doing business and goes to Ireland next week.[21] Lord Mansfield has told Mr Hume that C. Townshend had engaged since the *peerage*[22] to be useful to them in Opposition,[23] and as a proof of the probability of it and the ingratitude of his temper, he has[24] since wrote to my brother saying the King had given it unasked, though my brother himself carried the message from him saying he would resign if it was not granted.[25]

17. Commander-in-chief of the army since Aug. 1766 (Namier and Brooke iii. 104).

18. 'It will not be possible for the arrangement [Barrington's appointment as chancellor of the Exchequer] to take place, till the return of a letter to Lord Granby, whose concurrence the King wishes, before he can appoint any one to succeed your Lordship' (Grafton to Barrington, 12 Sept., Barrington, op. cit. 114).

19. Which accounts for Hertford and Conway not yet knowing of North's acceptance of the chancellorship. On Saturday, 12 Sept., Grafton was intercepted by a messenger with North's letter of acceptance as he headed out of town to Euston, and stopped momentarily to write letters to the King, Barrington, and North (Grafton, op. cit. 167–8), but evidently not to Hertford or Conway. Grafton's letter to the King is printed in Fortescue, op. cit. i. 504–5, and his letter to Barrington in Barrington, op. cit. 118–19.

20. See Coke, *Journals*, ii. 124–8 *et seq.*

21. See *ante* 14 Sept. 1767, n. 9.

22. Granted his wife 19 Aug.; see *ante* ca 20 Aug. 1767, n. 8.

23. In a memorandum of 17 Sept., Lord Townshend wrote that Theobald Taaffe, the notorious swindler and professional gambler, 'acquainted me that my brother Charles had carried on just before his death a negotiation through him to Mr Rigby and thence to the Duke of Bedford, Lord Temple, and Mr Grenville, by which the second was to have been first lord of the Treasury, my brother secretary of state and direction of the House of Commons, Duke of Bedford and Mr Grenville would support but no places' (printed Sir Lewis Namier and John Brooke, *Charles Townshend*, 1964, p. 183).

24. Hertford originally wrote 'had,' and then wrote a dark 's' and 'since' over the 'd.'

25. 'On the very day his wife kissed hands for a barony, Townshend had threatened Conway to resign unless the

Lord Chatham is said to be recovered;[26] Mrs Pitt, his sister, says he was neither so ill nor is now so well as has been reported, but that she knows enough of his constitution to follow it round the year, as it is very politically disposed, and that her knowledge of it makes her conclude he will be very well during the months of September and October; that in November his health will be more doubtful, and will be absolutely determined by the meeting of Parliament[27] from the state of the times. That her brother does not delight in halcyon days, but chooses rather times of difficulty, and therefore will choose retirement or public life, as matters may be easy or confused and worthy of his attention. In the meantime I do not find he communicates at all with Administration, but the Chancellor[28] is gone to the Bath and must learn something of him.[29] His Lordship has sold chief part of the Pynsent estate,[30] and I hear did it by letter of attorney to Lady Chatham.[31]

The anecdote you tell me from Paris[32] is curious, and may correspond with Mrs Pitt's ideas.

S[ir] E. Walpole has declined Yarmouth after your example,[33] and I hear one of the Walpoles will succeed him.[34] The vacancy you have made, Lord Buckingham tells me will be more uncertain; your con-

---

peerage was granted. The very next day he told Conway that the peerage had been offered by the King' (*Mem. Geo. III* iii. 73–4).

26. A false report; see *ante* 9 Sept. 1767, n. 12 and MANN vi. 552, n. 14.

27. 24 Nov. (*Journals of the House of Commons* xxxi. 421).

28. Lord Camden.

29. While at Bath, Camden wrote to Lady Chatham at Burton Pynsent 'to inquire after my Lord's health'; see his letter, 25 Sept., printed *Chatham Corr.* iii. 284–5.

30. In order to repurchase Hayes, which he had sold to Thomas Walpole in Nov. 1765; Chatham felt that his re-establishment at Hayes was essential to the recovery of his health. Thomas Walpole, naturally reluctant at first to part with Hayes, finally agreed (in a letter of 30 Oct.), rather than risk having Chatham's ill health imputed to him. See *Mem. Geo. III* iii. 30–3; Basil Williams, *Life of . . . Pitt*, 1913, ii. 241–2; *Chatham Corr.* ii. 328, iii. 289–92; Namier and Brooke iii. 599.

31. See *ante* 9 Sept. 1767 and n. 14.

32. See *ante* 9 Sept. 1767.

33. HW had written to William Langley, mayor of King's Lynn, 13 March 1767, informing him of his intention 'of not offering my service again to the town of Lynn, as one of their representatives in Parliament,' and Sir Edward announced his intention of retiring in the *Cambridge Journal* 8 Aug. 1767: 'For three or four years past I have not attended my duty in Parliament as I ought to do; and with that disposition I am by no means a fit representative of so considerable a trading town as [Great] Yarmouth. The indulgence of my friends there has been very great; which I must not abuse any longer' (quoted Namier and Brooke iii. 595). The current Parliament was dissolved 10 March 1768 (*Journals of the House of Commons* xxxi. 666).

34. Sir Edward was succeeded by his cousin, the Hon. Richard Walpole (1728–98), 3d son of 'Old Horace' Walpole, 1st Bn Walpole of Wolterton; he was returned unopposed for the borough 16 March 1768 and sat for it until 1784 (Namier and Brooke i. 340–1, iii. 598).

stituents have not yet taken your advice, but are in the midst of confusion.[35] Mr Walpole[36] has left them for some time, and his interest has suffered so much from the attendance of the other candidates[37] that Lord Walpole[38] was alarmed. He is now gone down, and will I suppose make it up by means equally out of your prescription.[39] The Duke of Northumberland has told me today that Lord Carlisle[40] is supposed in the North to have given his interest, both in Cumberland and Carlisle, against Government.[41] I will not be

35. HW, hearing that 'a warm contest is expected,' had hoped 'by an early declaration' of his retiring 'to preserve the integrity and peace' of King's Lynn (HW to Langley 13 March 1767), presumably by leaving the field clear for the uncontested return of the other two candidates (see n. 37 below). However, on 18 March Thomas Walpole, M.P. Sudbury 1754–61, Ashburton 1761–8, 'offered himself a candidate for . . . King's Lynn . . . in the room of his cousin the Hon. Horace Walpole' (*Daily Adv.* 24 March *sub* Norwich, 21 March; Thomas Walpole to the Mayor, Recorder, Aldermen, etc. of Lynn, 18 March 1767, printed in *The Lynn Magazine*, 1768, p. 6), thus reopening the contest. See n. 39 below.

36. Thomas Walpole.

37. Sir John Turner (1712–80), 3d Bt, lord of the Treasury 1762–5; and Crisp Molineux (1730–92), sheriff of Norfolk 1767–8. Turner, a follower of Grenville, had been M.P. for King's Lynn since 1739; Molineux, a friend of Wilkes and admirer of Chatham, was making his maiden bid for a Parliamentary seat (Namier and Brooke i. 341, iii. 146, 570).

38. Horatio Walpole (1723–1809), 2d Bn Walpole of Wolterton, 1757; cr. (1806) E. of Orford, n.c.; Thomas Walpole's brother, who had been M.P. for King's Lynn 1747–57 (ibid. iii. 597).

39. The contest for King's Lynn was marked by the apathy of Thomas Walpole and his sponsor, Lord Orford, and the treachery of Sir John Turner. In the contest for the borough Walpole remained neutral, Molineux and Turner having originally agreed to ask for one vote for themselves and one for Walpole. However, throughout the contest Turner campaigned for single votes only; had Molineux done likewise, Walpole would have

been returned at the bottom of the poll. As it turned out, for honouring his agreement Molineux was returned at the bottom (21 March 1768) with 159 votes, while Walpole and Turner emerged victorious with 200 and 174 votes. Walpole continued M.P. for King's Lynn until 1784 and Turner until 1774. Molineux, with Lord Orford's assistance, eventually became M.P. for Castle Rising 1771–4, and in 1774 succeeded Turner as M.P. for King's Lynn, Turner declining to stand; he continued M.P. there until 1790. See ibid. i. 341, iii. 146–7, 570, 598–601; *Lynn Magazine* pp. 60–73.

40. Frederick Howard (1748–1825), 5th Earl of Carlisle, 1758.

41. Carlisle, who was just departing on his Grand Tour, had not yet declared himself; however, he had been approached by the Duke of Portland to support the latter's candidates against those of Sir James Lowther, who had the support of Government, in the Cumberland election, and on 22 Sept. Carlisle's guardian, Sir William Musgrave, wrote him: 'You are now called upon in a very positive manner, both by the Duke of P[ortland] and Mr Howard [Philip Howard of Corby, a kinsman of Lord Carlisle] to declare yourself in consequence of some engagements you are supposed to have entered into several months ago with the Duke . . . [whose side] have been very attentive, and seem to rely on your promise' (Hist. MSS Comm., 15th Report, App. pt vi, *Carlisle MSS*, 1897, p. 213; Brian Bonsall, *Sir James Lowther and Cumberland and Westmorland Elections 1754–1775*, Manchester, 1960, pp. 79–80). After another prompting by Musgrave, Carlisle declared himself for Portland in October (ibid. 80; *Carlisle MSS* pp. 215, 217).

named, but if you see George Selwyn[42] and he is as desirous as he was of getting the green ribband[43] for his Lordship, the sooner he gives directions upon the point, if it is yet time, the better.[44]

Mr Harris, my brother-in-law, is in a very low-spirited unhappy way to himself, the physicians see no danger;[45] my sister feels great unhappiness and wishes him in town.

I long to see you here and so does my brother; my house is a melancholy place without you; pray come away.[46] I will do the best I can till you come, but you will make us all happier, easier and more satisfied when we can take your advice and assistance with us.

I will not enter into any farther particulars as I hope to see you soon, and am, with the best wishes and compliments of all my family, dear Horry,

Most truly and affectionately yours,

HERTFORD

I beg my compliments to all who remember me at Paris.
Lord North accepts.[47]

To HERTFORD, Monday 21 September 1767

Missing; listed in 'Paris Journals' (DU DEFFAND v. 385) as sent 'by Mr Caswall' (probably Timothy Caswall [ca 1733–1802], M.P.).

42. Who was on his way to Paris with Carlisle and Lord March; they arrived 20 Sept., and HW visited them the same day ('Paris Journals,' DU DEFFAND v. 321).

43. Of Knight of the Thistle.

44. Selwyn was negotiating both to get a green ribbon for Carlisle, and a place for Lord March; see J. H. Jesse, *George Selwyn and his Contemporaries*, 1882, ii. 183, 193–4. Though Carlisle declared against Government in the Cumberland election (n. 41 above), it was not held against him by Grafton, who, Musgrave wrote to Carlisle 16 Oct., 'has no objection to your giving your interest as you proposed, and thinks it a sufficient answer to any

person that though you wish very well to Government, yet in this instance you have done what you thought most for your honour, and the advancement of your own family interest' (*Carlisle MSS* p. 217). Carlisle was made K.T. 23 Dec. 1767, and invested at Turin 27 Feb. 1768 (W. A. Shaw, *Knights of England*, 1906, i. 79; see also Jesse, op. cit. ii. 277–8).

45. He died 5 Oct. (*ante* 9 Sept. 1767, n. 11).

46. HW left Paris 8 Oct., reaching London 12 Oct. ('Paris Journals,' DU DEFFAND v. 324).

47. The Exchequer; see above.

To Conway, Monday 21 September 1767

Missing; listed in 'Paris Journals' (DU DEFFAND v. 385) as sent 'by Mr Caswall.'

To Hertford, Sunday 27 September 1767

Missing; listed in 'Paris Journals' (DU DEFFAND v. 385).

To Conway, Wednesday 30 September 1767

Missing; listed in 'Paris Journals' (DU DEFFAND v. 385).

From Conway, June 1768

Missing; answered *post* 16 June 1768.

To Conway, Thursday 16 June 1768

Printed from the MS now WSL; first printed Wright v. 205–8. For the history of the MS see *ante* 29 June 1744 OS; it was marked by HW for inclusion in *Works,* but was not included.
Endorsed: Mr Walpole 16 June 68.

Strawberry Hill, June 16, 1768.

I AM glad you have writ to me,[1] for I wanted to write to you, and did not know what to say. I have been but two nights in town, and then heard of nothing but Wilkes, of whom I am tired to death,[2] and of T[homas] Townshend;[3] the truth of whose story I did not

1. Conway's letter is missing.
2. Wilkes, outlawed in Nov. 1764 (see *ante* 25 Nov. 1764, n. 39), had returned to England in February, unsuccessfully contested London (25 March) in the general election for Parliament, and then been returned head of the poll for Middlesex (28 March). Surrendering to his outlawry in the Court of King's Bench,

he was acquitted by Lord Mansfield on a technical point 8 June, but his prior convictions for publishing the *North Briton* No. 45 and the *Essay on Woman* were upheld 18 June. Mob support for Wilkes at his election and after led to extensive rioting. See Namier and Brooke i. 329–32, iii. 640; MANN vii. 5–33 *passim.*
3. I.e., 'young Tommy' Townshend

know;[4] and indeed the tone of the age has made me so uncharitable, that I concluded his ill-humour was put on, in order to be mollified with the reversion of his father's[5] place, which I know he has long wanted;[6] and the destination of the Pay Office has been so long notified,[7] that I had no notion of his not liking the arrangement. For the new Paymaster,[8] I could not think him worth writing a letter on purpose. By your letter and the enclosed,[9] I find Townshend has been very ill-treated, and I like his spirit in not bearing such neglect and contempt, though wrapped up in £2700 a year.[10]

What can one say of the Duke of G[rafton] but that his whole conduct is childish, insolent, inconstant and absurd? nay ruinous. Because we are not in confusion enough, he makes everything as bad as possible, neglecting on one hand, and taking no precautions on the other. I neither see how it is possible for him to remain minister, nor whom to put in his place. No government, no police,[11] London and Middlesex distracted,[12] the colonies in rebellion,[13] Ireland ready

(1733–1800) (ante 17 Nov. 1763, n. 9). See next note.

4. Upon the death 5 June of George Cooke, who was joint paymaster general with Townshend, Grafton had appointed Richard Rigby sole paymaster without first informing Townshend, who learned of the arrangement only upon being ordered to kiss hands for Rigby's place of joint vice-treasurer of Ireland. Offended at this discourtesy, Townshend resigned. See Namier and Brooke iii. 555; *Bedford Corr.* iii. 400–1; J. H. Jesse, *George Selwyn and his Contemporaries,* 1882, ii. 324.

5. Hon. Thomas Townshend (1701–80), M.P. Winchelsea 1722–7, Cambridge University 1727–74.

6. The elder Thomas was teller of the Exchequer, one of the richest government sinecures, from 1727 till his death (Namier and Brooke iii. 554; *Journals of the House of Commons* xxxviii. 755). A member of the Opposition, he supported his son's resolution to resign, and reportedly made him a present of £10,000 (Henry Strachey to Clive 14 June 1768, Clive MSS, cited Namier and Brooke iii. 555). However, the younger Thomas never obtained the reversion of his father's sinecure.

7. Rigby had been promised the entire Pay Office upon being reappointed joint

vice-treasurer of Ireland in January. See ibid. iii. 354, 357.

8. Rigby.

9. Missing; perhaps a copy of Camden's letter to Grafton 9 June, explaining Townshend's reasons for resigning; see ibid. iii. 555.

10. For joint vice-treasurer of Ireland; see n. 4 above.

11. HW wrote to Mann, 4 Aug. 1768, in reference to the attack of a mob of coal-heavers in April on the house of John Green, that 'it is pretty astonishing . . . that a house should be besieged for thirteen hours together in the capital, and no notice taken of it, though a justice of peace passed by at the time!' (MANN vii. 39).

12. Widespread rioting during the spring by the Wilkes mobs, coal-heavers, sawyers, and other groups threatened a state of anarchy in parts of London and Middlesex until the 12th of June, when a detachment of Guards put down a disturbance caused by the coal-heavers, who had been the chief offenders. After this, the riots began to subside. See ibid. vii. 20–39 *passim; Mem. Geo. III* iii. 136–49 *passim;* GM 1768, xxxviii. 195, 197, 242–5, 298–9; George F. Rudé, *Wilkes and Liberty,* Oxford, 1962, pp. 45–53, 97–8.

13. Against the duties proposed by Charles Townshend the year before and

to be so,[14] and France arrogant and on the point of being hostile![15] Lord Bute accused of all and dying of a panic;[16] George Grenville wanting to make rage desperate;[17] Lord Rockingham, the Duke of Portland[18] and the Cavendishes[19] thinking we have no enemies but Lord Bute[20] and Dyson,[21] and that four mutes[22] and an epigram[23] can set everything to rights; the Duke of Grafton like an apprentice,

imposed by 7 Geo. III, c. 46 (see Sir Lewis Namier and John Brooke, *Charles Townshend*, 1964, pp. 172–9; Owen Ruffhead, *Statutes at Large*, 1763–1800, x. 369–72). The *Daily Adv.* reported 25 May, *sub* Edinburgh, 20 May, that 'by a letter from New York, dated the 8th of April, it appears that . . . in several other places of the continent, they are much displeased with the custom house officers, and at Boston they have threatened to pull down the custom house'; and 1 June, *sub* Gloucester, 30 May, that 'intelligence is received from Boston . . . that the people have refused to pay the custom house duties, and have solicited, by circular letters, all the colonies upon the continent, to join in this resolution.'

14. The Irish Parliament had in May rejected a proposal presented by the lord lieutenant in April for an augmentation of the troops on the Irish establishment. See *Journals of the House of Commons . . . Ireland* xiv. 526–30, 532; *Calendar of Home Office Papers . . . 1766–1769*, ed. J. Redington, 1879, pp. 326–7, 330–1.

15. Against Corsica; see MANN vii. 31 and nn. 18, 21.

16. In August he felt compelled to go to Barèges for his health (ibid. vii. 42, n. 8). See n. 23 below.

17. HW had written to Mann, 2 Dec. 1767, that 'George Grenville is distracted that the ministers will not make America rebel, that he may be minister' (ibid. vi. 567). Actually, with the accession of the Bedfords to the administration later that month, Grenville's hopes for returning to office vanished, and he was content henceforth to let his man of business, Thomas Whately, look after what remained of their group in the House (Namier and Brooke ii. 544).

18. A follower of Rockingham.

19. Also followers of Rockingham.

20. Portland's dislike for Bute was compounded by Bute being father-in-law of Sir James Lowther, Portland's adversary in the Cumberland election (*ante* 17 Sept. 1767, n. 41), who was currently attempting to disprove Portland's title to certain estates in that county. See Namier and Brooke i. 243–5, iii. 57.

21. Jeremiah Dyson (*ante* 20 April 1764), currently lord of Trade and a principal adviser of Grafton. Though an office-holder in the Rockingham administration, he had continually embarrassed Rockingham by opposing administration measures and attempting to trip up ministers on points of order; such actions led Rockingham to ask for his dismissal, which was not effected. See Namier and Brooke ii. 371–3.

22. Presumably a satiric reference to Rockingham, who was a hesitant speaker, Portland, and the Cavendishes (Lords John and George; Lord Frederick was politically the least consequential of the three brothers; see Namier and Brooke ii. 201).

23. Perhaps the epigram 'To the Earl of B.' printed in the *Lynn Magazine*, 1768, p. 108:
'O B⸺ the author of our presents ills
Think e'er it be too late of poor Lord Squills [i.e. Squillace]:
Now that your neighbour's house is all on fire,
Gang your ways, cheeld, and whilst you can, retire:
Lest Prince's Guards be found too weak to save,
And thy own Peace too soon inscribe thy grave.'
Along with this epigram a longer attack is printed, beginning: 'Say B—te—born Anarchy, Confusion say, / Persists the Thane the same dark game to play?' and recommending at the end that 'gracious B[entin]ck reign' in Bute's stead, i.e. Portland (ibid. 107–8).

thinking the world should be postponed to a whore[24] and a horse-race; and the Bedfords not caring what disgraces we undergo, while each of them has £3000 a year and three thousand bottles of claret and champagne!—Not but that I believe these last good folks are still not satisfied with the satisfaction of their wishes. They have the favour of the Duke of Grafton, but neither his confidence nor his company, so that they can neither sell the places in his gift, nor his secrets. Indeed they have not the same reasons to be displeased with him as you have, for they were his enemies and you his friend —and therefore he embraced them and dropped you;[25] and I believe would be puzzled to give a tolerable reason for either.

As this is the light in which I see our present situation, you will not wonder that I am happy to have nothing to do with it. Not that were it more flourishing, I would ever meddle again. I have no good opinion of any of our factions, nor think highly of either their heads or their hearts. I can amuse myself much more to my satisfaction— and had I not lived to see my country at the period of its greatest glory, I should bear our present state much better. I cannot mend it and therefore will think as little of it as I can. The Duke of Northumberland asked me to dine at Sion tomorrow, but as his vanity of governing Middlesex[26] makes him absurdly meditate to contest the county,[27] I concluded he wanted my interest here, and therefore excused myself, for I will have nothing to do with it.

I shall like much to come to Park Place, if your present company stays, or if the Fitzroys or the Richmonds are there; but I desire to be excused from the Cavendishes, who have in a manner left me off, because I was so unlucky as not to think Lord Rockingham as great a man as my Lord Chatham, and Lord John[28] more able than either. If you will let me know when they leave you, you shall see me: but they would not be glad of my company, nor I of theirs.

24. His mistress, Nancy Parsons (*ante* 27 Aug. 1764).

25. The Bedfords came into office in December (see MANN vi. 568–72), and Conway resigned as secretary of state in January, a move he had long been wishing to make (see *ante* 9 Aug. 1767, n. 3). In February he was named colonel of the 4th Dragoons (*Army Lists*, 1769, p. 32).

26. He had been lord lieutenant of the county since 1762.

27. The death of George Cooke 5 June (n. 4 above) had left vacant one of the

seats for Middlesex, but no candidate stood for the seat on Northumberland's interest. At the by-election in December, the Court-favoured candidate, Sir William Beauchamp Proctor, was defeated by Wilkes's protégé, John Glynn. See Namier and Brooke i. 331–2.

28. Cavendish. HW had called him 'obstinate' and 'conceited' to Hertford *ante* 12 May 1765, and in *Mem. Geo. III* ii. 18 described him as 'a kind of heresiarch that sought to be adored by his enthusiastic disciples . . .'

My hay and I are drowned;[29] I comfort myself with a fire, but cannot treat the other with any sun, at least not with one that has more warmth than the sun in a harlequin farce.

I went this morning to see the Duchess of Grafton, who has got an excellent house[30] and fine prospect, but melancholy enough, and so I thought was she herself: I did not ask wherefore.[31]

I go to town tomorrow to see the *Devil Upon Two Sticks,*[32] as I did last week, but could not get in.[33] I have now secured a place in my niece Cholmondeley's[34] box, and am to have the additional entertainment of Mrs Macaulay[35] in the same company, who goes to see herself represented,[36] and I suppose figures herself very like Socrates.[37]

I shall send this letter by the coach, as it is rather free-spoken, and Sandwich[38] may be prying.

Mr Chute[39] has found the subject of my tragedy,[40] which I thought

29. HW had written to Montagu 15 June 1768 that 'the deluge . . . began here . . . on Monday last [13 June], and then rained near eight and forty hours without intermission. My poor hay has not a dry thread to its back' (MONTAGU ii. 262).

30. Formerly Lord Grosvenor's, at Combe, Surrey (Dr William Hunter's evidence at her trial in *Trials for Adultery,* 1779–80, Vol. IV).

31. Separated from the Duke since 1765 (see *ante* 3 Dec. 1764, n. 12), she was with child by Lord Ossory; a daughter, Lady Anne, was born 23 Aug. (OSSORY i. 58, n. 1). HW, in his MS 'foul copy' of *Mem. Geo. III,* 'from the beginning of his second Parliament,' p. 17, writes that 'the Duke of Grafton being assured that the Duchess was with child, resolved to acquaint her that he knew, and was determined to prove it. This notification he pressed both Lord Hertford and Mr Conway to carry to her; both declined an office so unworthy of a gentleman (for he had couched his letters in the harshest terms). . . . He then pressed the task on his secretary Mr Stonehewer. . . . A footman was at last forced to be the messenger.' After a trial, the Duke divorced the Duchess by Act of Parliament 23 March 1769, and the Duchess married Lord Ossory three days later.

32. A comedy by Samuel Foote, first

acted at the Haymarket 30 May (*London Stage* Pt IV, iii. 1336); HW's copy is Hazen, *Cat. of HW's Lib.,* No. 1810:28:7.

33. The play, which was very popular, had been performed the previous week on Monday, Wednesday, and Friday (6, 8, 10 June) (*London Stage* Pt IV, iii. 1338); HW, who wrote to Cole, Mme du Deffand and Mann from SH 6 and 9 June, probably tried to attend the performance of 10 June (see COLE i. 143; DU DEFFAND ii. 82; MANN vii. 28).

34. Mary Woffington (ca 1729–1811), m. (1746) Rev. Hon. Robert Cholmondeley, HW's nephew; sister of Margaret ('Peg') Woffington, the actress (OSSORY ii. 109, n. 10).

35. Catherine Sawbridge (1731–91), m. 1 (1760) George Macaulay, M.D.; m. 2 (1778) William Graham; historian; HW's occasional correspondent.

36. By the character of Mrs Margaret Maxwell.

37. The play satirizes her republican ideas, but is directed mainly against the medical profession. See Mary M. Belden, *The Dramatic Work of Samuel Foote,* New Haven, 1929, pp. 125–30.

38. Currently joint postmaster-general.

39. Whom HW had visited in London the previous week (MONTAGU ii. 263).

40. *The Mysterious Mother,* which deals with the subject of double incest. HW had finished it 15 March ('Short Notes,'

happened in Tillotson's[41] time, in the Queen of Navarre's[42] tales;[43] and what is very remarkable, I had laid my plot at Narbonne and about the beginning of the Reformation, and it really did happen in Languedoc, and in the reign of Francis I[44]—is not this singular?

I hope your canary hen was really with egg by the bluebird, and that he will not plead that they are none of his and sue for a divorce.[45] Adieu!

Yours ever,

H. W.

From CONWAY, ca Sunday 7 August 1768

Missing; answered *post* 9 Aug. 1768.

To CONWAY, Tuesday 9 August 1768

Printed from *Works* v. 136–8.

Strawberry Hill, August 9, 1768.

YOU are very kind, or else you saw into my mind, and knew that I have been thinking of writing to you, but had not a penful of matter. True, I have been in town,[1] but I am more likely to

GRAY i. 43), and began printing 50 copies at the SH Press 14 June (*Journal of the Printing Office at Strawberry Hill*, ed. Toynbee, 1923, p. 13).

41. John Tillotson (1630–94), Abp of Canterbury, 1691. HW writes in his postscript to the play, that 'I had heard, when very young, that a gentlewoman, under uncommon agonies of mind, had waited on Archbishop Tillotson, and besought his counsel,' etc. (*Works* i. 125).

42. Marguerite d'Angoulême (1492–1549), m. (1527) Henri d'Albret, King of Navarre.

43. The 30th tale of the *Heptaméron*, first published in 1558. However, the story exists in versions both earlier and later than Marguerite of Navarre's; see CHAT-

TERTON 165 and nn. 2–5; Topham Beauclerk to HW 19 Aug. 1775.

44. Marguerite of Navarre was sister of Francis I; she sets the tale in the reign of Louis XII, Francis I's immediate predecessor.

45. Presumably an allusion to Sir Charles and Lady Sarah Bunbury. Lady Sarah was with child by her lover, Lord William Gordon; in December she gave birth to a daughter, and in February 1769 she went off with Lord William. However, her husband did not divorce her until 1776. See *Leinster Corr.* i. 539 *et seq.*; Coke, *Journals*, ii. 304; Namier and Brooke ii. 138.

_____

1. HW had written to Mann from Arlington Street 4 Aug. (MANN vii. 39).

learn news here; where at least we have it like fish, that could not find vent in London. I saw nothing there but the ruins of loo, Lady Hertford's cribbage, and Lord Botetourt, like patience on a monument, smiling in grief. He is totally ruined,[2] and quite charmed. Yet I heartily pity him. To Virginia he cannot be indifferent: [3] he must turn their heads somehow or other.[4] If his graces do not captivate them, he will enrage them to fury; for I take all his *douceur* to be enamelled on iron.[5]

My life is most uniform and void of events, and has nothing worth repeating. I have not had a soul with me, but accidental company now and then at dinner. Lady Holderness, Lady Ancram, Lady Mary Coke,[6] Mrs Anne Pitt, and Mr Hume, dined here the day before yesterday. They were but just gone, when George Selwyn, Lord Bolinbroke, and Sir William Musgrave,[7] who had been at Hampton Court, came in, at nine at night, to drink tea. They told me, what I was very glad to hear, and what I could not doubt, as they had it from the Duke of Grafton himself, that Bishop Cornwallis[8] goes to Canterbury. I feared it would be Terrick;[9] but it seems he had secured all the back stairs, and not the great stairs. As the last head of the Church[10] had been on the midwife line,[11] I suppose goody Lyttelton had hopes;[12] and as he had been president of an atheistical

2. By 'schemes about mines' (Coke, *Journals*, ii. 323). See *Mem. Geo. III* iii. 107–8.

3. He had been appointed governor of Virginia 29 July (MANN vii. 44, n. 22).

4. The Virginia House and Council had recently alarmed the British Government by adopting a remonstrance to Parliament flatly denying the right of Parliament to levy any kind of tax for revenue on the colonies (*Journals of the House of Burgesses of Virginia*, 1766–1769, pp. 168–71; see also MANN vii. 43, n. 18).

5. HW writes in *Mem. Geo. III* iii. 156 that 'in the two years that he lived to govern them, his soothing flattering manners had so wrought on the province, that his death was bewailed with the most general and affectionate concern.'

6. See her *Journals*, ii. 330–1.

7. (1735–1800), 6th Bt; antiquary (COLE i. 57, n. 2).

8. Hon. Frederick Cornwallis (1713–83), Bp of Lichfield, 1750. He was appointed Archbishop of Canterbury 12 Aug. (*Lloyd's Evening Post* 12–15 Aug., xxiii.

157), succeeding Archbishop Secker, who had died 3 Aug. HW writes in *Mem. Geo. III* iii. 158 that he 'was preferred to the primacy by . . . Grafton, who had a friendship for the Bishop's nephew, Earl Cornwallis,' and describes him as 'a prelate of inconsiderable talents, but a most amiable, gentle, and humane man.' It appears from a letter of Grafton to the King 7 Aug. (printed George III's *Corr.*, ed. Fortescue, ii. 37) that John Thomas (1696–1781), Bp of Winchester, had first choice, but turned the primacy down.

9. Richard Terrick (*ante* 5 April 1764 *bis*, n. 16). HW writes in *Mem. Geo. III* iii. 158–9 that 'Terrick of London, the most time-serving of the clergy, was sorely disappointed in missing the first mitre of England,' and mentions, ibid. i. 331, his 'assiduity of back-stairs address.'

10. Thomas Secker, Archbishop of Canterbury (HW).

11. See *ante* 28 Sept. 1762, n. 36.

12. Charles Lyttelton, Bishop of Car-

club,[13] to be sure Warburton did not despair.[14] I was thinking it would make a good article in the papers, that three bishops had supped with Nancy Parsons[15] at Vauxhall, in their way to Lambeth. I am sure _____[16] would have been of the number; and _____,[17] who told the Duke of Newcastle, that if his Grace had commanded the Blues at Minden[18] they would have behaved better, would make no scruple to cry up her chastity.

The King of Denmark[19] comes on Thursday;[20] and I go tomorrow to see him. It has cost three thousand pounds to new-furnish an apartment for him at St James's; and now he will not go thither, supposing it would be a confinement.[21] He is to lodge at his own minister Dieden's.[22]

Augustus Hervey, thinking it the *bel air*,[23] is going to sue for a divorce from the Chudleigh.[24] He asked Lord Bolingbroke t'other day, who was his proctor,[25] as he would have asked for his tailor. The nymph has sent him word, that if he proves her his wife he must pay her debts; and she owes sixteen thousand pounds.[26] This obstacle thrown in the way, looks as if she was not sure of being Duchess

lisle, had been a lawyer before turning to the Church. HW jokes about Lyttelton's ambitions in MONTAGU ii. 137–8, 145.

13. HW makes this charge against Secker in *MS Poems*, p. 109, and in *Mem. Geo. II* i. 65. 'Here is my evidence. Mr Robyns said he had known him an atheist, and had advised him against talking so openly in coffee-houses. Mr Stevens, a mathematician, who lives much in the house with Earl Powlett, says, Secker made him an atheist at Leyden, where the club was established' (ibid. i. 65, n. 1).

14. HW believed Warburton to be an infidel; see *ante* 17 Nov. 1763, n. 52.

15. Grafton's mistress, to curry favour with Grafton.

16. Deleted · in *Works;* probably Terrick.

17. Also deleted in *Works;* probably Warburton.

18. Where Lord George Sackville was disgraced by failing to bring them up.

19. Christian VII.

20. 11 Aug. See HW to Mann 13 Aug. 1768, MANN vii. 41–3; *Mem. Geo. III* iii. 159–61.

21. However, according to Count Welderen, George III insisted (Coke, op. cit.

ii. 333), and consequently Christian VII did stay at St James's, 'where he has levees, but goes and is to go everywhere' (HW to Mann 13 Aug. 1768, MANN vii. 41).

22. Wilhelm Christopher von Diede (1732–1807), Danish minister to England 1767–76 (ibid. vii. 402, n. 10).

23. Word had spread that Grafton was going to divorce his Duchess; see *ante* 16 June 1768, n. 31; Coke, op. cit. ii. 304–5. Also, earlier in the year Lord Bolingbroke had divorced his wife (see n. 25 below).

24. See below, n. 28. Hervey's reason for seeking a divorce was that he had fallen in love with a physician's daughter at Bath (MANN vii. 93 and n. 5).

25. Bolingbroke had divorced his wife, the former Lady Diana Spencer, by Act of Parliament 10 March 1768 for *crim. con.* with Topham Beauclerk.

26. This report is contradicted in Coke, op. cit. ii. 347, *sub* 27 Aug.: 'Mr Harvey is really going to sue for a divorce, but he told Lady Blandford that the answer which it was reported Miss Chudleigh had sent to his letter, was invention, for he had received none.'

of Kingston.[27] The lawyers say, it will be no valid plea;[28] it not appearing that she was Hervey's wife, and therefore the tradesmen could not reckon on his paying them.

Yes, it is my Gray, Gray the poet, who is made professor of modern history; and I believe it is worth £500 a year.[29] I knew nothing of it till I saw it in the papers;[30] but believe it was Stonehewer[31] that obtained it for him.

Yes again; I use a bit of alum half as big as my nail, once or twice a week, and let it dissolve in my mouth.[32] I should not think that using it oftener could be prejudicial. You should inquire; but as you are in more hurry than I am, you should certainly use it oftener than I do. I wish I could cure my Lady A. too.[33] Ice-water has astonishing effect on my stomach, and removes all pain like a charm. Pray, though the one's teeth may not be so white as formerly, nor t'other look in perfect health, let the Danish King see such good specimens of the last age—though, by what I hear, he likes nothing but the very present age.[34]—However, sure you will both come and look at him: not that I believe he is a jot better than the apprentices that flirt to Epsom in a timwhiskey;[35] but I want to meet you in town.

I don't very well know what I write, for I hear a caravan on my stairs, that are come to see the house: Margaret is chattering, and the dogs barking; and this I call retirement! and yet I think it preferable to your visit at Becket.[36] Adieu! Let me know something more of

27. She was 'married' to the Duke 8 March 1769.

28. In Michaelmas Term 1768 Elizabeth Chudleigh brought a suit of jactitation in the Consistory Court against Hervey, and on 10 Feb. 1769 the Court declared her to be free from any matrimonial contract (MANN vii. 93, nn. 8, 9). This ruling was overturned in her famous trial for bigamy before the House of Lords in 1776, when it was declared that she had indeed been married to Hervey since 1744. See *post* 12 Dec. 1775.

29. Grafton nominated him Regius Professor of Modern History at Cambridge, the warrant being signed 28 July; the post was worth £400 a year, out of which he had to provide a French and an Italian teacher. See Gray, *Corr.*, ed. Toynbee and Whibley, Oxford, 1935, iii. 1033–5, 1037–41, 1048, 1253–9.

30. E.g., *Daily Adv.* 2 Aug.; *St James's Chronicle* 30 July – 2 Aug.

31. Richard Stonehewer (ca 1728–1809), under-secretary of state 1765–6; auditor of excise 1772–89; a friend of Gray who was also Grafton's friend and private secretary (OSSORY ii. 15, n. 3). See HW to Warton 20 Sept. 1768.

32. To strengthen his teeth; see below, and MONTAGU ii. 276.

33. Lady Mary Coke records, op. cit. ii. 299, *sub* 29 June, that 'Lady Ailesbury came to town to consult Sir William Duncan, having been very ill.'

34. Presumably an allusion to the King's young favourite, Count Holck (see *post* 25 Aug. 1768); or to 'Støvlet Katrine' the tailor's daughter (CHUTE 327, n. 15).

35. 'A kind of high light carriage' (OED).

36. Lord Barrington's seat in Berkshire.

your motions, before you go to Ireland, which I think a strange journey, and better compounded for:[37] and when I see you in town I will settle with you another visit to Park Place.

Yours ever,

Hor. Walpole

From Conway, ca Tuesday 23 August 1768

Missing; answered *post* 25 Aug. 1768.

To Conway, Thursday 25 August 1768

Printed from the MS now WSL; first printed Wright v. 220–1. For the history of the MS see *ante* 29 June 1744 OS.
Endorsed: Mr Walpole 25 Aug. 1768.

Arlington Street, Aug. 25, 1768.

I AM heartily glad you do not go to Ireland; it is very well for the Duke of Bedford, who, as George Selwyn says, is going to be made a mamamouchi.[1] Your brother sets out for Ragley on Wednesday next,[2] and that day I intend to be at Park Place, and from thence shall go to Ragley on Friday.[3] I shall stay there three or four days and then go to Lord Strafford's for about as many; and shall call on George Montagu on my return, so as to be at home in a fortnight, an infinite absence in my account.[4] I wish you could join in with any

37. That is, it would be better if he could settle his Irish business without actually having to go there; 'compound' in this sense means 'to discharge any liability or satisfy any claim by a compromise whereby something lighter or easier is substituted' (OED, 'compound,' *v.* 13b). Just what Conway's business was in Ireland at this time has not been determined; in any case, he did not go (see *post* 25 Aug. 1768).

———

1. The mock Turkish title proposed to be conferred upon M. Jourdain in Act IV,

scene iii of Molière's *Bourgeois gentilhomme.* HW had applied it to Newcastle upon his being installed as chancellor of Cambridge University in 1749 (see MANN iv. 72 and n. 7); Bedford was installed as chancellor of Dublin University 9 Sept. (GM 1768, xxxviii. 443).

2. 31 Aug.

3. See HW's 'Journey to Weston, Ragley, Warwick Castle [etc.] . . . Sept. 2, 1768' in *Country Seats* 62–7.

4. HW returned to SH 19 Sept. (HW to Thomas Warton 20 Sept. 1768).

part of this progress, before you go to worship the treasures that are pouring in upon your daughter by the old Damer's[5] death.

You ask me about the harvest—you might as well ask me about the funds. I thought the land flowed with milk and honey.[6] We have had forty showers, but they have not lasted a minute each; and as the weather continues warm, and my lawn green,

I bless my stars, and call it luxury.[7]

They tell me there are very bad accounts from several colonies, and the papers are full of their remonstrances;[8] but I never read such things. I am happy to have nothing to do with them, and glad you have not much more. When one can do no good, I have no notion of sorrowing one's self for every calamity that happens in general. One should lead the life of a coffee-house politician, the most real patriots that I know; who amble out every morning to gather matter for lamenting over their country. I leave mine, like the King of Denmark, to ministers and Providence, the latter of which like an able chancellor of the Exchequer to an ignorant or idle First Lord, luckily does the business. That little King has had the gripes,[9] which have addled his journey to York.[10] I know nothing more of his motions.[11] His favourite[12] is fallen in love with Lady Bel Stanhope, and the Monarch himself demanded her for him. The mother[13] was not averse, but Lady Bel very sensibly refused[14]—so unfortunate are favourites the instant they set their foot in England. He is jealous of Sackville,[15] and says, *ce gros noir n'est pas beau:*[16] which implies

5. John Damer (ca 1673 – Aug. 1768) of Ireland was great-uncle of the Hon. John Damer who m. (15 June 1767) Anne Seymour Conway (MANN vi. 498 and nn. 11–13). His estates devolved upon Lord Milton, Damer's father.

6. The London newspapers for the spring and summer of 1768 mention frequent and violent storms which did much harm to crops.

7. 'Blesses his stars, and thinks it luxury' (Addison, *Cato,* I. iv).

8. For instance, the *London Chronicle* 20–3 Aug., xxiv. 182, *sub* 23 Aug., carries a report that the Massachusetts Assembly 'have unanimously refused to submit to any tax or imposition whatever from Great Britain, and . . . sent their resolu-

tion to the other colonies,' and the *Chronicle* 23–5 Aug., xxiv. 185–6, *sub* 24 Aug., reprints messages and correspondence relating to this resolution.

9. 'From having eat too much fruit' (Coke, *Journals,* ii. 343).

10. To see the races (MANN vii. 48).

11. He was well enough to journey to Cambridge 29 Aug. (ibid. vii. 48, n. 6).

12. Frederik Vilhelm Conrad (1745–1800), Count (Greve) Holck (ibid. vii. 42 and n. 7).

13. Lady Harrington.

14. She married Charles William Molyneux, Vct Molyneux, 3 Dec.

15. John Frederick Sackville (1745–99), 3d Duke of Dorset 1769.

16. The Duchess of Devonshire wrote

that he thinks his own whiteness and pertness charming. Adieu! I shall see you on Wednesday.

From Henrietta Seymour Conway, September 1768

Printed for the first time from a photostat of BM Add. MSS 23219, f. 29. Dated by HW's missing reply 4 Oct. acknowledged *post* 9 Oct. 1768.

Sir,

THE honour and favour of your card, bearing date January 27th 1759,[1] I keep as a relic, valuable for its antiquity, but much more so for the politeness, strength and sincerity of the expressions it contains. The heart which breathes such sentiments must be replete of them and, indeed, can entertain none of a different nature.

Shall I repeat the words? No; that would be an injustice done to your modesty. Such they are as leave me no room to imagine you would decline doing me a good office if in your power. Without hesitation, therefore, I proceed to beg your interest in and influence on my brother, General Conway, or wherever else you may have any, towards procuring advancement (I had almost said common justice) for Captain Robert Molesworth,[2] who has been about 24 years in the service[3] and is only a lieutenant of Dragoons in Ireland with a captain's brevet.

Both my brothers are well informed of all the circumstances of his case; wherefore I shall only add that it is (in my opinion) peculiarly hard; that he has a wife[4] in Yorkshire[5] and five fine children;[6] that he cannot bear the expense of moving them to distant quarters

of Dorset in 1777: 'I always have looked upon him as the most dangerous of men, for with that beauty of his he is so unaffected and has a simplicity and persuasion in his manner that makes one account very easily for the number of women he has had in love with him' (*Anglo-Saxon Review*, 1899, i. 240).

1. Missing.

2. (1729–1813), 5th Vct Molesworth 1793; Cornet 1745 and Lt 1752 in the 5th (or Royal Irish) Dragoons; Capt. in the Army (*Army Lists* 1769, p. 33).

3. See below, n. 7.

4. Mary Anne Alleyne (ca 1730–1819), m. (1761) Robert Molesworth.

5. They apparently lived at Lascelles Hall in Kirkheaton, where their son William was born (see next note).

6. He was succeeded as 6th Vct Molesworth by his only surviving son and heir, William Molesworth (1763–1815); an apparent daughter, Eleanor Molesworth, 'dau. of Robert M. Esq.; and cousin to Lord M.' died unmarried at Nottingham in 1784 (GM 1784, liv pt ii. 798).

every year; and that he is in all respects deserving of your compassionate assistance.[7]

Having thus addressed you it cannot be necessary to add that you could not more sensibly oblige, Sir,

Your most obedient humble servant,

H. SEYMOUR CONWAY

My hopes and wishes are constant and fervent that you enjoy an uninterrupted state of good health.

To HENRIETTA SEYMOUR CONWAY,
Tuesday 4 October 1768

Missing; answered *post* 9 Oct. 1768.

From HENRIETTA SEYMOUR CONWAY,
Sunday 9 October 1768

Printed for the first time from a photostat of BM Add. MSS 23219, f. 30. *Address:* Honourable Horatio Walpole.

Chichester (Sussex), Oct. 9th 1768.

Sir,

THE honour you did me on the 4th instant[1] affords a fresh proof of your great goodness and humanity; which will indulge me in observing that you overlooked a material circumstance in my last, namely, that Captain Robert Molesworth is on the *Irish Establish-*

---

7. None was forthcoming; in 1776 Molesworth wrote to Lord Dartmouth asking for a small pension to aid him in his distress, observing that 'I . . . was four and twenty years an officer . . . I sold out, at the reduced price, when my increasing family prevented me from be-ing able to bear the expenses of an officer. I am now . . . given up to the ministry of the Gospel' (Hist. MSS Comm., 15th Report, App. pt i, *Dartmouth MSS*, Vol. III, 1896, pp. 226–7).

1. Missing.

ment, wherein (if I am not mistaken) the Marquis of Granby[2] does not interfere.

The Lord Lieutenant of Ireland[3] is undoubtedly the proper person to be applied to on this occasion: and when I troubled you for your interest in my brother I did not *then* recollect how nearly you are *related* to his Lordship;[4] therefore begged of you to influence the General so far as to procure a favourable recommendation to Lord Townshend. This alteration of the case occasions you a second address;[5] *earnestly* begging you to employ your good offices in an affair which *really* merits and possibly may require your utmost efforts, without loss of time: for Captain Molesworth is unfortunately much oppressed and distressed.

He is lieutenant of Dragoons in General Yorke's[6] regiment in Ireland and has had rank of captain by brevet these five or six years past:[7] wherefore his length of service and present rank seems to entitle him to a company of foot, either by vacancy or obtaining leave to sell his lieutenancy and purchasing the company.[8]

It would be unnatural and ungrateful in me to entertain the least doubt of my good brother's intentions to serve me when in his power, having always found him most willing and ready; but I make great allowances for his having many of his own friends to oblige and for the perplexity of various business. If I am so happy as to succeed in this application I never will trouble him with any other, wherefore hope he will join his interest to yours.

I hope that this affair in which I am so deeply interested is now put into a track of more probable success; and beg that you will kindly suppress my former application to my brother, which I confess has too much of an appearance of ill-grounded and undesigned suspicion.

My zeal, indeed, in this affair, which I have much at heart, prompted me to leave no stone unturned: and I flatter myself that your friendly endeavours will neither be wanting nor ineffectual.

2. Commander-in-chief of the Army 1766–70.

3. Townshend (*ante* 9 Aug. 1767, n. 2).

4. HW's aunt, Dorothy Walpole, married (1713) Charles, 2d Vct Townshend, who by a previous marriage was grandfather of the present Viscount, so that HW and he were not directly related.

5. No letter from HW to Townshend at this time has been found.

6. Hon. Sir Joseph Yorke (*ante* 29 June 1756, n. 13), the British ambassador to Holland; Col. 5th Dragoons 1760–87; Lt-Gen. 1760.

7. Since 13 April 1763 (*Army Lists,* 1769, p. 33).

8. See *ante* Sept. 1768, n. 7.

After presuming to give you thus much trouble, you will easily give me credit when I profess that I am and always must remain, Sir,

Your most obliged and most obedient humble servant,

H. SEYMOUR CONWAY

From HERTFORD, Thursday 27 October 1768

Printed for the first time from a photostat of BM Add. MSS 23219, f. 32.

London, October 27th 1768.

Dear Horry,

THE report about Monsieur de Choiseuil's disgrace is not true;[1] I suppose it was calculated to serve some jobbing purposes in the City if it was truly said to have been written by some considerable merchants at Paris. Corsica however labours with difficulties; the French do not advance as they expected.[2] They are said to have sent for 20 battalions more to reduce it,[3] and his enemies may perhaps employ any ill success in this expedition, which is of his own forming, against him. I called at your door last night hoping to have found you in town. I am sorry your gout is returned,[4] but flatter myself we shall converse with you at latest on Saturday.

Yours ever most sincerely,

HERTFORD

1. 'It was yesterday [19 Oct.] reported that the Duke de Choiseul had resigned, and that the Duke de Nivernois succeeded him as prime minister' (Whitehall Evening Post 18–20 Oct.). HW had written to Mann 24 Oct. 1768 (MANN vii. 62) that 'we have rumours here that the rebuffs in Corsica have shaken the Duke of Choiseul's credit considerably, which tottered before by the King's [Louis XV's] apprehension of that invasion producing a war.' Choiseul did not fall until 1770 (ibid. vii. 85, n. 9).

2. 'The French have received a total defeat in Corsica' (London Chronicle 8–11 Oct., xxiv. 350; see MANN vii. 62, n. 11).

3. 'The Marquis de Chauvelin has declared himself unable to act against the Corsicans till he receives a reinforcement of at least 10 or 12 battalions' (London Chronicle 22–5 Oct., xxiv. 394). Corsica was reduced in 1769.

4. HW wrote to Mann from SH 24 Oct. 1768 that 'I have been confined these three weeks with the gout in both feet' (MANN vii. 61).

From Hertford, Monday ca 14 November 1768

Printed from a photostat of BM Add. MSS 23219, f. 38; first printed in L. W. Conolly, 'Horace Walpole, Unofficial Play Censor,' *English Language Notes*, 1971, ix. 42.

Grosvenor Street, Monday past 3.

Dear Horry,

I AM prevented calling upon you this morning. Be so good to cast your eye upon the new play of *The Hypocrite*[1] and tell me if it is not too loose and indelicate for the Lord Chamberlain to send to the stage in its present state.

Yours ever,

Hertford

From Hertford, Monday 20 February 1769

Printed from a photostat of BM Add. MSS 23219, f. 33; first printed in L. W. Conolly, 'Horace Walpole, Unofficial Play Censor,' *English Language Notes*, 1971, ix. 43.
Address: To the Honourable Hor. Walpole.

Monday, February 20th 1769.

My dear Horry,

FORGIVE me for desiring you to read a very bad play[1] with some caution. It is proposed to be brought upon the stage if the Lord Chamberlain consents. You know his office, and he thinks many of the lines wrote for the times and some of them liable to just objection.[2]

Yours ever,

Hertford

1. By Isaac Bickerstaffe (ca 1735–?1812), first performed at Drury Lane 17 Nov. 1768 (*London Stage* Pt IV, iii. 1368; HW's MS note in his copy, now wsl, Hazen, *Cat. of HW's Lib.*, No. 1810: 13:9).

———

1. 'The Fatal Discovery' (HW's MS note), by John Home (1722–1808) first acted at Drury Lane 23 Feb. 1769 (*London Stage* Pt IV, iii. 1387; HW's MS note is in his copy, now wsl, Hazen, *Cat. of HW's Lib.*, No. 1810:14:5).

2. 'The MS of the play sent to Hertford for licensing has survived in the Huntington Library's Larpent Collection, but it

From HERTFORD, Thursday 13 April 1769

Printed for the first time from a photostat of BM Add. MSS 23219, f. 35.

April 13th 1769.

Dear Horry,

BE so good to read the enclosed letters[1] and tell me if you approve my answer. I do not know Sandby;[2] the King must be spoke to and I cannot apply without some reason, and any other than the true one would be discovered to my discredit in the Closet.

Yours, etc.,

HERTFORD

From HERTFORD, Friday 30 June 1769

Printed for the first time from a photostat of BM Add. MSS 23219, f. 36.

London, June 30th 1769.

Dear Horry,

MY Lady is gone to Ranelagh and has left me her commission to try to engage you to come and play at loo here next Tuesday. I undertake it most willingly and wish I may succeed.

The town is very empty but I think full and sociable enough.

The subject of conversation is the City address,[1] the election of aldermen[2] and the effects they may produce. One immediate con-

shows no evidence of having been censored' (Conolly, op. cit. 43 and n. 3). See A. E. Gipson, *John Home: A Study of His Life and Works*, New Haven, 1917, pp. 143–8.

1. Missing; presumably a letter from Grafton and Hertford's reply (see next note).

2. Presumably Paul Sandby (1725–1809), painter. HW writes in *Last Journals* ii. 113: 'Lord Hertford, Lord Chamberlain . . . promised the reversion [of surveyor of the King's pictures] to Paul Sandby, at the Duke of Grafton's request, when first

lord of the Treasury.' See MASON i. 342 and n. 6.

———

1. A petition of the livery of London to the Crown, protesting the expulsion of Wilkes from the House as M.P. for Middlesex earlier in the year, and the seating of Henry Lawes Luttrell in his place; it was presented 5 July (see MANN vii. 132 and n. 5; Namier and Brooke i. 333–4).

2. James Townsend and John Sawbridge, both Wilkes supporters, were elected aldermen of London at this time, Townsend for Bishopsgate Ward 23 June, and Sawbridge for Langbourn Ward 1

sequence is said to be Lord Chatham's recovery and intention of appearing soon at the King's levee.[3]

Yours ever most sincerely,

HERTFORD

To Conway, Friday 7 July 1769

Printed from *Works* v. 138–9.

Strawberry Hill, Friday, July 7, 1769.

YOU desired me to write, if I knew anything particular. How particular will content you? Don't imagine I would send you such hash as the Livery's petition.[1] Come; would the apparition of my Lord Chatham satisfy you? Don't be frightened: it was not his ghost. He, he himself *in propria persona,* and not in a strait waistcoat, walked into the King's levee this morning,[2] and was in the Closet twenty minutes after the levee;[3] and was to go out of town tonight again.[4] The deuce is in it if this is not news. Whether he is to be king, minister, lord mayor, or alderman, I do not know;[5] nor a word more than I have told you. Whether he was sent for to guard St James's gate, or whether he came alone, like Almanzor,[6] to storm it, I cannot tell:[7] by Beckford's violence I should think the latter.[8] I

July (A. B. Beaven, *Aldermen of . . . London,* 1913, ii. 134; see also Namier and Brooke iii. 410, 537).

3. See *post* 7 July 1769.

1. See *ante* 30 June 1769, n. 1.
2. After a seclusion of over two years; his last audience had been on 12 March 1767 (MANN vi. 497, n. 3).
3. 'About a quarter of an hour' (Chatham to Temple 7 [8] July, *Grenville Papers* iv. 427).
4. He returned in the evening to Hayes (*Daily Adv.* 8 July).
5. See 'Last Audience of Lord Chatham. Extract from the Duke of Grafton's MS memoirs . . . "July 7, 1769"' (based on information furnished presumably by George III) in Lord Mahon's *History of England,* 1836–54, Vol. V, App. pp. xxxii–iv. Chatham spoke of the 'em-

barrassing difficulties' he had had while holding office in his 'infirm state,' of his doubts 'whether his health would ever again allow him to attend Parliament,' and of his concern about the East India Company; he also made some 'other observations on the head of India.' See John Brooke, *King George III,* 1972, p. 156.

6. The hero of Dryden's *Conquest of Granada;* HW compares Chatham to Almanzor also *ante* 8 July 1758 and 17 Nov. 1763.
7. 'The Duke of Grafton had got notice the night before and had apprised the King' (HW's 'Journal . . . 1769,' *sub* 7 July).
8. Alderman William Beckford, Chatham's friend, had been one of the committee presenting the petition of the livery of London (GM 1769, xxxix. 362–3).

am so indifferent what he came for, that I shall wait till Sunday to learn; when I lie in town on my way to Ely.[9] You will probably hear more from your brother before I can write again. I send this by my friend Mr Granger,[10] who will leave it at your park-gate as he goes through Henley home. Good night: it is past twelve, and I am going to bed.

Yours ever,

Hor. Walpole

From Hertford, Saturday 15 July 1769

Printed for the first time from a photostat of BM Add. MSS 23219, f. 37. *Address:* To the Honourable Hor. Walpole.

London, July 15th 1769.

Dear Horry,

THE Princess of Wales is very sensible of all your attention to her,[1] and I am desired to say that the greatest compliment you can pay her is to allow her to send for the keys when she has time to go to Strawberry, as she wishes much to see it.[2]

Nothing of consequence transpires from the conversation between Lord Chatham and his Majesty; possibly much was not said, and possibly what was said may not be told.

Yours ever,

Hertford

---

9. HW went to Ely with William Cole, where, at the request of Bishop Mawson, he gave advice concerning the east window of the Cathedral and the removal of the organ to a side door; he was back at SH by 15 July (Cole i. 178 and n. 2).

10. Author of the *Biographical History of England* (HW). Rev. James Granger (1723–76), HW's correspondent; see ibid. i. 177 and n. 5.

1. Not ascertained.

2. There is no record of her visiting SH at this time; Lady Mary Coke wrote of her in her *Journals* iii. 103, *sub* 3 July, that she 'lives altogether in town, and never lies a night at Kew; all she sees of those delightful gardens are Tuesday and Saturday mornings when the King and Queen breakfast with her.'

To Hertford, ca Saturday 2 September 1769

Missing; listed in 'Paris Journals' (du Deffand v. 389), as sent 'by Edmondson' (possibly Joseph Edmondson [d. 1786], herald).

To Lady Ailesbury, Saturday 9 September 1769

Missing; listed in 'Paris Journals' (du Deffand v. 389) as sent 'by the post.'

From Lady Hertford, Sunday 10 September 1769

Printed for the first time from a photostat of BM Add. MSS 23218, f. 28.

Ragley, September the 10th.

Dear Mr Walpole,

IT seems odd that the only time I address myself to you is to give you trouble, but I must beg you to give orders to have two gold single-cased watches made for Lady Beauchamp[1] and me. Henry bought one of the sort I wish to have when he was at Paris;[2] one Griegson[3] made it, who is a person that may be heard of at Juvemier's,[4] a famous watch-maker, but I don't know where either of them live. The price is to be eighteen louis each: an H and an Earl's coronet upon one, a B and a Viscount's coronet upon the other. As they cannot be finished while you stay, I would have them finished as soon as possible and sent to Monsieur de Francès,[5]

1. Hon. Alice Elizabeth Windsor (1749–72), daughter of the 2d Vct Windsor, m. (4 Feb. 1768) Lord Beauchamp. A 'great heiress' (HW to Mann 21 Jan. 1767, Mann vi. 480), she was sister-in-law to Lord Mount Stuart, Lord Bute's son; Gilly Williams wrote to Selwyn, 5 Dec. 1766, that Hertford made the match 'to secure his Chamberlain's staff' (J. H. Jesse, *George Selwyn and his Contemporaries*, 1882, ii. 96).

2. HW had arrived at Paris 21 Aug., remaining there until 5 Oct. ('Paris Journals,' du Deffand v. 324–33).

3. Perhaps Pierre (?Peter) Gregson, later clockmaker to Louis XVI; see G. H. Baillie, *Watches: Their History, Decoration and Mechanism*, 1929, pp. 219, 365, Illust. 31.7 and idem, *Watchmakers and Clockmakers of the World*, 1929, p. 154.

4. Not further identified; he is not listed by Baillie, *Watches*, p. 365, as one of the most prominent watchmakers at Paris 1750–1800.

5. Jacques Batailhe de Francès (ca 1724–88), French chargé d'affaires at London with the rank of minister plenipotentiary June 1769 – ca 1771 (Mann vii. 218, n. 8).

who will give me leave to have them brought over by his courier. Mr Panshaw[6] must pay for the watches when they are done. Henry's watch goes vastly well, and I hope Griegson (who is an Englishman) will take care to make ours as good.

Col. Burgoyne[7] carries this to London, and as his chaise is at the door, I must not add a word more, but that we shall be very happy to see you in England. Accept the best wishes of this family, and believe me, dear Mr Walpole,

Most faithfully yours,

I. H.

Since I wrote the above we have changed our mind, and beg to have no letters and coronets upon our watches, but a vase or anything Mr Griegson thinks will look well upon the case.

To HERTFORD, Thursday 28 September 1769

Missing; listed in 'Paris Journals' (DU DEFFAND v. 389) as sent 'by Colonel Philipson,' presumably Lt-Col. Richard Burton Phillipson (?1723–92) (Namier and Brooke ii. 165).

From CONWAY, November 1769

Missing; acknowledged *post* 14 Nov. 1769.

6. Isaac Panchaud (1726–89), Paris banker (OSSORY i. 271, n. 3).

7. Either Col. John Burgoyne (1723–92) (*ante* 28 Sept. 1762) or his younger cousin Lt-Col. John Burgoyne (1739–85), 7th Bt of Sutton Park, Beds, 1780 (MONTAGU ii. 295, n. 2); the latter is reported by Montagu to HW 18 Sept. 1769 (ibid. ii. 295) as having just visited with him at Adderbury for a week.

To Conway, Tuesday 14 November 1769

Printed from *Works* v. 139–40.

Strawberry Hill, Tuesday Nov. 14, 1769.

I AM here quite alone, and did not think of going to town till Friday for the opera, which I have not yet seen.[1] In compliment to you and your Countess I will make an effort, and be there on Thursday; and will either dine with you at your own house, or at your brother's; which you choose. This is a great favour, and beyond my Lord Temple's journey to dine with my Lord Mayor.[2] I am so sick of the follies of all sides, that I am happy to be at quiet here, and to know no more of them than what I am forced to see in the newspapers; and those I skip over as fast as I can.

The account you give me of Lady Cecilia[3] was just the same as I received from Paris. I will show you a very particular letter I received by a private hand from thence;[4] which convinces me that I guessed right, contrary to all the wise, that the journey to Fontainebleau would overset Monsieur de Choiseul. I think he holds but by a thread, which will snap soon.[5] I am labouring hard with the Duchess[6] to procure the Duke of Richmond satisfaction in the favour he has asked about his duchy;[7] but he shall not know it till it is com-

---

1. *L'Olimpiade*, a pasticcio, was performed at the King's Opera House Saturday, 18 Nov. (*London Stage* Pt IV, iii. 1437).

2. In the second mayoralty of William Beckford (HW); Beckford was sworn in as lord mayor of London for the second time 9 Nov. HW wrote in his 'Journal . . . 1769,' *sub* 9 Nov.: 'The lord mayor's feast was attended by none of the great officers but the Chancellor, nor by any of the aldermen attached to the Court,' but 'Lord Temple, Lord Shelburne and Calcraft were there.' See GM 1769, xxxix. 555; *Grenville Papers* iv. 478; Namier and Brooke ii. 77.

3. Lady Cecilia Margaret Lennox (1750–69), sister of the Duke of Richmond. Mme du Deffand wrote to HW 23 Oct. 1769 *sub* 24 Oct. that 'La Milady Cécile n'est point morte' (DU DEFFAND ii. 292); Charles James Fox wrote to Selwyn 25 Oct. that 'Lady Cecilia is as she was;

Frouchin [Tronchin] visits her, but does not give any hopes' (J. H. Jesse, *George Selwyn and his Contemporaries*, 1882, ii. 399). She died 12 Nov. (Mme du Deffand to HW 15 Nov. 1769, DU DEFFAND ii. 306).

4. Mme du Deffand to HW 2 Nov. 1769; see next note.

5. Mme du Deffand wrote to HW 2 Nov. 1769 that 'le grand-papa [Choiseul] paraît de très bonne humeur, cependant il n'est pas sans inquiétude; la dame [Mme du Barry] ne dissimule plus sa haine pour lui . . . il reçoit journellement de petits dégoûts' (ibid. ii. 297). HW comments in *Mem. Geo. III* iv. 15: 'At Fontainebleau, hostilities were carried very high, but came to no decision. It was known, that though the Duc de Choiseul had stayed so long with the mistress, he had rather exasperated than softened her.'

6. The Duchess of Choiseul (HW).

7. Of Aubigné (HW); HW had written

pleted, if I can be so lucky as to succeed. I think I shall, if they do not fall immediately.

You perceive how barren I am, and why I have not written to you. I pass my time in clipping and pasting prints; and do not think I have read forty pages since I came to England. I bought a poem called *Trincalo's Trip to the Jubilee;*[8] having been struck with two lines in an extract in the papers,[9]

> And the ear-piercing fife,
> And the ear-piercing wife—

Alas! all the rest, and it is very long,[10] is a heap of unintelligible nonsense, about Shakespeare, politics, and the Lord knows what. I am grieved that, with our admiration of Shakespeare, we can do nothing but write worse than ever he did. One would think the age studied nothing but his *Love's Labour[s] Lost,* and *Titus Andronicus.* Politics and abuse have totally corrupted our taste. Nobody thinks of writing a line that is to last beyond the next fortnight. We might as well be given up to controversial divinity. The times put me in mind of the Constantinopolitan empire; where, in an age of learning, the subtlest wits of Greece contrived to leave nothing behind them, but the memory of their follies and acrimony. Milton did not write his *Paradise Lost* till he had outlived his politics. With all his parts, and noble sentiments of liberty, who would remember him for his barbarous prose? Nothing is more true than that extremes meet. The licentiousness of the press makes us as savage as our Saxon ancestors, who could only set their marks; and an outrageous pursuit of

to the Duchesse 3 Nov. (DU DEFFAND ii. 304, v. 390; the letter is missing), presumably about Richmond's desire to have this duchy recognized by the King and registered by the Parliament of Paris, currently considered impossible 'à cause de sa religion' (Mme du Deffand to HW 2 Nov. 1769, DU DEFFAND ii. 297); recognition and registration did not take place until 1776.

8. By Edward Thompson (?1738–86); HW's copy is Hazen, *Cat. of HW's Lib.,* No. 3222:10:13. It is a satirical ode on the Stratford Jubilee, held by Garrick in Shakespeare's memory in Sept.; see GM 1769, xxxix. 421–3, 458; Christian Deelman, *The Great Shakespeare Jubilee,* New York, 1964, p. 275 *et passim;* Johanne M. Stockholm, *Garrick's Folly,* New York, 1964, pp. 130–5 *et passim.*

Regarding the Jubilee and the masquerade proposed to be held at it, Hertford wrote Garrick 20 July 1769, 'If you continue in that choice and opinion I think I may now venture to say you may do it consistently with the respect and attention you always incline to testify. His Majesty is, as far as I can learn, averse to the encouragement of masquerades, and particularly in his capital, but he is not supposed or obliged to know what passes at so remote a distance, and Stratford is not within the jurisdiction of his Chamberlain' (A. W. Thibaudeau, *Catalogue of the [Alfred Morrison] Collection of Autograph Letters and Historical Documents,* 1883–97, ii. 291).
9. *London Chronicle* 7–9 Nov., xxvi. 449–50.
10. 47 pp., quarto.

individual independence, grounded on selfish views, extinguishes genius as much as despotism does. The public good of our country is never thought of by men that hate half their country. Heroes confine their ambition to be leaders of the mob. Orators seek applause from their faction, not from posterity; and ministers forget foreign enemies, to defend themselves against a majority in Parliament. When any Cæsar has conquered Gaul, I will excuse him for aiming at the perpetual dictature. If he has only jockeyed somebody out of the borough of Veii or Falernum, it is too impudent to call himself a patriot or a statesman. Adieu!

To CONWAY, Friday 12 January 1770

Missing. HW was with Conway at the Duke of Richmond's Thursday 11 January in the evening. 'The Duke of Richmond was so struck by the violence of Sir G[eorge] Saville's behaviour [10 Jan. in the House of Commons], that he desired Mr Conway to call in the evening to talk it over' (HW, 'Journal . . . 1770,' *sub* 11 Jan.). HW entered in his 'Journal . . . 1770' the next day, *sub* 12 Jan.: 'I was so uneasy at the conduct of Sir Geo. Saville, that early in the morning I wrote to Mr Conway to beg he would go directly to the D. of Grafton and represent the danger of inflaming, by dismissing the Chancellor [Lord Camden], which would probably be followed by the resignation of Lord Granby, and thus in case of insurrection or rebellion there would be a popular chief and who might make a schism in the army.' See *post* 22 Jan. 1770, nn. 2, 5.

From CONWAY, Monday 22 January 1770

Printed for the first time from the MS, now WSL. For the history of the MS, see *ante* 9 Aug. 1767.
Address: To the Hon. Horatio Walpole.
Endorsed (by HW): Jan. 23d 1770.
Memoranda (by HW):[1]
                    [in pencil]
          Chancellor[2]   Solicitor-Gen.[3]

1. Made after his visit to Conway (see text of letter) for his 'Journal . . . 1770,' *sub* 22 Jan.; also, most of these items are mentioned in his letter to Mann 22 Jan. 1770, MANN vii. 178–81.
2. This office and the following ones were mentioned by Grafton as being vacant in his conversation with Conway the morning of 22 Jan., when he announced his intention of resigning, which was the 'pressing' affair Conway wished to discuss with HW (HW, 'Journal . . . 1770,' loc. cit.; *Mem. Geo. III* iv. 40–1). Charles Yorke, appointed lord chancellor in the room of Lord Camden 17 Jan., had died suddenly 20 Jan. (MANN vii. 178–9).
3. John Dunning (*ante* 3 Dec. 1764, n. 28) resigned as solicitor-general (MANN vii. 175, n. 14).

Attorney to Queen[4]	2 Lds of Admiralty[9]
Commander-in-Chief	Vice-treasurer of Ireland[10]
M[aste]r of Ordnance[5]	237–121[11]
Privy Seal[6]	[in ink]
Vice-chamb[erlain] to King[7]	Ld Rock. Gen. Warrants.[12]
2 Lds of Bedchamber[8]	Ld Chath[am]. Eagle's Wing.[13]

Little Warwick Street, Monday, past 5.

My dear Friend,

I BEG I may see you for a little while as soon after dinner as convenient: it is for a little conversation on a matter very pressing and of great consequence.[14] Yours ever,

H.S.C.

To CONWAY, ca Tuesday 23 January 1770

Missing; answered *post* 24 Jan. 1770.

4. Richard Hussey (*ante* 25 Nov. 1763, n. 14) resigned as attorney-general to Queen Charlotte (MANN vii. 180).

5. Lord Granby resigned as commander of the army and master of the Ordnance (ibid. vii. 174–5). See *post* 24 Jan. 1770.

6. Lord Bristol resigned as Privy Seal (MANN vii. 173).

7. Lord Jersey resigned as vice-chamberlain; he was succeeded by the Hon. Thomas Robinson, later 2d Bn Grantham (GM 1770, xl. 95).

8. Lord Coventry and the Duke of Manchester resigned as lords of the Bedchamber (MANN vii. 173; *Court and City Register* 1769, p. 75; 1770, p. 71).

9. Sir Piercy Brett (ca 1710–81), Kt, and Sir George Yonge (1733–1812), 5th Bt, resigned as lords of the Admiralty (HW, 'Journal . . . 1770,' loc. cit.; Namier and Brooke ii. 115, iii. 673).

10. James Grenville (*ante* 12 Oct. 1761,

n. 14) resigned as joint vice-treasurer of Ireland (MANN vii. 180, n. 19).

11. The vote by which Sir Fletcher Norton was elected speaker of the House 22 Jan. (HW, 'Journal . . . 1770,' loc. cit.; MANN vii. 180).

12. In speaking to the Lords 22 Jan., Rockingham 'in the list of grievances . . . omitted the greatest of all, *general warrants*—for he was now acting with Mr Grenville' (HW, 'Journal . . . 1770,' loc. cit.; see also Cobbett, *Parl. Hist.* xvi. 741–5).

13. In his speech 22 Jan. Chatham said 'he would never touch prerogative, he would not come near it, he would not [pull] a feather from that master wing of the eagle' (HW, 'Journal . . . 1770,' loc. cit.; *Mem. Geo. III* iv. 40; see also Cobbett, op. cit. xvi. 747–55).

14. The intended resignation of the Duke of Grafton; see above, n. 2.

To CONWAY, Wednesday 24 January 1770

Missing. HW wrote in his 'Journal . . . 1770,' *sub* 24 Jan.: 'Mr Burke called on me. . . . I drew from him an acknowledgment that his party [Rockingham's] would be content without a dissolution, provided some act of Parliament was passed to take away from the House of Commons the power of incapacitation. Of this I immediately sent word to Mr Conway, that in case of a change he might acquaint the King that Lord Rockingham would not insist on a dissolution.'

From CONWAY, Wednesday 24 January 1770

Printed for the first time from the MS, now WSL. For the history of the MS, see *ante* 9 Aug. 1767.

Address: To the Honourable Horatio Walpole.

Endorsed (by HW): Jan. 24 1770.

I HAVE not much to remark now on the subject of your letter.[1]— Anything that sounds unfriendly from the Duke of R[ichmond] would mortify me much indeed, but I hope it was not meant so.— As to the fact I find he is in part right, in respect to the value of the office.—There are no perquisites that I know of—but the *salary* of Master-General and Lieutenant-General differ only 400 as he says[2]— one 1500, the other 1100—but there is the company of cadets[3] to

1. Missing.

2. HW wrote in his 'Journal . . . 1770,' *sub* 19 Jan.: 'When it was first apprehended that Lord Granby would resign [see *ante* 22 Jan. 1770, n. 5], I did not doubt but the Mastership of the Ordnance, if not the command of the Army, would be given to Mr Conway [currently lieutenant-general of the Ordnance]. Fearing this would involve him deeper with the Bedfords [amended to 'the administration' in HW's MS 'foul copy' of *Mem. Geo. III* for 1770, p. 9, and to 'the Court' in his MS 'fair copy,' p. 9], and desirous that he should preserve his character of disinterestedness, I begged him to accept neither, as it would not become him to profit of the spoils of Lord Granby, with whom he had lived in friendship, and as it would certainly make him very un-

popular. He said that he was overjoyed that this was my opinion, as it was strongly his own, and he would certainly adhere to that plan. Accordingly, when the King offered him the Ordnance, he desired to be excused accepting it, his friendship to Lord Granby would not allow it; but he offered to do the whole business without taking the salary, if his Majesty would be pleased to appoint no Master; he thought he could make advantageous improvements in the office, and Lord Granby would be less desperate, if he saw his posts not filled up. . . . His Majesty consented to his plan, and it was settled too to appoint no commander-in-chief.'

3. At the Royal Military Academy at Woolwich; the master-general of Ordnance was also governor of this academy

which I must of necessity be Captain which has a pay of 500 that comes with it unless I actually refuse the common establishment.—I did not know all this myself till I saw Sir Ch. Fredrick.⁴—I always understood the Master-Generalship was about double the Lieutenant-Generalship—so you see this difference of pay is not worth bragging about, nor the 500 I believe worth refusing—but in reality it now grows a thing of a day indeed, the Duke of G[rafton] resigning.⁵—I was sorry it turned out so and forgot to tell you yesterday. The rest of his discourse I think was not much. I agree with you in your remarks however; but am almost certain the Duke of G. is unalterable. And the——'s⁶ obstinacy may produce a dreadful scene.

Yours sincerely. I will call if I can but I expect a thousand people.

From HERTFORD, Thursday 8 March 1770

Printed for the first time from a photostat of BM Add. MSS 23219, f. 42. *Address:* To the Honourable Horatio Walpole.

March 8th 1770.

Dear Horry,

MY brother does not intend moving about the *Whisperer* or *Parliamentary Spy*,¹ so you need give yourself no farther trouble.

Yours ever,

HERTFORD

(see *Court and City Register*, 1769, pp. 201, 204; Sir John Smyth, *Sandhurst*, 1961, pp. 27–40).

4. Surveyor-General of the Ordnance (*ante* 25 Feb. 1740, n. 19).

5. However, 'on the 25th his Grace talked of going on if the Attorney-General De Grey would accept the Great Seal,' but he resigned 'on the evening of the 27th'; it was not known generally 'till very late on the 30th when Lord North was declared the successor' (*Mem. Geo. III* iv. 42, 47).

6. Left blank by Conway. Presumably he is referring to the King and his obstinate aversion to the Opposition; on the 22d he had gone to the King, and 'hinted at trying Lord Rockingham, but the King said he knew the disposition of Lord Rockingham and his friends, and would not hear of them. He was as thoroughly averse to Lord Chatham . . .' (ibid. iv. 41).

———

1. Weekly papers attacking the King, Bute, the Princess Dowager, the King's ministers, and Parliament; the most recent numbers (published 3 and 6 March, respectively), contained vicious attacks on the Princess (see MANN vii. 195–6 and nn.

From CONWAY, Tuesday 20 March 1770

Printed for the first time from the MS, now WSL. For the history of the MS, see *ante* 9 Aug. 1767.

Address: To the Hon. Hor. Walpole.

Endorsed (by HW): March 20, 1770.

Little War[wick] Street, Tuesday morning.

ALL passed quietly and was indeed a cool day,[1] except a little scolding and giving the lie between Beckford, and Harley[2]— the plan of *the aldermen* was not to have spoke. Beckford and Sawbridge[3] did *only on provocation*.[4]

The question was a resolution that, to *deny the validity of the proceedings of Parliament etc.* was *unwarrantable, tending to etc.*

1–4). On 16 March Sir William Meredith in the House of Commons 'complained of Junius, the Whisperer, and the Parliamentary Spy; the Solicitor-General said a prosecution was begun against the first' (HW, 'Journal . . . 1770,' *sub* 16 March). In February 1771 one of the vendors of the *Whisperer* was sentenced to twelve months' imprisonment (Sir Henry Cavendish, *Debates of the House of Commons*, ed. Wright, 1841, i. 514).

1. 19 March, when the 'Address, Remonstrance, and Petition of the Lord Mayor, Aldermen and Livery of . . . London, to the King's Most Excellent Majesty,' calling for the dissolution of Parliament and the removal of the King's 'evil' ministers, and the King's answer to the same were taken into consideration by the House of Commons (see MANN vii. 196–7, nn. 5, 13; Sir Henry Cavendish, *Debates of the House of Commons*, ed. Wright, 1841, i. 535; *Journals of the House of Commons* xxxii. 810). The Address, prompted by the King's ignoring petitions against the expulsion of Wilkes from the House (see *ante* 30 June 1769, n. 1), had been presented to the King at St James's 14 March by the Lord Mayor (Beckford) and sheriffs (James Townsend and John Sawbridge) (MANN vii. 196–7 and nn. 7–9, 14).

2. Hon. Thomas Harley (*ante* 9 Dec. 1763, n. 23). On 15 March 'Beckford Lord Mayor, the two Sheriffs and Alderman Trecothick all avowed warmly and openly their share in the Remonstrance. Harley attacked Beckford violently as the disturber of the City's peace, and strong altercation proceeded, in which Harley had much the better' (HW, 'Journal . . . 1770,' *sub* 15 March). See Cavendish, op. cit. i. 520–1, 526–7; Cobbett, *Parl. Hist.* xvi. 875–6.

3. John Sawbridge (1732–95), M.P. Hythe 1768–74, London 1774–80, 1780–95; sheriff of London 1769–70, alderman 1769, lord mayor 1775–6. See *ante* 30 June 1769, n. 2.

4. 'Lord Barrington said . . . [the Remonstrance] was so far from being an act of the City of London, that it could not properly be said to be the act of the poor people to whom it was once read, but of a set of Catilines only, who had no view but to draw all men from law and allegiance. Mr Beckford . . . was stung by this keen reproach, and to recriminate, said, that there were people out of the City, who were ready to cut throats, and had an army at hand for that purpose. Mr Sawbridge also felt himself wounded, and said, he knew of no conspirators but those who received the public revenues' (Cobbett, op. cit. xvi. 899).

etc.[5]—not violent—moved by Sir T[homas] Clavering[6] and Sir E[dward] Blackett.[7]—All the Cavendish, Greenville, Shelburne etc. against—but Barré has not said a word.—Division 284–126 on the *previous question*[8]—a second resolution[9] I did not stay.—It was between one and two.[10]

The Solicitor-General[11] shone. Burke *au contraire.*[12] Lord Beauchamp well.[13]—I did not speak.[14]

Yours etc.,

H. S. C.

From Conway, July 1770

Missing; implied *post* 12 July 1770.

5. 'To deny the legality of the present Parliament, and to assert that the proceedings therefore are not valid, is highly unwarrantable, and has a manifest tendency to disturb the peace of the Kingdom, by withdrawing his Majesty's subjects from their obedience to the laws of the realm' (Cavendish, op. cit. i. 535; *Journals of the House of Commons,* loc. cit.).

6. (1719–94), 7th Bt; M.P. St Mawes 1753–4, Shaftesbury 1754–60, Durham Co. 1768–90. See Cavendish, loc. cit., and Namier and Brooke ii. 217.

7. (1719–1804), 4th Bt; M.P. Northumberland 1768–74. See Cavendish, op. cit. i. 535–6 and Namier and Brooke ii. 94.

8. Dowdeswell moved the previous question, 'that the said proposed question be now put,' observing that the right of the subject to petition was indubitable, and that all prosecutions for petitioning were illegal; the motion was carried 284–127 (*Journals of the House of Commons,* loc. cit.; Debrett's *History, Debates, and Proceedings of Both Houses of Parliament,* 1792, v. 279; see also Cavendish, op. cit. i. 537–9).

9. By Sir Thomas Clavering for an address to the King against the remonstrance; it was voted by the House the next day 248–94, and agreed to 21 March (MANN vii. 199–200 and nn. 4, 7).

10. According to HW's 'Journal . . . 1770,' *sub* 19 March, 'the House sat till past two, when . . . the . . . previous question . . . was rejected'; and Lord Temple wrote to Lady Chatham 20 March that he stayed 'in the House of Commons till three o'clock this morning' (*Chatham Corr.* iii. 431). See also Debrett, loc. cit., and *Journals of the House of Commons,* loc. cit.

11. John Dunning, who had resigned as solicitor-general in Jan., but continued to officiate until he was replaced by Edward Thurlow (*ante* 22 Jan. 1770, n. 3), 'made a great figure against the Court,' defending the remonstrance (HW's 'Journal . . . 1770,' loc. cit.). 'The Solicitor-General (Mr Dunning) spoke in this debate on the side of the minority. His speech, which continued near an hour and a half was one of the finest pieces of argument and eloquence ever heard in the House' (Debrett, loc. cit.).

12. Burke also defended the remonstrance; part of his speech is in Cavendish, op. cit. i. 542–5.

13. He had spoken against the remonstrance on 15 March. See ibid. i. 526.

14. For Conway's remarks 15 March, condemning the remonstrance, see ibid. i. 534–5; Cobbett, op. cit. xvi. 888–92.

To Conway, Thursday 12 July 1770

Printed from *Works* v. 141–2. The opening sentence answers a pleasantry in a missing letter.

Arlington Street, July 12, 1770.

REPOSING under my laurels![1] No, no, I am reposing in a much better tent, under the tester of my own bed. I am not obliged to rise by break of day and be dressed for the Drawing-Room; I may saunter in my slippers till dinner-time, and not make bows till my back is as much out of joint as my Lord Temple's.[2] In short, I should die of the gout or fatigue, if I was to be Polonius to a princess for another week.[3] Twice a day we made a pilgrimage to almost every heathen temple[4] in that province that they call a garden; and there is no sallying out of the house without descending a flight of steps[5] as high as St Paul's. My Lord Besborough would have dragged me up to the top of the column,[6] to see all the kingdoms of the earth; but I would not, if he could have given them to me. To crown all, because we live under the line, and that we were all of us giddy young creatures, of near threescore, we supped in a grotto in the Elysian fields,[7] and were refreshed with rivers of dew and gentle showers that dripped from all the trees; and put us in mind of the heroic ages, when kings and queens were shepherds and shepherdesses, and lived in caves, and were wet to the skin two or three times a day. Well! thank heaven, I am emerged from that Elysium, and once more in a Christian country!—Not but, to say the truth, our pagan landlord and landlady were very obliging,[8] and the party went off much better than I expected. We had no very

1. That is, the laurels at SH.

2. In HW's letter to Montagu 7 July 1770 describing the party he said, 'the Earl you know is bent double' (MONTAGU ii. 314–15).

3. Mr Walpole had been for a week at Stowe, the seat of Earl Temple, with a party invited to meet her Royal Highness the late Princess Amelia (HW). He was there 2–7 July; he had been invited by the Princess herself while at Park Place the end of June. See HW to Strafford 9 July 1770, CHUTE 338–9; Coke, *Journals*, iii. 252–4.

4. For the numerous temples and other buildings at Stowe, see MONTAGU ii. 44, n. 7; *Stowe: A Description*, 1768, *passim* (HW's copy now WSL, Hazen, *Cat. of HW's Lib.*, No. 2387 : 4).

5. 'Fifty stone stairs' (HW to Montagu 7 July 1770, MONTAGU ii. 315).

6. 'Lord Cobham's Pillar'; see *Stowe*, p. 29.

7. See MONTAGU ii. 314–15; Coke, op. cit. iii. 253; *Stowe*, p. 26 and facing p. 19.

8. 'Nobody can do the honours of their house with more ease and propriety then Lord and Lady Temple' (Coke, op. cit. iii. 253).

recent politics, though volumes about the Spanish war;[9] and as I took care to give everything a ludicrous turn as much as I could, the Princess was diverted, the six days rolled away, and the seventh is my sabbath; and I promise you I will do no manner of work, I, nor my cat, nor my dog, nor anything that is mine. For this reason, I entreat that the journey to Goodwood[10] may not take place before the 12th of August, when I will attend you. But this expedition to Stowe has quite blown up my intended one to Wentworth Castle:[11] I have not resolution enough left for such a journey. Will you and Lady A. come to Strawberry before or after Goodwood? I know you like being dragged from home as little as I do; therefore you shall place that visit just when it is most convenient to you.

I came to town the night before last, and am just returning. There are not twenty people in all London. Are not you in despair about the summer? It is horrid to be ruined in coals in June and July. Adieu!

Yours ever,

Hor. Walpole

---

9. In early June accounts reached England of the Spanish having ordered the British to evacuate Port Egmont, in the Falkland Islands; the garrison there capitulated 10 June, though news of this did not reach England until September (see *Daily Adv.* 7, 8 June; *Grenville Papers,* iv. 507, 518; Mann vii. 239–40, nn. 1, 2).

During the ensuing months England was close to war with Spain; see *post* 29 Dec. 1770 and n. 11.

10. The Duke of Richmond's seat.

11. The seat of Lord Strafford; in his letter to Strafford 9 July 1770 (Chute 339) HW deferred his visit indefinitely.

From HERTFORD, Monday 23 July 1770

Printed for the first time from a photostat of BM Add. MSS 23219, f. 44.
Address: To the Honourable Horatio Walpole at Strawberry Hill near Twickenham, Middlesex. Free Hertford.
Postmark: FREE 23 IY.

London, July 23d 1770.

Dear Horry,

IN the midst of my affliction I cannot omit acquainting you that I have lost my dear daughter Sarah.[1] She died on the 18th after having struggled some days with an obstinate fever. She was seven or eight months gone with child.[2]

Yours ever most truly,

HERTFORD

From HERTFORD, Wednesday 25 July 1770

Printed for the first time from a photostat of BM Add. MSS 23219, f. 46.

London, July 25th 1770.

Dear Horry,

YOU are always good and friendly to us, and be assured we are most sensible of it. Do not think of coming to town till your engagements are satisfied. Time will assist in composing our spirits, and we shall be fitter for our friends next week, though there is no moment that we shall not be always happy and ready to receive you. I have some little thoughts of going into Suffolk for a few days if I can quit Lady Hertford, who is well in health.[1] I am ever, dear Horry,

Most truly and most affectionately yours,

HERTFORD

1. Lady Sarah Frances Seymour Conway, married Robert Stewart, later Lord Londonderry, in 1766 (*ante* 21 May 1766), died 18 July at Dublin (GM 1770, xl. 345; GEC).
2. She had had two prior children, Alexander Francis, b. 1767, d. young, and Robert, b. 18 June 1769, the famous Lord Castlereagh, who succeeded his father as 2d M. of Londonderry in 1821 (ibid.; see *post* 23 Oct. 1786).

1. I.e., though sad in spirit.

From Lady Hertford, Saturday 4 August 1770

Printed for the first time from a photostat of BM Add. MSS 23219, f. 102.
Address (by Lord Hertford): To the Honourable Horatio Walpole at Strawberry Hill near Twickenham, Middlesex. Free Hertford.
Postmark: FREE 4 AV.

Saturday the 4th.

Dear Mr Walpole,

P RAY be so indulgent as to come to town next Tuesday the 7th, to dine and pass the day here with Lady Mary Coke.[1] This day I imagine is warm enough for you. I received yesterday a very kind friendly letter from the Duke of G[rafton][2] which has made me forget it was long in coming.[3] I am always

Most faithfully yours,

I. H.

From Hertford, Tuesday 7 August 1770

Printed from a photostat of BM Add. MSS 23219, f. 47; first printed in John Forster, *Historical and Biographical Essays,* 1858, ii. 410.

London, August 7th 1770.

Dear Horry,

B E SO GOOD to cast your eye over the piece[1] enclosed herewith which Mr Foote has sent to me,[2] and acquaint me if you do not think with me that the political part of it is too strong and that the

1. Who wrote in her *Journals,* iii. 267–8, *sub* Tuesday, 7 Aug.: 'I dined in town at Lord Hertford's: tis the first time I have seen him since his daughter's death, which seems to have affected him very much. He was at times so dejected, that it quite hurt me. Lady Hertford continues very low.' As she does not mention HW, he was probably not present.
2. Lady Hertford's nephew.
3. Presumably it was an overdue letter

of condolence on the death of her daughter, Grafton's cousin.

———

1. Apparently Charles Macklin's *Man of the World,* sent for licensing on 2 Aug. (L. W. Conolly, 'Horace Walpole, Unofficial Play Censor,' *English Language Notes,* 1971, ix. 44).
2. As manager of the Little Theatre in the Haymarket, Foote was submitting other people's plays to the Lord Chamberlain as well as his own (ibid.).

piece should be returned to him to be softened and altered before it can be licensed.[3] I remain, dear Horry,

Ever truly yours,

Hertford

To Lady Hertford, September 1770

Missing; answered *post* 8 Sept. 1770.

From Lady Hertford, Saturday 8 September 1770

Printed for the first time from a photostat of BM Add. MSS 23219, f. 96.

Ragley,[1] Saturday the 8th.

Dear Mr Walpole,

I WAS shocked when I first opened your letter[2] today, as I was sure you must be very ill by writing so differently from what you usually do, but I must say I was much relieved when I found it was only the gout, and that it was the ingenious performance of your left hand.[3] I hope you won't be confined long,[4] as I know how impatient you will be under that restriction in the present fine weather. We are at present entirely a family party; Miss Lloyd[5] was with us three days, and went to Trentham[6] yesterday.

Mr and Mrs Vernon[7] etc. dined with us today, and arrived before two, though we don't dine till four, which fatigued me dreadfully and put me in mind of our famous visit to Lady Archer's.[8]

3. The play was not licensed until 1781; see Dougald MacMillan, 'The Censorship in the Case of Macklin's *The Man of the World,*' *Huntington Library Bulletin,* No. 10, 1936, pp. 79–101.

1. 'Lord and Lady Hertford set out for Warwickshire on Thursday [30 Aug.] for nineteen days' (Coke, *Journals,* iii. 278, *sub* 28 Aug.).

2. Missing.

3. 'At Lady Blandford's I heard that Mr Walpole was confined to his bed; the gout in both his feet and his right hand' (ibid. iii. 283, *sub* 9 Sept.).

4. HW's current fit, which began at the end of August, lasted into October (Mann vii. 236; Montagu ii. 322).

5. Presumably Rachel Lloyd, housekeeper at Kensington Palace (*ante* 1 Nov. 1764).

6. The seat of Lord Gower.

7. Not identified.

8. Catherine Tipping (d. 1754), m. (1726) Thomas Archer, cr. (1747) Bn Archer. See *ante* 14 Aug. 1760 and n. 1; 7 April 1765.

We intend being in town on Friday sennight;[9] in the meantime do let us know you are well.

Yours etc.

I. H.

On 24 Oct. 1770 Conway succeeded Lord Granby as colonel of the Royal Horse Guards, 'the most agreeable post in the army' (HW to Mann 12 Nov. 1770, MANN vii. 246 and n. 8). At the same time he withdrew from the Cabinet after five years of continuous service, the longest term of any member of the North Ministry at that time (Namier and Brooke ii. 246; HW's 'Journal . . . 1770,' *sub* Nov.).

From HERTFORD, Thursday 15 November 1770

Printed for the first time from a photostat of BM Add. MSS 23219, f. 48.
Address: To Hor. Walpole Esq., Arlington Street.
Memoranda (by HW):[1] sings[2]
                            English, Latin[3]
                            Quaker[4]
                            Sermon[5]

Northumberland House, Thursday.

Dear Horry,

THE Princess d'Ascow[6] dines here. The Duke and Duchess of Northumberland desire you will come after dinner and enjoy her in any way flattering to yourself.

Yours ever,

HERTFORD

9. 21 Sept.

1. For the continuation of his letter to Mann 12 Nov. 1770 *sub* 'Friday morning [16 Nov.]' (MANN vii. 248–50).
2. 'The Princess Daschioff . . . sings tenderly and agreeably with a pretty voice,' etc. (ibid. vii. 248–9).
3. 'She speaks English a little, understands it easily . . . and she knows Latin' (ibid. vii. 249).
4. HW tells an anecdote of the Princess at a Quaker's meeting, ibid. vii. 249–50.
5. 'The discourse which is said to be very eloquent, the Princess has translated into French, and Dr Hinchliffe . . . is to publish it in English' (ibid. vii. 249). This 'discourse' was a sermon preached on the tomb of Peter the Great at St Petersburg on the occasion of the recent Russian naval victory over the Turks (ibid. and nn. 24–5, 27).
6. Ekaterina Romanovna Vorontsova (1743–1810), m. (ca 1758–60) Mikhail Il-

To Conway, Tuesday 25 December 1770

Printed from *Works* v. 142.

Arlington Street, Christmas Day.

IF poplar-pines ever grow, it must be in such a soaking season as this. I wish you would send half a dozen[1] by some Henley barge to meet me next Saturday at Strawberry Hill, that they may be as tall as the Monument[2] by next summer. My cascades give themselves the airs of cataracts, and Mrs Clive looks like the sun rising out of the ocean. Poor Mr Raftor[3] is tired to death of their solitude; and as his passion is walking, he talks with rapture of the brave rows of lamps all along the streets, just as I used formerly to think no trees beautiful without lamps to them, like those at Vauxhall.

As I came to town but to dinner, and have not seen a soul, I do not know whether there is any news. I am just going to the Princess,[4] where I shall hear all there is. I went to *King Arthur*[5] on Saturday,[6] and was tired to death, both of the nonsense of the piece and the execrable performance, the singers being still worse than the actors.[7] The scenes are little better (though Garrick boasts of rivalling the French opera), except a pretty bridge, and a Gothic church with windows of painted glass.[8] This scene, which should be a barbarous

larionovich Dashkov; friend of Catherine the Great (ibid. vi. 65, n. 13). She had come to England in early October to put her son to school (ibid. vii. 242 and n. 12).

1. The first poplar-pine (or, as they have since been called, Lombardy poplar) planted in England is that at Park Place, on the bank of the river near the great arch. It was a cutting brought from Turin by the late Lord Rochford in his carriage, and planted by General Conway's own hand (Mary Berry). See OSSORY ii. 480 and n. 25.

2. The Monument, in Monument Yard, Fish Street Hill, designed by Christopher Wren and erected 1671–7 to commemorate the Great Fire of London, 1666, was 202 feet tall.

3. James Raftor (d. 1790), actor; brother of Mrs Clive. W. Whitehead wrote to Lord Nuneham 30 Oct. 1770: 'Raftor has left the stage; Mrs Clive has very kindly taken him to live entirely with her [at

Little Strawberry Hill], and I hear he is excessively happy at it' (MS letter quoted Cunningham ii. 458, n. 1).

4. The late Princess Amelia (HW).

5. Dryden's dramatic opera, *King Arthur; or, The British Worthy*, revived at Drury Lane 13 Dec. with alterations by Garrick, the music by Purcell and Thomas Augustine Arne (1710–78), with a new overture by Arne (*London Stage* Pt IV, iii. 1517–18; Sir George Grove, *Dictionary of Music and Musicians*, 5th edn, ed. Blom, 1954–61, i. 208, 212).

6. 22 Dec.; see *London Stage* Pt IV, iii. 1519.

7. For a list of the actors and singers, see ibid. iii. 1517–18. William Hopkins, in his MS Diary, 1769–76 (cited ibid. iii. 1518), notes that 'Miss Hayward played Emmeline very bad.'

8. 'This masque was got up in a superb manner . . . and greatly applauded' (Hopkins Diary, cited ibid.).

temple of Woden, is a perfect cathedral, and the devil[9] officiates at a kind of high mass! I never saw greater absurdities.

Adieu!

To Conway, Saturday 29 December 1770

Printed from *Works* v. 143–4.

Arlington Street, Dec. 29, 1770.

THE trees[1] came safe: I thank you for them: they are gone to Strawberry, and I am going to plant them. This paragraph would not call for a letter, but I have news for you of importance enough to dignify a dispatch. The Duc de Choiseul is fallen! The express from Lord Harcourt[2] arrived yesterday morning;[3] the event happened last Monday night,[4] and the courier set out so immediately, that not many particulars are yet known. The Duke was allowed but three hours to prepare himself, and ordered to retire to his seat at Chanteloup:[5] but some letters say, *Il ira plus loin.* The Duc de Praslin is banished too,[6] and Châtelet[7] is forbidden to visit Choiseul. Châtelet was to have had the marine; and I am sure is no loss to us.[8] The Chevalier de Muy[9] is made secretary of state *pour la guerre;* and it is concluded that the Duc d'Aiguillon is prime minister, but was not named so in the first hurry.[10] There! there is a revolution!

9. I.e., Merlin.

1. The Lombardy poplars (HW).
2. Then ambassador at Paris (HW).
3. See MANN vii. 257, n. 1.
4. 24 Dec.
5. Mme du Deffand heard that the original order delivered 24 Dec. to Choiseul, was for him 'de se rendre à Chanteloup'; when Choiseul asked permission to wait until Wednesday, he was told (at supper, Monday night) to leave before noon on Tuesday. HW, who had not yet received Mme du Deffand's account, dated 26 Dec. 1770 'à 10 heures du matin,' was at this time receiving the opinions of Francès, the French Resident (see below, and MANN vii. 257, n. 2).
6. By 'une simple lettre de cachet, qui

l'exile à sa terre de Vaux-Praslin près de Melun' (*Mercure historique,* 1771, clxx. 113).
7. Louis-Marie-Florent (1727–93), Comte (Duc, 1777) du Châtelet; ambassador to England 1767–70 (OSSORY i. 39, n. 18; *Dictionnaire de biographie française,* 1933– , xi. 1197–9). He was a protégé of Choiseul (ibid. xi. 1197; see also *post* ca 23 July 1771, n. 7).
8. HW calls him 'our bitter enemy' to Mann 29 Dec. 1770, MANN vii. 258.
9. Louis-Nicolas-Victor de Félix (1711–75), Comte du Muy; Maréchal de France, 1775. He declined the post at this time, but filled it in 1774–5 (ibid. n. 8).
10. He became minister for foreign affairs in June 1771 (ibid. vii. 265 and n. 18).

there is a new scene opened! Will it advance the war? Will it make peace?[11] These are the questions all mankind is asking. This whale has swallowed up all gudgeon questions. Lord Harcourt writes, that the d'Aiguillonists had officiously taken opportunities of assuring him, that if they prevailed it would be peace;[12] but in this country we know that opponents turned ministers *can* change their language. It is added, that the morning of Choiseul's banishment, the King said to him, 'Monsieur, je vous ai dit que je ne voulais pas la guerre.'[13] Yet how does this agree with Francès's[14] eager protestations that Choiseul's fate depended on preserving the peace?[15] How does it agree with the comptroller-general's[16] offer of finding funds for the war, and of Choiseul's proving he could not?[17]—But how reconcile half the politics one hears? De Guisnes[18] and Francès sent their excuses to the Duchess of Argyll[19] last night; and I suppose the Spaniards too, for none of them were there.—Well! I shall let all this bustle cool for two days; for what Englishman does not sacrifice anything to go his Saturday out of town?—And yet I am very much interested in this event; I feel much for Madame de Choiseul, though nothing for her *Corsican* husband;[20] but I am in the utmost anxiety for my dear old friend,[21] who passed every evening with the Duchess,

11. England and Spain were on the verge of a war over the Falkland Islands (see *ante* 12 July 1770, n. 9); however, peace was confirmed in January. See MANN vii. 266 and n. 1, 268 and nn. 11, 12, *et passim*.

12. 'Lord Harcourt wrote that the d'Aiguillonists had for some time officiously whispered him, that it would be peace, if they should prevail' (HW, 'Journal . . . 1770,' *sub* 28 Dec.).

13. On 23 Dec., Louis XV is said to have written to Charles III of Spain that 'my minister would have war, but I will not' (M. C. Morison, 'The Duc de Choiseul and the Invasion of England, 1768–70,' *Transactions of the Royal Historical Society*, 1910, 3d ser. iv. 105).

14. Then the chargé des affaires from the French Court in London (HW), which he had been until the arrival of the Comte de Guines in Nov. (*ante* 10 Sept. 1769, n. 5; n. 18 below).

15. 'Francès had with vehemence declared to our ministers here, that Choiseul's preservation depended on his mak-

ing peace' (HW, 'Journal . . . 1770,' loc. cit.).

16. Abbé Joseph-Marie Terray (1715–78), controller-general 1769–74.

17. 'Choiseul had defeated [it] by proving the impossibility of the comptroller-general du Terray's plan of raising funds for the war' (ibid.). The terms of the financial edict are given in the *Mercure historique*, 1771, clxx. 106–11.

18. Adrien-Louis de Bonnières (1735–1806), Comte and (1776) Duc de Guines, French ambassador to England 1770–6. He had presented his credentials 29 Nov. (MANN vii. 256, n. 16).

19. Elizabeth, Dowager Duchess of Hamilton (*ante* 23 June 1752 OS, n. 24) had become Duchess of Argyll 9 Nov. upon the succession of her second husband, Col. John Campbell, as the 5th Duke.

20. 'I cannot possibly feel for her husband; Corsica is engraved in my memory, as I believe it is on your heart' (HW to Mann 29 Dec. 1770, MANN vii. 258).

21. Madame la Marquise du Deffand (HW).

and was thence in great credit; and what is worse, though nobody I think can be savage enough to take away her pension, she may find great difficulty to get it paid[22]—and then her poor heart is so good and warm, that this blow on her friends, at her great age,[23] may kill her. I have had no letter, nor had last post[24]—whether it was stopped, or whether she apprehended the event, as I imagine—for everybody observed, on Tuesday night, at your brother's, that Francès could not open his mouth. In short, I am most seriously alarmed about her.

You have seen in the papers the designed arrangements in the law.[25] They now say there is some hitch; but I suppose it turns on some demands, and so will be got over by their being granted.[26]

Mr Mason,[27] the bard, gave me yesterday the enclosed memorial,[28] and begged I would recommend it to you. It is in favour of a very ingenious painter.[29] Adieu! the sun shines brightly; but it is one o'clock, and it will be set before I get to Twickenham.

Yours ever,

HOR. WALPOLE

22. The late Queen Marie Leszczyńska had procured for Mme du Deffand a pension of 6,000 livres a year, in recognition of her aunt's services to the Queen (DU DEFFAND i. 5, n. 19). Though Mme du Barry threatened the following March to stop her pension if she visited the Duke and Duchess of Choiseul, it was apparently continued until her death (ibid. iii. 43–4 et passim).

23. She was 74 (ibid. v. 368, n. 23).

24. See above, n. 5.

25. The London papers for 27 Dec. announced that Henry Bathurst (post 7 Nov. 1774, n. 10) was to be lord chancellor, William De Grey (1719–81) chief justice of the Common Pleas, Alexander Wedderburn (1733–1805) attorney-general, James Wallace (1729–83) solicitor-general, and Edward Thurlow (ante 20 May 1765, n. 72) chief justice of Chester (Public Adv. 27 Dec.; Gazetteer and New Daily Advertiser 27 Dec.; Whitehall Evening Post 25–7 Dec., sub 27 Dec.; St James's Chronicle 25–7 Dec., sub 27 Dec., postscript; Namier

and Brooke ii. 308; iii. 593, 618). A meeting of Lord North and the parties concerned had been scheduled for 19 December to determine these posts (Geo. III's Corr., ed. Fortescue, ii. 188–9).

26. Bathurst was sworn in as lord chancellor 23 Jan., and De Grey kissed hands for his post 25 Jan.; however, Wedderburn became solicitor-general and Thurlow attorney-general, both kissing hands 25 Jan., while Wallace received no post at this time (MANN vii. 268–9 and n. 16; Namier and Brooke iii. 593).

27. William Mason (1725–97), divine; poet; HW's correspondent.

28. Missing.

29. Perhaps W. Stavely, 'a young carver of York,' whom Mason, himself an amateur artist, instructed in his 'new discovered art of oiling drawings in watercolours,' though this Stavely did not settle in London and exhibit at the Royal Academy until 1785 (HW, Anecdotes of Painting, Vol. V, ed. Hilles and Daghlian, New Haven, 1937, p. 80 and n. 20).

From Hertford, Monday 18 February 1771

Printed from a photostat of BM Add. MSS 23219, f. 50; first printed in L. W. Conolly, 'Horace Walpole, Unofficial Play Censor,' *English Language Notes*, 1971, ix. 44.

Address: To the Honourable Horatio Walpole, Arlington Street.

February 18th 1771.

Dear Horry,

YOU asked me after the new tragedy.[1] I have therefore sent it to you, that if you have any curiosity you may satisfy it. Pray return it me today. You will soon read it. The piece in my judgment is very very moderate. The moment is not a favourable one to produce it; some applications may be made,[2] and yet I dare say you will agree with me that it should be licensed.

Yours ever,

Hertford

From Conway, June 1771

Missing; answered *post* 17 June 1771.

1. Presumably *Clementina*, a blank verse tragedy by Hugh Kelly (1739–77), submitted for licensing 14 Feb., and first acted at Covent Garden 23 Feb. (Conolly, loc. cit.; *London Stage* Pt IV, iii. 1529). HW, in his copy, now wsL (Hazen, *Cat. of HW's Lib.*, No. 1810:17:3) wrongly identifies the author as Dr Thomas Francklin (1721–84); the play was produced and printed anonymously, since Kelly's last play *A Word to the Wise*, had been the occasion of rioting by the Wilkesites, who objected to Kelly as a newspaper hack for the ministry (DNB).

2. I.e., political applications; Hertford may have been thinking of such lines as 'O! for a curse, a quick dispatching curse,/ to blast the ruthless tyrant on his throne' (Act I); 'Your monarch . . . / Seeks to subvert our glorious constitution' (Act II); 'The people's voice, howe'er it sometimes errs,/ Means always nobly, and is raised by virtue' (Act IV); and 'The man is half a traitor to the state,/ who only serves it from a sordid motive' (Act IV). However, to be construed as anti-ministerial, these lines have to be taken superficially and out of context, and it is hardly likely, in any case, that Kelly, a ministerial hack, would intend them as such.

To Conway, Monday 17 June 1771

Printed from the MS, now WSL; first printed in Wright v. 298–300. For the
history of the MS, see *ante* 29 June 1744 OS; it was marked by HW for inclusion
in *Works*, but was not included.
Endorsed: Mr Walpole 17 June 1771.

Strawberry Hill, June 17, 1771.

I WAS very sure you would grant my request, if you could; and
I am perfectly satisfied with your reasons;[1] but I do not believe
the parties concerned[2] will be so too, especially the heads of the
family,[3] who are not so ready to serve their relations at their own
expense as gratis.[4] When I see you, I will tell you more, and what
I thought I had told you.

You tax me with four days in Bedfordshire;[5] I was but three at
most, and of those the evening I went and the morning I came away,
made the third day. I will try to see you before I go.[6] The Edg-
cumbes[7] I should like, and Lady Lyttelton, but Garrick does not
tempt me at all: I have no taste for his perpetual buffoonery, and
am sick of his endless expectation of flattery—but you, who charge
me with making a *long* visit to Lord and Lady Ossory—you do not
see the mote in your own eye; at least I am sure Lady Ailesbury
does not see that in hers. I could not obtain a single day from her
all last year, and with difficulty got her to give me a few hours this.
There is always an indispensable pheasantry that must be visited, or
something from which she cannot spare four-and-twenty hours.
Strawberry sets this down in its pocket-book and resents the neglect.

1. Conway's letter, implied here, is missing.
2. William O'Brien and his wife Lady
Susan; see n. 4 below.
3. Lords Holland and Ilchester; see
next note.
4. Apparently HW had been approached by Lord and Lady Holland to
influence Conway not to dismiss William
O'Brien, who had eloped with Lady Susan
Fox Strangways, daughter of Holland's
brother Lord Ilchester, in 1764 (see *ante*
12 April 1764), from a post under the
Ordnance which the family had procured
for him in America. The couple having

returned to England, O'Brien had refused to go back to his post, though ordered to do so, upon which Conway dismissed him. See *Last Journals* i. 142.
5. Where he stayed with Lord and
Lady Ossory; see below and his 'Journey
to Houghton Park, Ampthill, Hawnes
[Flitton], and Wrest. June 1771' in his
Country Seats 69–71.
6. To Paris; HW left London 7 July,
arriving 10 July ('Paris Journals,' DU DEF-
FAND v. 333–4).
7. George, 3d Bn Edgcumbe (*ante* 17
Sept. 1767), m. (1761) Emma Gilbert
(1729–1807).

At two miles from Houghton Park[8] is the mausoleum of the Bruces,[9] where I saw the most ridiculous monument of one of Lady Ailesbury's predecessors that ever was imagined—I beg she will never keep such company. In the midst of an octagon chapel is the tomb of Diana Countess of Oxford and Elgin.[10] From a huge unwieldy base of white marble rises a black marble cistern, literally a cistern that would serve for an eating room. In the midst of this to the knees stands her Ladyship in a white domino or shroud, with her left hand erect as giving her blessing. It put me in mind of Mrs Cavendish[11] when she got drunk in the bathing tub. At another church[12] is a kind of catacomb for the Earls of Kent: there are ten sumptuous monuments.[13] Wrest[14] and Hawnes[15] are both ugly places; the house at the former is ridiculously old and bad.[16] The state bedchamber (not ten feet high) and its drawing-room, are laced with Ionic fluted columns of spotted velvet, and friezes of patchwork.[17] There are bushels of deplorable earls and countesses.[18] The garden was exe-

8. Houghton Park House, owned by the Duke of Bedford; the Ossorys were occupying it temporarily at this time while repairs were being made at the Earl's own seat, Ampthill Park. See below; Ossory i. 44 and n. 5, 51 and n. 5; and Country Seats 69–70.

9. At Maulden (ibid. 70).

10. Lady Diana Cecil (ca 1596–1654), m. 1 (1624) Henry de Vere, 18th Earl of Oxford; m. 2 (1629) Thomas Bruce, 1st Earl of Elgin. She was a great fortune and celebrated beauty (GEC). The tomb was erected by her second husband (Country Seats, loc. cit.).

11. Elizabeth Cavendish (d. 1779), m. Richard Chandler, later Cavendish (ante 15 March 1762, n. 13). HW wrote to Lady Ailesbury 15 March 1762: 'I recommend to you the idea of Mrs Cavendish, when half-stark'; she was enormously fat (ibid.).

12. Flitton (Country Seats, loc. cit.).

13. 'In a side chapel which opens into three more mausoleums, plain but pretty are ten fine monuments of alabaster and marble, besides gravestones of other earls near the altar' (ibid.).

14. Wrest Park, the seat of the earls of Kent; see ibid. 70–1 and Montagu i. 4–5 and n. 3.

15. The seat of Lord Granville. Though

HW here describes Hawnes along with Wrest as 'ugly,' in Country Seats 70 he calls it 'a pretty good house, with a handsome new front.' Hawnes is now called Haynes Park (Dalrymple 139, n. 9).

16. 'A wretched low bad house built round a small court' (Country Seats, loc. cit.).

17. 'The ancient state bedchamber, now so ruinous that it is going to be pulled down, and the old drawing-room, are remarkable. The first is exceedingly low; but the furniture very singular; round the hangings are spotted velvet fluted Ionic pillars with a frieze of devices in patchwork. The same are in the drawing-room but enlivened with white festoons between the columns' (ibid. 71).

18. 'The hall is large with copies whole length of James I, the Queen of Scots and others. Lord Hardwicke and the Marchioness of Grey his wife, the heiress of Kent, have made a fine dining room, in which amongst other portraits are two whole lengths by Vandyck. . . . One is a fine and beautiful portrait of Anne daughter of the Earl of Devonshire and wife of Lord Rich, son of the Earl of Warwick, the admiral; the other is a much worse portrait, but very valuable of the old Whig Lord Wharton, father of

crable too,[19] but is something mended by Brown.[20] Houghton Park and Ampthill stand finely: the last is a very good house and has a beautiful park.[21] The other has three beautiful old fronts, in the style of Holland House, with turrets and loggias, but not so large— within, it is the worst contrived dwelling I ever saw.[22] Upon the whole I was much diverted with my journey. On my return I stayed but a single hour in London, saw no soul, and came hither to meet the deluge. It has rained all night and all day—but it is midsummer, consequently midwinter, and one can expect no better. Adieu!

Yours ever,

H. W.

To Hertford, ca Sunday 14 July 1771

Missing; listed in 'Paris Journals' (DU Deffand v. 393).

To Hertford, ca Wednesday 17 July 1771

Missing; listed in 'Paris Journals' (DU Deffand v. 393). The letter was 'not sent.'

the Marquis. There are numbers of portraits of the Greys, Lucas's and Crewes etc. but indifferent, and nothing valuable in the house but a large library' (ibid. 70–1).

19. 'The gardens were fine and very ugly in the old-fashioned manner with high hedges and canals, at the end of the principal one of which is a frightful temple designed by Mr Archer the groom porter' (ibid. 71).

20. Lancelot ('Capability') Brown (1715– 83), landscape gardener; architect. 'Mr Brown has much corrected this garden, and built a hermitage and cold bath in a bold good taste' (ibid.).

21. See ibid. 69–70 and *Transactions of the Society . . . of Arts, Manufactures, and Commerce*, 1785, iii. 6–12.

22. 'A bad and inconvenient house within' (*Country Seats* 69).

From HERTFORD, ca Tuesday 23 July 1771

Printed for the first time from a photostat of BM Add. MSS 23219, ff. 83–4. Presumably written in answer to HW's missing letter *ante* ca 14 July 1771, and dated conjecturally between that letter and HW's missing letter *post* ca 31 July 1771; in any case, it was written before the installation of Knights of the Garter on 25 July (see n. 12).

Dear Horry,

I HAVE spoke to the King as you desire in regard to Lady Mary Churchill,[1] and his Majesty has ordered me to assure both you and her that nothing more is necessary on her part; that her excuse is quite sufficient, graciously taken, and that she may stay as long as she pleases.[2] The King laughed at your idea about the Countess of Provence[3] and was entertained with the news you sent me from Paris.

I am sorry Guignes[4] is likely to be recalled. The King has made Lord Harcourt[5] say everything he could with propriety to prevent it, being much satisfied with his behaviour and conduct here.[6]

Châtelet is, I hear, a good courtier and knows the road perfectly to Madame de Barré.[7]

Lord Harrington sets out tomorrow morning for Paris with his second son;[8] I therefore send this letter by him. Lord Petersham[9] is in disgrace with him.

1. Who was in France with her husband; see 'Paris Journals,' DU DEFFAND v. 334–6.

2. She was on leave from her duties as housekeeper at Windsor Castle (see *ante* 1 Nov. 1764 and n. 17). See *post* 30 July 1771, *sub* 31 July.

3. Marie-Joséphine-Louise (1753–1810) of Savoy, m. (14 May 1771) Louis-Stanislas-Xavier, Comte de Provence, later Louis XVIII (DU DEFFAND iii. 77; MANN vii. 312, n. 19). HW's 'idea' may have been a joke about her ugliness; see ibid.

4. Guines, the French ambassador to London.

5. The English ambassador to Paris.

6. Guines continued as ambassador until 1776 (*ante* 29 Dec. 1770, n. 18).

7. Jeanne Bécu (1743–93), m. (1768) Guillaume, Comte du Barry; mistress of Louis XV. Mme du Deffand wrote to HW

6 Jan. 1772 that, in seeking an augmentation of the cash sum and pension to be paid to Choiseul for his resignation of the Swiss Guards, du Châtelet, 'ne trouvant point de facilité auprès de M. d'Aiguillon . . . se determina à parler à Mme du Barry, en qui il trouva plus de douceur et de facilité' (DU DEFFAND iii. 166).

8. Hon. Henry Fitzroy Stanhope (1754–1828). He was commissioned cornet in the 15th light dragoons, 1772, and eventually reached the rank of colonel in the Army (1794); he was also M.P. for Bramber 1782–4 (Namier and Brooke iii. 463).

9. Charles Stanhope (1753–1829), Harrington's first son and heir; styled Vct Petersham 1756–79; succeeded his father as 3d Earl of Harrington, 1779. He had been commissioned an ensign in the 2d Foot Guards, 1769, and eventually attained the rank of general (1803). He was

We have been in distress and alarms about Lady Beauchamp, but still we are flattered by the faculty that she is likely to do well;[10] her nerves have been much affected. Today she is something better and more composed; I do not know that they have ever positively seen danger, but in the mystery of physic and the human frame, they did not know what might happen. James[11] was called, but his powder did not immediately seem to hit the case, and Dr Hunter has again the management.

I am employed enough, as you may conceive, about the installation,[12] and shall be glad when it is over; if Lady Beauchamp does not prevent me, I mean to set out as I proposed for Ireland.[13]

Adieu, dear Horry; the best compliments of the family attend you, and I am

Ever sincerely and affectionately yours,

HERTFORD

There is a waterman's badge vacant, which I will reserve for your commands.[14] There came a young man[15] here in your name to ask it one Monday. I told him he was young, but that you would dispose of it.

M.P. for Thetford 1774, and Westminster 1776-9 (ibid. iii. 462-3).

10. She died the following February; see *post* 11 Feb. 1772.

11. Robert James (1705-76), M.D., whose fever powder and cure-all was HW's favourite remedy; see *ante* 15 March 1762, n. 8.

12. Of Knights of the Garter, held 25 July at Windsor Castle (GM 1771, xli. 333). See W. A. Shaw, *Knights of England*, 1906, i. 46-7.

13. He left 30 July and returned to

London 13 Sept. (*Daily Adv.* 31 July, 14 Sept.).

14. Evidently Hertford, as lord chamberlain, was in charge of the disposal of places among the watermen to the King, reserving this place for HW's disposal as an act of friendship. See Henry Humpherus, *History of the . . . Company of Watermen*, 1874, i. 5.

15. Not identified. In 1776 a royal waterman under HW's protection was in danger of impressment into the navy; see *post* 31 Oct. 1776 *bis*.

To Conway, Tuesday 30 July 1771

Printed from *Works* v. 144–7; listed in 'Paris Journals' (DU DEFFAND v. 393); sent by 'Lady M. Churchill.'

Paris, July 30, 1771.

I DO NOT know where you are, nor where this will find you, nor when it will set out to seek you, as I am not certain by whom I shall send it.[1] It is of little consequence, as I have nothing material to tell you, but what you probably may have heard.

The distress here is incredible, especially at Court. The King's tradesmen are ruined, his servants starving, and even angels and archangels cannot get their pensions and salaries, but sing Woe! woe! woe! instead of Hosannahs. Compiègne[2] is abandoned; Villiers-Coterets and Chantilly[3] crowded, and Chanteloup[4] still more in fashion, whither everybody goes that pleases; though, when they ask leave, the answer is, *Je ne le defends ni le permets*. This is the first time that ever the will of a king of France was interpreted against his inclination. Yet, after annihilating his parliament, and ruining public credit, he tamely submits to be affronted by his own servants. Madame de Beauveau[5] and two or three high-spirited dames defy this czar of Gaul. Yet they and their cabal are as inconsistent on the other hand. They make epigrams, sing vaudevilles against the mistress,[6] hand about libels against the Chancellor,[7] and have no more effect than a sky-rocket; but in three months will die to go to

---

1. See below, *sub* 31 July.

2. Where the Court had retired for the summer (*Gazette de Leyde* 23 July, 'Supplément,' 'suite des nouvelles de Paris du 15 juillet').

3. The country palaces of the Duke of Orléans and the Prince of Condé, who were in disgrace at Court [along with the other Princes of the Blood] for having espoused the cause of the parliament of Paris, banished by the Chancellor Maupou [in January] (HW); see DU DEFFAND iii. 15, vi. 181–2; MANN vii. 270 and nn. 4–7; É. Glasson, *Le Parlement de Paris*, 1901, ii. 355–9. The *Gazette de Leyde* 26 July, 'Supplément,' 'Paris . . . 19 juillet,' reported that 'les princes et princesses du sang . . . sont actuellement chez M. le

Duc d'Orléans à Villers-Cotterêts d'où ils iront le 25 à Chantilly.'

4. The country seat of the Duc de Choiseul, to which, on his ceasing to be first minister [in Dec.], he was banished by the King (HW); see *ante* 29 Dec. 1770.

5. Marie-Sylvie de Rohan-Chabot (1729–1807), m. 1 (1749) Jean-Baptiste-Louis de Clermont d'Amboise, Marquis de Renel; m. 2 (1764) Charles-Just de Beauvau, Prince de Beauvau (MANN vi. 341, n. 5; DU DEFFAND, *passim*). The Prince was dismissed as governor of Languedoc, 25 Aug. (DU DEFFAND iii. 91, n. 4).

6. Mme du Barry; see the verses sent by Mme du Deffand to HW in her letter of 8 May 1771, ibid. iii. 70.

7. Maupou (HW).

Court, and to be invited to sup with Madame du Barry. The only real struggle is between the Chancellor and the Duc d'Aiguillon. The first is false, bold, determined, and not subject to little qualms. The other is less known, communicates himself to nobody, is suspected of deep policy and deep designs, but seems to intend to set out under a mask of very smooth varnish; for he has just obtained the payment of all his bitter enemy La Chalotais's pensions and arrears.[8] He has the advantage too of being but moderately detested in comparison of his rival, and, what he values more, the interest of the mistress.[9] The Comptroller-General[10] serves both, by acting mischief more sensibly felt; for he ruins everybody but those who purchase a respite from his mistress.[11] He dispenses bankruptcy by retail, and will fall, because he cannot even by these means be useful enough. They are striking off nine millions from *la caisse militaire,* five from the marine, and one from the *affaires étrangères:*[12] yet all this will not extricate them. You never saw a great nation in so disgraceful a position. Their next prospect is not better: it rests on an *imbécile,*[13] both in mind and body.

July 31.

Mr Churchill and my sister set out tonight after supper, and I shall send this letter by them. There are no new books, no new plays, no new novels; nay, no new fashions. They have dragged old Mlle Le Maure[14] out of a retreat of thirty years,[15] to sing at the

8. Reported in the *Gazette de Leyde* 2 Aug., *sub* Paris, 26 July. As governor of Brittany, d'Aiguillon had been in constant conflict with La Chalotais, procureur-général of the parliament of Rennes and champion of that parliament against the central administration. Arrested on a charge of treason in 1765, La Chalotais was cleared of any crime by Louis XV in 1769, but remained suspended from his functions (see *ante* 5 Dec. 1765 and nn. 5–7).

9. Madame du Barry (HW).

10. The Abbé Terrai (HW).

11. The Baronne de la Garde (DU DEFFAND iii. 107, n. 20). HW writes in *Mem. Geo. III* iv. 222 that 'she was so notorious for the sale of offices, that her protector was forced to dismiss her'; this occurred in September (DU DEFFAND iii. 107).

12. The *Mercure historique,* Sept. 1771,

clxxi. 382 reported that 'le projet de réduction de dépense dans . . . [le departement] de la guerre continue de s'effectuer. Les compagnies d'infanterie nationale et étrangère, qui étaient à 63 hommes, viennent d'être réduites à 50 . . . La réduction dans la cavalerie suivra de près. . . . On travaille aussi à une grande réduction dans la marine; mais l'on assure qu'on n'en sera aucune dans le département de M. le duc de la Vrillière [the *affaires étrangères*].'

13. The Dauphin, afterwards Louis XVI.

14. Catherine-Nicole Le Maure (or Lemaure or Le More) (1704–86), opera singer, m. (1762) Bn de Montbruel (*Enciclopedia dello spettacolo*, Rome, 1954–62, vi. 1372).

15. She had quit the stage definitively in 1744 (ibid.).

Colisée,[16] which is a most gaudy Ranelagh, gilt, painted, and be-cupided like an opera, but not calculated to last as long as Mother Coliseum, being composed of chalk and pasteboard. Round it are courts of treillage, that serve for nothing, and behind it a canal, very like a horse-pond, on which there are fireworks and jousts. All together it is very pretty; but as there are few nabobs and nabobesses in this country, and as the middling and common people are not much richer than Job when he had lost everything but his patience, the proprietors are on the point of being ruined,[17] unless the project takes place that is talked of. It is, to oblige Corneille, Racine, and Molière[18] to hold their tongues twice a week, that their audiences may go to the Colisée.[19] This is like our Parliament's adjourning when senators want to go to Newmarket. There is a Monsieur Guillard[20] writing a history of the *rivalité de la France et de l'Angleterre.* —I hope he will not omit this parallel.

The instance of their poverty that strikes *me* most, who make political observations by the thermometer of baubles, is, that there is nothing new in their shops. I know the faces of every snuff-box and every teacup as well as those of Madame du Lac[21] and Monsieur

16. For her appearances there see Louis Petit de Bachaumont, *Mémoires secrets,* 1780–9, v. 280 *et seq.* HW had gone there with the Churchills 18 July ('Paris Journals,' DU DEFFAND v. 335). Opened the previous May, the Colisée covered the space between the Rues du Faubourg St-Honoré and du Colisée and the Avenues Matignon and des Champs-Élysées (Bachaumont, op. cit. v. 268; Grimm, *Correspondance,* ed. Tourneux, 1877–82, ix. 330–1; Félix, Marquis de Rochegude and M. Dumolin, *Guide pratique à travers le vieux Paris,* [1923], p. 263). For contemporary descriptions, see Grimm, op. cit. ix. 331–2; Emmanuel, Duc de Croÿ, *Journal inédit,* ed. Grouchy and Cottin, 1906, ii. 495–6; *Dictionnaire historique de la ville de Paris,* 1779, ii. 487–8; and le sieur Le Rouge, *Description du Colisée élevé aux Champs-Élysées sur les dessins de M. le Camus,* 1771, reprinted in *Revue universelle des arts,* ed. P. Lacroix and C. Marsuzi de Aguirre, 1863, xviii. 87–96.

17. See Grimm, op. cit. ix. 332–3. Bachaumont, op. cit. v. 280 *sub* 14 July reports that 'M. le duc de la Vrillière et Madame la marquise de Langeac contin-

uent à couvrir de la protection la plus éclatante les entrepreneurs du colisée, ou à retarder leur ruine absolue autant qu'il sera possible.' Mlle Le Maure was engaged by them as one means of doing the latter (ibid.); however, despite this and other expedients, the Colisée was finally closed in 1778, and demolished in 1780 (Grimm, op. cit. ix. 333, n. 1).

18. I.e., the Comédie-Française.

19. Neither Grimm nor Bachaumont mentions this plan; evidently it was not put into effect. See the list of performances Aug.–Dec. 1771 in H. Carrington Lancaster, *The Comédie Française 1701–1774,* Philadelphia, 1951, pp. 831–2 (*Transactions of the American Philosophical Society,* 2d ser., Vol. 41, Pt IV).

20. Gabriel-Henri Gaillard (1726–1806), historian, author of the *Histoire de la rivalité de la France et de l'Angleterre,* 11 vols, 1771–7. HW apparently purchased the first three-volume instalment at this time; in 1774 he obtained the four-volume continuation; four supplementary volumes completed the series in 1777 (Hazen, *Cat. of HW's Lib.,* Nos 3013, 3096).

21. China merchant, not further iden-

Poirier.[22] I have chosen some cups and saucers for my Lady A.,[23] as she ordered me, but I cannot say they are at all extraordinary. I have bespoken two cabriolets[24] for her, instead of six, because I think them very dear, and that she may have four more if she likes them. I shall bring too a sample of a baguette[25] that suits them. For myself, between economy and the want of novelty, I have not laid out five guineas—a very memorable anecdote in the history of my life. Indeed, the Czarina and I have a little dispute: she has offered to purchase the whole Crozat collection of pictures,[26] at which I had intended to ruin myself.[27] The Turks take her for it![28]—Apropos, they are sending from hence fourscore officers to Poland,[29] each of whom I suppose, like Almanzor,[30] can stamp with his foot and raise an army.[31]

As my sister travels like a Tartar princess with her whole horde,[32] she will arrive too late almost for me to hear from you in return to this letter, which in truth requires no answer, *vu que* I shall set out myself on the 26th of August.[33] You will not imagine that I am

tified; see DU DEFFAND *passim*, and F. J. B. Watson, 'Walpole and the Taste for French Porcelain,' in *Horace Walpole, Writer, Politician and Connoisseur*, ed. W. H. Smith, New Haven, 1967, pp. 185–94.

22. Simon-Philippe Poirier, china merchant (P. Verlet, 'Le commerce des objets d'art,' *Annales*, 1958, xiii. 25). See DU DEFFAND *passim*.

23. HW lists a sugar dish, basin and milk-pot 'for Lady Ailesbury' in his list of purchases, 1771, in 'Paris Journals,' DU DEFFAND v. 411.

24. A type of small arm-chair; 'Lady Ailesbury's cabriolets, case and packing,' are listed in ibid.

25. A small ornamental moulding of semicircular section (OED).

26. The collection of Louis-Antoine Crozat (ca 1699–1770), Baron de Thiers, uncle of the Duchesse de Choiseul (MANN vii. 350, n. 7).

27. HW, in his 'Anecdotes, 1771' in 'Paris Journals,' DU DEFFAND v. 372, lists a portrait of Cardinal Reginald Pole which he admired, but which was bought by Catherine the Great and brought to St Petersburg (ibid. iii. 178 and n. 16, 184, v. 372, n. 16). Crozat's heirs in September consented to sell to HW his com-

plete suit of armour of Francis I (MANN vii. 350 and n. 6).

28. Turkey, encouraged by France, who objected to Russia's interference in Polish affairs, had declared war on Russia in 1768. See ibid. vii. 70 and nn. 3, 4.

29. HW wrote to Mann 22 Oct. 1771 that while at Paris, he knew 'they were sending to Poland between twenty and thirty officers, headed by a Monsieur de Vieumenil [the Baron de Vioménil], reckoned one of their best military heads' (ibid. vii. 338 and n. 3). France was supporting the various Polish confederations (of Lithuania, Great Poland, and of Bar) in their fight against the Russians and the collaborator King Stanislas II (ibid. vii. 318, n. 6).

30. The hero of Dryden's *Conquest of Granada*.

31. Mann wrote to HW 24 Aug. 1771 that 'the confederates will in all probability not be able to hold out long for want of support from the Turks, who are beaten everywhere' (ibid. vii. 319). For subsequent developments in Poland's internal affairs and in the Russo-Turkish War, see MANN *passim*.

32. She had seven children.

33. He stayed until 2 Sept. ('Paris Journals,' DU DEFFAND v. 342).

glad to save myself the pleasure of hearing from you, but I would not give you the trouble of writing unnecessarily. If you are at home, and not in Scotland,[34] you will judge by these dates where to find me. Adieu!

Yours ever,

Hor. Walpole

PS. Instead of restoring the Jesuits,[35] they are proceeding to annihilate the Celestine, Augustines, and some other orders.[36]

To Hertford, ca Wednesday 31 July 1771

Missing; listed in 'Paris Journals' (du Deffand v. 393); sent by 'Lady M. Churchill.'

34. Presumably for a social visit with Lady Ailesbury's relations, though he may have had some business there as lieutenant-general of the Ordnance.

35. HW had written to Mann 6 July 1771 that 'we are told the Jesuits are restored in France' (Mann vii. 316). This rumour presumably arose from an ordinance passed by Louis XV on 15 June allowing all priests, including Jesuits, who had been banished from France since 1756 to return to the country; subsequently Jesuits were allowed to preach in certain Paris churches and elsewhere. However, despite French toleration of individuals of the Order, the amnesty granted them did not amount to a restoration of the Order itself; see Ludwig, Freiherr von Pastor, *History of the Popes,* Vol. 38, trans. E. F. Peeler, 1951, pp. 195, 200 and n. 1.

36. Since 1766 a *Commission des Réguliers,* composed of five archbishops and five *conseillers d'État,* had been labouring to reform the various religious orders in France; those orders failing to conform to an edict prepared by the Commission and passed in March 1768, stipulating the terms of the reform, were subject to suppression or union to other orders. Be-

tween 1768 and 1780, when the Commission was dissolved, nine orders in France were completely abolished, including 19 *maisons* of the Celestines, 14 of the order of Ste-Croix de la Bretonnerie, and nine of the order of St-Ruf, the last two orders being subdivisions of the Canons Regular of St Augustine; of 410 *maisons* of the Canons Regular, 69 were closed, while 64 establishments of the religious mendicants of the rule of St Augustine were closed out of a total of 336. (HW, in mentioning the Augustines, may be referring specifically to the *Grands-Augustins,* a subdivision of the religious mendicants of St Augustine, which had held a national chapter in May at which it had been agreed, 'sous la pression des commissaires,' that 44 out of 123 *maisons* of that order be closed.) Other orders completely suppressed were the *Bénédictines exempts,* the Camaldules, the Guillelmites, the Servites, the Brigittines, and the order of Grandmont. All in all, across France, 426 *maisons* were closed out of a total of 2,972. See Suzanne Lemaire, *La Commission des Réguliers 1766–1780,* 1926, pp. 55–6, 99, 173–4, 224–31, 244–8 *et passim.*

From Conway, August 1771

Missing; answered *post* 11 Aug. 1771.

To Conway, Sunday 11 August 1771

Printed from *Works* v. 147–8.

Paris, Aug. 11, 1771.

YOU will have seen, I hope, before now, that I have not neglected writing to you. I sent you a letter by my sister, but doubt she has been a great while upon the road, as they travel with a large family. I was not sure where you was, and would not write at random by the post.

I was just going out when I received yours[1] and the newspapers. I was struck in a most sensible manner, when, after reading your letter, I saw in the newspapers that Gray[2] is dead! So very ancient an intimacy, and, I suppose, the natural reflection to self on losing a person but a year older,[3] made me absolutely start in my chair. It seemed more a corporal than a mental blow; and yet I am exceedingly concerned for him, and everybody must be so for the loss of such a genius. He called on me but two or three days before I came hither;[4] he complained of being ill, and talked of the gout in his stomach—but I expected his death no more than my own—and yet the same death will probably be mine.—I am full of all these reflections—but shall not attrist you with them:—only do not wonder that my letter will be short, when my mind is full of what I do not give vent to. It was but last night that I was thinking how few persons last, if one lives to be old, to whom one can talk without

1. Missing.
2. Thomas Gray, the poet (HW). He died 30 July. HW wrote to Mason 9 Sept. 1771 (MASON i. 19) that he read of his death in the *Chronicle,* which could have been the *Morning, St James's* or *London Chronicle;* the last reported, 1–3 Aug., xxx. 120, that he died 'on Tuesday evening . . . of the gout in his stomach, at his rooms in Pembroke College, Cam-

bridge,' etc. Actually, it appears that he died of chronic kidney disease, terminating in uremia (GRAY ii. 190, n. 17).
3. Gray was born 26 Dec. 1716 OS, HW 24 Sept. 1717 OS.
4. HW wrote 'but four or five days' to Cole 12 Aug. 1771, and 'the day before' to Mason 9 Sept. 1771 (COLE i. 228; MASON, loc. cit.).

reserve. It is impossible to be intimate with the young, because they and the old cannot converse on the same common topics; and of the old that survive, there are few one can commence a friendship with, because one has probably all one's life despised their hearts or their understandings. These are steps through which one passes to the unenviable lees of life!

I am very sorry for the state of poor Lady Beauchamp. It presages ill. She had a prospect of long happiness. Opium is a very false friend.

I will get you Bougainville's[5] book.—I think it is on the Falkland Isles,[6] for it cannot be on those just discovered;[7] but as I set out tomorrow sennight,[8] and probably may have no opportunity sooner of sending it, I will bring it myself.[9] Adieu!

Yours ever,

Hor. Walpole

To Conway, ca Wednesday 14 August 1771

Missing; listed in 'Paris Journals' (du Deffand v. 393) as sent 'with a book,' 'by Mr Edmondson' (see *ante* ca 2 Sept. 1769), presumably Bougainville's *Voyage autour du monde* (see *ante* 11 Aug. 1771 and n. 5).

To Lady Hertford, ca Saturday 24 August 1771

Missing; listed in 'Paris Journals' (du Deffand v. 393) as sent 'by Mr Hanbury's servant.'

5. Louis-Antoine de Bougainville (1729–1811), navigator; author of *Voyage autour du monde*, published at Paris 15 May 1771, describing his circumnavigation of the globe 1766–9, during the course of which he discovered a number of islands, including les îles des Quatre-facardins, des Lanciers, de la Harpe, Duclos, Bourn-and, d'Oraison, etc. See Jean-Étienne Martin-Allanic, *Bougainville navigateur et les découvertes de son temps*, 1964, i. 639, 767, ii. 1251–2 *et passim*.

6. Bougainville had led an expedition there in 1763, described in *Journal his-torique du voyage fait aux îles Malouïnes*, by Antoine-Joseph Pernety (1716–1801), first published Berlin, 1769 (NBG; Bibl. Nat. Cat.; BM Cat.; Yale Cat.).

7. HW is presumably referring to the islands recently discovered in the South Seas by Capt. Cook, who had returned to England from a three-year voyage in June.

8. He left 2 Sept. (*ante* 30 July 1771, n. 33).

9. However, he apparently sent it by Edmondson 14 Aug.; see next letter.

To Lady Hertford, ca Wednesday 28 August 1771

Missing; listed in 'Paris Journals' (DU DEFFAND v. 393) as sent 'by Mr Davenport' (possibly Richard Davenport [ca 1705–71]; see ibid. i. 15, n. 29 *et passim*).

To Conway, Saturday 7 September 1771

Printed from *Works* v. 148–9.

Arlington Street, September 7, 1771.

I ARRIVED yesterday within an hour or two after you was gone,[1] which mortified me exceedingly; Lord knows when I shall see you. You are so active and so busy, and cast bullets and build bridges,[2] are *pontifex maximus*,[3] and, like Sir John Thorold[4] or Cimon,[5]

——— triumph over land and wave,[6]

that one can never get a word with you. Yet I am very well worth a general's or a politician's ear. I have been deep in all the secrets of France, and confidant of some of the principals of both parties. I know what is, and is to be, though I am neither priest nor conjurer— and have heard a vast deal about breaking carabiniers and grenadiers;[7] though, as usual, I dare to say I shall give a woeful account of both. The worst part is, that by the most horrid oppression and

1. HW 'got to London by two' ('Paris Journals,' DU DEFFAND v. 342).
2. As lieutenant-general of the Ordnance; HW is probably also alluding to Conway's improvement of the grounds at Park Place, where he had constructed a bridge in the 1760s which HW greatly admired; see *ante* 25 Nov. 1764 and n. 49, *post* 11 Nov. 1787, and next note.
3. The Pope; HW is here punning on the reputed etymological meaning of 'bridge-maker.' See OED *sub* 'Pontifex,' MANN viii. 48, ix. 589.
4. HW means Sir George Thorold (ca 1666–1722), cr. (1709) Bt; lord mayor of London 1719–20 (A. B. Beaven, *Aldermen of . . . London*, 1908–13, ii. 121; GEC, *Baronetage* v. 9).
5. (d. 449 B.C.), Athenian statesman and general.
6. ' 'Twas on the day when Thorold,

rich and grave, / Like Cimon, triumph'd both on land and wave' (Pope, *Dunciad*, i. 83–4). HW also alludes to this passage *ante* 16 Feb. 1741 OS and quotes it OSSORY i. 132 and MANN i. 451.
7. 'Le corps des grenadiers de France, de 2,500 hommes, commandé par le comte de Stainville, frère du duc de Choiseul, vient d'être supprimé, comme inutile et très dispendieux. Son entretien coûtait plus que celui de 12 régiments. . . . On assure que les mêmes raisons d'économie pourraient bien aussi faire réformer entièrement la gendarmerie, ainsi que le corps des carabiniers' (*Mercure historique*, Aug. 1771, clxxi. 269–70). The *ordonnance* suppressing the grenadiers, dated 4 Aug., is summarized in *Gazette de Leyde* 3 Sept. 'Supplément,' 'suite des nouvelles de Paris du 26 août.'

injustice their finances will very soon be in good order—unless some bankrupt turns Ravaillac,[8] which will not surprise me. The horror the nation has conceived of the King and Chancellor,[9] makes it probable that the latter, at least, will be sacrificed.[10] He seems not to be without apprehension, and has removed from the King's library a MS trial of a chancellor who was condemned to be hanged under Charles VII.[11] For the King, *qui a fait ses épreuves,* and not to his honour, you will not wonder that he lives in terrors.

I have executed all Lady A.'s commissions;[12] but mind, I do not commission you to tell her, for you would certainly forget it.

As you will no doubt come to town to report who burnt Portsmouth,[13] I will meet you here, if I am apprised of the day. Your niece's marriage[14] pleases me extremely. Though I never saw him till last night, I know a great deal of her future, and like his character.[15] His person is much better than I expected,[16] and far

---

8. François Ravaillac (1578–1610), the assassin of Henri IV of France, 1610. Cf. MANN iv. 287; BERRY ii. 117.

9. Maupeou.

10. He remained chancellor until the death of the King in 1774; see *post* 7 Sept. 1774.

11. (1403–61), King of France 1422–61. None of Charles's chancellors was tried and so condemned; see G. du Fresne de Beaucourt, *Histoire de Charles VII,* 1881–91, 6 vols, *passim.* HW may be thinking of Jacques Cœur (ca 1395–1456), noted merchant and *argentier du roi,* who in 1453 was convicted of various financial abuses and of *lèse-majesté;* the death penalty, however, was remitted, and he was sentenced to banishment and the confiscation of his property (ibid. v. 124–5; *Dictionnaire de biographie française,* 1933– , ix. 116–18). Another possibility is Guillaume Poyet (ca 1474–1548), chancellor under Francis I, who in 1545 was dismissed from his office and fined, a sentence whose lightness reputedly moved Francis to comment 'qu'il ne fut jamais si jeune, qu'il n'eût oui dire, qu'un chancelier perdant son office, devait perdre la vie'; in 1776 an *Histoire du procès du chancelier Poyet* was published 'à Londres' (see pp. 347, 350 of his *Histoire,* and NBG, *sub* 'Poyet').

12. See *ante* 30 July 1771 and nn. 23–5.

13. On 27 July 1770 a fire had broken out in the dockyard at Portsmouth,

causing some £150,000 damages (*Annual Register . . . 1771,* 1772, p. 13). Sabotage was immediately suspected, and an investigation was still going on at the time of this letter; the *Daily Adv.* 7 Sept. reported the examination 5 Sept. before the Lord Mayor and other magistrates of one Dudley, who professed to have information relating to the fire. 'The examination . . . lasted a considerable time; but the man made no discovery of any consequence.' He was then sent to Portsmouth, accompanied by a King's Messenger, 'to see if he can make the discoveries there which he has asserted he can' (ibid.). At Portsmouth, where he arrived 6 Sept., 'he gave information against a Romish priest, and a person who goes by the name of Captain,' but on 14 Sept. he 'was brought back to town; his information, it is said, amounts to nothing' (ibid. 9, 18 Sept.).

14. The marriage [10 Feb. 1772] of Lady Gertrude Seymour-Conway [*ante* 10 Oct. 1765] to Lord Villiers [George Mason Villiers (1751–1800), styled Vct Villiers], since [1782] Earl of Grandison (HW); see MANN vii. 381 and n. 19.

15. However, he had extravagant tastes, and HW wrote to Lady Ossory 8 Aug. 1777 that he 'has fashioned away all he has' (OSSORY i. 369; see also ibid. n. 13; Mary Granville, Mrs. Delany, *Autobiography and Correspondence,* ed. Lady Llanover, 1861–2, iv. 464, 490).

16. HW, apparently on hearsay, had

preferable to many of the fine young moderns. He is better than Sir Watkin Williams Wynn,[17] at least as well as the Duke of Devonshire,[18] and Adonis compared to the charming Mr Fitzpatrick.[19] Adieu!

To Conway, Tuesday 7 January 1772

Printed from *Works* v. 149–50.

Late Strawberry Hill, January 7, 1772.

YOU have read of my calamity without knowing it, and will pity me when you do. I have been blown up; my castle is blown up; Guy Fawkes has been about my house; and the fifth of November has fallen on the sixth of January! In short, nine thousand powder-mills broke loose yesterday morning on Hounslow Heath;[1] a whole squadron of them came thither, and have broken eight of my painted glass windows; and the north side of the castle looks as if it had stood a siege. The two saints in the hall[2] have suffered martyrdom! they have had their bodies cut off, and nothing remains but their heads. The two next great sufferers are indeed two of the least valuable, being the passage windows to the library and great parlour—a fine pane is demolished in the Round Room; and the window by the Gallery is damaged. Those in the Cabinet and Holbein Room, and Gallery, and Blue Room, and Green Closet, etc. have escaped. As the storm came from the northwest, the China Closet was not touched,

described him as 'homely' to Lord Ossory 23 June 1771 (Ossory i. 48); Lady Mary Coke wrote in her *Journals*, iii. 303, *sub* 18 Oct. 1770, that he was 'not handsome.'

17. (1748–89), 4th Bt, 1749; M.P. Shropshire 1772–4, Denbighshire 1774–89. His first wife, Lady Henrietta Somerset, had died in 1769, and he married secondly Charlotte Grenville 21 Dec. 1771 (Namier and Brooke iii. 671–2). His name, as well as Devonshire's and Fitzpatrick's, was restored by Wright, who presumably saw the MS of this letter.

18. Who married Lady Georgiana Spencer in 1774.

19. Hon. Richard Fitzpatrick (1748–

1813), M.P.; army officer; author of occasional verse. Brother of Lord Ossory, he was noted for his wit and charm; HW described him to Lady Ossory 6 Sept. 1778 as an 'irresistible Dorimant' (Ossory ii. 47). He never married.

1. About 2½ miles from SH. On the morning of 6 Jan. two powder mills belonging to Edmund Hill blew up; according to the *Daily Adv.* 8 Jan. 'there were seven distinct explosions.' See Ossory i. 74–6 and n. 12, and Mann vii. 365 and nn. 7–10.

2. St John and St Francis ('Des. of SH,' *Works* ii. 401).

nor a cup fell down. The bow-window of brave old coloured glass,[3] at Mr Hindley's,[4] is massacred; and all the north sides of Twickenham and Brentford are shattered. At London it was proclaimed an earthquake, and half the inhabitants ran into the street.[5]

As lieutenant-general of the Ordnance, I must beseech you to give strict orders that no more powder-mills may blow up. My aunt, Mrs Kerwood,[6] reading one day in the papers that a distiller's had been burnt by the head of the still flying off, said, she wondered they did not make an act of Parliament against the heads of stills flying off. Now, I hold it much easier for you to do a body this service; and would recommend to your consideration, whether it would not be prudent to have all magazines of powder kept under water till they are wanted for service. In the meantime, I expect a pension to make me amends for what I have suffered under the government. Adieu!

Yours, all that remains of me,

HOR. WALPOLE

From LADY HERTFORD, Tuesday 11 February 1772

Printed for the first time from a photostat of BM Add. MSS 23219, f. 54.
Address: To the Honourable Mr Walpole.

Tuesday night.

My dear Mr Walpole,

YOU cannot give marks of kindness to any friends that are more sensible of them than we all are. The distress of this day has exceeded anything I ever saw, and we have lost the most valuable friend that people ever had.[1] My son is in this house, and begs me to

3. A 'fine bow-window of ancient scripture histories' (HW to Lady Ossory 6 Jan. 1772, OSSORY i. 75); it appears in two illustrations in F. C. Hodgson, *Thames-Side in the Past*, 1913, facing pp. 214, 221, and the painted glass is also described ibid. 215–16.
4. Frederick Atherton Hindley (d. 1781), steward to the 4th E. of Radnor (d. 1757),

who left him his house and furniture at Twickenham (OSSORY i. 75, n. 16).
5. See ibid. i. 74–5.
6. Kyrwood; see *ante* 29 Aug. 1748 OS and n. 5.

———

1. Lady Beauchamp died 11 Feb., 'at Lord Beauchamp's house in Grosvenor Square' (*London Chronicle* 11–13 Feb., xxxi. 151).

say how much he is obliged to you for the kind offer of your house; but he intends going down to Lord Mountstewart's,[2] which I fear is the worst thing he can do for his spirits. If you are out about three tomorrow, and[3] you are so kind as to call, I will let you know if there is any change in our plans.

Your most faithful and most obliged friend,

I. H.

From LADY HERTFORD, Wednesday 12 February 1772

Printed for the first time from a photostat of BM Add. MSS 23219, f. 160.
Address: To the Honourable Hor. Walpole.

Wednesday.

Dear Mr Walpole,

AS you are so good as to give leave, we have prevailed upon my son to go to Strawberry Hill instead of going to Lord Mount Stewart's. He proposes setting out this evening after it is dark. His brothers will go with him, and three or four servants. You may depend upon it that no prejudice shall be done to you, and we shall look upon it as an everlasting mark of your friendship, your kindness to us upon this occasion.

Yours most faithfully,

I. H.

[1]If you are so good to write a note to Mrs Margaret,[2] we will send a servant down with it directly.

I believe from the hurry of this day[3] that I must ask you to call here in the evening instead of the morning after eight o'clock.

2. John Stuart (1744–1814), styled Vct Mount Stuart; 4th E. of Bute, 1792; cr. (1796) M. of Bute; m. (1766) Charlotte Jane Windsor, sister of Lady Beauchamp. Lady Beauchamp's mother, the Dowager Lady Windsor (see *post* 24 March 1772, n. 2), may well have been staying with the Mount Stuarts, which would have added still more to the oppressiveness of the atmosphere.

3. Written over 'if' in the MS.

1. The second sentence of this postscript is squeezed into the upper right corner of the MS.

2. Margaret Young, HW's housekeeper at SH.

3. Lord Hertford was particularly hurried, as he not only had to make arrangements for Lady Beauchamp's funeral (20 Feb.), but as lord chamberlain also had to arrange for the funeral of the Princess

To Lord Beauchamp, Tuesday 24 March 1772

Printed for the first time from the MS, now WSL. The MS, once in the possession of John Wilson Croker, was sold by a descendant of his at Sotheby's 25 Feb. 1946, lot 225 to Maggs, and resold March 1946 to WSL.

Memorandum (by Croker?): To Lord Beauchamp. (2nd Marquis of Hertford) whose first Lady (Alicia Windsor) died *s.p.* Feb. 11, 1772.

Arlington Street, March 24, 1772.

I WAS so touched with your grief, my dear Lord, last night, that I had not power to ask you in what manner you wished I should execute your orders. Yet I could not go to bed till I had expressed in some degree what I felt for you. It is true I have not satisfied myself or done justice to the subject—but I send you this sketch[1] as a proof how earnest I am to obey you. If you like the Epitaph better in prose, I will write it so. Have no scruple of finding fault with, or rejecting what I send you, which was the work of but an hour and half—I wish I could say anything more satisfactory, but words are no cordial for affliction so reasonable as yours: Time, stronger than Reason, can only lessen your concern. I am most sincerely

Your obedient humble servant,

Hor. Walpole

[Enclosure]
Epitaph on Lady Beauchamp

Fair fleeting Shade, was then thy sweetness lent,
Like passing Flow'rs, but for a moment's scent?
Was Youth with Virtue, Grace with Fortune join'd,
A pleasing Form with a celestial Mind,
Not to instruct, attract, endear, and bless?
Could such a Gift be giv'n, but to distress?

Dowager, who had died 8 Feb. and was buried 15 Feb.; in addition, the marriage of his daughter Lady Gertrude to Lord Villiers had just taken place 10 Feb. (see *ante* 7 Sept. 1771, n. 14). On this day (12 Feb.) Hertford wrote to the King, asking that the Vice-Chamberlain be allowed to officiate in his place at the Princess's funeral, saying that 'my son has made it his earnest and anxious request that I should not appear in public till after Lady Beauchamp is buried'; his request was denied. See MANN vii. 379, 381 and n. 21.

———

1. See enclosure; it is printed here for the first time.

Ah! hapless Mother,[2] 'reft of half thy store![3]
Ah! Man of sorrows—Husband now no more!
Of all fair Beauchamp's Virtues what remains
To calm your griefs, and mitigate your pains?
What charm must lull your woes, what words beguile?
—Her angel Patience, her submissive Smile.
All Life's best joys, all Pleasure's dulcet train
She knew to value—but she knew were vain.
Yes, in that awful hour, when Death and Love,
When meek Regret with pious Firmness strove,
'Twixt Love and Heav'n stern Duty's law she weigh'd,
Wish'd to delay—but call'd by God, obey'd.

From CONWAY, ca Saturday 20 June 1772

Missing; acknowledged *post* 22 June 1772, *sub* 23 June.

To CONWAY, Monday 22 June 1772

Printed from *Works* v. 150–2.

Strawberry Hill, Monday, June 22, 1772.

IT is lucky that I have had no dealings with Mr Fordyce;[1] for, if he had ruined me, as he has half the world, I could not have *run* away. I tired myself with walking on Friday; the gout came on Saturday in my foot; yesterday I kept my bed till four o'clock, and my

2. Alice Clavering (1705–76), m. (1735 or 37) Herbert Windsor, 2d Vct Windsor of Blackcastle, 1738.

3. An elder sister, Charlotte Jane, Vcts Mount Stuart, survived Lady Beauchamp (see *ante* 11 Feb. 1772, n. 2).

1. Alexander Fordyce (d. 1789), a partner in Neale, James, Fordyce, and Down 'of Threadneedle Street, bankers,' whose bank stopped payment on 10 June. For-

dyce absconded the same day for France; his debts were first reported as 'upwards of £300,000,' and a commission of bankruptcy against him was published in the *London Gazette* No. 11256, 9–13 June. His bankruptcy was followed by numerous others, and HW mentions to Mann 1 July 1772, *sub* 3 July, the suicides of two men 'ruined by these failures.' See MANN vii. 418 and n. 3, 420 and nn. 12, 13.

room all day—but, with wrapping myself all over with bootikins, I have scarce had any pain—my foot swelled immediately, and today I am descended into the blueth and greenth; and though you expect to find that I am paving the way to an excuse, I think I shall be able to be with you on Saturday.[2] All I intend to excuse myself from, is walking. I should certainly never have the gout, if I had lost the use of my feet. Cherubims that have no legs, and do nothing but stick their chins in a cloud and sing, are never out of order. Exercise is the worst thing in the world, and as bad an invention as gunpowder.

Apropos to Mr Fordyce, here is a passage ridiculously applicable to him, that I met with yesterday in the letters of Guy Patin:[3] 'Il n'y a pas longtemps qu'un auditeur des comptes nommé Monsieur Nivelle fit banqueroute; et tout fraîchement, c'est-à-dire depuis trois jours, un trésorier des parties casuelles, nommé Sanson, en a fait autant; et pour vous montrer, qu'il est vrai que *res humanæ faciunt circulum,*[4] comme il a été autrefois dit par Plato et par Aristote, celui-là s'en retourne d'où il vient. Il est fils d'un paisan;[5] il a été laquais de son premier métier,[6] et aujourd'hui il n'est plus rien, sinon qu'il lui reste une assez belle femme.'[7]—I do not think I can find in Patin or Plato, nay, nor in Aristotle,[7a] though he wrote about everything, a parallel case to Charles Fox's: there are advertised to be sold more annuities of his and his society, to the amount of five hundred thousand pounds a year![8] I wonder what he will do next, when he has sold the estates of all his friends!

---

2. HW wrote to Cole 17 June 1772 that 'I am going to Park Place, then to Ampthill and then to Goodwood' (COLE i. 256); he left Sunday, 28 June (see below, *sub* 'Tuesday noon,' and COLE i. 264).

3. Gui Patin (1602–72), physician and author; HW's copy of his *Nouvelles lettres, tirées du Cabinet de Mr Charles Spon,* Amsterdam, 1718, is Hazen, *Cat. of HW's Lib.,* No. 1257. The passage he quotes is from Patin's letter to Spon of 29 May 1648; see Patin's *Lettres,* ed. Reveillé-Parise, 1846, i. 397–8.

4. 'Human affairs make a circle,' i.e. revolve in cycles; the sentiment, a commonplace one in classical thought, is expressed by Aristotle in his *Physics* 223b 25–6, and by Herodotus I. 207; it has not been traced in Plato.

5. Fordyce was the son of George Fordyce of Broadford, merchant and provost of Aberdeen (DNB).

6. Fordyce was for some time in the hosiery trade at Aberdeen (ibid.)

7. Fordyce married (1770) Lady Margaret Lindsay (1753–1814), second daughter of the fifth Earl of Balcarres (*Scots Peerage* i. 528–9; GM 1814, lxxxiv pt ii. 612).

7a. Plato and Aristotle do not appear in HW's library.

8. Fox needed money to cover heavy gambling debts; HW writes in *Last Journals* i. 12 that in Feb. he had 'sat up playing hazard at Almack's from Tuesday evening 4th, till five in the afternoon of Wednesday 5th. . . . losing £11,000,' and that subsequently he and his brother lost £32,000 in three nights.

I have been reading the most delightful book in the world, the lives of Leland,[9] Tom Hearne, and Antony Wood.[10] The last's diary makes a thick volume in octavo. One entry is, 'This day Old Joan began to make my bed.'[11] In the story of Leland is an examination of a freemason,[12] written by the hand of King Henry VI[13] with notes by Mr Locke.[14] Freemasonry, Henry VI and Locke, make a strange heterogeneous olio; but that is not all. The respondent, who defends the mystery of masonry, says it was brought into Europe by the Venetians[15]—he means the Phenicians[16]—and who do you think propagated it? Why, one Peter Gore[17]—and who do you think that was?—One Pythagoras, Pythagore.[18]—I do not know whether it is not still more extraordinary, that this and the rest of the nonsense in that account made Mr Locke determine to be a freemason:[19] so would I too, if I could expect to hear of more Peter Gores.

Pray tell Lady Lyttelton that I say she will certainly kill herself if she lets Lady A. drag her twice a day to feed the pheasants; and you make her climb cliffs and clamber over mountains. She has a tractability that alarms me for her; and if she does not pluck up a spirit and determine never to be put out of her own way, I do not know what may be the consequence. I will come and set her an

9. John Leland (ca 1506–52), antiquary.

10. *The Lives of Those Eminent Antiquaries John Leland, Thomas Hearne, and Anthony à Wood*, 2 vols, Oxford, 1772, advertised 5 June 1772 as to be published 'on Tuesday the 16th instant' (*Daily Adv.* 5 June); William Huddesford of the Ashmolean Library 1755–72 (*ante* 27 May 1762, n. 2) was the author of the life of Leland and editor of the work (COLE i. 255, nn. 8, 9; MASON i. 40, n. 25). HW's copy, which he got 17 June, is Hazen, op. cit., No. 2875.

11. 'July 1 [1678]. Old Jone began to make my bed' (*Lives* ii. 276).

12. Ibid. i. 67–8, Appendix No. vii. 96–103.

13. (1421–71), King of England 1422–61, 1470–1.

14. John Locke (1632–1704), philosopher.

15. 'The Venetians, whoo beynge grate Merchaundes, comed ffyrste ffromme the Este ynn Venetia, ffor the commodytye of Marchaund-ysynge beithe Este and Weste, bey the redde and Myddle londe Sees (ibid. Appendix No. vii. 98).

16. 'In the times of monkish ignorance, 'tis no wonder that the Phenecians should be mistaken for the Venetians,' etc. (ibid. n. 6).

17. 'Peter Gower, a Grecian, journeyedde ffor Kunnynge [knowledge] yn Egypte, and yn Syria . . . and Wynnynge Entraunce yn al Lodges of Maconnes, he lerned muche, and retournedde . . . and marked many Maconnes, some whereoffe dyd journeye yn Fraunce . . . wherefromme . . . the Art passed yn Engelonde' (ibid. 98–9).

18. See ibid. 98, n. 7.

19. 'I know not what effect the sight of this old paper may have upon your Lordship; but for my own part I cannot deny, that it has so much raised my curiosity, as to induce me to enter myself into the fraternity, which I am determined to do (if I may be admitted) the next time I go to London' (Locke to Earl of ——, 6 May 1696, ibid. 102).

example of immovability. Take notice, I do not say one civil syllable to Lady A. She has not passed a whole day here these two years. She is always very gracious, says she will come when *you* will fix a time, as if *you* governed, and then puts it off whenever it is proposed, nor will spare one single day from Park Place—as if other people were not as partial to their own Park Places! Adieu!

Yours ever,

HOR. WALPOLE

Tuesday noon.

I wrote my letter last night; this morning I received yours,[20] and shall wait till Sunday, as you bid me, which will be more convenient for my gout, though not for other engagements; but I shall obey the superior, as *nullum tempus occurrit regi et podagræ.*[21]

From LADY HERTFORD, Friday 31 July 1772

Printed for the first time from a photostat of BM Add. MSS 23219, f. 59.
Address (in Hertford's hand): Honourable Hor. Walpole, Twickenham, Middlesex. Free Hertford.
Postmark: 31 IY FREE.

Friday evening.

Dear Sir,

I HAVE just called at your house, and find you do not come to town till Sunday. I have engaged you for that evening to Madame de Welderen, and on Monday you are to go with us to *The Nabob*[1]

---

20. Missing.
21. 'No time runs against the King and the gouty foot,' HW's humorous expansion of the English common law maxim *nullum tempus occurrit regi*, signifying that the rights of the Crown are not voided by any lapse of time; see Sir Edward Coke, *The Second Part of the Institutes of the Laws of England*, 1642, p. 273. The Nullum Tempus Act of 1769 (9 Geo. III c. 16) had abridged this regulation in

the case of land grants (Owen Ruffhead, *Statutes at Large*, 1763–1800, x. 540–3).

---

1. A comedy by Samuel Foote, introduced at the Haymarket 29 June; see *London Stage* Pt IV, iii. 1647–51; Mary M. Belden, *Dramatic Work of Samuel Foote*, New Haven, 1929, pp. 146–52. HW's copy of the play, Hazen, *Cat. of HW's Lib.*, No. 1810 : 28 : 6, is now WSL; it has several notes in HW's hand.

and new farce.² If you have any orange flowers, pray bring them to me.³

Yours faithfully,

I. H.

From HERTFORD, Thursday 27 August 1772

Printed for the first time from a photostat of BM Add. MSS 23219, f. 61.

London, August 27th 1772.

Dear Horry,

LORD Arbermarle¹ is better and it is said out of danger from this attack, but that I doubt. I have again this day repeated to the King my most ardent wishes that something could be done with his approbation for my brother's satisfaction; in short it is not in my power to do more.² I am, dear Horry,

Always most truly and affectionately yours,

HERTFORD

2. *Cupid's Revenge: An Arcadian Pastoral,* 'a new dramatic pastoral farce' by Francis Gentleman (1728–84), music by James Hook (1746–1827), first performed 27 July; the performance of 3 Aug. was postponed because of the indisposition of one of the singers, and Edward Ravenscroft's *The Anatomist* was performed instead (*London Stage* Pt IV iii. 1648; DNB; Sir George Grove, *Dictionary of Music and Musicians,* 5th edn, ed. Blom 1954–61, iv. 348, 350). HW's copy of the play, Hazen, op. cit. No. 1810 : 18 : 13, with a note by HW is now WSL.

3. HW wrote to Mann from 'Arlington Street,' 3 Aug. 1772, and the next day set out on a visit to Yorkshire (MANN vii. 425 and n. 18, also n. 1).

———

1. *Sic* in MS. His ill health ended in death 13 Oct. (*post* 22 Oct. 1772, n. 1).

2. Conway had incurred the King's displeasure in March by his opposition to the Royal Marriage Bill, inspired by the marriages of the Duke of Cumberland to Mrs Horton and the Duke of Gloucester to Lady Waldegrave (see MANN vii. 390

and nn. 1–3), and the King had determined to disgrace him by appointing Lord Townshend, about to be recalled from Ireland, master-general of the Ordnance, despite the fact that Conway had declared earlier that he would not serve as lieutenant-general under a junior officer. Hertford had offended Conway and HW by taking the King's side and urging Conway to end his opposition to the Bill; finding Conway and HW adamant, he was persuaded to intercede with the King in his brother's behalf and to find some means of mitigating the impending disgrace. 'By little and little, and by ranging on my side his wife, who did not admire the approaching diminution of their income, I had softened Conway's mind so far as to make him bear the mention of an equivalent. In the interim Lord Albemarle was known to be in a hopeless state of health: he was governor of Jersey; on that I fixed my eye, and Lord Hertford, and other friends of Conway, hinted it both to the King and Lord North' (*Last Journals* i. 141–9 *passim*). See *post* 10, 22 Oct. 1772.

To Hertford, ca Thursday 17 September 1772

Two letters, missing; described in *Last Journals* i. 136: 'I wrote to Lord Hertford a letter, which I meant he should show to the King, couched in the most
respectful terms, in which I stated my own ignorance of the marriage [of the
Duke of Gloucester to Lady Waldegrave] till owned, but said that, concluding
the new Duchess's family could not be very welcome at St James's, I should not
presume to present myself there without leave. I mentioned having waited on
the Duke as a duty, due for the honour he had done the family and to the
tenderness I had always felt for my niece, whom were I to abandon, I should
expect his Majesty's own paternal affections would make him despise me. This
letter I enclosed in a cover, in which I told Lord Hertford plainly that, if it
was expected I should not see my niece, I was determined rather to give up
going to St James's.' HW goes on to say that 'Lord Hertford was too good a
courtier, I believe, to show even the ostensible letter; he did, in my name, ask
whether I might go to Court and to the Duke and Duchess of Gloucester too.
The King . . . replied *he chose everybody should take their own part*. Mine
was soon taken . . . and I went no more to St James's' (ibid. i. 136–7). The
marriage of the Duke to Lady Waldegrave 6 Sept. 1766 had been formally notified to HW by Sir·Edward Walpole 19 May 1772, and to the King by the Duke
14 Sept. 1772 (MANN vii. 437); HW waited on the Duke 17 Sept. (ibid. vii. 433–4
and nn. 4–5; *Last Journals* i. 130–5).

From Hertford, ? late September 1772

Missing; enclosed by HW in his letter to the Duchess of Gloucester 15 Nov.
1772. The Duchess suspected that Hertford 'had been officious at procuring the
general prohibition' of herself and the Duke (*Last Journals* i. 151); HW wrote
to her that 'his letter . . . which I here enclose, will convince you Lord Hertford
could not think for one moment that he should make his court to his Majesty by
inflaming the difference between him and the Duke of Gloucester' (FAMILY 86).

To Hertford, October 1772

Missing; answered *post* 10 Oct. 1772.

From LADY HERTFORD, Thursday ?8 October 1772

Printed for the first time from a photostat of BM Add. MSS 23219, f. 100.
Address: To the Honourable Mr Walpole.

Thursday evening.

My dear Mr Walpole,

I F I had known before Sunday how weak and ill you were, I should have begged as hard not to see you, as you have done, to be kept quiet.[1] The gout like the toothache never sounds terrible, and I was in hopes you only complained because you suffered wholesome pain. I am sincerely grieved you have been so seriously ill, but I hope you will soon be better, and that you will once in your life act rationally and neither drink cold water or lie in a wet room. If you have any commands in London pray employ me, and if we can be of any use at Strawberry Hill, pray send us a summons and we will obey it with alacrity. I am

Most sincerely yours,

I. H.

From HERTFORD, Saturday 10 October 1772

Printed for the first time from a photostat of BM Add. MSS 23219, ff. 62–3.

London, October 10th 1772.

Dear Horry,

W E are much obliged to you for taking, in the literal sense, the pain of writing.[1] We were not informed or aware that you had been so ill; the maid at your house in town spoke of it as a slight attack, and we are very sorry it has been so serious: Lady Hertford and my daughter Frances[2] intended, as we thought of it before, to have paid you a visit by way of inquiry, but they will now wait your

1. HW wrote to Mason 13 Oct. 1772: 'I have been in my bed this fortnight with the gout in every limb, and have not the use of either hand or foot' (MASON i. 51). HW's fit did not abate until the new year.

1. HW's letter is missing.
2. Lady Frances Seymour Conway (1751–1820), m. (1775) Henry Fiennes Pelham Clinton, styled Earl of Lincoln, heir apparent of the Duke of Newcastle.

return to London. I am going into Suffolk, and hope to see you better, in town and free from pain when I return; in the meantime, if you should grow worse, have the charity for us to acquaint us with it and not leave us in ignorance, behaving like brutes and with a seeming indifference for a friend's pains.

My brother when he left town was uneasy upon some information he had picked up that there was a doubt about his intention of re-signing,[3] in case the appointment of Lord Townshend[4] took place, and desired I would use all the proper means in my power to unde-ceive the world in that respect, which I have done, and in particular Lord North, by means of a joint friend,[5] that it might not have the appearance of menace and indispose him to serve us with his good offices. Lord North expressed great concern for my brother's resolu-tion, and said he was afraid that no arrangement could now be made to prevent Lord Townshend's appointment. This you will ob-serve in the way it has been communicated is not a formal notice, and it will remain for my brother to decide when he shall wait upon Lord North to acquaint him in form with it. In my opinion there does not seem to be any very immediate occasion, as Lord Harcourt[6] is not to be at Holyhead till the 30th,[7] and Lord Townshend talks of staying in Ireland some time after, to give every man who does not intend it an opportunity of fighting him for the errors of his government;[8] and whenever my brother does it, I hope for his own sake and character that he will be induced to say that he means to resign with as much respect as possible to the King, and as little injury as possible to the public service, and therefore is very ready to do the business till my Lord's appointment or that Lord North has made his arrangements. By this means a little time may be given if they can and are disposed to do anything to prevent it.

I am, dear Horry,

Very faithfully and sincerely yours,

HERTFORD

3. As lieutenant-general of the Ord-nance.

4. As master-general of the Ordnance; see *ante* 27 Aug. 1772, *post* 22 Oct. 1772.

5. Not identified.

6. Townshend's successor as lord lieu-tenant of Ireland; he had kissed hands for the post 9 Oct. (*Daily Adv.* 10 Oct.).

7. He did not embark from Holyhead until 28 Nov. (*London Gazette* No. 11307, 5–8 Dec., *sub* Dublin Castle, 30 Nov.).

8. 'At his giving up his government he affected a delay of eight days, to give time, when become a private man, to those who resented any part of his be-haviour to call him to account; but Dr Lucas [see *ante* 13 Jan. 1766], who had challenged him, was dead' (*Last Jour-*

From HERTFORD, Thursday 22 October 1772

Printed for the first time from a photostat of BM Add. MSS 23219, f. 64.

London, October 22d 1772.

Dear Horry,

I AM concerned to hear, upon my return to town, both from my Lady and my brother, that you have been so much out of order and are still so weak. I intended to have gone down to you, but my brother has forbid me, saying you are in a state not to choose it. I hope you will hear from my brother that everything has passed lately entirely to his satisfaction,[1] both with the King and Lord North, and I flatter myself he stands better now with respect to his future prospects than I thought practicable some time ago, within so short a time and the unfavourable situation in which his affairs stood. In the meantime the Government is a convenient thing and his mind seems easy and relieved.

I have sent you a brace of partridges, hoping at this time they may be agreeable, and am, dear Horry,

Very truly and affectionately yours,

HERTFORD

To LADY HERTFORD, Thursday 29 Oct. 1772

Missing; answered *post* 30 Oct. 1772.

nals i. 145). After greeting Harcourt upon his arrival in Dublin 30 Nov. and officially turning the government over to him, he delayed his departure until 8 Dec., reaching London 12 Dec. (*London Gazette* loc. cit.; No. 11309, 12–15 Dec., *sub* Dublin Castle, 8 Dec.; *Daily Adv.* 14 Dec.).

1. On this day 'Gen. Conway attended the levee at St James's, and resigned his place as lieutenant-general of the Ordnance' (*Daily Adv.* 23 Oct.); at the same time 'the King has been pleased to grant unto the Right Honourable Henry Seymour Conway . . . the office of governor and captain of the Isle of Jersey and Castle of Gouray' (*London Gazette* No. 11294, 20–24 Oct., *sub* St James's, 22 Oct.). He kissed hands for the post 23 Oct., succeeding Lord Albemarle, who had died 13 Oct. (*Daily Adv.* 16, 24 Oct.); he was succeeded as lieutenant-general by Sir Jeffery Amherst (ibid.). The appointment of Lord Townshend as master-general of the Ordnance, which had moved Conway to resign as lieutenant-general, was announced in the *Daily Adv.* 5 Nov.; Townshend kissed hands for the post upon his arrival from Ireland 14 Dec. (ibid. 15 Dec.).

From LADY HERTFORD, Friday 30 October 1772

Printed for the first time from a photostat of BM Add. MSS 23219, f. 99.

Friday night.

Dear Mr Walpole,

LADY Mary Coke and a large party dined and stayed here the whole evening yesterday,[1] which made it impossible for me to answer your kind note[2] by your servant. I know General Bur[goyne] has got the parcel you mention for you,[3] and I will desire him to send it to me, and you must let me know your commands about it. I am very happy to hear you are better, but your amendment is not half so quick as we wish it. I hope as soon as it is possible you will come to town, as I am sure you will recover faster in London than in the country at this time of year, and I should like to think I could be of use to you. *The* seven guineas[4] have been sealed up a great while.

Yours most faithfully,

I. H.

1. '*Thursday* [29 Oct.] . . . At half-an-hour after four I went to Lord Hertford's and at five we went to dinner. The present embroiled state of the north of Europe was the conversation after dinner; opinions were very freely given,' etc. (Coke, *Journals*, iv. 138).

2. Missing.

3. Burgoyne had been in France, visiting the Choiseuls at Chanteloup, and Mme du Deffand had sent back by him a parcel of effilage (unravellings) for HW out of which to make a coat. See DU DEFFAND i. 45, iii. 269–70, 272, 276 *et passim*.

4. Perhaps a gambling debt owed by Lady Hertford to HW.

From LADY HERTFORD, Monday 16 November 1772

Printed for the first time from a photostat of BM Add. MSS 23219, f. 97.
Address: To the Honourable Mr Walpole at Strawberry Hill near Isleworth, Middlesex.
Postmark: 16 NO (apparently an error for 17 Nov.).

Monday night, 11 o'clock.

My dear Mr Walpole,

LET me in a few words entreat you to come to town.[1] Your cough is worse, your gout is not lessened, and I hear your apothecary[2] says you cannot mend till you change the air. Don't fear London because of busy visitors, for we shall all wish you so much to be quiet that we won't one of us enter your door till you are stronger. My Lord comes to town tomorrow.

Yours most affectionately,

I. H.

From LADY AILESBURY, ca Sunday 27 December 1772

Missing; answered *post* 29 Dec. 1772.

To LADY AILESBURY, Tuesday 29 December 1772

Printed from the MS now WSL. First printed in part *Works* v. 564–5 and in full Toynbee viii. 221–3 and *Supp.* ii. 142–3. For the history of the MS see *ante* 23 Aug. 1760.

Arlington Street, Dec. 29, 1772.

I SHOULD not even thank you, dear Madam, so soon for your very kind letter,[1] as I have nothing to tell you, if it was not to join my tears to your Ladyship's for the death of dear little Colas![2]

1. HW did not go to town until late December. See MANN vii. 450; *post* 29 Dec. 1772.
2. Perhaps Stirling Gilchrist (d. 1791), surgeon and apothecary at Twickenham.

See MORE 205 and n. 1; BERRY i. 369 and n. 1.

———

1. Missing.
2. Evidently a pet.

I am not so ungrateful to him as not to lament his murder very sincerely. I think you have worse luck with your favourites than anybody.

Mrs Damer really appears to me better, but I shall not be satisfied till her night-sweats are gone. She is very good and comes to me often, though I preach to her. She is not yet gone to Goodwood,[3] but goes this week. I think it a cold house, but the air is certainly dry and wholesome, and the journey is good for her. You shall hear from me the moment she returns. Lady Lyttelton does, as your Ladyship suspected, find my house cold: I have not seen her this week till this morning; she is all over cramps and rheumatisms and Mr de Prie.[4] Indeed, Madam, I want you and Mr Conway in town: Christmas has dispersed all my company, and left nothing but a loo-party or two—which in truth you would be as impatient to be at, as they are. If all the fine days were not gone out of town too, I should take the air in a morning; but I am not yet nimble enough, like old Mrs Nugent,[5] to jump out of a post-chaise into an assembly.

You have a woeful taste, my Lady, not to like Lord Gower's bon mot; it is perfection: the next I tell you, shall be one of Lady Egremont's[6] own, which I dare to say you will admire. I am almost too indignant to tell you of a most amusing book in six volumes, called *Histoire philosophique et politique du commerce des deux Indies.*[7] It tells one everything in the world, how to make conquests, invasions, blunders, settlements, bankruptcies, fortunes, etc.; tells you

3. Seat of the Duke of Richmond in Sussex.

4. Louis de Prie (1734–82), Marquis and Comte de Prie de Bourbon-Lairey. HW had met him at Paris in 1766 (DU DEFFAND v. 293, 298).

5. See *ante* 8 Nov. 1752, 11 Sept. 1765.

6. Alicia Maria Carpenter (d. 1794), m. 1 (1751) Charles Wyndham, 2d E. of Egremont; m. 2 (1767) Hans Moritz, Graf von Brühl.

7. *Histoire philosophique et politique des établissements et du commerce des Européens dans les deux Indes,* by the Abbé Guillaume-Thomas-François Raynal (1713–96). The Bibl. Nat. Cat. lists editions published at 'Amsterdam,' 1770 and 1772, both volumes in octavo (see A. Feugère, *Bibliographie critique de . . . Raynal,* Angoulême, 1922, pp. 15–21).

Mme du Deffand mentioned the *Histoire* to HW 27 March 1772, *sub* 29 March, as a 'livre nouveau qui fait assez de bruit' (DU DEFFAND iii. 210; see also Louis Petit de Bachaumont, *Mémoires secrets,* 1780–9, vi. 111–12 and Grimm, *Correspondance,* ed. Tourneux, 1877–82, ix. 487). Since the work was published anonymously, HW presumably did not yet know that Raynal was the author; Mme du Deffand informed him 5 Jan. 1773 that 'tout le monde dit qu'il est de l'Abbé Raynal' (DU DEFFAND iii. 308). HW had met Raynal several times in Paris 1765–6 ('Paris Journals,' ibid. v. 267, 279, 289, 299, 302), and entertained him at SH in 1777 (DALRYMPLE 136; OSSORY i. 357). See *post* 12 Nov. 1774. HW's copy does not appear in the SH accounts.

the natural and historical history of all nations; talks commerce, navigation, tea, coffee, china, mines, salt, spices; of the Portuguese, English, French, Dutch, Danes, Spaniards, Arabs, caravans, Persians, Indians, of Louis XIV and the King of Prussia; of La Bourdonnois,[8] Dupleix[9] and Admiral Saunders;[10] of rice and women that dance naked; of camels, ginghams and muslin; of millions of millions of livres, pounds, rupees, and gowries;[11] of iron, cables, and Circassian women;[12] of Law[13] and the Mississippi; and against all governments and religions. This and everything else is in the two first volumes. I cannot conceive what is left for the four others. And all is so mixed, that you learn forty new trades, and fifty new histories in a single chapter. There is spirit, wit and clearness—and if there were but less avoirdupois weight in it, it would be the richest book in the world in materials—but figures to me are so many ciphers, and only put me in mind of children that say, an hundred hundred hundred millions. However it has made me learned enough to talk about Mr Sykes[14] and the secret committee,[15] which is all that anybody talks of at present—and yet Mademoiselle Heinel[16] is arrived.

8. Bertrand-François Mahé de la Bourdonnais (1699–1753), celebrated naval officer in the East Indies (*La Grande Encyclopédie*, 1886–1902, xxi. 694–5; L. Roubaud, *La Bourdonnais*, 1932, pp. 3, 215 *et passim*).

9. Joseph-François Dupleix (1697–1763), governor of Pondicherry 1741–54 (Mann vi. 211, n. 18).

10. HW must mean Admiral Sir Charles Saunders (ca 1713–75), K.B., but Raynal is referring to Thomas Saunders (fl. 1732–55), governor of Madras 1750–5 (C. E. Buckland, *Dictionary of Indian Biography*, 1906, p. 376); see the edition of the *Histoire* published at The Hague, 1774, ii. 127.

11. A variant form of 'cowries,' the porcelain-like shells of a certain species of small gastropod found abundantly in the Indian Ocean and used as small money in the East Indies; see OED.

12. The Circassians, inhabitants of a region in the western Caucasus, were noted for their physical beauty and used to sell their most desirable girls into Turkish harems.

13. John Law (1671–1729), adventurer and financier; controller-general of French finance 1720. His unsuccessful plan for French colonization of the Louisiana Territory (1717) became known as 'the Mississippi Scheme' or 'The System'; see Dalrymple 167 and n. 9.

14. Francis Sykes (1732–1804), the East India Company's resident at Murshidabad 1765–8 during Warren Hastings's leave of absence in England; cr. (1781) Bt; M.P. Shaftesbury 1771–5, 1780–4, Wallingford 1784–1804. On 18 Dec., Samuel Wilks, Examiner of the Indian Correspondence and Records 1769–85, testified before the House that Sykes, by means of a tax arbitrarily laid on the natives without the Company's knowledge, had received 60,000 rupees a year 'for his table . . . his dress . . . and . . . his moonshee' (Mann vii. 451, nn. 9–12).

15. Appointed 26 Nov. by the House 'to inquire into the state of the East India Company'; see ibid. vii. 441–2 and nn. 6–7, 451 and n. 8.

16. Anne-Frédérique Heinel (1753–1808), m. (1792) Gaetano Appolino Baldassare Vestris; dancer (Ossory i. 66, n. 15). 'The celebrated Mad. Heinel, engaged for this season of operas at the King's Theatre, arrived from Paris last Friday night

This is all I know, and a great deal too, considering I know nothing—and yet were there either truth or lies, I should know them, for one hears everything in a sick room. Good night both!

From HERTFORD, Saturday 1 May 1773

Printed from a photostat of BM Add. MSS 23219, f. 65; first printed in L. W. Conolly, 'Horace Walpole, Unofficial Play Censor,' *English Language Notes,* 1971, ix. 45.

G[rosvenor] Street, May 1st 1773.

Dear Horry,

MR Capel,[1] who inspects the theatrical pieces for the office, has reported that the subject of *Tamerlane*,[2] the new proposed opera, may be thought too like the present state of our royal family to be licensed. I have looked it over and do not agree with him; however let me beg you will pass your eyes carefully upon it and then give me your opinion.

I have sent *Tamerlane* and another opera which was licensed last year[3] that seems to me in the argument to be just as objectionable, and no observation or objection were ever made that I have heard of. I shall see you here, I hope, this evening. Yours, dear Horry,

Very truly,

HERTFORD

[25 Dec.]' (*Public Advertiser* 28 Dec.). This was her second season at the London opera; she made her début 5 Jan. in 'a new serious grand ballet with a new chacone' introduced into the last act of J. A. Hasse's *Artaserse* (*London Stage* Pt IV, iii. 1684).

1. Edward Capell (1713–81), editor and Shakespearian scholar; deputy-inspector of plays and groom of the privy chamber. HW's copy of his *Prolusions; or Select Pieces of Ancient Poetry,* 1760, is Hazen, *Cat. of HW's Lib.,* No. 2003.

2. *Tamerlano,* 'a new serious opera' by

Antonio Sacchini (1730–86). Presumably HW saw nothing objectionable in it for it was first performed 6 May (*London Stage* Pt IV, iii. 1720; *Enciclopedia dello spettacolo,* Rome, 1954–62, viii. 1362–3; Sir George Grove, *Dictionary of Music and Musicians,* 5th edn, ed Blom, 1954–61, vii. 347).

3. Three new operas had been performed the year before, all by Pietro Guglielmi (1728–1804): *Il Carnevale di Venezia, L'Assemblea,* and *Demetrio* (*London Stage* Pt IV, iii. 1600, 1619, 1643; *Enciclopedia dello spettacolo* vi. 32, 34; Grove, op. cit. iii. 840).

From HERTFORD, Wednesday 26 May 1773

Printed for the first time from a photostat of BM Add. MSS 23219, f. 66.
Address: To the Honourable Horatio Walpole.

G[rovesnor] Street, May 26th 1773.

Dear Horry,

I CALLED this morning on coming from Council to acquaint you that the two Dukes' marriages[1] were this day reported to be legal and ordered to be entered accordingly in those books.[2] The Duke of Gloucester's from the depositions you mentioned to me,[3] with the addition of one from the Bishop of Exeter;[4] the Duke of Cumberland's was all in the most perfect form.

Yours ever,

HERTFORD

1. The Duke of Gloucester had married Lady Waldegrave 6 Sept. 1766, and Cumberland, Mrs Anne (Luttrell) Horton 2 Oct. 1771.

2. The council books. The Duke of Gloucester had requested authentication of the forthcoming delivery of his Duchess (she was delivered of a daughter, Sophia Matilda of Gloucester, 29 May); the King's reply, 17 May, was that 'your marriage, as well as the birth of the child, shall be properly inquired into.' The Archbishop of Canterbury, the Lord Chancellor and the Bishop of London were sent to examine the proofs of Gloucester's marriage 23 May, and of Cumberland's 24 May;

they made their report in full council before the King 26 May. See MANN vii. 483 and nn. 1, 3–7; *Last Journals* i. 205–29 *passim.*

3. Gloucester had declared his marriage at Florence 'on his death bed, as he believed,' to his equerries, Colonels Charles Rainsford (1728–1809) and Nathaniel Heywood (d. 1808), 'who have taken their oaths of it' (HW to Mann 29 May 1773, MANN vii. 484, also 333, n. 11, 353, n. 12; *Last Journals* i. 218–19).

4. The Duchess had owned the marriage to him 1 March 1772 'at the Deanery of Windsor' (ibid. i. 219–20; MANN vii. 484).

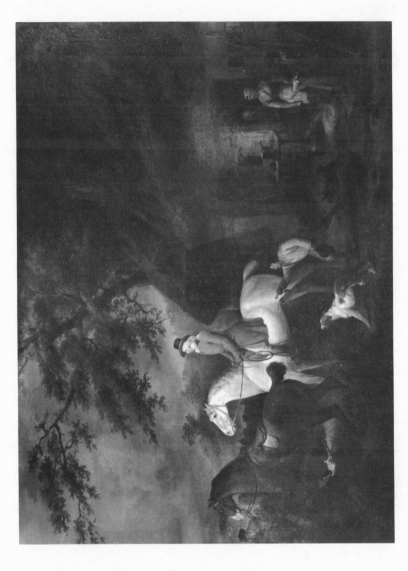

HON. FRANCIS SEYMOUR CONWAY, MARQUESS OF
HERTFORD, BY GEORGE MORLAND

From HERTFORD, Monday 21 June 1773

Printed for the first time from a photostat of BM Add. MSS 23219, f. 68.
Memoranda (by **HW**):
>Ld Walpole
>[?Buccky]
>Mr Coppinger[1]

Grosvenor Street, June 21st 1773.

Dear Horry,

MR Sharpe[2] tells me that you have determined to sell Lord Orford's horses and to give away his dogs.[3] If the latter be certainly and positively so, I will beg you to reserve for me two of his best pointers, which I shall of course take care of, use properly as I am a sportsman, and return for my Lord's use again at any time in case he recovers.[4] But I beg, as Lord Orford's friend, that it may not be done for me, as he might hereafter blame me, except it is a determined plan, as Mr Sharpe has told me, in which case the dogs would be better with me than in other hands. Pray do not mention this as an idea of mine, if I am misinformed, for the same reason. I am going to Portsmouth[5] and Mr Sharpe told me no time was to be lost, which makes me write. I am always, dear Horry,

Very truly and affectionately yours,

HERTFORD

1. Presumably Fysh Coppinger, lawyer, admitted Lincoln's Inn, 1751 (*Records of . . . Lincoln's Inn*, 1896, i. 439). A letter from him 5 July ?1772 to Sir Edward Walpole, promising to take care of a furniture transaction, is now WSL; see also Sir Edward Walpole to HW 5 May 1770, FAMILY 59.

2. Joshua Sharpe (d. 1788), lawyer and legal adviser to the Countess of Orford, Lord Orford's mother (*ante* 24 Oct. 1756, n. 2).

3. Lord Orford was suffering from an attack of insanity which had begun in January and lasted till the end of the year (see FAMILY, Appendix 6), and HW was undertaking the management of his affairs, Orford's mother being in Italy (see *post* 30 Aug. 1773). HW wrote to Lord Ossory, in his letter to Lady Ossory 26 June 1773, that 'I am advised to let . . .

[Mr Philip Burlton] sell Lord Orford's horses in this July meeting [at Newmarket]; and his mares, fillies, etc. in October'; this plan was followed (OSSORY i. 131, n. 4, 133 and nn. 16–17). For his dogs, see next note.

4. HW wrote to Lord Townshend 24 Aug. 1773 that 'I had determined to part with nothing that could give Lord Orford pleasure, but on condition that every individual should be restored to him, if I am so happy as to see him recover. With this view I have reserved his five best pointers . . .' The rest of his dogs, a 'very superior' collection, were sold or given away; see also HW to Thomas Walpole 4 Sept. 1773, FAMILY 95 and n. 3; MANN vii. 540 and n. 6.

5. Where the King was going to review the fleet; see ibid. vii. 491 and nn. 16–17.

TO CONWAY, Monday 30 August 1773

Printed from *Works* v. 152–3.

Arlington Street, August 30, 1773.

I RETURNED last night from Houghton, where multiplicity of business detained me four days longer than I intended,[1] and where I found a scene infinitely more mortifying than I expected;[2] though I certainly did not go with a prospect of finding a land flowing with milk and honey. Except the pictures, which are in the finest preservation,[3] and the woods, which are become forests, all the rest is ruin, desolation, confusion, disorder, debts,[4] mortgages, sales, pillage, villainy, waste, folly, and madness. I do not believe that five thousand pounds would put the house and buildings into good repair. The nettles and brambles in the park are up to your shoulders; horses have been turned into the garden, and banditti lodged in every cottage.[5] The perpetuity of livings that come up to the park pales[6] have been sold[7]—and every farm let for half its value.[8] In short, you know how much family pride I have—and consequently may judge how much I have been mortified!—Nor do I tell you half, or *near* the worst circumstances.[9] I have just stopped the torrent—and that is all. I am very uncertain whether I must not fling up the trust;[10] and some of the difficulties in my way seem

1. He wrote to Lord Nuneham 17 Aug. 1773 that he intended to set out for Houghton 'on Thursday [19 Aug]' (CHUTE 463; see also OSSORY i. 139–40).

2. HW describes the devastation at Houghton also in his letters to Lady Ossory 1 Sept. 1773, to Mann 2 Sept. 1773, to Mason 3 Sept. 1773 (OSSORY i. 140–1; MANN vii. 510–11; MASON i. 103), and to Thomas Walpole 4 Sept. 1773.

3. For the famous collection of pictures at Houghton, see HW's *Ædes Walpolianæ* (*Works* ii. 237–78); they were sold by Lord Orford to Catherine the Great in 1779 (MANN viii. 502).

4. 'My Lord has contracted debts of every kind, and when the bills are all come in, I think they will exceed forty-four thousand pounds, independently of the debts of his father and grandfather, which leaves him infinitely poorer than a

beggar' (HW to Thomas Walpole 4 Sept. 1773, FAMILY 95).

5. 'A crew of banditti were harboured in the house, stables, town, and every adjacent tenement' (HW to Lady Ossory 1 Sept. 1773, OSSORY i. 141).

6. I.e., fences.

7. 'He has sold the perpetuity of the livings of Harpley and Bircham, and was on the point of selling that of Massingham' (HW to Thomas Walpole 4 Sept. 1773, FAMILY 95).

8. 'I have already increased one, as you will see by the enclosed, above an hundred and forty pounds' (ibid. 96).

9. 'He has been plundered in the grossest manner by every species of dependant; and some of his *friends* I doubt have not spared him even since his misfortune began' (ibid. 95).

10. Chiefly because of Lady Orford's

unsurmountable, and too dangerous not to alarm even my zeal; since I must not ruin myself, and hurt those for whom I must feel too, only to restore a family that will end with myself, and to retrieve an estate, from which I am not likely ever to receive the least advantage.

If you will settle with the Churchills your journey to Chalfont,[11] and will let me know the day, I will endeavour to meet you there; I hope it will not be till next week. I am overwhelmed with business —but indeed I know not when I shall be otherwise! I wish you joy of this endless summer.

To Lady Ailesbury, Sunday 3 October 1773

Printed from the copy by Mrs Philip Lybbe Powys in her MS Book of Extracts, owned in 1960 by Anthony Powys-Lybbe, Esq., and kindly transcribed for the editors by Miss Ursula Powys. First printed in Ursula Powys, 'Recreations of a Georgian Family,' *Country Life,* 24 March 1960, cxxvii. 642.

The date of the day and month is determined by HW's saying that he had been 'at church this morning' and by the collect he quotes, which is for the seventeenth Sunday after Trinity at the morning service, when the second lesson was Mark 4. In 1773 the seventeenth Sunday after Trinity fell on 3 October.

Strawberry Hill, 1773.

I'VE been at church this morning, Madam, which is not my custom so often as it ought to be,[1] but to show you how attentive I was, I have (as good boys do) brought away the text. After the prayer, 'Prevent us not, O Lord, etc., that in all our *work begun, continued* and *ended,* etc.,'[2] the preacher[3] said,

failure to send him a letter authorizing his undertaking the management of her son's affairs; however, HW received 'a satisfactory, and even flattering, letter from Lady Orford' 9 Sept. (HW to Mann 9 Sept. 1773, MANN vii. 514).

11. The Churchills' house, Bucks.

1. John Pinkerton reports that HW, whose religious views were vaguely deistical, once told him: 'I go to church sometimes, in order to induce my servants to go to church. I am no hypocrite. I do not go in order to persuade them to believe what I do not believe myself. A good

moral sermon may instruct and benefit them. I only set them an example of listening, not of believing' (*Walpoliana,* 1799, i. 76).

2. 'Lord, we pray thee that thy grace may always prevent and follow us, and make us continually to be given to all good works; through Jesus Christ our Lord. Amen' (Collect for the seventeenth Sunday after Trinity, *Book of Common Prayer*).

3. Probably George Costard (1710–82), M.A. (Oxford) 1733, vicar of Twickenham 1764–82 (DNB), though he was not a 'doctor' (see below); the curate was James

'In the 4th chapter of St Mark's Gospel at the 3rd, 4th, 5th, 6th, 7th and 8th verse[4] you will find these words:

3rd. Hearken, behold there came in a *sower* to *sow*.

4th. And it came to pass, as *she* sowed, some stitches fell on a *farm yard,* and the fowls of the air came and dwelt therein.

5th. And some fell on stony ground, where there was not much earth and immediately it was *hung* up, because it had no depth of earth.

6th.[5] And some fell among *reeds,* and the reeds grew up and almost choked a stork and a setting dog that fought therein.

7th. And some fell on good grounds and did yield *fruit* and flowers that sprang up, and some brought forth *dogs* and horses and sheep, and some brought forth men thirty years old and some sixty, and some a woman *spinning* an hundred years old.

8th. He that hath eyes to see, let him see.'

I wished I could repeat the discourse which the Doctor *canvassed* very ably, but I was mightily pleased with his saying that it was easier for a *Campbell*[6] to go through the eye of a needle than for the wicked and slothful to imitate the good sower in the Gospel.[7]

I am,

Your Ladyship's most faithful humble servant,

H. W.

Lacy (ca 1742–76), M.A., who held his post from 1765 till his death (R. S. Cobbett, *Memorials of Twickenham,* 1872, p. 126; Foster, *Alumni Oxon.*). For a portrait of Costard, see Edward Ironside, *History and Antiquities of Twickenham,* 1797, facing p. 123.

4. Each verse alludes to some picture of her Ladyship's worsted work, of which there are twenty-two now hung up in the drawing-room at Park Place. 1784 (MS note of Mrs Philip Lybbe Powys). One of them (in the possession of Commander Colin Campbell-Johnston), showing a basket of flowers, some grapes and a parrot, is illustrated in Ursula Powys, loc. cit.; they were bequeathed to Mrs Damer, and of them 'seven are in the possession of various descendants' (ibid.). For the worsted-work pictures of Lady Ailesbury at SH, see *ante* 16 Sept. 1757 and 1 Sept. 1764.

5. This and the following two verses parody verses 7–9 in the original; verse 6 is omitted.

6. A pun, of course, on Lady Ailesbury's family name before marriage.

7. See Matthew 19. 24.

To Conway, Thursday 23 June 1774

Printed from *Works* v. 153–4.

Strawberry Hill, June 23, 1774.

I HAVE nothing to say—which is the best reason in the world for writing; for one must have a great regard for anybody one writes to, when one begins a letter neither on ceremony nor business. You are seeing armies,[1] who are always in fine order and great spirits when they are in cold blood: I am sorry you thought it worthwhile to realize what I should have thought you could have seen in your mind's eye. However, I hope you will be amused and pleased with viewing heroes, both in their autumn and their bud. Vienna will be a new sight;[2] so will the Austrian eagle and its two heads.[3] I should like *seeing* too, if any fairy would present me with a chest that would fly up into the air by touching a peg, and transport me whither I pleased in an instant: but roads, and inns, and dirt are terrible drawbacks on my curiosity. I grow so old, or so indolent, that I scarce stir from hence; and the dread of the gout makes me almost as much a prisoner, as a fit of it. News I know none, if there is any. The papers tell me the City was to present a petition to the King against the Quebec Bill yesterday; and I suppose they will tell me tomorrow whether it was presented.[4] The King's Speech[5] tells

1. Mr Conway was now on a tour of military curiosity through Flanders, Germany, Prussia, and part of Hungary (HW). His tour was prompted by an invitation from Sir Robert Murray Keith (*ante* 27 March 1764, n. 1), envoy to Vienna 1772–92, to visit him there (Keith, *Memoirs and Correspondence*, ed. Mrs Gillespie Smyth, 1849, ii. 5–12); he left London 8 June, accompanied by David Scott (d. 1792). Capt.-Lt in the Royal Artillery (*Army Lists* 1775, p. 171; *Scots Magazine* 1792, liv. 413), who kept a record of their travels in his MS 'Journal of a Military Tour of the Continent with Gen. Conway 8 June – 12 Nov. 1774' (Bodl. MS Eng. Hist. C 282); see Appendix 9. Conway wrote to Hertford from Brussels 20 June (MS now WSL), describing their itinerary thus far: they had visited garrisons, fortifications and battlefields at

Dunkirk, Cassel, St-Omer, Arras, Douai, Lille, Fontenoy, etc.

2. Conway was there 31 July – 14 Aug. (Appendix 9); see *post* 18 Aug. 1774 and n. 3.

3. I.e., Maria Theresa and her son Joseph II, who were joint Empress and Emperor of Austria.

4. 'The bill for the future government of Quebec ['for making more effectual provision for the government of the province of Quebec'] having passed both Houses, lies also ready for the royal assent [22 June]; but previous to his Majesty's going to the House of Peers, a petition [printed GM 1774, xliv. 247–8] will be presented to him by the Lord Mayor, aldermen, and commons of the City of London, relative to the said bill' (*Daily Adv.* 22 June). Among other things, the bill provided for toleration of Roman Catholics,

me, there has nothing happened between the Russians and the Turks.[6] Lady Barrymore[7] told me t'other day, that nothing was to happen between her and Lord Egremont.[8] I am as well satisfied with these negatives, as I should have been with the contrary. I am much more interested about the rain, for it destroys all my roses and orange-flowers, of which I have exuberance; and my hay is cut, and cannot be made. However, it is delightful to have no other distresses. When I compare my present tranquillity and indifference with all I suffered last year,[9] I am thankful for my happiness, and enjoy it— unless the bell rings at the gate early in the morning—and then I tremble, and think it an express from Norfolk.[10]

It is unfortunate, that when one has nothing to talk of but one's self, one should have nothing to say of one's self. It is shameful too to send such a scrap by the post. I think I shall reserve it till Tuesday.[11] If I have then nothing to add, as is probable, you must content yourself with my good intentions, as I hope you will with this speculative campaign. Pray, for the future remain at home and build bridges: I wish you were here to expedite ours to Richmond, which they tell me will not be passable these two years.[12] I have done looking so forward. Adieu!

and the petition requested that the King refuse his assent, objecting 'that the Roman Catholic religion, which is known to be idolatrous and bloody, is established' by it (GM 1774, xliv. 248). However, the King gave his assent, and the bill was enacted as 14 Geo. III c. 83 (*Daily Adv.* 23 June; *Journals of the House of Commons* xxxiv. 820; Owen Ruffhead, *Statutes at Large*, 1763–1800, xii. 184–7). See also *Annual Register . . . 1774*, 1775, pp. 74–8.

5. 22 June, closing the current session of Parliament.

6. 'Nothing material has happened, since your meeting, with respect to the war between Russia and the Porte' (*Journals of the House of Commons* xxxiv. 821). However, see *post* 18 Aug. 1774, n. 23.

7. Lady Amelia Stanhope (*ante* 5 May 1753, n. 25), a niece of Lady Hertford, m. (1767) Richard Barry, 6th Earl of Barrymore, who died in 1773.

8. George O'Brien Wyndham (1751–1837), 3d E. of Egremont, m. (1801) Elizabeth Ilive (or Iliffe), his mistress. Lady Mary Coke wrote in her *Journals*,

iv. 365–6, *sub* 18 June, that 'Lady Blandford cannot persuade herself Lord Egremount intends to marry Lady Barrymore, but nobody else doubts of it'; apparently, Lord Egremont was attached to her, and it was rumoured that he had even proposed, but his friends disapproved of the match, and she herself was against it (see ibid. 367, 376, 429).

9. During the illness of his nephew Lord Orford (HW); see *ante* 21 June, 30 Aug. 1773.

10. To bring him news of the relapse of his nephew.

11. 'Letters to all parts of Europe are dispatched from London every Tuesday and Friday' (*Court and City Register*, 1774, p. 128).

12. In 1772 and 1773 petitions from the inhabitants of Richmond and Twickenham had been presented to the House in favour of erecting a bridge in lieu of the ferry between those two localities; on 6 May 1773 a bill was introduced 'for building a bridge across the river of Thames, from Richmond . . . Surrey, to the opposite shore in . . . Middlesex,' and on 1

From Conway, July 1774

Missing; mentioned *post* 18 Aug. 1774.

From Beauchamp, Saturday after 21 July 1774

Printed for the first time from a photostat of BM Add. MSS 23219, f. 178. The letter was presumably written sometime after the first printing of HW's *Description of . . . Strawberry Hill,* 1774, and before the printing of the Appendix to the *Description* in 1781 (see n. 3; Hazen, *SH Bibl.* 107, 109); the letter is dated after 21 July in 1774 since on that date HW announced to Cole the completion of 'the catalogue of my collection' (COLE i. 338).

Saturday, 3 o'clock.

Dear Sir,

ACCEPT the two little boxes of china which my servant will deliver to you. They have not the smallest degree of value except as specimens of two manufactories,[1] which I need not tell you when you have opened the boxes, are still in an infant state.[2]

Yours ever, dear Sir,
Most sincerely

BEAUCHAMP

The Brunswic china is not yet come.[3]

July 1773 it was enacted as 13 Geo. III c. 83 (*Journals of the House of Commons* xxxiii. 491, 576, xxxiv. 78, 300–1, 389; Ruffhead, op. cit. xi. 891–8; H. Humpherus, *History of the . . . Company of Watermen,* [1874], ii. 299, 304). The estimated cost was £25,000, and the first stone was laid 24 Aug. 1774; the bridge was completed in Dec. 1777 (ibid. 304; *London Chronicle* 23–5 Aug. 1774, xxxvi. 186; *London Magazine* 1779, xlviii. 417). For a plate and short account of the bridge, see ibid. ———

1. Brunswick and Frankenthal; see postscript and n. 3.
2. Porcelain factories had been estab-

lished at Fürstenberg in Brunswick in 1747, and at Frankenthal in 1755 (George Savage, *18th-Century German Porcelain,* 1958, pp. 140, 156). 'Until 1770, when the paste and glaze was much improved, the body [of porcelain at Fürstenberg] was difficult to work,' while at Frankenthal 'in 1774 a new source of clay was exploited. This was cheaper and less satisfactory, and the quality greatly deteriorated in consequence' (ibid. 145, 159). For examples of Fürstenberg and Frankenthal porcelain figures, see ibid. plates 97–101, 109–13.

3. After this postscript HW has written: 'The two figures of Frankendahl [Frankenthal] porcelain,' and in a copy of his

To Conway, Thursday 18 August 1774

Printed from *Works* v. 154–6.

Strawberry Hill, August 18, 1774.

IT is very hard, that because you do not get my letters,[1] you will not let me receive yours, who do receive them. I have not had a line from you these five weeks.[2] Of your honours and glories Fame has told me;[3] and for aught I know, you may be a *veldt-marshal* by this time, and despise such a poor cottager as me. Take notice, I shall disclaim you in my turn, if you are sent on a command against Dantzick, or to usurp a new district in Poland.[4]

I have seen no armies, kings or empresses, and cannot send you such august gazettes; nor are they what I want to hear of. I like to hear you are well and diverted; nay, have pimped towards the latter, by desiring Lady Ailesbury to send you Monsieur de Guisnes's[5] invitation to a military fête at Metz.[6] For my part, I wish you was

Description of . . . Strawberry Hill, 1774, now WSL: 'Added since [to the collection in the China Room] . . . A group of two figures, and five single cupids, of Hessian [*sic*] and Brunswick porcelain, presents from Francis Lord Beauchamp' (p. 20); this addition is noted in his Appendix, 1781, to the *Description*, p. 122. The Brunswick group, described in the sale catalogue as 'five small figures of boys, representing the senses,' was sold SH xii. 113 to B. E. Willoughby, Esq., for £2.

---

1. See next note.

2. Conway's letter is missing; he wrote to Hertford from Hanover 2 July, noting that 'I have been disappointed in not finding any letters for me here . . . at Brunswick I hope I shall be more lucky' (MS now WSL).

3. Alluding to the distinguished notice taken of General Conway by the King of Prussia (HW). Conway wrote to Hertford from Berlin 17 July that Frederick II gave him 'a most flattering gracious audience [15 July, at Potsdam] of near half an hour, talking of a great variety of things,' etc. and from Vienna 3 Aug. that 'this morning I had the honour of an audience from the Emperor [Joseph II] whose re-

ception was the most gracious, flattering and pleasing imaginable'; he was presented to Maria Theresa 4 Aug. (MS now WSL; see also Appendix 9; MANN viii. 28 and n. 25).

4. The first partition of Poland, by Russia, Prussia, and Austria, had taken place in 1772 (see ibid. vii. 419, nn. 8–9), and the Prussians and Austrians had since made encroachments on the remaining Polish territories (*Annual Register . . . 1774*, 1775, pp. 17–18); the *London Chronicle* 2–4 Aug., xxxvi. 118, *sub* The Hague, 29 July, reported that the Austrians had 'extended their limits on the side of Moldavia much farther than they at first pretended to have any right to; and the Prussians have lately extended their line as far as the town of Sochazew, within eight [28] miles of Warsaw.' The Prussians had also reportedly besieged Danzig; a letter from there, dated 28 July (printed ibid. 16–18 Aug., xxxvi. 168), announced the lifting of this siege. See Frederick II, *Politische Correspondenz*, Berlin, 1879–1939, xxxv. 417 *et passim*.

5. The French ambassador at London (*ante* 29 Dec. 1770, n. 18).

6. To see the review of the French regiment of carabineers, then commanded by

returned to your plough. Your Sabine farm[7] is in high beauty. I have lain there twice within this week, going to and from a visit to George Selwyn near Gloucester: a tour as much to my taste as yours to you. For fortified towns I have seen ruined castles.[8] Unluckily, in that of Berkeley I found a whole regiment of militia in garrison,[9] and as many young officers as if the Countess[10] was in possession, and ready to surrender at indiscretion. I endeavoured to comfort myself by figuring that they were guarding Edward II.[11] I have seen many other ancient sights without asking leave of the King of Prussia:[12] it would not please me so much to write *to* him, as it once did to write *for* him.[13]

They have found at least seventy thousand pounds of Lord Thomond's.[14] George Howard[15] has decked himself with a red ribband,

Monsieur de Guisnes (HW); actually, Guines was commander of the regiment of Navarre (NBG; La Chenaye-Desbois iii. 515; *Répertoire . . . de la Gazette de France*, ed. de Granges de Surgères, 1902–6, ii. 620). Conway wrote to Hertford from Nuremberg 25 Sept. that 'I am . . . unfortunately too late for the military sights in France at Metz' (MS now WSL), but he later saw Guines at Paris (*post* 12 Nov. 1774).

7. Park Place (HW).

8. Berkeley and Thornbury Castles. HW described his tour to Cole 15 Aug. 1774 (COLE i. 340–5) and in *Country Seats* 75–6.

9. 'I found . . . [Lord Berkeley] in the midst of all his captains of the militia' (HW to Cole 15 Aug. 1774, COLE i. 343); see also *post* 7 Sept. 1774.

10. Deleted in *Works*; restored by Wright. HW wrote to Mann 16 Nov. 1778 of the Dowager Countess of Berkeley, who had married Robert Nugent (d. 1788) in 1757: 'There is nothing so black of which she is not capable. Her gallantries are the whitest specks about her' (MANN viii. 422). Nugent had disavowed a child she bore in 1761 (*ante* 14 July 1761, n. 5).

11. (1284–1327), King of England 1307–27. 'At the top of the house is a small retired chamber in which tradition says Edward II was murdered, and very probably, for it is only to be approached by a small kind of bridge and near it is a flight of steps to a gate, at which probably a guard was set on him' (*Country Seats*, loc. cit.).

12. Conway had requested, and been granted, the privilege of attending Frederick II at his camps in Silesia at the end of August: he had 'an hint . . . from an officer about him that if I had an inclination to see the Silesian camps next month and asked it I should not be refused. . . . I asked, and had a very gracious consent' (Conway to Hertford 17 July, MS now WSL; see also Appendix 9; *post* 27 Sept. 1774, n. 1).

13. Alluding to the letter to Rousseau in the name of the King of Prussia (HW); see *ante* 12 Jan. 1766.

14. Percy Wyndham Obrien. He was the second son of Sir Charles [Sir William] Wyndham, the chancellor of the Exchequer to Queen Anne, and took the name of Obrien pursuant to the will of his uncle the Earl of Thomond in Ireland (HW). He had died 21 July; HW described him to Mann 3 Aug. 1774 as 'possessed of near ten thousand a year and fifty thousand in money' (MANN viii. 25). Because 'he could not bring himself to make a will . . . the whole real estate falls to his nephew, Lord Egremont' (ibid.); it had been expected that Egremont's next brother, the Hon. Percy Charles Wyndham, would be his heir (OSSORY i. 198 and nn. 7, 8).

15. (1718–96), army officer; M.P.; governor of Chelsea Hospital 1768–95; invested K.B. 3 Aug. 1774. His career seems to have been at various times closely connected with Conway's; he had served with him at Fontenoy and Culloden, on the expedition to Rochefort in 1757, and in

money and honours!—Charming things! and yet one may be very happy without them.

The young Mr Coke[16] is returned from his travels in love with the Pretender's Queen,[17] who has permitted him to have her picture. What can I tell you more? Nothing. Indeed, if I only write to post-masters, my letter is long enough.[18] Everybody's head but mine is full of elections. I had the satisfaction at Gloucester, where G. Selwyn is canvassing,[19] of reflecting on my own wisdom: *Suave mari magno turbantibus æquora ventis*,[20] etc. I am certainly the greatest philosopher in the world, without ever having thought of being so: always employed, and never busy; eager about trifles, and indifferent to everything serious. Well, if it is not philosophy, at least it is content. I am as pleased here with my own nutshell, as any monarch you have seen these two months astride his eagle— not but I was dissatisfied when I missed you at Park Place, and was peevish at your being in an Aulic[21] chamber. Adieu!

Yours ever,

Hor. Walpole

PS. They tell us from Vienna that the peace is made between Tisiphone[22] and the Turk:[23] is it true?

Germany under Lord Granby 1760–2; was made field marshal with him in 1793; and succeeded him as governor of Jersey in 1795; also, Wraxall, in his *Historical and Posthumous Memoirs*, 1884, iii. 202, re-cords that Howard succeeded Conway as commander-in-chief in 1783, though this appointment does not seem to have actu-ally taken place. See Namier and Brooke ii. 645–6; W. A. Shaw, *Knights of England*, 1906, i. 172.

16. Thomas William Coke (1754–1842), cr. E. of Leicester, 1837; his name was deleted in *Works* but restored by Wright. He had just returned from his Grand Tour, begun in 1771 (Namier and Brooke ii. 234).

17. Luise Maximiliane of Stolberg-Gedern (1752–1824), m. (1772) Charles Edward Stuart, the 'Young Pretender'; styled Countess of Albany.

18. The fear of his letters being opened by foreign postmasters was always present in HW's mind.

19. Selwyn had been M.P. for Glouces-ter since 1754; in this election he and Charles Barrow were returned unopposed 7 Oct. (ibid. i. 290–1).

20. 'It is pleasant, when the winds stir the water on the great sea, [to watch from land another's toil]' (Lucretius, *De rerum natura* II. 1). HW quoted this passage also to Mann 6 Nov. 1769 and 6 Oct. 1774, and paraphrased it to Cole 24 Nov. 1780 (Mann vii. 151, viii. 48; Cole ii. 245).

21. 'Courtly'; the Aulic Council was the personal council of the Emperor of Aus-tria.

22. Catherine II of Russia.

23. 'This day at noon a courier arrived here with the news of peace between Russia and the Porte having been con-cluded on the 17th of July, at the head-quarters at Buyak Canarochi' (*London Gazette* No. 11483, 13–16 Aug., *sub* Vienna, 3 Aug., reprinted *London Chroni-cle* 16–18 Aug., xxxvi. 161). The peace was signed 10/21 July at Kücük Kainardje (Mann viii. 33, n. 7).

From Conway, ca Sunday 21 August 1774

Missing; answered *post* 7 Sept. 1774. Presumably written about the same time as Conway's letter to Hertford 21 Aug. (MS now wsl); see *post* 7 Sept. 1774 and nn.

To Conway, Wednesday 7 September 1774

Printed from *Works* v. 156–8.

Strawberry Hill, Sept. 7, 1774.

I DID not think you had been so like the rest of the world, as, when you pretended to be visiting armies, to go in search of gold and silver mines![1] The favours of courts and the smiles of emperors and kings, I see, have corrupted even you, and perverted you to a nabob. Have you brought away an ingot in the calf of your leg? What abomination have you committed? All the gazettes in Europe have sent you on different negotiations:[2] instead of returning with a treaty in your pocket, you will only come back with bills of exchange. I don't envy your subterraneous travels,[3] nor the hospitality of the Hungarians.[4] Where did you find a spoonful of Latin about

1. Conway had visited the gold and silver mines and furnaces at Schemnitz and Kremnitz in Hungary, 16–17 Aug. (Conway to Hertford 21 Aug., MS now wsl; Sir Robert Murray Keith, *Memoirs and Correspondence*, ed. Mrs Gillespie Smyth, 1849, ii. 16–17; Appendix 9).

2. Mann had written this to HW 23 Aug. 1774: 'The newspapers have given him great commissions' (MANN viii. 33). The GM Aug. 1774, xliv. 384 reported that 'General Conway is charged with an important commission at the two principal courts of Germany. At Berlin he has already concluded his business; but at the Court of Vienna he is still negotiating.' The *London Chronicle* 4–6 Aug., xxxvi. 128, had printed an 'extract of a letter from Berlin, July 26,' in which it was stated that 'the subject of the General's commission to his Majesty, is reported to be the treaties which are now nearly con-cluded between Prussia and Hanover, about exchanging some lands, and settling the demand of arrears, which the former has upon the latter'; see also *Mercure historique* 1774, clxxvii. 201–2, 355–6. However, there seems to be no evidence for such negotiations.

3. At Schemnitz Conway was conducted 'into the side of a mountain by a large gallery near a league long' and shown 'the branches from this gallery, the veins how they worked and followed them,' etc.; after this he descended into 'one of the longest and deepest shafts, which is 153 toises [about 300 meters]' (David Scott, 'Journal of a Military Tour of the Continent with Gen. Conway,' p. 123; see also Keith, op. cit. ii. 16–18).

4. Conway wrote to Hertford 21 Aug. that 'the whole air of people and country' were 'very different from any we had seen. Their appearance in many parts is wild

you?[5] I have not attempted to speak Latin these thirty years, without perceiving I was talking Italian thickened with terminations in *us* and *orum*. I should have as little expected to find an Ovid in those regions;[6] but I suppose the gentry of Presbourg[7] read him for a fashionable author, as our 'squires and their wives do the last collections of ballads that have been sung at Vauxhall and Marybone. I wish you may have brought away some sketches of Duke Albert's[8] architecture. You know I deal in the works of royal authors, though I have never admired any of their own buildings, not excepting King Solomon's temple. Stanley[9] and Edmondson in Hungary![10] What carried them thither? The chase of mines too? The first, per-

almost to barbarism, but their behaviour extremely the reverse, and in general the politeness and peculiar attention showed us throughout the journey almost incredible.'

5. Scott observed in his 'Journal' that in Hungary 'most of the polite people speak Latin,' and that in dining with a certain 'noble Hungarian Protestant,' Conway carried on 'a long conversation' in that language (pp. 122, 127).

6. Perhaps Dávid Baróti Szabó (1739–1819), whose odes, epistles, etc., in Hungarian, but based on classical models, first appeared in 1773; the movement he founded reflected Greek and Roman authors rather than French neo-classicists (József Szinnyei, *Magyar írók*, Budapest, 1891–1914, i. 607–10; *Magyar életrajzi lexikon*, Budapest, 1967–, i. 122–3; Constant von Wurzbach, *Biographisches Lexikon des Kaiserthums Oesterreich*, Vienna, 1856–91, i. 162–3; J. H. Schwicker, *Geschichte der ungarischen Literatur*, Leipzig, 1889, pp. 248–9).

7. Present-day Bratislava in Czechoslovakia; then the capital of Hungary (see next note).

8. Albrecht Kasimir August (1738–1822), Duke of Saxe-Teschen, son-in-law of Maria Theresa and Viceroy of Hungary (OSSORY ii. 291, n. 15). In going to the mines at Schemnitz and Kremnitz, Conway 'passed by Presburg, the capital of Hungary and residence of Duke Albert, who lives in the castle or palace finely situated on an hill over the Danube. He draws well, has furnished a whole room with his drawings, and the house chiefly

from designs of his own. Another is filled with very pretty paintings of his' (Conway to Hertford 21 Aug.).

9. Mr Hans Stanley (HW); however, see next note.

10. 'We have two strangers here [at Pest] besides ourselves: young Stanley and Edmonstone' (Conway to Hertford 21 Aug.). Despite HW's identification in *Works* (n. 9 above), which may be actually Mary Berry's (see Manuscripts and Bibliography), and despite his description below, the 'young' seems definitely to rule out Hans Stanley, who was 52 at the time (see Namier and Brooke iii. 468); in his missing letter which HW is answering, Conway may have named Stanley without describing him further, leading to HW's confusion. A better possibility is the Hon. Thomas Stanley (?1753–79), younger brother of the 12th Earl of Derby; he took his M.A. at Cambridge in 1773, and may have been on his travels at this time; in 1775 he became a cornet in the 16th light dragoons (ibid. iii. 473; Venn, *Alumni Cantab.*). 'Edmondson' is perhaps Archibald Edmonstone (b. *post* 1753, d. 1780), ensign in the 1st foot guards, 1770, or his brother William Archibald (b. *post* 1754, living 1801), sons of Sir Archibald Edmonstone, 1st Bt (Namier and Brooke ii. 380; GEC, *Baronetage* v. 170 and n. 'c'; *Army Lists* 1775, p. 49); one of them was apparently a classmate of Stanley at Eton 1768–70 (R. A. Austen-Leigh, *Eton College Register 1753–1790*, Eton, 1921, pp. 176, 494).

haps, waddled thither obliquely, as a parrot would have done whose direction was to Naples.[11]

Well, I am glad you have been entertained, and seen such a variety of sights. You don't mind fatigues and hardships, and hospitality, the two extremes that to me poison travelling. I shall never see anything more, unless I meet with a ring that renders one invisible. It was but the other day, that, being with George Selwyn at Gloucester, I went to view Berkeley Castle,[12] knowing the Earl[13] was to dine with the Mayor of Gloucester.[14] Alas! when I arrived, he had put off the party to enjoy his militia a day longer, and the house was full of officers. They might be in the Hungarian dress, for aught I knew; for I was so dismayed, that I would fain have persuaded the housekeeper that she could not show me the apartments; and when she opened the hall, and I saw it full of captains, I hid myself in a dark passage, and nothing could persuade me to enter, till they had the civility to quit the place. When I was forced at last to go over the castle, I ran through it without seeing anything, as if I had been afraid of being detained prisoner.

I have no news to send you: if I had any, I would not conclude, as all correspondents do, that Lady A. left nothing untold. Lady P[owis] is gone to hold mobs at Ludlow, where there is actual war, and where a *knight*,[15] I forget his name, one of their friends, has been *almost cut in two* with a scythe.[16] When you have seen all the other armies in Europe, you will be just in time for many election battles—perhaps for a war in America, whither more troops are going. Many of those already sent have deserted;[17] and to be sure the prospect there is not smiling.[18] Apropos, Lord M[ahon] whom Lord

11. HW wrote of Hans Stanley after his death: 'Awkward he was, and brayed' (to Mason 29 Jan. 1780, MASON ii. 8).

12. A rare instance of HW repeating himself to the same correspondent; see *ante* 18 Aug. 1774.

13. Frederick Augustus Berkeley (1745–1810), 5th E. of Berkeley.

14. John Jefferis, mayor of Gloucester 1769 and 1774 (COLE i. 343, n. 24).

15. Not identified.

16. For the Montgomeryshire election, see *post* 27 Sept. 1774, n. 8.

17. 'Yesterday [7 Sept.] arrived a mail from New York . . . *Boston, New England, July* 25. On the 15th instant Gen.

Gage issued the following notice: . . . "Whereas some soldiers have deserted his Majesty's service, belonging to the regiments lately arrived from Great Britain and Ireland: This is to give notice, that all soldiers who deserted from said corps previous to the tenth day of this instant month of July, shall receive their pardons, upon surrendering themselves before or on the tenth day of August next ensuing [etc.]"' (*London Chronicle* 6–8 Sept., xxxvi. 238, *sub* 8 Sept.).

18. On 22 July the Pennsylvania House of Representatives, 'taking into their most serious consideration the unfortunate differences which have long subsisted be-

S[tanhope] his father will not suffer to wear powder because wheat is so dear, was presented t'other day[19] in coal black hair and a white feather: they said *he had been tarred and feathered.*

In France you will find a new scene.[20] The Chancellor[21] is sent, a little before his time, to the devil. The old parliament is expected back.[22] I am sorry to say I shall not meet you there.[23] It will be too late in the year for me to venture, especially as I now live in dread of my biennial gout, and should die of it in a *hôtel garni,* and forced to receive all comers—I, who you know lock myself up when I am ill, as if I had the plague.

I wish I could fill my sheet, in return for your five pages.[24] The only thing you will care for knowing is, that I never saw Mrs D[amer] better in her life, nor look so well. You may trust me, who am so apt to be frightened about her.[25]

From CONWAY, ca Monday–Tuesday 12–13 September 1774

Missing; presumably the 'seven large' sides answered *post* 27 Sept. 1774. Conway wrote to Hertford from Prague 12 Sept.: 'H. Walpole can tell you my history from Breslau [Conway had written to Hertford from there 4 Sept.]' and 13 Sept.: 'I have just writ . . . ['H. Walpole] a long letter' (MSS now WSL).

tween Great Britain and the American colonies, and which have been greatly increased by the operation and effects of divers late acts of the British Parliament,' resolved 'that there is an absolute necessity that a congress of deputies from the several colonies be held as soon as conveniently may be to consult together upon the present unhappy state of the colonies,' etc. (ibid., *sub* 'Philadelphia, July 27').

19. Mahon and his parents had returned to England in July from Geneva, where he had been receiving his education since 1764; he had turned 21 on 3 Aug., proposed to Lady Hester Pitt, daughter of Lord Chatham, later in September (they were married in December), and unsuc-

cessfully contested Westminster in October (Ghita Stanhope and G. P. Gooch, *Life of Charles Third Earl Stanhope,* 1914, p. 20 *et passim;* for his contesting Westminster, see also *post* 27 Sept. 1774 and 16 Oct. 1774, nn. 17, 18).

20. Upon the death of Louis XV [10 May] (HW); see MANN viii. 1, n. 1.

21. Maupeou; see ibid. viii. 34, n. 2.

22. See ibid. viii. 35, n. 4.

23. Conway was to meet Lady Ailesbury and Mrs Damer at Paris in October; see subsequent letters.

24. Conway's letter is missing.

25. Mrs Damer tended to be sickly; see *ante* 29 Dec. 1772; HW to Mann 7 Sept. 1781, 7 May 1785, MANN ix. 183–4, 576, etc.

To Conway, Tuesday 27 September 1774

Printed from *Works* v. 158–60.

Strawberry Hill, September 27, 1774.

I SHOULD be very ungrateful indeed if I thought of complaining of you, who are goodness itself to me: and when I did not receive letters from you, I concluded it happened from your eccentric positions. I am amazed, that, hurried as you have been, and your eyes and thoughts crowded with objects, you have been able to find time to write me so many and such long letters, over and above all those to Lady A., your daughter, brother, and other friends. Even Lord Strafford brags of your frequent remembrance. That your superabundance of royal beams would dazzle you, I never suspected.[1] Even I enjoy for you the distinctions you have received—though I should hate such things for myself, as they are particularly troublesome to me, and I am particularly awkward under them, and as I abhor the King of Prussia, and, if I passed through Berlin, should have no joy like avoiding him—like one of our countrymen, who changed horses at Paris, and asked what the name of that town was? All the other civilities you have received I am perfectly happy in. The Germans are certainly a civil well-meaning people, and I believe one of the least corrupted nations in Europe. I don't think them very agreeable; but who do I think are so? A great many French women, some English men, and a few English women—exceedingly few French men. Italian women are the grossest, vulgarest of the sex. If an Italian man has a grain of sense, he is a buffoon—so much for Europe.

I have already told you, and so must Lady A., that my courage

1. Conway was especially overwhelmed by Frederick II's reception of him at his camp near Breslau, 31 Aug.–3 Sept.: I 'can't say how much in my particular [*sic*] I am obliged to his Majesty for his extraordinary reception and distinction shown me throughout . . . Each day after the manœuvre and giving the orders of the day he held a little levee . . . at which . . . he not only talked to me, but literally to nobody else at all . . . he also called me up and spoke to me several times on horseback when he was out' (Conway to Hertford 4 Sept., MS now WSL; see also Sir Robert Murray Keith, *Memoirs and Correspondence*, ed. Mrs Gillespie Smyth, 1849, ii. 23). Frederick wrote to Maltzan, the Prussian minister at London, 5 Sept.: 'J'ai eu de nouveau occasion en Silésie de voir le général Conway et de lui faire éprouver mes bontés. . . . J'espère qu'il sera content des attentions que j'ai eues pour lui' (Frederick II, *Politische Correspondenz*, Berlin, 1879–1939, xxxvi. 4).

fails me, and I dare not meet you at Paris. As the period is arrived when the gout used to come, it is never a moment out of my head. Such a suffering, such a helpless condition as I was in for five months and a half two years ago, makes me tremble from head to foot. I should die at once if seized in a French inn; or what, if possible, would be worse, at Paris, where I must admit everybody.—I, who you know can hardly bear to see even you when I am ill, and who shut myself up here, and would not let Lord and Lady Hertford come near me—I, who have my room washed though in bed, how could I bear French dirt? In short, I, who am so capricious, and whom you are pleased to call a philosopher, I suppose because I have given up everything but my own will—how could I keep my temper, who have no way of keeping my temper but by keeping it out of everybody's way! No, I must give up the satisfaction of being with you at Paris. I have just learnt to give up my pleasures, but I cannot give up my pains, which such selfish people as I, who have suffered much, grow to compose into a system, that they are partial to because it is their own. I must make myself amends when you return: you will be more stationary, I hope, for the future; and if I live I shall have intervals of health. In lieu of me you will have a charming *succedaneum*, Lady Harriet Stanhope.[2] Her father,[3] who is more a hero than I, is packing up his decrepit bones, and goes too. I wish she may not have him to nurse, instead of diverting herself.

The present state of your country is, that it is drowned and dead drunk; all water without and wine within. Opposition for the next elections[4] everywhere, even in Scotland; not from party, but as laying out money to advantage. In the headquarters, indeed, party is not out of the question: the day after tomorrow will be a great bustle in the City for a lord mayor,[5] and all the winter in Westminster, where Lord Mahon and Humphrey Cotes oppose the Court.[6] Lady Powis is saving her money at Ludlow and Powis Castles by keeping open-house day and night against Sir Watkin Williams,[7] and fears she

2. Her name was deleted in *Works* but restored by Wright.

3. The Earl of Harrington.

4. The next general election for Parliament, scheduled for early 1775, took place sooner than expected, since on 30 Sept. the King dissolved the current one and ordered the issuing of writs of summons for the new one 1 Oct., returnable 29 Nov. (Mann viii. 44, n. 1). HW learned of

the forthcoming dissolution later this day (*Last Journals* i. 375).

5. When Mr Wilkes was elected (HW). The poll for lord mayor of London opened 29 Sept.; see *Daily Adv.* 30 Sept. and *post* 16 Oct. 1774, n. 10.

6. See *post* 16 Oct. 1774 and nn. 17–19.

7. I.e., Sir Watkin Williams Wynn; see next note.

shall be kept there till the general election.[8] It has rained this whole month, and we have got another inundation. The Thames is as broad as your Danube, and all my meadows are under water. Lady Browne[9] and I, coming last Sunday night from Lady Blandford's, were in a piteous plight.[10] The ferry-boat[11] was turned round by the current, and carried to Isleworth. Then we ran against the piers of our new bridge,[12] and the horses were frightened. Luckily my cicisbea was a Catholic, and screamed to so many saints, that some of them at the nearest alehouse came and saved us, or I should have had no more gout, or what I dreaded I should; for I concluded we should be carried ashore somewhere, and be forced to wade through the mud up to my middle. So you see one may wrap one's self up in flannel and be in danger, without visiting all the armies on the face of the globe, and putting the immortality of one's chaise to the proof.

I am ashamed of sending you but three sides of smaller paper in answer to seven large[13]—but what can I do? I see nothing, know nothing, do nothing. My castle is finished,[14] I have nothing new to read, I am tired of writing, I have no new or old bit for my printer.[15] I have only black hoods around me;[16] or, if I go to town, the family-party[17] in Grosvenor Street. One trait will give you a sample of how I pass my time, and made me laugh, as it put me in mind of you, at least as it was a fit of absence, much more likely to have happened to you than to me. I was playing at eighteen-penny tredille with the Duchess of Newcastle and Lady Browne, and certainly not much interested in the game. I cannot recollect nor conceive what I was thinking of, but I pushed the cards very gravely to the Duchess, and

8. The two leading families in Montgomeryshire were the Wynns of Wynnstay and the Herberts of Powis Castle, and in the 1774 election Sir Watkin Williams Wynn supported the candidacy of his cousin, Watkin Williams, the incumbent, against that of William Mostyn Owen, put forward by Lady Powis; after a bitter campaign Owen was returned 14 Oct. by a vote of 700 to 624 (Namier and Brooke i. 466, iii. 242, 644, 671; see also *Collections . . . Relating to Montgomeryshire*, 1875, viii. 8–13).

9. Frances Sheldon (1714–90), m. 1 (1736) Henry Fermor; m. 2 Sir George Browne, 3d Bt, 1751; HW's correspondent (Ossory ii. 37, n. 26).

10. See HW to Craufurd 26 Sept. 1774.

11. From Richmond to Twickenham.

12. Under construction to take the place of the ferry; see *ante* 23 June 1774 and n. 12.

13. Missing.

14. HW was to add the 'Beauclerk Tower' to the house in 1776 (W. S. Lewis, 'Genesis of Strawberry Hill,' *Metropolitan Museum Studies*, 1934, v pt i. 82).

15. The printing of the *Description of . . . Strawberry Hill* had been completed ca July, and nothing more was printed till the following June (Cole i. 338; HW's *Journal of the Printing Office at Strawberry Hill*, ed. Toynbee, 1923, p. 17).

16. 'By age and situation I live at this time of year with nothing but old women' (HW to Craufurd 26 Sept. 1774).

17. Lord Hertford's.

said, *Doctor,* you are to deal. You may guess at their astonishment, and how much it made us all laugh. I wish it may make you smile a moment, or that I had anything better to send you. Adieu, most affectionately.

Yours ever,

Hor. Walpole

To Hertford, Tuesday 27 September 1774

Missing. Immediately after learning of the forthcoming dissolution of Parliament (see *ante* 27 Sept. 1774, n. 4), HW 'wrote to Lord Hertford, earnestly pressing him to sound the Duke of Grafton on his brother's situation immediately [Grafton was Conway's sponsor as M.P. for Thetford], and telling him, if the Duke was adverse, that I depended on his finding a borough for his brother: but thinking him in Suffolk, as he was, I ordered the servant to deliver the letter to Lady Hertford, who was warmer in zeal, and had more weight with her nephew [Grafton] than her husband did' (*Last Journals* i. 381). See *post* 2 Oct. 1774.

To Lady Ailesbury, Tuesday 27 September 1774

Missing. 'I . . . wrote to Lady Ailesbury to insist on Lady Hertford's dispatching a messenger [with HW's letter to Hertford 27 Sept. 1774] immediately, which she did' (*Last Journals* i. 381).

To Conway, Wednesday 28 September 1774

Printed from *Works* v. 160–3.

Strawberry Hill, Sept. 28, 1774.

LADY Ailesbury brings you this,[1] which is not a letter, but a paper of directions, and the counterpart of what I have written to Madame du Deffand.[2] I beg of you seriously to take a great deal of

1. Mr Conway ended his military tour at Paris, whither Lady Ailesbury and Mrs Damer went to meet him, and where they spent the winter together (HW).

2. Missing.

notice of this dear old friend of mine. She will perhaps expect more attention from *you,* as my friend, and as it is her own nature a little, than will be quite convenient to you: but you have an infinite deal of patience and good nature, and will excuse it. I was afraid of her importuning Lady A., who has a vast deal to see and do, and therefore I have prepared Madame du D. and told her Lady A. loves amusements, and that, having never been at Paris before, she must not confine her: so you must pay for both—and it will answer: and I do not, I own, ask this only for Madame du Deffand's sake, but for my own, and a little for yours. Since the late King's death she has not dared to write to me freely, and I want to know the present state of France exactly, both to satisfy my own curiosity, and for her sake, as I wish to learn whether her pension, etc. is in any danger from the present ministry, some of whom are not her friends.[3] She can tell you a great deal if she will—by that I don't mean that she is reserved, or partial to her own country against ours—quite the contrary; she loves me better than all France together—but she hates politics; and therefore, to make her talk on it, you must tell her it is to satisfy me, and that I want to know whether she is well at Court, whether she has any fears from the government, particularly from Maurepas[4] and Nivernois;[5] and that I am eager to have Monsieur de Choiseul and *ma grand'maman* the Duchess restored to power.[6] If you take it on this foot easily, she will talk to you with the utmost frankness and with amazing cleverness. I have told her you are strangely absent, and that, if she does not repeat it over and over, you will forget every syllable: so I have prepared her to joke and be quite familiar with you at once.[7] She knows more of personal

3. Her pension was continued.

4. Who, disgraced by Louis XV in 1749, was recalled from exile by a letter of 12 May from Louis XVI, in which the King asked him 'de m'aider de vos conseils'; he was named chef du conseil des finances in 1776 (*ante* 5 Dec. 1765, n. 15; MANN viii. 13, n. 5; DU DEFFAND iv. 315, 317).

5. Maurepas' brother-in-law; he did not hold office under Louis XVI at this time, but in 1781 was rumoured to be Maurepas' successor as chef du conseil des finances, and in 1787 became a member of the conseil d'état du roi as ministre d'état (MANN ix. 212 and n. 13; *Répertoire . . .*

de la Gazette de France, ed. de Granges de Surgères, 1902–6, iii. 506).

6. They never were; Choiseul had returned to Paris in June, and was received 'neither well nor ill' by the King (Stormont to Rochford 15 June, S.P. 78/292, f. 153; DU DEFFAND iv. 62).

7. Mme du Deffand wrote to HW 28 Oct. 1774, after Conway's arrival at Paris: 'Selon l'idée que vous m'en aviez donnée, je le croyais grave, sévère, froid, imposant; c'est l'homme le plus aimable, le plus facile, le plus doux, le plus obligeant, et le plus simple que je connaisse. Il n'a pas ces premiers mouvements de sensibilité qu'on trouve en vous, mais aussi n'a-t-il pas votre humeur' (ibid. iv. 107).

characters, and paints them better than anybody: but let this be between yourselves, for I would not have a living soul suspect that I get any intelligence from her, which would hurt her; and therefore I beg you not to let any human being know of this letter, nor of your conversations with her, neither English nor French.

Madame du Deffand hates *les philosophes,* so you must give them up to her. She and Madame Geoffrin are no friends: so, if you go thither, don't tell her of it. Indeed you would be sick of that house, whither all the pretended *beaux esprits* and *faux savants* go, and where they are very impertinent and dogmatic.

Let me give you one other caution, which I shall give Lady A. too. Take care of your papers at Paris, and have a very strong lock to your *porte-feuille.* In the *hôtels garnis* they have double keys to every lock, and examine every drawer and paper of the English that they can get at. They will pilfer too whatever they can.—I was robbed of half my clothes there the first time,[8] and they wanted to hang poor Louis to save the people of the house who had stolen the things.[9]

Here is another thing I must say. Madame du Deffand has kept a great many of my letters, and, as she is very old, I am in pain about them. I have written to her to beg she will deliver them up to you to bring back to me, and I trust she will.[10] If she does, be so good to take great care of them. If she does not mention them, tell her just before you come away, that I begged you to bring them; and if she hesitates,[11] convince her how it would hurt me to have letters written in very bad French, and mentioning several people, both

8. See *ante* 2 Oct. 1765 and n. 54.

9. In investigating the robbery 'M. Buot, *deputy lieutenant de police . . .* and another . . . endeavoured to throw the suspicion of the robbery on Louis, and would not hear a word against the people of the house where I had lodged, but said it was a *genéalogie des plus honnêtes';* the Commissary also 'threw suspicions on Louis,' but HW had caught Mme Menard, the mistress of the hotel, in a lie, and 'an Irish servant to an officer in that house . . . told me he had had a waistcoat . . . stolen from him in that very house not a year before' ('Paris Journals,' du Deffand v. 267–9).

10. HW, in returning from Paris in Oct. 1769, had brought back with him his letters to Mme du Deffand written up to that time; Conway brought back the letters since then on his return to England in Feb. 1775. Most of these letters and those of March–Sept. 1780, sent back to HW by Wiart, Mme du Deffand's secretary, were presumably destroyed after HW's death by Mary Berry, his literary executrix; Mme du Deffand herself destroyed his letters from Feb. 1775 to March 1780 (ibid. i. p. xliii, ii. 279, iv. 126, 152, 156, v. 69, 249); only five written in January 1775 have survived (now WSL).

11. She was somewhat annoyed at HW's 'méfiance,' writing him in her letter of 28 Oct. 1774 that 'il y a longtemps que Wiart a ses instructions' that his letters be returned to him in the event of her death, but assured him in her letter of 29 Dec. 1774 that 'jamais, non jamais, je ne serai l'occasion de vous causer le plus petit chagrin' (ibid. iv. 108, 126).

French and English, fall into bad hands, and, perhaps, be printed. Let me desire you to read this letter more than once, that you may not forget my requests, which are very important to me; and I must give you one other caution, without which all would be useless. There is at Paris a Mlle de l'Espinasse,[12] a pretended *bel esprit,* who was formerly an humble companion of Madame du Deffand; and betrayed her and used her very ill.[13] I beg of you not to let anybody carry you thither. It would disoblige my friend of all things in the world, and she would never tell you a syllable; and I own it would hurt me, who have such infinite obligations to her, that I should be very unhappy if a particular friend of mine showed her this disregard. She has done everything upon earth to please and serve me, and I owe it to her to be earnest about this attention. Pray do not mention it: it might look simple in me, and yet I owe it to her, as I know it would hurt her: and at her age, with her misfortunes, and with infinite obligations on my side, can I do too much to show my gratitude, or prevent her any new mortification? I dwell upon it, because she has some enemies so spiteful that they try to carry all English to Mademoiselle de l'Espinasse.

I wish the Duchess of Choiseul may come to Paris while you are there; but I fear she will not: you would like her of all things.[14] She has more sense and more virtues than almost any human being. If you choose to see any of the *savants,* let me recommend Monsieur Buffon.[15] He has not only much more sense than any of them, but is an excellent old man, humane, gentle, well-bred, and with none of the arrogant pertness of all the rest. If he is at Paris, you will see a good deal of the Comte de Broglie at Madame du Deffand's.[16] He is not a genius of the first water, but lively and sometimes agreeable. The Court, I fear, will be at Fontainebleau, which will prevent your seeing many, unless you go thither.[17] Adieu! at Paris! I leave the rest

12. Julie-Jeanne-Éléonore de Lespinasse (1732–76), Mme du Deffand's companion 1754–64 and afterwards her rival (ibid. i. 289, n. 11).

13. In 1764 Mme du Deffand discovered that Mlle de Lespinasse was holding a secret salon in her own room where Mme du Deffand's friends were accustomed to assemble before she was ready to receive them, and as a consequence Mlle de Lespinasse was dismissed (Marquis de Ségur, *Julie de Lespinasse,* [1905], pp. 142–8).

14. See *post* 31 Dec. 1774.

15. Jean-Louis Le Clerc (1707–88), Comte de Buffon, the naturalist. HW had met him at Paris in 1766 ('Paris Journals,' DU DEFFAND v. 306); HW's copy of his *Histoire naturelle* is Hazen, *Cat. of HW's Lib.,* No. 2152.

16. HW had met the Comte at Paris in 1766 and 1771 ('Paris Journals,' DU DEFFAND v. 304, 335).

17. See *post* ca 4 Nov. 1774.

of my paper for England, if I happen to have anything particular to tell you.

From HERTFORD, Saturday 1 October 1774

Printed for the first time from a photostat of BM Add. MSS 23219, f. 40.

Grosvenor Street, Saturday.

Dear Horry,

I HAVE seen Mr Boone[1] and Mr Moon[2] this morning. The latter has had no application from any quarter whatever,[3] and seems doubtful whether Lord Orford's interest at Callington has not been too long neglected even to elect one.[4] The only chance is that,[5] and he offers to go down and see if Lord Orford honours a son of mine with his countenance.[6]

In consequence I have written the enclosed letter[7] to Lord Orford, which I shall send if you approve it. I am, dear Horry,

Yours sincerely,

HERTFORD

1. Charles Boone (ante 14 Aug. 1762, n. 17), M.P. (on Lord Orford's interest) Castle Rising 1757–68, 1784–96, Ashburton 1768–84. He was returned again for Ashburton unopposed 11 Oct. (The other seat was controlled by Robert Palk, who had a powerful 'natural interest' in the borough; see Namier and Brooke i. 249–50, iii. 245.)

2. William Moone (ca 1725–97), clerk in the Exchequer ca 1770–97 and Lord Orford's steward (OSSORY i. 135 and n. 8).

3. To fill the vacant seats at Callington.

4. I.e., one member. The Orford interest at Callington had been weakened by Lady Orford's insistence on keeping a share in the management of the borough, although she lived in Italy, and Lord Orford himself was neglectful of their interest there; see Namier and Brooke i. 225–6; MANN viii. 46–7.

5. However, see next note.

6. Hertford means his son Henry, who had been M.P. for Coventry on the corporation interest since 1766. In the current

election Hertford refused to let him stand again there. The ostensible reason was an affront Hertford had received from the corporation in 1769 when they reversed his election as recorder of Coventry, but more compelling reasons were Hertford's unpopularity there and the declining power of the corporation, which led him to anticipate his son's defeat if he stood again. However, HW wrote to Mann 6 Oct. 1774 that Orford had dispatched 'Mr Skreene' for Callington; William Skrine, an incumbent for the borough, and John Dyke Acland, also an Orford candidate, were returned unopposed 13 Oct. On 27 Dec. Henry replaced Herbert Mackworth, who chose to sit for Cardiff Boroughs, as M.P. for Midhurst on the government interest (MANN viii. 46; Namier and Brooke i. 225–6, 395–6, 400–1, iii. 91; Last Journals i. 390; T. W. Whitley, Parliamentary Representation of . . . Coventry, Coventry, 1894, pp. 168, 169, 171).

7. Missing.

To Hertford, Saturday 1 October 1774

Printed for the first time from a photostat of BM Add. MSS 23219, f. 41. This is HW's draft of his reply to the preceding letter, and is written on the preceding letter; presumably the reply was sent the same day.

My dear Lord,

I CAN only repeat what I said last night to your Lordship that having in consequence of a message from the Duke of P[ortland] sent his Grace word what measures I thought best for him to take about Lord O[rford]'s[1] boroughs, I must entreat your Lordship as I did last night to consult the Duke of P. first, as I should seem to be acting a double part, if I gave any advice without his Grace's knowledge.[2] I do beg that you will do so, not only for my sake, but as at this moment nothing could be so fatal as any disagreement in the party;[3] and should the Duke reproach me, I must avow that I had told your Lordship what answer I had sent to his Grace.[4] If he should approve it, I certainly should be glad one of your sons was the person.

Yours most sincerely,

H. W.

To Hertford, Sunday 2 October 1774

Missing; not sent. It was written in anger at Hertford's refusal to see him the night before, when HW had called to urge him to seek a seat for Conway in Parliament in case Grafton failed to bring him in; for HW's account of the episode (in *Last Journals* i. 390–1), see Appendix 10.

1. After 'O.'s' the word 'measures' has been crossed out in the MS.

2. Portland, a member of the Rockingham opposition, was currently sounding various boroughs on behalf of himself, Rockingham, and other friends (see Edmund Burke, *Correspondence*, Vol. III, ed. G. H. Guttridge, Cambridge, 1961, pp. 23, 29, 34–6, 40–2 *et passim*). He had attempted unsuccessfully to capture Callington in 1768, but apparently did not contest any of Orford's boroughs this time (see Namier and Brooke i. 225–6).

3. Presumably the Rockingham party,

the chief faction of the Opposition; see next note.

4. HW must mean that he wished to avoid any disagreement between Portland, a Rockinghamite, and Conway, who had been secretary of state in Rockingham's first administration, and was apparently still counted upon as a Rockingham supporter, though in fact he had for some time been pursuing an independent political line; HW and Hertford might be construed by Portland as acting in Conway's interest against his own.

From LADY HERTFORD, Sunday 2 October 1774

Missing. HW's account in *Last Journals* continues: 'As I expected, Lady Hertford wrote, said Lord Hertford had been angry at her not telling him I wanted to speak with him, and that, seeing his distress, and that there was no hurry, as the answer was not come from Euston [i.e., from the Duke of Grafton, declaring whether or not he intended bringing Conway again into Parliament], she had deferred telling him, thinking his business would be over; but that it lasted till half-an-hour past two. She added, "As soon as he comes from church, he goes to *Kew*, and will call on you when he comes back." ' HW 'did not believe the excuses, though with regard to Lady Hertford they were pretty true,' and Hertford's 'going to Kew *before* he saw me appeared indubitable evidence of a plot' between Hertford, the King, and Grafton to keep Conway out of Parliament (Conway had earlier in the year opposed government measures with respect to America) (*Last Journals* i. 382, 391–2; Namier and Brooke ii. 246).

To LADY HERTFORD, Sunday 2 October 1774

Missing. 'I sent a very civil note to Lady Hertford for all her goodness to me, but telling her that, after the indignity with which her Lord had treated both his brother and me, I could never enter his house again or have any friendship with him' (*Last Journals* i. 392). That afternoon Lady Hertford came to HW to remonstrate with him over his 'injustice,' and that night 'the Earl came to me,' and 'at last promised to lay down any sum to bring his brother into Parliament, and we parted very good friends' (ibid. i. 392–5). See next letter.

To CONWAY, Monday 3 October 1774

Missing. 'As I meant to keep them [Hertford and Conway] well together, I wrote by Lady Ailesbury, who went next day to Paris, a very moderate letter to Mr Conway, did justice to Lady Hertford, excused Lord Hertford, said nothing hard of the Duke of Grafton and took all the blame I could on myself' (*Last Journals* i. 396). Hertford informed HW 3 Oct. of Grafton's decision not to run Conway in the current elections; Thetford, his pocket borough, he reserved for his brother Charles Fitzroy and his uncle Charles Fitzroy Scudamore, while he conceded Bury St Edmunds to Sir Charles Davers and Augustus John Hervey. However, when Hervey was called to the upper House 18 March 1775, Grafton successfully ran Conway against William Hervey in the by-election for Hervey's place (27 March) (ibid. i. 395; Namier and Brooke i. 342, 378; see also *Last Journals* i. 449–50).

From Conway, Thursday 6 October 1774

Missing; written from Strasbourg; answered *post* 16 Oct. 1774.

To Conway, Sunday 16 October 1774

Printed from *Works* v. 163–5.

Strawberry Hill, Sunday, October 16, 1774.

I RECEIVED this morning your letter of the 6th from Strasburg;[1] and before you get this you will have had three from me by Lady Ailesbury.[2] One of them[3] should have reached you much sooner; but Lady A. kept it, not being sure where you was. It was in answer to one[4] in which you told me an anecdote, which in this last you ask if I had received.[5]

Your letters are always so welcome to me, that you certainly have no occasion for excusing what you say or do not say.[6] Your details amuse me, and so would what you suppress; for, though I have no military genius or curiosity, whatever relates to yourself must interest me. The honours you have received, though I have so little taste for such things myself, gave me great satisfaction; and I do not know whether there is not more pleasure in *not* being a prophet in one's own country, when one is almost received like Mahomet in every other. To be an idol at home, is no assured touchstone of merit. Stocks and stones[7] have been adored in fifty regions, but do not bear transplanting. The Apollo Belvedere and the Hercules Farnese[8] may lose their temples, but never lose their estimation, by travelling. Elections, you may be sure, are the only topic here at present—

1. Missing; Conway also wrote to Hertford from Strasbourg 6 Oct. (MS now WSL).

2. Those of 27 and 28 Sept., and the missing letter of 3 Oct. Lady Ailesbury, Mrs Damer, and Lady Harriet Stanhope left for Paris 4 Oct., arriving there 9 Oct.; Conway arrived 19 Oct., meeting them at the Hôtel de Danemark (*Last Journals* i. 396; Appendix 9).

3. That of 27 Sept.

4. The missing letter of ca 12–13 Sept.

5. HW does not allude to the anecdote in his letter of 27 Sept.

6. Conway was also apologetic to Hertford 6 Oct.: 'I have writ you so many long letters, I wish this may not be the most tiresome of all.'

7. A contemptuous phrase for 'gods of wood and stone'; see OED, *sub* 'stock,' sb.[1] 1d.

8. See MANN i. 249, n. 3.

I mean in England—not on this quiet hill, where I think of them as little as of the spot where the battle of Blenheim was fought.[9] They say there will not be much alteration, but the phoenix will rise from its ashes with most of its old plumes, or as bright. Wilkes at first seemed to carry all before him, besides having obtained the mayoralty of London at last.[10] Lady Hertford told me last Sunday,[11] that he would carry twelve members. I have not been in town since, nor know anything but what I collect from the papers; so, if my letter is opened, M. de Vergennes[12] will not amass any very authentic intelligence from my *dispatches*.

What I have taken notice of, is as follows: For the City Wilkes will have but three members:[13] he will lose Crosby;[14] and Townsend[15] will carry Oliver.[16] In Westminster, Wilkes will not have one;[17] his Humphrey Cotes is by far the lowest on the poll;[18] Lord Percy and Lord T. Clinton[19] are triumphant there. Her Grace of Northumberland[20] sits at a window in Covent Garden, harangues the mob, and is 'Hail, fellow, well met!' At Dover, Wilkes has

9. Conway wrote to Hertford 6 Oct. that he had ridden 'all over the field of Blenheim and examined it thoroughly'; this occurred 27 Sept. (Appendix 9). See his observations on the battle in his letter to Sir Robert Murray Keith 19 Nov. in Keith's *Memoirs and Correspondence*, ed. Mrs Gillespie Smyth, 1849, ii. 27.

10. He had been returned at the head of the poll for the mayoralty in 1772 and 1773, but was rejected both times by the court of aldermen. This year, returned again at the head of the poll 6 Oct., he was declared duly elected 8 Oct. (*Daily Adv.* 7, 10 Oct.).

11. See Coke, *Journals*, iv. 411.

12. Charles Gravier de Vergennes (1719–87), Chevalier, 1774; cr. (1779) Comte de Vergennes; minister of foreign affairs 1774–87 (MANN vii. 264, n. 16; viii. 17, n. 45).

13. Out of four places.

14. Brass Crosby (1725–93), M.P. Honiton 1768–74; lord mayor of London 1770–1. He finished sixth in the poll 18 Oct. Wilkes's successful candidates were John Sawbridge (first in the poll), George Hayle (second) and Frederick Bull (fourth) (Namier and Brooke i. 329).

15. James Townsend (1737–87), M.P. West Looe 1767–74, Calne 1782–7; lord mayor of London 1772–3. Once a follower of Wilkes, he had become his active enemy (Namier and Brooke iii. 537–8; *ante* 30 June 1769, n. 2, and 20 March 1770, n. 1).

16. Richard Oliver (1735–84), M.P. London 1770–80. Also a former follower of Wilkes, he had joined Townsend in opposition to him (Namier and Brooke iii. 224); he was returned third in the poll (ibid. i. 329).

17. His candidates were Lord Mahon, Lord Mountmorres, and Humphrey Cotes (ibid. i. 335).

18. As of 14 Oct. Cotes had polled only 81 votes, as compared with the next lowest total (Lord Mahon's) of 1200 (*Daily Adv.* 15 Oct.); he finished 26 Oct. with only 130 votes (ibid. 27 Oct.; Namier and Brooke loc. cit.).

19. Lord Thomas Pelham Clinton 1752–95; styled E. of Lincoln 1779–94; 3d D. of Newcastle-under-Lyme, 1794; army officer; M.P. Westminster 1774–80, East Retford 1781–94. He and Percy were returned at the head of the poll with 4774 and 4994 votes, respectively (ibid.).

20. Percy's mother.

carried one,[21] and probably will come in for Middlesex himself with Glynn.[22] There have been great endeavours to oppose him, but to no purpose.[23]—Of this I am glad, for I do not love a mob so near as Brentford; especially as my road[24] lies through it. Where he has any other interest I am too ignorant in these matters to tell you.[25] Lord John Cavendish is opposed at York, and at the beginning of the poll had the fewest numbers.[26] Charles Fox, like the ghost in *Hamlet*, has shifted to many quarters; but in most the cock crew, and he walked off.[27] In Southwark, there has been outrageous rioting; but I neither know the candidates, their connections, nor success.[28] This, perhaps, will appear a great deal of news at Paris: here, I dare to say, my butcher knows more.

I can tell you still less of America. There are two or three more ships with forces going thither,[29] and Sir William Draper as second in command.[30]

Of private news, except that Dyson[31] has had a stroke of palsy, and will die, there is certainly none;[32] for I saw that shrill *Morning*

21. John Trevanion (ca 1740–1810), M.P. Dover 1774–84, 1789–1806. He was returned unopposed, together with a government candidate, 11 Oct. (ibid. i. 445).

22. John Glynn (1722–79), M.P. Middlesex 1768–79. He and Wilkes were returned unopposed 20 Oct. (ibid. i. 331, 334).

23. See ibid. i. 334.

24. To London.

25. Nathaniel Polhill, a Wilkesite, was returned head of the poll for Southwark (see n. 28 below), while Sir Watkin Lewes, also a Wilkesite, was defeated at Worcester (Namier and Brooke i. 77, 425–6, iii. 40).

26. Cavendish and Charles Turner, both Rockingham candidates and the incumbents, were opposed by Martin Bladen Hawke, M.P. Saltash 1768–74, who came of an old Yorkshire family. According to a 'letter from York, Oct. 11,' printed *Daily Adv.* 14 Oct., at the end of the first day's poll Hawke led with 110 votes to Turner's 63 and Cavendish's 57; however, by the end of the voting (10 Oct.) Turner and Cavendish had emerged triumphant with 828 and 807 votes to Hawkes's 647 (Namier and Brooke i. 441, 443).

27. He was elected M.P. for Malmesbury 8 Oct. (ibid. i. 417).

28. Nathaniel Polhill, a Wilkesite, and

Henry Thrale, a government candidate, were returned 18 Oct. over Sir Abraham Hume, another government candidate, and William Lee (ibid. i. 387, ii. 652, iii. 306, 528).

29. 'Orders are come down for the *Asia* of 64 guns, *Scarborough* frigate, and *Falkland* sloop of war, to proceed to Boston as soon as possible. . . . Orders came down last night for 300 marines to get themselves in readiness to embark for America, and 300 from Plymouth; likewise the *Raisonable, Somerset,* and a frigate to get in readiness for the same' ('Extract of a letter from Gosport . . . Oct. 13,' printed *Daily Adv.* 17 Oct.). The same *Advertiser* also printed an 'extract of a letter from Chatham, Oct. 12,' announcing the dispatching of 'a detachment of marines . . . consisting of 150 men, exclusive of officers . . . from hence to Portsmouth, to be embarked in the ships now fitting out at that port for Boston.'

30. He is included in a list of generals for commands in America made out by the King at this period (Geo. III's *Corr.,* ed. Fortescue, iii. 162); however, he did not go to America.

31. Jeremiah Dyson.

32. Lord North wrote to the King 14 Oct.: 'Poor Mr Dyson was this morning

Post, Lady Greenwich, two hours ago, and she did not know a paragraph.

I forgot to mention to you M. de Maurepas. He was by far the ablest and most agreeable man I knew at Paris:[33] and if you stay, I think I could take the liberty of giving you a letter to him; though, as he is now so great a man,[34] and I remain so little an one, I don't know whether it would be quite so proper—though he was exceedingly good to me, and pressed me often to make him a visit in the country.—But Lord Stormont can certainly carry you to him—a better passport.[35]

There was one of my letters[36] on which I wish to hear from you. There are always English coming from Paris, who would bring such a parcel; at least you might send me one volume at a time, and the rest afterwards: but I should not care to have them ventured by the common conveyance. Madame du Deffand is negotiating for an enamel picture for me;[37] but if she obtains it, I had rather wait for it till you come.[38] The books I mean, are those I told you Lady A. and Mrs D. would give you a particular account of, for they know my mind exactly. Don't reproach me with not meeting you at Paris. Recollect what I suffered this time two years; and if you can have any notion of fear, imagine my dread of torture for five months and a half! When all the quiet of Strawberry did but just carry me through it, could I support it in the noise of a French hotel! and, what would be still worse, exposed to receive all visits? for the French, you know, are never more in public than in the act of death. I am like animals, and love to hide myself *when I am dying.* Thank God, I am now two days beyond the crisis when I expected my dreadful periodic visitant, and begin to grow very sanguine

attacked by a stroke of palsy, has lost the use of one side, and lies most dangerously ill at his house in Clifford Street' (Fortescue, op. cit. iii. 145). However, he survived until 1776.

33. See *ante* 5 Dec. 1765.

34. As Louis XVI's chief adviser; see *ante* 28 Sept. 1774, n. 4.

35. Stormont was British ambassador at Paris 1772–8 (D. B. Horn, *British Diplomatic Representatives 1689–1789,* 1932, pp. 24–5).

36. That of 3 Oct.; see *post* 29 Oct.

37. A miniature portrait of Mme

d'Olonne by Petitot which HW first saw in 1765; its owner, the collector Pierre-Jean Mariette, had died 10 Sept., and Mme du Deffand was negotiating with his heirs to purchase it for HW (DU DEFFAND iv. 95, n. 6, 96–8, 102, v. 269).

38. Mme du Deffand did not obtain it until Dec. 1775, when she purchased it for 3200 livres; it was brought over to HW by Horace Saint Paul the following March (ibid. iv. 245, 280). See 'Des. of SH,' *Works* ii. 475; it was sold SH xiv. 53 for £141 15*s.* to P. and D. Colnaghi for Robert Holford.

about the virtue of the bootikins. I shall even have courage to go tomorrow to Chalfont[39] for two days, as it is but a journey of two hours. I would not be a day's journey from hence for all Lord Clive's diamonds. This will satisfy *you*. I doubt Madame du Deffand is not so easily convinced: therefore pray do not drop a hint before her of blaming me for not meeting you; rather assure her you are persuaded it would have been too great a risk for me at this season. I wish to have her quite clear of my attachment to her; but that I do not always find so easy. You, I am sure, will find her all zeal and *empressement* for you and yours. Adieu!

To Lady Ailesbury, ca Thursday 20 October 1774

Missing. 'Mais vous, vous ne me parlez point de votre santé, vous mandez à la Milady que vous avez eu quelque ressentiment de goutte' (Mme du Deffand to HW 26 Oct. 1774, du Deffand iv. 105). Mme du Deffand was presumably mistaken about the gout; see *post* 7 Nov. 1774.

From Lady Ailesbury, ca Thursday 20 October 1774

Missing; mentioned *post* 29 Oct. 1774.

From Conway, Sunday 23 October 1774

Missing; answered *post* 29 Oct. 1774.

39. Seat of the Churchills.

To Conway, Saturday 29 October 1774

Printed from *Works* v. 165–8.

Strawberry Hill, October 29, 1774.

I HAVE received your letter of the 23d,[1] and it certainly overpays
me, when you thank instead of scolding me, as I feared.[2] A
passionate man has very little merit in being in a passion, and is
sure of saying many things he repents, as I do. I only hope you
think that I could not be so much in the wrong for everybody; nor
should have been perhaps even for you, if I had not been certain I
was the only person, at that moment, that could serve you essentially:
and at such a crisis, I am sure I should take exactly the same part
again, except in saying some things I did, of which I am ashamed![3]
I will say no more now on that topic, nor on anything relating to it,
because I have written my mind very fully, and you will know it soon.
I can only tell you now, that I approve extremely your way of
thinking, and hope you will not change it before you hear from
me, and know some material circumstances. You and Lady A. and
I agree exactly, and she and I certainly consider only *you*. I do not
answer her last,[4] because I could not help telling you how very kindly
I take your letter. All I beg is, that you would have no delicacy about
my serving you any way. You know it is a pleasure to me: anybody
else may have views that would embarrass you; and therefore, till
you are on the spot, and can judge for yourself (which I always insist
on, because you are cooler than I, and because, though I have no
interests to serve, I have passions which equally mislead one), it
will be wiser to decline all kind of proposals and offers. You will
avoid the plague of contested elections and solicitations; and I see
no reasons, at present, that can tempt you to be in a hurry.[5]

You must not expect to be Madame du Deffand's first favourite.
Lady Ailesbury has made such a progress there, that you will not
easily supplant her. I have received volumes in her praise.[6] You

1. Missing.
2. Conway was replying to HW's missing letter *ante* 3 Oct. 1774, in which he 'took all the blame' he could on himself for his recent conduct towards Hertford (see *ante* 27 Sept. 1774 *bis*, 2, 3 Oct. 1774).
3. 'A great deal of very intemperate in-

vective,' spoken in anger to Lady Ailesbury after their failure to see Hertford the night of 1 Oct. (Appendix 10).
4. Missing.
5. See *ante* 3 Oct. 1774.
6. 'Je ne saurais vous dire combien Mme Ailesbury me plaît' (Mme du Def-

CAROLINE CAMPBELL
Countess of Ailesbury,
from the original Bust in Marble
executed by her Daughter
the Hon.ble Anne Damer
1789.

James Roberts del.

John Jones sculp.

have a better chance with Madame de Cambis,[7] who is very agreeable; and I hope you are not such an English husband as not to conform to the manners of Paris while you are there.

I forgot to mention one or two of my favourite objects to Lady A. Nay, I am not sure she will taste one of them, the Church of the Celestines.[8] It is crowded with beautiful old tombs:[9] one of Francis II[10] whose beatitude is presumed from his being husband of the martyr Mary Stuart.[11] Another is the first wife of John, Duke of Bedford,[12] the regent of France. I think you was once there with me formerly.[13] The other is Richelieu's tomb, at the Sorbonne[14]—but that everybody is carried to see. The Hôtel de *Carnavalet*,[15] near the Place Royale, is worth looking at, even for the façade, as you drive by.[16] But of all earthly things the most worth seeing is the house at Versailles, where the King's pictures, not hung up, are kept.[17] There is a treasure past belief, though in sad order, and piled one against another. Monsieur de Guerchy once carried me thither;[17a] and you may certainly get leave. At the Luxembourg are some hung up, and

fand to HW 16 Oct. 1774, DU DEFFAND iv. 101). Mme du Deffand's most fulsome praise of Lady Ailesbury is in her letter to HW 28 Oct. 1774: 'Milady Ailesbury est certainement la meilleure des femmes, la plus douce, et la plus tendre. . . . Son humeur me paraît très égale, sa politesse noble et aisée' (ibid. iv. 108).

7. Gabrielle-Françoise-Charlotte d'Alsace-Hénin-Liétard (1729–1809), m. (1755) Jacques-François-Xavier-Régis-Ignace, Vicomte de Cambis (ibid. i. 311, n. 9 *et passim*).

8. In the Rue du Petit-Musc, near the Bastille. The church was sacked in the Revolution and demolished in 1849; HW had visited it in 1739, 1765 and 1766, and again in 1771 (GRAY i. 163 and n. 14; 'Paris Journals,' DU DEFFAND v. 271, 308, 337).

9. Most of them are now in the Louvre (Marquis de Rochegude and Maurice Dumolin, *Guide pratique à travers le vieux Paris*, 1923, p. 135); they are described at length in Hurtaut and Magny, *Dictionnaire historique de la ville de Paris*, 1779, ii. 102–19.

10. (1544–60), K. of France 1559–60.

11. Queen of Scots; they were married in 1558. The 'tomb' is a votive column with a bronze urn on top, now in the basilica of St-Denis; one of three inscriptions on the pedestal of the column proclaims: '. . . tanto veræ fidei assertori, generosam Christi martyrem Mariam Stuard conjugem habuisse, quædam fuit veræ immortalitatis assertio' (ibid. ii. 108; Rochegude and Dumolin, loc. cit.; see also Cole's *Journal of My Journey to Paris in . . . 1765*, ed. Stokes, 1931, p. 225).

12. John (1389–1435), cr. (1414) D. of Bedford; regent of France, 1422; m. (1423) Anne (d. 1432) of Burgundy. The French and Latin epitaph on her tomb, which is described ibid. 221, is given in Hurtaut and Magny, op. cit. ii. 104; her statue is now in the Louvre (Rochegude and Dumolin, loc. cit.).

13. In 1739 (GRAY i. 163; connecting note between *ante* 24 March and ca 8 Nov. 1739 NS).

14. See GRAY i. 165, n. 31.

15. Where Madame de Sévigné resided (HW).

16. HW had purchased an oil of the Hôtel by Raguenet in 1766 which he hung in the Breakfast Room at SH (DU DEFFAND ii. 30, n. 10, v. 304, n. 267).

17. See *ante* 2 Oct. 1765.

17a. In 1765; see ibid.

one particularly is worth going to see alone: it is the Deluge by Nicolo Poussin,[18] as Winter.[19] The three other seasons[20] are good for nothing—but the Deluge is the first picture in the world of its kind.[21] You will be shocked to see the glorious pictures at the Palais Royal[22] transplanted to new canvases, and new painted and varnished, as if they were to be scenes at the opera—at least, they had treated half a dozen of the best so, three years ago,[23] and were going on. The Prince of Monaco[24] has a few fine, but still worse used; one of them shines more than a looking-glass.[25] I fear the exposition of pictures[26] is over for this year; it is generally very *diverting*.[27] I, who went into every church of Paris, can assure you there are few worth it, but the Invalids[28]—except the *scenery* at St-Roch,[29] about one or two o'clock at noon, when the sun shines; the Carmelites,[30] for the Guido[31] and the portrait of Madame de la Valière[32] as a Magdalen;[33] the Val de Grâce,[34] for a moment; the *treasure* at Notre

18. (1594–1665).

19. Winter or the Flood, one of the Four Seasons, painted for the Duc de Richelieu between 1660 and 1664; now in the Louvre (Anthony Blunt, *The Paintings of Nicolas Poussin: A Critical Catalogue*, 1966, pp. 9–10).

20. Spring or the Earthly Paradise, Summer or Ruth and Boaz, and Autumn or the Spies with the Grapes from the Promised Land (ibid.). All four paintings are reproduced in idem, *Nicolas Poussin*, New York, 1967, plates 242–5.

21. It has been 'praised by men of such different tastes as Diderot, Delacroix, and Turner' (idem, *Paintings of . . . Poussin*, p. 9).

22. Listed Hurtaut and Magny, op. cit. iii. 739–46.

23. HW had visited the Palais Royal in July 1771 ('Paris Journals,' du Deffand v. 336).

24. Honoré-Camille-Léonor Goyon-de-Matignon de Grimaldi (1720–95), Prince de Monaco.

25. See 'Paris Journals,' ibid. v. 335; Chute 344–5.

26. At the Louvre.

27. He means from their extreme bad taste (Mary Berry). HW had called the pictures 'in general, tawdry and hard' in 1765 ('Paris Journals,' du Deffand v. 261).

28. Described Hurtaut and Magny, op. cit. iii. 362–7; see also Cole, op. cit. 148–9, 151.

29. In the Rue St-Honoré.

30. In the Rue d'Enfer.

31. Guido Reni's 'Annunciation'; see Ossory i. 261 and nn. 31, 32.

32. Françoise-Louise de la Baume le Blanc (1644–1710), Duchesse de la Vallière; mistress of Louis XIV.

33. 'La Madeleine Repentante,' painted by Charles Le Brun (1619–90) ca 1656–7 for the Carmelites in the Rue d'Enfer; it was removed in 1792 to the convent of the Petits-Augustins, and in 1793 to the Musée Central des Arts; it is presently in the Louvre (Henry Jouin, *Charles Le Brun et les arts sous Louis XIV*, 1889, pp. 83, 493–4; [Versailles. Musée National], *Charles Le Brun . . . [catalogue de l'exposition au] château de Versailles . . . 1963*, Versailles, 1963, p. 25; reproduction facing p. 67). The tradition that the painting is of Mlle de la Vallière *en Madeleine* is incorrect; though she retired at the age of 30 to the convent of the Carmelites in the Rue d'Enfer, this was in 1674, some 17 or 18 years after the painting was executed (ibid. 25; Jouin, op. cit. 493; nbg; this corrects du Deffand v. 264, n. 48).

34. A Benedictine abbey in the Rue St-Jacques. HW noted in 1765 that there was 'nothing remarkable' there ('Paris Journals,' ibid. v. 265); the church is described Hurtaut and Magny, op. cit. i. 122–8.

Dame; the Sainte-Chapelle, where in the ante-chapel are two very large enamelled portraits;[35] the tomb of Condé at the Great Jesuits in the Rue St-Antoine,[36] if not shut up; and the little church of St-Louis in the Louvre,[37] where is a fine tomb[38] of Cardinal Fleury,[39] but large enough to stand on Salisbury Plain.[40] One thing some of you *must* remember, as you return; nay, it is better to go soon to St-Denis, and Madame du Deffand must get you a particular order to be shown (which is never shown without) the effigies of the kings.[41] They are in presses over the treasure which is shown,[42] and where is the glorious antique cameo cup;[43] but the countenance of Charles IX[44] is so horrid and remarkable, you would think he had died on the morrow of the St-Barthélemi, and waked full of the recollection.[45] If you love enamels and exquisite medals, get to see

35. HW presumably means the 'enamel pictures . . . [of] Francis I and Queen . . . kneeling above 8 inches diameter; well done and preserved,' in one of 'two little altars' in the Sainte-Chapelle, mentioned 'Paris Journals,' DU DEFFAND v. 276.

36. The *maison professe* of the Jesuits in Paris from 1580 till their expulsion from France in 1763; convent of Saint-Louis-la-Couture from 1768 to 1790 (Rochegude and Dumolin, op. cit. 115). Cole, visiting the church in Nov. 1765, observed (op. cit. 293–4): 'The heart of the Prince of Condé is in an urn, held by angels, under the arch which communicates with the side chapel where Lewis 13 his heart is preserved; which arch is the east side of St Ignatius's chapel. This is one of the finest things I saw at Paris.'

37. A new church, consecrated in 1744, situated near the Louvre and later destroyed (DU DEFFAND v. 280, n. 153).

38. A mausoleum.

39. André-Hercule de Fleury (1653–1743), cardinal; minister of Louis XV.

40. HW describes the mausoleum in 'Paris Journals' (ibid. v. 280) as 'gigantic beyond all proportion.' Fleury is represented 'expirant entre les bras de la Religion. La France désignée par son écusson, exprime ses regrets: derrière le piedestal, s'élève une pyramide, qui porte une urne, du pied de laquelle descend une grande draperie, dont l'artiste [Jean-Baptiste le Moine] se sert pour dérober presqu'entièrement la figure hideuse de la Mort qui se présente au Cardinal' (Hurtaut and Magny, op. cit. iii. 422).

41. HW had seen them with Cole 22 Nov. 1765: 'Mr Walpole had been informed . . . [of] several wax figures of some of the later Kings of France, and asked one of the monks for leave to see them, as they were not commonly shown, or much known: accordingly, in 4 cupboards, above those in which the jewels, crosses, busts, and curiosities were kept, were 8 ragged figures of so many monarchs of this country, to Lewis 13, which must be very like, as their faces were taken off in wax immediately after their decease' (Cole, op. cit. 306).

42. Illustrated and described in M. Félibien, *Histoire de l'abbaye royale de Saint-Denys,* 1706, pp. 536–44 and plates 1–5.

43. The so-called 'coupe des Ptolomées,' allegedly made by order of Ptolemy II (309–247 B.C.), King of Egypt; it is now in the Bibliothèque Nationale, Cabinet des Médailles (*Abbot Suger on the Abbey Church of St-Denis and its Art Treasures,* ed. E. Panofsky, Princeton, N.J., 1946, p. xiv; Félibien, op. cit. 544–5 and plate 6). Cole describes it as 'a curious cup or vase of one entire oriental agate' (op. cit. 320); Gray remarks in a letter to West 12 April 1739 (he had seen the cup with HW on their way to Paris) that 'the beauty of the stone and sculpture upon it (representing the mysteries of Bacchus) [is] beyond expression admirable' (Gray, *Correspondence,* ed. Toynbee and Whibley, Oxford, 1935, i. 102).

44. (1550–74), King of France 1560–74.

45. Charles IX had given his consent

the collection of a Monsieur d'Henery,[46] who lives in the corner of the street where Sir John Lambert[47] lives—I forget its name. There is an old man[48] behind the Rue de Colombier, who has a great but bad collection of old French portraits; I delighted in them, but perhaps you would not. *I*, you may be sure, hunted out everything of that sort. The convent and collection of St-Germain,[49] I mean that over against the Hôtel du Parc Royal,[50] is well worth seeing[51]—but I forget names strangely.—Oh! delightful—Lord Cholmondeley[52] sends me word he goes to Paris on Monday: I shall send this and my other letter[53] by him. It was him I meant; I knew he was going, and had prepared it.

Pray take care to lock up your papers in a strong box that nobody can open. They imagine you are at Paris on some commission,[54] and there is no trusting French hotels or servants. America is in a desperate situation. The accounts from the Congress are not expected before the 10th, and expected very warm.[55] I have not time to tell you some manœuvres against them that will make your blood curdle.[56] Write to me when you can by private hands, as I will to you. There are always English passing backwards and forwards.

to the St Bartholomew's Day Massacre of French Huguenot leaders (24 Aug. 1572), chiefly plotted by his mother, Catherine de' Medici.

46. Michelet d'Ennery (1709–86), numismatist; collector (du Deffand iv. 136, v. 325).

47. (1728–99), 3d Bt.

48. M. Doumenil in the Rue des Marais; not further identified ('Paris Journals,' ibid. v. 313).

49. St-Germain-des-Prés.

50. HW's Paris hotel; see Cole, op. cit. 52.

51. See 'Paris Journals,' du Deffand v. 290; Hurtaut and Magny, op. cit. i. 96–100.

52. George James Cholmondeley (1749–

1827), styled Vct Malpas, 1764–70; 4th Earl of Cholmondeley, 1770; cr. (1815) Marquess of Cholmondeley; HW's great-nephew.

53. To Mme du Deffand, missing; see *post* 23 Nov. 1774.

54. See *ante* 7 Sept. 1774, n. 2.

55. See Mann viii. 61 and n. 15; *post* 15 Dec. 1774.

56. Besides the usual ships preparing to sail for Boston, the *Daily Advertiser* 31 Oct. reported *sub* Boston, 24 Sept., that Gen. Gage had had 'four 24-pounders and eight nine-pounders' placed at the fortifications in the avenues, and trenches dug around the town, as protective measures.

From Lady Ailesbury, ca Tuesday 1 November 1774

Missing. Lady Mary Coke writes in her *Journals*, iv. 423, *sub* 5 Nov. that HW 'has had two letters' from Lady Ailesbury; the first is mentioned *ante* 29 Oct. 1774, while this one was presumably answered by HW's letter to Lady Ailesbury *post* 7 Nov. 1774.

From Conway, ca Friday 4 November 1774

A fragment of a letter otherwise missing; printed from *Works* v. 170, n. 2. See *post* 12 Nov. 1774, n. 13, for another possible fragment from this letter.

ON St Hubert's[1] Day in the morning I had the honour of being presented to the King:[2] 'twas a good day and an excellent deed. You may be sure I was well received, the French are so polite! and their Court so polished!—The Emperor[3] indeed talked to me every day; so did the King of Prussia regularly and much:[4] but that was not to be compared to the extraordinary reception of his Most Christian Majesty, who, when I was presented, did not stop, nor look to see what sort of an animal was offered to his notice, but carried his head as it seemed somewhat higher, and passed his way.[5]

1. (ca 655–727), Bishop of Liège. His feast is 3 Nov.

2. At Fontainebleau. Mme du Deffand wrote to HW 31 Oct. 1774 that Conway, presumably with Lady Ailesbury and Mrs Damer, was to set out for Fontainebleau 1 Nov. and return 4 Nov.; she wrote 6 Nov. 1774 that 'vos Miladys ont été passer deux jours [presumably 2–3 Nov.] à Fontainebleau . . . elles ont parfaitement réussi,' omitting any mention of Conway's reception there (DU DEFFAND iv. 110, 112).

3. Joseph II. For his gracious reception of Conway at Vienna 3 Aug., see *ante* 18

Aug. 1774, n. 3; he also treated Conway with distinction at his camp at Pest 19–25 Aug., (Conway to Hertford 21, 31 Aug., MSS now WSL); see also David Scott, 'Journal of a Military Tour of the Continent with Gen. Conway,' pp. 129–39.

4. See *ante* 18 Aug. 1774, n. 3, 27 Sept. 1774, n. 1.

5. See Conway's further remarks on his presentation in his letter to Sir Robert Murray Keith 19 Nov. in Keith's *Memoirs and Correspondence*, ed. Mrs Gillespie Smyth, 1849, ii. 30.

To Lady Ailesbury, Monday 7 November 1774

Printed from the MS now WSL. First printed, with omissions, *Works* v. 565–7; first printed in full Toynbee ix. 81–4 and *Supp.* ii. 144–6. For the history of the MS see *ante* 23 Aug. 1760; it was marked by HW for inclusion in *Works*.
Address: À Madame Madame la Comtesse d'Ailesbury.

Strawberry Hill, Nov. 7, 1774.

I HAVE written such tomes to Mr Conway, Madam, and have so nothing new to write, that I might as well methinks begin and end like the Lady to her husband, 'Je vous écris parce que je n'ai rien à faire, je finis parce que je n'ai rien à vous dire.'[1] Yes, I have two complaints to make, one of your Ladyship, the other of myself. You tell me nothing of Lady Harriot:[2] have you no tongue or the French no eyes? or are her eyes employed in nothing but seeing? What a vulgar employment for a fine woman's eyes after she is risen from her toilet! I declare I will ask no more questions—what is it to me whether she is admired or not? I should know how charming she is though all Europe were blind, I hope I am not to be told by any barbarous nation upon earth what beauty and grace are!

For myself I am guilty of the gout in my elbow; the left, witness my handwriting—whether I caught cold by the deluge in the night, or whether the bootikins like the water of Styx can only preserve the parts they surround, I doubt they have saved me but three weeks, for so long my reckoning has been out.[3] However as I feel nothing in my feet, I flatter myself that this Pindaric transition[4] will not be a regular ode, but a fragment, the more valuable for being imperfect.

Now for my gazette. Marriages, nothing done. Intrigues, more in the political than civil way. Births, under par since Lady Berkeley left off breeding.[5] Gaming, low water. Deaths, Lord Morton,[6] Lord Wentworth,[7] Duchess Douglas.[8] Election stock, more buyers than

1. Recounted in *Walpoliana* i. 4.
2. Stanhope, who accompanied Lady Ailesbury to Paris; see *ante* 16 Oct. 1774, n. 1 and *post* 12, 23 Nov. 1774.
3. See *ante* 16 Oct. 1774.
4. See Dalrymple 61; Chatterton 297; Berry i. 175.
5. A standing joke of HW's, alluding to the triplets she bore to Lord Berkeley in

1748; see *ante* 29 Aug. 1748 OS, 14 July 1761.
6. Sholto Charles Douglas (1732–25 Sept. 1774), 15th Earl of Morton, 1768. He died at Taormina, in Sicily.
7. Edward Noel (1715–31 Oct. 1774), 9th Bn Wentworth, 1745; cr. (1762) Vct Wentworth.
8. Died 24 Oct.

sellers. Promotions, Mr Wilkes as high as he can go[9]—apropos he was told Lord Chancellor[10] intended to signify to him that the King did not approve the City's choice; he replied, 'Then I shall signify to his Lordship that I am at least as fit to be Lord Mayor as he to be Lord Chancellor'[11]—this being more gospel than everything Mr Wilkes says, the formal approbation was given.[12]

Mr Burke has succeeded at Bristol,[13] and Sir James Peachey[14] will miscarry in Sussex.[15] I fear it costs the Duke[16] a great sum[17]—but what care you, Madam, about our Parliament; you will see the *rentrée* of the old one,[18] with songs and epigrams into the bargain. We do not shift our Parliaments with so much gaiety. Money in one hand, and abuse in t'other—those are all the arts we know. *Wit and a gamut* I don't believe ever signified a Parliament, whatever the glossaries may say,[19] for they never produce pleasantry and harmony[20]—perhaps you may not taste this Saxon pun, but I know it will make the Antiquarian Society die with laughing.

Expectation hangs on America. The result of the General Assem-

9. As lord mayor of London.

10. Henry Bathurst (1714–94), cr. (1771) Bn of Apsley; 2d E. Bathurst, 1775; lord chancellor 1771–8.

11. HW records in *Mem. Geo. III* iv. 174 that the legal profession punned on Lord Apsley's ignorance, calling him 'Lord *Absque*'; Wraxall says of him that he 'may probably be considered as the least able lawyer to whom the Great Seal of this country was confided, in the course of the eighteenth century' (*Historical Memoirs of His Own Time*, 1836, ii. 203).

12. 3 Nov. (*Daily Adv.* 4 Nov.).

13. He was returned for Bristol 3 Nov. with Henry Cruger (Namier and Brooke i. 283–6).

14. (1723–1808), 4th Bt, 1765; cr. (1794) Bn Selsey; M.P. Seaford 1755–68.

15. He finished third and last in the poll 20 Oct. (ibid. i. 388); see n. 17.

16. Of Richmond.

17. In supporting Sir Thomas Spencer Wilson against Peachey. The Duke and Thomas Pelham, the leading patrons in the county, had promised to be neutral, agreeing that they and their adherents would give one vote to Richmond's brother, Lord George Lennox, while the other two candidates, Peachey and Sir Thomas Spencer Wilson, were to contest the re-

maining seat unaided (ibid.). However, Richmond, at least, appears not to have observed the neutrality; Lady Mary Coke, who was for Peachey, writes in *Journals,* iv. 425, *sub* 6 Nov., that 'the Duke of Richmond has behaved most shamefully: he promised a neutrality, since which his Grace's servants have voted for Sir Thomas Willson, and the Duchess took a meal man into her coach because he was a friend to Sir Thomas.' John Baker Holroyd wrote on 25 Nov. 1774 to congratulate Wilson on having freed the country from 'lordly nominations,' presumably referring to the support Peachey received from the Court (Namier and Brooke, loc. cit., iii. 255–6); it was perhaps in opposition to this outside support that Richmond took up Wilson's cause, Wilson having been nominated by an assembly of Sussex freeholders (ibid. iii. 646–7).

18. The old Parliament of Paris, banished in 1771, was restored by a *lit de justice* of 12 Nov. (Mann viii. 55, n. 5).

19. The Witenagemot was the assembly of the Witan, the King's council of wise men in Anglo-Saxon times; the term has been used by transference to denote the assembly of modern parliaments (OED).

20. HW by 'gamut' means the musical gamut or scale; see ibid.

bly[21] is expected in four or five days. If one may believe the papers, which one should not believe, the other-side-of-the-waterists are not *doux comme des moutons*,[22] and yet we do intend to eat them. I was in town on Monday;[23] the Duchess of Beaufort[24] graced our loo, and made it as rantipole[25] as a Quaker's meeting.[26] Loois Quinze[27] I believe is arrived by this time, but I fear without quinze louis.

Your herb-snuff and the four glasses are lying in my warehouse, but I can hear of no ship going to Paris.[28] You are now at Fontainebleau,[29] but not thinking of Francis I, the Queen of Sweden[30] and Monaldeschi.[31] It is terrible that one cannot go to courts that are gone! You have supped with the Chevalier de Boufflers;[32] did he act everything in the world, and sing everything in the world, and laugh at everything in the world?[33] Has Madame de Cambis sung to you 'Sans dépit, sans légèreté?'[34] Has Lord Cholmondeley delivered my packet?[35] I hear I have hopes of Madame d'Olonne.[36] Gout or no gout I think I shall be little in town till after Christmas. My elbow

21. I.e., the Continental Congress; see *post* 15 Dec. 1774.

22. For instance, the *Daily Adv.* 5 Nov. printed 'the instructions given to the deputies [from North Carolina] in General Congress,' expressing that colony's 'steady adherence to the first law of nature, a firm and resolute defence of our persons and properties against all unconstitutional encroachments whatsoever.'

23. 31 Oct.

24. Elizabeth Berkeley (ca 1719–99), m. (1740) Lord Charles Noel Somerset (d. 1756), 4th Duke of Beaufort, 1745.

25. 'Wild, disorderly, rakish' (OED).

26. HW alludes elsewhere to her stiff, formal manner; see especially BERRY i. 86–7 and n. 19.

27. This was a cant name given to a lady of their society who was very fond of, and had lost much money at loo (Mary Berry), here presumably Lady Powis, who had been at her seat in Montgomeryshire supporting the candidacy of William Mostyn Owen for Parliament (see *ante* 27 Sept. 1774), and was now in town playing loo. Lady Mary Coke wrote of her, op. cit. iv. 426, *sub* 8 Nov.: 'Lady Powis paid me the ten guineas she owed me before I was in Yorkshire. . . . She won nine and twenty; and played with so

much prudence that she will not lose the sums she has done.'

28. HW's packet arrived 1 Dec., together with 'quatre petits cornets' for Mme du Deffand (Mme du Deffand to HW, 4 Dec. 1774, DU DEFFAND iv. 116).

29. See *ante* ca 4 Nov. 1774.

30. Christina (1626–89), Queen of Sweden 1644–54.

31. Marchese Gian Rinaldo Monaldeschi (d. 1657), equerry to Queen Christina; executed for treachery by other members of her entourage at Fontainebleau in 1657 (Georgina Masson, *Queen Christina*, New York, 1969, pp. 270, 289–93 *et passim*).

32. Stanislas-Jean de Boufflers (1737–1815), Chevalier de Boufflers; Marquis de Remiencourt (DU DEFFAND *passim*).

33. See *post* 12, 23 Nov. 1774.

34. The first words of a favourite French air (Mary Berry); see DU DEFFAND iii. 137, 152, iv. 338; *post* 23 Nov. 1774.

35. See ibid.

36. An enamel portrait by Petitot of Catherine-Henriette d'Angennes (1634–1714), m. (1652) Louis de la Trémoïlle, Comte d'Olonne; Mme du Deffand wrote to HW 31 Oct. 1774: 'Ne croyez pas que j'oublie la miniature . . . j'espère que nous l'obtiendrons' (DU DEFFAND iv. 111). See *ante* 16 Oct. 1774, nn. 37–8.

makes me bless myself that I am not at Paris. Old age is no such uncomfortable thing, if one gives one's self up to it with a good grace, and don't drag it about

> To midnight dances and the public show.[37]

If one stays quietly in one's own house in the country, and cares for nothing but one's self, scolds one's servants, condemns everything that is new, and recollects how charming a thousand things were formerly that were very disagreeable, one gets over the winters very well, and the summers get over themselves.

Lady Villiers[38] is returned to Henley, and Lord Hertford says, grown fat. I long for more journals of you; Madame du D[effand] tells me when you are there, but that is not sufficient.

PS. Since I wrote my letter, a person came in, and told me with a face of very grave concern that there was happened a great political event—Mr Bradshaw[39] was dead!—I had much ado to keep from laughing out. Apropos, my footman David[40] fell off the coachbox t'other night, and was near being killed.

From Conway, ca Tuesday 8 November 1774

Missing; presumably the second of the two letters answered *post* 12 Nov. 1774.

---

37. Pope, 'Elegy to the Memory of an Unfortunate Lady,' l. 58.

38. Hertford's daughter Lady Gertrude, m. (1772) George Mason Villiers, Vct Villiers.

39. Thomas Bradshaw (1733–6 Nov. 1774), M.P.; secretary to the Treasury 1767–70; a lord of the Admiralty 1772–4. HW calls him in *Last Journals* i. 407 a 'low but useful tool of Administration.' For the circumstances of his death, see *post* 12 Nov. 1774 and n. 4.

40. David Monnerat (d. 1785), HW's Swiss footman.

To Conway, Saturday 12 November 1774

Printed from *Works* v. 168–71.

Strawberry Hill, November 12, 1774.

I HAVE received a delightful letter from you of four sheets,[1] and another since.[2] I shall not reply to the campaigning part (though much obliged to you for it), because I have twenty other subjects more pressing to talk of. The first is to thank you for your excessive goodness to my dear old friend[3]—she has some indiscretions, and *you must not have any to her;* but she has the best heart in the world, and I am happy, at her great age, that she has spirits enough not to be always upon her guard. A bad heart, especially after long experience, is but too apt to overflow *inwardly* with prudence. At least, as I am but too like her, and have corrected too few of my faults, I would fain persuade myself that some of them flow from a good principle—but I have not time to talk of myself, though you are much too partial to me, and give me an opportunity; yet I shall not take it.

Now for English news, and then your letter again.

There has been a great mortality here; though death has rather been *prié* than a volunteer. Bradshaw, as I told Lady Ailesbury last post, shot himself.[4] He is dead, totally undone. Whether that alone was the cause, or whether he had not done something worse, I doubt. I cannot conceive that, with his resources, he should have been hopeless—and to suspect him of delicacy, impossible!

A ship is arrived from America, and I doubt with very bad news,[5] for none but trifling letters have yet been given out—but I am here, see nobody that knows anything, and only hear by accident from people that drop in. The sloop that is to bring the result of the General Assembly is not yet come. There are indeed rumours, that

1. Presumably Conway's letter to HW ca 4 Nov. 1774.
2. Missing.
3. Mme du Deffand.
4. HW repeats this allegation in *Last Journals* i. 407, citing overwhelming debts as the motive behind the shooting; see also Lady Mary Coke, *Journals*, iv. 426; Thomas Hutchinson, *Diary and Letters*, ed. P. O. Hutchinson, 1883–6, i. 288–9, 303. However, the *London Chronicle* 5–8 Nov., xxxvi. 447, simply reports his death 'after a few days' illness,' while C. W. Cornwall wrote to Charles Jenkinson 7 Nov. that he 'died of a fever' (BM Add. MSS 38470, f. 146, quoted Namier and Brooke ii. 110).
5. See MANN viii. 56, n. 10.

both the non-importation and even non-exportation have been decreed;[6] and that the flame is universal. I hope this is exaggerated! yet I am told the stocks will fall very much in a day or two.[7]

I have nothing to tell Lady Ailesbury, but that I hear a deplorable account of the opera.[8] There is a new puppet-show at Drury Lane, as fine as scenes can make it, called *The Maid of the Oaks,*[9] and as dull as the author could not help making it.

Except M. D'Hérouville I know all the people you name.[10] C.[11] I doubt by things I have heard formerly, may have been a *concussionnaire.*[12] The Duke, your *protecteur,*[13] is mediocre enough: you would have been more pleased with his wife. The Chevalier's[14] bon mot is excellent, and so is he. He has as much *bouffonnerie* as the Italians, with more wit and novelty. His impromptu verses often

6. 'Letters from Philadelphia gave an account that the Congress had agreed on a non-importation, to commence the first day of December next' ('Extract of a letter from New York, Oct. 5,' printed *Public Adv.* 11 Nov.). See *post* 15 Dec. 1774.

7. A false rumour; see 'Prices of Stocks' for Nov. in GM 1774, xliv. 544.

8. Lady Mary Coke reports, op. cit. iv. 425, *sub* 8 Nov., that 'almost everybody' went to the opera that night, where they heard *Armida,* 'a new serious opera' by Antonio Sacchini (*London Stage* Pt IV, iii. 1847–8 and index). Despite the 'deplorable account' HW heard, the opera ran through April for a total of 13 performances; 'alterations, a new duet, and new songs by several eminent masters' were introduced into the performance of 7 Jan. 1775 (ibid. iii. 1847–86 *passim*).

9. By Gen. John Burgoyne, first performed 5 Nov. (ibid. iii. 1846). 'This piece is got up in a most superb manner. The scenery is beyond description fine' (William Hopkins, MS Diary, 1769–76, quoted ibid.). 'The fable . . . [is] too simple and artificial, as well as its *dénouement* too stale and insipid, to prove either interesting or entertaining. . . . Had it not appeared obvious that the whole was intended as a mere vehicle for a splendid spectacle, we do not suppose . . . that the author's labours would have been tolerated. The very excellent scenery, however . . . preserved this piece from that damnation which, as a dramatic production,

it richly merited' (*Westminster Magazine,* Nov. 1774, ii. 601). See also Hans Graf, *The Dramatic Works of General John Burgoyne,* Berne, 1915, pp. 15–21.

10. Mrs Toynbee identifies Hérouville as Antoine de Ricouart (ca 1713–82), Comte d'Hérouville de Claye. However, since Mme du Deffand had written to HW 10 March 1771 of this Hérouville's appointment as 'directeur des troupes' (DU DEFFAND iii. 41), and HW had met a 'M. Hérouville,' probably this one, at the Richmonds' in Paris in 1766 ('Paris Journals,' ibid. v. 294), HW means either that he does not know Hérouville well enough to give his impressions of him, or that the M. d'Hérouville in question is another man whom he had never met, perhaps the Comte's half-brother, Antoine-Jean de Ricouart (1722–86), Marquis d'Hérouville, who was also an army officer. See La Chenaye-Desbois xvii. 52–4; *Répertoire . . . de la Gazette de France,* ed. de Granges de Surgères, 1902–6, ii. 666.

11. Not identified.

12. An embezzler of public funds.

13. The Duc de la Valière, of whom Mr Conway had said [presumably in one of the letters HW is answering] that, when presented to him, 'his reception was what might be called good, but rather *de protection* [i.e., patronizing]' (Mary Berry). This was Louis-César de la Baume le Blanc (1708–80), Duc de la Vallière (DU DEFFAND *passim*).

14. De Boufflers (*ante* 7 Nov. 1774).

admirable. Get Madame du Deffand to show you his 'Embassy to the Princess Christine,'[15] and his verses on his eldest uncle,[16] beginning, *Si Monsieur de Veau*.[17] His second uncle[18] has parts, but they are not so natural. Madame de Caraman is a very good kind of woman, but has not a quarter of her sister's[19] parts. Madame de Mirepoix is *the* agreeable woman of the world, when she pleases—but there must not be a card in the room. Lord ———[20] has acted like himself; that is, unlike anybody else. You know, I believe, that I think him a very good speaker;[21] but I have little opinion of his judgment and knowledge of the world, and a great opinion of his affectation and insincerity. The Abbé Raynal, though he wrote that fine work on the *commerce des deux Indes*,[22] is the most tiresome creature in the world.[23] The first time I met him[24] was at the dull Baron d'Olbach's:[25] we were twelve at table: I dreaded opening my mouth in French, before so many people and so many servants: he began questioning me, cross the table, about our colonies, which I understand as I do Coptic. I made him signs I was deaf. After dinner he found I was not, and never forgave me. Mademoiselle Raucoux[26] I never saw till you told me Madame du Deffand said she was *démoniaque sans chaleur!* What painting! I see her now. Le Kain[27] sometimes pleased

15. Marie-Christine (1735–82), Abbess of Remiremont, dau. of Friedrich Augustus of Saxony, King of Poland (du Deffand i. 40, n. 4). The verses, and an account of their composition, may be found in Lætitia Matilda Hawkins, *Memoirs*, 1824, ii. 207–9; Gaston Maugras, *Les dernières années du Roi Stanislas*, 1906, p. 361; Nesta H. Webster, *The Chevalier de Boufflers*, 1916, pp. 30–1.

16. The Prince de Beauvau.

17. 'Si Monsieur de Vaux / Était un peu plus beau, / Que Monsieur de Beauvau / Fût un peu moins beau,' etc. The *impromptu* plays on the contrast in appearance between his uncle, who was uncommonly handsome, and a Monsieur de Vaux, who was very plain, and on the similarity of their names (Hawkins, op. cit. ii. 210–11). Copies of these verses in Wiart's hand are in a quarto notebook entitled by Wiart, 'Œuvres de Mr Le Chevalier de Boufflers,' which was bequeathed by Mme du Deffand to HW and is now wsl (Hazen, *Cat. of HW's Lib.*, No. 2545).

18. Ferdinand-Jérôme de Beauvau

(1723–90), Prince de Craon (Mann du Deffand *passim*).

19. Mme de Cambis.

20. Probably Lord Shelburne, who was at Paris in October (see du Deffand iv. 100).

21. See, for instance, *Last Journals* i. 411.

22. See *ante* 29 Dec. 1772.

23. HW calls him an 'eternal talker' in 'Paris Journals,' du Deffand v. 279, and 'an impertinent and tiresome old gossip' at the time of his visit to SH in 1777 (Ossory i. 357).

24. 6 Oct. 1765 ('Paris Journals,' du Deffand v. 267).

25. Paul-Henri Thiry (1723–89), Baron d'Holbach; encyclopedist (ibid. *passim*).

26. Françoise-Marie-Antoinette-Joseph Saucerotte (1756–1815), called Mlle Raucourt; actress. She made her début at the Comédie-Française 23 Dec. 1772; HW saw her 18 Sept. 1775 (*Enciclopedia dello spettacolo*, Rome, 1954–62, viii. 744–6; 'Paris Journals,' du Deffand v. 349). This corrects ibid. iii. 312, n. 7.

27. Henri-Louis Caïn or Kaïn (1729–

me, oftener not. Molé[28] is charming in genteel, or in pathetic comedy, and would be fine in tragedy, if he was stronger. Préville[29] is always perfection. I like his wife[30] in affected parts, though not animated enough. There was a delightful woman who did the Lady Wishforts,[31] I don't know if there still, I think her name Mademoiselle Drouin;[32] and a fat woman,[33] rather elderly, who sometimes acted the *soubrette*.[34] But you have missed the Dumenil,[35] and Caillaut![36] What irreparable losses! Madame du Deffand, perhaps—I don't know —could obtain your hearing the Clairon[37]—yet the Dumenil was infinitely preferable.

I could now almost find in my heart to laugh at you for liking Boutin's[38] garden. Do you know, that I drew a plan of it, as the completest absurdity I ever saw. What! a river that wriggles at right angles through a stone gutter, with two tansy puddings that were dug out of it, and three or four beds in a row, by a corner of the wall, with samples of grass, corn, and of *en friche,*[39] like a tailor's paper of patterns! And you like this! I will tell Park Place—Oh! I had forgot your audience in dumb show[40]—well, as Madame de

78), called LeKain or Le Kain, of the Comédie-Française 1750–78 (*Enciclopedia dello spettacolo*, vi. 1364–7). This corrects the identifying footnotes in DU DEFFAND, MONTAGU, and MASON.

28. François-René Molé (1734–1802), of the Comédie-Française 1760–91 (*Enciclopedia dello spettacolo*, vii. 691–2).

29. See *ante* 9 March 1765, n. 15.

30. Madeleine - Michelle - Angélique Drouin (1731–94), called Mme Préville; m. (1750) Pierre-Louis Dubus, called Préville (*Enciclopedia dello spettacolo* viii. 456).

31. A character in Congreve's *Way of the World.*

32. Françoise-Jeanne-Élisabeth Gaultier (1720–1803), m. 1 (1744) Charles Martel, actor; m. 2 Jean-Jacques-François Drouin, dancer; of the Comédie-Française 1742–80 (*Enciclopedia dello spettacolo* iv. 1029–30; *Dictionnaire de biographie française,* 1933– , xi. 821–2). HW calls her 'Mlle Gautier' in 'Paris Journals,' Nov. 1765, where he notes her acting 'admirably' the widow's part in *Le Baron d'Albikrac*, 'like Lady Wishfort' (DU DEFFAND v. 272 and n. 106, 275).

33. Not identified.

34. Lady's-maid.

35. See *ante* 26 March 1765, n. 18; actually, she did not quit the stage until 1776.

36. Joseph Caillot (1733–1816), actor and singer, of the Comédie-Italienne 1760–72 (*Enciclopedia dello spettacolo* ii. 1476; *Dictionnaire de biographie française* vii. 867–8). Conway, Lady Ailesbury and Mrs Damer saw him perform at Versailles in December (DU DEFFAND iv. 127 and n. 3). This corrects the identifying notes in DU DEFFAND and MASON.

37. See *ante* 9 March 1765, n. 14. She had quit the Comédie-Française in 1766, but still gave private performances.

38. Simon-Charles Boutin (d. 1794) (DU DEFFAND iv. 378, n. 3). HW sent a plan of the garden, 'laid out in our taste,' to Lady Ossory in his letter of 11 Aug. 1771 (reproduced OSSORY i. 56); see also HW to Chute 5 Aug. 1771, CHUTE 125.

39. A 'slip . . . of weeds, very rural' (OSSORY loc. cit.); generally, uncultivated land.

40. His presentation to Louis XVI 3 Nov., when the King passed him by without saying a word; see *ante* ca 4 Nov. 1774.

Sévigné said, 'Le roi de Prusse, c'est le plus grand roi du monde'[41] still. My love to the old Parliament:[42] I don't love new ones.

I went several times to Madame de Monconseil's,[43] who is just what you say. Mesdames de Tingri[44] and de la Vauguion[45] I never saw: Madame de Noailles[46] once or twice, and enough. You say something of Madame Mallet,[47] which I could not read; for, by the way, your brother and I agree that you are grown not to write legibly: is that lady in being? I knew her formerly. Madame de Blot[48] I know, and Monsieur de Paulmy[49] I know, but for heaven's sake who is Col. Conway?[50] Mademoiselle Sanadon[51] is *la sana donna*,[52] and not Mademoiselle *Celadon*,[53] as you call her. Pray assure my good Monsieur Schoualow[54] of my great regard: he is one of the best of beings.

41. See *ante* 2 Oct. 1765, n. 15.

42. Restored by Louis XVI on this day (12 Nov.) (*ante* 7 Nov. 1774, n. 18).

43. Claire-Cécile-Thérèse-Pauline Rioult de Douilly (1706–87), m. (1725) Étienne-Louis-Antoine Guignot, Marquis de Monconseil. HW had been first introduced to her in 1739, and had visited her in 1766 and 1769 (HW's 'Marginal Notes written in . . . Memoirs of Chesterfield,' *Philobiblon Society Miscellanies*, 1867–8, xi. 63; 'Paris Journals,' DU DEFFAND v. 296–7, 332); he wrote in his 'Marginal Notes,' p. 62, that she 'was a most intriguing and interested woman, and dipped in all kinds of cabals.'

44. Éléonore-Josèphe-Pulchérie des Laurents (b. 1745), m. (1765) Charles-François-Christian de Montmorency-Luxembourg, Prince de Tingry (DU DEFFAND iii. 32, n. 3).

45. Antoinette-Rosalie de Pons (1751–1824), m. (1766) Paul-François de Quélen de Stuer de Caussade, Marquis (later Duc) de Saint-Maigrin, later Duc de la Vauguyon (ibid. i. 219, n. 5).

46. Anne-Claudine-Louise d'Arpajon (d. 1794), m. (1741) Philippe de Noailles, Marquis d'Arpajon, Comte de Noailles, later Duc de Mouchy and Maréchal de France. HW saw her at Hénault's in 1766 ('Paris Journals,' ibid. v. 307).

47. Probably Lucy Elstob (ca 1716–95), m. (1742) David Mallet (d. 1765), poet (DNB, *sub* 'Mallet'; Mallet, *Ballads and Songs*, ed. F. Dinsdale, 1857, pp. 41–2, 57–61). She was much at Paris, and died there (ibid.); HW had known her husband

(CHATTERTON 25; see also Francis Hardy, *Memoirs of . . . Earl of Charlemont*, 1812, i. 235; David Hume, *Letters*, ed. Greig, Oxford, 1932, i. 434, 466).

48. Marie-Cécile-Pauline Charpentier d'Ennery (b. ca 1734), m. (1749) Gilbert de Chauvigny, Baron de Blot. HW had supped with her at Mme de Luxembourg's in 1766 ('Paris Journals,' DU DEFFAND v. 304).

49. Marc-Antoine-Réne de Voyer (1722–87), Marquis de Paulmy; academician (ibid. i. 42, n. 8 *et passim*).

50. An officer in the French service (HW). There were three Col. Conways in the French service at this time: James Conway (1711–87), 1st Count Conway, an Irishman who in his youth had emigrated to France and joined Clare's Irish regiment; and his sons Thomas Conway (1733 or 1735 – ca 1800), 2d Count Conway, colonel, 1772, and James Conway (1741–95), Vct Conway, colonel, 1770 (Richard Hayes, *Biographical Dictionary of Irishmen in France*, Dublin, 1949, pp. 41–3; de Granges de Surgères, op. cit. ii. 73; BERRY ii. 71, n. 24; *Dictionnaire de biographie française*, ix. 550).

51. A lady who lived with Madame du Deffand (HW); she was niece of Père Noël Sanadon, the Latin scholar; see DU DEFFAND i. 366 *et passim*.

52. Here, 'the sensible woman.'

53. The swain in D'Urfé's pastoral romance *Astrée* (1607), and also in Thomson's *The Seasons: Summer* (1727); HW's name in the 'Quadruple Alliance' at Eton.

54. Shuvalov (*ante* 9 March 1765, n. 4, 7 April 1765).

I have said all I could, at least all I should. I reserve the rest of my paper for a postscript; for this is but Saturday, and my letter cannot depart till Tuesday: but I could not for one minute defer answering your charming volumes, which interest me so much. I grieve for Lady Harriet's[55] swelled face, and wish for both their sakes she could transfer it to her father.[56] I assure her I meant nothing by desiring you to see the verses to the Princess Christine,[57] wherein there is very profane mention of a pair of swelled cheeks.[58] I hear nothing of Madame d'Olonne.[59]—Oh! make Madame du Deffand show you the sweet portrait of Madame de Prie,[60] the Duke of Bourbon's[61] mistress.[62] Have you seen Madame de Monaco, and the remains of Madame de Brionne?[63] If you wish to see Mrs A———,[64] ask for the Princesse de Ligne. If you have seen Monsieur de Maurepas, you have seen the late Lord Hardwicke.[65] By your not naming him, I suppose the Duc de Nivernois is not at Paris. Say a great deal for me to M. de Guisnes. You will not see my passion, the Duchess de Châtillon.[66] If you see Madame de Nivernois, you will think the Duke of Newcastle is come to life again.[67] Alas! where is my postscript?

55. Lady Harriet Stanhope, afterwards married to Lord Foley, was at this time at Paris with her father the Earl of Harrington (HW).

56. Whom HW describes *ante* 27 Sept. 1774 as 'decrepit.'

57. By the Chevalier de Boufflers (HW). See above, n. 15.

58. 'Avec une joue enflée, / Je débarque tout honteux; / La Princesse boursoufflée, Au lieu d'une, en avait deux' (Hawkins, op. cit. ii. 208).

59. The beautiful enamel miniature of Madame d'Olonne, now at Strawberry Hill (HW). See *ante* 16 Oct. 1774, nn. 37–8.

60. Agnès Berthelot de Pleneuf (1698–1727), m. (1713) Louis, Marquis de Prie (du Deffand *passim*).

61. Louis-Henri (1692–1740), Duc de Bourbon.

62. This portrait is now at Strawberry Hill (HW); see *post* 26 Dec. 1774, 15 Jan. 1775.

63. Who had been a great beauty in her youth (*ante* 5 May 1753, n. 12).

64. Probably Elizabeth Holford (ca 1734–73), m. (before 1758) Dr Anthony Askew, physician and book-collector. HW wrote to Selwyn 31 Jan. 1766 that 'the 'Princess of Ligne is the very image of Mrs Askew' (Selwyn 214 and n. 23).

65. He means from their personal resemblance (HW). HW notes their resemblance also in his letter to Selwyn 31 Jan. 1766 (ibid. ii. 214).

66. Adrienne-Émilie-Félicité de la Baume le Blanc (1740–1812), m. (1756) Louis-Gaucher, Duc de Châtillon (du Deffand *passim*). Mme du Deffand wrote to HW 16 Oct. 1774 that she was now 'la plus intime amie' of Mlle de Lespinasse, Mme du Deffand's rival (ibid. iv. 102).

67. 'The Duchess of Nivernois makes amends for the instructive prattle of the Duke of Newcastle' (HW to Selwyn 1 Jan. 1766, loc. cit.; see also More 76).

To LADY AILESBURY, ca Tuesday 15 November 1774

Missing. This letter and *ante* 7 Nov. 1774 were answered *post* 23 Nov. 1774; in this one HW announced the 'retreat' of his gout.

From CONWAY, ca Saturday 19 November 1774

Missing. 'I some days ago sent Mr Walpole an imperfect sketch [of the *lit de justice* 12 Nov., restoring the old Parliament banished in 1771], which I desired him to communicate to you' (Conway to Hertford 22 Nov. 1774, MS now WSL); Conway also mentions the *lit de justice* in his letter to Keith 19 Nov. in Keith's *Memoirs and Correspondence*, ed. Mrs Gillespie Smyth, 1849, ii. 30. See *post* 27 Nov. 1774, n. 4.

From CONWAY, ca Tuesday 22 November 1774

Missing; a 'letter of six pages' answered *post* 27 Nov. 1774. Tentatively dated the same as Conway's letter to Hertford 22 Nov. (MS now WSL), in which Conway also sent a copy of the *procès verbal* of the *lit de justice* of 12 Nov.

From LADY AILESBURY, Wednesday 23 November 1774

Printed from the MS now WSL; first printed Toynbee *Supp.* iii. 237–41. For the history of the MS see *ante* 23 Aug. 1760.
Address: To the Honourable Horatio Walpole in Arlington Street, London.

Paris, November 23, 1774.

I AM unpardonable not to have thanked you before for two letters[1] I have received from you since I wrote,[2] the last of which made me particularly happy by informing me that the formidable enemy appeared to be upon the retreat.[3]

Madame du Deffands is in perfect health and spirits and a few days

1. *Ante* 7 Nov. 1774 and the missing letter *ante* ca 15 Nov. 1774.
2. *Ante* ca 1 Nov. 1774.
3. HW had complained *ante* 7 Nov. 1774 of the gout in his elbow.

ago went to *La Chasse d'Henri Quatre*,[4] *aux français*, and supped out afterwards; by the by that same *Chasse* is nothing but a *réchauffée* of the *King and the Miller of Mansfeild*,[5] and most of the scenes word for word literally translated from the English;[6] there is one indeed upon the famous story of the King and Sulli,[7] 'Lève-toi on croira etc.'[8] but all together it is but a poor performance not worth sending you, and would not go down if it was not acted by the best performers, Brizars,[9] Préville, Belcores[10] and Madame Doligni;[11] here it is applauded up to the skies. There is another *aux italiens* upon the same subject,[12] new also and much more ridiculous, which you'll easily believe when I tell you Henri Quatre sings a trio with Maréchal Biron,[13] and Maréchal d'Aumont,[14] writes letters and makes his will set to music.[15] The Battle of Ibery[16] is heard at a

4. *La Partie de chasse de Henri IV*, by Charles Collé (1709–83), performed at the Comédie-Française 16 Nov. (Louis Petit de Bachaumont, *Mémoires secrets*, 1780–9, vii. 235; see also Grimm, *Correspondance*, ed. Tourneux, 1877–82, x. 508–9; DU DEFFAND i. 285, 286, 289, ii. 154, iv. 116; *Enciclopedia dello spettacolo*, Rome, 1954–62, iii. 1075–6; *Dictionnaire de biographie française*, 1933– , ix. 259–60).

5. By Robert Dodsley (1703–64), first performed at Drury Lane in 1737 (*London Stage* Pt III, ii. 634).

6. An exaggeration; however, compare the opening scene in Dodsley's play where the King meets the miller in Sherwood Forest with Act II, scene xi in Collé's play.

7. Maximilien de Béthune (1559–1641), Duc de Sully; Henri IV's prime minister.

8. 'Relevez-vous donc . . . ces gens-là qui vous voient . . . vont croire que je vous pardonne' (Act I, scene vi). Sully, in his *Mémoires*, Amsterdam and Paris, 1638–62, ii. 358, writes that after denying calumnies made against him by his enemies, he begged the King: 'Me permettez . . . que je me jette à vos pieds et vous embrasser les genoux, comme à mon Roi bien aimé,' but the King prevented him, saying: 'Je ne voudrais pour rien du monde, que ceux qui nous regardent, creussent que vous eussiez commis aucune faute qui meritast une telle soumission.' HW's copy of the *Mémoires*, 'Londres, 1747,' is Hazen, *Cat. of HW's Lib.*, No. 1016.

9. Jean-Baptiste Britard (1721–91), called Brizard, of the Comédie-Française 1757–86 (*Enciclopedia dello spettacolo* ii. 1134–5; *Dictionnaire de biographie française* vii. 375).

10. Jean-Claude-Gilles Colson (1725–78), called Bellecour, of the Comédie-Française 1750–78 (*Enciclopedia* ii. 193; *Dictionnaire* v. 1322–3). This corrects DU DEFFAND v. 18, n. 3.

11. Louise-Adélaïde Berthon de Maisonneuve (1746–1823), called Mlle Doligny or d'Oligny, of the Comédie-Française 1763–83 (*Enciclopedia* iv. 816–17; *Dictionnaire* v. 445–6).

12. *Henri IV, ou la bataille d'Ivry, drame lyrique en trois actes mêlés d'ariettes*, words by Barnabé Farmain de Rozoi (1743–92), music by Johann Paul Ægidius Martini (1741–1816), presented for the first time at the Comédie-Italienne 14 Nov. (Grimm, op. cit. x. 509–10; Bachaumont, op. cit. vii. 233–5; NBG sub 'Rozoi'; Sir George Grove, *Dictionary of Music and Musicians*, ed. Blom, 1954–61, v. 597–8).

13. Charles de Gontaut (1562–1602), Duc de Biron, Maréchal de France (*Dictionnaire de biographie française*, vi. 520–2).

14. Jean d'Aumont (1522–95), Maréchal de France (ibid. iv. 634–5). The trio is sung at the end of Act II, scene iv.

15. Act II, scene iii.

16. Ivry, fought in 1590, when Henri IV led the Huguenots to victory over the Catholic League.

distance,[17] the cannon and the shouts of the victorious, during which a fine symphony is played,[18] and a duo is sung[19] by two ladies[20] whose son and lover[21] are supposed to be engaged. Ridiculous as this may seem, between the music, the acting of Clerval,[22] and the singing of Madame Trial,[23] the whole was so touching that Madame de Cambis and I cried several times during the performance. I am afraid you'll think I am grown very silly.

Mr Conway will tell you how well pleased we are here upon the whole, and that we have thoughts of staying some time longer; indeed he hates the idea of going to London, after the disagreeable usage he has met with,[24] and I hate it for his sake. Madame du Deffands makes it her business to amuse me,[25] but nothing pleases me so much as her conversation, in which there is wit, good sense and good-humour mixed, so equally mixed that you can't say which predominates. The old Maréchale de Luxemburg[26] likes me very well, but Mr Conway much better, and indeed he rivals me with several others, particularly Madame de Mirpoix, and the Princesse de Beauveau, who are both you know very agreeable. Madame de Beauveau has I think more eloquence in her conversation, than I ever met with in any woman, but to be sure none of the ladies here have the least tincture of our miserable *mauvaise honte,* for which I envy them most exceedingly. Madame de Cambise is our intimate acquaintance, and we seldom pass a day without seeing her. She is uncommonly sensible and lively, and sings 'Sans dépit et sans légèreté' charmingly.[27]

The Chevalier de Boufflers is my admiration, but does not take to

17. During the *entr'acte* between Acts II and III, and scene i of Act III.
18. In the *entr'acte;* 'c'est l'endroit le mieux senti de la part du musicien' (Bachaumont, op. cit. vii. 235).
19. Act III, scene i.
20. La Marquise de Lenoncourt and Eugénie.
21. Le Chevalier de Lenoncourt.
22. Jean-Baptiste Guignard (1735 – 1795 or 7), called Clairval, of the Comédie-Italienne 1762–92 (*Enciclopedia dello spettacolo* iii. 924–5; *Dictionnaire de biographie française* viii. 1343–4). He played the rôle of Henri IV (Grimm, op. cit. x. 510; Bachaumont, op. cit. vii. 235).
23. Marie-Jeanne Milon (1746–1814), soprano, m. (1769) Antoine Trial, tenor;

of the Comédie-Italienne 1766–86 (*Enciclopedia* ix. 1114–15). She presumably played the rôle of Eugénie.
24. An allusion to Grafton's failure to support him again for Parliament in the October elections (*ante* 27 Sept. *bis,* 2, 3 Oct. 1774).
25. See *ante* 29 Oct. 1774 and n. 6; du Deffand iv. 115, 117.
26. Madeleine-Angélique de Neufville (1707–87), m. 1 (1721) Joseph-Marie, Duc de Boufflers; m. 2 (1750) Charles-François-Frédéric de Montmorency-Luxembourg (d. 1764), Duc de Luxembourg, Maréchal de France (du Deffand i. 12, n. 9 *et passim*).
27. See *ante* 7 Nov. 1774 and n. 34.

me so much as I could wish, but I intend to take some pains to bring it about, though I fear I shall not succeed; I am actually making a book of his bons mots; I'll tell you two which I hope you have not heard. One day eating some very tough mutton, somebody remarked the pains he took to chew, 'It is true,' says he, 'it is *un combat entre les voraces, et les coriaces.*'[28] King Stanislaus sitting to him for his picture, very fat and near fourscore, observed that he was but an unworthy model for a painter; the Chevalier said, 'Il est vrai, Sire, que votre Majesté est un modèle plutôt pour les rois que pour les peintres.' I am sadly afraid Mr Conway has told you these already, but there is one more I am sure he has not, as it passed only a few nights ago; Monsieur and Madame de Viry[29] supped at Madame du Deffand's, and the Chevalier not having seen them before was amazed at their appearance; he said they could not be called properly 'homme et femme, mais le mâle et la femelle de Viry.'[30]

Lady Harriot is sitting by, and desires me to say a thousand kind things to you, and thanks for all you have said of her; one cannot say too much; she is very much admired, but there's nobody here worthy her admiration. Lord Cholmondely never went near Madame du Deffand though he had a letter from you to carry,[31] and Mrs Cholmondely[32] had mentioned him to her; I was vexed at this.

I had almost forgot to thank you for your Saxon pun,[33] which may very well be placed in my book of bons mots. Madame du Deffand's machine for holding toasts was only a toasting fork; and your little grate, for she calls it *petite grille,*[34] is in high favour. Pray send me the snuff and the glasses, I am very impatient to have them.[35] I cannot say a word more, for this is waited for.

Most affectionately yours,

C. Ailesbury

28. Between voracity and the toughness of the meat. This is an echo of the three Horatii and the three Curatii in Corneille's *Horace.*

29. Francesco Maria Giuseppi Giustino (1736–1813), Conte di Viry; Sardinian minister to Paris 1773–7; m. (1761) Henrietta Jane Speed (Mann viii. 328, n. 14; *ante* 28 Nov. 1761, n. 30).

30. Boufflers presumably means that both looked more like animals than humans. Mme de Viry was described as a 'witty amazon' by Admiral Sir John Thomas Duckworth (1748–1817), who knew her in his youth (Gray, *Correspondence,* ed. Toynbee and Whibley, Oxford, 1935, i. 332, n. 1).

31. See *ante* 29 Oct. 1774.

32. Lord Cholmondeley's aunt.

33. See *ante* 7 Nov. 1774.

34. A toast-rack, brought over by Mrs Damer as a gift from HW to Mme du Deffand (see du Deffand iv. 101, 104).

35. See *ante* 7 Nov. 1774 and n. 28.

To Conway, Sunday 27 November 1774

Printed from *Works* v. 172–5.

Arlington Street, November 27, 1774.

I HAVE received your delightfully plump packet with a letter of six pages,[1] one from Madame du Deffand,[2] the *Éloges*,[3] and the *Lit de Justice*.[4] Now observe my gratitude: I appoint you my resident at Paris; but you are not to resemble all our ministers abroad, and expect to live at home, which would destroy *my Lord Castlecomer's* views[5] in your staying at Paris. However, to prove to you that I have some gratitude that is not totally selfish, I will tell you what little news I know, before I answer your letter; for English news, to be sure, is the most agreeable circumstance in a letter from England.

On my coming to town yesterday, there was nothing but more deaths—don't you think we have the plague? the Bishop of Worcester,[6] Lord Breadalbane,[7] Lord Strathmore.[8] The first fell from his horse, or with his horse, at Bath, and the bishopric was incontinently given to Bishop North.[9]

---

1. Missing.

2. Presumably the letter of 15 Nov. 1774; see next note.

3. 'Je vous envoie les éloges de La Fontaine, l'un par La Harpe, l'autre par Chamfort' (Mme du Deffand to HW 15 Nov. 1774, DU DEFFAND iv. 114). These were written by Jean-François de la Harpe and Sébastien-Roch Nicolas (1741–94), called Chamfort, in competition for a prize offered by the Académie de Marseille. Chamfort was awarded the prize 25 Aug., and HW wrote to Mme du Deffand 25 Nov. 1774 that he much preferred Chamfort's effort (*Dictionnaire de biographie française*, 1933– , viii. 275; Grimm, *Correspondance*, ed. Tourneux, 1877–82, x. 480; Chamfort, *Éloge de la Fontaine*, 1774; DU DEFFAND loc. cit.). HW's copies of the *Éloges* are Hazen, *Cat. of HW's Lib.*, No. 2050 : 25.

4. Conway also sent a copy of 'the history of the Parliament, or *Procès Verbal* of the whole transaction as far as

regards the Grande Chambre' along with his letter to Hertford 22 Nov. 1774 (MS now WSL). The *procès verbal* of the *lit de justice* of 12 Nov., restoring the Parliament banished by Louis XV in 1771, which fills 90 pages in quarto (*Mercure historique* 1774, clxxvii. 654n.) is printed in abridged form ibid. 654–87.

5. See *ante* 15 Oct. 1758, n. 12.

6. Dr James Johnson (1705–74), Bp of Gloucester 1752–9, of Worcester 1759–74. See n. 9 below.

7. John Campbell (1696–1782), 3d E. of Breadalbane, 1752. 'It is reported that advice is received of the death of the Earl of Breadalbane, lately elected one of the 16 peers for Scotland' (*London Chronicle* 26–9 Nov., xxxvi. 519). This was a false report.

8. John Lyon (after 1767 Bowes) (1737–76), 7th E. of Strathmore, 1753; also a false report.

9. Hon. Brownlow North (1741–1820), Bp of Lichfield 1771–4, of Worcester 1774–81,

America is still more refractory, and I doubt will outvote the Ministry. They have picked General Gage's[10] pocket of three pieces of cannon, and intercepted some troops that were going to him.[11] Sir William Draper is writing plans of pacification in our newspapers;[12] and Lord Chatham flatters himself that he shall be sent for when the patient is given over;[13] which I don't think at all unlikely to happen. My poor nephew[14] is very political too: so we shall not want mad-doctors. Apropos, I hear Wilkes says he will propose Mackreth[15] for speaker.

The Ecclesiastical Court are come to a resolution that the Duchess of Kingston is Mrs Hervey;[16] and the sentence will be public in a fortnight. It is not so certain that she will lose the estate.[17] Augustus[18] is not in a much more pleasant predicament than she is. I saw Lord

of Winchester 1781–1820; half-brother of Lord North. HW writes in *Last Journals* i. 410: 'Dr Johnson, Bishop of Worcester, had a fall from his horse in the streets of Bath on the 24th or 25th, and it was thought had fractured his skull. The King immediately named Dr North . . . his successor; but on the 26th news came that Johnson was still alive, which made the precipitation ridiculous; however, he died of the hurt [26 Nov.].' See MANN viii. 63, nn. 28–9.

10. Hon. Thomas Gage (1719 or 20– 1787), Lt-Gen., 1770, Gen., 1782; commander-in-chief in North America 1763– 73, May 1774 – Oct. 1775; governor of Massachusetts Bay 1774 – Oct. 1775 (J. R. Alden, *General Gage in America*, Baton Rouge, La, 1948, *passim*). This corrects the identifying notes in MASON, OSSORY and MANN.

11. These incidents have not been traced. In September 1774, patriots deterred carpenters that Gage wished to have build barracks in Boston from coming there (Thomas Gage, *Correspondence*, ed. Carter, New Haven, 1931–3, i. 376); in December, rebels carried off cannon from the King's fort in Portsmouth, New Hampshire (see L. H. Gipson, *British Empire before the American Revolution*, New York, 1936–70, xii. 170–1 and sources cited there).

12. 'Thoughts of a Traveller upon our American Disputes' by 'Viator,' printed

Public Advertiser 23, 24, 25 Nov., and *London Chronicle* 22–4, 24–6 Nov., 29 Nov. – 1 Dec., xxxvi. 497, 508, 524, reprinted as a separate pamphlet for J. Ridley, 1774, 27 pp.

13. See Basil Williams, *Life of William Pitt*, 1913, ii. 295–303; *post* 22 Jan. 1775.

14. George Walpole, Earl of Orford (HW).

15. Robert Mackreth (?1725–1819), Kt 1795; M.P. Castle Rising 1774–84, Ashburton 1784–1802. An ex-waiter and manager of White's, he had been returned to Parliament by Orford, who allegedly owed him a large sum of money (see Namier and Brooke iii. 89). George III wrote to North 27 Nov. 'I have heard a report that Mr Wilkes is to propose Mackreath for Speaker. . . . Might it therefore not be prudent to get him on Tuesday morning [29 Nov., the opening day of the new Parliament] to vacate his seat, and not to mention it but in case the motion should be made' (George III's *Corr.*, ed. Fortescue, iii. 154). Mackreth was not proposed; Sir Fletcher Norton was unanimously re-elected Speaker (*Journals of the House of Commons* xxxv. 5).

16. A false report; see *ante* 9 Aug. 1768, *post* 12 Dec. 1775, MANN viii. 62, n. 24.

17. The Duke, who died without an heir in 1773, willed his entire estate to her; the will was not overturned.

18. Augustus Hervey, to whom she was first married (HW).

Bristol[19] last night: he looks perfectly well, but his speech is much affected, and his right hand.[20]

Lady Lyttelton, who, you know, never hears anything that has happened, wrote to me two days ago,[21] to ask if it would not be necessary for *you* to come over for the meeting of the Parliament.[22] I answered,[23] very gravely, that to be sure you ought: but though *Sir James Morgan* threatened you loudly with a petition, yet, as it could not be heard till after Christmas, I was afraid you would not be persuaded to come sooner. I hope she will inquire who *Sir James Morgan* is, and that people will persuade her she has made a confusion about Sir James Peachey. Now for your letter.

I have been in the *chambre de parlement,* I think they call it the *grande chambre;* and was shown the corner in which the monarchs sit, and do not wonder you did not guess where it was they sat. It is just like the dark corner, under the window, where I always sat in the House of Commons. What has happened, has passed exactly according to my ideas. When one king breaks one parliament, and another another, what can the result be but despotism? or of what else is it a proof?[24] If a Tory king displaces his father's Whig lord chamberlain, neither lord chamberlain has the more or the less power over the theatres and court-mournings and Birthday balls. All that can arrive is, that the people will be still more attached to the old parliament, from this seeming restitution of a right[25]—but the people must have some power before their attachment can signify a straw. The old parliament too may sometime or other give itself more airs on this confession of right; but that too cannot be but in a minority, or when the power of the crown is lessened by reasons that have nothing to do with the parliament. I will answer for it,

---

19. Hervey's brother.

20. HW wrote to Mann 11 Nov. 1774 that 'Lord Bristol has been struck with a palsy that has taken away the use of all his limbs' (ibid. viii. 55). He died 18 March 1775.

21. Her letter is missing.

22. 29 Nov.

23. Also missing.

24. Conway wrote to Hertford 22 Nov.: 'I believe you will not perceive in . . . [the *procès verbal* of the *lit de justice* of 12 Nov.] any great symptoms of an improvement in their constitution, any great steps made in favour of French

liberty; it breathes regal power and despotism throughout.' Louis XVI proclaimed that in restoring the old parliament, 'je ne perds point de vue, que leur tranquillité et leur bonheur exigent, que je conserve mon autorité dans toute sa plénitude' (*Mercure historique* clxxvii. 656).

25. 'Yet are people pleased in general who aim at liberty here, because the ancient parliament is recalled, because it is done without new provisions, and because they think it may do something by its influence towards restraining ministers hereafter' (Conway to Hertford 22 Nov.).

they will be too *grateful* to give umbrage to their restorer. Indeed I did not think the people would be so quick-sighted at once, as to see the distinction of old and new was without a difference. Methinks France and England are like the land and the sea; one gets a little sense when the other loses it.

I am quite satisfied with all you tell me about my friend.[26] My intention is certainly to see her again, if I am able;[27] but I am too old to lay plans, especially when it depends on the despot gout to register or cancel them. It is even melancholy to see her, when it will probably be but once more; and still more melancholy, when we ought to say to one another, in a different sense from the common, *à revoir!* However, as mine is a pretty cheerful kind of philosophy, I think the best way is to think of dying, but to talk and act as if one was not to die; or else one tires other people, and dies before one's time. I have truly all the affection and attachment for her that she deserves from me, or I should not be so very thankful as I am for your kindness to her. The Choiseuls will certainly return at Christmas,[28] and will make her life much more agreeable. The Duchess has as much attention to her as I could have; but that will not keep me from making her a visit.

I have only seen, not known, the younger Madame de Boufflers.[29] For her musical talents,[30] I am little worthy of them—yet I am just going to Lady Bingham's[31] to hear the Bastardella,[32] whom, though the first singer in Italy, Mrs Yates[33] could not or would not

---

26. Mme du Deffand.

27. HW went the following August (see *post* 9, 17 Aug. 1775).

28. See *post* 31 Dec. 1775.

29. Amélie-Constance Puchot des Alleurs (ca 1750–1825), m. (1768) Louis-Édouard, Comte de Boufflers (DU DEFFAND ii. 58, n. 14 *et passim*).

30. She sang and played the harp (ibid. iv. 363, 469).

31. Margaret Smith (d. 1814), m. (1760) Sir Charles Bingham, 7th Bt, cr. (1776) Bn and (1795) E. of Lucan.

32. Lucrezia Aguiari or Agujari (1743–83), called La Bastardella or La Bastardina in allusion to her being the natural child of a nobleman (Sir George Grove, *Dictionary of Music and Musicians*, ed. Blom, 1954–61, i. 73; *Enciclopedia dello spettacolo*, Rome, 1954–62, i. 186–7). Mozart

wrote to his sister from Bologna, 24 March 1770, that she 'has (1) a beautiful voice, (2) a marvellous throat, (3) an incredible range' (*Letters*, ed. Emily Anderson, 1938, i. 179), while Charles Burney comments in his *General History of Music* (ed. F. Mercer, 1935, i. 883) that 'the lower part of her voice was full, round, of an excellent quality, and its compass . . . beyond any one who had then heard. . . . Her shake was open and perfect, her intonation true, her execution marked and rapid; and her style of singing . . . grand and majestic.'

33. Mary Ann Graham (1728–87), m. (ca 1756) Richard Yates; actress; joint-manager of the Opera 1773–7 (Michael Kelly, *Reminiscences of . . . the King's Theatre and . . . Drury Lane*, 1826, ii. 359).

agree with;[34] and she is to have twelve hundred pounds for singing twelve times at the Pantheon,[35] where, if she had a voice as loud as Lord Clare's,[36] she could not be heard. The two bons mots you sent me are excellent; but, alas! I had heard them both before: consequently your own, which is very good too, pleased me much more. M. de Stainville I think you will not like:[37] he has sense, but has a dry military harshness, that at least did not suit me—and then I hate his barbarity to his wife.[38]

You was very lucky indeed to get one of the sixty tickets.[39] Upon the whole, your travels have been very fortunate, and the few mortifications amply compensated. If a duke[40] has been spiteful when your back was turned, a hero-king[41] has been all courtesy. If another king[42] has been silent, an emperor[43] has been singularly gracious. Frowns or silence may happen to anybody: the smiles have been addressed to you particularly.—So was the ducal frown indeed—but would you have earned a smile at the price set on it?[44] One cannot do right and be always applauded—but in such cases are not frowns tantamount?

As my letter will not set forth till the day after tomorrow, I reserve the rest for any additional news, and this time *will* reserve it.[45]

---

34. To sing at the opera (HW).

35. A 'winter Ranelagh' in Oxford Road, opened in 1772 (Mann vii. 210 and n. 9). Burney writes, op. cit. ii. 882, that 'the proprietors of the Pantheon ventured to engage the Agujari, at the enormous salary of £100 a night, for singing two songs only!'

36. HW mentions that Clare 'roared' in Parliament *ante* 15 Nov. 1755.

37. Conway wrote to Hertford 22 Nov. that 'M. de Stainville has got me leave to see the gallery of fortifications and will carry me there on Thursday [24 Nov.].'

38. Upon a suspicion of gallantry, she was confined for life (HW). Thomassine-Thérèse de Clermont d'Amboise (b. 1746), m. (1761) Jacques-Philippe de Choiseul, Comte de Stainville. After learning of her affair with Clairval, the actor (*ante* 23 Nov. 1774, n. 22), Stainville had her confined for life in a convent at Nancy (1767) (du Deffand i. 217 and n. 3).

39. To the *lit de justice* 12 Nov. Conway wrote to Hertford 22 Nov.: 'You may imagine I thought myself fortunate in

getting a ticket, when there were but about sixty given in all for French and foreigners. Your old friend Sarsfield [see *ante* ca 20 Aug. 1767] bought it, but I understand I rather owe it to the Prince de Beauvau . . . and Prince Tingri.'

40. Grafton; see n. 44 below.

41. Frederick II of Prussia.

42. Louis XVI of France.

43. Joseph II of Austria.

44. I.e., going back on his principles. HW felt that Grafton failed to bring Conway into Parliament again because Conway had differed with him over America and the Royal Marriage Bill (*Last Journals* i. 379–80). However, Grafton had understandably reserved his pocket borough Thetford for his brother and uncle, while he presumably felt it pointless to propose Conway, a stranger who was out of the country, for Bury, where he had a contest (see *ante* 3 Oct. 1774; Namier and Brooke ii. 246). In any case, Grafton did return Conway on the first vacancy in his boroughs (ibid.).

45. See *ante* 12 Nov. 1774.

St Parliament's Day, 29th,[46] after breakfast.

The speech is said to be firm, and to talk of the *rebellion* of our province of Massachusets.[47] No sloop is arrived yet to tell us how to call the rest.[48] Mr Van[49] is to move for the expulsion of Wilkes;[50] which will distress, and may produce an odd scene. Lord Holland[51] is certainly dead; the papers say, Robinson[52] too, but that I don't know:—so many deaths of late make report kill to right and left.

To Lady Ailesbury, Tuesday 13 December 1774

Missing; mentioned *post* 15 Dec. 1774.

To Conway, Thursday 15 December 1774

Printed from *Works* v. 175–6.

Arlington Street, December 15, 1774.

AS I wrote to Lady Ailesbury but on Tuesday,[1] I should not have followed it so soon with this, if I had nothing to tell you but of myself. My gouts are never dangerous, and the shades of them not important. However, to dispatch this article at once, I will tell you, that the pain I felt yesterday in my elbow made me think all former

46. The new Parliament opened this day.

47. The King's speech of 30 Nov., printed *Journals of the House of Lords* xxxiv. 269, expresses the King's 'firm and steadfast resolution to withstand every attempt to weaken or impair the supreme authority of this legislature over all the dominions of his crown'; it also refers to 'a most daring spirit of resistance and disobedience to the law . . . in the province of the Massachusetts Bay,' but does not use the word 'rebellion,' which appears however in George III's letter to North of 18 Nov.: 'The New England governments are in a state of rebellion' (Fortescue, op. cit. iii. 153).

48. See *post* 15 Dec. 1774.

49. Charles Van (d. 1778), M.P. Brecon 1772–8.

50. No such motion was made. In Feb. 'Vann, a strange man, urged the imputation of blasphemy against Wilkes, having in a bravado the last winter vowed to do so' (*Last Journals* i. 438; see also Cobbett, *Parl. Hist.* xviii. 376).

51. Stephen Fox, 2d Lord Holland; for various alleged dates of his death, see Ossory i. 219, n. 13.

52. John Robinson (1727–1802), M.P. Westmorland 1764–74, Harwich 1774–1802; joint secretary to the Treasury 1770–82. He had been ill, and the *Daily Adv.* 29 Nov. and other papers reported his death at Bath, but the *London Chronicle* 26–9 Nov., xxxvi. 520, refuted this report, 'that gentleman being better.'

————

1. His letter is missing.

pain did not deserve the name. Happily the torture did not last above two hours; and, which is more surprising, it is all the real pain I have felt; for though my hand has been as sore as if flayed, and that both feet are lame, the bootikins demonstrably prevent or extract the sting of it, and I see no reason not to expect to get out in a fortnight more. Surely, if I am laid up but one month in two years, instead of five or six, I have reason to think the bootikins sent from heaven.

The long expected sloop is arrived at last,[2] and is indeed a *man of war!* The General Congress[3] have voted,

A non-importation.[4]

A non-exportation.[5]

A non-consumption.[6]

That, in case of hostilities committed by the troops at Boston, the several provinces will march to the assistance of their countrymen.[7]

2. 'Yesterday [13 Dec.] arrived a mail from New York, brought by the *St Paul,* Capt. Gordon' (*London Chronicle* 13–15 Dec., xxxvi. 572); the same day Lord Dartmouth (secretary for the colonies) sent to Thomas Hutchinson, governor of Massachusetts Bay who had come to London in June, an 'account of the packet's arrival from New York, and of the Congress at Philadelphia, that they had agreed upon non-importation, non-exportation, and non-consumption,' etc. (Thomas Hutchinson, *Diary and Letters,* ed. P. O. Hutchinson, 1883–6, i. 323).

3. Which had met at Philadelphia 5 Sept. – 26 Oct. with delegates from 12 colonies (*Journals of the Continental Congress,* Washington, 1904–37, i. 13–114 *passim*).

4. Agreed upon 27 Sept. (ibid. i. 43). The 'Association' of the Congress, signed 20 Oct., printed ibid. 75–81, *London Chronicle* 15–17 Dec., xxxvi. 578–9, declared: 'From and after the first day of December next, we will not import, into British America, from Great Britain or Ireland, any goods, wares, or merchandise whatsoever,' etc. (*Journals* i. 76; *London Chronicle* xxxvi. 578).

5. Agreed upon 30 Sept. (*Journals* i. 51–2): 'The earnest desire we have, not to injure our fellow subjects in Great Britain, Ireland or the West Indies, in-duces us to suspend a non-exportation, until the tenth day of September, 1775; at which time, if the said acts and parts of acts of the British Parliament herein after mentioned are not repealed, we will not, directly or indirectly, export any merchandise or commodity whatsoever to Great Britain, Ireland, or the West Indies, except rice to Europe' (ibid. i. 77; *London Chronicle* loc. cit.).

6. Agreed upon 27 Sept. (*Journals* i. 43): 'From this day [20 Oct.], we will not purchase or use any tea, imported on account of the East India Company, or any on which a duty hath been or shall be paid; and from and after the first day of March next, we will not purchase or use any East India tea whatever; nor will we . . . purchase or use any of those goods, wares, or merchandise, we have agreed not to import, which we shall know, or have cause to suspect, were imported after the first day of December' (ibid. i. 77; *London Chronicle* loc. cit.).

7. The Congress resolved, 8 Oct., that it 'approved of the opposition by the inhabitants of the Massachusetts Bay, to the execution of the late acts of Parliament; and if the same shall be attempted to be carried into execution by force, in such case, all America ought to support them in their opposition' (*Journals* i. 58).

That the cargoes of ships now at sea shall be sold on their arrival, and the money arising thence given to the poor at Boston.[8]

That a letter, in the nature of a petition of rights, shall be sent to the King;[9] another to the House of *Commons*;[10] a third to the people of England;[11] a demand of repeal of all the acts of Parliament affecting North America passed during this reign, as also of the Quebec Bill:[12] and these resolutions not to be altered till such repeal is obtained.[13]

Well, I believe you do not regret being neither in Parliament nor in administration! As you are an idle man, and have nothing else to do, you may sit down and tell one a remedy for all this. Perhaps you will give yourself airs, and say you was a prophet, and that prophets are not honoured in their own country.—Yet, if you have any inspiration about you, I assure you it will be of great service—we are at our wit's end—which was no great journey.—Oh! you conclude Lord Chatham's crutch will be supposed a wand, and be sent for—they might as well send for *my* crutch; and they should not have it;

8. 'In case any merchant, trader, or other person, shall import any goods or merchandise, after the first day of December, and before the first day of February next, the same ought forthwith . . . to be either reshipped . . . stored . . . or . . . sold . . . and in the last-mentioned case . . . the profit, if any, [is] to be applied towards relieving and employing such poor inhabitants of the town of Boston, as are immediate sufferers by the Boston Port Bill' ('Association,' ibid. i. 78–9, *London Chronicle* xxxvi. 579).

9. The petition of the Congress, signed 26 Oct., is printed *Journals* i. 115–21. See *post* 26 Dec. 1774 and nn. 18–22.

10. There was no separate address to the House of Commons; various documents by or relating to the Congress were laid before the House 19 Jan. (*Journals of the House of Commons* xxxv. 64–6).

11. An address 'to the people of Great Britain,' printed *Journals of the Continental Congress* i. 82–90, *London Chronicle* 17–20, 20–22 Dec., xxxvi. 591, 593–4.

12. 'Such parts of the several acts of Parliament passed since the close of the last war, as impose or continue duties on tea, wine, molasses, syrups, [etc.] . . . im-

ported into America, and extend the powers of the admiralty courts beyond their ancient limits, deprive the American subject of trial by jury, [etc.] . . . and . . . the four acts, passed the last session of Parliament, viz. that for stopping the port and blocking up the harbour of Boston—that for altering the charter and government of the Massachusetts Bay— and that which is entitled "An act for the better administration of justice, etc." —and that "for extending the limits of Quebec, etc."' ('Association,' *Journals* i. 79–80; *London Chronicle* 15–17 Dec., xxxvi. 579). For the Quebec Bill, see *ante* 23 June 1774 and n. 4; the Congress also prepared an address 'to the inhabitants of the province of Quebec' (printed *Journals* i. 105–13, *London Chronicle* 22–4, 24–7 Dec., xxxvi. 605, 609), informing them of their resolution that 'we should consider the violation of your rights by the act for altering the government of your province, as a violation of our own,' and inviting them 'to accede to our confederation' (*Journals* i. 112–13; *London Chronicle* 24–7 Dec., xxxvi. 609).

13. 'Association,' loc. cit.

the stile is a little too high to help them over. His Lordship is a little
fitter for raising a storm than laying one, and of late seems to have
lost both virtues. The Americans at least have acted like men,[14] gone
to the bottom at once, and set the whole upon the whole. Our conduct has been that of pert children: we have thrown a pebble at a
mastiff, and are surprised it was not frightened. Now we must be
worried by it, or must kill the guardian of the house, which will be
plundered the moment little master has nothing but the old nurse to
defend it. But I have done with reflections; you will be fuller of them
than I.

From CONWAY, ca Tuesday 20 December 1774

Missing. Several letters, answered *post* 26 Dec. 1774, and presumably received
after HW had written and sent his missing letter to Conway *post* 23 Dec. 1774.
In them Conway mentions his visit to Montmorency, where he, Lady Ailesbury
and Mrs Damer were staying apparently 15–17 Dec. (DU DEFFAND iv. 119).

To CONWAY, Friday 23 December 1774

Missing. 'Votre lettre du 23 qu'il [Conway] me traduisit en grande partie,
m'apprend que votre goutte est bien forte, vous n'aviez plus de douleurs, dites-
vous, mais votre faiblesse est extrême' (Mme du Deffand to HW 29 Dec. 1774,
DU DEFFAND iv. 125). HW wrote to Mann 23 Dec. 1774: 'You will perceive by
the change of writing that my hand hath lost its cunning. . . . The gout . . .
has . . . bound me hand and foot above a fortnight. However . . . the wounds
have not been deep, nor will the scars I think remain long. Yet for these last
five days I have been very ill, less by the gout than by its consequential weakness, which has chiefly affected my breast' (MANN viii. 66).

14. Chatham expressed his approval of
their conduct in a letter of 24 Dec. to
Stephen Sayre: 'I have not words to express my satisfaction, that the Congress
has conducted this most arduous and delicate business, with such manly wisdom
and calm resolution, as do the highest
honour to their deliberations. Very few
are the things contained in their resolves,
that I could wish had been otherwise'
(*Chatham Corr.* iv. 368).

From Conway, Sunday 25 December 1774

Missing; received 30 Dec.; answered *post* 31 Dec. 1774.

From Lady Ailesbury, ca Sunday 25 December 1774

Missing. 'La Milady m'a dit vous avoir écrit une lettre de sept pages, et qu'elle vous a rendu compte de tout ce qui pouvait vous intéresser' (Mme du Deffand to HW 29 Dec. 1774, DU DEFFAND iv. 126). HW received this letter along with Mme du Deffand's letter of 23–5 Dec. 1774: 'Celle de Milady Ailesbury, que je reçus avec, ne me plût nullement. Elle dit que vous vous êtes tellement épuisée à votre fête [Mme du Deffand's soirée of 24 Dec. for the Choiseuls], que vous en avez pensé mourir' (HW to Mme du Deffand 4 Jan. 1775, ibid. iv. 131).

To Conway, Monday 26 December 1774

Printed from *Works* v. 176–9.

Arlington Street, December 26, 1774.

I BEGIN my letter today, to prevent the fatigue of dictating two tomorrow.[1] In the first and best place, I am very near recovered; that is, though still a mummy,[2] I have no pain left, nor scarce any sensation of gout except in my right hand, which is still in complexion and shape a lobster's claw. Now, unless anybody can prove to me that three weeks are longer than five months and a half, they will hardly convince me that the bootikins are not a cure for fits of the gout, and a very short cure, though they cannot prevent it: nor perhaps is it to be wished they should; for, if the gout prevents everything else, would not one have something that does? I have but one single doubt left about the bootikins, which is, whether they do not weaken my breast: but as I am sensible that my own spirits do half

1. HW also dictated a letter to Mme du Deffand 26 Dec. 1774 (DU DEFFAND iv. 124–5).

2. That is, though still swathed in the bootikins.

the mischief, and that, if I could have held my tongue, and kept from talking and dictating letters, I should not have been half so bad as I have been, there remains but half due to bootikins on the balance: and surely the ravages of the last long fit, and two years more in age, ought to make another deduction. Indeed, my forcing myself to dictate my last letter to you[3] almost killed me; and since the gout is not dangerous to me if I am kept perfectly quiet, my good old friend[4] must have patience, and not insist upon letters from me but when it is quite easy to me to send them.[5] So much for me and my gout. I will now endeavour to answer such parts of your last letters[6] as I can in this manner, and considering how difficult it is to read *your* writing in a dark room.

I have not yet been able to look into the French harangues[7] you sent me. Voltaire's verses to Robert Covelle[8] are not only very bad, but very contemptible.

I am delighted with all the honours you receive,[9] and with all the amusements they procure you, which is the best part of honours. For the glorious part, I am always like the man in Pope's Donne,

Then happy he who shows the tombs, said I.[10]

3. *Ante* 23 Dec. 1774 (missing).
4. Mme du Deffand.
5. Mme du Deffand had written to HW 18 Dec. 1774: 'Si vous voulez m'obliger, vous donnerez de vos nouvelles deux fois la semaine, une à moi, l'autre à votre cousin' (DU DEFFAND iv. 121). HW replied 26 Dec. 1774: 'Vous oubliez la première de toutes les règles, qui est, que c'est le malade qu'on doit ménager, et non pas le malade qui doit ménager ceux qui se portent bien' (ibid. iv. 124).
6. Missing.
7. Not found. Perhaps they were speeches delivered upon the occasion of the opening of the new parliament of Paris 28 Nov.; one delivered that day by the advocate-general Séguier 'reçut de grands applaudissements,' while another, delivered 29 Nov. by M. Target, 'fut aussi fort applaudi' (*Mercure historique* Dec. 1774, clxxvii. 690 and n., 691). The *Gazette de Leyde* 9 Dec., 'Supplément,' *sub* 'Versailles, le 1 décembre,' prints a complimentary 'harangue' of M. d'Aligre addressed to Louis XVI at Versailles 27

Nov. on behalf of deputations from the parliament and the cour des aides, assembled to compliment the King upon his accession to the throne.
8. A goldsmith of Geneva, who in 1764 had refused to beg forgiveness of God on his knees before the Genevan Consistory for having fathered an illegitimate child by Catherine Ferboz; Voltaire espoused his cause and celebrated him in *La Guerre civile de Genève, ou les amours de Robert Covelle. Poëme héroïque* (1768). See Jean-P. Ferrier, 'Covelle, Voltaire, et l'affaire de la génuflexion,' *Bulletin de la Société d'Histoire et d'Archéologie de Genève*, Geneva, 1943–6, viii. 217–25; Voltaire, *Œuvres complètes*, ed. Moland, 1877–85, ix. 515–55.
9. Mme du Deffand wrote to HW 17 Dec. 1774 that Conway and his ladies 'plaisent généralement à tout le monde; ils doivent être contents de l'empressement qu'on leur marque' (DU DEFFAND iv. 119).
10. 'Then, happy man who shows the tombs! (said I)' (Pope, *Satires of Donne*, Satire IV, l. 102).

That is, they[11] are least troublesome there.[12] The *Serenissimé*[13] you met at Montmorency[14] is one of the least to my taste; we quarrelled about Rousseau, and I never went near him after my first journey. Madame du D[effand] will tell you the story, if she has not forgotten it.[15]

It is supposed here, that the new proceedings of the French parliament[16] will produce great effects: I don't suppose any such thing. What America will produce I know still less; but certainly something very serious. The merchants have summoned a meeting for the second of next month,[17] and the petition from the Congress to the King is arrived.[18] The heads have been shown to Lord Dartmouth;[19] but I hear one of the agents is against presenting it:[20] yet it is thought it will be delivered,[21] and then be ordered to be laid before

11. Kings and princes.

12. An allusion, presumably, to Conway's snub by Louis XVI at Fontainebleau 3 Nov. (*ante* ca 4 Nov. 1774); he had also been ill-received by the Princes of the Blood; see his letter to Keith 19 Nov. in Keith, *Memoirs and Correspondence*, ed. Mrs Gillespie Smyth, 1849, ii. 30.

13. The Prince de Conti (HW).

14. The seat of Mme de Luxembourg; Conway, Lady Ailesbury and Mrs Damer were there ca 15–17 Dec. (DU DEFFAND loc. cit.).

15. See *ante* 20 Jan. 1766, n. 8.

16. Which had opened 28 Nov. (n. 7 above).

17. On 4 Jan. there was 'a numerous meeting of the North American merchants, tradesmen and others concerned in American commerce,' at which it was decided to petition Parliament against the late measures of administration (*Daily Adv.* 6 Jan. 1775; *Last Journals* i. 417; Edmund Burke, *Correspondence*, Vol. III, ed. G. H. Guttridge, Cambridge, 1961, pp. 95, 97–8). See *post* 22 Jan. 1775.

18. See *ante* 15 Dec. 1774, n. 9. A copy of the petition was sent to Benjamin Franklin, agent for Massachusetts, New Jersey and Pennsylvania, as representing the colonial agents in London; he wrote of its receipt to Edmund Burke 19 Dec. (Burke, op. cit. 80–1).

19. The petition was delivered to him by Franklin, William Bollan, and Arthur

Lee, the last two also being agents for Massachusetts (Franklin to Charles Thomson 5 Feb. 1775 in Franklin, *Writings*, ed. A. H. Smyth, New York, 1905–7, vi. 303; Burke, op. cit. 81, n. 1).

20. Rather, three of the agents, Burke, representing New York, Paul Wentworth, New Hampshire, and Thomas Life, Connecticut, 'declined being concerned in it, and without consulting each other gave the same reason, viz. that they had no instructions relating to it from their constituents' (Franklin to Thomson 5 Feb. 1775, loc. cit.; see also Burke, op. cit. 81 and n. 1, 188–9, 196–8). According to a memorandum endorsed 'Mr Pownall' and dated 20 Dec. in Hist. MSS Comm., 11th Report, App. pt v, *Dartmouth MSS*, Vol. I, 1887, p. 372, Wentworth was particularly vehement against the petition, saying it 'is an assertion of all their claims in a very high tone and with very offensive expressions.'

21. Dartmouth, after perusing it, declared that 'he found nothing in it improper for him to present, and, afterwards sending for us, he informed us, that he had presented the petition to his Majesty, who had been pleased to receive it very graciously' (Franklin to Thomson 5 Feb. 1775, Franklin, op. cit. vi. 303–4). The petition was presented to the King on or before 24 Dec. (Arthur Lee to Richard H. Lee 22–6 Dec., in Peter Force, *American Archives*, 4th ser. i [Washington, 1837]. 1058).

Parliament.[22] The whole affair has already been talked of there on the army and navy days;[23] and Burke, they say, has shone[24] with amazing wit and ridicule on the late inactivity of Gage,[25] and his losing his cannon and straw;[26] on his being entrenched in a town with an army of observation;[27] with that army being, as Sir William Meredith had said, an asylum for magistrates, and to secure the port.[28] Burke said, he had heard of an asylum for debtors and whores, never for magistrates;[29] and of ships, never of armies, securing a port.[30] This is all there has been in Parliament, but elections. Charles Fox's place did not come into question.[31] Mr _____,[32] who is one of the

22. The King commanded Dartmouth to tell Franklin, Bollan, and Lee that the petition 'contained matters of such importance, that, as soon as they met, he would lay it before his two Houses of Parliament' (Franklin to Thomson 5 Feb. 1775, Franklin, op. cit. vi. 304). Franklin goes on to note that 'it came down among a great heap of letters of intelligence from governors and officers in America, newspapers, pamphlets, handbills, etc., from that country, the last in the list, and was laid upon the table with them, undistinguished by any particular recommendation of it to the notice of either House' (ibid.). It is listed in *Journals of the House of Commons* xxxv. 66, last among papers presented to the House relating to the American colonies 19 Jan., as 'No. 149. Petition of sundry persons, on behalf of themselves and the inhabitants of several of his Majesty's colonies in America: Received 21 December 1774'; in *Journals of the House of Lords* xxxiv. 290 it is the penultimate item, No. 148, among the papers presented 20 Jan.

23. See Cobbett, *Parl. Hist.* xviii. 54–68.

24. In the debate on continuing the land tax at three shillings a pound, 20 Dec. (ibid. xviii. 71–3).

25. 'It is, indeed, an absurdity without parallel; a warlike Parliament, and a patient forbearing general' (ibid. xviii. 72).

26. 'The account we have is, that the General . . . had cannon sent to him, but they were stolen . . . and that his straw has been burnt, and his brick and mortar destroyed' (ibid. xviii. 73). Gage had written to Dartmouth 17 Oct. that 'moderation and forbearance has been put to the test, by burning the straw, and sinking boats

with bricks, coming for the use of the troops,' and that he hoped 'we may be able to prevent' twelve pieces of cannon then en route from London 'from falling into bad hands' (Gage, *Correspondence*, ed. C. E. Carter, New Haven, 1931–3, i. 379).

27. 'The General is . . . besieged . . . and . . . in fine, Sir, your army is turned out to be a mere army of observation' (Cobbett, loc. cit.).

28. Burke asserted that the army was 'of no other use but as an asylum for magistrates,' to which Meredith retorted that 'the troops . . . were for the protection of the magistrates, the protection of the property and trade of the merchants, and the enforcing of the Acts,' the last being accomplished by the port being 'blocked up' (ibid.).

29. 'He had often heard of such places for thieves, rogues and female orphans; but it was the first time he ever heard of an asylum for magistrates' (ibid.).

30. 'As to the blocking up an harbour . . . to him this mode of blockade seemed rather novel' (ibid.).

31. He had been returned unopposed for Malmesbury 8 Oct. (*ante* 16 Oct. 1774, n. 27).

32. Perhaps David Hartley (ca 1730–1813), M.P. Kingston-upon-Hull 1774–80, 1782–4, described in *Last Journals* i. 412, n. 1, as 'much versed in finances . . . friend of Lord Rockingham . . . and . . . now in Parliament for the first time.' He spoke for the first time in Parliament 5 Dec. (ibid. i. 412; Cobbett, op. cit. xviii. 44), and though another speech of his 20 Dec. is described ibid. xviii. 69 as 'mild, sensible,' Wraxall mentions 'the intoler-

new elect, has opened, but with no success. There is a seaman, Lutt-rell,[33] that promises much better.

I am glad you like the Duchess de Lauzun:[34] she is one of my fa-vourites. The Hôtel du Châtelet promised to be very fine, but was not finished when I was last at Paris.[35] I was much pleased with the person that slept against St-Lambert's[36] poem:[37] I wish I had thought of the nostrum, when Mr ———,[38] a thousand years ago, at Lyons, would read an epic poem to me just as I had received a dozen letters from England. St-Lambert is a great jackanapes, and a very tiny genius. I suppose the poem was *The Seasons*,[39] which is four fans[40] spun out into a Georgic.[41]

If I had not been too ill, I should have thought of bidding you hear midnight mass on Christmas Eve in Madame du Deffand's tri-bune, as I used to do.[42] To be sure, you know that her apartment was part of Madame du Montespan's,[43] whose arms are on the back of

able length' and 'dullness of his speeches' (*Historical and Posthumous Memoirs*, ed. Wheatley, 1884, iii. 124), and Anthony Storer calls him a 'boar' (Hist. MSS Comm., 15th Report, App. pt vi, *Carlisle MSS*, 1897, p. 315).

33. Hon. John Luttrell (later Luttrell Olmius) (ca 1740–1829), 3d E. of Carhamp-ton 1821; M.P. Stockbridge 1774–5, 1780–5; Capt. R. N. 1762 (John Hardy, *Chronologi-cal List of the Captains*, 1779, p. 52). He spoke 12 and 13 Dec. in the debate on the navy estimates (Cobbett, op. cit. xviii. 55, 58–9).

34. Amélie de Boufflers (1751–94), m. (1766) Armand-Louis de Gontaut, Comte (later Duc) de Biron, Duc de Lauzun (DU DEFFAND i. 24, n. 20 *et passim*).

35. HW visited it in Sept. of 1775 ('Paris Journals,' ibid. v. 348). It was in the rue de Grenelle, Faubourg Saint-Germain, and in 1776 'vient d'être achevé. Son grand extérieur est frappant, et la distribution des appartements mérite d'être vue' (*Al-manach parisien*, [?1776], p. 110). The ar-chitect was Mathurin Cherpitel (1736–1809); the building in 1968 housed the Ministère du Travail (*Dictionnaire de biographie française*, 1933– , viii. 1028; *The Blue Guides: Paris*, ed. S. Rossiter, 1968, p. 50).

36. Jean-François de Saint-Lambert (*ante* 10 Oct. 1765, n. 20).

37. See below.

38. Identified by Wright and subsequent

editors as Thomas Seward (1708–90), poet and divine. He was travelling tutor to Lord Charles Fitzroy, 4th son of the 2d D. of Grafton, who died in Italy in July 1739; he presumably met HW at Lyons on his return to England in Sept. or Oct. of that year (see OSSORY ii. 422–3 and nn. 7, 9; GM 1739, ix. 439; *ante* connecting note between 24 March OS and ca 8 Nov. 1739 NS).

39. First published in 1769.

40. Eighteenth-century fans were com-monly decorated with pastoral scenes.

41. The poem, written in alexandrine couplets, fills 163 pages in the 1769 'Am-sterdam' [Paris] duodecimo edition. HW wrote to Mme du Deffand 21 March 1769 corroborating her opinion that it was a 'plat ouvrage! point de suite, point d'imagination, une philosophie froide et déplacée; un berger et une bergère qui re-viennent à tous moments; des apostrophes sans cesse,' etc. (DU DEFFAND ii. 213). For other contemporary opinions of the poem, see Luigi de Nardis, *Saint-Lambert: Scienza e paesaggio nella poesia del Settecento*, Rome, 1961, pp. 131–41.

42. HW records having done this on Christmas Eve of 1765 in 'Paris Journals,' DU DEFFAND v. 289.

43. Françoise-Athénaïs de Rochechouart (1641–1707), m. (1663) Henri-Louis de Pardaillan de Gondrin, Marquis de Monte-span; mistress of Louis XIV.

the grate in Madame du Deffand's own bedchamber.[44] Apropos, ask
her to show you Madame de Prie's picture, M. le Duc's[45] mistress—
I am very fond of it[46]—and make her tell you her history.[47]

I have but two or three words more. Remember my parcel of letters from Madame du D[effand][48] and pray remember this injunc-
tion, not to ruin yourselves in bringing presents. A very slight fair-
ing[49] of a guinea or two obliges as much, is more fashionable, and
not a moment sooner forgotten than a magnificent one; and then
you may very cheaply oblige the more persons: but as the sick fox,
in Gay's *Fables*, says (for one always excepts oneself),

A chicken too might do me good—[50]

I allow you to go as far as three or even five guineas for a snuff-box
for me: and then, as George Grenville told the King, when he asked
for the reversion of the Light House for two lives, and the King reproached him with having always advised him against granting re-
versions; he replied, 'Oh Sir, but if your Majesty will give me this,
I will take care you shall never give away another.'[51]

Adieu, with my own left hand,

Hor. Walpole

44. 'Mme du Deffand's tribune . . . is
in the chapel of the nuns of St-Joseph,
founded by Mme de Montespan, whose
arms are on the back of Mme du Deffand's
chimney' (du Deffand, loc cit.). Actually,
Mme de Montespan was not the foundress
of the convent, but a benefactress, in
recognition of which she was accorded the
rights and privileges reserved 'aux mem-
bres fondateurs,' including the privilege
of lodging there (Henri Carré, *Madame de
Montespan*, 1939, pp. 219–20). Mme du
Deffand 'occupait le petit appartement'
of Mme de Montespan, 'au-dessous de la
grande. . . . Le petit appartement avait
une tribune qui donnait dans la chapelle'
(HW's note to Mme du Deffand's MS
Recueil de lettres, du Deffand i. 12, n. 11;
see also ibid. vi. 3–4).

45. De Bourbon.

46. See *ante* 12 Nov. 1774, *post* 15 Jan.
1775.

47. Mme de Prie was sent to Courbé-
pine in Normandy, 12 June 1726, when
her lover, the Duc, was disgraced. 'Mme

du Deffand told me . . . at first she bore
her banishment well, but finding no hopes,
grew desperate, acted illness, and made
them give her emetics and opium, which
were bad for fits that she was subject
to, and so killed herself' ('Paris Journals,'
du Deffand v. 275; ibid. v. 214, n. 1).

48. See *ante* 28 Sept. 1774.

49. Literally, a present given at or
brought from a fair; by transference, a
complimentary gift of any kind (OED).

50. John Gay, Fable XXIX ('The Fox
at the Point of Death') l. 50. HW quotes
this and the two preceding lines to Mann
22 Dec. 1772 (Mann vii. 450).

51. Cf. *Mem. Geo. III* ii. 145 and n. 1.
Grenville records in his 'Diary,' *sub* 13
Aug. 1764: 'Mr Grenville . . . took an opportunity to apprize his Majesty that there
was a grant of a Light House in the disposal of the Treasury, which was to expire in four years, held now by Lord
Leicester's executors. He humbly asked
of his Majesty to bestow this upon him as
a provision for his younger children. . . .

To Conway, Saturday 31 December 1774

Printed from *Works* v. 179–82.

Arlington Street, December 31, 1774.

NO child was ever so delighted to go into breeches, as I was this morning to get on a pair of cloth shoes as big as Jack Harris's:[1] this joy may be the spirits of dotage—but what signifies whence one is happy? Observe too that this is written with my own *right* hand, with the bootikin actually upon it, which has no distinction of fingers: so I no longer see any miracle in Buckinger,[2] who was famous for writing without hands or *feet* (as if it was indifferent which one uses, provided one has a pair of either). Take notice, I write so much better without fingers than with, that I advise *you* to try a bootikin. To be sure, the operation is a little slower; but to a prisoner, the duration of his amusement is of far more consequence than the vivacity of it.

Last night I received your very kind, I might say *your* letter *tout court,* of Christmas Day.[3] By this time I trust you are quite out of pain about me. My fit has been as regular as possible; only, as if the bootikins were post-horses, it made the grand tour of all my limbs in three weeks. If it will always use the same expedition, I am content it should take the journey once in two years. You must not mind my breast: it was always the weakest part of a very weak system; yet did not suffer now by the gout, but in consequence of it; and would not have been near so bad, if I could have kept from talking and dictating letters. The moment I am out of pain I am in high spirits; and though I never take any medicines, there is one thing absolutely necessary to be put into my mouth—a gag. At present the town is so empty that my tongue is a sine-cure.

The King was graciously pleased to grant it' (*Grenville Papers* ii. 512). However, HW notes, loc. cit., that 'when Grenville notified the boon at the Treasury, he learned, to his inexpressible mortification, that the reversion was already engaged.'

1. Who also suffered from gout in the feet; see *ante* 7 Aug. 1760, 25 May 1766, Ossory ii. 525.

2. Matthew Buckinger (originally Buchinger) (b. 1674, d. 1737–9), German dwarf, born without hands or feet, who developed remarkable abilities, including the ability to write diminutively. See ibid. i. 94, n. 1, and for specimens of his calligraphy, GM 1791, lxi pt i plate 2 opp. p. 417, and C. J. Smith, *Historical and Literary Curiosities*, 1847, plate 56.

3. Missing.

I am well acquainted with the Bibliothèque du Roi,[4] and the medals, and the prints.[5] I spent an entire day in looking over the English portraits, and kept the librarian without his dinner till dark night, till I was satisfied.[6] Though the Choiseuls will not *acquaint* with you,[7] I hope their Abbé Barthélemi[8] is not put under the same quarantine. Besides great learning, he has infinite wit and *polissonnerie*, and is one of the best kind of men in the world. As to the grandpapa,[9] *il ne nous aime pas nous autres*, and has never forgiven Lord Chatham. Though exceedingly agreeable himself, I don't think his taste exquisite.—Perhaps I was piqued; but he seemed to like Wood better than any of us.[10] Indeed I am a little afraid that my dear friend's impetuous zeal may have been a little too prompt in pressing you upon them *d'abord:*[11]—but don't say a word of this—it is her great goodness.—I thank you a million of times for all yours to her:—she is perfectly grateful for it.

The Chevalier's verses are pretty enough.[12] I own I like Saurin's[13]

4. Now the Bibliothèque Nationale.

5. Several of which HW mentions in 'Paris Journals, Anecdotes 1766,' DU DEFFAND v. 358; see also FAMILY 280–1.

6. HW first visited the Bibliothèque 5 April 1766, and on 1 Oct. 1767 visited it again with George Selwyn, returning after dinner ('Paris Journals,' ibid. v. 311, 323). The King's librarian 1741–70 was Armand-Jérôme Bignon (1711–72), while Hugues-Adrien Joly (1718–1800) was curator of the prints from ca 1750 (NBG; *Dictionnaire de biographie française,* 1933–   , vi. 434; *Almanach royal, passim*).

7. Mme du Deffand wrote to HW 29 Dec. 1774 that the Choiseuls, who had come to Paris in Dec., would not see Conway or Lady Ailesbury except 'par rencontre chez moi ou ailleurs; ils se sont fait une loi de ne point recevoir d'étrangers' (DU DEFFAND iv. 126). In Feb. she prevailed upon the Duchess to receive Conway and Lady Ailesbury; however, by then it was too late; the Conways were miffed, and 'ils ne voulurent pas en profiter.' The Duchess, afraid that she may have offended HW by her recalcitrance, made Mme du Deffand promise to excuse her 'le mieux qu'il me serait possible': Mme du Deffand's excuse was that

the Duchess's 'déférence pour son mari est extrême' (ibid. iv. 155).

8. The author of the *Voyage du jeune Anacharsis* (HW). Jean-Jacques Barthélemy (1716–95), Abbé; antiquarian; writer; curator of the King's medals; a devoted friend of the Choiseuls (DU DEFFAND *passim; Dictionnaire de biographie française* v. 666–8).

9. A name given to the Duc de Choiseul by Madame du Deffand (HW). See DU DEFFAND i. 11, n. 2 for an explanation.

10. See *ante* 9 Sept. 1767 and n. 20.

11. Mme du Deffand had written to HW 4 Dec. 1774 of her having no doubts that Conway and Lady Ailesbury 'ne soient fort fêtés par M. et Mme de Choiseul; par la grand'maman, j'en suis sûre' (DU DEFFAND iv. 115).

12. Verses written by the Chevalier de Boufflers, to be presented by Mme du Deffand to the Duke and Duchess of Choiseul. They are mere *vers de société*, and would not be tolerable out of the society for which they were written (Mary Berry).

13. Bernard-Joseph Saurin, dramatist and occasional poet (*ante* 29 Nov. 1765, n. 15). The verses, addressed to 'Monsieur de Malesherbes, premier président de la cour des aides,' are printed *Works* v. 181, n. 2.

much better than you seem to do. Perhaps I am prejudiced by the curse on the Chancellor[14] at the end.[15]

Not a word of news here. In a sick-room one hears all there is, but I have not heard even a lie: but as this will not set out these three days,[16] it is to be hoped some charitable Christian will tell a body one. Lately indeed we heard that the King of Spain had abdicated;[17] but I believe it was some stock-jobber that had deposed him.

Lord George Cavendish, for my solace in my retirement, has given me a book, the history of his own Furness Abbey, written by a Scotch ex-Jesuit.[18] I cannot say that this unnatural conjunction of a Cavendish and a Jesuit has produced a lively colt; but I found one passage worth any money. It is in an extract of a constable's[19] journal kept during the civil war; and ends thus: 'And there was never heard of such troublesome and distracted times as these five years have been, *but especially for constables.*'[20] It is so natural, that *inconvenient to my Lord Castlecomer* is scarce a better proverb.[21]

Pray tell Lady A. that though she has been so very good to me,[22] I address my letters to you rather than to her, because my pen is not always upon its guard, but is apt to say whatever comes into its nib; and then if she peeps over your shoulder, I am *censé*[23] not to know it. Lady Harriet's wishes have done me great good: nothing but a father's gout could be obdurate enough to resist them.[24] My Mrs D[amer] says nothing to me; but I give her intentions credit, and lay her silence on you.

14. Maupeou.

15. 'Mais disons que le diable emporte/ On sait bien qui!' (ibid.).

16. Tuesday, 3 Jan., was the next post day for Europe (*Court and City Register* 1775, p. 125).

17. 'An evening paper says, that an express arrived yesterday from Spain, with an account that the King of Spain has retired from the sovereignty, and that the Prince of Asturias [his eldest son, the future Charles IV] has assumed the reins of government' (*Daily Adv.* 28 Dec.). This was a false rumour.

18. *The Antiquities of Furness; or, an Account of the Royal Abbey of St Mary . . . near Dalton in Furness, belonging to . . . Lord George Cavendish,* 1774, by

Thomas West (1720–79), a Scottish Jesuit on the English mission stationed at Titcup Hall, near Dalton in Furness (DNB). The book is dedicated to Lord George; HW's copy is Hazen, *Cat. of HW's Lib.*, No. 258.

19. Thomas Park of Millwood, high constable of Furness 1642–7 (West, op. cit. li).

20. Ibid. lii.

21. See *ante* 15 Oct. 1758, n. 12, 27 Nov. 1774.

22. Presumably an allusion to her missing letter of 'sept pages' *ante* ca 25 Dec. 1774.

23. Supposed.

24. An allusion to the decrepit state of Lady Harriet's father, Lord Harrington (*ante* 27 Sept. 1774).

January 1, 1775; and a Happy New Year!

I walk! I walk! walk alone!—I have been five times quite round my room today, and my month is not up! The day after tomorrow I shall go down into the dining-room;[24a] the next week to take the air; and then if Mrs _____[25] is very pressing, why, I don't know what may happen. Well! but you want news—there are none to be had. They think there is a ship lost with Gage's dispatches.[26] Lady Temple gives all her diamonds to Miss Nugent.[27] Lord Pigot[28] lost 400 pounds the other night at Princess Amelia's.[29] Miss Davis[30] has carried her cause against Mrs Yates,[31] and is to sing again at the opera.[32] This is all my coffee-house furnished this morning.

From CONWAY, January 1775

Missing; answered *post* 15 Jan. 1775, *sub* 17 Jan. Probably sent by Sir Thomas Clarges, 3d Bt, who was to leave Paris ca 7 Jan., and had arrived in London by 13 Jan. (DU DEFFAND iv. 129, 137).

24a. I.e., the Refectory or Great Parlour.

25. Left blank in all previous editions, but very possibly Mrs Clive.

26. There seems to have been no such accident; the *Daily Adv.* 3 Jan. reports the arrival 29 Dec. 'at Plymouth' of 'his Majesty's schooner, the St *Laurance* . . . express from Boston,' while the *London Chronicle* 29–31 Dec., xxxvi. 630, reports that late the night of 29 Dec. 'an express arrived at Lord Suffolk's office . . . from . . . General Gage.' The *Daily Adv.* 4 Jan. prints a proclamation of Gen. Gage and other news from America, presumably received by the above-mentioned ship.

27. Hon. Mary Elizabeth Nugent (d. 1812), m. (16 April 1775) George Grenville, 2d E. Temple, 1779, cr. (1784) M. of Buckingham. Grenville was heir of the present Lord Temple, his uncle. Lady

Mary Coke writes in her *Journals*, iv. 450, *sub* 27 Dec., that Lady Temple 'acts very nobly: she gives all her fine jewels to the future Mrs Greenville, and entails them in the family' (see also ibid. iv. 446, 448).

28. George Pigot (1719–77), cr. (1766) Bn Pigot.

29. Lady Mary Coke mentions ibid. iv. 450, *sub* 28 Dec., the 'high play' introduced there at this time by 'Mrs [the Hon. Caroline] Howe.'

30. Cecilia Davies (ca 1750–1836), called 'L'Inglesina' and 'l'Inghilesina'; soprano singer (MANN vii. 547, n. 10).

31. See *ante* 27 Nov. 1774 and n. 33.

32. She had sung there during the 1773–4 season, but did not return until 1777 (*London Stage* Pt IV, iii. 1743–4, 1831, 1910; Pt V, i. 53).

To Conway and Lady Ailesbury,
Sunday 15 January 1775

Printed from *Works* v. 182–6.

Arlington Street, January 15, 1775.

YOU have made me very happy by saying your journey to Naples is laid aside. Perhaps it made too great impression on me; but you must reflect, that all my life I have satisfied myself with your being perfect, instead of trying to be so myself. I don't ask you to return, though I wish it: in truth, there is nothing to invite you. I don't want you to come and breathe fire and sword against the Bostonians, like that second Duke of Alva[1] the inflexible Lord George Germain;[2] or to anathematize the Court and all its works, like the incorruptible B[urke] who scorns lucre, except when he can buy an hundred thousand acres from naked Caribs for a song.[3] I don't want you to do anything like a party man. I trust you think of every party as I do, with contempt, from Lord Chatham's mustard-bowl[4] down to Lord Rockingham's hartshorn. All perhaps will be tried in their turns; and yet, if they had genius, might not be mighty enough to save us—from some ruin or other I think nobody can, and what signifies an option of mischiefs?

An account is come of the Bostonians having voted an army of sixteen thousand men, who are to be called *minute men,* as they are to be ready at a minute's warning.[5] Two directors or commissioners, I

1. Fernando Álvarez de Toledo (1508–82), Duque d'Alba or d'Alva; Spanish general notorious for his suppression of the revolt against King Philip II's authority in the Netherlands (1567).

2. For Germain's advocacy of firm measures against the American rebels, see Namier and Brooke iii. 394–5.

3. Burke's younger brother, Richard, had, according to a memorial of his read at the Treasury 2 July 1773, purchased certain lands from the 'red' Caribs in St Vincent in 1770 (Burke, *Correspondence,* Vol. II, ed. L. S. Sutherland, Cambridge, 1960, p. 453, n. 3). An unfavourable account of the 'adventurers' who were said to have cheated the 'red' Caribs into selling large tracts of land, appeared in

the *Public Advertiser* 20 March 1771 in a letter from St Vincent dated 6 Jan., and the government subsequently disputed the legality of these purchases (Burke, op. cit. 227 and n. 3, 307 and n. 3). Edmund's loyal support of his brother aroused the suspicion that he was involved in the speculation, and HW wrote to Mason 23 March 1774 that 'Mr Burke . . . has a tolerable stake in St Vincent's' (MASON i. 142 and n. 21; see also *Last Journals* i. 419). On 21 Nov. 1775 the Treasury declared Richard's claim to the lands in question null and void (Burke, op. cit. 524).

4. See *ante* 6 Feb. 1764, n. 25.

5. 'In this province they have established what they call Minute-Men; that

don't know what they are called, are appointed.[6] There has been too a kind of mutiny in the 5th regiment. A soldier was found drunk on his post. Gage, in this time of *danger,* thought rigour necessary, and sent the fellow to a court martial. They ordered 200 lashes. The General ordered them to improve their sentence. Next day it was published in the *Boston Gazette.*[7] He called them before him, and required them on oath to abjure the communication: three officers refused. Poor G. is to be scapegoat, not for this, but for what was a reason against employing him, incapacity.[8] I wonder at the precedent! Howe is talked of for his successor.[9]—Well, I have done with *you!*—Now I shall go gossip with Lady A.

You must know, Madam, that near Bath is erected a new Parnassus, composed of three laurels, a myrtle tree, a weeping-willow, and a view of the Avon, which has been new-christened Helicon. Ten years ago there lived a Madam Riggs,[10] an old rough humourist who passed for a wit; her daughter who passed for nothing, married to a Captain Miller,[11] full of good-natured officiousness. These good folks were friends of Miss Rich,[12] who carried me to dine with them at

is, a body of men ready to turn out and take the field at a minute's warning ('Extract of a letter received in London, from an officer at Boston, dated December 17, 1774,' in Peter Force, *American Archives,* 4th ser. i [Washington, 1837]. 1050; see also the address of the first Massachusetts Provincial Congress 'to the freeholders and other inhabitants of . . . Massachusetts Bay,' dated 'Cambridge, Dec. 10, 1774,' printed *Boston Gazette* 12 Dec. and reprinted *Gazetteer and New Daily Advertiser* 14 Jan.). On 21 Feb. 1775 the Massachusetts Committee of Safety voted that the Committee of Supplies should 'purchase all kinds of warlike stores, sufficient for an army of 15,000 men to take the field' (minute of the Committee of Safety, printed Force, op. cit. i. 1367).

6. Possibly a reference to the appointment 8 Dec. of Col. John Thomas (1724–76) and Col. William Heath (1737–1814) as general officers of the militia. However, they were apparently subordinate general officers; on 27 Oct. the Provincial Congress had appointed Jedediah Preble, Artemas Ward, and Col. Seth Pomeroy to be first, second, and third in

command (*Journals of each Provincial Congress of Massachusetts in 1774 and 1775,* ed. W. Lincoln, Boston, 1838, pp. 35, 65; *Dictionary of American Biography*).

7. This report did not appear in the *Gazette,* and no other account has been found of this 'mutiny.'

8. Gage was not relieved of his command at this time, but, in July, George III decided to recall him; see Mason i. 219, nn. 15–16.

9. He sailed for Boston at the head of reinforcements for Gage in April (*London Chronicle* 20–2 April, xxxvii. 382), and in October succeeded Gage as commander-in-chief in America.

10. Margaret Pigott (ca 1714–88), m. Edward Riggs (Mann viii. 197, n. 17).

11. Anna Riggs (1741–81), m. (1765) John Miller (after ca 1765 Riggs Miller) (d. 1798), Capt. 113th Ft 1761; ret. 1763; cr. (1778) Bt; M.P. Newport 1784–90 (ibid. viii. 197, nn. 14, 16; Namier and Brooke iii. 138).

12. Daughter of Sir Robert Rich, and sister to the second wife of George Lord Lyttelton (HW).

Batheaston, now Pindus.[13] They caught a little of what was then called taste, built and planted, and begot children, till the whole caravan were forced to go abroad to retrieve.[14] Alas! Mrs Miller is returned a beauty, a genius, a Sappho, a tenth muse, as romantic as Mademoiselle Scuderi, and as sophisticated as Mrs Vesey. The Captain's fingers are loaded with cameos, his tongue runs over with virtu; and that both may contribute to the improvement of their own country, they have introduced *bouts-rimés* as a new discovery.[15] They hold a Parnassus fair every Thursday,[16] give out rhymes and themes, and all the flux of quality at Bath contend for the prizes. A Roman vase dressed with pink ribbands and myrtles receives the poetry,[17] which is drawn out every festival: six judges of these Olympic games retire and select the brightest compositions, which the respective successful acknowledge, kneel to Mrs Calliope Miller, kiss her fair hand, and are crowned by it with myrtle, with—I don't know what. You may think this a fiction, or exaggeration.—Be dumb, unbelievers! The collection is printed, published—[18] yes, on my faith! there are *bouts-rimés* on a buttered muffin, by her Grace the Duchess of Northumberland;[19] receipts to make them by Corydon the venerable, alias George Pitt;[20] others very pretty, by Lord Palmerston;[21] some by Lord Carmarthen;[22] many by Mrs Miller her-

13. HW describes the visit to Montagu 22 Oct. 1766 (MONTAGU ii. 233).

14. Mrs Riggs, the Millers and their infant daughter went to France in 1770; at Paris a son was born, John Edward Augustus Miller (later Riggs Miller) (1770–1825), 2d Bt, 1798 (Ruth A. Hesselgrave, *Lady Miller and the Batheaston Literary Circle*, New Haven, 1927, p. 3).

15. 'Here [at Batheaston] it was imagined . . . to naturalize a little Gallic institution, which has been productive of much wit and pleasantry to that light and sprightly nation . . . called *Bouts Rimés*' (*Poetical Amusements at a Villa Near Bath*, Bath, 1775, p. iii).

16. 'Every other Thursday' (ibid. viii).

17. A 'vase . . . found by a labouring man in 1769 at Frescati, near the spot where is supposed formerly to have stood the Tusculanum of Cicero . . . is at present the receptacle of all the contending poetical morsels' (ibid. vii-viii; the vase is illustrated in the frontispiece).

18. 12 Jan. (OSSORY i. 221, n. 1); HW's copy, now WSL, is Hazen, *Cat. of HW's Lib.*, No. 2420. HW kept it locked in the Glass Closet, doubtless because of a long satirical note on a fly-leaf.

19. HW wrote to Lady Ossory 19 Jan. 1775 that 'the Duchess . . . has got very jollily through her task' (OSSORY i. 225). Her contribution, printed *Poetical Amusements* pp. 10–11, ends: 'I should prefer a butter'd muffin./A muffin, Jove himself might feast on,/If eat with Miller at Batheaston.'

20. Ibid. 15–16.

21. HW mentions 'one very pretty copy by Lord Palmerston' to Lady Ossory 19 Jan. 1775 (loc. cit.); of Palmerston's six contributions, five are *bouts rimés*, while the sixth is a longer poem on the subject, 'Beauty' (*Poetical Amusements* pp. 12–13, 52–7, 60, 61, 62–3).

22. Francis Godolphin Osborne (1751–99), styled Marquess of Carmarthen 1761–89; 5th Duke of Leeds 1789. He contrib-

self,[23] that have no fault but wanting metre; and immortality promised to her without end or measure.[24] In short, since folly, which never ripens to madness but in this hot climate, ran distracted, there never was anything so entertaining, or so dull—for you cannot read so long as I have been telling.

January 17.

Before I could finish this, I received your dispatches by Sir T[homas] Clarges,[25] and a most entertaining letter in three tomes.[26] It is being very dull not to be able to furnish a quarter so much from your own country—but what can I do? You are embarked in a new world, and I am living on the scraps of an old one, of which I am tired. The best I can do is to reply to your letter, and not attempt to amuse you when I have nothing to say. I think the Parliament meets today or in a day or two[27]—but I hope you are coming—your brother says so, and Madame du Deff[and] says so;[28] and sure it is time to leave Paris, when you know ninety of the inhabitants.[29] There seems much affectation in those that will not know you;[30] and affectation is always a littleness—it has been even rude;[31] but to be sure the rudeness one feels least is that which is addressed to one before there has been any acquaintance.

Ninon[32] came, because, on Madame du D.'s mentioning it, I concluded it a new work, and am disappointed. I can say this by heart.[33]

uted three *bouts rimés,* printed ibid. 4, 24–5.

23. She contributed three *bouts rimés,* and four longer poems.

24. There are five laudatory poems expressly addressed to her, and numerous others containing her praises.

25. (1751–82), 3d Bt.

26. Missing.

27. It met 19 Jan. (*Journals of the House of Commons* xxxv. 62).

28. 'Vos parents iront, je crois, la semaine prochaine à Saint-Cyr; après quoi leur départ sera bien proche' (Mme du Deffand to HW 11 Jan. 1775, du Deffand iv. 133).

29. 'Savez-vous combien il [Conway] connaît déjà de personnes dans Paris? Quatre-vingt-six. Il n'est nullement sauvage' (idem to idem 3 Jan. 1775, ibid. iv. 131).

30. The Duke de Choiseul (HW); also possibly the Princes of the Blood (*ante* 26 Dec. 1774, n. 12, 31 Dec. 1774).

31. Perhaps an allusion to Conway's encounter with the Prince de Conti at Montmorency in December; see *ante* 26 Dec. 1774.

32. The Life of Ninon de l'Enclos (HW). See next note.

33. Mme du Deffand had sent HW her copy of *Mémoires sur la vie de mademoiselle de Lenclos* by Antoine Bret (1717–92), Amsterdam, 1751, bound with *Mémoires et lettres pour servir à l'histoire de la vie de mademoiselle de L'Enclos,* ed. —— Douxménil (d. 1777), Rotterdam, 1751 (du Deffand iv. 121, n. 3 and corrigendum). However, HW already owned a copy of the Douxménil *Mémoires* (Hazen, *Cat. of HW's Lib.,* No. 988 : 2), upon which he had based his article in *The World,* No. xxviii, 12 July 1753. See du Deffand iv. 121–2, 125, 128–9, 136.

The picture of Madame de Prie,[34] which you don't seem to value, and so Madame du D. says, I believe I shall dispute with you: I think it charming, but when offered to me years ago, I would not take it— it was now given to you a little *à mon intention.*[35]

I am sorry that, amongst all the verses you have sent me, you should have forgotten what you commend the most, *Les Trois exclamations;*[36] I hope you will bring them with you. Voltaire's[37] are intolerably stupid, and not above the level of officers in garrison. Some of M. de Pezay's[38] are very pretty, though there is too much of them; and in truth I had seen them before.[39] Those on Madame de la Valière pretty too, but one is a little tired of Venus and the Graces. I am most pleased with your own[40]—and if you have a mind to like them still better, make Madame du D. show you mine,[41] which are neither French, nor measure, nor metre. She is unwilling to tell me so;[42] which diverts me. Yours are really genteel and new.

I envy you the Russian anecdotes[43] more than M. de Chamfort's

34. It is now at Strawberry Hill (HW). See *ante* 12 Nov., 26 Dec. 1774, and next note.

35. Mme du Deffand wrote to HW 3 Jan. 1775, *sub* 4 Jan.: 'Je donnai hier à votre cousin le portrait de Mme de Prie; j'y pensai mettre la condition que c'était en cas que vous n'en eussiez point d'envie; il ne me parut pas lui faire grand plaisir, j'imagine qu'il vous le céderait sans peine' (DU DEFFAND iv. 129–30). The picture was hung beside the window in the Red Bedchamber ('Des. of SH,' *Works* ii. 438); withdrawn SH xxii. 52, it was sold at Christie's, 14 May 1920, Lot 97, for 72 guineas to C. Brunner of Paris (DU DEFFAND iv. 130, n. 6).

36. An epigram on Jean-Baptiste-Antoine Suard (1733–1817), journalist; not found (ibid. iv. 131; NBG).

37. Presumably his verses to be sung at Mme du Deffand's Christmas Eve party for the Choiseuls, enclosed in his letters to her of 2 and 5 Dec. 1774; she had requested them in a letter of 24 Nov. 1774, and wrote to HW 11 Dec. 1774 that they were 'de la plus grande platitude'; see also her letter to Voltaire 9 Dec. 1774 (Voltaire, *Correspondence*, ed. Besterman, Geneva, 1953–65, lxxxix. 122, 133–4, 135–6, 151–2; DU DEFFAND iv. 118).

38. Alexandre-Frédéric-Jacques de Mas-

son (1741–77), Marquis de Pezay (ibid. *passim*).

39. Mme du Deffand had sent HW verses to her by Pezay in her letter of 22 June 1774.

40. They were . . . sent with a *porcelaine déjeuné* to the Vicomtesse de Cambis at the beginning of the new year, when it was the universal custom at Paris to interchange small presents known by the name of *étrennes* (Mary Berry). They are printed *Works* v. 185, n. 1.

41. HW's verses for Mme de Choiseul (missing); see DU DEFFAND iv. 133.

42. 'Ceux [verses] que le sentiment dicte sont à l'abri de la critique' (Mme du Deffand to HW 11 Jan. 1775, ibid.). HW reproaches her for her 'ménagement poli pour mes couplets' in his letter of 19 Jan. 1775 (ibid. iv. 138).

43. The account of the revolution in Russia which placed Catherine II on the throne, by M. de la Rulhière, now published. Mr Conway had heard it read in manuscript in a private society (Mary Berry). Mme du Deffand mentioned the account in her letter to HW 10 Dec. 1769, *sub* 13 Dec. (DU DEFFAND ii. 319); it was *Anecdotes sur la révolution de Russie, en l'année 1762,* by Claude-Carloman de Rulhière (1735–91), poet, formerly secretary of the French embassy in Russia, who had circulated the account in manu-

fables,[44] of which I know nothing; and as you say no more, I conclude I lose not much. The stories of Sir Charles[45] are so far not new to me, that I heard them of him from abroad after he was mad:[46] but I believe no mortal of his acquaintance ever heard them before; nor did they at all correspond with his former life, with his treatment of his wife,[47] or his history with Mrs Woffington,[48] *qui n'était pas dupe.* I say nothing on the other stories you tell me of billets dropped,[49] *et pour cause.*

I think I have touched all your paragraphs, and have nothing new to send you in return. In truth, I go nowhere but into private rooms; for I am not enough recovered to re-launch into the world, when I have so good an excuse for avoiding it. The bootikins have done wonders; but even two or three such victories will cost too dear. I submit very patiently to my lot. I am old and broken, and it never was my system to impose upon myself when one can deceive nobody else. I have spirits enough for my use, that is, amongst my friends and cotemporaries: I like young people and their happiness for everything but to live with; but I cannot learn their language, nor tell them old stories, of which I must explain every step as I go. Politics, the proper resource of age, I detest—I am contented, but see few that are so—and I never will be led by any man's self-interest. A

script after his return to France in 1765. Catherine's emissaries vainly sought to suppress it, and it was printed after her death in 1797 (ibid. ii. 319–20, n. 7).

44. HW presumably means Chamfort's *contes*, which were apparently not published until after his death, in 1795 (see his *Œuvres*, ed. Ginguené, Paris, 1795, 4 vols; Bibl. Nat. Cat.; BM Cat.).

45. Sir Charles Hanbury Williams (HW).

46. He was confined for insanity after his return from his embassy to St Petersburg in 1758 (SELWYN 322).

47. Lady Frances Coningsby (d. 1781), m. (1732) Sir Charles Hanbury Williams. HW writes in his account of Sir Charles that Sir Charles had 'poxed' her; they separated permanently in 1742 (ibid. 312 and n. 15; Lord Ilchester and Mrs Langford-Brooke, *Life of Sir Charles Hanbury-Williams*, 1929, pp. 55–7).

48. Whom he kept as his mistress the winter of 1744 (SELWYN 52, n. 42).

49. This alludes to circumstances Mr Conway mentions as having taken place at a ball at Versailles (HW). The Comte de Mercy-Argenteau wrote to Maria Theresa 19 Jan.: 'Il est arrivé un petit événement au bal de la reine le 2 de ce mois. Un jeune homme nommé le marquis de Douvetot [César-Louis-Marie-François-Ange (1749–1825), Vicomte de Houdetot] trouva dans la salle du bal un billet: c'était une déclaration d'une femme à son amant. Le jeune homme eut l'imprudence . . . de faire lire ce billet à d'autres jeunes gens, et il s'ensuivit des soupçons sur plusieurs femmes et beaucoup de propos. La reine en ayant été instruit fit imposer silence sur cette aventure, et punit la légèreté du marquis de Douvetot en lui faisant défendre de reparaître aux bals de la cour' (*Correspondance secrète entre Marie-Thérèse et le comte de Mercy-Argenteau*, ed. Arneth and Geffroy, 1874, ii. 287–8; see also Louis Petit de Bachaumont, *Mémoires secrets*, 1780–9, vii. 262–3; A. Révérend, *Titres . . . de la restauration*, 1901–6, iv. 11).

great scene is opening, of which I cannot expect to see the end; I am pretty sure not a happy end—so that, in short, I am determined to think the rest of my life but a postscript: and as this has been too long an one, I will wish you good night, repeating what you know already, that the return of you three is the most agreeable prospect I expect to see realized. Adieu!

From CONWAY, Thursday 19 January 1775

Missing. 'Je viens de reçevoir une lettre de M. Conway du 19 par un jeune seigneur anglais [not identified]. Il dit qu'ils seront de retour au temps fixé, mais j'ignore quel est ce temps fixé. Il me parle d'une grande révolution qui va se faire dans la mode de s'habiller chez vous, et par conséquent chez nous. Il dit qu'il s'agit de se mettre comme les chevaliers du St-Esprit' (HW to Mme du Deffand 27 Jan. 1775, DU DEFFAND iv. 144; see also ibid. n. 6a).

To CONWAY, Sunday 22 January 1775

Printed from the MS now WSL; first printed Wright v. 410–12. For the history of the MS, see *ante* 29 June 1744 OS; it was marked by HW for inclusion in *Works,* but was not included.

Address: À Monsieur Monsieur le General Conway chez Monsieur Panchaud Banquier, rue St Sauveur à Paris.

Postmark: DANGLETERRE.

Endorsed: Mr H. W. 22 January 75.

34. 16

Jan. 22, 1775.

AFTER the magnificent overture for peace from Lord Chatham, that I announced to Madame du D.,[1] you will be most impatient for my letter. *Ohimè!*[2] You will be sadly disappointed. Instead of drawing a circle with his wand round the House of Lords, and ordering them to pacify America on the terms he prescribed before they ventured to quit the circumference of his commands, he brought a ridiculous uncommunicated, unconsulted motion for addressing the King immediately to withdraw the troops from Boston

1. See HW to Mme du Deffand 19 Jan.   2. 'Alas!' (Italian).
1775, DU DEFFAND iv. 138–9.

as an earnest of lenient measures.[3] The Opposition stared and shrugged; the courtiers stared and laughed. His own two or three adherents left him,[4] except Lord Camden[5] and Lord Shelburne,[6] and except Lord Temple, who is not his adherent, and was not there.[7] Himself was not much animated, but very hostile, particularly on Lord Mansfield, who had taken care not to be there.[8] He talked of three millions of Whigs in America,[9] and told the Ministers they were checkmated and had not a move left to make.[10] Lord Camden was as strong.[11] Lord Suffolk was thought to do better than ever,[12] and Lord Lyttelton's declamation was commended as usual.[13] At last, Lord Rockingham, very punily, and the Duke of Richmond joined and supported the motion,[14] but at eight at night it was rejected by 68 to 18, though the Duke of Cumberland voted for it.[15]

3. He moved in the Lords 20 Jan. 'That an humble address be presented to his Majesty . . . That, in order to open the ways towards an happy settlement of the dangerous troubles in America, by beginning to allay ferments, and soften animosities there . . . immediate orders may be dispatched to General Gage for removing his Majesty's forces from the town of Boston,' etc. (*Journals of the House of Lords* xxxiv. 290; Cobbett, *Parl. Hist.* xviii. 149–50, n.; see also Basil Williams, *Life of William Pitt*, 1913, ii. 304–6).

4. 'Lord Coventry and Lord Grosvenor, usually followers of Lord Chatham, [voted] in the majority' (*Last Journals* i. 422).

5. See nn. 8, 11 below.

6. His speech is reported Cobbett, op. cit. xviii. 162–3.

7. 'Lord Temple, who had again veered to the Stamp Act, was absent' (*Last Journals*, loc. cit.).

8. Chatham and Lord Camden inveighed against involuntary taxation and the Declaratory Act; 'the lawyer both . . . aimed at was pitifully absent' (ibid. i. 421; Cobbett, op. cit. xviii. 153–4n, 156–7, 164–6).

9. 'This glorious spirit of Whiggism animates three millions in America' (ibid. 154n), that is, the entire population.

10. 'They cannot, my Lords, they cannot stir a step; they have not a move left; they are checkmated' (ibid. 155n).

11. His speech is reported ibid. 164–5.

12. Secretary of state for the north, he 'condemned the conduct of the Americans in the most determined and unreserved terms' (ibid. 160); his speech is reported ibid. 160–2.

13. Lyttelton 'disclaimed all personal connection with administration,' but 'said he supported them, because he imagined and believed them to be right' (ibid. 164). HW mentions the 'dazzling facility of his eloquence' in *Last Journals* i. 372.

14. Their speeches are reported Cobbett, op. cit. xviii. 167.

15. 'At eight at night the motion was thrown out by 68 votes and 9 proxies to 18. The Duke of Cumberland voted in the minority' (*Last Journals* i. 422). For lists of the minority see Cobbett, op. cit. xviii. 168 and *London Chronicle* 21–4 Jan., xxxvii. 78. Chatham's son William gives a very different account of the debate in a letter to Lady Chatham 21 Jan.: 'Nothing prevented his [Chatham's] speech from being the most forcible that can be imagined, and administration fully felt it . . .'; also, Benjamin Franklin, who heard the debate, wrote (in the third person) to Lord Stanhope 23 Jan. in reference to Chatham's speech: 'Dr Franklin is filled with admiration of that truly great man! He has seen, in the course of life, sometimes eloquence without wisdom, and often wisdom without eloquence: in the present instance, he sees both united, and both, as he thinks, in the highest degree possible' (*Chatham Corr.* iv. 376, 385–6).

This interlude would be only entertaining, if the scene was not so totally gloomy. The Cabinet have determined on civil war, and regiments are going from Ireland and our West Indian islands.[16] On Thursday the plan of the war is to be laid before both Houses.[17] Tomorrow the merchants carry their petition,[18] which, I suppose, will be coolly received, since, if I hear true, the system is to cut off all traffic with America at present—as, you know, we can revive it when we please.—There! there is food for meditation! Your reflections, as you understand the subject better than I do, will go farther than mine could—will the French you converse with, be civil and keep their countenances?

George Damer[19] t'other day proclaimed your departure for the 25th but the Duchess of Richmond received a whole cargo of letters from ye all on Friday night, which talk of a fortnight or three weeks longer.[20] Pray remember it is not decent to be dancing at Paris, when there is a civil war in your own country. You would be like the country esquire who passed by with his hounds as the battle of Edgehill began.[21]

24th.

I am very sorry to tell you the Duke of Gloucester is dying.[22] About three weeks ago the physicians[23] said it was absolutely neces-

16. 'At the very eve of the meeting [19 Jan.] of the Parliament the warlike part of the Cabinet prevailed, and four more regiments were ordered for Boston' (*Last Journals* i. 420). Lord Dartmouth wrote to Gen. Gage 27 Jan.: 'Orders have been given this day for the immediate embarkation of . . . seven hundred marines, and of three regiments of infantry, and one of light dragoons, from Ireland' (Thomas Gage, *Correspondence*, ed. Carter, New Haven, 1931–3, ii. 180); the regiments, all from Ireland, were the 17th Light Dragoons, and the 35th, 49th, and 63d Foot (*Public Adv.* 27 Jan.). For the subsequent history of this embarkation, see MANN viii. 74, n. 2.

17. According to HW, *Last Journals* i. 421, Lord Suffolk was the source of this information in his speech 20 Jan. (see n. 12 above); however, no 'plan' appears in the journals of the two Houses. See MANN viii. 75, n. 3.

18. See below, *sub* 24 Jan.

19. (1746–1808), Mrs Damer's brother-in-law; styled Vct Milton 1792–8; 2d E. of Dorchester, 1798.

20. Conway, Lady Ailesbury and Mrs Damer left Paris 10 Feb., and after a side trip to Flanders, arrived in London 21 Feb. (DU DEFFAND iv. 156, 162, 163; *Daily Adv.* 23 Feb.).

21. A favourite story of HW's; see, e.g., *ante* 5 May 1765.

22. On a detached card, now WSL, HW has made notes concerning the Duke's illness: '21. Duke very ill. 23. Physicians despaired. . . . 25. Duke better.' According to the *London Chronicle,* his complaint was thought to be 'an abscess of the lungs' (24–26 Jan., xxxvii. 88). HW gives a circumstantial account of this illness and some of the underlying causes of it in *Last Journals* i. 504–7.

23. See MANN viii. 74, n. 1.

sary for him to go abroad immediately. He dallied, but was actually preparing. He now cannot go—and probably will not live many days, as he has had two shivering fits, and the physicians give the Duchess no hopes.[24] Her affliction and courage are not to be described; they take their turns as she is in the room with him or not. His are still greater—his heart is broken, and yet his firmness and coolness amazing. I pity her beyond measure; and it is not a time to blame her having accepted an honour which so few women could have resisted, and scarce one ever has resisted.

The London and Bristol merchants carried their petitions yesterday to the House of Commons.[25] The Opposition contended for their being heard by *the* committee of the whole House who are to consider the American papers,[26] but the Court sent them to *a* committee,[27] after a debate till nine at night, with nothing very remarkable, on divisions of 197 to 81, and 1‹92›[28] to 65.[29] Lord Stanley[30] spoke for the first time; his voice and manner pleas‹ed b›ut his matter was not so successful.[31]

Dowds‹we›ll[32] is dead and Tom Hervey[33]—the latter sent for his wife,[34] and o‹nly then› acknowledged her. Don't forget to inform me when my letters ‹must› stop. Your brother has made his peace in Cavendish Square.[35] Adieu!

24. 'The physicians who gave no hopes yesterday [24 Jan.], say tonight, that they never saw any mortal symptoms' (HW to Mann 25 Jan. 1775, ibid. viii. 74).

25. The petitions, one from London and two from Bristol, asking for reconciliation with America, are printed in *Journals of the House of Commons* xxxv. 71–3. See also *Last Journals* i. 423; *London Chronicle* 21–4, 24–6 Jan., xxxvii. 80, 82; Cobbett, op. cit. xviii. 168–81.

26. On 26 Jan.; the papers had been laid before the House 19 Jan. (*Journals of the House of Commons* xxxv. 66, 81).

27. Dubbed by Burke the committee of 'oblivion' or 'silent committee' (Cobbett, op. cit. xviii. 177); Richard Burke wrote to Richard Champion 24 Jan. that the petitions, by being sent to another committee, 'were in effect rejected' and 'neither can or will have the smallest effect upon the American deliberation or the consequent measures' (Fitzwilliam MSS, N. R. S., quoted in Burke, *Correspondence*, Vol. III, ed. Guttridge, Cambridge, 1961, p. 106).

28. At this point there are several torn places in the MS; conjectural readings are supplied in angular brackets.

29. On the first two petitions; there was no division on the third.

30. Edward Smith Stanley (1752–1834), styled Lord Stanley or Lord Strange 1771–6; 12th E. of Derby, 1776; M.P. Lancashire 1774–6.

31. See Ossory i. 231 and n. 5.

32. William Dowdeswell, M.P. (*ante* 22 Jan. 1764, n. 85). The report of his death was premature; he died at Nice 6 Feb. (Namier and Brooke ii. 335).

33. Hon. Thomas Hervey, eccentric pamphleteer (*ante* 2 Sept. 1758, n. 8). The date of his death is variously given as 10, 16, 18 and 20 Jan. (Ossory i. 231, n. 6; Sedgwick ii. 136).

34. Ann Coghlan (d. 1786), m. (1744) Thomas Hervey, who publicly disowned and berated her in a newspaper advertisement and pamphlet before their reconciliation on his death-bed (Ossory i. 231, n. 7).

35. Where Princess Amelia had her town house; it is not known how Hertford displeased her.

From Beauchamp, Friday 9 June 1775

Printed for the first time from a photostat of BM Add. MSS 23219, f. 70.

Stanhope St,[1] June 9th.

Dear Sir,

I AM particularly desired to get a copy of Mr Fitzpatrick's *Town Eclogue*,[2] and am told that you have the only copy extant of it in your possession; if that is the case, I shall be much obliged to you if you will lend it to me for a few hours, and I will return it immediately with many acknowledgments. I remain ever, dear Sir,

Your very affectionate and obliged servant,

BEAUCHAMP

To Conway, Sunday 9 July 1775

Printed from *Works* v. 186–7.

Strawberry Hill, July 9, 1775.

THE whole business of this letter would lie in half a line. Shall you have room for me on Tuesday the 18th? I am putting myself into motion that I may go farther.[1] I told Madame du Deffand how you had scolded me on her account, and she has charged me to thank you, and tell you how much she wishes to see you too.[2] I would give anything to go—but the going!—However, I really think I

1. In Mayfair; Beauchamp had moved there apparently within the past year or so from his former house in Grosvenor Square (*Court and City Register* 1775, p. 55; 1776, p. 55).

2. *Dorinda, a Town Eclogue*, by the Hon. Richard Fitzpatrick (*ante* 7 Sept. 1771, n. 19). HW wrote to Mason 27 May 1775: 'I am to have a . . . copy of verses by Fitzpatrick, which I expect to like much,' and 12 June 1775: 'I shall send you soon Fitzpatrick's *Town Eclogue*, from my own furnace. . . . PS. Here is the *Eclogue*' (MASON i. 202, 205, 207). In June HW printed 300 copies of the poem at the SH Press (*Journal of the Printing-Office at Strawberry Hill*, ed. Toynbee, 1923, p. 18; see also Hazen, *SH Bibl.* 112–14).

1. To Nuneham, whither he had been invited by Lord Nuneham (see HW to Nuneham 14 June, 18 July 1775, CHUTE 469–71). He wrote to Lady Ossory 23 July 1775 that 'on Wednesday [26 July] I go to Park Place and Nuneham,' and mentions his visit in his letter to her 3 Aug. 1775 (OSSORY i. 242, 247).

2. See Mme du Deffand to HW 1 July 1775 (DU DEFFAND iv. 202).

shall[3]—but I grow terribly affected with a *maladie de famille,* that of taking root at home.

I did but put my head into London on Thursday, and more bad news from America.[4] I wonder when it will be bad enough to make folks think it so, without going on! The stocks indeed begin to grow a little nervous,[5] and they are apt to affect other pulses. I heard this evening here that the Spanish fleet is sailed, and that we are not in the secret whither[6]—but I don't answer for Twickenham gazettes, and I have no better. I have a great mind to tell you a Twickenham story; and yet it will be good for nothing, as I cannot send you the accent in a letter. Here it is; and you must try to set it to the right emphasis. One of our Maccaronis is dead, a Captain Mawhood,[7] the tea-man's[8] son. He had quitted the army, because his comrades called him Captain Hyson,[9] and applied himself to learn the classics and free-thinking; and was always disputing with the parson of the parish[10] about Dido and his own soul. He married Miss Paulin's warehouse,[11] who had six hundred a year; but, being very much out of conceit with his own canister, could not reconcile himself to her riding-hood[12]—so they parted beds in three nights. Of late he has taken to writing comedies, which everybody was welcome to hear

3. He did, on his last visit; see subsequent letters.

4. An 'account of another skirmish between Gage's men and the provincials at Hogg Island' (*Last Journals* i. 469). See Ossory i. 239 and nn. 7, 9.

5. They declined slightly between 29 May and 28 June, but during July there was little change (Mason i. 211, n. 7).

6. In May, HW records, 'apprehensions were felt that the Spaniards, who had a large fleet ready to sail, were meditating some blow' (*Last Journals* i. 459). Fear and speculation continued until the end of July, when news arrived that 'the great Spanish armament, on which attention had hung so long, had [after setting sail from Cartagena 23 June] at last attacked Algiers [8 July, in an attempt to put an end to piracy there] and was repulsed with great loss;—it retired' (ibid. i. 472). See Ossory i. 239, n. 1; Mann viii. 119, n. 4 *et passim.*

7. James Mawhood (d. 1775); sub-brigadier and cornet in the 1st troop of Horse Guards, 1758; brigadier and lieutenant, 1763 (*Army Lists* 1759, p. 13; 1765, p. 13). He is last listed in the *Army Lists* for 1767, p. 17.

8. Presumably Collet Mawhood, druggist and teaman opposite the New Exchange, Strand, in 1751, succeeded in the business in or before 1767 by James Randall (Sir Ambrose Heal's collection of tradesmen's cards).

9. 'Hyson' is a species of green tea from China (OED).

10. Presumably George Costard, vicar of Twickenham 1764–82 (*ante* 3 Oct. 1773, n. 3).

11. The Paulins seem to have been a family of mercers in Tavistock St, Covent Garden, one of whom is described in 1731 as a warehouse mercer (Sir Ambrose Heal's collection of tradesmen's cards). According to GM 1768, xxxviii. 590, 'James Mawhood, Esq.' in Dec. 1768 married 'Mrs Paulin,' who is, however, described as being 'of Kensington gravel pits.'

12. I.e., 'womanhood'; see OED *sub* 'riding-hood.'

him read, as he could get nobody to act them. Mrs Mawhood has a friend, one Mrs V————,[13] a mighty plausible good sort of body, who feels for everybody, and a good deal for herself, is of a certain age, wears well, has some pretensions that she thinks very reasonable still, and a gouty husband.[14] Well! she was talking to Mr Raftor[15] about Captain Mawhood a little before he died. 'Pray, Sir, does the Captain ever communicate his writings to Mrs Mawhood?'—'Oh dear, no, Madam; he has a sovereign contempt for her understanding.'— 'Poor woman!—And pray, Sir,—give me leave to ask you: I think I have heard that they very seldom sleep together?'—'Oh, never, Madam! Don't you know all that?'—*'Poor woman!'*—I don't know whether you will laugh; but Mr Raftor, who tells a story better than anybody,[16] made me laugh for two hours. Good night.

To CONWAY, Wednesday 9 August 1775

Printed from the MS now WSL; first printed Wright v. 423–4. For the history of the MS, see *ante* 29 June 1744 OS; it was marked by HW for inclusion in *Works,* but was not included.
Endorsed: Mr W.—10 Aug. 75.

Strawberry Hill, Aug. 9, 1775.

WELL! I am going *tout de bon*[1]—and heartily wish I was returned.[2] It is a horrid exchange, the cleanness and verdure, and tranquillity of Strawberry, for a beastly ship, worse inns, the *pavé* of the roads bordered with eternal rows of maimed trees,[3] and the racket of a *hôtel garni!* I never dote on the months of August and September, enlivened by nothing but Lady Greenwich's speaking trumpet[4]—but I do not want to be amused—at least never at the

13. Presumably Mrs Henry Vaughan (d. ?1789) (see next note; GM 1789, lix pt i. 88); not further identified.
14. Henry Vaughan (d. 1775) of Twickenham, a friend of the Duke of Newcastle (Hist. MSS Comm., 15th Report, App. pt vi, *Carlisle MSS,* 1897, p. 747). See Lady Hertford to HW *post* 8 Sept. 1775.
15. James Raftor, brother of Mrs Clive (*ante* 25 Dec. 1770, n. 3).
16. 'In the talent of relating a story he was unrivalled' (MS note of Lord Nuneham, quoted Cunningham ii. 458, n. 1).

1. 'In earnest.'
2. He set out for Paris 16 Aug. (*post* 17 Aug. 1775).
3. HW wrote to Conway *ante* 11 Sept. 1765, *sub* 12 Sept.: 'For a French absurdity, I have observed that along the great roads they plant walnut trees, but strip them up for firing.'
4. He calls her a 'shrill *Morning Post' ante* 16 Oct. 1774.

expense of being put in motion. Madame du Deffand I am sure may be satisfied with the sacrifice I make to her.

You have heard to be sure of the war between your brother and Foote;[5] but probably not how far the latter has carried his impudence. Being asked why Lord Hertford[6] had refused to license his piece,[7] he replied, 'Why, he asked me to make his youngest son[8] a boxkeeper, and because I would not, he stopped my play.' The Duchess of Bristol[9] offered to buy it off, but Foote would not take her money,[10] and swears he will act her in Lady Brumpton,[11] which to be sure is very applicable.

I am sorry to hear Lord Villiers is going to drag my Lady[12] through all the vile inns in Germany—I think he might go alone.[13]

George Onslow told me yesterday that the American Congress had sent terms of accommodation, and that your brother told him so— but a strange fatality attends George's news, which is rarely canonical; and I doubt this intelligence is far from being so. I shall know more tomorrow[14] when I go to town to prepare for my journey on Tuesday.[15] Pray let me hear from you, enclosed to Monsieur Panchaud.

I accept with great joy Lady Ailesbury's offer of coming hither in October, which will increase my joy in being at home again. I intend to set out on my return the 25th of next month.[16]

Sir Gregory Page[17] has left Lord Howe eight thousand pounds at present and twelve more after his[18] aunt Mrs Page's[19] death.

---

5. Samuel Foote, the playwright.

6. As lord chamberlain.

7. *A Trip to Calais*, in which the Duchess of Kingston was to have been lampooned as 'Lady Kitty Crocodile' (Mason i. 218, n. 8); see below, n. 10.

8. Hon. George Seymour-Conway (later Lord George Seymour) (1763–1848) (*ante* 20 Aug. 1763, n. 1).

9. That is, the Duchess of Kingston, who was in fact Countess of Bristol.

10. See Mason i. 218, n. 9 and C. E. Pearce, *The Amazing Duchess*, [1911], ii. 169. The Duchess subsequently applied successfully to Hertford to prevent the play's being licensed (Mason i. 218). It was altered and acted in 1776 as *The Capuchin; A Trip to Calais* was not printed in its original form until 1778, after Foote's death, and was never acted.

11. A bigamous lady in Steele's *The Funeral*.

12. Lord Hertford's daughter.

13. See Lady Hertford to HW *post* 8, 25 Sept. 1775.

14. See below, *sub* 10 Aug.

15. He left on Wednesday, 16 Aug. (above, n. 2).

16. He did not leave Paris until 12 Oct. (*post* 6 Oct. 1775).

17. (ca 1695–4 Aug. 1775), 2d Bt (Ossory ii. 137, n. 12).

18. Howe's.

19. Hon. Judith or Juliana Howe (ca 1701–80), 2d dau. of Scrope, 1st Vct Howe, by his 2d marriage, m. (1725) Thomas Page (d. 1763), younger brother of Sir Gregory Page (ibid. i. 144, n. 26; GEC, *Baronetage* v. 24, n. 'c'). GM 1775, xlv. 407 reports that Sir Gregory 'has left

Thursday 10th.

I cannot find any grounds for believing that any proposals are come from the Congress. On the contrary, everything looks as melancholy as possible.[20] Adieu!

To Lady Ailesbury, Thursday 17 August 1775

Printed from the MS now WSL; first printed *Works* v. 567–8. For the history of the MS see *ante* 23 Aug. 1760; it was marked by HW for inclusion in *Works*.
Address: To the Countess of Ailesbury, at Park Place near Henley, Angleterre.
Postmark: 19 AV. DOVER.

From t'other side of the water,[1] Aug. 17th 1775.

INTERPRETING your Ladyship's orders in the most personal sense as respecting the dangers of the sea, I write the instant I am landed. I did not in truth set out till yesterday morning at eight o'clock,[2] but finding the roads, horses, postilions, tides, winds, moons and Captain Factors[3] in the pleasantest humour in the world, I embarked almost as soon as I arrived at Dover[4] and reached Calais befor the sun was awake[5]—and here I am for the sixth time of my life, with only the trifling distance of seven and thirty years between my

the bulk of his immense fortune to Sir Gregory Turner, Bt,' who was his great-nephew and took the name of Page before that of Turner by royal licence of 15 Nov. (GEC, *Baronetage* v. 24, n. 'd,' 78).

20. However, Edmund Burke had written to John Almon 6 Aug. thanking him for 'your early communication of the intelligence you have' regarding an 'opening towards a reconciliation on the part of America,' and Almon in his *Memoirs* states that 'this letter related to the petition brought from the American Congress by Mr Penn'; if so, Almon must have received some information which anticipated the arrival of Richard Penn, Jr (ca 1735–1811) 13 Aug. with the so-called 'olive branch petition' (Burke, *Correspondence,* Vol. III, ed. Guttridge, Cambridge, 1961, pp. 184, 188). This petition, the original of which is reproduced in facsimile in B. F. Stevens, *Facsimiles of*

Manuscripts in European Archives Relating to America, 1889–98, v. No. 454, begged the King to use his influence to revoke the acts of his ministers which stood in the way of reconciliation. It was presented to Lord Dartmouth 1 Sept., but the King refused to see it (Hist. MSS Comm., 14th Report, App. pt x, *Dartmouth MSS,* Vol. II, 1895, p. 358; GM 1775, xlv. 433).

1. Calais (see below).

2. '*Aug. 16.* Set out from Arlington Street at 10 minutes past 8' ('Paris Journals,' DU DEFFAND V. 342).

3. James Peter Fector (1723–1814) of Dover (ibid. iii. 307, n. 2; MONTAGU ii. 282, n. 1 and addendum).

4. HW 'arrived at Dover a quarter before seven' and 'embarked at half an hour past twelve at night' ('Paris Journals,' loc. cit.).

5. 'At six in the morning' (ibid.).

first voyage and the present.[6] Well, I can only say in excuse, that I am got into the land of Strulbrugs, where one is never too old to be young, and where *la béquille du père Barnabas*[7] blossoms like Aaron's rod, or the Glastonbury thorn.

Now to be sure I shall be a little mortified, if your Ladyship wanted a letter of news, and did not at all trouble your head about my navigation. However, you will not tell one so; and therefore I will persist in believing that this good news will be received with transport at Park Place, and that the bells of Henley will be set a-ringing. The rest of my adventures must be deferred till they have happened, which is not always the case of travels. I send you no compliments from Paris, because I have not got thither, nor delivered the bundle which Mr Conway sent me. I did, as your Ladyship commanded, buy three pretty little medallions in frames of filigraine for our dear old friend.[8] They will not ruin you, having cost not a guinea and half, but it was all I could find that was genteel and portable; and as she does not measure by guineas but attentions, she will be as much pleased as if you had sent her a dozen acres of Park Place. As they are in bas-relief too, they are feelable, and that is a material circumstance to her—Indeed I wish the Diomède had even so much as a pair of Nankin![9]

Adieu, *toute la chère famille!* I think of October[10] with much satisfaction; it will double the pleasure of my return.

6. HW first set out for Paris in March 1739 (*ante* connecting note between 24 March OS and ca 8 Nov. 1739 NS).

7. A popular French tune, mentioned by HW also to Lady Ossory 4 Nov. 1786 (Ossory ii. 534).

8. Mme du Deffand.

9. Trousers (specifically, trousers made of nankeen, or yellow cotton cloth; see OED *sub* 'Nankeen').

10. I.e., of Lady Ailesbury's proposed visit to SH in October.

To Lady Ailesbury, Sunday 20 August 1775

Printed from the MS now wsl; first printed *Works* v. 568–9. For the history of the MS see *ante* 23 Aug. 1760.

Address: To the Countess of Ailesbury, at Park Place, near Henley, Angleterre.

Postmark: 25 AV.

Paris,[1] Aug. 20, 1775.

I HAVE been sea-sick to death, I have been poisoned by dirt and vermin, I have been stifled by heat, choked by dust, and starved for want of anything I could touch; and yet, Madam, here I am perfectly well, not in the least fatigued,[2] and thanks to the rivelled parchments, formerly faces, which I have seen by hundreds, I find myself almost as young as when I [c]am[e] hither first in the last century. In spite of my whims and delicacy and laziness, none of my grievances have been mortal; I have borne them as well as if I set up for a philosopher like the sages of this town. Indeed I have found my dear old woman so well, and looking so much better than she did four years ago, that I am transported with pleasure, and thank your Ladyship and Mr Conway for driving me hither. Madame du Deffand came to me the instant I arrived,[3] and sat by me while I stripped and dressed myself, for, as she said, since she cannot see, there was no harm in my being stark. She was charmed with your present, but was so kind as to be so much more charmed with my arrival, that she did not think of it a moment. I sat with her till half an hour after two in the morning, and had a letter from her before my eyes were open again. In short, her soul is immortal and forces her body to bear it company.

This is the very eve of Madame Clotilde's[4] wedding; but Monsieur Turgot,[5] to the great grief of Lady Maryc,[6] will suffer no cost,

1. Where HW arrived 19 Aug. ('Paris Journals,' du Deffand v. 343).

2. See below, n. 16.

3. 'At half an hour after six' (du Deffand loc. cit.).

4. Marie - Adélaïde - Clotilde - Xavière, sister of Louis XVI, m. (by proxy 21 Aug. 1775) Charles Emmanuel, Prince of Piedmont, later Charles Emmanuel IV of Sardinia (*ante* 2 Oct. 1765, n. 21; Ossory i. 254).

5. Anne-Robert-Jacques Turgot (1727–81), Baron de l'Aulne; controller-general of finance 1774–6 (Mann viii. 26, n. 17).

6. Lady Mary Coke, who had arrived at Paris from England 31 July (Coke, 'MS Journals' 1 Aug.). In imitation of royalty she had taken to signing her name 'Maryc' (with the 'c' at the end passing for a flourish) after the death of the Duke of York (1767), George III's brother, whom

but one banquet,[7] one ball[8] and a play at Versailles.[9] Count Virri[10] gives a banquet,[11] a *bal masqué*[12] and a firework;[13] I think I shall see little but the last, from which I will send your Ladyship a rocket in my next letter.[14] Lady Mary, I believe, has had a private audience of the ambassador's leg,[15] but *en tout bien et honneur,* and only to satisfy her ceremonious curiosity about any part of royal nudity. I am just going to her, as she is to Versailles,[16] and I have not time to add a word more to the vows of your Ladyship's

Most faithful

H. W.

To LADY HERTFORD, ca Saturday 26 August 1775

Missing; listed in 'Paris Journals' (DU DEFFAND v. 395).

To CONWAY, ca Tuesday 29 August 1775

Missing; listed in 'Paris Journals' (DU DEFFAND v. 395) as sent 'by French servant.'

she claimed had married her. See MASON i. 402–3; MANN vii. 530, 550, n. 9 *et passim.*

7. The night of the wedding (OSSORY loc. cit.).

8. A *bal paré* 22 Aug. (ibid. and n. 20).

9. *Le Connétable de Bourbon,* by Jacques-Antoine-Hippolyte (1743–90), Comte de Guibert, acted at Versailles 26 Aug. (ibid. i. 256–7 and n. 46).

10. Viry, the Sardinian minister to France (*ante* 23 Nov. 1774, n. 29), who on 8 Aug. 'made a *formal demand* of the French King of his sister, Madame Clotilde, for the Prince of Piedmont' (James Harris, E. of Malmesbury, *Letters,* 1870, i. 315; Coke, 'MS Journals' 3 Aug.).

11. 23 Aug. (OSSORY i. 256 and n. 41).

12. 25 Aug. (ibid. i. 256 and nn. 43, 45).

13. Which preceded the masquerade (ibid. n. 45).

14. HW did not attend the firework or masquerade, but did go to the *bal paré,* Viry's banquet, and the play (ibid. i. 254, 256, nn. 44, 45, 257, n. 51).

15. She visited Mme de Viry 1 Aug., and dined with her and the ambassador 3 Aug. ('MS Journals' 1, 3 Aug.). HW is alluding humorously to an apocryphal account of the marriage of Henry VIII and Anne of Cleves: according to this account, which he repeats to Montagu 26 Aug. 1749, Sir Anthony Browne stood proxy for the King, and symbolically consummated the marriage by putting his leg into bed with Anne. This method of 'consummating' a proxy marriage was actually employed for the match between the Princess Mary and Louis XII of France (MONTAGU i. 99 and nn. 29, 30).

16. 'Mr Walpole come to me at five o'clock in good looks and spirits; at seven I set out for Versailles and arrived at nine' (Coke, 'MS Journals' 20 Aug.).

To Conway, Friday 8 September 1775

Sent 10 Sept. ('Paris Journals,' DU DEFFAND v. 396) with a letter for Mrs Damer; printed from *Works* v. 187–9.

Paris, September 8, 1775.

THE delays of the post, and its departure before its arrival,[1] saved me some days of anxiety for Lady A., and prevented my telling you how concerned I am for her accident;[2] though I trust by this time she has not even pain left. I feel the horror you must have felt during her suffering in the dark, and on the sight of her arm; and though nobody admires her needlework[3] more than I, still I am rejoiced that it will be the greatest sufferer—however, I am very impatient for a farther account. Madame du Deffand, who you know never loves her friends by halves, and whose impatience never allows itself time to inform itself, was out of her wits because I could not explain exactly how the accident happened, and where. She wanted to write directly, though the post was just gone; and as soon as I could make her easy about the accident, she fell into a new distress about her fans for Madame de Marchais,[4] and concludes they have been overturned and broken too.[5] In short, I never saw anything like her—she has made engagements for me till Monday sennight;[6] in which are included I don't know how many journeys into the country;[7] and as nobody ever leaves her without her engaging them for another time, all these parties will be so many polypuses, that will shoot out into new ones every way. Madame de Jonsac,[8] a great friend of mine, arrived the day before yesterday, and Madame du Deffand has pinned her down to meeting me at her house four

---

1. I.e., the departure of the post for England before the arrival of the post from there with the news of Lady Ailesbury's accident.

2. Lady Ailesbury had been overturned in her carriage at Park Place, and dislocated her wrist (HW).

3. See *ante* 3 Oct. 1773, n. 4.

4. Élisabeth-Josèphe de la Borde (ca 1725–1808), m. 1 (1747) Gérard Binet, Baron de Marchais; m. 2 (1781) Charles-Claude Flahaut, Comte de la Billarderie d'Angiviller. See below.

5. They arrived by 6 Oct.; see *post* 6 Oct. 1775.

6. 18 Sept.

7. HW visited Mme de Boufflers' English garden at Auteuil and supped at M. Necker's at St-Ouen 9 Sept. ('Paris Journals,' DU DEFFAND v. 347–8).

8. Élisabeth-Pauline-Gabrielle Colbert (d. 1786), m. (1736) François-Pierre-Charles Bouchard d'Esparbez de Lussan, Marquis de Jonzac. HW first met her in Nov. 1765, and saw her frequently thereafter on his trips to Paris (ibid. i. 3, n. 4, v. 270 *et passim*).

times before next Tuesday,[9] all parentheses, that are not to interfere with our other suppers; and from those suppers I never get to bed before two or three o'clock. In short, I need have the activity of a squirrel, and the strength of a Hercules, to go through my labours—not to count how many *demêlés* I have had to *raccommode,* and how many *mémoires* to present against Tonton,[10] who grows the greater favourite the more people he devours. As I am the only person who dare correct him, I have already insisted on his being confined in the Bastille every day after five o'clock. T'other night[11] he flew at Lady Barrymore's[12] face, and I thought would have torn her eye out; but it ended in biting her finger. She was terrified; she fell into tears. Madame du Deffand, who has too much parts not to see everything in its true light, perceiving that she had not beaten Tonton half enough, immediately told us a story of a lady, whose dog having bitten a piece out of a gentleman's leg, the tender dame, in a great fright, cried out, 'Won't it make my dog sick?'

Lady Barrymore has taken a house.[13] She will be glutted with conquests: I never saw anybody so much admired.[14] I doubt her poor little head will be quite overset.

Madame de Marchais is charming: eloquence and attention itself.[15] I cannot stir for peaches, nectarines, grapes and bury[16] pears.[17] You would think Pomona was in love with me. I am not so transported with N——— cock and hen.[18] They are a tabor and pipe that I do not understand. He mouths and she squeaks, and neither articu-

9. 12 Sept.; HW records in 'Paris Journals' meeting Mme de Jonzac at Mme du Deffand's 7, 8 and 10 Sept. and visiting her at her own lodgings 11 Sept. (ibid. v. 347–8).

10. A favourite dog of Madame du Deffand's (HW), bequeathed at her death to HW; see *post* 6 May 1781.

11. Probably 6 Sept.; see 'Paris Journals,' DU DEFFAND V. 347.

12. Lady Amelia Stanhope (*ante* 5 May 1753, n. 25), m. Richard Barry (d. 1773), 6th E. of Barrymore.

13. Lady Mary Coke wrote in her 'MS Journals' 5 Sept. that 'Lady Barrymore . . . has taken a house, and stays all the winter.'

14. 'She is now reckoned like the Queen' (ibid. 22 Sept.).

15. See HW's humorous description of her to Selwyn 16 Sept. 1775 (SELWYN 265).

16. 'Beurré,' a mellow variety of pear (OED).

17. Her devoted friend, the Comte de la Billarderie d'Angiviller, whom she married in 1781 (n. 4 above), was directeur des bâtiments, jardins, etc. du roi and 'lui fournit toutes sortes de fruits en abondance' (*Almanach royal* 1775, p. 434; DU DEFFAND iv. 217, 232).

18. Probably the Neckers: Jacques Necker (1732–1804), Swiss banker at Paris, m. (1764) Suzanne Curchod (1739–94). HW had met them several times since his arrival at Paris, and Mme du Deffand wrote to him 22 May 1776, *sub* 26 May, at the time of their visit to SH: 'Ils ne vous plaisent pas beaucoup, je le vois bien' (ibid. iv. 318).

lates. M. d'Entragues[19] I have not seen. Upon the whole, I am much more pleased with Paris than ever I was; and, perhaps, shall stay a little longer than I intended.[20] The Harry Grenvilles[21] are arrived. I dined with them at Madame de Viry's,[22] who has completed the conquest of France by her behaviour on Madame Clotilde's wedding, and by the fêtes she gave.[23] Of other English I wot not, but grieve the Richmonds do not come.

I am charmed with Doctor Bally;[24] nay, and with the King of Prussia—as much as I can be with a northern monarch. For your Kragen,[25] I think we ought to procure a female one, and marry it to Ireland, that we may breed some new islands against we have lost America.[26] I know nothing of said America. There is not a Frenchman that does not think us distracted.

I used to scold you about your bad writing,[27] and perceive I have written in such a hurry and blotted my letter so much, that you will not be able to read it: but consider how few moments I have to myself. I am forced to stuff my ears with cotton to get any sleep.—However, my journey has done me good. I have thrown off at least fif-

19. Louis-César de Crémeaux (d. 1781), Marquis d'Entragues. HW had met him often on his previous trips to Paris, and this time saw him first at Mme de Mirepoix's 10 Sept. ('Paris Journals,' ibid. v. 348 et passim).

20. 'I think I shall stay here a month longer' (HW to Mason 6 Sept. 1775 sub 10 Sept., MASON i. 223).

21. [Hon.] Henry Grenville [1717–84], brother to the first Earl Temple. He married [1757] Miss Margaret Banks, the celebrated beauty (HW). See ante ca 15 Feb. 1752 OS, n. 33; Namier and Brooke ii. 545.

22. The former Henrietta Speed (ante 28 Nov. 1761, n. 30), the friend of Gray; wife of the Sardinian ambassador to France; the dinner in question took place 6 Sept. ('Paris Journals,' DU DEFFAND v. 347 and n. 19).

23. See ante 20 Aug. 1775. Lady Mary Coke notes in her 'MS Journals' 23 Aug. that 'the Ambassadress did the honours better than I ever saw them done' at the wedding banquet given by Viry.

24. William Baylies (1724–87), M.D., 1748; physician to Frederick II of Prussia. 'It is related of him, that when he was first introduced to the late King of Prussia, to whom much had been said of his medical skill, the King observed to him, "that to have acquired so much experience he must necessarily have killed a great many people." To which the Doctor replied, Pas tant que votre Majesté' (GM 1787, lvii pt ii. 838).

25. Presumably the 'Kraken,' a mythical sea-monster of enormous size, said to have been seen at times off the coast of Norway (OED). The name was first brought into general notice by Erik Pontoppidan (1698–1764), in his Første Forsøg paa Norges naturlige Historie, Copenhagen, 1752–3, translated into English and published at London, 1755, as The Natural History of Norway (see Pt II, pp. iv and 210–18). In 1770 the results of an inquiry by Charles Douglas 'as to the existence of the aquatic animals, called Kraakens,' were read to the Royal Society (Philosophical Transactions, 1770, lx. 39, 41).

26. According to Pontoppidan, the kraken had often been mistaken for a floating island; see The Natural History of Norway, Pt II, pp. 214–15.

27. For instance, see ante 26 Dec. 1774.

teen years. Here is a letter for my dear Mrs D[amer] from Madame de _____,[28] who thinks she dotes on you all. Adieu!

PS. I shall bring you two *éloges* of Marshal Catinat,[29] not because I admire them, but because I admire him, because I think him very like you.

From LADY HERTFORD, Friday 8 September 1775

Printed for the first time from a photostat of BM Add. MSS 23219, ff. 71–2.

London, Friday, September the 8th.

Dear Mr Walpole,

I HAVE no inducement for writing today but gratitude, for London is bereft of all its inhabitants, and if there is any news here there is nobody to impart it. I am become almost as great a traveller as yourself, for I have been ten days in Warwickshire[1] since I saw you, and the day after tomorrow I go to Sudborne to stay about the same time.[2] I had rather pass those days at Paris, to do the honours of it to you, and to satisfy my own curiosity, for there are many things there I should like to see again, and some people who were so good to me I can never[3] forget them.

Your poor housemaid[4] lamented you had suffered so much by being sick at sea; but I hope all the bad effects ceased upon landing, as your letter to me[5] (I flattered myself) was wrote when you was in

28. Identified by Wright and subsequent editors as Mme de Cambis, for whom Mrs Damer 's'était prise . . . d'une grande passion' (Mme du Deffand to HW, 13 Sept. 1772, DU DEFFAND iii. 267). She met HW at Mme du Deffand's and supped with him 8 Sept. ('Paris Journals,' ibid. v. 347) when she presumably gave him this letter, which is missing.

29. Nicolas Catinat (1637–1712), maréchal de France (*Dictionnaire de biographie française*, 1933– , vii. 1424–5). Mme du Deffand wrote to the Duchess de Choiseul 31 Aug.: 'Il n'est plus question aujourd'hui que des éloges de Catinat: celui de La Harpe, qui a remporté le prix [offered by the Académie Française]; celui de M.

de Guibert, qui a eu le premier accessit, et celui de l'abbé d'Espagnac, qui a eu le second' (Mme du Deffand, *Correspondance*, ed. Ste-Aulaire, 1866, iii. 192). For these *éloges* and their authors, see OSSORY i. 258, n. 1.

———

1. At Ragley, the Hertfords' country seat there.

2. See *post* 25 Sept. 1775.

3. 'Not' crossed out in the MS.

4. Mary, in Arlington St (see OSSORY i. 75, 84, 330); not further identified. HW wrote her a letter from Paris ca 29 Aug. 1775 (missing) ('Paris Journals,' DU DEFFAND v. 396).

5. *Ante* ca 26 Aug. 1775 (missing).

good spirits. Our weather lately has been hot and wet, which is exactly what disagrees the most with my feelings, and I fear with the corn. Lord and Lady Villiers are determined to set out the 1st of October for Vienna,[6] and as they are to go by Frankfort, I am told the road is so bad that they will meet with very great difficulties; but it is all fixed, therefore we prudently say no more.[7] We fear much for her health, and I believe could have prevailed with Lord Villiers to have left her,[8] but Lady Grandison[9] said, if she did not go with her son, she should have a much worse opinion of her.[10] The Beau Richard[11] is come from Jamaica[12] and is gone into Suffolk with my Lord;[13] and is grown so robust in his figure, that I think he may venture to have his teeth cleaned without any risk of his getting cold.

The Vine and her daughter[14] I hear are set out upon a tour in France for a few weeks. They went this morning, and she signified to her friend that she wished to be out of the way till a certain wedding was over, which she has fixed is to be very soon, though I know if it ever is, will not be [for] a great while; but this is a subject we don't talk upon at present, and I talk upon very few with her except upon loo, as she has such absurd ideas. The Prince of Hesse[15] is arrived, and my Lord, who has seen him several times, likes him very

6. Lord Villiers apparently had been there before during the winter of 1770–1 (Coke, *Journals* iii. 303).

7. Lady Mary Coke met them at Rochester 2 Oct. on her return to England from Paris (Coke, 'MS Journals' 2 Oct.). 'They propose staying a month at Vienna, and then going to Paris for a very little while, and being back in England by the second meeting of the Parliament [i.e., after the Christmas recess; Villiers was M.P. for Ludlow]' (ibid.; Namier and Brooke iii. 586).

8. Lady Mary Coke wrote, loc. cit., that Lord Villiers 'seems to me the most complaisant husband that ever was.'

9. Lady Elizabeth Villiers (d. 1782), m. 1 (1739) Aland John Mason; m. 2 (1763) Gen. Charles Montagu; cr. (1746) Vcts Grandison and (1767) Vcts Villiers and Cts Grandison, s.j.

10. Lord Villiers was a pampered only child (Namier and Brooke loc. cit.).

11. Fitzherbert Richards (*ante* 9 Feb. 1765, n. 12).

12. Cf. George Selwyn to Lord Carlisle 11 Oct. 1775, where he describes Richards as 'un mélange d'irlandais et de créol' (Hist. MSS Comm., 15th Report, App. pt vi, *Carlisle MSS,* 1897, p. 294); Richards apparently had property in the 'Sugar Islands' (ibid. 537).

13. See *post* 25 Sept. 1775.

14. Perhaps Lady Harrington and her daughter Lady Harriet Stanhope, though it was Lord Harrington and Lady Harriet who went to Paris; see HW to Selwyn 16 Sept. 1775 (SELWYN 264) and *post* 6 Oct. 1775. The nickname 'Vine' might refer to her gallantries; cf. HW to Conway *ante* 19 Sept. 1760 where HW jokes about Lady Ailesbury's curling 'like a vine' with Mr Alexander.

15. Georg Wilhelm (1743–1821), son of George II's dau., Princess Mary, by Frederick II, Landgrave of Hesse-Cassel; Landgrave of Hesse-Cassel as Wilhelm IX, 1785; arrived in London at the Princess Amelia's, Cavendish Square, 30 Aug. (OSSORY i. 277, n. 12).

much.[16] He intends staying here the whole winter, and therefore proposes asking H. R. H. to take a house, and not remain at Cavendish House. You must not tell the good story about Mrs Vaughan[17] any more, for her husband died last night,[18] and I hear she is almost distracted.

I have not heard for some days of Lady Ailesbury, but I believe she still has very little use of her arm,[19] as the swelling continued a great while and I fancy is not yet gone off. Our Parliament meets the 26th of October.[20] There has been no news of consequence from Boston since you went. I found Ragley in great beauty, but wetter than I ever saw it, as they had not had a dry day there since Whitsunday,[21] though London and its environs had so fine a summer till August.

Mr Selwyn is at Richmond with the child,[22] and foregoes the joy of going to Castle Howard[23] for her sake. Lord March is not quite in his good graces at present,[24] for they have been three weeks there, and he has not made them one visit, though he has made a great many to a beautiful kitty[25] in London.

I now reckon summer almost over (which I rejoice at) as Drury Lane playhouse opens tomorrow sennight.[26] Pray write to me soon

16. Lady Mary Coke describes him in her 'MS Journals' 22 Nov. as 'in his manner very polite, and seems to be liked by everybody.'

17. Mrs Henry Vaughan (ante 9 July 1775, n. 13).

18. 'Last Friday [8 Sept.] [sic] died, at his house at Twickenham, H[enry] Vaughan, Esq.' (Daily Adv. 12 Sept.; GM 1775, xlv. 455).

19. See ante 8 Sept. 1775.

20. The King's proclamation ordering the meeting of Parliament on that date is printed Daily Adv. 8 Sept.

21. 4 June in 1775.

22. Maria Emily Fagnani ('Mie Mie') (1771–1856), m. (1798) Francis Charles Seymour-Conway, styled E. of Yarmouth, 3d M. of Hertford 1822, the Hertfords' grandson. Legally the daughter of Giacomo, Marchese Fagnani, who had m. (1767) Costanza Brusati, she was in reality probably the Marchesa's daughter by Lord March. Selwyn virtually adopted her soon after her birth (SELWYN 263, n. 7).

23. Yorkshire, seat of Lord Carlisle.

Selwyn wrote to Carlisle from Richmond 1 Sept., excusing himself from visiting him at Castle Howard on account of business; however, his primary concern was presumably to look after Mie Mie (see Carlisle MSS, pp. 286–7, 291, 747).

24. Selwyn had apparently quarrelled with March about bringing Mie Mie to Richmond; see ibid. 286, 291, 747.

25. Presumably Catherine ('Kitty') Frederick (d. ?1777), courtesan, 'the favourite mistress of the Duke of Queensberry' (Horace Bleackley, Ladies Fair and Frail, 1925, p. 282; portrait facing p. 284; see also MS note cited in Musgrave's Obituary, ed. Armytage, 1899–1901, ii. 369; F. O'Donoghue and H. M. Hake, Catalogue of Engraved British Portraits . . . in the British Museum, 1908–25, ii. 258; J. C. Smith, British Mezzotinto Portraits, 1884, iii. 1268).

26. 16 Sept.; actually, Drury Lane opened 23 Sept. with a performance of Richard Cumberland's The Brothers (London Stage Pt IV, iii. 1912).

and tell me some more Paris news, and then set out yourself to inform me of more.

Herbert Lodge[27] is very neat and has a very fine view of[28] one side, but it does not look like a place that had cost six thousand pounds. You won't envy me at Sudborne, as you don't admire it more than I do; and if it was not for the pleasure of seeing my Lord there, I should certainly not go. It is time to release you, and I should have thought it more kind not to have troubled you with a letter if I had not wanted to tell you how much obliged I was to you for writing to me. I am at all times

Most faithfully yours,

I. H.

Have you met with anything half so clever at Paris as Priscilla Plaw?[29]

To LADY HERTFORD, ca Sunday 10 September 1775

Missing; listed in 'Paris Journals' (DU DEFFAND v. 396).

To LADY AILESBURY, ca Tuesday 19 September 1775

Missing; listed in 'Paris Journals' (DU DEFFAND v. 396).

To LADY HERTFORD, ca Tuesday 19 September 1775

Missing; listed in 'Paris Journals' (DU DEFFAND v. 396).

27. Apparently a new dwelling of Lady Powis 'in Putney Lane, between Barnes and Wimbledon Common' (Lady Hertford to HW *post* 24 Aug. 1776 *bis*).

28. *Sic* in MS.
29. See HW to Lady Ossory 3 Aug. 1775, OSSORY i. 246–7.

FROM LADY HERTFORD, Monday 25 September 1775

Printed for the first time from a photostat of BM Add. MSS 23219, ff. 73–5.

London, September the 25th 1775.

Dear Mr Walpole,

I MET with a disappointment today, for it was reported you was to be here in a day or two,[1] and this evening your maid[2] called to say you did not set out till the 10th; but I am within this half hour put into good humour again by your kind letter,[3] which next to seeing you, always is a great satisfaction to me. I have not time to tell you what parts of it entertain me the most, and shall reserve all my curiosity about Paris till we meet; but I am rejoiced to hear you have seen so much of Madame de Praslin,[4] for she was always so good to me that I only see her perfections. I have many requests to get over some *point d'Argentan* men's ruffles; may I therefore ask you to get some female friends to choose some for me, for they are always the best judges of lace. They must be of the newest patterns, and from five to seven guineas a pair, and I will desire Mr Panchaud[5] to pay you the money for them. You must bring them for me, and like-wise twelve pair of embroidered shoes not made up, without gold or silver. They cost 50 sols[6] a pair. They will take up very little room or I would not trouble you to bring them. I should be glad to have them of different colours, all worked with white silk. Am I intelligible?[7]

I returned on Wednesday[8] from Sudborne, and my Lord comes

1. See *ante* 9 Aug. 1775.
2. Mary (*ante* 8 Sept. 1775 *bis*, n. 4). HW wrote to her cà 19 and 21 Sept. 1775 ('Paris Journals,' DU DEFFAND v. 396); the second letter went by 'Morgan' 21 Sept., who also carried HW's letter to Lady Ossory 12–21 Sept. 1775, in which HW announced *sub* 16 Sept. that he had promised to stay at Paris 'till the tenth of next month' (OSSORY i. 264).
3. Presumably *ante* ca 19 Sept. 1775 (missing).
4. Wife of the Duc de Praslin, secretary of state for foreign affairs during Hertford's Paris embassy (see *ante* 19 Nov., 7

Dec. 1763, 9 March 1765). HW had seen her most recently on 18 Sept. ('Paris Journals,' DU DEFFAND v. 349).
5. Isaac Panchaud, banker.
6. Two shillings (*Gentleman's Guide . . . through France*, 1788, p. 7).
7. In his list of 'things sent to England Sept. 28. 1775,' HW notes '2 candlesticks —Lady Hertford' costing 13 louis; there are no other items listed as expressly for her, though he does mention '2 pair of lace ruffles 6 louis' in his 'Money laid out, 1775' ('Paris Journals,' DU DEFFAND v. 413–14).
8. 20 Sept.

from thence on Thursday.[9] I left him, Henry,[10] and Mr Richards,[11] choosing their mayor.[12] Lord Beauchamp has been a month at Lord Irwin's[13] in Yorkshire; and though we have not yet announced it to anybody, I must tell you the satisfaction we feel at its being fixed that he is to marry Miss Ingram.[14] Her education has been such as to give us great hopes of her turning out just what we would wish his wife to be,[15] and her disposition is as perfect as her person. She is not seventeen[16] and therefore rather too young for him,[17] but she is so composed[18] for her age, and is so fond of reading and amusing herself in a rational way, that I have no fear of her youth being any disadvantage; and she has an exceeding good guide in Lady Irwin, who is one of the most sensible women I ever conversed with. He is very happy with the choice, and likes her more and more every day.

Poor Lady Villiers sets out next Tuesday,[19] and is very low and uncomfortable. Lady Barrymore[20] and Massareene[21] are to pass the winter in London,[22] so that you will still have your Monday's loo.[23] Everybody admires the Prince of Hesse.[24] I saw Lady Mary Somer-

9. 28 Sept.

10. The Hertfords' son, Henry Seymour-Conway.

11. Fitzherbert Richards (*ante* 8 Sept. 1775 *bis* and n. 11).

12. For Orford; one Joseph Probart was elected in Sept. to serve Oct. 1775–Sept. 1776 (information kindly supplied by W. R. Sergeant, Esq., Archivist, Ipswich and East Suffolk Record Office, County Hall, Ipswich, England).

13. Charles Ingram (1727–78), 9th Vct Irvine, 1763. Beauchamp was still at Lord Irvine's the middle of October (Coke, 'MS Journals' 13 Oct.).

14. Hon. Isabella Anne Ingram Shepheard (1760–1834), eldest dau. of Lord Irvine, m. (20 May 1776) Lord Beauchamp. See next letter.

15. 'Lady Hertford thinks Miss Engram has been so well educated that she will not be in the style of the young ladies of the present times' (Coke, loc. cit.).

16. She was not yet sixteen.

17. Beauchamp was 32.

18. The last five words have been written over (?) 'for she is naturally.'

19. 3 Oct.; however, see *ante* 8 Sept. 1775 *bis* and n. 7.

20. Hon. Margaret Davys (*ante* 20 April 1764, n. 26), m. James Barry (d. 1751), 5th E. of Barrymore.

21. Anne Eyre (*ante* 11 March 1764, n. 25), m. Clotworthy Skeffington (d. 1757), 1st E. Massereene. She and Lady Barrymore were close companions; Lady Mary Coke called them 'the two Irish countesses' (*Journals*, iv. 155, 433, 437).

22. Lady Mary Coke wrote in her 'MS Journals' 15 Sept. that 'Mr Craufort [Craufurd] is come here [Paris] from the Spa, and tells me Lady Barrymore and Lady Massereene have changed their minds, and instead of passing the winter at Brusselles, return to England and pass the winter in London.' However, she added 12 Oct. that they 'have again changed their minds and now talk of passing the winter in the south of France.' Lady Hertford may have got her information from Lady Strafford, to whom Lady Mary's 'MS Journals' are addressed.

23. HW, in his letter to Nuneham 6 Dec. 1773, calls Lady Barrymore and Lady Massereene 'my dear sisters in loo' (CHUTE 468); he mentions loo on Monday to Lady Ailesbury *ante* 7 Nov. 1774.

24. See *ante* 8 Sept. 1775 *bis* and n. 16.

set[25] on Friday. She has not been very well, but I am sure not very ill, as the Duchess[26] was in great spirits. I have not had time to go to Park Place yet, but I hope Lady Ailesbury is quite recovered, for I heard she was in town last week and went to the magic lantern,[27] which I believe is like the booths at Sadler's Well. There have been no letters from Boston for some time, but as we cannot expect to hear much that is good, we may as well remain ignorant. I don't know where Mr Selwyn is, but I suppose he is upon Richmond Hill, in the child's cradle.[28] I have played at loo but once since you went, and yet I am alive and am not impatient for its beginning again. Mrs Howe[29] and Miss Harvey[30] have passed three weeks at Phillis Court,[31] which is astonishing, as they neither of them are without a habitation. Lady Grandison says the Comtesse de W.[32] is the most agreeable woman in the world to live with.

Mr Seymour[33] has brought over a French lady,[34] who lives with him and his daughters,[35] and I hear he will certainly marry her. Pray find out at Paris who and what she is, for we are curious to know.[36]

25. Lady Mary Isabella Somerset (1756–1831), m. (26 Dec. 1775) Charles Manners, styled M. of Granby, 4th D. of Rutland, 1779.

26. Presumably her mother, the Dowager Duchess of Beaufort (ante 7 Nov. 1774, n. 24). Mann wrote to HW 25 Jan. 1772 of the Duchess's taking up residence that winter at Pisa with Lady Mary and her grand-daughter to seek out 'good air to fortify the constitution of her children against the dangerous age, at which she has lost three daughters by consumption' (MANN vii. 372 and n. 17).

27. An optical instrument for projecting an image upon a screen or wall; Smollett mentions in *The Adventures of Ferdinand Count Fathom*, 1753, 'the travelling Savoyards who stroll about Europe, amusing ignorant people with the effects of a magick-lanthorn' (OED).

28. Mie Mie's. Selwyn was at Richmond 23 Sept., when he wrote to Lord Carlisle that he had been to Court the day before, but had come back to Richmond for dinner, despite invitations to dine in town, because 'Mie Mie *l'emporta*, and so away I came' (Hist. MSS Comm., 15th Report, App. pt vi, *Carlisle MSS*, 1897, p. 292).

29. Presumably the Hon. Caroline Howe

(ante 19 Sept. 1758, n. 20), m. John Howe.

30. Not identified.

31. A manor in Henley-on-Thames, Oxon (see James Granger to HW 30 Jan. 1772). It belonged to Sambrooke Freeman (ante 21 Oct. 1756, n. 3; J. S. Burn, *History of Henley-on-Thames*, 1861, pp. 253–4, 267, 281).

32. Perhaps the Countess van Welderen, wife of the Dutch envoy to England (ante 20 July 1761, n. 3).

33. Henry Seymour (ante 23 June 1752 OS, n. 3), a cousin of Lord Hertford and Conway.

34. Anne-Louise-Thérèse de la Martellière de Chançay (1741–1821), m. 1 (1763) Guillaume de Panthou (ca 1692–1768), m. 2 (5 Oct. 1775) Henry Seymour (OSSORY i. 119, n. 14). Seymour's first wife, Lady Caroline Cowper, whom he married in 1753, had died 2 June 1773 (ibid. i. 119, n. 12).

35. Caroline Seymour (b. 1755), m. (16 Sept. 1775) William Danby, and Georgiana Seymour (b. 1756), m. (1794) Félicité-Jean-Louis-Étienne de Durfort, called Comte Louis de Durfort (MANN viii. 94, n. 7; Sir John Bernard Burke, *Peerage*, 1928, p. 2137; La Chenaye-Desbois iii. 118, vii. 156).

36. Lady Mary Coke wrote in her 'MS

You are to bring me six pair of men's point ruffles; and may I add one more commission, which is a silk umbrella, as I intend by degrees to become a walker again.

Your companions will be angry that I have kept you so long from them and that I have told you no news that you can entertain them with. London is still very empty, but not quite so bad as it was. I must add one word, to tell you that old Miss Maccartney[37] has got such an influence over old Lord Harcourt[38] that the way to get jobs done in Ireland is to pay court to her.[39] She will have a large fortune,[40] and it is thought if she gets possession of it he will marry her. I don't now wonder the Nunehams[41] don't go over this winter.[42] My best respects to my French and English friends with you. I don't grieve for the Comte de Broglio.[43] I am

Most faithfully yours,

I. H.

There will be no end to my giving you trouble till I seal my letter, for I have just now recollected I want twelve roots for cleaning the

Journals' 15 Oct. that Seymour 'made his acquaintance with the lady in the hotel at Paris where he lodged. . . . They say . . . that she is of a good family in Normandy, a widow lady about thirty years of age, handsome and agreeable.' However, she and Seymour later separated (Namier and Brooke iii. 423).

37. Alice Macartney (?living 1799), sister of Fanny Greville, the poetess; she had an evil reputation as a troublemaker (SELWYN 45, n. 4; for her possibly living in 1799, see Mrs Philip Lybbe Powys, *Passages from the Diaries*, ed. E. J. Climenson, 1899, p. 327).

38. Lord lieutenant of Ireland.

39. Lady Louisa Conolly wrote to the Duchess of Leinster 7 Dec. that Miss Macartney's 'influence with Lord Harcourt is really something ridiculous. There are various conjectures about the *connection*, but I am persuaded that he imagines she can be useful to him in politics and fancies he gets a great deal of intelligence from her. That part I don't doubt, for as she loves meddling, she tells him a *great deal*, I dare say. The dirty court people pay her would make you sick, she is absolutely upon the footing of Madame

Pompadour, and has as great levées as a minister could have' (*Leinster Corr.* iii. 168).

40. Her father, James Macartney, had died in 1770, leaving his estates in Ireland to her and her surviving sisters (Mrs Greville and Catherine Macartney) (John Lodge and Mervyn Archdall, *Peerage of Ireland*, 1789, vii. 91). It is not clear if this is the inheritance being referred to.

41. George Simon Harcourt, Vct Nuneham (*ante* 15 Feb. 1764, n. 100), m. (1765) Hon. Elizabeth Venables Vernon (1746–1826).

42. Lady Louisa Conolly, in her letter to the Duchess of Leinster 11 July 1776, after reporting Miss Macartney's remark that Lord Harcourt had once wanted to marry the Duchess, wrote: "'Tis a matter of doubt with many whether she [Miss Macartney] is not married to him herself, but I hope not for the sake of the Nunehams and Colonel [William] Harcourt [afterwards 3d E. Harcourt], who all hate her' (*Leinster Corr.* iii. 210).

43. Presumably Charles-François de Broglie (1719–81), Comte de Broglie. He had been implicated in 'la procédure, connue sous le nom d'affaire de la Bastille'

teeth[44] and twelve yards of broad and twelve yards of narrow of white *gros grain* ribbon. I am shocked; I really put myself in mind of the lady at Petersham.[45]

From HERTFORD, Saturday 30 September 1775

Printed for the first time from a photostat of BM Add. MSS 23219, f. 76.

Grosvenor Street, September 30th 1775.

Dear Horry,

FROM the very long friendship I have experienced on your part, I am assured of the interest you take in the happiness of my family. I cannot therefore even leave it to Lady Hertford to do, but must privately send this short letter to meet you when you arrive from Paris, and to acquaint you that my eldest son has the fairest prospect of satisfaction in matrimony by having obtained Lord and Lady Irwin's consent to marry Miss Ingram, their eldest daughter.[1]

I am going to Clumber[2] and cannot therefore see you on your arrival. I am, dear Horry,

Always very truly and affectionately yours,

HERTFORD

from which a letter signed 3 May 1775 by Muy and Vergennes solicited his pardon. Though Louis XVI in letters of 2 and 25 May cleared him, this may not have been generally known at the time of this letter (La Chenaye-Desbois iv. 293–7).

44. Mme du Deffand wrote HW 15 Sept. 1776 that the French did not know what these were (DU DEFFAND iv. 358.)

45. Presumably Lady Harrington; Petersham Lodge, Richmond, was the Harringtons' seat.

1. Hertford apparently did not know that Lady Hertford had told HW this *ante* 25 Sept. 1775.

2. Clumber Park in Nottinghamshire, the seat of the Duke of Newcastle. Hertford's daughter Lady Frances Seymour-Conway (*ante* 10 Oct. 1772, n. 2) had married (21 May 1775) Henry Fiennes Pelham Clinton, styled Lord Lincoln, Newcastle's son and heir apparent.

To Conway, Friday 6 October 1775

Printed from *Works* v. 189–91. Sent 7 Oct. 'by M. Bourdieu's servant' ('Paris Journals,' DU DEFFAND v. 396).

Paris, October 6, 1775.

IT will look like a month since I wrote to you; but I have been coming, and am. Madame du Deffand has been so ill, that the day she was seized[1] I thought she would not live till night.[2] Her Herculean weakness, which could not resist strawberries and cream after supper, has surmounted all the *ups* and *downs* which followed her excess; but her impatience to go everywhere and do everything has been attended with a kind of relapse,[3] and another kind of giddiness: so that I am not quite easy about her, as they allow her to take no nourishment to recruit, and she will die of inanition, if she does not live upon it. She cannot lift her head from the pillow without *étourdissements;* and yet her spirits gallop faster than anybody's, and so do her repartees. She has a great supper tonight for the Duc de Choiseul,[4] and was in such a passion yesterday with her cook about it, and that put Tonton into such a rage, that *nos dames de Saint-Joseph* thought the devil or the philosophers were flying away with their convent! As I have scarce quitted her, I can have had nothing to tell you. If she gets well, as I trust, I shall set out on the 12th;[5] but I cannot leave her in any danger—though I shall run many myself, if I stay longer. I have kept such bad hours with this *malade,* that I have had alarms of gout; and bad weather, worse inns, and a voyage in winter, will ill suit me. The fans[6] arrived at a propitious moment, and she immediately had them opened on her bed, and felt all the patterns, and had all the papers described. She was all satisfaction and thanks, and swore me to do her full justice to Lady A. and Mrs D. Lord Harrington and Lady Harriet are arrived;[7] but have announced and persisted in a strict invisibility.

1. 20 Sept. ('Paris Journals,' DU DEFFAND v. 350; Coke, 'MS Journals' 20 Sept.).

2. 'Mme du Deffand . . . was taken ill, and Mr Walpole very much alarmed . . . however it took a turn that was favourable and she grew better in the evening' (ibid.).

3. Presumably 3 Oct., when HW wrote in 'Paris Journals': 'Mme du Deffand . . . ill again and in bed' (DU DEFFAND v. 352).

4. See ibid. *sub* 6 Oct. and Mme du Deffand to the Duchesse de Choiseul 7 Oct., in her *Correspondance,* ed. Marquis de Sainte-Aulaire, 1866, iii. 199–200.

5. See below, *sub* 7 Oct.

6. For Mme de Marchais, who came to see them 7 Oct. (*ante* HW to Conway 8 Sept. 1775; 'Paris Journals,' loc. cit. *sub* 7 Oct.).

7. From the Spa (Coke, 'MS Journals' 24 Sept.).

I know nothing of my *chère patrie,* but what I learn from the *London Chronicle;* and that tells me, that the trading towns are suing out *lettres de noblesse,* that is, entreating the King to put an end to commerce, that they may all be gentlemen.[8] Here agriculture, economy, reformation, philosophy, are the bon ton even at Court. The two nations seem to have crossed over and figured in; but as people that copy take the bad with the good, as well as the good with the bad, there was two days ago a great horse-race in the plain de Sablon,[9] between the Comte d'Artois,[10] the Duc de Chartres, Monsieur de Conflans,[11] and the Duc de Lauzun.[12] The latter won by the address of a little English postilion, who is in such fashion, that I don't know whether the Academy will not give him for the subject of an *éloge.*

The Duc de Choiseul, I said, is here; and as he has a second time put off his departure,[13] *cela fait beaucoup de bruit.* I shall not be at all surprised if he resumes the reins, as (forgive me a pun) he has the *Reine* already.[14] Messieurs de Turgot and Malesherbes[15] cer-

---

8. 'Is it credible that five or six of the great *trading* towns have presented addresses against the Americans?' (HW to Mann 10 Oct. 1775, Mann viii. 132). Between 14 Sept. and 3 Oct. the *London Chronicle* printed or mentioned addresses from Manchester, Lancaster, Liverpool, Leicester, Poole, Coventry, and Exeter (xxxviii. 266–322), and between 3 and 10 Oct., addresses also from Beverley, Bristol, Gloucester, Suffolk, Taunton, King's Lynn, Warwick, Great Yarmouth and Montrose (xxxviii. 329–46). The address from Montrose contained the following passage: 'We are happy in acquainting your Majesty that the trade and manufactures in this town and neighbourhood have not in the smallest degree been hurt or affected by the American ports being shut against us' (xxxviii. 346).

9. Reported in the *Gazette de Leyde* 20 Oct., *sub* Paris 13 Oct.; 'La reine s'y est trouvée à cheval.'

10. Charles-Philippe (1757–1836), Comte d'Artois; K. of France as Charles X 1824–30. Mme du Deffand wrote to HW 16 March 1777: 'Le Comte d'Artois . . . fait continuellement des courses et perd tous ses paris' (du Deffand iv. 418).

11. Louis-Gabriel de Conflans d'Armentières (1735–89), Marquis de Conflans (ibid. i. 237, n. 7).

12. Armand-Louis de Gontaut (1747–93), Comte de Biron and Duc de Lauzun 1766; Duc de Biron 1788 (Mann ix. 211, n. 9).

13. Mme du Deffand wrote to the Duchesse de Choiseul 7 Oct. that 'le grand-papa nous quitte demain' (Mme du Deffand, op. cit. iii. 200).

14. He never returned to power. The Comte de Mercy-Argenteau, Austrian ambassador at Paris, wrote to Maria Theresa 19 Oct.: 'Il est vrai que depuis un certain temps . . . [le] parti du duc de Choiseul a montré dans les occasions un esprit d'intrigue du plus mauvais genre. . . . Le baron de Besenval est un des grands ouvriers du parti susdit; sa faveur auprès de la reine continue.' In a second letter of the same date he writes: 'La reine commence à prendre en grand affection la princesse de Guéménée . . . amie du duc de Choiseul' (*Correspondance secrète entre Marie-Thérèse et le Comte de Mercy-Argenteau,* ed. Arneth and Geffroy, 1874, ii. 389–90). However, upon the death of the Comte du Muy, minister of war, 10 Oct., the Queen failed to support the Choiseul party's nominee for his successor (ibid. ii. 389, n. 1; Mann viii. 133, n. 7).

15. Chrétien-Guillaume de Lamoignon de Malesherbes (1721–94), first president of the Cour des Aides until 12 July 1775;

tainly totter[16]—but I shall tell you no more till I see you; for, though this goes by a private hand, it is so private, that I don't know it, being an English merchant's,[17] who lodges in this hotel, and whom I do not know by sight: so perhaps I may bring you word of this letter myself. I flatter myself Lady A.'s arm has recovered its straightness and its cunning.

Madame du Deffand says I love you better than anything in the world. If true, I hope you have not less penetration: if you have not, or it is not true, what would professions avail?—So I leave that matter in suspense. Adieu!

October 7.

Madame du Deffand was quite well yesterday; and at near one this morning I left the Duc de Choiseul, the Duchess de Grammont, the Prince and Princess of Beauveau, Princess of Poix,[18] the Maréchale de Luxembourg, Duchess de Lauzun, Ducs de Gontaut[19] et de Chabot,[20] and Caraccioli,[21] round her chaise longue; and she herself was not a dumb personage. I have not heard yet how she has slept, and must send away my letter this moment, as I must dress to go to dinner with Monsieur de Malesherbes at Madame de Villegagnon's.[22] I must repose a great while after all this living in company; nay, intend to go very little into the world again, as I do not admire the French way of burning one's candle to the very snuff in public. Tell Mrs D. that the fashion now is to erect the *toupée* into a high detached tuft of hair, like a cockatoo's crest; and this *toupée* they call *la physionomie*—I don't guess why.

My *laquais* is come back from Saint-Joseph's, and says Marie de

minister of the King's Household 1775–6, 1787–8 (ibid. viii. 133, n. 5).

16. HW wrote to Mann 10 Oct. 1775: 'Messieurs de Turgot and Malesherbes are philosophers in the true sense, that is, legislators—but as their plans tend to serve the public, you may be sure they do not please interested individuals' (ibid. viii. 133). Turgot, controller-general of finance, was dismissed and Malesherbes resigned in May 1776 (DU DEFFAND iv. 311).

17. Not identified; the letter actually went 'by M. Bourdieu's servant' (above, headnote).

18. Anne-Louise-Marie de Beauvau (1750–1833), m. (1767) Philippe-Louis-Marc-Antoine de Noailles, Prince de Poix (MANN vi. 342, n. 7).

19. Charles-Antoine-Armand de Gontaut

(1708–1800), Duc de Gontaut (DU DEFFAND ii. 288, n. 5).

20. Louis-Antoine-Auguste de Rohan-Chabot (1733–1807), Duc de Chabot, Duc de Rohan, 1791 (ibid., *passim*).

21. 'Caracciolo' in 'Paris Journals' (ibid. v. 352): Domenico Caracciolo (*ante* 7 Dec. 1763, n. 2), currently Neapolitan ambassador to France. Jérôme-Marie Champion de Cicé (1735–1810), Bishop of Rodez, also supped with Mme du Deffand ('Paris Journals,' loc. cit.).

22. Jeanne-Marguerite Batailhe de Montval (1731–1821), m. 1 (1755) — Durand, Marquis de Villegagnon; m. 2 (1787) Hon. Thomas Walpole (OSSORY ii. 587, n. 25). See HW to Mason 25 Oct. 1775, MASON i. 226.

Vichy[23] has had a very good night and is quite well.[24]—Philip,[25] let my chaise be ready on Thursday.[26]

To Lady Ailesbury, Tuesday 12 December 1775

Printed from the MS now WSL. First printed (with omissions) *Works* v. 569; first printed in full Toynbee ix. 294 and *Supp.* ii. 148. For the history of the MS see *ante* 23 Aug. 1760; it was marked by HW for inclusion in *Works*.
Address: To the Countess of Ailesbury, at Park Place near Henley.
Postmark: RD 12 DE.

Arlington Street, Dec. 12, 1775.

DID you hear that scream?[1]—don't be frightened, Madam; it was only the Duchess of Kingston last Sunday was sevennight at chapel:[2] but it is better to be prepared, for she has sent word to the House of Lords that her nerves are so bad she intends to scream for these two months, and therefore they must put off her trial.[3] They are to take her throes into consideration today;[4] and that there may be sufficient room for the length of her veil and train and attendants,[5] have a mind to treat her with Westminster Hall.[6] I hope

23. The maiden name of Madame du Deffand (HW).
24. She wrote to Mme de Choiseul 7 Oct. 'à 7 heures du matin' that 'je suis en état . . . de vous dire moi-même que je me porte mieux' (Mme du Deffand, op. cit. iii. 199).
25. Mr Walpole's valet de chambre (HW), Philip Colomb (d. 1799), who had been in HW's service since ca 1767 (MANN viii. 211, n. 5).
26. HW left Paris Thursday, 12 Oct., arriving back in London Tuesday, 17 Oct. ('Paris Journals,' DU DEFFAND v. 353).

———

1. An echo, perhaps, of a passage in Mme de Sévigné's letter to her daughter dated Livry 28 Oct. 1676: 'O good God! Did not you hear the scream I gave? The whole forest has repeated it . . .' (*Letters from the Marchioness de Sévigné to her Daughter*, 1763, v. 180). The original is: 'Eh, bon Dieu! n'avez-vous point entendu le cri que j'ai fait? Tout la forêt l'a répeté . . .' (Mme de Sévigné, *Lettres*, ed. Monmerqué, 1862–6, v. 121).

2. The *Daily Adv.* 4 Dec. reported her as 'suddenly taken ill in the Chapel Royal, St James's, during the time of divine service,' and GM 1775, xlv. 602, *sub* 3 Dec., as 'suddenly seized with a fainting fit during divine service . . . and carried home speechless.'
3. For bigamy, originally appointed 20 Nov. for 18 Dec. in the House of Lords (*Journals of the House of Lords* xxxiv. 512). The Duchess petitioned the Lords 11 Dec. 'to postpone the . . . trial for two months,' pleading 'a very severe illness' (ibid. xxxiv. 527).
4. On 12 Dec. the trial was put off to 24 Jan., and again on 20 Dec. to 28 Feb. (ibid. xxxiv. 531, 539).
5. See MANN viii. 187, 192.
6. So moved 14 Dec. For further particulars of the Duchess and her trial at this time, see ibid. viii. 149–51 and nn. 1–4, 6–10. She was finally tried 15–22 April in Westminster Hall, and found guilty (ibid. viii. 192, n. 4, 195–6).

so, for I should like to see this *comédie larmoyante;* and besides, I conclude, it would bring your Ladyship to town: you shall have timely notice.

There is another comedy infinitely worth seeing, Monsieur Le Tessier.[7] He is Préville, and Caillaud,[8] and Garrick and Weston[9] and Mrs Clive all together, and as perfect in the most insignificant part as in the most difficult. To be sure it is hard to give up loo in such fine weather when one can play from morning till night. In London Pam[10] can scarce get a house till ten o'clock. Mrs Howe[11] and Miss Loyd[12] are in waiting at Althorpe,[13] and Lady Powis still *hors de combat.*[14] If you happen to see the General your husband, make my compliments to him, Madam: his friend the King of Prussia is going to the devil and Alexander the Great.[15]

From HERTFORD, Friday 19 January 1776

Printed for the first time from a photostat of BM Add. MSS 23219, f. 77.

London, January 19th 1776.

Dear Horry,

I COULD not write to you yesterday;[1] my day was employed in adjusting ranks and taking out young people to dance, a matter of duty, not of choice, so I hope it carries its excuse with it.

7. Antoine-A. Le Texier (ca 1737–1814), actor (OSSORY i. 277, n. 14; first name and birth-date kindly supplied by Miss Patricia Sigl in a letter to WSL 5 Feb. 1966).

8. Joseph Caillot (*ante* 12 Nov. 1774, n. 36).

9. Thomas Weston (1737–76), actor.

10. The knave of clubs, the highest trump in five-card loo (OED).

11. Hon. Caroline Howe, m. John Howe.

12. Rachel Lloyd.

13. Althorp Park, Northants, the seat of Earl Spencer. HW wrote to Lady Ossory 30 Dec. 1773, alluding to the departure of her three half-sisters: 'Lady Spenser could as soon keep up her drawing-room without Mrs Howe and Miss Loyd' (OSSORY i. 178).

14. She had been ill in November, but on 3 Jan. 1776 lost about 100 guineas at loo at Princess Amelia's (Coke, 'MS Journals,' 14–22 Nov. 1775, 3 Jan. 1776).

15. In Oct. Frederick wrote to Prince Henry of Prussia that 'j'ai essuyé l'accès de goutte le plus violent que j'aie eu de ma vie,' and by the end of November had suffered, by his count, thirteen more *accès* (*Politische Correspondenz*, Berlin, 1879–1939, xxxvii. 249, 325). However, his malady 'n'a pas été dangereuse,' and by the middle of December there remained of it only 'une grande faiblesse' (Frederick to the Dowager Queen of Denmark 17 Dec., ibid. xxxvii. 353). See OSSORY i. 280, n. 11; MANN viii. 149, n. 7.

———

1. The day 'appointed for celebrating her Majesty's birthday' (*Daily Adv.* 19 Jan.).

Our ball and appearance were much as usual. Some people of rank and some even in office at St James's were absent, but it was[2] covered by the crowd, and looked and lasted as long as ever.[3]

I made your excuses to the Princess.[4] She loves attentions, seemed sensible of yours, and I think you will be *fêté* with many an invitation when the snow will allow you to return.

My brother and Lady Ailesbury are in town;[5] we are to play at loo together here this evening.

I remain, dear Horry,

Always very truly and affectionately yours,

HERTFORD

To LADY HERTFORD, ca Saturday 10 February 1776

Missing; answered *post* ?10 Feb. 1776.

FROM LADY HERTFORD, Saturday ?10 February 1776

Printed for the first time from a photostat of BM Add. MSS 23219, f. 173. *Address:* The Honourable Mr Walpole.

Saturday.

I REJOICE to see that you are able to write a kind long note[1] again, and I should certainly have seen you before this time if I had not known that you was low and I was sure you wished to talk but little.[2] I won't say one word about the coach but that I will take great care of it. I believe you had better not send to Mrs Conway,[3]

2. MS, 'it is was.'
3. 'There were present a much greater number of the nobility and gentry . . . than was expected, considering the badness of the roads' (*Daily Adv.* loc. cit.). Lady Mary Coke wrote in her 'MS Journals' 17 Jan. that 'this is the eleventh day it has snowed,' and HW in *Last Journals* i. 516: 'The year began with a remarkable snow and frost that lasted a month.'
4. Presumably Princess Amelia.

5. They came to town 15 Jan. (Coke, loc. cit.).

———

1. Missing.
2. 'I am, and have been this week confined to my bed with the gout in six or seven different places' (HW to Mason 6 Feb. 1776, MASON i. 240).
3. Anne Delmé (d. 1804), m. (1773) Hon. (after 1793, Lord) Robert Seymour-Conway (1748–1831), 3d son of Lord Hert-

for there is great disappointment felt in that house, just at this time, with great reason, for Mr Delmé,[4] after making the strongest professions, has left them only six thousand pounds. He has left an immense fortune to Mr Delmé[5] and his second son.[6]

Yours ever,

I. H.

From CONWAY, ca Friday 28 June 1776

Missing; answered *post* 30 June 1776.

To CONWAY, Sunday 30 June 1776

Printed from *Works* v. 191–3.

Strawberry Hill, June 30, 1776.

I WAS very glad to receive your letter,[1] not only because always most glad to hear of you, but because I wished to write to you, and had absolutely nothing to say till I had something to answer. I have lain but two nights in town since I saw you,[2] have been else constantly here, very much employed, though doing, hearing, knowing exactly nothing. I have had a Gothic architect[3] from Cambridge to design me a gallery, which will end in a mouse, that is, in an hexagon closet of seven feet diameter.[4] I have been making a beauty-

ford; M.P.; army officer (OSSORY i. 125, nn. 7–8).

4. John Delmé (d. 7 Feb. 1776), of Rowdeford House, Wilts; Mrs Seymour-Conway's uncle (GM 1776, xlvi. 95; *Vict. Co. Hist. Wilts* vii. 219).

5. Peter Delmé (1748–89), Mrs Seymour-Conway's brother; M.P. Morpeth 1774–89. 'By the decease of an uncle, he suceeded to . . . the vast sum of £140,000' (*English Chronicle* 1780 or 1781, cited Namier and Brooke ii. 313).

6. Emilius Henry Delmé (later Delmé Radcliffe) (1774–1832) (R. A. Austen-Leigh, *Eton College Register 1753–1790*, Eton,

1921, p. 155); the eldest son, John Delmé (1772–1809) (ibid. 155–6), would of course have his own fortune. A third son, James Frederick (b. 1775) (ibid. 155), was apparently not provided for.

1. Missing.

2. HW was in town 19–21 June (OSSORY i. 292).

3. James Essex (1722–84), architect and builder; designer of the Beauclerk Tower and the Offices at SH (ibid. i. 294, n. 7).

4. The Beauclerk Tower, 9 ft 5 in. in diameter, was HW's last addition to the house itself at SH (W. S. Lewis, 'Genesis

room,[5] which was effected by buying two dozen of small copies of Sir Peter Lely,[6] and hanging them up; and I have been making hay, which is not made, because I put it off for three days, as I chose it should adorn the landscape when I was to have company; and so the rain is come, and has drowned it.—However, as I can even turn calculator when it is to comfort me for not minding my interest, I have discovered that it is five to one better for me that my hay should be spoiled than not; for, as the cows will eat it if it is damaged, which horses will not, and as I have five cows and but one horse, is not it plain that the worse my hay is, the better? Do not you with your refining head go, and, out of excessive friendship, find out something to destroy my system. I had rather be a philosopher than a rich man; and yet have so little philosophy, that I had much rather be content than be in the right.

Mr Beauclerk and Lady Di.[7] have been here four or five days—so I had both content and exercise for my philosophy. I wish Lady A. was as fortunate! The Pembrokes, Churchills, Le Texier, as you will have heard, and the Garricks, have been with us. Perhaps, if alone, I might have come to you—but you are all too healthy and harmonious. I can neither walk nor sing—nor, indeed, am fit for anything but to amuse myself in a sedentary trifling way. What I have most certainly not been doing, is writing anything: a truth I say to you, but do not desire you to repeat. I deign to satisfy scarce anybody else. Whoever reported that I was writing anything, must have been so totally unfounded, that they either blundered by guessing without reason, or knew they lied—and that could not be with any kind intention; though saying I am going to do what I am not going

of Strawberry Hill,' *Metropolitan Museum Studies*, 1934, v pt i. 61, 82).

5. 'I have turned the little yellow bedchamber below stairs into a beauty room' (HW to Lady Ossory 20 June 1776, Ossory i. 294); HW's description of it is in 'Des. of SH,' *Works* ii. 418–20.

6. (1618–80), painter; 'nineteen small heads, in oil, of the Court of Charles II (except Sacharissa), copied by Jarvis [Charles Jervas or Jarvis (ca 1675–1739)] for himself, and bought with his house at Hampton by Mr [Edward] Lovibonde [(1724–27 Sept. 1775)], at whose sale these and the three foregoing [three watercolours by Charles Beale, one after Van

Dyck and two after Lely], were purchased' (ibid. ii. 419; Ossory i. 294, nn. 12–13). Lovibonde's sale took place 27–28 May, 'by auction by Mr Skinner . . . on the premises at Hampton' (*Daily Adv.* 10–28 May); HW also purchased a painting of Cowley by Lely, which he hung in the Breakfast Room (Ossory i. 294 and n. 11).

7. These names were deleted by Mary Berry, but restored by Wright. Topham Beauclerk (1739–80) m. (1768) Lady Diana Spencer. HW was having the Beauclerk Tower constructed to house her drawings for *The Mysterious Mother* (see Ossory i. 289 and n. 18, 294–5).

to do, is wretched enough. Whatever is said of me without truth, anybody is welcome to believe that pleases. In fact, though I have scarce a settled purpose about anything, I think I shall never write any more. I have written a great deal too much, unless I had written better, and I know I should now only write still worse. One's talent, whatever it is, does not improve at near sixty—yet, if I liked it, I dare to say a good reason would not stop my inclination:—but I am grown most indolent in that respect, and most absolutely indifferent to every purpose of vanity. Yet without vanity I am become still prouder and more contemptuous. I have a contempt for my country-men that makes me despise their approbation. The applause of slaves and of the foolish mad is below ambition. Mine is the haughtiness of an ancient Briton, that cannot write what would please this age, and would not if he could. Whatever happens in America, this coun-try is undone. I desire to be reckoned of the last age, and to be thought to have lived to be superannuated, preserving my senses only for myself and for the few I value. I cannot aspire to be tra-duced like Algernon Sydney,[8] and content myself with sacrificing to him amongst my *lares*. Unalterable in my principles, careless about most things below essentials, indulging myself in trifles by system, annihilating myself by choice, but dreading folly at an unseemly age, I contrive to pass my time agreeably enough, yet see its termination approach without anxiety. This is a true picture of my mind; and it must be true, because drawn for you, whom I would not deceive, and could not if I would. Your question on my being writing drew it forth, though with more seriousness than the report deserved—yet talking to one's dearest friend is neither wrong nor out of season. Nay, you are my best apology. I have always contented myself with your being perfect, or, if your modesty demands a mitigated term, I will say, unexceptionable. It is comical, to be sure, to have always been more solicitous about the virtue of one's friend than about

8. Algernon Sidney or Sydney (1622–83), patriot; HW's hero; executed for his complicity in the Rye House plot, 1683. HW is alluding to a letter of 14 Dec. 1679 from the French ambassador, Barillon, to Louis XIV, printed in the second volume of Sir John Dalrymple's *Memoirs of Great Britain and Ireland*, 1771–3, pp. 255–64, stating that Sidney had taken bribes from the French. In *Last Journals* i. 272–3 HW states that the charge of bribery was 'pre-tended to be drawn from Barillon's papers at Versailles; a source shut up to others, and actually opened to Sir John by the in-tercession of even George III. . . . What must ['the designs of this reign'] . . . be when George III encourages a Jacobite wretch to hunt in France for materials for blackening the heroes who withstood the enemies of Protestan[t]ism and liberty!' See MASON i. 66–7, nn. 2–3.

one's own—yet I repeat it, you are my apology—though I never was
so unreasonable as to make you answerable for my faults in return:
I take them wholly to myself—but enough of this. When I know my
own mind, for hitherto I have settled no plan for my summer, I will
come to you. Adieu!

From HERTFORD, Monday 15 July 1776

Printed for the first time from a photostat of BM Add. MSS 23219, f. 78.

London, July 15th 1776.

Dear Horry,

LAST night at Lady Drogheda's I met Lady Villiers on her return
from Henley, and she gave me very sincere concern and anxiety
by telling me that my brother had been out of order.[1] She said at
the same time that he was now much better, and in a manner quite
well, but her way of talking of the complaint left a sort of doubt
about the cause and foundation of the disorder.

I sent there early this morning and have received the enclosed letter from him.[2] I hope it is nothing but the effect of cold.[3]

Yours, dear Horry,

Very affectionately,

HERTFORD

From CONWAY, ca Tuesday 16 July 1776

Missing; alluded to *post* 20 July 1776.

To HERTFORD, ca Thursday 18 July 1776

Missing; answered *post* 20 July 1776.

1. '13th [July]. General Conway had a
slight paralytic stroke in his face, occasioned by catching cold' (*Last Journals* i.
565). See below and subsequent letters.
2. Missing.
3. Lady Hertford told Lady Mary Coke

17 July that Conway 'had heated himself
with playing at skittles, and 'tis thought
the cold air struck him and occasioned a
blight on one side his face' (Coke, 'MS
Journals,' 17, 21 July).

From HERTFORD, Saturday 20 July 1776

Printed for the first time from a photostat of BM Add. MSS 23219, f. 79.

London, July 20th 1776.

Dear Horry,

I THANK you for the letter[1] I have just received. I rejoice that my brother does not think his complaint of the nervous kind and tendency;[2] he did not write so distinctly to me.[3]

I offered to dine with him any day he chose, but as he has not answered that letter, he may perhaps wish me to defer it a little, and therefore I do not go; if he mentions it and you should go,[4] that doubt has been my only reason for not having been there.

You must have heard that Lady Tyrconnel[5] has very simply made an unnecessary elopement with a Mr Lorrain Smith;[6] a Frenchwoman would have been satisfied with the liberties this town and age allow. I am, dear Horry,

Most truly yours,

HERTFORD

1. Missing.
2. Since Conway's face 'was drawn awry, Lady Ailesbury was alarmed and begged him to go to town for advice: he consented and is assured it is not paralytic' (Coke, 'MS Journals' 17 July).
3. Conway's letter to HW implied here is missing.
4. HW visited Conway 22 July and reported to Cole in his letter of 24 July 1776: 'Mr Conway is in no manner of danger, is better, his head nor speech are affected, and the physicians, who barely allow the attack to be of the paralytic nature, are clear it is local in the muscles of the face' (COLE ii. 18).
5. Lady Frances Manners (1753–92), m. (1772) George Carpenter, 2d E. of Tyrconnel. See next note.
6. Charles Loraine Smith (1751–1835), M.P. Leicester 1784–90. Lady Mary Coke wrote in her 'MS Journals' 21 July that

'the first report said she had eloped with a Mr Smith: that circumstance is now denied, but that she has eloped from her husband is acknowledged by all her friends, who say that she and her Lord had been agreed some time to separate, and that the articles of separation were actually drawing.' According to Lady Mary, ibid. 22 Sept. and 13 Oct., Lady Tyrconnel was with child by Smith, and was 'hurrying on the divorce, in hopes it may pass time enough for her to marry Mr Lorreign Smith before she is brought to bed, that the child may be legitimated.' The divorce took place by Act of Parliament 16 May 1777 (*Journals of the House of Commons* xxxvi. 513); however, Lady Tyrconnel on 27 Oct. 1777 married Philip Leslie (otherwise Anstruther) (b. 1747), a merchant in Boulogne, who, according to the *Scots Peerage* vi. 445, was the man she had eloped with in the first place.

From HERTFORD, Saturday ?3 August 1776

Printed for the first time from a photostat of BM Add. MSS 23219, ff. 80–1.

London, Saturday night.

Dear Horry,

I WAS vastly happy to find my brother much better than I expected, and if you was to see him now, I am persuaded you
would enjoy yourself more than your affection for him now admits
of, thinking as you do about him.[1] He has no stare remaining; his
mouth is still contracted, but in a small degree, and the muscles in
his face have in great measure recovered their usual action, particularly those about the eyes, which he tells me he feels returning to
their tone every day. In short his countenance is returning, I flatter
myself, to that state where you and I have so long seen it with friendship and affection, and I am happy, after what I expected, to differ
with General Johnson[2] in finding it vastly better than I could have
flattered myself after hearing of a paralytic stroke. I met Dr Mickel-
son[3] there, and he told me this morning that he was of opinion the
complaint was local, occasioned by cold or repelling the humour in
his face,[4] and not a matter which affected his general constitution;
that his blood when he took it from him upon his first being attacked was that of a man in health and of a strong constitution, that
the colour of the cheek and of the part affected was not pale, nor
was my brother sick, weak, or heavy and sleepy; the common symptoms, therefore, of palsy did not accompany his case; and as he is
growing every day so much better, I hope in God he will get entirely
well, and that we shall suffer no otherways from this attack than
from the suspicion it may leave upon our minds whether there is
not a paralytic disposition in his constitution. His speech is now
very near perfect; his head as clear as I ever saw it; his spirits good
and his strength great, for he walked as freely with me today by his
own choice and direction as if he had had no complaint. He is at the
same time extremely disposed to follow advice except in the taking
a dish or two of tea, which he thinks will not hurt him.

1. HW, upon visiting Conway 22 July, had been 'shocked . . . to find him more changed than I expected' (HW to Cole 24 July 1776, COLE ii. 18).
2. Gen. James Johnston, a close friend of Conway (ante 6 Feb. 1764, nn. 41, 44).
3. Probably Thomas Michaelson (d. 1780), M.D. who died at Reading, a few miles from Park Place (GM 1780, l. 103).
4. See ante 15 July 1776 and nn. 1, 3.

I imagine he may be easily diverted from going to Mount Edge-combe;[5] he spoke very doubtfully about it last night, and today they have had a letter from Lady Mary Churchill saying she could not go with them, possibly by your management, and you will do well to continue to prevent such a journey being undertaken or resolved in his present circumstances.

I met Lord John Cavendish on the road, who sees his case as I apprehend it from him in a favourable light, and very differently from General Johnson, and I have told you my opinion as it strikes me. I wish it may give you satisfaction and that your judgment can be convinced, putting the General's opinion with your first view of him, that I do not flatter myself too soon and too strongly with his present amendment. We passed the evening at Lady Grandison's, and I think none of the company are now inclined to think ill of his case.[6]

Adieu, dear Horry; I scratch down my thoughts upon him very hastily, and am

Always very truly and affectionately yours,

HERTFORD

From HERTFORD, Thursday 15 August 1776

Printed for the first time from a photostat of BM Add. MSS 23219, f. 82.

London, August 15th 1776.

Dear Horry,

I HAVE just sent a letter to my son Henry at Park Place, desiring him, as he may do it less abruptly, to acquaint my brother and Lady Ailesbury that their son-in-law Mr John Damer[1] shot himself this morning at three o'clock.

He did it in a most profligate and abandoned way at a tavern[2] in Covent Garden, the particulars of which I can tell you when we

---

5. Near Plymouth, the seat of Lord Edgcumbe. The visit was postponed until the next year; see *post* 16 Sept. 1777.

6. 'I am glad to find that everybody thinks I was too much alarmed' (HW to Lady Ossory 4 Aug. 1776, OSSORY i. 309).

1. Hon. John Damer (1744–76), eldest son of Lord Milton, m. (1767) Anne Seymour-Conway (COLE ii. 21, n. 5).

2. The Bedford Arms (HW to Mann 20 Aug. 1776, MANN viii. 234).

meet; they are not fit for the public ear, and if possible³ still less for that of his relations.⁴ I am, dear Horry,

Always very truly and affectionately yours,

HERTFORD

From CONWAY, late Thursday or early Friday, 15 or 16 August 1776

Missing. 'I have had a very calm letter from him [Conway] on the occasion [of Damer's suicide]' (HW to Lady Ossory 15 Aug. 1776, *sub* 16 Aug., OSSORY i. 314).

From LADY AILESBURY, Thursday 22 August 1776

Printed from the MS now WSL; first printed Toynbee *Supp.* ii. 151–2. For the history of the MS see *ante* 23 Aug. 1760.

Park Place, Thursday.

My dear Mr Walpole,

I CANNOT be longer silent, when I have so many thanks to return you, for the part you have taken in this melancholy event, and your very kind offer of putting off the promised journey to Brighthelmstone; which I hope to profit by, though not exactly according to our first intentions, for our tour into Norfolk we shall be obliged to give up, for the reasons I am going to explain to you.¹ Mr Conway has this day received a letter from Mrs Damer, acquainting us, that Lord Milton is resolved to pay none of his late son's debts,² and that she after everything is sold for that purpose will set

---

3. 'If possible' inserted above the line in the MS.

4. He shot himself after supping with 'four common women' and a 'blind fiddler'; see MANN loc. cit.

---

1. HW wrote to Lady Ossory 13 July 1776 that he intended to go to Brighthelmstone (Brighton) for the sea air, and

15 Aug. 1776: 'I shall not go to Brighthelmstone. . . . I have asked my nephew's leave to show them [the Beauclerks] Houghton, and to Mr Conway and Lady Ailesbury' (OSSORY i. 304, 313). Before HW received this letter, the Beauclerks had already declined (ibid. i. 319).

2. HW wrote to Mann 11 Aug. 1776 that Damer and his two brothers (George and

HON. ANNE SEYMOUR DAMER, BY RICHARD COSWAY

aside part of her own income to make up a sum to discharge the just ones; and offers at the same time to come and live with us for at least the first year.[3] This last circumstance is the best remedy to alleviate the uneasiness the first has caused us, and you may imagine how happy I shall be to have her under my protection! I will make no comments to you upon this affecting scene, and only tell you a bare matter of *fact* which I know you love; however I shall wish to expatiate more at large upon it hereafter, and hope you will give me an opportunity as soon as it is convenient to you, and perhaps you will meet Mrs Damer here, who I expect in a few days.

Mr Conway is very well, and his face considerably better. The Duchess of Richmond has left us today. We are quite alone and see no company yet, and my mind is too much taken up to wish it.

Yours most affectionately,

C. AILESBURY

Lionel) had contracted a debt of £70,000 (MANN viii. 230 and n. 13); Lady Mary Coke wrote in her 'MS Journals' 5 Sept. that Damer's debt alone, according to his father, was £60,000.

3. HW, in his letter to Mann 11 Aug. 1776, implied that the debts of all three Damer brothers were due to gambling, but wrote to Mann 20 Aug. 1776 that Damer's 'brothers have gamed, he never did' (MANN viii. 235), and Lady Mary Coke wrote, loc. cit., that Lord Milton 'looked upon Mrs Damer as the cause of all.' 'He insists on selling her jewels, which are magnificent, for discharge of just debts. This is all the hurt he can do her; she must have her jointure of £2500

a year' (HW to Mann 20 Aug. 1776, loc. cit.). Lady Sarah Lennox wrote to Lady Susan O'Brien 19 Sept. that 'Lord Milton has taken her diamonds, furniture, carriages, and *everything* away to pay the debts with,' and that 'she is to live with . . . [Conway] for a year in order to save one year's income . . . towards the payment of Mr Damer's debts' (*Life and Letters of Lady Sarah Lennox*, ed. Lady Ilchester and Lord Stavordale, 1902, i. 251); Lady Louisa Conolly wrote to the Duchess of Leinster 17 Sept. that 'Mrs Damer has given up £1,500 a year of her jointure to pay his debts, and intends to live with her father and mother upon the remaining £1000' (*Leinster Corr.* iii. 227).

From LADY HERTFORD, Saturday 24 August 1776

Printed for the first time from a photostat of BM Add. MSS 23219, f. 164. The month and year for this and the two subsequent extant letters have been determined by the passages in Lady Mary Coke's 'MS Journals' cited *post* 2 Sept. 1776, nn. 1, 3.

Address: To the Honourable Mr Walpole.

Saturday, the 24th.

Dear Mr Walpole,

AS you was so good as to give us leave, we will wait upon you to-morrow or Monday evening, whichever is the most convenient to you; lie at Strawberry Hill that night,[1] and the next morning go to see Hampton Court and Claremont,[2] and dine at one of these places; and perhaps you will accompany us. We shall trouble you with Bell[3] and the two boys;[4] and one bed always serves these gentlemen. I must propose another thing which is to be put in practice, only upon Lady Powis's own terms, which is that she and Lady Harriot[5] should sup with you, but not to lie at your house, but at the inn at Twickenham,[6] and that if you don't consent to this, that they won't come at all. If any part of this scheme is inconvenient to you, pray let me know it, and we[7] will come to you some other time. Pray determine the day for us, and when you have fixed you must be so good as to order two bedchambers at the inn for Lady Pow. and Lady Harriot, and she does not mind their not being good. We beg not to have any loo.

Yours ever,

I. H.

R. S. V. P.

1. 'That night' inserted above the line in the MS.

2. Seat of the late Duke of Newcastle.

3. Lady Isabella Rachel Seymour-Conway (b. 1755), the Hertfords' youngest daughter, m. (1785) George Hatton (OSSORY ii. 283, n. 7).

4. Presumably the Hertfords' youngest sons, George (1763–1848) and William (1760–1837), who were at Harrow 1775–6 and 1770–6, respectively (Namier and Brooke iii. 424, 426); the Hertfords' next youngest son, Hugh (1759–1801), had been in the Royal Navy since 1770 and was

commissioned a lieutenant this year (ibid. iii. 425).

5. Lady Henrietta Antonia Herbert (1758–1830), daughter of Lady Powis, m. (1784) Edward Clive, 2d Bn Clive, cr. (1804) E. of Powis.

6. The George Inn, near the intersection of London Street and Church Street, as shown in 'A Plan of Twickenham . . . from an Actual Survey by Samuel Lewis, 1784,' the back endpaper to MORE.

7. 'I' crossed out and 'we' written above it in the MS.

To LADY HERTFORD, Saturday 24 August 1776

Missing; presumably written in response to the preceding and answered by the following.

From LADY HERTFORD, Saturday 24 August 1776 *bis*

Printed for the first time from a photostat of BM Add. MSS 23219, f. 182.
Address (in Hertford's hand): To the Honourable Horatio Walpole, Strawberry Hill, Twickenham, Middlesex. Free Hertford.
Postmark: 24 AV FREE.

Saturday, 9 o'clock.

Dear Mr Walpole,

LADY Powis says you are so good to her, that she cannot refuse; but then she insists upon making her terms, and that you will meet us at Herbert Lodge at dinner on Monday, and we will all return to Strawberry Hill together. It is in Putney Lane, between Barnes and Wimbledon Common. We must play a great deal at[1] whist in the evening, so that you must consider if you will admit us upon those terms, or if you will call in Lady Browne or anybody to your assistance. Pray don't put us in your best chintz bed, as I am in the secret, and know Sir Robert died in it.[2] Don't you wish us hanged?

Yours ever,

I. H.

1. Written over 'of' in the MS.
2. 'The Red Bedchamber . . . a chintz bed, in which Sir Robert Walpole died in Arlington Street' (*Description of . . . Strawberry Hill,* 1774, p. 38).

From LADY HERTFORD, Monday 2 September 1776

Printed for the first time from a photostat of BM Add. MSS 23219, f. 166.
Address: To the Honourable Hor. Walpole at Strawberry Hill near Twicken-
ham, Middlesex.
Postmark: 2 SE.

London, Monday, September the 2d.

Dear Sir,

I WAS afraid of giving you offence, or else I should have wrote on
Wednesday to tell you how much we all felt obliged to you for
letting us pass two days so agreeably with you.[1] My Lord is at Oatlands[2] and I have not seen a creature these two days, and therefore
cannot tell you if there is any news; and I only write from wishing
to know if there are any hopes of seeing you in town before Friday,
as we are to set out that day for Sudborne.[3] I hope you was not
washed away with the rain of last night. I am ever,

Most faithfully yours,
I. H.

To LADY HERTFORD, ca Thursday 3 October 1776

Missing; answered *post* 3 Oct. 1776.

1. 'Lady Powis and Lady Hertford lodged two nights at Strawberry Hill' (Coke, 'MS Journals' 5 Sept.).
2. Surrey, the seat of Lord Lincoln.
3. 'I've had a note from Lady Hertford, to tell me she goes to my Lord's house in Suffolk tomorrow [6 Sept.] for a fortnight' (ibid.).

From Lady Hertford, Thursday 3 October 1776

Printed for the first time from a photostat of BM Add. MSS 23219, f. 168. The year has been determined by the references to Lady Drogheda's illness in Lady Mary Coke's 'MS Journals' cited below, n. 3.

Address (in Hertford's hand): To the Honourable Hor. Walpole, Twickenham, Middlesex. Free Hertford.

Postmark: 3 OC FREE.

Thursday, October the 3d.

Dear Mr Walpole,

I AM this moment come from Court and am to go at six o'clock to Kew; therefore I can only thank you for your kind note,[1] and have the pleasure of[2] telling you in a very few words that Lady D[rogheda] has had very little fever since Monday, and we flatter ourselves is going on very well, but her pulse is not quite quiet yet.[3] What day will you be in town?[4]

Yours ever faithfully,

I. H.

From Conway, ca Tuesday 29 October 1776

Missing; answered *post* 31 Oct. 1776.

1. Missing.
2. Written over 'in' in the MS.
3. Lady Mary Coke wrote in her 'MS Journals' 24 Sept.: 'Lady Drogheda continues ill: I called at the door and the servant said she was not out of danger,'

and 14 Oct.: 'Lady Drogheda is recovering and goes out every day to take the air.'

4. HW wrote to Mason from Arlington Street 8 Oct. 1776 (Mason i. 276).

To Conway, Thursday 31 October 1776

Printed from *Works* v. 193–5.

Thursday, 31.

THANK you for your letter.[1] I send this by the coach. You will have found a new scene[2]—not an unexpected one by you and me, though I do not pretend I thought it so near.[3] I rather imagined France would have instigated or winked at Spain's beginning with us.[4] Here is a solution of the Americans declaring themselves independent.[5] Oh! the folly, the madness, the guilt of having plunged us into this abyss! Were we and a few more endued with any uncommon penetration?—No—they who did not see as far, *would* not. I am impatient to hear the complexion of today. I suppose it will on the part of administration have been a wretched farce of fear daubed over with airs of bullying. You, I do not doubt, have acted like yourself, feeling for our situation, above insulting, and unprovoked but at the criminality that has brought us to this pass.[6] Pursue your own path, nor lean to the court that may be paid to you on either side, as I am sure you will not regard their being displeased that you do not go as far as their interested views may wish.

If the Court should receive any more of what they call good news, I think the war with France will be unavoidable. It was the victory at Long Island,[7] and the frantic presumption it occasioned, that has ripened France's measures[8]—and now we are to awe them by press-

1. Missing.
2. On the opening of the Parliament in the year 1776 (HW); the new session began 31 Oct. (*Journals of the House of Commons* xxxvi. 3).
3. HW means war with France over America; see HW to Mann 1 Nov. 1776, MANN viii. 252–4.
4. Over Portugal; see ibid. viii. 253 and n. 4.
5. News of the American declaration of independence 4 July had been printed in the *London Gazette* No. 11690, 6–10 Aug.; the full text of the Declaration was printed in the London papers 16 and 17 Aug. (MANN viii. 230, n. 8).
6. In the Commons debate 31 Oct. on the Address of Thanks to the King, which condemned the actions of the rebels and

condoned the administration's measures against them, 'General Conway said, he should be very sorry any part of his conduct were construed as disrespectful to his Majesty; no person bore his Majesty higher respect; but the Address was so entirely against his sentiments, so often declared in that House, that he must vote against it' (Cobbett, *Parl. Hist.* xviii. 1431; see also *Last Journals* i. 584–5). The Address was carried 232–83 (ibid.; *Journals of the House of Commons* xxxvi. 6).
7. The defeat of the rebel army on Long Island by Gen. Howe's forces 27 Aug., news of which was printed in a *London Gazette Extraordinary* 10 Oct. (MANN viii. 248, n. 1).
8. HW wrote to Mann 1 Nov. 1776 that 'the agent of the colonies [Silas Deane] is

ing[8a]—an act that speaks our impotence!—which France did not want to learn![9]

I would have come to town, but I had declared so much I would not, that I thought it would look as if I came to enjoy the distress of the ministers—but I do not enjoy the distress of my country. I think we are undone—I have always thought so—whether we enslaved America or lost it totally—so we that were against the war could expect no good issue. If you do return to Park Place tomorrow, you will oblige me much by breakfasting here: you know it wastes you very little time.

I am glad I did not know of Mrs D.'s sore throat till it is almost well. Pray take care and do not catch it.

Thank you for your care of me: I will not stay a great deal here, but at present I never was better in my life—and here I have no vexatious moments. I hate to dispute; I scorn to triumph myself, and it is very difficult to keep my temper when others do. I own I have another reason for my retirement, which is prudence. I have thought of it late, but at least I will not run into any new expense. It would cost me more than I care to afford to buy a house in town,[9a] unless I do it to take some of my money out of the stocks, for which I tremble a little. My brother[10] is seventy; and if I live myself, I must not build too much on his life; and you know, if he fails, I lose the most secure part of my income.[11] I refused from Lord Holland, and last year from Lord North, to accept the place for my own life;[12] and

openly countenanced at Versailles, and it is past a doubt that they are assisted and traded with' (ibid. viii. 253–4).

8a. See *post* 31 October 1776 *bis*, n. 3.

9. Vergennes, the French minister of foreign affairs, had told Deane in July that 'considering the good understanding between the two Courts of Versailles and London, they could not *openly* encourage the shipping of warlike stores' (Deane to Secret Committee of Continental Congress 18 Aug., *Deane Papers*, ed. Isham, New York, 1887–90, i. 198–9, cited MANN viii. 254, n. 9).

9a. HW's house in Arlington Street was left to him by Sir Robert Walpole for the unexpired term of the lease, to 1781. It appears that the lease was not entirely paid for, and HW's nephew Lord Orford did not agree to discharge this debt until 1778 (OSSORY ii. 62 and n. 8).

10. Sir Edward.

11. £1400 a year, his share of Sir Edward's patent place as Collector of Customs (MANN x. 52).

12. 'I refused the reversion for myself . . . when Lord Holland was secretary of state [1755–6] and offered to obtain it for me' (HW to Montagu 14 July 1770, MONTAGU ii. 317). 'When he united with the Duke of Newcastle, he had offered . . . to procure the reversion . . . to be confirmed for my own, provided I would be upon good terms with the Duke' (*Mem. Geo. III* i. 167). HW had written to Montagu 14 July 1770 to apprize Lord North of the value of the place so that he might bestow it upon one of his own sons (MONTAGU ii. 316–17); in HW's 'Account of My Conduct Relative to the Places I Hold under Government,' he mentions that 'from Lord North I always re-

having never done a dirty thing, I will not disgrace myself at fifty-nine. I should like to live as well as I have done; but what I wish more, is to secure what I have already saved for those I would take care of after me. These are the true reasons of my dropping all thoughts of a better house in town,[13] and of living so privately here. I will not sacrifice my health to my prudence; but my temper is so violent, that I know the tranquillity I enjoy here in solitude, is of much more benefit to my health, than the air of the country is detrimental to it. You see I can be reasonable when I have time to reflect; but philosophy has a poor chance with me when my warmth is stirred—and yet I know, that an angry old man out of Parliament, and that can do nothing but be angry, is a ridiculous animal.

From HERTFORD, Thursday 31 October 1776

Printed for the first time from a photostat of BM Add. MSS 23219, f. 85.

London, October 31st 1776.

Dear Horry,

I SPOKE to Lord Sandwich[1] last night, who told me he would not accept the name of the waterman[2] from me himself, but that if he would apply by petition to the Admiralty, setting forth his case and that he was waterman to the King, his badge would be a plea for his release.[3]

Lord Sandwich is very nice not to take the name from me; I suppose I am to imagine he never does such things, as the trade for granting protections at the Admiralty is a very lucrative one to some of the parties there.

ceived justice and civility' in the payment of his fee as usher of the Exchequer (*Works* ii. 369, n. 1).

13. See *post* 23 Oct. 1778.

1. First lord of the Admiralty.
2. Not identified; see *ante* ca 23 July 1771.
3. From impressment into the navy. On 28 Oct. press-warrants were signed by the Board of Admiralty; the press gangs started work on the 29th, and Lady Mary Coke wrote in her 'MS Journals' 30 Oct. that 'last night . . . seventeen hundred [were] taken' (see MANN viii. 252–3 and n. 3). Watermen were 'always . . . allowed by the lords of the Admiralty protections from being impressed . . . except on very urgent occasions. . . . These protections were generally limited according to the rank of the employer' (H. Humpherus, *History of the . . . Company of Watermen*, [1874], i. 6). On 1 Nov. warrants of protection to the watermen of peers and peeresses were issued by the company (ibid. ii. 324).

I do not know where to find or send to the waterman or any of his family, as the woman who brought your letter left no direction. You must therefore take that trouble, and the sooner the better, lest the man should in the meantime be sent on board a ship-of-war.

The general prospect is gloomy enough; America is sufficient without the danger of a foreign war. Yours, dear Horry,

Always most truly,

HERTFORD

To CONWAY, ca Thursday 3 – Thursday 10 July 1777

Several letters, missing; alluded to *post* 10 July 1777.

To CONWAY, Thursday 10 July 1777

Printed from *Works* v. 195–6.

Strawberry Hill, July 10, 1777.

DON'T be alarmed at this thousandth letter in a week.[1] This is more to Lady Hamilton[2] than to you. Pray tell her I have seen *Monsieur la Bataille d'Agincourt.*[3] He brought me her letter[4] yesterday: and I kept him to sup, *sleep* in the modern phrase, and breakfast here this morning; and flatter myself he was, and she will be, content with the regard I paid to her letter.

The weather is a thought warmer today, and I am as busy as bees

1. The other letters are missing.
2. The first wife of Sir William Hamilton, envoy extraordinary at the court of Naples (HW). Catherine Barlow (d. 1782), m. (1758) Sir William Hamilton, K.B. (DU DEFFAND iv. 345, n. 6; *ante* 29 Aug. 1757, n. 3).
3. M. le Chevalier d'Azincourt, a French antiquary, long settled in Italy (HW). Jean-Baptiste-Louis-Georges Seroux d'Agincourt (1730–1814), archæologist and numismatist, author of *Histoire de l'art par les monuments*, 6 vols, Paris, 1823 (NBG; Yale Cat.; BM Cat.; Bibl. Nat. Cat.; *Enciclopedia italiana*, Rome, 1929–39, xxxi. 445). HW is of course punning on the Battle of Agincourt, and perhaps alluding to Agincourt's military experience (in his youth he had belonged to a regiment of cavalry).
4. Missing.

are about their hay. My *hayssians*[5] have cost me as much as if I had hired them of the Landgrave.[6]

I am glad your invasion[7] is blown over. I fear I must invite those flat-bottomed vessels hither, as the Swissess Necker[8] has directed them to the port of Twickenham. Madame de Blot is too fine, and Monsieur Schomberg[9] one of the most disagreeable, cross, contemptuous savages I ever saw. I have often supped with him at the Duchess de Choiseul's,[10] and could not bear him; and now I must be *charmé* and *pénétré* and *comblé* to see him: and I shall act it very ill, as I always do when I don't do what I like. Madame Necker's letter[11] is as affected and *précieuse,* as if Marmontel[12] had written it for a Peruvian milk-maid.[13] She says I am a philosopher, and as like Madame de Sévigné as two peas—who was as unlike a philosopher as a gridiron. As I have none of Madame de Sévigné's natural easy wit, I am rejoiced that I am no more like a philosopher neither, and still less like a *philosophe;* which is a being compounded of D'Urfey[14] and Diogenes, a pastoral coxcomb and a supercilious brute.

5. Hessians (HW). HW makes the same pun in his letter to Mason 4 Aug. 1777 (Mason i. 326).

6. Of Hesse-Cassel, Friedrich Wilhelm II (1720–85); by a treaty of 15 Jan. 1776 he had agreed to provide England with more than 12,000 troops (Mann viii. 175, n. 11).

7. A party of French nobility then in England, who were to have made a visit at Park Place (HW).

8. Mme Necker, wife of Jacques Necker, Swiss banker at Paris, recently appointed directeur des finances (*ante* 8 Sept. 1775, n. 18; du Deffand iv. 455).

9. Gottlob-Louis Schomberg (d. ca

1792), Comte de Schomberg (ibid. iii. 245, n. 1).

10. HW records doing so on one occasion in his 'Paris Journals' 5 Sept. 1769, ibid. v. 328.

11. Missing.

12. Jean-François Marmontel (1723–99), author.

13. An allusion to his historical novel, *Les Incas,* Paris, 1777, a copy of which HW sent to Mason with the comment, 'I have *seen* but not read one syllable of Marmontel's *Yncas,* nor ever will' (HW to Mason 18 April 1777, Mason i. 301; Hazen, *Cat. of HW's Lib.,* No. 4011).

14. Honoré d'Urfé (1568–1625), author of the pastoral romance, *L'Astrée,*

To Conway, Tuesday 16 September 1777

Printed from *Works* v. 196–7.

Tuesday evening, Sept. 16, 1777.

I HAVE got a delightful plaything, if I had time for play. It is a new sort of camera-obscura[1] for drawing the portraits of persons, or prospects, or insides of rooms, and does not depend on the sun or anything. The misfortune is, that there is a vast deal of machinery and putting together, and I am the worse person living for managing it. You know I am impenetrably dull in everything that requires a grain of common sense. The inventor[2] is to come to me on Friday, and try if he can make me remember my right hand from my left. I could as soon have invented my machine as manage it; yet it has cost me ten guineas, and may cost me as much more as I please for improving it. You will conclude it was the dearness tempted me. I believe I must keep an astronomer, like Mr Beauclerc,[3] to help me to play with my rattle. The inventor, who seems very modest and simple, but I conclude an able flatterer, was in love with my house, and vowed nothing ever suited his camera so well. To be sure, the painted windows and the prospects, and the Gothic chimneys, etc. etc. were the delights of one's eyes, when no bigger than a silver penny.[4] *You* would know how to manage it, as if you had never done anything else. Had not you better come and see it? You will learn how to conduct it, with the pleasure of correcting my awkwardness and *unlearnability*. Sir Joshua Reynolds and West[5] have each got one; and the Duke of Northumberland is so charmed with the invention, that I dare say he can talk upon and explain it till I should understand ten times less of the matter than I do. Remember, nei-

1. The machine called a delineator (HW). See HW to Mason 21 Sept. 1777 (Mason i. 328–9) and the description of the machine in *British Patents,* progression number 1183, cited ibid., n. 1.

2. William Storer (fl. 1777–85), optician, of Saham Toney, near Swaffham, Norfolk (ibid. i. 329, n. 2).

3. Topham Beauclerk's astronomer has not been identified. HW, in his MS 'Notes to Mr Daniel Lysons's *Environs of London,* Volume the Third' (now WSL), p. 2, mentions that Beauclerk had an observatory at his villa at Muswell Hill which was sold at his death (1780).

4. No drawings made of SH with the 'delineator' have been discovered. A camera obscura was sold SH xix. 27*.

5. Benjamin West (1738–1820), the painter.

ther Lady A. nor you, nor Mrs D. have seen my new divine closet,[6] nor the billiard-sticks with which the Countess of Pembroke and Arcadia[7] used to play with her brother Sir Philip;[8] nor the portrait of *la belle* Jennings[9] in the state bedchamber. I go to town this day sennight for a day or two;[10] and as, *to be sure,* Mount Edgecumbe has put you out of humour with Park Place,[11] you may deign to leave it for a moment. I never did see Cotchel,[12] and am sorry. Is not the old wardrobe there still? There was one from the time of Cain; but Adam's breeches and Eve's under-petticoat were eaten by a goat in the ark. Good night.

From CONWAY, October 1777

Missing; answered *post* 5 October 1777.

6. The Beauclerk Tower; HW announced the completion of it to Lady Ossory 6 July 1777 (OSSORY i. 364).

7. Mary Sidney (1561–1621), m. (1577) Henry Herbert, 2d E. of Pembroke, 1570. In letters to Lady Ossory 15 Aug. 1782 and 16 July 1793 HW calls her 'the Arcadian' and 'the Countess of Arcadia,' alluding to her brother Sir Philip having written the *Arcadia* for her (ibid. ii. 351 and n. 10, iii. 184).

8. Sir Philip Sidney (1554–86), Kt; poet. 'Two ivory billiard-sticks, engraved; they belonged to H. Herbert Earl of Pembroke, and have his crest a wyvern holding a bloody hand, and the bear and ragged staff for his third wife, the famous Mary, sister of Sir Philip Sidney . . . from the collection of Mr Gostling at Canterbury' ('Des. of SH,' *Works* ii. 502). William Gostling (1696–1777), antiquary, died at Canterbury 9 March (GM 1777, xlvii. 147). The billiard-sticks were kept in the glass closet in the Great North Bedchamber, and were sold SH xvi. 89, together with 'an ancient ivory busk' to W. M. Smith for £3 17s. 6d.

9. Frances Jennings (ca 1649–1731), 'la belle Jennings' of Gramont's *Mémoires* (*ante* 31 Jan. 1756, n. 12). 'Frances, daughter of Richard Jennings . . . copy by [John] Milbourn [fl. 1773–95] from the original at Lord Spencer's' ('Des. of SH,' *Works* ii. 495–6; BERRY i. 113, n. 5), sold SH xx. 106 to Hor. Rodd for £8 8s.

10. HW mentions his visit to Lady Ossory 29 Sept. 1777 (OSSORY i. 383).

11. HW heralds Conway's, Lady Ailesbury's, and Mrs Damer's visit to Mount Edgcumbe, seat of Lord Edgcumbe, in his letter to Lady Ossory 24 Aug. 1777 (ibid. i. 375; see also n. 33), and mentions the beauty of the place in his letter to her 16 Aug. 1780 (ibid. ii. 211).

12. [Cotehele,] the old residence of the family of Edgecumbe, 12 miles distant from Mount Edgecumbe (HW); an early Tudor mansion, it has been preserved as far as possible by the Edgcumbe family in its original condition (*The Blue Guides: England,* ed. F. Muirhead, 1924, p. 181). For a description and illustrations of Cotehele House, see H. A. Tipping, *English Homes,* Periods I and II, Vol. II, 1937, pp. 69–90; however, no mention of the 'old wardrobe' has been found.

To Conway, Sunday 5 October 1777

Printed from *Works* v. 197–9.

October 5, 1777.

YOU are exceedingly good, and I shall assuredly accept your proposal in the fullest sense, and, to ensure Mrs D., beg I may expect you on Saturday next the 11th. If Lord and Lady William Campbell[1] will do me the honour of accompanying you, I shall be most happy to see them, and expect Miss Caroline.[2] Let me know about them, that the state bedchamber may be aired.

My difficulties about removing from home arise from the consciousness of my own weakness. I make it a rule, as much as I can, to conform wherever I go. Though I am threescore today, I should not think that an age for giving everything up; but it is for whatever one has not strength to perform. You, though not a vast deal younger, are as healthy and strong, thank God, as ever you was: and you cannot have ideas of the mortification of being stared at by strangers and servants, when one hobbles, or cannot do as others do. I delight in being with you, and the Richmonds, and those I love and know; but the crowds of young people, and Chichester folks, and officers, and strange servants, make me afraid of Goodwood,[3] I own. My spirits are never low, but they will seldom last out the whole day; and though I dare to say I appear to many capricious, and different from the rest of the world, there is more reason in my behaviour than there seems. You know in London I seldom stir out in a morning, and always late; and it is because I want a great deal of rest. Exercise never did agree with me: and it is hard if I do not know myself by this time; and what has done so well with me will probably suit me best for the rest of my life. It would be ridiculous to talk so much of myself, and to enter into such trifling details, but *you* are the person in the world that I wish to convince that I do not act merely from humour or ill-humour; though I confess at the same time that I want your *bonhommie,* and have a disposition not to care at all for people that I do not absolutely like. I could say a

1. Lady Ailesbury's brother and his wife (*ante* 27 Aug. 1764, n. 50).
2. Miss Caroline Campbell [1764–89],

eldest daughter of Lord William Campbell (HW). See Ossory ii. 50, n. 10.
3. Richmond's seat, 3 miles NE of Chichester.

great deal more on this head, but it is not proper; though, when one has pretty much done with the world, I think with Lady Bland-ford that one may indulge one's self in one's own whims and par-tialities in one's own house. I do not mean, still less to profess, re-tirement, because it is less ridiculous to go on with the world to the last, than to return to it: but in a quiet way it has long been my purpose to drop a great deal of it. Of all things I am farthest from not intending to come often to Park Place, whenever you have little company; and I had rather be with you in November than in July, because I am so totally unable to walk farther than a snail. I will never say any more on these subjects, because there may be as much affectation in being over-old, as folly in being over-young. My idea of age is, that one has nothing really to do but what one ought, and what is reasonable. All affectations are pretensions; and pretending to be anything one is not, cannot deceive when one is known, as everybody must be that has lived long. I do not mean that old folks may not have pleasures, if they can; but then I think those pleasures are confined to being comfortable, and to enjoying the few friends one has not outlived. I am so fair as to own, that one's duties are not pleasures. I have given up a great deal of my time to nephews and nieces, even to some I can have little affection for. I do love my nieces, nay like them; but people above forty years younger are cer-tainly not the society I should seek. They can only think and talk of what is, or is to come; I certainly am more disposed to think and talk of what is past: and the obligation of passing the end of a long life in sets of totally new company is more irksome to me than pass-ing a great deal of my time, as I do, quite alone. Family love and pride make me interest myself about the young people of my own family—for the whole rest of the young world, they are as indifferent to me as puppets or black children. This is my creed, and a key to my whole conduct, and the more likely to remain my creed, as I think it is *raisonné*. If I could paint my opinions instead of writing them, and I don't know whether it would not make a new sort of alphabet, I should use different colours for different affections at different ages.[4] When I speak of love, affection, friendship, taste, lik-ing, I should draw them rose colour, carmine, blue, green, yellow,

4. This whimsical appropriation of colours to affections of the mind, can appear apposite only to those acquainted with Mr Walpole's particular opinion of particular colours (Mary Berry). HW's 'al-phabet of six colours' is expounded in his letter to Lady Ossory 4 Jan. 1781 (ibid. ii. 261–3).

for my cotemporaries: for newcomers, the first would be of no colour; the others, purple, brown, crimson, and changeable. Remember, one tells one's creed only to one's confessor, that is *sub sigillo*. I write to you as I think: to others as I must. Adieu!

From HERTFORD, ca Friday 27 March 1778

Missing. 'On the 27th [March], on calling out the militia [because of the critical state of affairs with respect to France; see MANN viii. 367, n. 10], which Lord Orford's insanity would not permit him commanding [see *post* 5 April 1778], Lord Weymouth [secretary of state for the south] wrote to Lord Hertford, by the King's order, to say he had a mind to appoint three deputy lieutenants [of Norfolk], whom he named, but would not fix till he knew they would be agreeable to the Walpole family, which Lord Hertford was desired to inquire' (*Last Journals* ii. 153).

To HERTFORD, ca Friday 27 March 1778

Missing; HW's 'very respectful answer' to the preceding (*Last Journals* ii. 153). Hertford put the letter into the hands of George III, and HW subsequently asked that it be returned; see Hertford to George III 30 March 1778 (Appendix 11; FAMILY 336).

To HERTFORD, Sunday 5 April 1778

Printed from a photostat of the MS in the Royal Archives, Windsor Castle. First printed in Geo. III's *Corr.*, ed. Fortescue, iv. 97.

April 5, 1778.

My dear Lord,

SIR John Wodehouse[1] has been with me again, and has been with my nephew, but has had no success in dissuading him from sending both battalions to Norwich.[2] I find all the Norfolk gentlemen

---

1. (1741–1834), 6th Bt, of Kimberley, Norfolk; cr. (1797) Bn Wodehouse of Kimberley; M.P. Norfolk 1784–97.

2. For quartering (see below); Lord Orford, lord lieutenant of Norfolk 1757–91 and colonel of the Norfolk militia 1758–91, had resumed command of the regiment after his recovery from his

now in town equally alarmed at this measure; and as there is no time to be lost, I believe, if I may presume to say so, that it will be necessary to have it intimated to Lord Orford that his Majesty wishes to have that disposition altered, the greatest inconveniencies being apprehended; and that both battalions should be quartered, as they used to be, at Yarmouth and Dereham. Perhaps this being intimated by Lord Townshend from his Majesty might be a proper channel.[3] However, it was my duty to state these apprehensions; my nephew is so impetuous that I fear nothing but his Majesty's name will control him.[4] I am in great pain at the thought of his commanding the militia at all at present himself, both as it will hurry him too much, and as I fear he will only exhibit scenes that are surely not fit for the public eye.[5]

I never saw Sir John Wodehouse till Thursday last, but he appears a most amiable sensible gentleman, and expresses so much tenderness for my nephew, and at the same time such prudent attention to the public that I cannot doubt but his apprehensions are well founded. I am going to sleep out of town to compose my own mind a little, that is much agitated with these distresses, but shall be back tomorrow by dinner, if you have any commands for, my dear Lord,

Your most obedient

Hor. Walpole

From Lady Ailesbury, June 1778

Missing; mentioned *post* 25 June 1778.

second attack of insanity, announced in his letter to Lord Hertford 31 March 1778, printed in Fortescue, op. cit. iv. 89.

3. Townshend was master-general of the Ordnance and a neighbour of Orford's in Norfolk; see Selwyn 169, n. 2 and Townshend to HW 30 Nov. 1791.

4. HW wrote to Lady Ossory 28 Feb. 1789 that at this time 'the King . . . commanded me to prevent [Orford's 'marching to Norwich at the head of the Norfolk

militia'] and . . . I could not' (Ossory iii. 47–8; see also n. 7). In Aug. Lord Hertford wrote to the King begging him to remove a company of Norfolk militia from Orford (Fortescue, op. cit. iv. 190–2).

5. According to HW, Orford wrote in the orderly book at Norwich 'that if the French should land on any part of the coast, the magistrates were to burn the suburbs of that city, which would then be impregnable' (Ossory iii. 47–8).

To Lady Ailesbury, Thursday 25 June 1778

Printed from the MS now WSL. First printed (with omissions) *Works* v. 570; first printed in full Toynbee x. 267–8 and *Supp.* ii. 158–9. For the history of the MS see *ante* 23 Aug. 1760; it was marked by HW for inclusion in *Works*. The first page is reproduced in W. S. Lewis, *Horace Walpole,* New York, 1961, facing p. 112.

Address: To the Countess of Ailesbury at Park Place near Henley.
Postmark: Isleworth 26 IV.

Strawberry Hill, June 25, 1778.

I AM quite astonished, Madam, at not hearing of Mr Conway's being returned![1] What is he doing? Is he revolting and setting up for himself like our nabobs in India? or is he forming Jersey, Guernsey, Alderney and Sark into the United Provinces in the compass of a silver penny? I should not wonder if this was to be the fate of our distracted empire, which we seem to have made so large, only that it might afford to split into separate kingdoms. I told Mr C. I should not write any more, concluding he would not stay a twinkling; and your Ladyship's last[2] encouraged my expecting him. In truth I had nothing to tell him if I had written.

I am impatient too to know how poor Lord William does, and if you have better hopes of him.[3] I long to hear that my dear Mrs Damer is well again. I hope it was nothing at all serious.

I have been in town but one single night[4] this age, as I could not bear to throw away this phoenix June. It has rained a good deal this morning, but only made it more delightful. The flowers are all Arabian—I have found but one inconvenience, which is, the hosts of cuckoos; one would not think one was in Doctors Commons.[5] It

1. 'On Tuesday last [30 June] General Conway arrived at his house in Warwick Street, Charing Cross, from taking his survey of the forts and garrisons in the islands of Jersey and Guernsey . . . and yesterday waited on his Majesty at the levee, and made report of the same' (*Public Advertiser* 2 July). Conway was governor of Jersey from 1772 till his death (see MANN ix. 111, n. 5). 'Le 13 juin 1778, le Général Conway, gouverneur, assiste à une séance de la Cour Extraordinaire ou du Samedi. . . . Le 17 juin . . . il est présent à une séance des États, qui lui expriment leur reconnaissance de ce qu'il

a bien voulu visiter l'île dans ce temps critique; ils le remercient aussi de tout ce qu'il a déjà fait, depuis son arrivée, pour la défense du pays' (J. A. Messervy, 'Liste des gouverneurs . . . de l'île de Jersey,' *Société jersiaise, Bulletins,* 1902–5, v. 12–13).
2. Missing.
3. Lord William Campbell, Lady Ailesbury's brother, died 4 Sept. (OSSORY ii. 50, n. 8).
4. 19 June (MANN viii. 388).
5. Location of the Bishop's or Consistory Court, where divorces were adjudged (ibid.

is very disagreeable that the nightingales should sing but half a dozen songs, and the other beasts squall for two months together.

Pray, Madam, tell Lady Lyttelton, for I know she is at Park Place, that I begged Mr Churchill[6] to ask her to meet them and the Cadogans[7] here—not that she would have met them, for they could not come, but are gone a-camping.

Lady H[ertford] sent me word Lord Irwin is dead[8]—I want to know if the borough comes to Lord B[eauchamp].

Poor Mrs Clive has been robbed again in her own lane, as she was last year, and has got the jaundice, she thinks with the fright. I don't make a visit without a blunderbuss;[9] so one might as well be invaded by the French. Though I live in the centre of ministers, I do not know a syllable of politics—and though within hearing of Lady Greenwich, who is but two miles off,[10] I have not a word of news to send your Ladyship. I live like Berecynthia[11] surrounded by nephews and nieces; big and little I have fifteen near me; yet Park Place is full as much in my mind, and I beg for its history.

Your most faithful,

H. W.

To Hertford, July 1778

Missing; answered Hertford to HW *post* 8 July 1778.

i. 452, n. 23); HW's writing 'not' is an apparent slip.

6. Charles Churchill, HW's brother-in-law.

7. Hon. Charles Sloane Cadogan (*ante* 20 April 1764, n. 11), 3d Bn Cadogan, 1776, m. (1777) Mary Churchill (*ante* 6 July 1754, n. 5), dau. of Charles Churchill; see FAMILY 152–3.

8. Lord Irvine, Beauchamp's father-in-law (see *ante* 25 Sept. 1775), died without male issue 19 June, when the borough of Horsham, of which he owned the majority of burgages, devolved upon his widow. Upon her death in 1807 Beauchamp (then Lord Hertford) inherited the burgages, which he sold in 1811 to Charles, 11th

Duke of Norfolk, who had begun buying up the non-Irvine property in 1778 with a view to contesting the Irvine interest there (W. Albery, *Parliamentary History of . . . Horsham*, 1927, pp. 114, 128, 252–4 *et passim*).

9. That is, his footman who went with him in his carriage carried one.

10. HW calls her a 'shrill *Morning Post*' *ante* 16 Oct. 1774.

11. A surname of Cybelé, the Asiatic goddess of procreation, who was worshipped, among other places, upon Mount Berecyntus in Phrygia (*Harper's Dictionary of Classical Literature and Antiquities*, ed. H. Thurston Peck, New York, 1923, pp. 205, 1370–1).

To Hertford, ca Wednesday 8 July 1778

Missing; answered *post* 10 July 1778.

To Conway, Wednesday 8 July 1778

Printed from *Works* v. 199–200.

July 8, 1778.

I HAVE had some conversation with a ministerial person,[1] on the subject of pacification with France;[2] and he dropped a hint, that as we should not have much chance of a good peace, the Opposition would make great clamour on it. I said a few words on the duty of ministers to do what they thought right, be the consequence what it would. But as honest men do not want such lectures, and dishonest will not let them weigh, I waived that theme, to dwell on what is more likely to be persuasive, and which I am firmly persuaded is no less true than the former maxim; and that was, that the ministers are *still* so strong, that if they could get a peace that would save the nation, though not a brilliant or glorious one, the nation in general would be pleased with it, and the clamours of the Opposition be insignificant.

I added, what I think true too, that no time is to be lost in treating; not only for preventing a blow, but from the consequences the first misfortune would have. The nation is not yet alienated from the Court, but it is growing so; is grown so enough, for any calamity to have violent effects. Any internal disturbance would advance the hostile designs of France. An insurrection from distress would be a double invitation to invasion; and, I am sure, much more to be dreaded, even personally, by the ministers, than the ill-humours of Opposition for even an inglorious peace. To do the Opposition justice, it is not composed of incendiaries. Parliamentary speeches raise

1. Not identified.
2. On 26 June 'Lord and Lady Hertford made me a visit . . . and confirmed the account I had received . . . of the engagement between two of [Admiral] Keppel's frigates and three of the French. . . . Lord H. thinks the war now determined by them, and I need not say, has most gloomy apprehensions' (HW to Lady Ossory 27 June 1778, Ossory ii. 22–3; see also HW to Mann 7 July 1778, Mann viii. 390–1 and n. 3).

no tumults; but tumults would be a dreadful thorough bass to speeches. The ministers do not know the strength they have left (supposing they apply it in time), if they are afraid of making any peace. They were too sanguine in making war; I hope they will not be too timid of making peace.

What do you think of an idea of mine, of offering France a neutrality? that is, to allow her to assist both us and the Americans.[3] I know she would assist only them: but were it not better to connive at her assisting them, without attacking us, than her doing both? A treaty with her would perhaps be followed by one with America. We are sacrificing all the essentials we *can* recover, for a few words; and risking the independence of this country, for the nominal supremacy over America. France seems to leave us time for treating. She made no scruple of begging peace of us in '63, that she might lie by and recover her advantages. Was not that a wise precedent? Does not she *now* show that it was? Is not policy the honour of nations? I mean, not morally, but has Europe left itself any other honour? And since it has really left itself no honour, and as little morality, does not the morality of a nation consist in its preserving itself in as much happiness as it can? The invasion of Portugal by Spain in the last war, the partition of Poland, have abrogated the law of nations. Kings have left no ties between one another. Their duty to their people is still allowed. He is a good king that preserves his people; and if temporizing answers that end, is it not justifiable? You, who are as moral as wise, answer my questions. Grotius[4] is obsolete. Dr Joseph[5] and Dr Frederic,[6] with four hundred thousand commentators, are reading new lectures—and I should say, thank God, to one another, if the four hundred thousand commentators were not in worse danger than they.[7] Louis XIV is grown a casuist

3. France and America had signed a Treaty of Amity and Commerce and a Treaty of Alliance at Paris 6 Feb.; the treaties were ratified by the Continental Congress 4 May (ibid. viii. 354–5, n. 3).

4. Huigh de Groot (Hugo Grotius) (1583–1645), Dutch jurist and humanist. HW had his *De jure belli ac pacis* (originally published 1625, revised 1631), Amsterdam, 1720 (Hazen, *Cat. of HW's Lib.*, No. 2207:16).

5. The Emperor of Germany (HW), Joseph II of Austria.

6. Frederic II King of Prussia (HW).

7. Joseph and Frederick were in disagreement about Bavaria, Joseph 'claiming part of the domains of the late Elector of Bavaria' (HW's note on his letter to Mann 17 March 1778, MANN viii. 365, n. 10); according to GM 1778, xlviii. 189, *sub* 30 April, 'foreign gazettes say that his Prussian Majesty's army in Silesia, of which the King is to put himself at the head, amounts to 200,000 men,' while Maria Theresa wrote to Mercy-Argenteau 7 July that Frederick's army was 'plus fort de 40,000 hommes que nous' (*Correspondance secrète entre Marie-Thérèse et le*

compared to those partitioners. Well, let us simple individuals keep our honesty, and bless our stars that we have not armies at our command, lest we should divide kingdoms that are at our *bienséance!*[8] What a dreadful thing it is for such a wicked little imp as man to have absolute power!—But I have travelled into Germany, when I meant to talk to you only of England; and it is too late to recall my text. Good night.

From HERTFORD, Wednesday 8 July 1778

Printed for the first time from a photostat of BM Add. MSS 23219, ff. 86–7.

London, July 8th 1778.

Dear Horry,

THIS country is at present most certainly in a very perilous state, and you have as properly pointed out the various ways by which it may be relieved or must be defended.[1]

The French would not let the opportunity slip of distressing us by assisting the Americans, but if that point can be obtained without war I think she would yet be glad to avoid it. How that is to be done after what has passed is difficult to say; the crisis is come and must be soon determined. There are no means that I see but through Spain, and I do not pretend to judge of *her* real views and inclinations.[2] The ministers must I think be disposed to seize any measure that could lead decently to reconcilement in our present circumstances, if they have resolution enough to risk their places in spite of the clamour which might attend it from Opposition. I have

Comte de Mercy-Argenteau, ed. Arneth and Geffroy, 1874, iii. 220). *The Daily Adv.* 7 July carried a report, *sub* Leyden, 1 July, that 'the two armies in Germany . . . will take the field the 12th instant'; however, the dispute was settled without a battle by the Peace of Teschen, 1779 (see MANN viii. 400, n. 9, 454, n. 11).

8. Convenience.

———

1. HW's letter, evidently very similar to the one he wrote to Conway 8 July, is missing.

2. 'It was yesterday [7 July] reported, that proposals for preventing an open rupture with France, under the mediation of the Spanish Court are now under consideration' (*Daily Adv.* 8 July). HW wrote in *Last Journals* ii. 190, *sub* 10 July 1778, that the 'great Duchess [of Tuscany, Maria Louisa] told Mrs Ann Pitt, at Florence, that her father [the King of Spain] had written to her that he condemned the protection France gave to the Americans, and that he would not join in it'; HW received this information from Mann in the latter's letter of 28 April 1778 (see MANN viii. 375).

as you know fortunately no seat in the Cabinet, nor do I ever converse otherways with them than by accident; if I saw them oftener or conversed more with them, my voice would probably have but little weight. My opinion however is clear for peace, if it can be decently obtained, and first with America, where I should not be so nice about the terms if I could exclude France from being a party to the treaty. That power has grievously offended us as a nation, but we have in some measure softened the blow by the capture of her frigates.[3] I wish therefore, as you say, that we could agree; we can scarce ever be upon worse terms or in worse circumstances for war than at present, and I would therefore put off the evil day.

Russia is the only power perhaps that wishes us well,[4] but I doubt she may be fully employed about her own affairs and in her own quarrel.[5] Every circumstance seems untoward except the time which the French have given us so genteelly, but if they cannot make peace they will I suppose take every method they can to ruin us, and I imagine from your letter that an invasion may be attempted.

I am going for a few days or weeks, as I like it, to Tunbridge, but I shall not go there or elsewhere with the indifference you so justly blame in the country at large. I remain, dear Horry,

Most truly and affectionately yours,

HERTFORD

Your nephew I hear has had a brush upon the coast with some smugglers. He has taken the prize for which they contended, but with the loss of 6 or 7 militiamen, which they wish to conceal.[6]

---

3. In the skirmish between British and French frigates mentioned *ante* 8 July 1778, n. 2, and in a second engagement 19 June, the British captured three frigates and disabled a fourth (OSSORY ii. 23, n. 3).
4. See MANN viii. 127, 324, and *Last Journals* ii. 46.
5. Hertford presumably means with Turkey; the *London Chronicle* 19–21 March, xliii. 274, had reported that 'when the last dispatches left Petersburgh, a courier was arrived with advice, that a fresh treaty of accommodation was opened,

which, it was hoped, would prevent the renewal of a war with the Turks, but that otherwise every preparation was making to begin a vigorous campaign.'
6. A detachment of Orford's militia camped at Southwold fought a battle with smugglers trying to make a landing under cover of a bombardment by a 12-gun cutter; reinforcements came in and all the goods were seized (letter of K. Gobbet, 18 July 1778, WO. 1/1000, cited in J. R. Western, *The English Militia in the Eighteenth Century*, 1965, p. 433).

From HERTFORD, Friday 10 July 1778

Printed for the first time from a photostat of BM Add. MSS 23219, f. 88.

London, July 10th 1778.

Dear Horry,

VERY far from tiring, you instruct and entertain me whenever you employ your pen with me. I shall however, in this letter proposed for the post, say little in answer to your last.[1]

I am concerned for what you have heard spoke with so little reserve; I wish I could remedy or prevent it. Every principle would incline me to it.

We are going this evening to our temporary villa upon Mount Ephraim.[2]

The Jamaica fleet is safely arrived[3] and the Spanish ambassador[4] with his family is expected on Monday or Tuesday;[5] d'Escarano[6] goes tomorrow to Dover to meet him, but yet I fear we shall have war. I remain, dear Horry,

Very truly and affectionately yours,

HERTFORD

1. Missing.
2. 'Eprhaim' in the MS; a hamlet in Sussex, 15 miles beyond Tunbridge Wells (see preceding letter). No other mention has been found of Hertford's 'temporary villa' there.
3. On 8 July 'advice was received that the Jamaica fleet, bound to London, is safe arrived in the Channel' (*Daily Adv.* 9 July). The West India fleet arrived about the same time; HW wrote in *Last Journals* ii. 189 that 'it was very astonishing that France had not endeavoured to intercept them [the two fleets]; not only for the great blow it would have been to our trade, but as out of them the government

got 1300 sailors to man more men-of-war.'
4. Pedro Francisco Luján Silva y Góngora (1727–94), 6th Marqués de Almodóvar; cr. (1780) Duque de Almodóvar; ambassador to England 1778–9 (OSSORY ii. 60, n. 13).
5. He arrived on Monday, 13 July; see *post* 18 July 1778.
6. The Caballero d'Escarano; secretary of the Spanish embassy in London ca 1772–9 and chargé d'affaires there from the departure and death of the Principe di Masserano in 1777 till the arrival of Almodóvar; not further identified (*Court and City Register* 1772–9, *passim*; MANN viii. 328 and n. 16).

To Conway, Saturday 18 July 1778

Printed from *Works* v. 201-2.

Saturday, July 18, 1778.

YESTERDAY evening the following notices were fixed up in Lloyd's Coffee House:

That a merchant[1] in the City had received an express from France,[2] that the Brest fleet, consisting of 28 ships of the line,[3] were sailed, with orders to burn, sink, and destroy.[4]

That Admiral Keppel was at Plymouth,[5] and had sent to demand three more ships of the line[6] to enable him to meet the French.

On these notices the stocks sunk 3½ per cent.[7]

An account I have received this morning from a good hand[8] says, that on Thursday[9] the Admiralty received a letter from Admiral Keppel, who was off the Land's End,[10] saying, that the *Worcester*[11] was in sight; that the *Peggy*[12] had joined him, and had seen the

1. 'Mr Cazalet, a merchant in the City' (*London Packet* 15-17 July), presumably Peter Cazalet (d. 1788), 'merchant in Austin Friars' (GM 1788, lviii pt i. 368; see also Baldwin's *New Complete Guide . . . City of London*, 1768, p. 104).

2. 'Dated July 14 . . . occasioned by a letter received . . . from Monsieur de Sartine [minister of the marine]' (*London Chronicle* 16-18 July, xliv. 62); the express was from Cazalet's 'brother, who is now at Boulogne,' who received Sartine's account 'from the intendant of the marine at that port' (*London Packet* 15-17 July).

3. 32, including two 50-gun ships, the *Amphion* and the *Fier;* see *London Chronicle*, loc. cit,; *Proceedings at Large of the Court-Martial . . . of . . . Augustus Keppel, Admiral of the Blue*, 1779, p. 125; *Gazette de Leyde* 21 July, *sub* 'Paris, le 13 juillet'; *Sandwich Papers* ii. 10-11. The fleet also consisted of 9 frigates, listed ibid. ii. 11 and two smaller ships.

4. 'The Brest fleet sailed on the 8th instant . . . with positive orders to attack, seize, and take all ships belonging to the King of England, or any of his subjects' (*London Chronicle*, loc. cit.). In a letter of 10 July to the Duc de Penthièvre, Louis XVI authorized the issuance of

letters of marque and reprisals against British ships (*Gazette de Leyde* 28 July; English text in *Daily Adv.* 27 July).

5. 'Off the harbour' (ibid. 18 July, *sub* 'Plymouth, July 14'); he had sailed from St Helens the 9th, and sailed from Plymouth the 16th (ibid. 21 July, *sub* 'Plymouth, July 16'; *Sandwich Papers* ii. 122, 372).

6. See below.

7. On 17 July India stock fell from 136 to '131¼ a 132'; the next day the rest of the market also dipped, though not as steeply (*Daily Adv.* 16, 17, 18 July).

8. Not identified.

9. 16 July.

10. 'On Wednesday [15 July] some dispatches were brought to the Admiralty office from Admiral Keppel, who, with the fleet under his command, were at the time of writing in Torbay' (ibid. 17 July).

11. A third rate, of 64 guns, Capt. M. Robinson. She had sailed from Portsmouth 10 July, and joined the fleet 14 July (*London Evening Post* 7-9 July; *Daily Adv.* 14 July; *Sandwich Papers* ii. 113, n. 1; *Court and City Register*, 1778, p. 144).

12. A cutter sent by Keppel 23 July from near Ushant, with a letter to the

Thunderer[13] making sail for the fleet; that he was waiting for the *Centaur*, *Terrible*, and *Vigilant*;[14] and that having received advice from Lord Shuldham[15] that the *Shrewsbury*[16] was to sail from Plymouth on Thursday, he should likewise wait for her.[17] His fleet will then consist of 30 ships of the line;[18] and he hoped to have an opportunity of trying his strength with the French fleet on our own coast: if not, he would seek them on theirs.[19]

The French fleet sailed on the 7th, consisting of 31[20] ships of the line, 2 fifty-gun ships, and 8 frigates.[21]

This state is probably more authentic than those at Lloyd's.

Thus you see how big the moment is! and, unless far more favourable to us in its burst than good sense allows one to promise, it must leave us greatly exposed. Can we expect to beat without considerable loss?—and then, where have we another fleet? I need not state the danger from a reverse.

Admiralty (Keppel to Stephens 23, 24 July, in *Proceedings*, pp. 121, 182).

13. A third rate, of 74 guns, Capt. the Hon. Robert B. Walsingham; she sailed from Portsmouth 10 July, and joined the fleet on the 15th (ibid., Appendix, p. 8; *Daily Adv.* 14 July; *Sandwich Papers*, loc. cit.; *Court and City Register*, 1778, p. 149).

14. The *Centaur*, of 74 guns (Capt. Phillips Cosby), and the *Vigilant*, of 64 guns (Capt. Robert Kingsmill), joined the fleet the 17th, and the *Terrible*, of 74 guns (Capt. Sir Richard Bickerton), off Ushant on the 19th (*Proceedings*, loc. cit.; *Sandwich Papers*, loc. cit.; *Court and City Register*, 1778, pp. 149–50, 1779, p. 150). All three were to have sailed from Portsmouth the afternoon of 11 July (*Daily Adv.* 14, 17 July; *Geo. III's Corr.*, ed. Fortescue, iv. 177–8).

15. Molyneux Shuldham (ca 1717–98), cr. (1776) Bn Shuldham [I]; vice-admiral 1775; admiral 1787; commander-in-chief at Plymouth 1777–82; M.P. Fowey 1774–84.

16. A third-rate, of 74 guns, Capt. John Ross (*Court and City Register*, 1778, pp. 144, 149).

17. She joined Keppel's fleet with the *Centaur* and *Vigilant* off the Lizard on the 17th; see *Sandwich Papers*, ii. 107, 113n, 123; *Daily Adv.* 21 July, *sub* 'Plymouth, July 16.'

18. 'On the ninth of July, finding my

fleet made up to twenty-four ships of the line of battle with four frigates and two fireships I sailed again [from St Helens] . . . trusting to such reinforcement as I was given to expect would join me at Plymouth, off the Lizard, and at sea, by several reinforcements . . . the fleet was made up to thirty sail of the line' (Keppel's speech, in *Proceedings*, p. 125; see also the list of Keppel's fleet in Fortescue, op. cit. iv. 177; summary of Keppel's orders, *sub* 9 July, in *Sandwich Papers* ii. 372; 'List of Admiral Keppel's fleet, who are now sailed to watch the motions of the French fleet in Brest water,' in *Public Advertiser* 14 July; and 'Order of Battle, as it stood 27th July 1778,' in *Proceedings*, Appendix, p. 8).

19. Before he sailed 9 July, Keppel 'was authorized to extend his station from between Brest and Ushant as far as Scilly and the Lizard' ('Summary of Orders to Admiral Keppel 1778,' in *Sandwich Papers* ii. 372–3). Keppel wrote to Sandwich 17 July from 'off the Lizard' that 'a battle with the French fleet must depend upon them; if they are eager, I shall endeavour to get them a little from their own coast, but I am apprehensive they will not allow me to lead them from their land' (ibid. ii. 123). See *post* ?19 July 1778, n. 1.

20. This date and figure were reported in the *Daily Adv.* 16 July.

21. See above, nn. 3, 4.

The Spanish ambassador certainly arrived on Monday.[22]

I shall go to town on Monday for a day or two;[23] therefore, if you write tomorrow, direct to Arlington Street.

I add no more: for words are unworthy of the situation; and to blame now, would be childish. It is hard to be gamed for against one's consent; but when one's country is at stake, one must throw one's self out of the question. When one is old, and nobody, one must be whirled with the current, and shake one's wings like a fly, if one lights on a pebble. The prospect is so dark, that one shall rejoice at whatever does not happen, that may. Thus I have composed a sort of philosophy for myself, that reserves every possible chance. You want none of these artificial aids to your resolution. Invincible courage and immaculate integrity are not dependent on the folly of ministers or on the events of war. Adieu!

From HERTFORD, Sunday ?19 July 1778

Printed for the first time from a photostat of BM Add. MSS 23219, f. 89.

Tunbridge, Sunday evening.

ALAS, dear Horry, the die, the deep die is I fear cast. The Brest fleet as well as Keppel's are I hear at sea, and a few days may determine the fate of this Empire.[1] It is too late to negotiate, and we must look up to the God of armies for protection. I wish we deserved better.

The French have I hear already taken two of our trading ships, though not West Indiamen,[2] and they fear for the *Lively* frigate.[3]

22. 'On Monday night [13 July] his Excellency the Marquis de Almadovor, the new Spanish ambassador, arrived in town from Madrid . . . and yesterday he notified his arrival to the secretary of state [for the south, Lord Weymouth] in that quality' (*Daily Adv.* 15 July). On 17 July he 'had an audience of his Majesty to deliver his letters of credence' (ibid. 18 July).

23. HW was in town 22 and 23 July (MASON i. 421 and n. 8).

1. On 23 July Keppel's fleet sighted the French (*Sandwich Papers* ii. 10, 127, n. 1,

373), and on 27 July an inconclusive action was fought off Ushant, for which see MASON i. 425, nn. 1–3 and OSSORY ii. 31, nn. 1–4.

2. The *Daily Adv.* 16 July, *sub* 'Newcastle, July 11,' reported that 'by letters from France, which arrived at Sunderland on Tuesday last [7 July], we are informed, that several vessels belonging to that port, which had been stopped at Dunkirk, are made prizes of, and that their masters had left them on the above account.'

3. A 6th rate, of 20 guns, Capt. Robert Biggs. Keppel wrote to Sandwich from

The Brest fleet is likewise superior in numbers, though our ships are larger.[4] We have thought of America till England is in danger. I am, dear Horry,

Very truly and affectionately yours,

Hertford

From Conway, ca Wednesday 19 August 1778

Missing; acknowledged *post* 21 Aug. 1778.

To Conway, Friday 21 August 1778

Printed from *Works* v. 202–3.

Strawberry Hill, August 21, 1778.

I THINK it so very uncertain whether this letter will find you, that I write it merely to tell you I received yours[1] today.

I recollect nothing particularly worth seeing in Sussex that you have not seen (for I think you have seen Coudray[2] and Stansted,[3] and I know you have Petworth),[4] but Hurst Monceaux[5] near Battle;[6]

St Helens 7 July that 'the *Lively* is now the frigate that I am in doubt about, I wish she was safe in.' She was captured 9 July outside Brest by the *Iphigénie* frigate and *Curieuse* corvette, and retaken in the Channel 29 July 1781 by the *Perseverance* (*Sandwich Papers* ii. 109, n. 1, 113; *Court and City Register*, 1779, pp. 146, 152).

4. Actually, by the time the two fleets closed, each had 30 ships of the line, since the *Duc de Bourgogne* and the *Alexandre* had left the French fleet (*Sandwich Papers* ii. 10–11, 373, n. 1). The British fleet had a considerable superiority in the number of guns and size of the ships (ibid.).

1. Missing.

2. Cowdray, near Midhurst, the seat of Vct Montagu. HW went there in 1749 and 1774; it was destroyed by fire in 1793.

See Montagu i. 98–9; *Country Seats* 76; Berry ii. 15; H. A. Tipping, *English Homes*, Period II, Vol. I, 1924, pp. 139–48.

3. Stanstead Park, about seven miles NW of Chichester. HW went there in 1770, when it belonged to the 2d E. of Halifax (du Deffand ii. 455, n. 1). See D. G. C. Elwes and C. J. Robinson, *History of the Castles, Mansions and Manors of Western Sussex*, 1876, p. 225; M. E. Macartney, *English Houses . . . in the Seventeenth and Eighteenth Century*, 1908, p. 23.

4. Petworth House, seat of Lord Egremont. See Montagu i. 97–8; Charles Latham, *In English Homes*, 1904–9, iii. 199–211.

5. Hurstmonceaux Castle; see HW to Bentley 5 Aug. 1752 OS (Chute 137–40).

6. HW describes Battle Abbey ibid. 140.

and I don't know whether it is not pulled down.[7] The site of Arundel Castle[8] is fine, and there are some good tombs of the Fitzalans[9] at the church,[10] but little remains of the castle; in the room of which is a modern brick house;[11] and in the late Duke's[12] time the ghost of a giant walked there his Grace said[13]—but I suppose the present Duke[14] has laid it in the Red Sea—of claret.[15]

Besides Knowle[16] and Penshurst,[17] I should think there were several seats of old families in Kent worth seeing; but I do not know them. I poked out Summer Hill[18] for the sake of the *Babylonienne*[19] in Grammont; but it is now a mere farm-house. Don't let them persuade you to visit Leeds Castle,[20] which is not worth seeing.[21]

You have been near losing me and half a dozen fair cousins today. The Goldsmiths' Company dined in Mr Shirley's[22] field, next to

7. Hurstmonceaux Castle was unroofed and pillaged in 1777 by Mrs Robert Hare to provide building materials for a new house designed by Wyatt (ibid., n. 66; A. J. C. Hare, *Memorials of a Quiet Life,* New York, n.d., i. 84–6).

8. Seat of the Duke of Norfolk.

9. Earls of Arundel.

10. Now called the Fitzalan Chapel; the monuments, described in Mark Tierney, *History of . . . Arundel,* 1834, ii. 618–29, were damaged during alterations in 1782 (Montagu i. 97, n. 12).

11. 'A new indifferent apartment clapped up for the Norfolks, when they reside there for a week or a fortnight' (ibid. i. 96).

12. Edward Howard (1686–1777), 9th D. of Norfolk (*ante* 12 Feb. 1756, n. 21).

13. HW repeats this anecdote in his letters to Lady Ossory 30 Sept. 1791 and to Mary Berry 16 Aug. 1796 (Ossory iii. 127; Berry ii. 206).

14. Charles Howard (1720–86), 10th D. of Norfolk, 1777.

15. HW calls the 10th Duke 'drunken' in his letter to Lady Ossory 29 Sept. 1777 (Ossory i. 384; see also ibid. ii. 467; Mann vi. 483, vii. 194), and makes a similar remark about a 'Red Sea of claret' in his letter to Mary Berry 16 Aug. 1796 (loc. cit.).

16. Knole, seat of the Duke of Dorset, described by HW in his letter to Bentley 5 Aug. 1752 OS (Chute 132–5), revisited by HW in 1780 (Ossory ii. 223–4; *Country Seats* 77).

17. Penshurst Place, the seat of the Sidneys, described HW to Bentley 5 Aug. 1752 OS (Chute 141–2).

18. See ibid. 135–6. HW's drawing of it is in his copy of Gramont, now wsl (ibid. 136, n. 53).

19. Lady Margaret de Burgh (d. 1698), daughter of 1st M. of Clanricarde, from whom she inherited Summer Hill (E. Hasted, *History . . . of Kent,* 2d edn, Canterbury, 1797–1801, v. 234); m. 1 (1660) Charles Maccarty, styled Vct Muskerry; m. 2 (1676) Robert Villiers, self-styled Vct Purbeck; m. 3 Robert Feilding. She was very ugly, and was called 'the Princess of Babylon' from a costume she wore at a masquerade to which she had been invited as a joke (Anthony Hamilton, *Mémoires du Comte de Grammont,* SH, 1772, pp. 96–7, 105).

20. Described and illustrated in Tipping, op. cit., Period I, Vol. I, 1921, pp. 201–19.

21. 'Never was such disappointment! There are small remains: the moat is the only handsome object,' etc. (HW to Bentley 5 Aug. 1752 OS, Chute 145). The Castle was extensively restored and rebuilt in the 19th century (ibid., n. 133).

22. Hon. George Shirley (1705–87) (du Deffand iii. 88, n. 3). For his property in Twickenham, see Chute 358 and nn. 13–14; 'A Plan of Twickenham . . . by Samuel Lewis, 1784,' the back endpaper to More. Pope's property was currently owned by Welbore Ellis (R. S. Cobbett, *Memorials of Twickenham,* 1872, p. 285).

Pope's. I went to Ham[23] with my three Waldegrave nieces[24] and Miss Keppel,[25] and saw them land, and dine in tents erected for them from the opposite shore. You may imagine how beautiful the sight was in such a spot and in such a day! I stayed and dined at Ham, and after dinner Lady Dysart with Lady Bridget Tollemache[26] took our four nieces on the water to see the return of the barges,[27] but were to set me down at Lady Browne's.[28] We were, with a footman and the two watermen, ten in a little boat. As we were in the middle of the river, a larger boat full of people drove directly upon us on purpose. I believe they were drunk. We called to them, to no purpose; they beat directly against the middle of our little skiff— but, thank you, did not do us the least harm—no thanks to them. Lady Malpas was in Lord Strafford's garden,[29] and gave us for gone. In short, Neptune never would have had so beautiful a prize as the four girls.

I hear an express has been sent to _____ to offer him the Mastership of the Horse. I had a mind to make you guess, but you never can—to Lord Exeter.[30]

Pray let me know the moment you return to Park Place.

Shirley's 'freehold and copyhold villa and estate, containing twenty-five acres of rich land, on the banks of the Thames, at Twickenham, adjoining the villa of the late Alexander Pope,' were sold by auction, at his decease, in 1788 (notice cited by Cunningham vii. 109, n.).

23. Ham House, near Petersham, Surrey, across the Thames from SH; seat of Lord Dysart.

24. The three daughters of HW's niece, the Duchess of Gloucester, by her first marriage: (1) Lady Anna Horatia Waldegrave (1762–1801), m. (1786) Hon. Hugh Seymour-Conway, later Lord Hugh Seymour, Hertford's son; (2) Lady Charlotte Maria Waldegrave (ante 26 Oct. 1761, n. 11); (3) Lady Elizabeth Laura Waldegrave (1760–1816), m. (1782) George Waldegrave, styled Vct Chewton, 4th E. Waldegrave, 1784.

25. Anna Maria Keppel (1759–1836), daughter of the Bishop of Exeter and Mrs Keppel, HW's niece, m. (1790) William Stapleton (OSSORY i. 382, n. 2).

26. Lady Bridget Henley (d. 1796), m. 1 (1761) Hon. Robert Fox-Lane; m. 2 (1773)

Hon. John Tollemache (1750–77), Lord Dysart's brother (ibid. i. 108, n. 2, 164, n. 7).

27. 'To see the Goldsmith's barge that was coming with a shoal of boats' (HW to Lady Ossory 29 Aug. 1778, ibid. ii. 47). 'The new-built barge belonging to the goldsmiths' company' on 22 Aug. 'ran foul of a coal-barge and was greatly damaged' (London Chronicle 29 Aug.–1 Sept., xliv. 216).

28. A 'pretty cottage' called 'Riverside'; she lived there until 1785 (Cobbett, op. cit. 248; OSSORY ii. 472).

29. For Strafford's house at Twickenham, see CHUTE 279, n. 11; OSSORY i. 192, n. 1. HW owned 'three small messuages adjoining to Lord Strafford's garden in Twickenham' (HW's will, SELWYN 366).

30. Brownlow Cecil (1725–93), 9th E. of Exeter. The Mastership of the Horse had been rendered vacant by the death 12 Aug. of Peregrine, 3d D. of Ancaster; however, Ancaster was succeeded in Dec. by the Duke of Northumberland (Daily Adv. 7 Dec.).

To HERTFORD, ca Thursday 27 August 1778

Missing; answered *post* 29 Aug. 1778.

From HERTFORD, Saturday 29 August 1778

Printed for the first time from a photostat of BM Add. MSS 23219, f. 90.

Tunbridge, August 29th 1778.

INDEED, dear Horry, I have no doubt of the goodness of your information and judgment in regard to our present condition.[1]

I long as you may imagine on every account to see this country in
a safer state, and shall be happy with any opportunity that may arise
within my very limited powers of contributing to it. I thank you for
your intelligence and inquiries after us. We propose being in London next week. I am, dear Horry,

Always most truly and faithfully yours,

HERTFORD

To HERTFORD, ca Friday 4 September 1778

Missing; answered *post* 6 Sept. 1778.

1. HW's letter is missing; in his letter to Lady Ossory 29 Aug. 1778 he wrote: 'The American war draws indeed to an end; the [British] fleet and the relics of the army may very possibly be taken in a net [at New York]. . . . Perhaps by Christ-mas we shall know what law France and Spain will dictate to us. Our eyes will open, but it will be too late' (OSSORY ii. 44).

From HERTFORD, Sunday 6 September 1778

Printed for the first time from a photostat of BM Add. MSS 23219, f. 91.

London, Sunday past 3.

Dear Horry,

I THINK there is great good sense in what your letter[1] says, and there may be a foundation for the apprehension you express, though I do not believe there is any such present intention in the Court of Spain;[2] however in these cases private opinion should not weigh, and every possible security should be preserved.

I hope Keppel has orders not to run to the southward,[3] for every reason, but it is too late now to interpose with anything I could say if I was ever so well authorized to do it.

The reports of yesterday, but all unauthenticated, were that the Brest fleet was gone to Cales,[4] that it was gone back into their own port, and that it was beat by Keppel who fell in the action.[5] The last account from himself[6] was that he was off Ushant and had neither heard of nor seen anything of them.[7] Perhaps they may have gone towards Rochfort to be joined by the ships from that port.[8]

We intend going tomorrow into Suffolk. I am, dear Horry,

Always yours,

HERTFORD

1. Missing.
2. HW wrote to Lady Ossory 6 Sept. 1778: 'The Duke [of Gloucester] fears the plan [of the French] is to draw Mr Keppel southward till he falls into the jaws of the Spanish squadron, or is enclosed between them and the French' (OSSORY ii. 48). Keppel, who had put his fleet into Plymouth after the Battle of Ushant 27 July (ante ?19 July 1778, n. 1), had set sail again 23 Aug. (MANN viii. 408–9, n. 4).
3. His orders were to engage the French fleet but not to leave the 'Channel approaches unguarded unless he received definite information of the enemy' (W. M. James, The British Navy in Adversity, 1926, p. 137).
4. Presumably Calais, though 'Cales' was the old form for 'Cadiz.'
5. 'On Saturday evening [5 Sept.] it was reported at the west end of town that advice had been received of an engagement between Admiral Keppel's fleet and the Brest squadron, that 11 of the French were taken and four sunk, and that Admiral Keppel was killed in the action; but as no advices of the kind have been received at any of the public offices, it was not credited' (Daily Adv. 7 Sept.).
6. 'Yesterday [4 Sept.] some private dispatches were received at St James's from Admiral Keppel, brought by a cutter, arrived at Falmouth, which were laid before his Majesty' (ibid. 5 Sept.).
7. Keppel 'was off Ushant from the 28th to the 31st but saw nothing of the French fleet' (James, loc. cit.). He returned to Portsmouth 25 Oct. without having made contact (MANN viii. 420 and n. 12).
8. For the Brest fleet's whereabouts at this time, see post 2 Oct. 1778, n. 7.

From HERTFORD, ca October 1778

Missing; mentioned *post* 2 Oct. 1778.

From HERTFORD, Friday 2 October 1778

Printed for the first time from a photostat of BM Add. MSS 23219, ff. 92–3.

Sudborne Hall, October 2d 1778.

Dear Horry,

I HAVE received a letter from Mrs Keppel[1] which I enclose to you;[2] my answer you may see in her hands. It will I hope satisfy her perfectly in regard to Mr Drummond's[3] lodgings, though it is more guarded in the expression than the one I wrote to you,[4] lest she should show it and the example might operate against the directions I have given, and expose me to the King's censure. The lodgings she mentions are considered I believe as a royal apartment, and will consequently not be given by the King's permission to any person whatever. I am besides under two positive engagements of some years' standing which are not yet discharged, from the number of requests of that sort which were upon the list.

His Majesty in addition to all the rest is become of late, from the expenses and abuses committed in his palaces, so averse to all applications of the sort that I am not very fond of naming the subject to him, and the repairs etc. have been taken for some considerable time past, and before I was Chamberlain,[5] out of the office where I serve, and put into the hands of the Treasury, so that when an apartment is given, the favour of having them repaired and put in order must be solicited at the Treasury. All I can say is that whenever I am free,

---

1. HW's niece, widow of Frederick Keppel, Bp of Exeter, who died 27 Dec. 1777 (*ante* 21 July 1758, n. 26; FAMILY 156, n. 2).

2. Her letter is missing.

3. Not identified. Widowed the previous year (above, n. 1), Mrs Keppel may have wanted a permanent apartment in Hampton Court Palace vacated by this man; she was 'comfortable' in lodgings there in June

(Mrs Keppel to Anne Clement 17 June 1778, MS now WSL). By 1782 she was living at Stud House, Hampton Court (CHUTE 628, n. 2). Hampton Court Palace was a royal palace in which officials and indigent gentry (such as HW's niece Lady Malpas) were accommodated.

4. Missing.

5. Hertford became lord chamberlain in 1766.

if I should continue so long in office, there is no person I shall be more happy to oblige than a person for whom you are interested, being, dear Horry,

Very truly and affectionately yours,

HERTFORD

I have just received a letter from my daughter Drogheda at Spa, in which she surprises me by saying that Madame de Guéméné,[6] who is there, had just received a letter from Paris informing her that the Brest fleet was in the Spanish seas.[7]

From HERTFORD, Saturday 10 October 1778

Printed for the first time from a photostat of BM Add. MSS 23219, f. 94.
Address: To the Honourable Hor. Walpole, Strawberry Hill, Twickenham, Middlesex. Free Hertford.
Postmark: 10 OC FREE.

London, October 10th 1778.

Dear Horry,

I HAVE this morning received the enclosed letter[1] from my brother, which I think it right to communicate to you, though I do not see any direct step that we can take in opposition to what he says.[2] I remain, dear Horry,

Very truly and affectionately yours,

HERTFORD

6. Marie-Louise-Henriette-Jeanne de La Tour d'Auvergne (d. 1781), m. (1743) Jules-Hercule-Mériadec de Rohan, Prince de Guéménée (DU DEFFAND vi. 405).

7. The Brest fleet had returned to Brest 18 Sept. after cruising a month between there and Cape Finisterre (on the northwest tip of Spain) (GM 1778, xlviii. 492; W. M. James, *The British Navy in Adversity*, 1926, p. 137).

———

1. Missing.
2. Not explained.

To Conway, Friday 23 October 1778

Printed from *Works* v. 203–4. The beginning of the letter is missing.

October 23, 1778.

————having thus told you all I know, I shall add a few words, to say I conclude you have known as much, by my not having heard from you. Should the Post Office or Secretary's Office set their wits at work to bring to light all the intelligence contained under the above hiatus, I am confident they will discover nothing, though it gives an exact description of all they have been about themselves.

My personal history is very short. I have had an assembly[1] and the rheumatism[2]—and am buying a house[3]—and it rains—and I shall plant the roses against my *treillage* tomorrow. Thus you know what I have done, suffered, am doing, and shall do. Let me know as much of you, in quantity, not in quality. Introductions to and conclusions of letters are as much out of fashion, as *to, at,* etc. on letters. This sublime age reduces everything to its quintessence: all periphrases and expletives are so much in disuse, that I suppose soon the only way of making love will be to say '*Lie down.*' Luckily, the lawyers will not part with any synonymous words, and will, consequently, preserve the redundancies of our language—*Dixi.*

From Conway, January 1779

Missing; implied *post* 9 Jan. 1779.

1. 8 Oct., for his grand-nieces, described in his letter to Mason 11 Oct. 1778 (MASON i. 445–8; see also OSSORY ii. 61, nn. 2–3).

2. 'My courtesy [at the assembly] was so general and flowing, that it produced a rheumatism, and a very painful one, but that is gone too and you shall hear no more of it' (HW to Lady Ossory 21 Oct. 1778, ibid. ii. 62). However, he was shortly afflicted with a severe fit of the gout; see next letter.

3. In Berkeley Square, his town house from 14 Oct. 1779 until his death. See OSSORY ii. 62, n. 11; *post* 28 Oct. 1779.

To Conway, Saturday 9 January 1779

Printed from *Works* v. 204–5.

Arlington Street, January 9, 1779.

YOUR flight to Bath would have much surprised me, if Mr C.[1] who, I think, heard it from Stanley,[2] had not prepared me for it.[3] Since you was amused, I am glad you went, especially as you escaped being initiated in Mrs Miller's follies at Batheaston,[4] which you would have mentioned.[5] She would certainly have sent some trapes of a muse to press you, had she known what good epigrams you write.

I went to Strawberry partly out of prudence, partly from ennui.[6] I thought it best to air myself before I go in and out of hot rooms here, and had my house thoroughly warmed for a week previously, and then only stirred from the red room to the blue on the same floor. I stayed five days, and was neither the better nor the worse for it. I was quite tired with having neither company, books, nor amusement of any kind. Either from the emptiness of the town, or that ten weeks of gout[7] have worn out the patience of all my acquaintance, but I do not see three persons in three days. This gives me but an uncomfortable prospect for my latter days: it is but probable that I may be a cripple in a fit or two more, if I have strength to go through them; and as that will be long life, one outlives one's acquaintance. I cannot make new acquaintance, nor interest myself at all about the young, except those that belong to me; nor does that go beyond contributing to their pleasures, without having much satisfaction in their conversation—but—one must take everything as it comes, and make the best of it. I have had a much happier life than I deserve, and than millions that deserve better. I should be very weak, if I could not bear the uncomfortableness of old age, when I can afford

1. Churchill, according to Wright and subsequent editors; however, another possibility is John 'Fish' Craufurd (*ante* 20 May 1765, n. 28), who visited HW 14 Jan. (Ossory ii. 85).

2. Hans Stanley.

3. 'Lady Aylesbury and Mr Conway are gone to the Bath not to drink the waters but to visit Lord Huntingdon' (Coke, 'MS Journals' 3 Jan. 1779).

4. See *ante* 15 Jan. 1775 and Ossory ii. 84–5.

5. Conway's letter, implied here, is missing.

6. HW was at SH 1–6 Jan. (see below; Mann viii. 432).

7. See HW to Lady Ossory 9 Nov. 1778 (Ossory ii. 69).

what comforts it is capable of. How many poor old people have none of them! I am ashamed whenever I am peevish, and recollect that I have fire and servants to help me!

I hear Admiral Keppel is in high spirits with the great respect and zeal expressed for him. In my own opinion, his constitution will not stand the struggle.[8] I am very uneasy too for the Duke of Richmond,[9] who is at Portsmouth, and will be at least as much agitated.[10]

Sir William Meredith has written a large pamphlet, and a very good one.[11] It is to show, that whenever the Grecian republics taxed their dependants, the latter resisted and shook off the yoke. He has printed but twelve copies:[12] the Duke of G.[13] sent me one of them. There is an anecdote of my father, on the authority of old Jack White,[14] which I doubt. It says, he would not go on with the excise scheme,[15] though his friends advised it.[16] I cannot speak to the particular event, as I was then at school;[17] but it was more like him to

---

8. The court martial of Keppel on charges of misconduct and neglect of duty at the Battle of Ushant 27 July 1778, preferred by Adm. Sir Hugh Palliser, his third in command there, had begun at Portsmouth 7 Jan.; see ibid. ii. 85, nn. 9–10.

9. Whom Lady Mary Coke reported in her 'MS Journals' 17 Dec. 1778 as being ill of a bloody flux; see also Lady Sarah Lennox to Duchess of Leinster 15 Dec. 1778, *Leinster Corr.* ii. 265–6.

10. Richmond and Keppel were cousins, and both members of the Opposition. In Feb. Keppel was honourably acquitted of all charges, a decision that met with great popular acclaim.

11. His 'Historical Remarks on the Taxation of Free States,' 82 pp., printed anonymously at London 16 Nov. 1778. See *Last Journals* ii. 232.

12. 30, according to DNB, but W. T. Lowndes, *The Bibliographer's Manual of English Literature*, 1864, iii. 1537 accepts HW's figure.

13. Gloucester, according to Wright and subsequent editors; Meredith was one of the Duke's 'particular friends' (*Last Journals* i. 371). HW's copy is not in his collection, 'Tracts of the Reign of George the 3d.'

14. John White (1699–1769), M.P. East Retford 1733–68. 'It was told me by an

intelligent and most respectable member of the last Parliament (Mr White, of Redford)' ('Historical Remarks,' p. 80).

15. Of 1733; see J. H. Plumb, *Sir Robert Walpole: The King's Minister*, 1960, pp. 233–71 *passim*.

16. 'The bill, having been opposed in every stage, was ordered to be reported. . . . On the evening before the report, Sir Robert summoned a meeting of the principal members who had supported the bill. . . . When Sir Robert had heard them all, he assured them ". . . in the present inflamed temper of the people, it could not be carried into execution without an armed force. That there would be an end of the liberty of England, if supplies were to be raised by the sword. If, therefore, the resolution was to go on with the bill, he would immediately . . . desire his Majesty's permission to resign his office. For he would not be the minister to enforce taxes, at the probable expense of blood"' ('Historical Remarks,' p. 81). The foregoing seems to be a garbled version of what really occurred; see Plumb, op. cit. 263–71. Sir Robert's primary motive for deciding to drop the bill was not fear of bloodshed, but fear of losing his majority in both the Lords and Commons (ibid. 267).

17. At Eton.

have yielded against his sentiments, to Mr Pelham[18] and his candid— or say, plausible and timid friends. I have heard him say, that he never did give up his opinion to such men, but he always repented it. However, the anecdote in the book would be more to his honour. But what a strange man is Sir William! I suppose now he has written this book, he will change his opinion, and again be for carrying on the war—or, if he does not know his own mind for two years together, why will he take places, to make everybody doubt his honesty? [19]

From HERTFORD, Saturday 8 May 1779

Printed for the first time from a photostat of BM Add. MSS 23219, f. 102. The enclosed letter is also printed for the first time from a photostat of ibid. f. 103.

Grosvenor Street, Saturday morn, 8 o'clock.

Dear Horry,

THE letter enclosed herewith came to me in the night long after I went to bed; I give you joy of it, though it does not quite answer the public wishes.[1] Will you enclose and send it to go by the coach to Lady Ailesbury, to save time, and do me justice by telling her the reasons, or shall I?

Yours ever,

HERTFORD

18. Henry Pelham; then paymaster-general and Sir Robert's right-hand man.
19. Meredith had been comptroller of the Household March 1774 – Dec. 1777; however, upon resigning his post, he denied that he had ever 'voted for any one measure that tended to create or to support this war' (Namier and Brooke iii. 130, 132).

———

1. Conway had set out for Jersey 3 May upon receiving confirmation of a French attack upon that island, in an express from Adm. Arbuthnot, who had sailed without orders for the relief of the island. However, by the time both Conway and Arbuthnot arrived, the attack had already been repulsed (1 May). Presumably Hertford means that the public would be disappointed that the French had not been more decisively defeated. See below and MANN viii. 471–3.

[Enclosure]

St James's, Friday night, 7 May 1779.

LORD Weymouth[2] presents his compliments to Lord Hertford, and has the honour to acquaint his Lordship that letters are just received at the Admiralty with an account that Admiral Arbuthnot[3] was yesterday near Torbay on his return to join his convoy there,[4] that he had left a sufficient naval force to protect the Islands,[5] and that the French were returned to St Cas or near that place according to accounts from Jersey of the 2d instant.[6]

To CONWAY, Saturday 22 May 1779

Printed from *Works* v. 205–6.

Arlington Street, May 22, 1779.

IF you hear of us no oftener than we of you, you will be as much behindhand in news as my Lady Lyttelton. We have seen a traveller that saw you in your island,[1] but it sounds like hearing of Ulysses.—Well! we must be content. You are not only not dethroned,

2. Secretary of state for the south. Hertford had asked him about the invasion Sunday, 2 May, when he said 'he did not believe it' (HW's unpublished memoranda [May 1779] for *Last Journals*, in the possession of Lord Waldegrave).

3. Marriot Arbuthnot (?1711–94), Rear-Adm. 1778, Adm. of the Blue 1793.

4. 'I . . . am now proceeding to Torbay, to rejoin the trade' (Arbuthnot to Philip Stephens, '*Europe*, at sea, May 6,' printed *London Gazette* No. 11976, 4–8 May, *sub* 'Admiralty Office, May 8'). Arbuthnot had been about to set out on a voyage to America at the head of a convoy of troop and merchant ships when he learned of the attack upon Jersey; he left the merchant ships at Tor Bay, proceeding to Jersey with the troops. He arrived back at Tor Bay 7 May, and the convoy embarked for America 24 May (Edmund Burke, *Correspondence*, Vol. IV,

ed. J. A. Woods, Cambridge, 1963, p. 69, n. 3).

5. 'Capt. [John] Ford of the *Unicorn* has, in my opinion, a force under his command sufficient for the protection of those islands: I therefore leave the direction of the King's service there in his hands' (Arbuthnot to Stephens 6 May, loc. cit.; *Court and City Register*, 1779, pp. 146, 151).

6. 'The Lieutenant-Governor of Guernsey [Lt-Col. Paulus Æmilius Irving] acquaints me, that a boat from Jersey arrived at Guernsey Sunday [2 May], and says that an armament attempted to land, but could not accomplish their design; that they then stood out to sea, and have returned either to St Cas Bay, or to Cape Frehel' (Arbuthnot to Stephens, loc. cit.; *Court and City Register*, p. 187).

1. Mr Conway was now at his government, Jersey (HW).

but owe the safety of your dominions to your own skill in fortification.[2] If we do not hear of your extending your conquests, why, it is not less than all our modern heroes have done, whom prophets have foretold and gazettes celebrated—or who have foretold and celebrated themselves. Pray be content to be cooped up in an island that has no neighbours, when the Howes[3] and Clintons,[4] and Dunmores[5] and Burgoynes[6] and Campbells[7] are not yet got beyond the great river—Inquiry![8] Today's papers say, that the *little* Prince of Orange[9] is to invade you again[10]—but we trust Sir James Wallace[11] has clipped his wings so close, that they will not grow again this season, though he is so ready to *fly*.

2. The French invaders were repelled by Lord Seaforth's regiment of foot and some 6000 Jersey militia, aided by artillery (MANN viii. 472 and nn. 13–14). In 1778 Conway had made a survey of the forts and garrisons of Jersey (*ante* 25 June 1778, n. 1).

3. On 17 Feb. Sir William Howe had moved for an inquiry in the House on the conduct of his brother and himself of the American war, saying, 'that imputations had been thrown on himself, and his brother, for not terminating the American war last campaign; the very contrary of which he would venture to say would appear, when an inquiry was instituted' (Almon's *Parliamentary Register*, 1775–80, xi. 241). See MANN viii. 439, n. 8, 474, nn. 21–2.

4. Lt-Gen. Sir Henry Clinton (1730–95), K.B., 1777, had in 1778 replaced Sir William Howe as commander-in-chief in America. In America at this time, he did not appear at the inquiry.

5. John Murray (1730–1809), 4th E. of Dunmore 1756, governor of Virginia 1770–6, where his measures had greatly antagonized the colonists. He did not testify.

6. Gen. John Burgoyne (*ante* 28 Sept. 1762, n. 12) had been defeated at Saratoga in Oct. 1777; he testified at length in his own behalf 20 May (Almon, op. cit. xiii. 124–42; Cobbett, *Parl. Hist.* xx. 780–803). See *post* 5 June 1779.

7. HW is presumably referring to Col. Archibald Campbell (1739–91), K.B. 1785, who returned to England a great favourite of the Court after leading a successful expedition against Savannah (see *Last Journals* ii. 255; Namier and Brooke ii. 179–80). He did not testify.

8. The Parliamentary inquiry which took place in the House of Commons on the conduct of the American war (HW).

9. The Prince of Nassau, who had commanded the attack upon Jersey, claiming relationship to the great house of Nassau, Mr Walpole calls *the little prince of Orange* (Mary Berry). Karl Heinrich Nicolaus Otto (1745–1808), Prince of Nassau-Siegen (MANN viii. 471, n. 4).

10. 'Certain advice has been received that the Prince of Nassau is determined upon another enterprise. . . . Regiments of volunteers are raising at St Maloes and Granville' (*Public Adv.* 21 May). However, there was no further attempt upon Jersey at this time.

11. (1731–1803), Kt, 1777, admiral. On 13 May, Wallace, who along with Arbuthnot had gone to the relief of Jersey, pursued a number of French vessels into Cancale Bay on the French coast, where he burned two frigates, captured a third plus a sloop and brig, scuttled a cutter, and silenced a battery of twelve-pounders on shore. 'From some of the prisoners we are informed, that these were the ships that were to cooperate with 2000 troops of the Prince of Nassau's, who are now encamped upon a small island called Sezambre, about two leagues from St Maloes' (letter of Wallace, enclosed in Capt. J. L. Gidoin's letter to Philip Stephens 14 May 1779, printed *London Gazette Extraordinary* 17 May).

Nothing material has happened since I wrote last—so, as every moment of a civil war is precious, everyone has been turned to the interest of diversion. There have been three masquerades,[12] an installation, and the ball of the Knights at the Haymarket[13] this week; not to mention Almack's festino,[14] Lady Spencer's, Ranelagh and Vauxhall,[15] operas and plays. The Duchess of Bolton[16] too saw masks—so many, that the floor gave way, and the company in the dining-room were near falling on the heads of those in the parlour, and exhibiting all that has not yet appeared in Doctors' Commons.[17] At the Knights' ball was such a profusion of strawberries, that people could hardly get into the supper-room.[18]—I could tell you more, but I do not love to exaggerate.

Lady A. told me this morning, that Lord Bristol has got a calf with two feet to each leg—I am convinced it is by the Duchess of Kingston, who has two of everything, where others have but one.[19]

12. Given 17, 18 and 20 May at the casino rooms of Mrs Cornelys, Carlisle House, and the King's Theatre in the Haymarket, described in the *Whitehall Evening Post* 15–22 May.

13. An installation of Knights of the Bath took place 19 May; 'in the evening a grand ball was given by the Knights, at the King's Theatre in the Haymarket, at which upwards of 1000 of the nobility, gentry, etc. were present' (*Daily Adv.* 21 May).

14. 'Almack's, Festino' in *Works*. A meeting of the 'nobility and gentry, subscribers to the assembly in King Street [Almack's],' was held 20 May (*Public Adv.* 20 May).

15. 'The gardens of this place were opened last night [17 May] for the first time this season, where by about the latter end of the evening about 2000 persons assembled' ('Vauxhall Intelligence,' *Whitehall Evening Post* 15–18 May, *sub* 18 May).

16. Katharine Lowther (ca 1736–1809), m. (1765) Lord Harry Powlett, 6th D. of Bolton, 1765.

17. Where, in the Consistory Court, trials for adultery were held; a 1792 print by Rowlandson, entitled 'Work for Doctors'-Commons,' shows a young couple on a sofa and two men peering at them from behind a screen (British Museum, *Catalogue of Prints and Drawings . . . Political and Personal Satires*, Vol. VI, ed. M. D. George, 1938, p. 962 [No. 8178]). 'From the number of the nobility, gentry, etc. assembled in masks at the Duke's . . . [of Bolton] house, in Southampton Row, on Monday evening [17 May], a main girder which supported the room gave a violent crash, and had not the company run out, and assistance been instantly administered, the whole house would probably have fallen in a few minutes. The ceiling in the room under that in which the company were assembled came down entirely, and there was every appearance of an approaching tumble of the entire fabric' (*Morning Chronicle*, cited *Whitehall Evening Post* 20–22 May, *sub* 21 May).

18. The report of the ball, ibid., mentions the 'admirable supper and dessert . . . the dessert . . . consisted of the choicest produce of Nature and Art, such as pineapples, strawberries, melons, cherries, iced creams, sweetmeats, etc., etc.'

19. Alluding to the Duchess's conviction for bigamy in 1776, and the rumour of her having had twins; see C. E. Pearce, *The Amazing Duchess*, [1911], i. 126, and Elizabeth Mavor, *The Virgin Mistress*, 1964, p. 49.

Adieu!—I am going to sup with Mrs Abington[20]—and hope Mrs Clive will not hear of it.

Yours ever,

HOR. WALPOLE

To Conway, Saturday 5 June 1779

Printed from *Works* v. 207–9.

Strawberry Hill, Saturday, June 5, 1779.

I WRITE to you more seldom than I am disposed to do, from having nothing positive to tell you, and from being unwilling to say and unsay every minute something that is reported positively. The confident assertions of the victory over D'Estaing[1] are totally vanished—and they who invented them, now declaim as bitterly against Byron,[2] as if he had deceived them—and as they did against Keppel. This day sennight[3] there was a great alarm about Ireland—which was far from being all invention, though not an absolute insurrection, as was said.[4] The case, I believe, was this: The Court, in order to break the volunteer army established by the Irish themselves,[5] endeavoured to persuade a body in Lady Blayney's[6] county of Monaghan to enlist in the militia—which they took indignantly. They said, they had great regard for Lady Blayney and Lord Clermont;[7] but to act under them, would be acting under the King, and

---

20. Frances Barton (1737–1815), m. (ca 1759) James Abington; actress.

———

1. Jean - Baptiste - Charles d'Estaing, Comte d'Estaing; naval officer (*ante* 9 Nov. 1764, n. 9); commander of the Toulon fleet stationed in the West Indies.

2. Hon. John Byron (1723–86), the grandfather of the poet; Vice-Adm. 1778. See MANN viii. 480–1 and nn. 2–4, and *post* 13 Sept. 1779.

3. 29 May.

4. A 'report is given us on the authority of the *General Advertiser,* which says, that "an insurrection has actually taken place in Ireland; that the people of that coun-

try, oppressed, ruined, starved, have risen up in their own relief, and finding themselves in no hopes of succour or protection from Government, seem determined on measures of a desperate nature." The news of this, they say, arrived yesterday [31 May]' (*St James's Chronicle* 29 May – 1 June, *sub* 'Postscript . . . June 1').

5. See MASON i. 468–9, n. 3.

6. Mary Cairnes (d. 1790), m. 1 (1724) Cadwallader Blayney, 7th Bn Blayney, 1706; m. 2 (1734) Col. John Murray (d. 1743), M.P. for co. Monaghan.

7. William Henry Fortescue (1722–1806), Lady Blayney's son-in-law, cr. (1770) Bn and (1776) Vct Clermont, and (1777) E. of

that was by no means their intention.[8] There have since been motions for inquiries what steps the ministers have taken to satisfy the Irish—and these they have imprudently rejected[9]—which will not tend to pacification. The ministers have been pushed too on the article of Spain, and could not deny that all negotiation is at an end —though they will not own farther.[10] However, the Spanish ambassador[11] is much out of humour. From Paris they write confidently of the approaching declaration;[12] and Lord Sandwich, I hear, has said in a very mixed company, that it was folly not to expect it.[13] There is another million asked, and given on a vote of credit;[14] and Lord

Clermont; M.P. Monaghan borough 1761–70, Gov. of co. Monaghan 1775–1806, and Custos Rot. co. Monaghan 1775–1805.

8. Lady Ossory wrote to George Selwyn 3 June 1779, presumably referring to the same incident, that 'Lord Clermont is going to pacify matters' (J. H. Jesse, *George Selwyn and his Contemporaries*, 1882, iv. 175). Lord Beauchamp, speaking in Parliament 15 June, said that 'rumours of an insurrection in the county of Monaghan arose only from the people of property in that county, each individual of whom bore their own expenses, proceeding to an election of their own officers' (Almon's *Parliamentary Register*, 1775–80, xiii. 403).

9. On 11 May Lord Rockingham moved in the Lords 'That this House, taking into consideration the distressed and impoverished state of . . . Ireland, and being of opinion, that it is consonant to justice and true policy, to remove the causes of discontent, by a redress of grievances . . . that an humble address be presented to his Majesty . . . to take the matter into his most serious consideration'; the motion was withdrawn but a similar one passed, with the reference to 'redress of grievances' omitted. On 27 May Rockingham complained that 'not one step had been taken in that important business,' and on 2 June Lord Shelburne moved that the House request the King 'to order to be laid before this House, "An account of such steps as have been taken in consequence of the address of this House of the 11th of May,"' and to continue the Parliament and call up

the Irish parliament, if necessary; this motion was defeated 61–32. In the Commons Lord Beauchamp on 26 May made a motion identical to that which had passed in the Lords on the 11th; this was also passed and then ignored. See *Journals of the House of Lords* xxxv. 732, 771; *Journals of the House of Commons* xxxvii. 420, 423; Cobbett, *Parl. Hist.* xx. 635–57, 662–75; Almon, op. cit. xiii. 151, xiv. 325–39, 372–80, 383–96; Edmund Burke, *Correspondence*, Vol. IV, ed. J. A. Woods, Cambridge, 1963, pp. 69–72, 81.

10. Lord North admitted in the Commons 2 June that 'the mediation of Spain certainly was at an end; the same friendly disposition towards us, however, apparently existed at the court of Madrid' (Cobbett, op. cit. xx. 830).

11. Almodóvar.

12. Not found; however, the *London Chronicle* 1–3 June, xlv. 526, carried a report *sub* 'Dublin, May 25,' that 'we are informed from very respectable authority, that the Spaniards intend to make an immediate junction with the French.'

13. See next letter.

14. On 1 June Lord North read to the Commons a message from the King, asking that 'this House will enable him to defray any extraordinary expenses incurred, or to be incurred, on account of military services' for the current year; on 2 June a committee of the whole House agreed to Lord North's motion for a vote of credit of one million pounds (*Journals of the House of Commons* xxxvii. 430, 433, 435; Cobbett, op. cit. xx. 828–35).

North has boasted of such mines for next year, that one would think he believed next year would never come.[15]

The inquiry[16] goes on, and Lord Harrington[17] did himself and Burgoyne honour. Barré[18] and Governor Johnstone[19] have had warm words, and Burke has been as frantic for the Roman Catholics as Lord George Gordon[20] against them. The Parliament, it is said, is to rise on the 21st.[21]

You will not collect from all this that our prospect clears up. I fear there is not more discretion in the treatment of Ireland than of America. The Court seems to be infatuated, and to think that nothing is of any consequence but a majority in Parliament—though they have totally lost all power but that of provoking. Fortunate it

15. In the debate on the budget 31 May, North declared 'that money would be had the next year with greater facility, and upon better terms. There were . . . good grounds for this expectation,' etc. (ibid. xx. 819–20).

16. Into the conduct of the American war (HW).

17. Charles Stanhope, 3d E. of Harrington (ante ca 23 July 1771, n. 9), had succeeded his father 1 April 1779. Aide-de-camp to Burgoyne in America, he testified in Burgoyne's behalf 1 June (Almon, op. cit. xiii. 188–204).

18. Col. Isaac Barré (ante 9 Dec. 1763, n. 6).

19. George Johnstone (1730–87), M.P. Cockermouth 1768–74, Appleby 1774–80, Lostwithiel 1780–4, Ilchester 1786–7; Gov. West Florida 1763–7. In the debate in the Commons 3 June on the King's message for a vote of credit, Johnstone called Barré a 'scaramouch'; Barré demanded an explanation, but the Speaker (Sir Fletcher Norton) put an end to the altercation (Cobbett, op. cit. xx. 834–5).

20. (1751–93), M.P. Ludgershall 1774–80; fomenter of the famous 'Gordon Riots' of 1780 (see post 13 June 1780). On 2 June he interrupted a debate in the Commons 'by informing the House of the victory the Kirk of Scotland had lately gained over Popery' (Cobbett, op. cit. xx. 831). This was in reference to the speech of the lord high commissioner, George, Earl of Dalhousie, to the general assembly of the Church of Scotland, which had

met at Edinburgh 20 May. In his speech Dalhousie said 'that he had his Majesty's command to assure the assembly, that his Majesty was determined to maintain the rights and privileges of the Church of Scotland . . . and would not countenance any attempt to alter the laws respecting Popery in this country' (Scots Magazine 1779, xli. 277–8); passage of the Catholic relief bill of 1778, easing restrictions on Catholics in England (see post 13 June 1780, n. 5), had led Scottish Protestants to fear that a similar bill would be passed affecting their own country. On 25 May the general assembly of the Church of Scotland passed a resolution declaring their steadfast opposition to 'a repeal of the laws now in force against Papists,' and approving the assurances sent them by the King (Scots Magazine xli. 279). Burke responded to Gordon's announcement by pointing 'the keenest satire against the bigotry and intolerance of the Scotch, but laid the greatest blame on Administration, for nearly giving up the dignity of Parliament, in the speech made by the lord high commissioner in the synod of the church of Scotland' (Cobbett, op. cit. xx. 831). See also ibid. xx. 622–3; Journals of the House of Commons xxxvii. 263–4, 373; Burke, Correspondence, iv. 83–8. Lord George's copy of the third edition, 1780, of Scotland's Opposition to the Popish Bill, magnificently bound for him by Scott of Edinburgh, is now wsl.

21. It did not rise until 3 July (Journals of the House of Commons xxxvii. 460).

had been for the King and kingdom, had the Court had no majority for these six years! America had still been ours!—and all the lives and all the millions we have squandered! A majority that has lost thirteen provinces by bullying and vapouring, and the most childish menaces, will be a brave countermatch for France and Spain, and a rebellion in Ireland! In short, it is plain that there is nothing a majority in Parliament can do, but outvote a minority; and yet by their own accounts one would think they could not do even that. I saw a paper t'other day that began with this Iricism, 'As the minority have lost us thirteen provinces, etc.' I know nothing the minority have done, or been suffered to do, but restore the Roman Catholic religion—and that too was by the desire of the Court.[22]

This is however the present style. They announced with infinite applause a new production of Tickell:[23]—it has appeared, and is a most paltry performance. It is called the *Cassette Verte* of M. de Sartine,[24] and pretends to be his correspondence with the Opposition. Nay, they are so pitifully mean as to laugh at Doctor Franklin,[25] who has such thorough reason to sit and laugh at them. What triumph it must be to him to see a miserable pamphlet all the revenge they can take! There is another, still duller, called *Opposition Mornings*,[26] in which you are lugged in.[27] In truth, it is a

22. HW writes also in *Last Journals* ii. 174 that 'the Court were . . . disposed to the Catholics.' See *post* 13 June 1780, n. 5.
23. Richard Tickell (1751–93), dramatist and pamphleteer.
24. Antoine-Raymond-Jean-Gualbert-Gabriel de Sartine (1729–1801), Comte d'Alby; lieutenant-general of police 1759–74; minister of the marine 1774–80 (NBG). HW's copy of *La Cassette verte de Monsieur de Sartine*, with the false imprint 'La Haye, Chez la veuve Whiskerfeld,' 1779, 71 pp., now WSL, is Hazen, *Cat. of HW's Lib.*, No. 1609:40:2; an English translation, *The Green Box of Monsieur de Sartine . . . from the French of the Hague Edition*, London, 1779, 71 pp., was reviewed and extracted in the *London Chronicle* 3–5 June, xlv. 529, with the comment: 'This truly humorous pamphlet is the production of Mr Tickell.' '*La Cassette verte. . . .* tire son nom d'une portefeuille de maroquin verte qu'a ce ministre, d'où l'on est censé avoir extrait les papiers qui ont fourni le canevas du livre. Ce

sont les conversations, aventures, anecdotes de l'ancien lieutenant-général de police, où les filles et les filoux jouent un très grand rôle. Ce cadre aurait pu fournir quelque chose de piquant, mais le fond est pitoyable et le style maussade' ('Extrait d'une lettre d'Amsterdam du 22 mai 1780' in Louis Petit de Bachaumont, *Mémoires secrets*, 1780–9, xv. 169).
25. The pamphlet contains two spurious letters of Franklin (pp. 31, 50–1).
26. Also by Tickell, under the pseudonym of 'Elizabeth O'Neil': *Opposition Mornings: With Betty's Remarks* [on the American war], 1779, 67 pp. HW's copy is Hazen, op. cit., No. 2966:7.
27. The pamphlet satirizes Conway's vaunted independence from faction. After studying an Opposition plan for a new administration, in which he is to be Master of the Ordnance, Conway proclaims '*That as he has been open to all parties, and influenced by none,* he hopes he shall not be thought inconsistent, if he endeavours to promote a general re-

compliment to any man to except him out of the number of those
that have contributed to the shocking disgraces inflicted on this undone country! When Lord Chatham was minister, he never replied
to abuse but by a victory.

I know no private news: I have been here ever since Tuesday,[28]
enjoying my tranquillity, as much as an honest man can do who sees
his country ruined. It is just such a period as makes philosophy
wisdom. There are great moments when every man is called on to
exert himself—but when folly, infatuation, delusion, incapacity and
profligacy fling a nation away, and it concurs itself, and applauds its
destroyers, a man who has lent no hand to the mischief, and can
neither prevent nor remedy the mass of evils, is fully justified in
sitting aloof and beholding the tempest rage, with silent scorn and
indignant compassion. Nay, I have, I own, some comfortable reflections. I rejoice that there is still a great continent of Englishmen
who will remain free and independent, and who laugh at the impotent majorities of a prostitute Parliament. I care not whether
General Burgoyne and Governor Johnstone cross over and figure in,
and support or oppose;[29] nor whether Mr Burke, or the superior of
the Jesuits, is high commissioner to the Kirk of Scotland.[30] My ideas
are such as I have always had, and are too plain and simple to
comprehend modern confusions; and, therefore, they suit with those
of few men. What will be the issue of this chaos, I know not, and,
probably, shall not see. I do see with satisfaction, *that what was
meditated* has failed by the grossest folly; and when one has escaped
the worst, lesser evils must be endured with patience.

After this dull effusion, I will divert you with a story that made
me laugh this morning till I cried. You know my Swiss David,[31] and
his incomprehensible pronunciation. He came to me, and said, 'Auh!
dar is Meses Ellis[32] wants some of your large flags to put in her great

conciliation, and bring about, if possible,
a plan of coalition' (pp. 62, 65–6).

28. 1 June.

29. Burgoyne had crossed over to the
Opposition in 1778 after being refused
the chance to defend his conduct in
America in a Parliamentary inquiry;
Johnstone had veered back to Government
after initially falling out with them over
their American policy (Namier and Brooke
ii. 144, 684–5).

30. See above, n. 20.

31. David Monnerat (*ante* 7 Nov. 1774,
n. 40).

32. Anne Stanley (ca 1725–1803), m.
(1765) Welbore Ellis, cr. (1794) Bn Mendip.
The Ellises lived at Twickenham in
Pope's villa (*ante* 21 Aug. 1778, n. 22;
Ossory ii. 105, n. 17); HW repeats this
anecdote to Lady Ossory 22 June 1779
(ibid. ii. 105).

O.' With much ado I found out that Mrs Ellis had sent for leave to take up some flags[33] out of my meadow for her grotto.

I hope in a few days to see Lady A. and Miss Jennings[34] here; I have writ to propose it.—What are your intentions? Do you stay till you have made your island impregnable?[35] I doubt it will be our only one that will be so.

To CONWAY, Wednesday 16 June 1779

Printed from *Works* v. 209–11.

Strawberry Hill, June 16, 1779.

YOUR Countess was here last Thursday,[1] and received a letter from you, that told us how slowly you receive ours. When you will receive this I cannot guess; but it dates a new era, which you with reason did not care to look at as possible. In a word, behold a Spanish war![2] I must detail a little to increase your wonder. I heard here the day before yesterday[3] that it was likely; and that night received a letter from Paris, telling me (it was of the 6th)[4] that Monsieur de Beauveau was going, they knew not whither, at the head of 25,000 men, with three lieutenant-generals and six or eight *maréchaux de camp* under him.[5] Yesterday I went to town, and

33. Or irises.

34. A friend and companion of Lady Ailesbury, presumably the Miss Jennings who wrote to Benjamin Franklin 20 March 1771 (MS in University of Pennsylvania Library) regarding a gift of seeds to her and 'Mr Conway.' Mentioned by Mrs Damer and Mrs Lybbe Powys as being at Park Place in 1795 (BERRY i. 369, n. 2), she is perhaps the 'Miss Susannah Jennings' who 'early in 1802 . . . died at the age of seventy-seven, and was brought from London to be buried at Shiplake' (Emily J. Climenson, *History of Shiplake*, 1894, p. 351); HW mentions in his 'Book of Materials,' 1771, p. 90, a 'Miss Jennings of Shiplake' who was taught paper mosaic by Mrs Delany, and in 'Des. of SH,' *Works* ii. 493, identifies a 'flower in paper mosaics' there as being by 'Miss Jennings.'

35. The *Daily Adv.* 29 May reported: 'In

consequence of some dispatches received from General Conway, governor of Jersey, orders are given for several pieces of cannon to be immediately sent to that island, and an additional number of troops.'

———

1. 10 June; she and Lady William Campbell stayed overnight (OSSORY ii. 104).

2. Earlier this day the Spanish ambassador had presented to Lord Weymouth the rescript of the King of Spain, declaring the end of Spanish neutrality in the American war and her readiness to support France against England; see MANN viii. 482–3 and nn. 1–2.

3. Perhaps from the Duke of Richmond; see OSSORY, loc. cit.

4. Mme du Deffand to HW 6 June 1779 (DU DEFFAND v. 146–7).

5. 'Nous envoyons 25,000 hommes je ne

T[homas] W[alpole] happened to call on me.—He, who used to be informed early, did not believe a word either of a Spanish war or a French expedition. I saw some other persons in the evening as ignorant. At night I went to sup at Richmond House. The Duke said the Brest fleet was certainly sailed, and had got the start of ours by twelve days;[6] that Monsieur de Beauveau was on board with a large sum of money, and with white and *red* cockades;[7] and that there would certainly be a Spanish war.[8] He added, that the Opposition were then pressing in the House of Commons to have the Parliament continue sitting,[9] and urging to know if we were not at the eve of a Spanish war; but the ministers persisted in the prorogation for tomorrow or Friday, and would not answer on Spain.[10]

I said I would make you wonder—but no—why should the Parliament continue to sit? Are not the ministers and the Parliament the same thing? And how has either House shown that it has any talent for war?

The Duke of R. does not guess whither the Brest fleet is gone.[11]— He thinks, if to Ireland, we should have known it by this time. He has heard that the Prince of Beauveau has said he was going on an expedition that would be glorious in the eyes of posterity.—I asked, if that might not mean Gibraltar?[12] The Duke doubts, but hopes it, as he thinks it no wise measure on their side; yet he was very melancholy, as you will be, on this heavy accession to our distresses.

Well! here we are, *aris et focis*[13] and all at stake! What can we be

---

sais où. Celui qui les commandera est nommé ainsi que trois lieutenants généraux, et six ou huit maréchaux de camp' (ibid.; for the names of the *lieutenants généraux* and the *maréchaux de camp,* see ibid. nn. 2–3). Mme du Deffand does not name the leader of the expedition, who was in fact Nöel de Jourda (1705–88), Comte de Vaux; HW may have heard a misrepresentation of the report that among the three *chefs d'escadre* of the Brest fleet (see below) was M. de Beausset (MANN viii. 484, n. 7).

6. The Brest fleet under Orvilliers sailed 3 June for a rendezvous with the Spanish fleet off the Sisarga Islands, while the English fleet under Sir Charles Hardy sailed 16 June to seek out the combined French and Spanish fleets (ibid. viii. 473, n. 17, 482, n. 7).

7. 'To show that a union had taken place between France and Spain' (*Public Adv.* 17 June).

8. 'Ireland is at present most thought of for the place in which the first act of hostilities will commence' (ibid.). See below.

9. See the 'Debate on Mr Thomas Townshend's Motion for an Address [to the King] to defer the Prorogation of Parliament . . . June 15,' in Cobbett, *Parl. Hist.* xx. 854–76.

10. See MANN viii. 483 and nn. 5–6; Parliament was not prorogued until 3 July (*ante* 5 June 1779, n. 21).

11. See above, n. 6.

12. See MANN viii. 484 and n. 8.

13. 'Altars and hearths,' from 'pro patria, pro liberis, pro aris atque focis suis': 'in defence of their country, their children, their altars, and their hearths' (Sallust, *Catiline,* lix. 5).

meaning? Unable to conquer America before she was assisted—scarce able to keep France at bay—are we a match for both, and Spain too? —What can be our view? nay, what can be our expectation? I sometimes think we reckon it will be more creditable to be forced by France and Spain to give up America, than to have the merit with the latter of doing it with grace.—But, as Cato says,

I am weary of conjectures—This must end them;[14]

that is, the sword:—and never, I believe, did a country plunge itself into such difficulties step by step, and for six years together, without once recollecting that each foreign war rendered the object of the civil war more unattainable; and that in both the foreign wars we have not an object in prospect. Unable to recruit our remnant of an army in America, are we to make conquests on France and Spain? They may choose their attacks: we can scarce choose what we will defend.

Ireland, they say, is more temperate than was expected. That is some consolation—yet many fear the Irish will be tempted to unite with America, which would throw all that trade into their convenient harbours: and I own I have apprehensions that the Parliament's rising without taking a step in their favour, may offend them. Surely at least we have courageous ministers. I thought my father a stout man:—he had not a tithe of their spirit.

The town has wound up the season perfectly in character by a fête at the Pantheon by subscription.[15] Le Texier managed it; but it turned out sadly. The company was first shut into the galleries to look down on the supper, then let to descend to it.[16] Afterwards they were led into the subterraneous apartment, which was laid with mould, and planted with trees, and crammed with nosegays:[17] but the fresh earth, and the dead leaves, and the effluvia of breaths made such a stench and moisture, that they were suffocated; and when they remounted, the legs and wings of chickens and remnants of ham (for the supper was not removed) poisoned them more. A druid in an arbour distributed verses to the ladies; then the Baccelli[18] and

14. Addison's *Cato*, V. i.

15. Held Monday evening, 14 June, and described in the *Public Adv.* 17 June.

16. 'The great room, in which the tables were laid, was kept locked; by this means the tables were seen from the galleries to great advantage. . . . At eleven the great room was opened' (ibid.).

17. 'When the company, which consisted of between five and six hundred, had supped, they were led down to the Tea Room, which was hung with bows representing a thick wood' (ibid.).

18. Giovanna (or Gianetta) Baccelli (d. 1801), principal dancer at the Opera (MORE 268, n. 8; see also *London Stage*

the dancers of the Opera danced;[19] and then danced the company;[20] and then it being morning, and the candles burnt out, the windows were opened; and then the stewed danced assembly were such shocking figures, that they fled like ghosts as they looked.—I suppose there will be no more balls unless the French land, and then we shall show we do not mind it.

Thus I have told you all I know. You will ponder over these things in your little distant island, when we have forgotten them. There is another person, one Doctor Franklin, who, I fancy, is not sorry that we divert ourselves so well.

To Conway, Saturday 3 July 1779

Missing; mentioned *post* 10 July 1779.

From Lady Ailesbury, ca Thursday 8 July 1779

Missing; answered *post* 10 July 1779.

To Lady Ailesbury, Saturday 10 July 1779

Printed from the MS now wsl. First printed, with omissions, *Works* v. 571–2; first printed in full Toynbee x. 446–8 and *Supp.* ii. 160–1. For the history of the MS see *ante* 23 Aug. 1760.

Saturday night, July 10, 1779.

I COULD not thank your Ladyship before the post went out today, as I was getting into my chaise to go and dine at Carshalton with my cousin T. Walpole,[1] when I received your kind inquiry[2]

Pt IV, iii. 1831, 1910; Pt V, i. *passim*, ii. 828; *Enciclopedia dello spettacolo,* Rome, [1954–62], i. 1207).

19. 'A group of dancers ['from the Opera House'] descended from the galleries, representing the Four Seasons. . . . Mr Simonet and Mrs Bachelli danced a *minuet de la cour*' (*Public Adv.* loc. cit.).

20. 'The young part of this brilliant assembly went to country dances, and continued till between five and six' (ibid.).

1. HW mentions the visit in his letter to Lady Ossory 14 July 1779 (Ossory ii. 110–11).

2. Missing.

about my eye. It is quite well again, and I hope the next attack of the gout will be anywhere rather than in that quarter.[3]

I did not expect Mr Conway would think of returning just now, though I am persuaded the French will not stoop to pick up such a minikin pin—but he is scrupulous even about appearances. As you have lost both Mrs Damer and Lady William,[4] I do not see why your Ladyship should not go to Goodwood.[5]

The Baroness's[6] increasing peevishness does not surprise me. When people will not weed their own minds, they are apt to be overrun with nettles. She knows nothing of politics, and no wonder talks nonsense about them. It is silly to wish three nations had but one neck, but it is ten times more absurd to act as if it was so, which the government has done—ay, and forgetting too that it has not a scimitar large enough to sever that neck, which they have in effect made *one*. It is past the time, Madam, of making conjectures—how can one guess whither France and Spain will direct a blow that is in their option. I am rather inclined to think that they will have patience to ruin us in detail. Hitherto France and America have carried their points by that manœuvre. Should there be an engagement at sea, and the French and Spanish fleets by their great superiority[7] should have the advantage, one knows not what might happen—yet, though there are such large preparations making on the French coast,[8] I do not much expect a serious invasion,[9] as they are sure they can do us more damage by a variety of other attacks, where we can make little resistance. Gibraltar and Jamaica can but be the immediate objects of Spain.[10] Ireland is much worse guarded than this island—nay, we must be undone by our expense, should the summer pass without any attempt. My cousin thinks they will try to destroy Portsmouth and Plymouth[11]—but I have seen nothing in the present French Ministry that looks like bold enterprise. We

3. HW had suffered from the 'gout' in his left eye for four or five days at the beginning of July; he suffered a recurrence in Aug. (ibid. ii. 106; Mann viii. 501).

4. Who were on their way to the Continent; see next letter.

5. Seat of the Richmonds.

6. Probably Lady Greenwich; see Ossory ii. 485 *et passim* for her 'superabundant fund of bad qualities.'

7. See Mann viii. 490–1 and nn. 2–3, and *post* 23 July 1779, n. 7.

8. See Mann viii. 496–7, n. 4.

9. However, one was planned; see A. T. Patterson, *The Other Armada*, Manchester, 1960, *passim*.

10. Spain instituted a naval blockade of Gibraltar 16 July; see Mann viii. 501, n. 5.

11. These were in fact the primary and secondary objectives of the enemy (Patterson, op. cit. 133 *et passim*).

are much more adventurous, that set everything to the hazard—but there are such numbers of Baronesses that both talk and act with passion, that one would think the nation had lost its senses. Everything has miscarried that has been undertaken, and the worse we succeed, the more is risked—yet the nation is not angry! How can one conjecture during such a delirium? I sometimes almost think I must be in the wrong to be of so contrary an opinion to most men— yet when every misfortune that has happened, had been foretold by a few, why should I not think I have been in the right? Has not almost every single event that has been announced as prosperous, proved a gross falsehood—and often a silly one? Are we not at this moment assured that Washington cannot possibly amass an army of above 8000 men?[12] and yet Clinton with twenty thousand men, and with the hearts, as we are told too, of three parts of the colonies, dares not show his teeth without the walls of New York![13]—Can I be in the wrong in not believing what is so contradictory to my senses? We could not conquer America when it stood alone. Then France supported it—and we did not mend the matter. To make it still easier, we have driven Spain into the alliance. Is this wisdom? Would it be presumption, even if one were single, to think that we must have the worst in such a contest? Shall I be like the mob, and expect to conquer France and Spain, and then thunder upon America—nay, but the higher mob do not expect such success. They would not be so angry at the House of Bourbon, if not morally certain that those kings destroy all our passionate desire and expectation of conquering America. We bullied, and threatened and begged, and nothing would do. Yet independence was still the word—now we rail at the two monarchs—and when they have banged us, we shall sue to them as humbly as we did to the Congress[13a]—all this my senses, such as they are, tell me has been and will be the case. What is worse, all Europe is of the same opinion—and though forty thou-

12. 'Washington's army does not consist of more than 8,000 effective men, including those on furlough and on different services. . . . He has asked for 10,000 additional troops for the ensuing campaign. Congress has begun the raising of some, but meet with small success' ('Extract of a letter from a Loyalist in Philadelphia to his friend in New York, dated April 3, 1779,' in *London Chronicle* 6–8 July, xlvi. 24).

13. However, the *London Gazette* No. 11994, 6–10 July, and *Whitehall Evening Post* 8–10 July, *sub* 10 July, carried reports of some of Clinton's forces foraying out of New York to capture rebel posts at Verplanck and Stonypoint.

13a. The peace proposal brought by the Carlisle Commission was presented to Congress 13 June 1778 and was rejected 17 June (Ossory ii. 28–9 and nn. 6, 8; Mann viii. 400).

sand Baronesses may be ever so angry, I venture to prophesy that we shall make but a very foolish figure, whenever we are so lucky as to obtain a peace—and posterity, that may have prejudices of its own, will still take the liberty to pronounce that its ancestors were a woeful set of politicians from the year 1774 to—I wish I knew when.

The Duke of Ancaster[14] is dead, and Lord Bolinbroke.[15] If I might advise I would recommend Mr Burrel[16] to command the fleet in the room of Sir Charles Hardy[17]—the fortune of the Burrells is powerful enough to baffle calculation.[18] Mr Burrel is Lord Great Chamberlain-Consort of England.[19] Good night, Madam.

PS. I have not written to Mr Conway since this day sevennight,[20] not having a teaspoonful of news to send him. I will beg your Ladyship to tell him so.

From Lady Ailesbury, ca Wednesday 21 July 1779

Missing; answered *post* 23 July 1779.

14. Robert Bertie (1756–8 July 1779), 4th D. of Ancaster, 1778. See Mann viii. 498–9.

15. 'On Thursday night [8 July] died of the dead palsy . . . Viscount Bolingbroke' (*Public Adv.* 10 July). This was a false report; however, he was ill, apparently of a 'palsy upon the brain,' and was confined in a madhouse in 1780 (Ossory ii. 107, n. 9; Mann ix. 11).

16. Peter Burrell (1754–1820), Kt, 1781, 2d Bt, 1787; cr. (1796) Bn Gwydir.

17. (ca 1714–80), Kt, 1755; Adm., 1770; M.P. See *ante* 16 June 1779, n. 6.

18. See Mann viii. 499.

19. Upon the death of Ancaster his hereditary office of Lord Great Chamberlain and barony of Willoughby de Eresby fell into abeyance between his two sisters, the elder of whom, Lady Priscilla Barbara Elizabeth Bertie (1761–1828), had married Burrell on 23 Feb. 1779. By patent dated 18 March 1780, she was declared to be Baroness Willoughby of Eresby, while in May 1781 it was declared that the office of Lord Great Chamberlain was to be shared between her and her sister; on 14 Aug. 1781 Burrell was appointed Deputy Lord Great Chamberlain.

20. HW's earlier letter is missing.

To Lady Ailesbury, Friday 23 July 1779

Printed from the MS now WSL; first printed *Works* v. 573–4. For the history of the MS see *ante* 23 Aug. 1760.

Address: To the Countess of Aylsbury, at Park Place near Henley.

Postmark: 24 IY.

Strawberry Hill, Friday night.

I AM not at all surprised, my dear Madam, at the intrepidity of Mrs Damer; she always was the heroic daughter of a hero.[1] Her sense and coolness never forsake her. I, who am not so firm, shuddered at your Ladyship's account.[2] Now that she has stood fire for four hours, I hope she will give as clear proofs of her understanding, of which I have as high opinion as of her courage, and not return in any danger.

I am to dine at Ditton[3] tomorrow, and will certainly talk on the subject you recommend—yet I am far, till I have heard more, from thinking with your Ladyship, that more troops and artillery at Jersey would be desirable.[4] Any considerable quantity of either, especially of the former cannot be spared at this moment, when so big a cloud hangs over this island, nor would any number avail if the French should be masters at sea. A large garrison would but tempt the French thither, were it but to distress this country; and what is worse would encourage Mr Conway to make an impracticable defence. If he is to remain in a situation so unworthy of him, I confess I had rather he was totally incapable of making any defence. I love him enough not to murmur at his exposing himself where his country and his honour demand him—but I would not have him measure himself in a place untenable against very superior force. My present comfort is, as to him, that France at this moment has a

1. The packet in which she was crossing from Dover to Ostend [with Lady William Campbell and the Duchess of Leinster] was taken by a French frigate after a running fight of several hours (Mary Berry); see also OSSORY ii. 113 and nn. 3, 6. She and the others were shortly released unharmed, continuing on their journey, Mrs Damer and presumably Lady William going to the Spa, and the Duchess to Aubigny (DU DEFFAND v. 160).

2. HW wrote to Lady Ossory 20 July

1779 that on 19 July 'Lady Ailesbury was come to me all terror and distress' about Mrs Damer being 'taken prisoner' (OSSORY ii. 113); the present letter, however, is probably a reply to a missing letter of Lady Ailesbury written since her visit.

3. The Hertfords' seat at Thames Ditton in Surrey.

4. Lady Ailesbury had been frightened by a false rumour that Conway and Jersey had been captured by the French (ibid. ii. 113 and nn. 5–6).

far vaster object. I have good reason to believe the government knows that a great army is ready to embark at St Malo's;[5] but will not stir till after a sea-fight, which we do not know but may be engaged at this moment.[6] Our fleet is allowed to be the finest ever set forth by this country—but it is inferior in number by seventeen ships[7] to the united squadron of the Bourbons. France, if successful, means to pour in a vast many thousands on us, and have threatened to burn the capital itself[8]—Jersey, my dear Madam, does not enter into a calculation of such magnitude. The moment is singularly awful—yet the vaunts of enemies are rarely executed successfully and ably. Have we trampled America under our foot?

You have too good sense Madam to be imposed upon by my arguments, if they are insubstantial. You do know, that I have had my terrors for Mr Conway—but at present they are out of the question from the insignificance of his island. Do not listen to rumours, nor believe a single one till it has been canvassed over and over. Fear, folly, fifty motives, will coin new reports every hour at such a conjuncture. When one is totally void of credit and power, patience is the only wisdom. I have seen dangers still more imminent. They were dispersed. Nothing happens in proportion to what is meditated. Fortune, whatever fortune is, is more constant than is the common notion—I do not give this as one of my solid arguments, but I have always encouraged myself in being superstitious on the favourable side. I never, like most superstitious people, believe auguries against my wishes. We have been fortunate in the escape of Mrs Damer and in the defeat at Jersey even before Mr Conway arrived, and thence I depend on the same future prosperity. From the authority of persons who do not reason on such airy hopes, I am seriously persuaded, that if the fleets engage, the enemy will not gain advantage without deep-felt loss, enough probably to dismay their invasion. Coolness may succeed, and then negotiation—surely, if we can weather the

5. Some 31,000 French troops were assembled at Le Havre and St-Malo; Lord North wrote to Lord Sandwich 18 July that 'immediate attention should be given to any attempt at invasion from St-Malo, Granville, and Havre' (*Sandwich Papers* iii. 48; A. T. Patterson, *The Other Armada*, Manchester, 1960, p. 151).

6. The object of the combined fleets was to cover the passage of the French troops in an attack upon England; however, no invasion took place and there was no further sea-fighting in home waters for the rest of the war.

7. Actually, 28 (MANN viii. 502, n. 7).

8. ' 'Tis with the greatest confidence asserted, that the French are absolutely determined to risk sixty thousand men in a descent upon England, and that the attack and destruction of the city of London is their real object' (*Public Adv.* 8 July). See *ante* 10 July 1779, n. 11.

summer, we shall, obstinate as we are against conviction, be compelled by the want of money to relinquish our ridiculous pretensions, now proved to be utterly impracticable; for with an inferior navy at home, can we assert sovereignty over America? It is a contradiction in terms and in fact. It may be hard of digestion to relinquish it, but it [is] impossible to pursue it. Adieu, my dear Madam, I have not left room for a line more.

To Hertford, ca Saturday 31 July 1779

Missing; answered *post* 2 Aug. 1779.

From Hertford, Monday 2 August 1779

Printed for the first time from a photostat of BM Add. MSS 23219, f. 104. Dated by the arrival of the Leeward Island and Mediterranean fleets.

London, Monday even.

Dear Horry,

I RECEIVED your letter[1] last night and sent it this morning to Windsor.[2] I could not do you or the contents of it so much justice in any other way, and I think your observation upon the expression in your friend's letter[3] just and very well worth every attention.

The Leeward Island fleet and that from the Mediterranean are arrived.[4] The French are so far ignorant or good to us; but perhaps

1. Missing.
2. 'Yesterday [1 Aug.] in the afternoon their Majesties . . . went from Kew to Windsor' (*Daily Adv.* 2 Aug.).
3. The only extant letter at this time to HW from a friend is Cole's letter of 24 July 1779 (Cole ii. 171–2), postmarked 27 July, the first paragraph of which deals with Lord Orford's intention of selling the pictures at Houghton to the Empress of Russia. The 'expression' upon which HW made his 'observation' may have been Cole's remark about the pictures being eventually 'forgotten,'

prompting HW to make a last minute plea that the King himself, who was a collector, purchase the pictures, to prevent their going out of the Kingdom; the *Whitehall Evening Post* 17–20 July wrote that 'Government have been sufficiently warned of this event, so that there is not an excuse left to them for suffering the most valuable collection in the kingdom to depart from it.' HW wrote to Mann 4 Aug. 1779 of 'the completion of the sale' (Mann viii. 502).
4. The *London Packet* 30 July – 2 Aug. announced the arrival of the Leeward

nothing will satisfy but the possession or positive ruin of our little island. Yours, dear Horry,

Always most truly and affectionately,

HERTFORD

From HERTFORD, Friday 3 September 1779

Printed for the first time from a photostat of BM Add. MSS 23219, f. 105. Dated by the arrival of the grand fleet at Spithead.
Address: To the Honourable Hor. Walpole.

Grosvenor Street, Friday 3 o'clock.

Dear Horry,

YOUR news of the French is I find about the town, but I do not believe it to be true.[1] Our grand fleet is all at Spithead.[2] Everything is quiet and I think likely to be so. I am unfortunately no subscriber to the Incurables.

Yours always most truly,

HERTFORD

To CONWAY, Monday 13 September 1779

Printed from *Works* v. 211–12.

Strawberry Hill, Sept. 13, 1779.

I AM writing to you at random; not knowing whether or when this letter will go: but your brother told me last night that an officer, whose name I have forgot, was arrived from Jersey, and

---

Island fleet, and the expected arrival of another fleet consisting of 'near 90 sail. From Oporto 44; from Lisbon 15; from Malaga 13; and the remainder from different ports in the Mediterranean.'

1. 'The only intelligence that at present transpires, is, that the combined fleets of France and Spain were in sight, and that a general engagement was hourly expected' (*Daily Adv.* 4 Sept.; see also *Sandwich Papers* iii. 87–91). There was no engagement.

2. Where it arrived 3 Sept. (MANN viii. 511, n. 7).

would return to you soon. I am sensible how very seldom I have written to you—but you have been few moments out of my thoughts. What *they* have been, you who know me so minutely may well guess, and why they do not pass my lips. Sense, experience, circumstances, can teach one to command one's self outwardly, but do not divest a most friendly heart of its feelings. I believe the state of my mind has contributed to bring on a very weak and decaying body my present disorders. I have not been well the whole summer; but for these three weeks much otherwise. It has at last ended in the gout, which, to all appearance, will be a short fit.[1]

On public affairs I cannot speak. Everything is so exaggerated on all sides, that what grains of truth remain in the sieve would appear cold and insipid; and the great manœuvres you learn as soon as I. In the naval battle between Byron and D'Estaing, our captains were worthy of any age in our story.[2]

You may imagine how happy I am at Mrs D.'s return, and at her not being at Naples, as she was likely to have been, at the dreadful explosion of Vesuvius.[3] Surely it will have glutted Sir William's rage for volcanos![4] How poor Lady Hamilton's nerves stood it I do not conceive.—Oh, mankind! mankind!—Are there not calamities enough in store for us, but must destruction be our amusement and pursuit?

I send this to Ditton,[5] where it may wait some days; but I would not suffer a sure opportunity to slip without a line. You are more obliged to me for all I do not say, than for whatever eloquence itself could pen.

PS. I unseal my letter to add, that undoubtedly you will come to the meeting of Parliament, which will be in October.[6] Nothing can

1. HW describes his illness more fully to Mason 14 Sept. 1779, MASON i. 463.

2. D'Estaing's fleet in the West Indies (see *ante* 5 June 1779, n. 1) had on 4 July taken Grenada, and on 6 July defeated Byron's squadron, which had come to the relief of the island; however, the victory was not attained without heavy losses, and both Byron and Major-Gen. James Grant, commander-in-chief of the British forces in the Leeward Islands and a witness of the action, testified to the 'determined bravery and gallantry of the whole squadron' (Byron to Philip Stephens 8 July, and Grant to Germain 8 July,

printed in *London Gazette* No. 12012, 7–11 Sept., reprinted *Daily Adv.* 13 Sept.; see also MANN viii. 515–16 and nn. 2–4).

3. 8 Aug.; see ibid. viii. 514–15 and n. 4.

4. Sir William Hamilton (*ante* 29 Aug. 1757, n. 3), the British envoy at Naples and an enthusiastic student of volcanos, sent a description of the eruption in his letter of 1 Oct. to Sir Joseph Banks, president of the Royal Society; the letter was read to the Society 16 Dec. (MANN viii. 514–15, nn. 3–4).

5. Where Lord Hertford had then a villa (HW).

6. On 16 Sept. Parliament was further

or ever did make me advise you to take a step unworthy of yourself.
—But surely you have higher and more sacred duties than the government of a molehill!

To LADY AILESBURY, before Thursday 14 October 1779

Missing; mentioned *post* 28 Oct. 1779.

To HERTFORD, ca Tuesday 26 October 1779

Missing; answered *post* 27 Oct. 1779.

From HERTFORD, Wednesday 27 October 1779

Printed for the first time from a photostat of BM Add. MSS 23219, f. 107.
Dated by HW, 'Oct. 27. 1779.'
Address: To the Honourable Hor. Walpole.

Thames Ditton, Wednesday 2 o'clock.

Dear Horry,

I AM much concerned that we cannot see you tomorrow, and
more so that pain confines you.[1] Your letter[2] looks nothing like a
finished campaign, and it is so circumstantial and so natural that I
believe it in contradiction to the commonly received opinion and,
I may add, to any intelligence our Ministers receive, for which I
have no great respect.[3] My brother has an order for a frigate whenever he chooses to employ it for his return, but he has not yet sent

---

prorogued until 7 Oct., but on that date it
was again prorogued until 25 Nov., when
it finally met (*Journals of the House of
Commons* xxxvii. 460–1). Conway arrived
back in London 21 Nov. (OSSORY ii. 142,
n. 13).

1. See *post* 28 Oct. 1779.

2. Missing.
3. HW wrote to Lady Ossory 27 Oct.
1779: 'I have reason to believe that the
combined fleets will again appear before
the conclusion of the campaign, though
the Government thinks not' (OSSORY ii.
129). See *post* 28 Oct. 1779.

for it. Lady Hertford desires her best compliments. I remain, dear Horry,

Ever yours sincerely,

HERTFORD

TO LADY AILESBURY, Thursday 28 October 1779

Printed from the MS now WSL; first printed Toynbee, *Supp.* i. 276–8. For the history of the MS see *ante* 23 Aug. 1760; it was marked by HW for inclusion in *Works*, but was not included.
Address: To the Countess of Ailesbury at Park Place near Henley.
Postmark: ISLEWORTH ⟨29⟩ OC.

Strawberry Hill, Thursday night.

I HAVE not written to your Ladyship for above a fortnight[1] from that most sovereign of reasons, that I had nothing to tell you. I was in town three days last week[2] and so fortunate as to find both your daughters,[3] and to see one or both every day. I returned hither on Monday, and for two days have been confined with the rheumatism in my arm, for I am grown to have such a regiment of disorders, that when one goes off duty, another *relieves* it—an excellent word I have chosen truly on the occasion! I was to have dined at Ditton today,[4] but could not get on my coat, so Lord and Lady Hertford called on me, and he told me that a sloop is ordered to bring Mr Conway over whenever he pleases—but I fear he will not send for it yet, for the combined fleets are said to be at sea, as well as ours;[5] and though the former will certainly not deign to stoop to pick up a minikin pin, Mr Conway I am sure will stay till they are returned to their own pincushion. What horrible times, Madam! That is, how horrible they make one! The wind blustered and tempested this morning, and I instantly wished it might sink the whole hostile squadrons—that is, forty or fifty thousand men! One grows quite righteous, when one corrects one's self, and only wishes the authors

1. HW's letter is missing.
2. HW wrote to Mason from Berkeley Square (see below) Thursday, 21 Oct. 1779, that he would 'return to Strawberry on Monday [25 Oct.]' (MASON i. 470).
3. The Duchess of Richmond and Mrs Damer.

4. See *ante* 27 Oct. 1779.
5. The English fleet had sailed from Spithead 22 Oct., but the combined fleet, which had put into Brest 15 Sept., did not sail again this year (see OSSORY ii. 131, nn. 7–8; A. T. Patterson, *The Other Armada*, Manchester, 1960, pp. 210–12).

of all these wars, whoever they are, at the bottom of the ocean. Ireland seems disposed to join in the grand ballet. They have forty thousand men in arms,[6] which may keep the peace, for what forty thousand *ask*, it is not civil to refuse, though we were so ill-bred as to affront three millions.

Lord Stormont kissed hands yesterday for Lord Suffolk's seals;[7] there was to have been more kissing, but I have some idle notion that there is a little hitch somewhere or other.[8]

After Sunday next, Berkeley Square will be my chief residence, though I shall probably come hither once a week as usual.[9] Mrs Damer is charmed with my new house. It is so cheerful, that when I came back, I thought even Strawberry less brilliant than it was wont to be—am not I an old simpleton with a young wife!

Adieu! my dear Madam. I will not wish Pharaoh and all his host buried in the Red Sea; but I do hope November will make the ocean too *cold* to hold navies[10]—and then, that the rest of the winter may restore peace—

> Peace my supreme delight, not Fleury's more,—

and yet I am not so sore as ministers.[11]

Your Ladyship's most devoted

H. W.

6. The Irish volunteers; see *ante* 5 June 1779, n. 5.

7. As secretary of state for the North; Henry Howard, 12th E. of Suffolk, had died 7 March, since which time Lord Weymouth, secretary of state for the south, had served as secretary for the north *pro tem.*

8. See MANN viii. 526, n. 10.

9. See *ante* 23 Oct. 1778, n. 3; HW had moved into his new house in Berkeley Square 14 Oct. (OSSORY ii. 124).

10. In fact, a French council of war held 3 Oct. advised in a memorandum to the French ministry that, if permitted to sail, the combined fleet would be exposed to great dangers from the November storms (Patterson, op. cit. 211–12).

11. 'Peace is my dear delight—not Fleury's more: / But touch me, and no minister so sore' (Pope, *First Satire of Second Book of Horace*, ll. 75–6).

DAME RAT, and her poor little Ones.

Pub.ᵈ March 12ᵗʰ 1792 by Hannah Humphry Bond Street

Gillray.   Sir Guilford Lamp St   Fox   The Guilford children

1792

From HERTFORD, Saturday 30 October 1779

Printed for the first time from a photostat of BM Add. MSS 23219, ff. 109–10.

Thames Ditton, October 30th 1779.

Dear Horry,

I HAVE just had three letters from my brother, one of which is gone to the King, a second to his attorney,[1] and the third is of the oldest date, and you will receive no satisfaction from it. In the one gone to the King, he says that having sent to look into Concale Bay[2] and St-Maloes,[3] and finding nothing offensive there, he should with the King's leave which he had received, return to England in the course of next week, and his letter is dated the 21st instant. We may therefore expect him every day.[4] He has done everything in his government which could be done, and more than any other man I believe could have effected. Your political news of Lord Gower etc. was well founded; he seems to be dissatisfied with Lord Stormont's appointment,[5] or else, which is more probable, sees the present system so weak and his own party so strong, that he will be minister;[6] and I think the present ministry is unlikely to last as it is, and that his Lordship's judgment and his friends' may be good in supposing, as I conclude he does, that though he may offend the King a little by his present conduct and sending away Lord North, yet his Majesty will prefer him and his party to a ministry entirely made from Opposition.

I am glad to hear you was abroad last night.

Yours always very sincerely,

HERTFORD

1. A 'Mr Sharpe,' perhaps Joshua Sharpe (*ante* 21 June 1773, n. 2); Conway mentions him in his letter to Hertford 27 Oct. 1779 (MS in Huntington Library) in connection with the Prize Commission at Jersey, and wrote to him 23 Dec. about the same (MS in University of Rochester Library).

2. Cancale Bay.

3. St-Malo.

4. In his letter to Hertford 27 Oct. Conway wrote 'I hope I may be in motion by the middle of this week, as I believe I told

you': however, on 3 Nov. he was present 'de nouveau à une séance des États' of Jersey, and he did not reach London until 21 Nov. (J. A. Messervy, 'Liste des gouverneurs . . . de l'île de Jersey,' *Société jersiaise, Bulletins*, 1902–5, v. 13; *ante* 13 Sept. 1779, n. 6).

5. HW wrote to Lady Ossory 1 Nov. 1779 that Gower, lord president of the Council, 'would not attend to swear in Lord Stormont, but walked in the Park during the solemnities' (OSSORY ii. 131).

6. Gower was dissatisfied with the North

From HERTFORD, Friday ?November or ?December ?1779

Printed for the first time from a photostat of BM Add. MSS 23219, f. 111.

T[hames] Ditton, Friday morn.

Dear Horry,

IF there was anything which appeared free in our accidental meeting last night, I hope the Duchess of Gloucester will not think it was want of respect or attention towards her R. H. on my part. I cannot as you know pay my respects to her personally,[1] and therefore it is more incumbent on me to behave properly at a distance. This principle would have diverted me even from speaking to your amiable nieces[2] and their company if I could have hid myself or turned decently from them, for I did not, till you came to me, know even where the Duchess was. In short, if I have done wrong, it was by accident and because I could not avoid it, for you may be assured I could mean or intend nothing disrespectful or inattentive. I remain, dear Horry,

Always very truly and affectionately yours,

HERTFORD

From HERTFORD, Saturday 25 December 1779

Printed for the first time from a photostat of BM Add. MSS 23219, f. 112. *Address:* To the Honourable Hor. Walpole.

Saturday, December 25th 1779.

Dear Horry,

SINCE I saw you yesterday I hear that Adams[1] and another of the Congress are coming to France in a French frigate, and the reason assigned for their coming is the decline of Franklin's credit in

ministry, and in Oct. was talking 'of turning out Lord North, and making a new ministry' (Anthony Storer to George Selwyn, in J. H. Jesse, *George Selwyn and his Contemporaries,* 1882, iv. 279). However, nothing came of this, and Gower resigned his office ca 20 Nov. (MANN viii. 526, n. 12; see also ibid. n. 10).

1. Since the Duchess was not received at Court.
2. The Duchess's three daughters.

―――

1. John Adams (1735–1826), 2d President of the United States.

the Congress.² If this be the case I am sorry to think we can expect little from thence but what the French leave for us, with their eyes open to the circumstances of us and them.

Yours ever,

HERTFORD

From HERTFORD, Monday 3 January 1780

Printed for the first time from a photostat of BM Add. MSS 23219, f. 114. Dated by the contents. HW echoes this letter in writing to Lady Ossory 3 Jan. 1780; see OSSORY ii. 154–5.

Address: To the Honourable Hor. Walpole.

Monday, 1 o'clock.¹

Dear Horry,

FIELDING² has brought in with him all the Dutch ships³ without any resistance being made.⁴ I do not yet know the particulars. I likewise hear that the back settlers in Carolina, to the number of

---

2. The *Daily Adv.* 25 Dec. reported 'by a gentleman lately arrived from Boston, we are informed, that . . . Mr Samuel [*sic*] Adams, with another member of the Congress, embarked in a frigate for France' and, *sub* 'Extract of a letter from Falmouth, Dec. 18,' 'two members of Congress were immediately to embark for England, by way of France, to endeavour to bring the Mother Country into terms of accommodation.' John Adams, appointed by Congress 27 Sept. to negotiate peace with Great Britain, had embarked for France on the *Sensible* 13 Nov. with his two sons, John Quincy, 6th President of the United States, and Charles, landing at Ferrol 8 Dec. and travelling to Paris by 5 Feb.; though the GM 1780, l. 41 and in the 'index to the essays,' etc. reported that he was to replace Franklin as minister plenipotentiary at Paris, Franklin, who had been appointed to that post 14 Sept. 1778, remained in it till the end of the war (*Dictionary of American Biography*). The report of two members of Congress departing for Paris may have been occasioned by the fact that originally

John Jay had been nominated along with Adams as a peace negotiator; Jay instead went to Spain as minister plenipotentiary (ibid.).

———

1. HW wrote Mann 4 Jan. 1780, 'it was but yesterday at noon that the notice [of Feilding's encounter with the Dutch fleet] arrived' (MANN ix. 4 and n. 8).

2. Charles Feilding (1740–83), Capt., R.N. 1760–83 (OSSORY ii. 154, n. 2).

3. On 31 Dec. off Portland, Feilding with a squadron of 8 ships of the line, 2 frigates and 10 smaller vessels intercepted 'a fleet of Dutch merchant ships, under convoy of the Admiral Count Byland, with a squadron of five ships and frigates of war' which had sailed from the Texel 27 Dec. (*London Gazette* No. 12045, 1–4 Jan.; MANN ix. 4, n. 10). Eight Dutch merchantmen, accompanied by three men-of-war, were brought into Plymouth (ibid. ix. 3 and nn. 4, 5; OSSORY ii. 154, n. 3).

4. Feilding requested permission to search the merchant ships; this was refused. There was an exchange of broadsides, and then the Dutch struck their

about 3,000, have risen since Prevost's[5] victory,[6] seized a town, and declared for the old Government.[7]

> Yours ever,
>
> HERTFORD

From HERTFORD, Tuesday 4 January 1780

Printed for the first time from a photostat of BM Add. MSS 23219, f. 116. Dated by the contents. HW wrote this news to Mann and to Mason on the same day (MANN ix. 3–4, MASON ii. 1–2). The letter is in Lady Hertford's hand, but apparently dictated by Hertford.

Address: Honourable Mr Walpole, Berkeley Square.

> Tuesday, 6 o'clock.

Dear Mr Walpole,

I AM afraid the true ships with the masts etc. are gone, and got into Brest;[1] whilst we have been catching doggers laden with hemp

colours (*London Gazette* loc. cit., OSSORY ii. 155–6, n. 9; for a full account see *London Chronicle* 1–4 Jan., xlvii. 16; *Sandwich Papers* iii. 11).

5. James Mark (Marcus) Prévost (d. 1781), 4th son of Augustin Prévost (1695–1740) of Geneva, Switzerland (Severo Mallet-Prévost, *Historical Notes . . . of the Mallet Family,* New York, 1930, pp. 84, 88). He was Maj. in the 60th Foot 1778, and Lt-Col. in America 1777 (*Army Lists* 1780, p. 131). After the victory at Briar Creek (see next note) he became Lt-Gov. of Georgia by proclamation of 4 March 1779 (*Facsimiles of Manuscripts in European Archives Relating to America 1773–1783,* ed. B. F. Stevens, 1889–95, xii. No. 1267). Prévost m. (1763) Theodosia Bartow of New Jersey, by whom he left two sons; he 'died of his wounds in Jamaica during the American War' (Mallet-Prévost, op. cit. 88; H. S. Parmet and M. B. Hecht, *Aaron Burr: Portrait of an Ambitious Man,* New York, 1967, pp. 39, 55–6).

6. At Briar Creek, near the junction of the creek with the Savannah River, where Lt-Col. James Mark Prévost defeated the American General John Ashe on 3 March 1779 (Maj.-Gen. Augustine Prévost's letter to Lord George Germain 5 March 1779 in *London Gazette* No. 11971, 17–20 April 1779; MANN viii. 464, n. 5).

7. HW writes this news to Lady Ossory 3 Jan. (OSSORY ii. 155). According to the *London Chronicle* 28–30 Dec. 1779, xlvi. 617, 'a large body of Highland emigrants (said to be about 3000 men) had assembled in the back settlements of Carolina, and made themselves masters of the town of Cambden' where the inhabitants of Charleston had stored their valuables in expectation of an attack by Maj.-Gen. Augustine Prévost (see also ibid. 4–6 Jan. 1780, xlvii. 24).

1. Feilding's object was to capture the Dutch ships carrying naval stores, i.e., masts and timbers, to the Brest fleet; see MASON ii. 2 and nn. 14, 15; MANN ix. 3–4 and n. 10. Feilding suspected a Dutch trick and wrote Lord Sandwich 31 Dec. 1779, 'that whilst this trifling convoy has come down Channel on our coasts, the ships of which your Lordship sent me an account have escaped on the French. . . . I am only sorry that the whole of what I expected to meet were not together' (*Sandwich Papers* iii. 113–14).

and iron,[2] and perhaps a quarrel with Holland at the same time.[3] It is too much to be outwitted by Holland; [4] or even by Paul Jones [5] through the medium of a Dutchman.

Yours ever,

Hertford

You are to suppose Lord Hertford writes this.[6]

---

2. According to the *London Chronicle* 6–8 Jan. (xlvii. 29, 30), the British 'found them to consist of about 30 sail of doggers, under convoy of one 50-gun ship, the *Admiral*, two 40-gun ships, and three large frigates, all Dutch. . . . the doggers were loaded with hemp, flax, and iron, some bound to Nantz, and others to Port L'Orient in France.'

3. The Cabinet Council on 28 Dec. 1779 discussed the danger of war with Holland and decided that the Dutch could not be permitted to supply the French without intervention; see Ossory ii. 156, n. 10. Sir Joseph Yorke about 14 Dec. warned the Stadtholder of 'the determination of our Court, at all events to persist in searching their ships' (*London Chronicle* 13–15 Jan., xlvii. 54; Ossory ii. 155, n. 7). Feilding's instructions of 12 Dec. stated that 'whereas . . . this measure is resolved as indispensably necessary, there is every reason to wish that it may not lead to such consequences as would disturb the friendship between Great Britain and the Republic' (*Sandwich Papers* iii. 10).

4. The *Gazetteer and New Daily Advertiser* 7 Jan. commented, 'It is confessed, even by the warmest ministerialists, that such is the fallen state of British policy, that we have been outwitted by our Belgian neighbours, the *heavy* Dutchmen. They carried their point, that of assisting their *friends,* the French; and at the same time have led us to the unpleasant alter-native, of either an immediate rupture, or causing Sir Joseph Yorke to make his *penance* in *sack-cloth* and *ashes,* in the eyes of all Europe, at the *feet* of the *High* and *Mighty Lords* the States General.'

5. John Paul Jones (1747–92), American naval officer (Mason i. 467, nn. 4, 6). The *Morning Chronicle* 4 Jan. reported, 'Paul Jones has escaped; it is imagined he crept along the French shore, as close as his ship could sail with any safety.' The *London Chronicle* 1–4 Jan. (xlvii. 16) stated, 'Paul Jones was not in company with the above [Dutch] fleet, as reported, but sailed out of the Texel in a foggy night about a fortnight ago in a single ship (the *Alliance*); and from the Dutch Admiral's account, went north about, to avoid the frigates that were cruising for him.' Jones with his squadron had taken shelter in the Texel 3 Oct. 1779, where he waited for the exchange of his English prisoners and the settlement of his prizes. On 27 Dec. in the American ship *Alliance* he escaped from the Texel, eluding the English warships, and sailed south through the English Channel; he was off Cape Finisterre 8 Jan. and reached Corunna 16 Jan. (Mrs Reginald de Koven, *The Life and Letters of John Paul Jones,* New York, 1913, ii. 8, 44, 55–6; Gardner W. Allen, *A Naval History of the American Revolution,* Boston, 1913, ii. 484–5).

6. See headnote.

From CONWAY, Saturday 3 June 1780

Printed for the first time from the MS, now WSL. For the history of the MS, see *ante* 9 Aug. 1767.

Endorsed (by HW): General Conway to Mr Horace Walpole. June 3d 1780.

Sat[urday], near 3.

I HAVE received a letter and communication of so extraordinary a kind and from so extraordinary a quarter this morning that I am very impatient to communicate it to you and talk with you upon it.[1] I would have come to you this moment but that I have just made a long and hot walk from the Tower[2] and am not sure of finding you at home. I shall dress now and then will either expect you here,[3] or come to you before my dinner abroad as you like best.[4]

Yours, etc.

H. S. C.

1. In *Last Journals, sub* 3 June (ii. 307–8), HW wrote, 'The same day happened a very extraordinary negotiation. General Conway received a letter from an inferior person, who said he was authorized to acquaint him that the King had a mind to make a change in the Administration, and would leave it entirely to General Conway to form a new one, his Majesty excepting but three persons whom he would not remove—the Chancellor, Lord Sandwich, and Lord George Germaine, the latter of whom the letter declared *had the King's confidence*, which Lord North had forfeited by his indolence and inactivity. . . . it was proposed to Mr Conway to meet Lord George Germaine at night, as by accident, at the letter-writer's house, who had a door into the Park. Mr Conway immediately sent for me. . . .'

2. Possibly in connection with providing military protection against the Gordon rioters. The inadequate police force against the mobs assembled around, and in, the Houses of Parliament on Friday 2 June was discussed in both Houses 3 June; see *Morning Chronicle* 5 June; *London Chronicle* 3–6 June, xlvii. 539–41; MASON ii. 53–4, n. 16; MANN ix. 53.

3. Conway lived in Little Warwick Street, Charing Cross (*Royal Kalendar*, 1780, p. 56).

4. HW went to Conway, when Conway 'showed me the letter, and asked my opinion. I said at once that it was the silliest plan I had ever seen of the sort, and that I thought he could not give in to it; that the proposed change was no real one, would render things worse, not better, for Lord George Germaine was much more unpopular than Lord North, whom the King was betraying; and that Mr Conway's friends would certainly not accede. . . . He said he had abstained from speaking till he had heard my opinion; and that he agreed with me in every point; that he did not like treating with Lord George Germaine, nor could approve of him; and then, dashing down the letter with warmth very unusual to him, he said, "And to think I would act a moment with Lord Sandwich!" ' (*Last Journals* ii. 308–9). Conway then 'wrote an answer . . . declining the negotiation' (ibid. ii. 309, 319).

From HERTFORD, Tuesday 13 June 1780

Printed for the first time from a photostat of BM Add. MSS 23219, f. 118. Dated by the contents (see below, n. 4). Hertford is apparently writing from London to HW at Strawberry Hill, where he went on Friday 9 June, returning 16 June (see OSSORY ii. 191, 193, and below, n. 8).

Dear Horry,

YOU will be rejoiced to hear that the report about a second attack on Jersey, which was near carrying my brother there, does not turn out to be a true one.[1] Lord Sandwich told me yesterday the Admiralty had received accounts from thence on Sunday.[2]

We are quiet here, but I believe we owe it to the military force.[3] I heard the examinations of the keepers of the prisons yesterday.[4] I

1. Lt-Gov. Moses Corbet wrote Lord Hillsborough from Jersey 31 May and again 6 June (in a letter endorsed 'R. 12th') regarding an 'armament . . . making at Saint-Malo,' 'most probably intended for this island' (S.P. 47/9, No. 81), and the newspapers reported Conway's setting out 9 June 'from his house in Warwick Street for Portsmouth, to embark for his Government of Jersey, on account of . . . advices . . . [of] a second attempt on that island' (Morning Chronicle 13 June; London Chronicle 10–13 June, xlvii. 561); but HW wrote Lady Ossory 16 June that 'the alarm was ill-founded' (OSSORY ii. 199 and n. 15).

2. 11 June; these accounts have not been found. Lloyd's Evening Post 16–19 June (xlvi. 584) and the Morning Chronicle 19 June reported dispatches being received 16 June 'from the islands of Jersey and Guernsey by a cutter which arrived from the above places on Thursday morning at Portsmouth; and on Saturday [17 June] a Council was held on the above, and a messenger sent off express with the necessary directions, in case of any visit from the French, which is seriously expected to happen, from the great preparations making at the contiguous ports.'

3. Hertford is referring to the Gordon Riots which began 2 June; for HW's accounts see OSSORY ii. 174–93 and MASON

ii. 51–60. According to the London Chronicle 10–13 June (xlvii. 561, 568), 'Orders are given for an additional regiment to be added to the troops already encamped in St James's Park. . . . The grand camp in Hyde Park consists of . . . nine . . . regiments. . . . The number of troops now in town exceeds 15,000.' The Public Advertiser 14 June commented, 'The Cities of London and Westminster were never so well guarded nor so peaceable as at present. In the night-time there is not the least noise heard in any of the streets, but everything is profoundly still.' Lord Mount Stuart wrote Col. Charles Stuart 12 June, 'We are now in as peaceful a situation here as ever London was. . . . What the rioters might not do if the military were removed, there is great difference of opinion' (A Prime Minister and his Son, ed. Hon. Mrs E. Montagu-Stuart-Wortley, 1925, p. 191).

4. 'I was at Council this morning [12 June], where all the principal keepers of prisons in London were very minutely examined about the late riots; some of them were justices of the peace—other magistrates were examined yesterday and the day before, in order to ground proofs against the delinquents, of whom many are apprehended' (ibid.). The Daily Adv. 13 June reported, 'The same day [12 June] a Privy Council was held at the Queen's

learnt from them that it had been a premeditated plan to burn and destroy, and I fear there is too much reason to think it has a deeper foundation than the repeal of the Popery Act would remove.⁵ What may happen in Ireland I cannot say;⁶ at present they are returning to their senses and do not mean to quarrel or at least to separate from us.⁷ The repeal of the Act in question would not be pleasing to the papists there.

Palace, at which all the great officers of state assisted.'

5. The anti-Catholic sentiment created by the Catholic relief bill of 1778, 18 Geo. III, c. 60, 'An Act for relieving his Majesty's subjects professing the popish religion from certain penalties and disabilities imposed on them' (Owen Ruffhead, *Statutes at Large*, 1763–1800, xiii. 290–1; MASON i. 395, n. 10), led to the mass meeting of the Protestant Association on 2 June 1780, after which Lord George Gordon presented to the House of Commons a 'petition, signed by nearly 120,000 of his Majesty's Protestant subjects, praying for a repeal of the Act passed the last session in favour of Roman Catholics' (Cobbett, *Parl. Hist.* xxi. 656; MASON ii. 51, n. 2); Conway's motion to consider the petitions was passed 6 June (OSSORY ii. 178, n. 40; 191 and nn. 33, 37). Lord Mount Stuart after the Council meeting 12 June agreed with Hertford that 'It seems to be the opinion that the Act (the pretended cause of all these disturbances) should not be repealed' (to Col. Charles Stuart 12 June, in Montagu-Stuart-Wortley, op. cit. 192), and Hertford the same day wrote John Hely Hutchinson that 'popery and religion . . . might be the motive with which the people were misled, but I cannot help suspecting that it has a political foundation, and has been supported and encouraged by foreign enemies' (quoted J. Paul de Castro, *The Gordon Riots*, 1926, p. 217; see also Montagu-Stuart-Wortley, op. cit. 193; MASON ii. 62 and n. 1; OSSORY ii. 199 and n. 11; *Last Journals* ii. 322; MANN ix. 66–7 and nn. 5–9).

6. Lord Hillsborough wrote the E. of Buckinghamshire, lord lieutenant of Ireland, 11 June, 'I think it fit to inform

your Excellency that Lord George Gordon in the course of his examination yesterday informed us that he had received a letter from the Protestants in and near Killarney in Ireland, desiring his Lordship's advice how they should behave as they were under great apprehensions from the Papists in that part' (quoted in De Castro, op. cit. 192–3).

7. In April, Henry Grattan had moved three resolutions declaring the rights of the Irish Parliament, and Barry Yelverton had moved to amend Poynings' Act (6 George I, c. 5) which stated the right of the British Parliament to make laws binding on Ireland; see Buckinghamshire's letters to Hillsborough 20, 21, 29 April 1780 in Henry Grattan, *Memoirs*, ed. Grattan, 1839–46, ii. 51–5, 78–80 and also ibid. ii. 44, 48–50. During May the Irish pressed for an Irish Mutiny Bill to replace the British Mutiny Act which controlled the army in Ireland; the Irish Bill was moved by Gervase Bushe 22 May, transmitted to England at the beginning of June, and passed the Commons 17 Aug. (*Journals of the House of Commons . . . Ireland*, xix. 419–20, 427, 432, 434, 436, 439, 495–6). It passed the Irish Lords in two days and received the royal assent 19 Aug. Although he could not stop the Irish Mutiny Bill, Buckinghamshire wrote Hillsborough 24 May, 'I have been careful that the minds of men should be impressed with just ideas of the consequences, injurious to Great Britain and fatal to this country, if the legislative authority of the one should be formally denied by the other; and the language of the day leads me to indulge a hope that the impression is made, and that prudence and moderation will resume their influence' (Grattan, op. cit. ii. 92).

We are beset with difficulties. Troops, peace and a little time may I hope produce a favourable change. Yours, dear Horry,

Most truly,

Hertford

You must know that the King is reconciled to his brothers of Gloucester and Cumberland.[8]

From Lady Hertford, Thursday 7 ?December ?1780

Printed for the first time from a photostat of BM Add. MSS 23219, f. 170.
Address: To the Honourable Hor. Walpole.

Thursday the 7th.

Sir,

WHEN I desired my Lord to ask you to dine with us tomorrow, I own it was with a view to treat Doctor Barnard[1] and Doctor Hunter, as I know they are both upon the list of your most devoted admirers; but since, I have recollected that you are so fond of dining at home[2] that you may perhaps be more inclined to that than to dine here, in which case I would give you up, though not without acknowledging it would be a great disappointment to me as

8. Who had had audiences with the King on 11 and 12 June (Mann ix. 63, n. 6). HW heard of the reconciliation 13 June at SH from his grandniece, Anna Maria Keppel, and on 15 June 'the Duchess [of Gloucester] herself sent me word of it, and desired me to come to town' (Ossory ii. 198); HW went to London 16 June, where Hertford told him that the King had received his brothers but refused to receive their Duchesses (see *Last Journals* ii. 313–19). *The Gazetteer and New Daily Advertiser* 16 June noted, 'It is said, the reason of the Duke of Gloucester's not being at Court yesterday was, that his Duchess will not consent to his Highness's appearing there, unless she is admitted in the same sphere,' and the *London Chronicle* 15–17 June (xlvii. 584)

reported, 'Yesterday morning [16 June] his Royal Highness the Duke of Gloucester was with his Majesty near two hours at the Queen's Palace; and on Thursday evening their Royal Highnesses the Duchesses of Gloucester and Cumberland paid a private visit to her Majesty, and were very graciously received.'

1. Probably Edward Barnard (1717–81), D.D. 1756; headmaster of Eton, 1756; provost, 1765.
2. HW wrote to Lady Ossory 27 Oct. 1779 about his 'seldom dining abroad,' and to Mann 3 March 1780, 'I have renounced dining abroad, and hide myself as much as I can' (Ossory ii. 130; Mann ix. 22).

well as to our guests. My Lord has no vacancy at the Hospital,[3] nor has no chance of getting a patient in these nineteen weeks; upon hearing this, my Lord sent to know who had vacancies and received the enclosed list.[4] I need not tell you that my Lord's best services are always at your command, and that he is unhappy when he cannot obey them. We shall still hope to see you tomorrow. I am

Most faithfully yours,

I. H.

To Conway, Tuesday 2 January 1781

Missing; mentioned *post* 3 Jan. 1781.

To Conway, Wednesday 3 January 1781

Printed from *Works* v. 213–14.

January 3, 1781.

AFTER I had written my note[1] to you last night, I called on ——,[2] who gave me the dismal account of Jamaica, that you will see in the *Gazette,*[3] and of the damage done to our shipping.[4] Admiral

3. Hertford, after being sworn of the Privy Council in 1763, would have been an ex-officio governor of the Royal Naval Hospital at Greenwich. He was also a vice-president of St George's Hospital ca 1771–94 (*Court and City Register, passim*), and HW had apparently inquired if a place was free for an unidentified patient he wished to place there.
4. Missing.

1. Missing.
2. Not identified.
3. The *London Gazette* No. 12149, 30 Dec. 1780 – 2 Jan. 1781 prints a letter of 20 Oct. from Maj.-Gen. John Dalling, Gov. of Jamaica, to Lord George Germain, which reports that 'On Monday the 2d instant, the weather being very close, the sky on a sudden became very much over-

cast, and an uncommon elevation of the sea immediately followed. Whilst the unhappy settlers at Savanna la Mar were observing this extraordinary phenomenon, the sea broke suddenly in upon the town, and on its retreat swept everything away with it, so as not to leave the smallest vestige of man, beast, or house behind. This most dreadful catastrophe was succeeded by the most terrible hurricane than ever was felt in this country, with repeated shocks of an earthquake, which has almost totally demolished every building in the parishes of Westmoreland, Hanover, part of St James's, and some part of Elizabeth's, and killed numbers of the white inhabitants as well as of the negroes.' See also Mason ii. 90 and n. 4.
4. A list of merchant ships lost in the hurricane at Jamaica is in the *Morning*

Rowley[5] is safe; but they are in apprehensions for Walsingham.[6] He told me too what is not in the *Gazette;* that of the expedition against the Spanish settlements, not a single man survives![7] The papers today, I see, speak of great danger to Gibraltar.[8]

Your brother[9] repeated to me his great desire that you should publish your speech,[10] as he told you. I do not conceive why *he* is so

Chronicle 4 Jan. and in *Lloyd's Evening Post* 3–5 Jan., xlviii. 19.

5. Joshua Rowley (1734–90), naval officer, cr. (1786) Bt (Mann vi. 578, ix. 105–6). The Admiralty office received 1 Jan. an express from Vice-Adm. Sir Peter Parker, commander-in-chief of his Majesty's ships and vessels at Jamaica, dated 6 Nov. 1780, which said, 'On the 26th Rear-Admiral Rowley arrived in the *Grafton* with the following ships, from convoying the Trade part of their way to Europe, viz. *Hector, Bristol, Trident* and *Ruby,* all of them disabled, and mostly dismasted' (*London Gazette* loc. cit.).

6. Hon. Robert Boyle Walsingham (1736–80), M.P.; Capt. R.N., 1757; commodore, 1780 (Ossory ii. 48, n. 4): he was lost in the hurricane.

7. On 4 Jan. HW wrote this news also to Mason and to Lady Ossory (Mason ii. 90–1 and n. 10; Ossory ii. 263 and n. 9), and in *Last Journals,* commented, 'On this the Government said not a word' (ii. 343). The expedition was sent by Gov. Dalling from Jamaica against Fort San Juan in Nicaragua in the spring of 1780, although Sir Peter Parker disapproved of decreasing the defences of the island by so many troops (*Sandwich Papers* iii. 150). A list of the forces sent out (totalling 1379) is in G. W. Bridges, *Annals of Jamaica,* 1828, ii. 470–1.

8. *Lloyd's Evening Post* 1–3 Jan., xlviii. 14, reported, 'On Monday [1 Jan.] a dispatch was received from Gibraltar. It is reported, that the activity and diligence of the Spaniards has increased so much lately, that almost every avenue is shut up for the procuring of provisions, and that out of ten Barbary vessels which sail for their relief, there is seldom above one that can so far elude the vigilance of the enemy as to effect an entry into the harbour. The garrison have already been put on allowance, and Governor Elliot expresses the strongest apprehensions for the

safety of the place if some mode of introducing a supply of necessaries is not immediately thought of. This will be difficult to effect, for the Governor farther states, that the Cadiz squadron is hovering in the environs, and makes it almost impossible for any victualling vessel to approach, if a force is not sent out to keep the enemy at a distance.' Gen. Eliott had written Lord Hillsborough 1 Dec. 1780, 'An ample supply of all ordnance engineer stores and ammunition must be sent, the daily expenditure very great by the constant firing to be kept up on the enemy's slow approach and on their gun boats. . . . At least two thousand more troops with camp necessaries are indispensably wanted. . . . The Spaniards will now persevere in the attack, sparing no expense— We must be supported from home' (W. O. 34/129, f. 18; *Morning Chronicle* 7 Jan.).

9. Deleted in *Works* but restored by Wright.

10. Introductory of a motion 'for leave to bring in a bill for quieting the troubles that have for some time subsisted between Great Britain and America, and enabling his Majesty to send out commissioners with full power to treat with America for that purpose' (HW). The speech, delivered 5 May 1780, is reported in Cobbett, *Parl. Hist.* xxi. 570–6; the bill which Conway proposed is printed ibid. 588–91. Conway's speech was published 23 Jan. 1781, according to HW's note in his copy (now wsl); see Mason ii. 96, n. 6. In *Last Journals, sub* 6 May 1780, HW wrote, 'General Conway moved for a bill for pacifying America. He had long meditated his plan, and had communicated it both to the Administration and Opposition. The former would not explain their intentions to him; the others were but part for it. . . . Charles Fox supported Conway warmly, but Lord George Germaine and Lord North opposed it, and even T. Pitt' (ii. 303).

eager for it; for he professes total despair about America. It looks to me as if there was a wish of throwing blame somewhere[11]—but I profess I am too simple to dive into the objects of shades of intrigues; nor do I care about them. We shall be reduced to a miserable little island; and from a mighty empire sink into as insignificant a country as Denmark or Sardinia! When our trade and marine are gone, the latter of which we keep up by unnatural efforts,[12] to which our debt will put a stop, we shall lose the East Indies as Portugal did;[13] and then France will dictate to us more imperiously than ever we did to Ireland, which is in a manner already gone too![14] These are mortifying reflections, to which an English mind cannot easily accommodate

11. The news of Cornwallis's retreat in South Carolina, which reached London 28 Dec. 1780, had destroyed the Administration's hopes of capturing the southern colonies (Charles, Lord Cornwallis, *Correspondence*, ed. C. Ross, 1859, i. 62–5, 69, 87; I. R. Christie, *The End of North's Ministry 1780–1782*, 1958, p. 243, n. 1; Hist. MSS Comm., *Stopford-Sackville MSS*, 1904–10, ii. 185–6). HW recorded this news in *Last Journals, sub* 30 Dec. (ii. 341) and commented, 'I saw a letter that came by that very mail from Colonel [Charles] O'Hara to General Conway, describing the embarrassed situation of Clinton, the aversion of the Carolinians, who were described here as returning to their allegiance, declaring he trembled for Lord Cornwallis . . . and professing his firm belief of the impossibility of our recovering America.' HW suggested in *Last Journals* that the Opposition was blamed: 'The people were told and believed that the Opposition encouraged America, and that several rich persons had been ruined by sending money thither. . . . and the Government that had precipitated us into all these calamities and had achieved nothing, was more popular' (ii. 342).

12. There were two classes of bounties which benefited the merchant marine and kept in active service a number of ships and seamen who could be called upon for the royal navy in time of war: (1) subsidies to fisheries for individual vessels fulfilling certain qualifications; and (2) bounties for naval stores, called 'the premium on naval stores,' for which the importers were required to give the navy an option to buy the supplies if needed

(J. E. D. Binney, *British Public Finance and Administration 1774–1792*, Oxford, 1958, pp. 135–7).

13. In the late 16th century the Dutch and English merchant vessels began to challenge the Portuguese monopoly of trade in the East Indies, and by 1633 Portugal had lost its control (F. C. Danvers, *The Portuguese in India*, New York, 1966, ii. 108–10, 237–40, 247, 331–3, 374–5). During the 18th century the power of the English East India Company increased so decisively that by 1761 the English were dominant (ibid. ii. 433–4 and n., 436, 440–2; MANN vi. 478–9, nn. 2, 4).

14. See *ante* 13 June 1780, n. 7. Although the Lord Lieutenant, Buckinghamshire, had manœuvred through the Irish House of Commons the Mutiny Bill and Sugar Bill as altered by the English Privy Council, Henry Grattan and other Irish leaders continued to work toward the legislative independence of the Irish Parliament (Buckinghamshire to Hillsborough 17 Aug., 19 Nov. 1780 in Henry Grattan, *Memoirs*, ed. Grattan, 1839–46, ii. 126–7, 169–70; see also ibid. ii. 191–3). During the summer of 1780 the Irish Volunteers were increased and strengthened, and they published resolutions supporting 'the strenuous, though unsuccessful efforts of the minority of the [Irish] House of Commons, in defence of our constitution and commerce' (ibid. ii. 129–31, 147–9; Rev. Patrick Rogers, *The Irish Volunteers and Catholic Emancipation*, 1934, pp. 51–4). The independence of the Irish Parliament was not achieved until 1782; see *post* 30 Oct. 1782.

itself—but, alas! we have been pursuing the very conduct that France would have prescribed, and more than with all her presumption she could have dared to expect. Could she flatter herself that we would take no advantage of the dilatoriness and unwillingness of Spain to enter into the war? [15] that we would reject the disposition of Russia to support us? [16] and that our still more natural friend Holland would be driven into the league against us? [17] All this has happened; and, like an infant, we are delighted with having set our own frock in a blaze!—I sit and gaze with astonishment at our frenzy—yet why? Are not nations as liable to intoxication as individuals? Are not predictions founded on calculation oftener rejected than the

15. The 'Declaración' delivered by the Spanish ambassador, Almodóvar, to Lord Weymouth 16 June 1779, presented Spain's grievances and reasons for entering the war 'notwithstanding the pacific dispositions of his Majesty, and even the particular inclination he has always had and expressed for cultivating the friendship of his Britannic Majesty' (translation in Journals of the House of Commons, xxxvii. 453–4; MANN viii. 482–3 and nn. 1, 5, 486 and n. 3, 492 and n. 7; ix. 32, n. 6; MASON ii. 65, n. 24; ante 16 June, 10 July 1779).

16. Catherine II's declaration of 28 Feb. 1780 OS to the Courts of London, Versailles, and Madrid stated Russia's five regulations for armed neutrality; see MANN ix. 39, n. 10. The British objected to the proposal because it would destroy their power to blockade a harbour; Stormont wrote the King 1 April 1780, 'The second article if adhered to would totally destroy all that has been so properly resolved with regard to the Dutch. . . . It strikes me . . . that the best method of answering this declaration will be to answer it in very civil general terms, and to instruct Sir J. Harris to take a fit opportunity of explaining the mistake upon which the second article proceeds, and the consequences to which it would lead highly pernicious to this country, and therefore contrary to her I. Majesty's friendly intentions' (Geo. III's Corr., ed. Fortescue, v. 38–9; Sir F. Piggott and G. W. T. Omond, Documentary History of the Armed Neutralities, 1919, pp. 209–11). But Sir James Harris was unable to block the Empress's agreements with Denmark, Sweden, and the United Provinces (Sir James Harris, Diaries and Correspondence, ed. Lord Malmesbury, 1844, i. 270–80, 283–4; Christie, op. cit. 16, 244–5; Piggott and Omond, op. cit. 233, 239, 247).

17. The Dutch claimed, under the Anglo-Dutch treaty of 1674, the right to carry naval stores and some other supplies in neutral ships to ports of countries at war with Britain. The British claimed that by the later Anglo-Dutch treaties of 1678 and 1716 the United Provinces were required to give naval and military assistance to Britain against any belligerent power. On 21 March 1780 Sir Joseph Yorke delivered a memorial to the States General of the United Provinces complaining that the Dutch had failed to provide any assistance and had continued to transport supplies to France, thus negating the British blockade of France (ibid. 146–8). Since the Dutch made no satisfactory answer to these remonstrances, the British on 17 April 1780 announced the suspension of Anglo-Dutch treaties and the determination to subject Dutch ships to search for contraband supplies (ibid. 148–50; Annual Register 1780, pp. 342–6). On 11 Oct. 1780 Lord Stormont wrote Yorke that if the Dutch acceded to the Russian proposal for armed neutrality, the British would have 'no alternative' but to treat them as an enemy; on 20 Oct. Yorke wrote that the Dutch had withdrawn their demand for a guarantee of their territories by Russia (quoted in Christie, op. cit. 245–6). On 20 Nov. the States General voted to join the armed neutrality (Ossory ii. 259, nn. 6, 8; MANN ix. 104–5; MASON ii. 89–90, n. 1).

prophecies of dreamers? Do we not act precisely like Charles Fox, who thought he had discovered a new truth in figures, when he preached that wise doctrine, that nobody could want money that would pay enough for it?—The consequence was, that in two years he left himself without the possibility of borrowing a shilling.[18] I am not surprised at the spirits of a boy of parts—I am not surprised at the people—I do wonder at Government, that games away its consequence. For what are we now really at war with America, France, Spain, and Holland?—Not with hopes of reconquering America, not with the smallest prospect of conquering a foot of land from France, Spain, or Holland—no; we are at war on the defensive, to protect what is left, or more truly to stave off, for a year perhaps, a peace that must proclaim our nakedness and impotence. I would not willingly recur to that womanish vision of, 'Something may turn up in our favour!' That something must be a naval victory that will annihilate at once all the squadrons of Europe—must wipe off forty millions of new debt—reconcile the affections of America, that for six years we have laboured to alienate—and that must recall out of the grave the armies and sailors that are perished—and that must make thirteen provinces willing to receive the law, without the necessity of keeping ten thousand men amongst them. The gigantic imagination of Lord Chatham would not entertain such a chimera. Lord ———[19] perhaps would say he did, rather than not undertake; or Mr Burke could form a metaphoric vision, that would satisfy no imagination but his own: but I, who am *nullius addictus jurare in verba*,[20] have no hopes either in our resources or in our geniuses, and look on my country already as undone!—It is grievous—but I shall not have much time to lament its fall!

18. HW compared the nation's financial imprudence to Charles Fox's also in a letter to Mann 15 Feb. 1775 (MANN viii. 81), and repeats anecdotes of Fox's dealings with money-lenders in *Last Journals* i. 7, 12; OSSORY i. 166 and n. 15; MANN vii. 530.

19. Not identified, but probably Lord North.

20. 'Nullius addictus jurare in verba magistri,' 'not addicted to swear in the words of any master' (Horace, *Epistolæ* I. i. 14).

From HERTFORD, Monday 8 January 1781

Printed for the first time from a photostat of BM Add. MSS 23219, f. 123. Dated by the contents; see below, n. 1 and MANN ix. 110.
Address: The Honourable Hor. Walpole.

Monday, past one.

Dear Horry,

OUR troubles are again to begin. An express[1] is just come that the French have landed 4500[2] on the island of Jersey and taken the Lieutenant-Governor;[3] an express[4] is gone to my brother to send him there. Alas, alas!

HERTFORD

1. On 8 Jan. Amherst received an express brought by Lt Jonathan Anderson of the 83d Foot at 3 A.M., and another brought by Lt Durell Saumarez of the 78th Foot at 4 A.M. (*London Chronicle* 6–9 Jan., xlix. 42; Amherst to Monckton 8 Jan., W.O. 34/236, f. 436). He also received a packet from Lt-Gov. P. Æ. Irving of Guernsey containing the first reports from Lt-Gov. Moses Corbet and Lt-Col. James Pipon of Jersey, all dated 6 Jan. (Irving to Amherst 6 Jan., W.O. 34/107, ff. 8, 10, 18); Amherst replied 8 Jan. to Irving, 'I have this morning received yours of the 6th which, I need not tell you surprised me very much. I could not suppose at the first moment, that the whole island could be in possession of the French, and a second account from Lt Anderson of the 83d regiment says they have landed 3,500 men and the Lt-Governor is taken prisoner, a very unlucky circumstance, but I must flatter myself there will be spirit enough in the troops to retake what the enemy may have surprised and to regain the full possession of the island' (W.O. 34/236, f. 434). Conway later wrote Hillsborough 2 Sept. that 'the earliest intelligence received by Government on that occasion' was brought by the corsair *Le Hazard* to Admiral Sir Thomas Pye at Portsmouth (S.P. 47/9). The arrival of the various expresses is reported in the *Morning Chronicle* and *Morning Herald* for 9 Jan.; see also Geo. III's *Corr.* ed. Fortescue, v. 180–1.

2. The early reports exaggerated the numbers of the French forces (see MANN ix. 110 and n. 2); Lt-Gov. Moses Corbet wrote Hillsborough from Jersey 9 Jan., 'Of this embarkation only 800 men landed, about 200 were drowned in boats among the rocks: they also lost their artillery; and about 300 with a major and some other officers remained on board their craft off the Bank du Viellet' (S.P. 47/9).

3. Moses Corbet (d. 1817), Lt-Gov. of Jersey 1771–81 (see MANN ix. 111, n. 3). Corbet wrote P. Æ. Irving 6 Jan. from Jersey, 'I am now to acquaint you that the French landed this morning about two o'clock between two posts so distant that the guards did not perceive them or probably the guards of the militia of the East Regiment on duty there were asleep . . . they marched across the roads and were in the market place by 6 o'clock this morning. I was taken prisoner about seven' (W.O. 34/107, f. 20). In his letter of 7 Jan. to Hillsborough Corbet says, 'I had just time to dispatch him [Capt. Clement Hemery] at a venture, to give notice of it to the 83d in Grouville Bay, and another messenger across the country to the 78th and the 95th and they were scarce gone from me when I was made a prisoner, and carried to the courthouse, where the French General was, who immediately proposed for me to enter into terms for the surrender of the island' (S.P. 47/9).

4. The express from the Council ordering Conway to Jersey 'went to him at Park

My son[5] is running to get leave to go with him.

From HERTFORD, Tuesday 9 January 1781

Printed for the first time from a photostat of BM Add. MSS 23219, f. 121.
Dated by the contents.
Address: Honourable Hor. Walpole.

Tuesday, 1 o'clock.[1]

Dear Horry,

I THINK you need now entertain no doubt for the future case of Jersey;[2] my brother will certainly proceed to see everything settled,[3] and to confirm the islanders in their spirited attachment to this drooping country.[4]

Place at eleven; he was in town by three, though with a broken arm not quite recovered, and set out in two hours for Portsmouth' (*Last Journals* ii. 343; OSSORY ii. 264–5). He conferred with Lord Hillsborough, as a note to Hillsborough 8 Jan. from Little Warwick St indicates, and wrote him from Portsmouth 9 Jan., 'On my arrival here I found nothing but the *Emeralde* frigate ready to sail immediately, on board of which I am going to embark. . . . PS. Past 9 A.M. The *Emeralde* will be ready to sail in about an hour and half' (S.P. 47/9). Amherst in a letter to Lt-Gen. Monckton 8 Jan. wrote, 'The intelligence has been sent to Gen. Conway, his health has been bad lately, what he may do on this occasion I do not know' (W.O. 34/236, ff. 436–7).

5. Hon. Robert Seymour-Conway (*ante* ?10 Feb. 1776, n. 3), aide-de-camp to Gen. Clinton in America, 1780 (see Namier and Brooke iii. 425). He sailed with Conway from Portsmouth; see *post* 14 Jan. 1781 and OSSORY ii. 269.

————

1. In *Last Journals*, sub 9 Jan. HW wrote, 'At noon an express from Guernsey that the troops in Jersey had rallied, attacked the French, gained a complete victory, taken 500 prisoners, and driven 400 into the sea' (ii. 343; see also MANN ix. 111).

2. A *London Gazette Extraordinary* 9

Jan. printed an extract from Lt-Gov. Moses Corbet's letter of 6 Jan. which described the recapture of Saint-Hélier by the English troops and the surrender of the French (MANN ix. 111, n. 6). Amherst had received this news the day before (*ante* 8 Jan. 1781, n. 1).

3. HW repeats this comment to Lady Ossory 9 Jan. (OSSORY ii. 265). Lt-Gen. Monckton wrote Amherst from Portsmouth 9 Jan., 'I had the honour to receive your Lordship's letter of yesterday, this morning at 4 o'clock by Lieut-Col. Staunton. General Conway arrived about seven, and went off to St Helens about half past ten o'clock, with a prospect of having a very short passage, the wind being very fair. The ships with the 14th and 97th regiments will not sail till the evening, if then. General Conway having desired to be assisted with tents, blankets, kettles, entrenching tools, and some other necessaries for the field, everything of this sort at Jersey being in Elizabeth Castle—I purpose forwarding by the ships which sail this evening—everything our stores can afford—which I hope will meet with your Lordship's approbation' (W.O. 34/107, f. 24). Conway was unable to reach Jersey, and his ship returned to Plymouth; see *post* 14 Jan. 1781, n. 5.

4. The *Morning Chronicle* 10 Jan. commented, 'The spirited and valiant conduct of the Jersey-men on Saturday last is a

Lord Stormont has already sent an express to Lady Ailesbury.[5]

Yours most truly,

HERTFORD

From HERTFORD, Thursday 11 January 1781

Printed for the first time from a photostat of BM Add. MSS 23219, f. 125.
Address: Honourable Hor. Walpole.

Thursday.

Dear Horry,

THE time will not allow us to hear of my brother's arrival there.[1] The French numbers which arrived on that coast were 12 hundred,[2] four [hundred] of which were drowned in landing; the rest succeeded in the surprise[3] as you know. They were afterwards

second instance of their loyalty to their Royal Master, their love of liberty, their zeal for their country's welfare, and their detestation of French government, which is but another phrase for despotism and tyranny. By their successful efforts, France has again been baffled in her hostile attempts against the island.' See also *London Chronicle* 11–13 Jan., xlix. 42. Thomas Pipon wrote Conway from Jersey 8 Jan., 'I am happy in transmitting to your Excellency this fresh proof of the loyalty of the inhabitants of this island, whom no danger or considerations could deter from their duty, but by the most determined courage manifested their firm attachment to his Majesty's person and government; and I make no doubt your Excellency will represent us in such light to his Majesty as to insure to this island the continuance of his royal favour and protection' (enclosure in Conway to Hillsborough 21 Jan. 1781, S.P. 47/9).

5. The *London Chronicle* 6–9 Jan. (xlix. 32) reported, 'We are happy to be able to inform our readers, that an express is just arrived from Jersey at Lord Stormont's office, with the agreeable intelligence that the militia and regular troops had assembled, and made a successful attack on

their invaders, and taken them prisoners. . . . An Extraordinary Gazette will appear this evening with the particulars.'

———

1. Conway's letter to Hillsborough 11 Jan. reporting his arrival at Plymouth did not reach London until 14 Jan. (see *post* 14 Jan. 1781, n. 5).

2. This estimate of the French forces was given in a report of the officers of the 83d and 95th regiments: 'The enemy . . . embarked 1200 men, 200 were drowned in landing and 200 sent back with their transports' (enclosure in Col. John Reid to Amherst 17 Jan., W.O. 34/107, f. 45). For various reports on the size of the French landing force see MANN ix. 110–11, n. 2.

3. The capture of Saint-Hélier. Conway wrote Hillsborough 10 Feb., 'The French troops were actually embarked and at sea in their boats no less than thirteen days, viz. from the 24th December till early on the 6th January following; the first 6 days in the open Road of Cancale, and the rest actually between the coast of France and the island of Jersey; and what almost passes all credibility, the whole of that time unperceived, because we had no cruiser or vessel of any kind out on dis-

defeated[4] and the commanding officer[5] killed; five hundred prisoners are already landed in England[6] and the business is happily and fortunately over, for they had five thousand destined for this expedition on the coast.[7] Yours, dear Horry,

In great haste,

HERTFORD

covery; which gave them the advantage of choosing the most favourable moment for their purpose of surprise, which nothing but such an entire neglect of any watch at sea could have made possible' (S.P. 47/9).

4. The report of the officers of the 83d and 95th regiments stated, 'Major Pierson had detached Captain Fraser with five companies to take a circle and endeavour to get possession of the town hill, which commands the market-place, which was done without any loss—The 78th and 95th regiments marched in columns, with each a regiment of militia and a fieldpiece; the attack was begun from the hill, which was immediately followed by the 78th and 95th with the militia and continued about fifteen minutes; about the middle of the action Major Peirson was killed. At last the enemy threw down their arms and run for shelter into the houses; the French General being wounded threw down his sword and waved a white handkerchief as a signal of surrender. On the colours of the 95th being planted in the square, the firing ceased' (enclosure in Col. John Reid to Amherst 17 Jan., W.O. 34/107, ff. 44–5).

5. Philippe - Charles - Félix Macquart (1744–81), Baron de Rullecourt; Chevalier (MANN ix. 127, n. 4). Lt-Gov. Moses Corbet wrote Hillsborough 7 Jan., 'The enemy finding themselves attacked on all sides gave way, the officers retiring into the court house; the General then took me by the arm, and obliged me to attend him in the midst of the fire, in the market place, saying that as the British troops had chosen to attack him, I should share his fate, and in a few minutes afterwards he was shot in the mouth; I led him back to the market house in the midst of the fire, by which he was wounded in two places, before I could get him in; I had two balls thro' my hat, but fortunately

was not hit' (S.P. 47/9, endorsed, 'R. 11th by Lt McRae').

6. The *London Packet* 10–12 Jan. and *Daily Advertiser* 13 Jan., *sub* Plymouth, reported the arrival of French prisoners from Jersey; see MANN ix. 111, n. 7, 115, n. 4. J.-B. Fuel, French surgeon, reported, 'Le 11, sont arrivés à Plymouth, dans divers paquebots, environ cent cinquante hommes de la légion de Luxembourg . . . qu'il est débarqué cinq cents hommes de la légion, tant à Plymouth qu'à Falmouth et autres ports du comté de Cornouailles' (La Rozière to M. de Ségur 18 Jan., in C. Hippeau, *Le Gouvernement de Normandie au xviie et au xviiie siècle*, Caen, 1863–9, Pt I, ii. 319). Corbet wrote Hillsborough from Jersey 9 Jan., 'I have the honour to send this by an officer [Col. George Scott] of the 83d who goes with a party to guard our last embarkation of the prisoners, which I send in two vessels hired for that purpose, upon the same terms as the transports hired by Government . . . which mode I hope may be approved of, as the number of prisoners required dispatch, our situation admitting of no such nuisance' (S.P. 47/9).

7. A second expedition of about 3000 men, stationed at Granville and St-Malo, was expected to reinforce de Rullecourt; see MANN ix. 128, n. 5; *post* 14 Jan. 1781. Corbet, in his letter to Hillsborough 9 Jan., wrote, 'I am with the King's officers examining their [the enemy's] papers, which are many; they give a very clear explanation of their plan against this island, and it appears evident, that this debarkation was merely intended to take post, and by signal of fire to be made the following night, get reinforced the next day, as I understand, by a legion of 1500 men and 4 battalions of a 1000 men each that were on purpose in the neighbourhood of Granville' (loc. cit., endorsed 'R. 15th via Plymouth').

From HERTFORD, Sunday 14 January 1781

Printed for the first time from a photostat of BM Add. MSS 23219, f. 127. HW wrote the news in this letter to Lady Ossory on 14 Jan. (OSSORY ii. 269) and to Mann on 18 Jan. (MANN ix. 115–16).

Address: Honourable Hor. Walpole.

Sunday.

Dear Horry,

I BELIEVE your mind may be perfectly easy. The French prisoners consider the attempt as quite over, since they did not succeed; if they had, the Chevalier de Luxembourg[1] was to have followed them with five of the best battalions in France.[2] The ship[3] in which my brother and son[4] were was in the worst weather imaginable for two nights, and in great danger. The wind forced them to Plimouth,[5] and they fear the cutter which sailed from Portsmouth is

1. Anne - Paul - Emmanuel - Sigismond de Montmorency-Luxembourg (b. 1742), younger son of the Duc d'Olonne, called 'le Chevalier de Montmorency-Luxembourg'; Lt-Col. in the Régiment Royal, cavalerie; captain of a compagnie des gardes du corps du Roi, 1767; Prince de Luxembourg, 1781; maréchal de camp; chevalier du Saint-Esprit, 1788 (La Chenaye-Desbois xiv. 394; Comte de Colleville and F. Saint-Christo, *Les Ordres du Roi*, [1925], pp. 49, 393; *Répertoire . . . de la Gazette de France*, ed. de Granges de Surgères, 1902–6, iii. 683). He did not intend to lead the expedition himself; see M. Perrot, *Deux expéditions insulaires françaises. Surprise de Jersey en 1781*, 1929, pp. 53, 56, and C. Hippeau, *Le gouvernement de Normandie au xviie et au xviiie siècle*, Caen, 1863–9, Pt I, ii. 301–8, 336–7. Conway wrote Sir Stanier Porten 11 Feb. 1781 that among the papers captured from the French were 'the instructions of the Count de Vaux relative to embarkations and descents; the letter from Paris apparently of the Chevalier de Luxembourgh to the Baron de Rullecour, though without signature; the journal of the Baron de Rullecour, and the *dernières réflexions* of the same' (S.P. 47/9). In *Last Journals* ii. 344, *sub* 9 Jan., HW mentions this 'letter from the Chevalier de Luxem-

bourg, expressing the eagerness of the French King for the expedition.'

2. The components of the second expedition which was ready to embark if de Rullecourt made a successful landing, are listed in Perrot, op. cit. 125–6, 129; see also *ante* 11 Jan. 1781, n. 7. The expedition was ordered to be abandoned by the Duc d'Harcourt 17 Jan. (see Hippeau, op. cit. ii. 306–18; Perrot, op. cit. 123–8, 132; MANN ix. 115).

3. The *Emeralde* frigate.

4. Lt-Col. Robert Seymour-Conway (*ante* 8 Jan. 1781, n. 5). He delivered Conway's letter of 11 Jan. to Hillsborough, which is endorsed, 'R. 14 by Lt-Col. Conway' (S.P. 47/9), brought the news of Conway's safety to HW on 14 Jan., and called on him again the next day to tell him about the voyage (OSSORY ii. 269–70).

5. Conway wrote Hillsborough 11 Jan. from Plymouth, 'Though I have nothing more material to inform your Lordship of than the arrival here of his Majesty's ship *Emeralde* in which I embarked, I think it my duty to trouble your Lordship with a line for that purpose. It was impossible for us to make the islands of Guernsey or Jersey with the winds and weather we had though Capt. Marshal I am certain from his great diligence and activity would have done anything he

lost.[6] Shocking misery; in the midst of all, our friends thank God are well.

Yours ever,

HERTFORD

From LADY AILESBURY, Monday 15 January 1781

Missing. Mentioned in the postscript of HW to Lady Ossory 14 Jan. 1781: 'Monday. Col. Conway was with me an hour this morning and has given me such an account of their voyage as makes me shudder; and I have since received a note from Lady Ailesbury to tell me her husband is in bed with the rheumatism and fatigue' (OSSORY ii. 270).

To HERTFORD, ca Monday 15 January 1781

Missing; answered *post* 17 Jan. 1781.

could for that purpose consistent with the safety of his M[ajesty]'s ship. After beating about therefore from the time we passed the Needles (which was about 5 on Tuesday evening) in hard gales of wind we were obliged to put in here this morning where the *R. Charlotte*, armed ship which had parted company with us in the gale yesterday, soon followed. Your Lordship will have [been] fully apprised of the happy issue of the silly attempt of the French on the island of Jersey, and as I thereby see no particular call for my immediate presence there, unless it be his Majesty's pleasure I should go, I pro-

pose coming soon to town and having the honour to pay my duty to him there' (S.P. 47/9). See also OSSORY loc. cit.; MANN loc. cit.

6. HW mentions the fears for this cutter in his letters to Lady Ossory 14 Jan. and to Mann 18 Jan. (OSSORY ii. 269; MANN loc. cit.). According to depositions enclosed in Conway to Hillsborough 2 Sept. 1781 (S.P. 47/9), the *Sprightly* cutter of Guernsey sailed from Portsmouth 8 Jan. towing the sailboat *Le Hazard;* the latter was lost but the *Sprightly* reached Guernsey 9 Jan.

From HERTFORD, Wednesday 17 January 1781

Printed for the first time from a photostat of BM Add. MSS 23219, f. 119.
Address: To the Honourable Hor. Walpole, Arlington Street [a slip for Berkeley Square].

Grosvenor Street, January 17th 1781.

Dear Horry,

I THANK you for your note[1] and hope in God there is no reason for alarm about my brother.[2] The King was vastly gracious about him, talked aloud about him at the levee[3] and spoke very properly about his illness, and as if it was acquired in his service at a time when he was not very fit for what he has undergone.

Yours ever,

HERTFORD

---

1. Missing.

2. HW expressed his concern about Conway in letters to Mann 18 Jan., to Lady Ossory 25 Jan., and to Mason 27 Jan., and finally went to visit Conway at Park Place from 28 Jan. until the 31st (MANN ix. 115–16, 119; OSSORY ii. 270–1, 272; MASON ii. 96, 99, 100). On 17 Jan. Conway wrote Hillsborough from Park Place, 'The situation I have found myself in for these three last days has thrown me into the greatest anxiety. It was my intention as I believe I informed your Lordship, after passing here in my road from Plymouth which is but twelve miles out of the way to have proceeded immediately to London in order to pay my duty to his Majesty and receive his commands but on the night of my arrival being seized with violent pain in the arm I had some time ago fractured and at the same time with a fever and rheumatic pains all over my body I have been unable for the first three days to stir from my bed, and even with difficulty to move in it. I have been up for a few hours today, and propose the first moment I am able to come to town' (S.P. 47/9, in Lady Ailesbury's hand, signed by Conway).

3. The *Morning Herald* 18 Jan. reported, 'Yesterday there was a levee at St James's, at which but few of the nobility, except the Duke of Montagu, Master of the Horse, and the ministers of state, were present; the Council was put off till Friday; Lords Amherst, Hillsborough, North, and Bellamont had separate conferences previous to his Majesty's going to the play.' According to the *London Chronicle* 16–18 Jan., xlix. 62, 'Last night [17 Jan.] their Majesties were at Drury Lane Theatre. . . attended by the Duke of Montague; the Earls of Waldegrave, Talbot, and Hertford; Lady Hertford, Miss Vernon, and Miss Jefferies.'

From LADY AILESBURY, Sunday 21 January 1781

Printed from the MS now WSL; first printed in Cunningham vii. 502–3. For the history of the MS see *ante* 9 Aug. 1767.

MR Conway is writing to you[1] at this present minute, much against my good-will and advice, but he is too much hurt with that brutal letter of Lord H[illsborough]'s[2] to be quiet till he gives you an account of it; I cannot express the anxiety and indignation I feel at finding him so ungratefully treated,[3] after all he has done and suffered for his duty. I need not recapitulate it to you, yet I can't help repeating his having passed four months in Jersey in '81,[4] and seven months last year,[5] and new-modelling all things with such success in the island as to have had the approbation and thanks of his Majesty.[6] On this occasion you know he rather flew than travelled, and at the peril of his life attempted to get to Jersey,[7] for which he

1. Actually to Hertford, as Lady Ailesbury says at the end of this letter; his letter of 21 Jan., now WSL, is printed in Cunningham vii. 501–2, n. 1, and was sent in the packet which Hertford mentions *post* 23 Jan. 1781.

2. Hillsborough's 'private' and official letters of 19 Jan. to Conway are now WSL (copies in S.P. 47/9), and printed in part in Cunningham vii. 500–1, n. 1. Hillsborough wrote, 'I have received the favour of your private letter dated from Park Place 17 instant [*ante* 17 Jan. 1781, n. 2], and am extremely sorry your intentions of coming to town have been prevented by so disagreeable a cause. The King is very far from wishing you to remove from Park Place a minute sooner than you can do it with perfect safety; and I am directed by his Majesty to send you a further leave of absence from your Government on account of the state of your health, as otherwise the circumstances of that island might seem to require your attendance.'

3. Conway wrote Hertford 21 Jan., 'I have, from the first, thought that there was something wrong at bottom. I had not from Lord Hillsborough the smallest word of approbation, or thanks, on my return, when I explained to him the state of my health from hence [*ante* 17 Jan. 1781, n.

2]. I received from him in return the cold formal letter . . . accompanied with a formal *leave of absence*, on account of my health, which his Lordship styles a *farther leave of absence*, though no leave of absence did actually exist, nor have I, nor any other governor of either island, I apprehend for these fifty years, had any *leaves of absence* at all, except when having voluntarily gone over to the island.'

4. A mistake for 1778; see *ante* 25 June 1778 and next note.

5. That is, 1779, when Conway was there, from May through Nov. (*ante* 8 May 1779, n. 1, 13 Sept. 1779, n. 6). In letters to Hillsborough 25 May 1780 and 10 Feb. 1781 Conway mentions his 'seven months' in Jersey in 1779, and his total of 'eleven months' residence' (S.P. 47/9).

6. The *London Chronicle* 23–5 Nov. 1779 (xlvi. 502) reported, 'On Tuesday evening Gen. Conway arrived in town from his government of Jersey, was yesterday at Court, and laid before his Majesty the state of that island on his departure, which is now so strongly fortified that they are under no apprehension of another visit from the French.'

7. See *ante* 8 Jan. 1781, n. 4; 14 Jan. 1781, n. 5.

has been laid up with a severe illness, which would have proved a dangerous one, had it not been taken in time; and now but beginning to recover, and just getting from his bed. Lord Hillsborough intimates that he is loitering his time away, whilst he should be upon his duty, and making it a favour that the King gives him *leaves* of absences,[8] which never was thought necessary to be given to a Governor before, and only to officers of inferior rank. I must complain to you, to unburthen myself, though Mr Conway will himself I am sure explain the whole affair. I am miserable too that musing over these things should affect his health and retard his recovery,[9] nay rather I am sure it will, for he slept less last night and seems weaker. Mr Mappleton[10] however is very well satisfied with his amendment, and all he finds fault with is that his pulse beats two strokes more than usually it does in a minute, which makes him apprehend the fever is not quite off, and his having a little cough; for as to the rheumatism it is very much diminished indeed; and I should hope the fever also very inconsiderable, as after he eat his chicken yesterday, he was neither hot, or his face flushed.

8. Conway in his reply to Hillsborough 21 Jan. wrote, 'I received the leave of absence which your Lordship tells me his Majesty was pleased to order during the continuance of my illness which I therefore presume I am rather to look upon [as] a formal order to repair to my Government as soon as my health permits for though your Lordship is pleased to call it a farther leave of absence I never was before honoured with any leave of absence in form nor as I imagine any governor of either of the islands for many years past and I must confess I was so conscious that the slightest hint of his Majesty's pleasure was sufficient at any time to make me set out at a moment's warning as the novelty of this form struck me with some apprehension that I might by some means inadvertently have incurred his Majesty's displeasure' (S.P. 47/9; Cunningham vii. 501, n. 1). Hillsborough replied 26 Jan., 'The King saw with satisfaction your zeal and activity in endeavouring to repair to the island, on the late alarming occasion, and I am much concerned that my signifying to you his Majesty's further leave of absence should have been so entirely misunderstood by you as to have given you any cause of uneasiness' (S.P. 47/9); but Hillsborough's letter to Amherst 10 Jan. shows his annoyance and the King's, 'that had the island been conquered much blame would with reason have been thrown on the neglect in letting so many officers be absent' (W.O. 34/171 f. 189).

9. Conway revealed his distress in his letter to Hertford 21 Jan.: 'I look upon this unnecessary and ostentatious leave of absence as, in effect, meant to destroy all idea of confidence in me, to cancel any merit I may have pretended to for my care and assiduity in that government, and to set me in the light of a person wanting the spur and goad of Government to keep me to my duty. . . . So that I seem from henceforth to be considered in the light of a residentiary governor, or other officer of inferior rank, wanting leaves of absence like a colonel and lieutenant-colonel of the garrison; in this situation you see, my dear brother, that his Lordship has contrived to set me agreeably on a seat of thorns.'

10. Presumably the chemist whom Conway later employed for his experiments with coke at Park Place; see *post* 17 Sept. 1782.

I find myself in an error, for I thought Mr Conway was writing to you, whilst he was writing to Lord Hertford,[11] to whom he begs you would go, to see Lord H.'s letter with his answer,[12] etc. By my persuasion, and finding writing fatigues him, he will not write to you today.

It will please you to hear Mr Conway is to try a few grains of James's Powder tonight.

I am affectionately yours,

C. A.

From HERTFORD, Tuesday 23 January 1781

Printed from the MS, now WSL; first printed in Cunningham vii. 500. For the history of the MS see *ante* 9 Aug. 1767.

Address: Honourable Horatio Walpole, Berkley Square.

Grosvenor Street, January 23d 1781.

Dear Horry,

THE extreme badness of the day may prevent my calling upon you; I therefore send you a very disagreeable packet[1] I received last night from my brother. I shall write today[2] and entreat him not to allow such a correspondent as Lord Hillsbro' to affect his feelings[3]

11. See above, n. 1.

12. Lord Hillsborough's 'private' letter of 19 Jan. and Conway's answer of 21 Jan. were enclosed in Conway's letter to Hertford 21 Jan. (see *post* 23 Jan. 1781).

---

1. Which included Hillsborough's official and private letters to Conway 19 Jan. (S.P. 47/9, printed Cunningham vii. 500–1, n. 1), Conway's answer 21 Jan. (ibid.) with two enclosures which Conway had received from Col. Thomas Pipon of Jersey (S.P. 47/9), and Conway's letter to Hertford 21 Jan. (Cunningham vii. 501–2, n. 1). See *ante* 21 Jan. 1781.

2. Hertford's letter is missing.

3. Conway in his letter of 21 Jan. to Hillsborough explained his failure to reach Jersey: 'Had it been possible to make the port of Dartmouth which we attempted, my purpose was to have gone immediately from thence by land to Ports-

mouth in order to embark on board the first ship that might be ready to carry me to Jersey. I had the same intention even when we were drove into Plymouth as the fierceness and obstinacy of the easterly winds which then blew seemed in the opinion of the sailors not to leave the smallest prospect of reaching the island from any western port, but meeting at Plymouth the officer who brought over the French prisoners from whom and others I had so distinct and certain an account of the total defeat of the French weak and ill-conducted expedition that I then changed my mind and thought it would be much more for his Majesty's service that I should have the honour of attending him to receive his commands in England . . .' (S.P. 47/9; Cunningham vii. 501, n. 1). Hillsborough answered 26 Jan., 'To remove all uneasiness that my letter may have occasioned in your mind, I have

and bring him to town before he can return with safety, for which the present weather does not seem calculated.[4]

Yours ever,

HERTFORD

To CONWAY, ca Tuesday 1 May 1781

Missing. HW wrote Conway *post* 6 May 1781, 'I told you in my last, that Tonton was arrived.' Tonton was delivered to HW by 30 April 1781, as HW wrote the Hon. Thomas Walpole on that day (FAMILY 196); see also COLE ii. 270.

From CONWAY, Thursday 3 May 1781

Missing; answered *post* 6 May 1781 in the postscript 8 May.

the pleasure to assure you that your conduct upon this occasion meets with his Majesty's approbation' (S.P. 47/9).

4. On 28 Jan. Conway was still at Park Place and wrote Hillsborough, 'I find myself now so far recovered of my disorder as to have a prospect of being able to come to town in the course of a few days, tho' on account of the extreme badness of the weather I have not yet been permitted to leave my room and am apprehensive, should I undertake the journey without having previously used myself to the air for a few days, I might be in danger of a relapse' (S.P. 47/9). On 10 Feb. he reported to Hillsborough from Park Place, 'I propose following this immediately to town where I shall be ready to receive your Lordship's commands finding my health now in a great measure reestablished' (ibid.). Conway stayed in London until 18 March, spent a few days at Park Place, and embarked for Jersey 24 March, arriving there 26 March (Conway to Hillsborough 17, 27 March, S.P. 47/9).

To Conway, Sunday 6 May 1781

Printed from *Works* v. 214–16.

Strawberry Hill, Sunday evening, May 6, 1781.

I SUPPED with your Countess on Friday at Lord Frederic Campbell's,[1] where I heard of the relief of Gibraltar by Darby.[2] The Spanish fleet kept close in Cadiz:[3]—however, he lifted up his leg, and just squirted contempt on them. As he is disembarrassed of his transports, I suppose their ships will scramble on shore rather than fight. Well, I shall be perfectly content with our fleet coming back in a whole skin. It will be enough to have out-quixoted Don Quixote's own nation.[4] As I knew your Countess would write the next day, I waited till she was gone out of town and would not have much to tell you—not that I have either; and it is giving myself an air, to pretend to know more at Twickenham than she can at Henley. Though it is a bitter north-east, I came hither today to look at my lilacs, though *à la glace,* and to get from pharaoh, for which there is a rage. I doted on it above thirty years ago; but it is not decent to sit up all night now with boys and girls.[5] My nephew, Lord Cholmondeley,[6] the banker *à la mode,* has been demolished. He and his associate Sir Willoughby Aston[7] went early t'other night to Brookes's, before C[harles] F[ox] and F[itzpatrick], who keep a bank there,[8]

1. Who lived in Craig's Court, Charing Cross (*Court and City Register,* 1781, p. 55).

2. George Darby (d. 1790), Vice-Adm., 1779. On 4 May the news reached London that Admiral Darby on 12 April had 'sent safe into Gibraltar 72 transports laden with provisions, ammunition, and stores . . . under a detachment of his squadron, while he remained with the rest at the entrance of the Straits' (*London Chronicle* 3–5 May 1781, xlix. 432; MANN ix. 147, nn. 1, 2).

3. Darby blocked the Spanish fleet in the Bay of Cadiz from which they did not venture to engage in battle in spite of their superiority of numbers (ibid. ix. 147, n. 2; *Last Journals* ii. 360).

4. Mann wrote Hillsborough 8 May that the Court of Spain was 'incensed against the French for not having sent ships to their assistance,' and on 12 May

wrote HW that Spain was determined to avenge the affront by taking Gibraltar (MANN ix. 147, n. 3, 149).

5. HW expresses similar sentiments to Mann 16 May 1781, where he says he has played 'but thrice, and not all night, as I used to do' (ibid. ix. 154).

6. Deleted in *Works,* but restored by Wright. Anthony Storer wrote Lord Carlisle 27 April 1781 that 'Lord Cholmondeley holds a . . . pharaoh bank' (Hist. MSS Comm., 15th Report, App. pt vi, *Carlisle MSS,* p. 477).

7. (ca 1748–1815), 6th Bt, 1772; deleted in *Works,* but restored by Wright. George Selwyn wrote Carlisle 21 May 1781, 'At Devonshire House there had been a bank held by Sir W. Aston and Grady, and that won 700 [guineas]' (*Carlisle MSS,* p. 484).

8. Selwyn wrote Carlisle 24 April 1781, 'Storer was out of spirits yesterday . . .

LORD FREDERICK CAMPBELL, BY SIR HENRY RAEBURN

were come. But they soon arrived, attacked their rivals, broke their bank, and won above £4000.[9] 'There,' said F[ox], 'so should all usurpers be served!'—He did still better; for he sent for his trades-men, and paid as far as the money would go.—In the mornings he continues his war on Lord North—but cannot break *that* bank.[10] The Court has carried a secret committee for India affairs[11]—and it is supposed that Rumbold[12] is to be the sacrifice:—but as he is near

he had been losing, like a simple boy, his money at Charles's and Richard's damned pharo bank, which swallows up everybody's cash that comes to Brooks's' (ibid. 476); and again on 4 May, 'Charles and Richard's bank is *florissante; elle baisse et se lève, mais elle ne laisse pas d'être une ressource immense'* (ibid. 479).

9. Storer wrote Carlisle 7 May 1781 of Charles Fox, 'His bank thrives prodi-giously, and, what is more, he has punted with the same success that he has held the bank. He won four thousand pounds of Lord Cholmondeley's bank. He is now in prodigious affluence' (ibid. 480; see also ibid. 483, 484).

10. In spite of Charles Fox's attacks in the House of Commons, Lord North still had a majority as well as the support of the King. Fox opposed North's motion on 30 April for a secret committee on Indian affairs (see next note), and HW wrote in *Last Journals* (ii. 359), 'Fox, in one of his capital speeches, was most justly severe on Lord North for inviting inquiries into the conduct of others, and preventing all scrutiny into his own, which had brought too many disgraces and losses on us. He arraigned, too, the pusillanimity of a late proclamation, in which we submitted to a neutrality in the Baltic, if the French did attack us there.' On 8 May Fox ac-cused North of continuing the American war from 'mean and sordid motives of avarice and self-interest, which evidently actuate the minister and all that numer-ous herd of placemen and pensioners who lived by his smiles, and were supported by his power' (Cobbett, *Parl. Hist.* xxii. 173-4). Of the same debate the *Morning Chronicle* 9 May reported, 'Mr Fox went into a variety of most shrewd comments on what Lord Fielding had said, relative to the late riots having saved Administra-tion, observing, that young men, how-ever attached to ministers, could not avoid speaking the truth. The noble Lord had truly said, that the riots and disorders of the last year were the grounds on which Administration stood, fit basis for such a building, *mater pulchra filia pulchrior!* proper mother for such a child!'

11. On Monday 30 April Lord North moved 'That a Committee of Secrecy be appointed, to inquire into the causes of the war that now subsists in the Carnatic, and of the present condition of the British possessions in those parts; and to report the same to the House, with their observations thereupon' (*Journals of the House of Commons* xxxviii. 430; reported in the *Daily Adv.* 2 May). 'Burke, Charles Fox, and others contended for its being only a *select* Committee. . . . The secret Committee was preferred on a division of 134 to 80' (*Last Journals* ii. 359).

12. Sir Thomas Rumbold (1736-91), cr. (1779) Bt, M.P.; Indian administrator (MANN ix. 119, n. 25); 'It [North's motion] was supposed to be chiefly aimed at Sir G. [*sic*] Rumbold' (*Last Journals* loc. cit.). According to the *Daily Adv.* 2 May, in answering North's motion Rumbold ob-served, 'He at first had his fears that Government would have acceded to pro-posals offered by the Company for the renewal of their charters, and that all further Parliamentary inquiry into the state of our India affairs would have thus been passed over. This was to him a matter of serious apprehension, lest, amidst the cries and prejudices which he found to prevail against him, on his re-turn to this country, he should be de-prived of an opportunity of fully and fairly vindicating himself as to every matter of accusation before that House and the public.' See also Cobbett, *Parl. Hist.* xxii. 122-5.

as rich as Lord Clive, I conclude he will escape by the same golden key.[13]

I told you in my last,[14] that Tonton[15] was arrived. I brought him this morning to take possession of his new villa; but his inauguration has not been at all pacific. As he has already found out that he may be as despotic as at Saint-Joseph's,[16] he began with exiling my beautiful little cat;—upon which, however, we shall not quite agree. He then flew at one of my dogs, who returned it, by biting his foot till it bled; but was severely beaten for it. I immediately rung for Margaret[17] to dress his foot; but in the midst of my tribulation could not keep my countenance; for she cried, 'Poor little thing, he does not understand my language!'—I hope she will not recollect too that he is a papist!

Berkeley Square, Tuesday, May 8.

I came before dinner, and find your long letter of the 3d.[18] You have mistaken Tonton's sex, who is a cavalier, and a little of the *mousquetaire* still; but if I do not correct his vivacities, at least I shall not encourage them like my dear old friend.

You say nothing of your health: therefore, I trust, it is quite re-established.[19] My own is most flourishing for me.

They say the Parliament will rise by the Birthday[20]—not that it seems to be any grievance or confinement to anybody. I hope you will soon come[21] and enjoy a quiet summer under the laurels of your own conscience. They are at least as spreading as anybody's else; and the soil will preserve their verdure forever. Methinks we

13. HW wrote Mann 18 Jan. 1781 that Rumbold's *'value* is estimated at a million' (MANN ix. 119). For his later investigation and trial see ibid. ix. 274, nn. 7, 8, and 400.

14. Missing.

15. Madame du Deffand's dog, which she left by will to Mr Walpole (HW); see *ante* 8 Sept. 1775.

16. Mme du Deffand's apartment in the convent of Saint-Joseph.

17. Mr Walpole's housekeeper (HW), Margaret Young.

18. Missing; Conway's letter to Hillsborough of 3 May is endorsed, 'Jersey 3 May 1781 General Conway R. 8th' (S.P. 47/9).

19. On 29 April 1781 Conway wrote Sir

William Hamilton, 'After all my *malheurs* I find myself in perfect health; living the wholesomest life in the world, in which business and exercise are the only ingredients; but the air is pure, the country pleasant; there is a pretty numerous garrison, and duty itself is a kind of pleasure' (printed in Percy Noble, *Park Place*, 1905, p. 115).

20. Monday 4 June. The *London Chronicle* 24–6 May (xlix. 504) reported, 'Parliament, it is said, will not rise till the second week in July, which is 36 weeks without the intervention of prorogation'; see also *Lloyd's Evening Post* 25–8 May (xlviii. 512). Parliament rose 18 July.

21. From Jersey (HW).

western powers might as well make peace, since we make war so clumsily.—Yet I doubt the awkwardness of our enemies will not have brought down our stomach. Well, I wish for the sake of mankind there was an end of their sufferings! Even spectators are not amused—the whole war has passed like the riotous murmurs of the upper gallery before the play begins—they have pelted the candle-snuffers, the stage has been swept, the music has played, people have taken their places—but the deuce a bit of any performance!—And when folks go home, they will have seen nothing but a farce, that has cost fifty times more than the best tragedy!

From CONWAY, ca Thursday 10 May 1781

Missing. HW wrote Conway *post* 28 May 1781, 'I have just received your second letter [ca 17 May]'; presumably Conway's first letter was written midway between his letters of 3 May and ca 17 May.

From CONWAY, ca Thursday 17 May 1781

Missing; Conway's 'second' letter, mentioned *post* 28 May 1781. Since Conway wrote Hillsborough 18 May 1781 a letter which is endorsed, 'Jersey 18th May 1781 Gen. Conway R. 29th,' it seems reasonable to assume that Conway's letter to HW would have taken the same amount of time to reach London (S.P. 47/9).

To CONWAY, Saturday 26 May 1781

Missing; mentioned *post* 28 May 1781.

To Conway, Monday 28 May 1781

Printed from *Works* v. 216–19.

Berkeley Square, May 28, 1781.

THIS letter, like an embarkation, will not set out till it has gotten its complement; but I begin it, as I have just received your second letter.[1] I wrote to you two days ago,[2] and did not mean to complain; for you certainly cannot have variety of matter in your sequestered isle: and since you do not disdain trifling news, this good town, that furnishes nothing else, at least produces weeds, which shoot up in spite of the *Scotch thistles*,[3] that have choked all good fruits. I do not know what Lady C[raven][4] designs to do with her play;[5] I hope, act it only in private; for her other[6] was murdered, and the audience did not exert the least gallantry to so pretty an authoress, though she gave them so fair an opportunity. For my own play,[7] I was going to publish it in my own defence, as a spurious edition was advertised here,[8] besides one in Ireland.[9]—My advertisement[10] has overlaid the former for the present, and that tempts me to suppress mine, as I have a thorough aversion to its appearance.[11] Still, I think I shall produce it in the dead of summer, that it

1. Both this and the first letter are missing.
2. Missing.
3. HW is presumably referring to the allegedly baneful influence of the Scots; see MANN viii. 448–9, ix. 62 and MASON ii. 105.
4. Lady Elizabeth Berkeley (1750–1828), m. 1 (1767) William Craven, 6th Bn Craven, 1769, from whom she was separated ca 1783; m. 2 (1791) Christian Friedrich Karl Alexander, Margrave of Brandenburg-Ansbach and Bayreuth; HW's correspondent (OSSORY i. 92, n. 4).
5. *The Silver Tankard,* a musical farce, about which she consulted HW 24 Nov. 1780 (ibid. ii. 241). It was first performed at the Little Theatre in the Haymarket 18 July 1781 and ran for six nights (ibid. ii. 241, n. 4; *London Stage* Pt V, i. 442–3). The *London Chronicle* 17–19 July, l. 63, reviews it favourably.
6. *The Miniature Picture,* performed 8 April 1780 by Lady Craven and her

friends at her own house, Benham Place, Berks; first acted at Drury Lane 24 May 1780. HW describes the reception of the second performance at Drury Lane 26 May, which he and Conway attended, in a letter to Mason 28 May 1780; see MASON ii. 43–5 and nn. 1, 2, 8; OSSORY ii. 182 and n. 10; *London Stage* Pt V, i. 344–7.
7. *The Mysterious Mother,* which was reprinted by Dodsley in May, but was not published; see MASON ii. 139–40 and nn. 19, 20, 143–4; Hazen, *SH Bibl.* 82–3. HW kept the whole impression except for some copies presented to his friends (OSSORY ii. 579 and n. 11).
8. No advertisements of a 'spurious edition' in London have been found.
9. No Irish edition appeared at this time; in 1791 an edition was published in Dublin (MASON ii. 148; Hazen, op. cit. 83).
10. In the *Public Advertiser* 30 April 1781, quoted MASON ii. 139, n. 18.
11. The *Morning Herald* 1 June reported, 'Mr Horace Walpole is said to

may be forgotten by winter; for I could not bear having it the subject of conversation in a full town. It is printed;[12] so I can let it steal out in the midst of the first event that engrosses the public; and as it is not quite a novelty, I have no fear but it will be still-born, if it is twin with any babe that squalls and makes much noise. —At the same time with yours I received a letter[13] from another cousin[14] at Paris, who tells me Necker[15] is on the verge; and in the postscript says, he has actually resigned.[16] I heard so a few days ago;[17] but this is a full confirmation. Do you remember a conversation at your house, at supper, in which a friend of yours[18] spoke very unfavourably of Necker, and seemed to wish his fall? In my own opinion, they are much in the wrong.[19] It is true, Necker laboured with all his shoulders to restore their finances; yet I am persuaded that his attention to that great object made him clog all their military operations. They will pay dearer for money; but money they will have—nor is it so dear to them; for, when they have gotten it, they have only not to pay.[19a] A Monsieur Joly de Fleury[20] is comptroller-

be yet undetermined about the publication of his tragedy, *The Mysterious Mother*. His friends wonder at the author's coyness of publication, all with reason agreeing with the good character of the work, that it is rather unequal, but on the whole it is to be pronounced good. *Plura nitent, quædam sunt reprehensione digna* ['More are flourishing which are worthy of reprehension'].'

12. See MASON ii. 148.

13. Missing; written ca 19 May 1781.

14. The Hon. Thomas Walpole, who was in Paris 1780–9, was a friend of Necker's (Namier and Brooke iii. 601; DU DEFFAND v. 180, 184, 198, 200–1, 211, 231).

15. Jacques Necker (*ante* 8 Sept. 1775, n. 18), Swiss banker, director-general of Finance 1777–81, 1788–90.

16. Necker's resignation, supposed to have been tendered 1 May, was at first refused by Louis XVI, but was accepted 19 May (MANN ix. 159, n. 2; Louis Petit de Bachaumont, *Mémoires secrets*, 1780–9, xvii. 179–80, 182–3, 188).

17. The news reached London 20 May; see a letter of intelligence 19 May from Paris, in Geo. III's *Corr.*, ed. Fortescue, v. 237–8. The *London Chronicle* 26–9 May (xlix. 505) reported, 'Monsieur Neckar,

the great French financier, it is said, has at last been dismissed. The reason generally assigned for this important event is, that it was utterly impossible for him to continue the war without laying new taxes, a measure which, he had pledged his honour to the King, he should never have occasion to adopt'; see also ibid. 29–31 May, 31 May – 2 June, xlix. 514, 528.

18. Not identified.

19. For HW's opinion of Necker's abilities, see *post* 15 July 1789; BERRY i. 45 and n. 33; MANN ix. 21, 159.

19a. A reference to the frequent bankruptcies and repudiation of debts by the French government in the 18th century.

20. Jean-François Joly de Fleury (1718–1802), appointed ministre des finances 24 May 1781, resigned in March 1783, when he was succeeded by Henri-François de Paule Le Fèvre d'Ormesson (NBG; *Répertoire . . . de la Gazette de France*, ed. de Granges de Surgères, 1902–6, iii. 770). 'On croit cependant M. Joly de Fleury peu au fait de la finance, n'ayant jamais travaillé dans cette partie, et n'ayant été qu'un instant intendant en Bourgogne: on suppose que son idée est de devenir ministre et d'entrer au conseil d'état, le seul dont il ne soit pas encore: il ne serait

general. I know nothing of him—but as they change so often, some able man will prove minister at last—and there they will have the advantage again.

Lord Cornwallis's courier, Mr Broderic,[21] is not yet arrived; so you are a little precipitate in thinking America so much nearer to being subdued, which you have often swallowed up as if you were a minister; and yet, methinks, that era has been so frequently put off, that I wonder you are not cured of being sanguine—or rather, of believing the magnificent lies that every trifling advantage gives birth to. If a quarter of the Americans had joined the royalists, that have been said to join, all the colonies would not hold them.[22] But, at least, they have been like the trick of kings and queens at cards; where one of two goes back every turn to fetch another. However, this is only for conversation for the moment. With such aversion to disputation, I have no zeal for making converts to my own opinion, not even on points that touch me nearer.

Thursday, May 31.

If you see the papers,[23] you will find that there was a warm debate

---

pas fâché non plus de devenir chancelier, ou du moins d'avoir les sceaux' (Bachaumont, op. cit. 186, 190–1, 201).

21. Hon. Henry Brodrick (1758–85), Capt. 55th Foot, America, 1777; Capt. and Lt-Col. Coldstream Foot Guards 1782–5 (R. A. Austen-Leigh, *Eton College Register 1753–1790*, Eton, 1921, p. 69; CM 1785, lv pt ii. 572; *Army Lists* 1779, p. 119; 1780, p. 126; 1785, pp. 11, 58). Cornwallis wrote to Lord Rawdon 17 March 1781, 'I shall send my aide-de-camp, Captain Brodrick, as soon as possible to England with the particulars'; and to Hon. Thomas Townshend 21 April, 'I send you H. Brodrick with another victory' (Charles, Lord Cornwallis, *Correspondence*, ed. C. Ross, 1859, i. 85, 92). He arrived in London 4 June (*London Gazette* No. 12195, 2–5 June).

22. In the summer and fall of 1780 there had been considerable hope of support from American loyalists, and Cornwallis had tried to organize them into useful militia; for example, he wrote Clinton 6 Aug. 1780, 'Our assurances of attachment from our poor distressed friends in North Carolina are as strong as ever'

(Cornwallis, op. cit. i. 54, 486–7, 489, 494–5; see also Lord Rawdon to Clinton 29 Oct. 1780, ibid. i. 62–3). But on 18 April 1781 Cornwallis wrote Lord George Germain, 'The principal reasons for undertaking a winter's campaign were—the difficulty of a defensive war in South Carolina, and the hopes that our friends in North Carolina, who were said to be very numerous, would make good their promises of assembling and taking an active part with us in endeavouring to re-establish his Majesty's government. Our experience has shown that their numbers are not so great as had been represented, and that their friendship was only passive' (ibid. i. 89). HW wrote in *Last Journals* sub 3 June 1781 (ii. 364) that 'the Carolinas were so hostile, though represented as ready to come over, that Cornwallis had not been able to get intelligence from a single person, nor could ever learn where the enemy was till he met them'; see also *ante* 3 Jan. 1781, n. 11.

23. E.g., the *London Chronicle* 29–31 May, xlix. 518–19; *Morning Herald* 31 May; *Lloyd's Evening Post* 30 May – 1 June, xlviii. 522–3; *Daily Adv.* 1 June.

yesterday on a fresh proposal[24] from Harley[25] for pacification with America; in which the ministers were roundly reproached with their boasts of the returning zeal of the colonies;[26] and which, though it ought by their own accounts to be so much nearer complete, they could not maintain to be at all effectual; though even yesterday a report was revived[27] of a second victory of Lord Cornwallis. This debate prevented another on the Marriage Bill,[28] which C[harles] F[ox] wants to get repealed, and which he told me he was going to labour.[29] I mention this from the circumstance of the moment

24. 'That leave be given to bring in a bill to invest the Crown with sufficient powers to treat, consult, and finally to agree, upon the means of restoring peace with the provinces of North America,' defeated 72–106 (*Journals of the House of Commons* xxxviii. 498).

25. Winchcombe Henry Hartley (?1740–94), of Bucklebury, Berks, and Little Sodbury, Glos; M.P. Berks 1776–84, 1790–4.

26. Charles Fox in 'a long and animated speech' said, 'The American war . . . was continued upon the opinion of men whose interest it promoted. Mr Galloway had told the House at their bar, that five-sixths of the people of America were in the interest of Great Britain, others had said nine-tenths; yet what had we been able to do, although those nine-tenths of the people had an army to assist them. . . . What, five-sixths of the people amicable, and yet not a blow struck in our behalf, ·not one visible symptom of loyalty through the continent' (Cobbett, *Parl. Hist.* xxii. 345, 350; see also *London Chronicle* 29–31 May, xlix. 518–19). Lord George Germain answered that the loyalists were unarmed, disorganized, scattered, and carefully watched (Cobbett, op. cit. xxii. 352–3).

27. In the *Daily Advertiser* 30 May: 'It was also reported, that advice has been received, that General Green having been reinforced by a body of troops under the command of Monsieur Fayette, a second battle had been fought between him and Lord Cornwallis, on March 27, in which the latter, after a desperate conflict, gained a complete victory.' See also *Lloyd's Evening Post* 28–30 May, xlviii. 520; *London Chronicle* 26–9 May, xlix. 512.

28. On 28 May Lord Beauchamp moved for leave to bring in 'a bill to remedy certain inconveniencies which have arisen' by means of 'an act, made in the twenty-sixth year of the reign of his late Majesty King George the Second [1753], entitled, "An Act for the better preventing of clandestine marriages"'; it was read a second time 30 May and a third time 7 June, when it was passed (*Journals of the House of Commons* xxxviii. 493, 498, 506). The bill was passed as amended by the House of Lords 2 July (*Journals of the House of Lords* xxxvi. 335, 340). See *ante* 24 May 1753; *London Chronicle* 24–6, 26–9 May, xlix. 499, 510–11).

29. On 28 May 'Mr Fox took an opportunity to speak a little of the Marriage Act: the late decision in the King's Bench [on the validity of marriages in certain cases] had demonstrated the absurdity of that statute, by showing that it bastardised one half of the nation. He felt a triumph, he owned, at this decision, which gave so signal an overthrow to the policy of that Act; and all he wanted to complete his triumph was, that those persons were now alive, who would not in 1751 [1753] believe that any possible inconvenience could attend their favourite bill. They would now see that Parliament would be obliged to pass a new act every seven years like an Act of Insolvency, to make those children legitimate which that ridiculous law was daily bastardising: But he hoped that this law would expire under the late decision' (*Lloyd's Evening Post* 28–30 May, xlviii. 514; Cobbett, *Parl. Hist.* xxii. 372–4). On 7 June Fox 'reprobated the intentions of the Marriage Act in very severe terms, and considered the whole as tyrannical and absurd, oppressive and ridiculous'; after Beauchamp's bill was passed,

when he told me so. I had been to see if Lady A. was come to town: as I came up St James's Street, I saw a cart and porters at Charles's door;[30] coppers[31] and old chests of drawers loading.—In short, his success at faro[32] has awakened his host of creditors—but unless his bank had swelled to the size of the Bank of England, it could not have yielded a sop apiece for each. Epsom[33] too had been unpropitious—and one creditor has actually seized and carried off his goods, which did not seem worth removing. As I returned full of this scene, whom should I find sauntering by my own door but C[harles]? He came up and talked to me at the coach window, on the Marriage Bill, with as much sang-froid[34] as if he knew nothing of what had happened.—I have no admiration for insensibility to one's own faults, especially when committed out of vanity. Perhaps the whole philosophy consisted in the commission. If *you* could have been as much to blame, the last thing you would bear well would be your own reflections. The more marvellous Fox's parts are, the more one is provoked at his follies, which comfort so many rascals

Fox made a motion to amend the Marriage Act (*Journals of the House of Commons* xxxviii. 507; Cobbett, *Parl. Hist.* xxii. 377–83). On 15 June Fox 'made his celebrated speech in favour of his motion' (ibid. 395); his bill was passed 27 June by the House of Commons, but rejected by the Lords on the motion for the second reading 12 July (*Journals of the House of Commons* xxxviii. 546; *Journals of the House of Lords* xxxvi. 356).

30. George Selwyn wrote Lord Carlisle 29 May 1781, 'For these two days past, all passengers in St James' Street have been amused with seeing two carts at Charles's door filling, by the Jews, with his goods, clothes, books, and pictures' (Hist. MSS Comm., 15th Report, App. pt vi, *Carlisle MSS*, p. 488). Anthony Storer wrote Carlisle 30 May, 'St James' Street at present is one of the most extraordinary scenes that ever was presented upon any theatre, or in any country. While Charles, Richard, and Hare are holding the pharaoh bank night and day, the bailiffs are ransacking Charles' house. . . . I went into the house when it was pulling to pieces, in order to inquire after the fate of the books, and I learnt that they were going

too to the Jews. While Charles was poor he had a comfortable house, now he is rich he is turned out of doors' (ibid.).

31. Vessels made of copper, particularly large boilers for cooking or laundry purposes; or copper mugs or vessels for liquor (OED).

32. HW seems at this time to have adopted the modern spelling of the word; see *ante* 6 May and *post* 3 June 1781 (*sub* 8 June), 20 Aug. 1782. In Kirgate's transcription of HW's letter to Mann 5 June 1763, HW has written 'faro' above the older spelling 'pharaoh' (MANN vi. 148 and n. 19).

33. Races at Epsom, Surrey, on 23, 24, 25, 26 May 1781 are listed in *Baily's Racing Register*, 1845, i. 512–13.

34. George Selwyn wrote Lord Carlisle 29 May 1781, 'Charles, with all Brooks's on his behalf, in the highest spirits. And while this execution is goin[g] on in one part of the street, Charles, Richard, and Hare are alternatively holding a bank of £3000 ostensible, and by which they must have got among them near £2000' (*Carlisle MSS*, loc. cit.); and again on 1 June, 'Charles's house is now going to be new painted, and entire new furniture to be put into it' (ibid. 491).

and blockheads; and make all that is admirable and amiable in him, only matter of regret to those who like him as I do.

I did intend to settle at Strawberry on Sunday;[35] but must return on Thursday, for a party made at Marlborough House for Princess Amelia.[36] I am continually tempted to retire entirely—and should—if I did not see how very unfit English tempers are for living quite out of the world. We grow abominably peevish and severe on others, if we are not constantly rubbed against and polished by them.[37] I need not name friends and relations of yours and mine as instances. My prophecy on the short reign of faro is verified already. The bankers[38] find that all the calculated advantages of the game do not balance pinchbeck *parolis* and debts of honourable women.—The bankers, I think, might have had a previous and more generous reason, the very bad air of holding a bank:[39]—but this country is as hardened against the *petite morale,* as against the greater.—What should I think of the world if I quitted it entirely?

35. 3 June; see *post* 3 June 1781, written at Strawberry Hill.

36. HW attended this party on 7 June, in honour of Princess Amelia's birthday, which was on 10 June; see *post* 3 June 1781 and n. 39. Lady Mary Coke was invited but declined ('MS Journals,' 3 June).

37. Cf. Shaftesbury, *Characteristicks,* 1723, i. 64 (HW's copy Hazen, *Cat. of HW's Lib.,* No. 55): 'We polish one another, and rub off our corners and rough sides, by a sort of *amicable collision.*'

38. Anthony Storer wrote Carlisle 24 May 1781, 'The pharaoh bankers are in excessive great fashion. They are sent for to hold banks. . . . Sir William Areton goes about with his strong box and his memorandum book. Each lady has her day set down in his book, exactly as if he was the physician, to wait upon them at such a particular hour' (*Carlisle MSS,* p.

486). George Selwyn wrote Carlisle 28 May 1781, 'The trade or amusement which engrosses everybody who lives in what is called the pleasurable world is pharon, and poor Mr Grady is worn out in being kept up at one Lady's house or another till six in the morning. Among these, Lady Spencer and her daughter the Duchess of D[evonshire] and Lady Harcourt are his chief punters' (ibid. 487).

39. Of Charles Fox's bank George Selwyn wrote Carlisle 11 June 1781, 'This pharo bank is held in a manner which, being so exposed to public view, bids defiance to all decency and police. The whole town as it passes views the dealer and the punters, by means of the candles, and the windows being levelled with the ground. The Opposition, who have Charles for their ablest advocate, is quite ashamed of the proceeding, and hates to hear it mentioned' (ibid. 496).

To Conway, Sunday 3 June 1781

Printed from *Works* v. 219–21.

Strawberry Hill, June 3, 1781.

YOU know I have more philosophy about *you* than courage; yet for once I have been very brave. There was an article in the papers last week that said, a letter from Jersey mentioned apprehensions of being attacked by 4,000 French.[1]—Do you know that I treated the paragraph with scorn?—No, no: I am not afraid for your island, when you are at home in it,[2] and have had time to fortify it, and have sufficient force.[3] No, no: it will not be surprised when you are there, and when our fleet is returned,[4] and Digby before Brest.[5]—

1. 'Yesterday some dispatches were received from Jersey, which mention, that the inhabitants there are under apprehensions of a visit from the French, as it has been reported there, that they intend to make an attack upon that island; that there are 4000 soldiers embarking on board of transports for that purpose, under convoy of several ships of the line. The militia and inhabitants however keep a continual watch, and are ready to give them a warm reception' (*Daily Adv.* 1 June). This report also appeared in *Lloyd's Evening Post* 30 May – 1 June, xlviii. 528, and *London Chronicle* 29–31 May, xlix. 520.

2. Conway's letters to Hillsborough during May do not mention a rumoured attack. His letter of 18 May (received the 29th) said, 'I have the pleasure to inform your Lordship that everything continues apparently very quiet in these quarters at present; there have been a few agues among the soldiers, . . . but in general the troops are very healthy, and in the beginning of next week I have ordered them all into their respective camps' (S.P. 47/9). His letter of 29 May (received 5 June) mentions 'the fleet being returned and no immediate symptoms of alarm appearing' (ibid.).

3. Conway frequently urged naval assistance for the security of Jersey, writing Hillsborough 18 May, 'I can only repeat what I have so often declared as my final opinion: that this island never

can be secure from surprises without the employment of some ships of this kind [cutters], not visiting occasionally but constantly attached to its service. Of which every day's experience and reflexion for these three years past with a settled attention to that object have more and more convinced me. We have now two cutters and two small luggers or row-boats employed in this way in the government's pay who keep a regular, and constant watch round the island' (S.P. 47/9). But the Admiralty was slow in taking action, and Conway wrote Hillsborough 13 July, 'We have in consequence of all this had no cutter at all for now these six weeks past; the ships of war very seldom visit this island, and without the Admiralty will send over cutters I now see no prospect at all of engaging any for this service' (ibid.).

4. The *Daily Adv.* 23 May reported the arrival of Admiral Darby and seventeen ships at Portsmouth 21 May and stated, 'Admiral Darby arrived yesterday [22 May] at twelve o'clock, at his house in Cavendish Square; after having brought in the fleet safe to their moorings, and detached ten ships of the line, under Admiral Digby, in search of Monsieur de la Motte Piquet, and for protection of the homeward-bound Jamaica fleet.'

5. 'Advice is received by the Flanders mail from Brest, that an English fleet, supposed to be under the command of Admiral Digby, is cruising so near Brest

However, with all my valour, I could not help going to your brother to ask a few questions—but he had heard of no such letter. The French would be foolish indeed if they ran their heads a third time against your rocks, when watched by the most vigilant of all governors. Your nephew George[6] is arrived with the fleet: my door opened t'other morning; I looked towards the common horizon of heads, but was a foot and a half below any face. The handsomest giant in the world made but one step cross my room; and, seizing my hand, gave it such a robust gripe, that I squalled; for he crushed my poor chalk-stones to powder.[7] When I had recovered from the pain of his friendly salute, I said, 'It must be George Conway: and yet is it possible?—Why, it is not fifteen months ago since you was but six feet high.'—In a word, he is within an inch of Robert[8] and Edward,[9] with larger limbs, almost as handsome as Hugh,[10] with all the bloom of youth; and—in short, another of those comely sons of Anak,[11] the breed of which your brother and Lady Hertford have piously restored for the comfort of the daughters of Sion. He is delighted with having tapped his warfare with the siege of Gibraltar, and burns to stride to America. The town, he says, is totally destroyed;[12]

harbour, that no ships, either going out or in, can escape them; and that the men of war lying there are in so bad a condition that they are not fit to go out and engage them' (*London Chronicle* 26–9 May, xlix. 512; see also *Lloyd's Evening Post* 30 May – 1 June, xlviii. 528).

6. Hon. George Seymour-Conway, 7th and youngest son of Lord Hertford (*ante* 20 Aug. 1763, n. 1); Ensign 39th Foot at Gibraltar, 1779; Lt 10th Foot, 1781; Capt. 23d Foot in America, 1782; half-pay, 1783; Capt. 1st Foot, 1796 (Namier and Brooke iii. 424; BERRY ii. 40, n. 11). On 24 July 1781 HW saw George and Hugh Seymour-Conway at Lady Hertford's seat at Thames Ditton, Surrey (OSSORY ii. 283).

7. Cunningham records a MS note by Croker: 'Lord George Seymour, then called Conway, has assured me that he never shook hands in his life with Walpole, and that all this is pure invention' (viii. 48, n. 2).

8. Hon. Robert Seymour-Conway, 3d son of Lord Hertford; at this time aide-de-camp to Sir Henry Clinton in America (*ante* 8 Jan. 1781, n. 5; OSSORY ii. 305–6 and n. 4).

9. Hon. Edward Seymour-Conway (1757–85), 4th son of Lord Hertford; rector of Sudbourne-cum-Orford, Suffolk; canon of Christ Church, Oxford, 1783 (OSSORY ii. 500, n. 33). The King appointed him to the living of Rendlesham in Suffolk 15 May 1781; but in March 1782 Hertford solicited 'a compensation to my son before he gave up his pretensions to the living' (Geo. III's *Corr.*, ed. Fortescue, v. 228–9, 231, 384–5).

10. Hon. Hugh Seymour-Conway, 5th son of Lord Hertford; at this time Capt. in the Royal Navy; he served on the expedition to relieve Gibraltar (*ante* 30 Nov. 1763, n. 5; MANN ix. 631–2; Namier and Brooke iii. 425).

11. See *ante* 18 Oct. 1763, n. 24.

12. Admiral Darby wrote Sandwich 22 April 1781, 'The town is beat down and often set on fire so that it is quite destroyed, many people killed by saving their effects' (*Sandwich Papers* iv. 35; MANN ix. 155–6). The *Daily Adv.* 22 May printed an 'Extract of a letter from a sea-officer' 22 April which said, 'Much damage is done to the town, many houses being knocked to pieces. Many are killed,

and between two and three hundred persons were killed.—Well! it is pity Lady Hertford has done breeding: we shall want such a race to re-people even the ruins we do not lose! The rising generation does give one some hopes.—I confine myself to some of this year's birds. The young William Pitt[13] has again displayed paternal oratory.[14] The other day,[15] on the commission of accounts,[16] he answered Lord North,[17] and tore him limb from limb. If C[harles] F[ox] could feel, one should think such a rival, with an unspotted character, would rouse him[18]—what, if a Pitt and Fox should again be rivals!—A still newer orator has appeared in the India business,[19] a Mr Banks,[20] and against Lord North too—and with a merit, that the

and the inhabitants are drove out to the southward of the Rock. . . . The goods now brought by the shipping are lying on the Rock, not a storehouse left standing to put them in'; see also ibid. 26 May; *London Chronicle* 24–6 May, xlix. 501.

13. Hon. William Pitt (1759–1806), the younger; M.P. Appleby 1781–4, Cambridge University 1784–1806; chancellor of the Exchequer 1782–3; first lord of the Treasury and chancellor of the Exchequer 1783–1801, 1804–6.

14. The *Morning Herald* 1 June gave a typically glowing account: 'Mr W. Pitt made a reply to Lord North, in which it was difficult to determine whether he distinguished himself most by the solidity of his reasoning, the manliness of his expression, or the grammatical purity and elegance of his language, from which he derived the greater credit, as his speech was by no means studied; but replied immediately to the arguments urged by the noble Lord.' See also the *Morning Chronicle* 1 June, *London Chronicle* 31 May – 2 June, xlix. 524–5, and Cobbett, *Parl. Hist.* xxii. 362–70.

15. 31 May.

16. A bill for continuing 'An Act for appointing and enabling commissioners to examine, take, and state, the public accounts of the kingdom . . .' (*Journals of the House of Commons* xxxviii. 501).

17. North opposed requiring that the commissioners of public accounts be members of the House of Commons, and favoured reappointing the present commissioners who were not members. Pitt argued that the control of public ex-

penditure was the duty of the House and should not be delegated to outsiders (*London Chronicle* 31 May – 2 June, xlix. 524–5; Cobbett, op. cit. xxii. 359–70). The motion 'that it be an instruction to the said committee, that they have power to make provision in the said bill, for removing the commissioners named by the said act, and for substituting other commissioners in their stead, who are members of the House of Commons' was defeated 42–98 (*Journals of the House of Commons*, loc. cit.).

18. After Pitt's maiden speech in the House 26 Feb. Fox generously complimented him (Fox, *Memorials and Correspondence*, ed. Lord John Russell, 1853, i. 262). Thomas Coutts wrote Charles Stuart 19 Nov. 1783, 'Mr Pitt's character is the great contrast to Mr Fox's. If he continues virtuous I think, in time, he will surmount, and perhaps do good' (*A Prime Minister and his Son*, ed. Hon. Mrs E. Montagu-Stuart-Wortley, 1925, p. 201).

19. On 1 June Lord North presented 'a bill for securing to the public the payment of three-fourths parts of the net profits of the East India Company at home, above the sum of £8 *per centum per annum* upon the capital stock of the said company, which have accrued' from 1 March 1778 to 1 March 1781 (*Journals of the House of Commons* xxxviii. 503; reported in Cobbett, op. cit. xxii. 531–5).

20. Henry Bankes (1756–1834), M.P. Corfe Castle 1780–1826, Dorset 1826–31. The *Morning Chronicle* said that 'Mr Powys . . . highly complimented Mr

very last crop of orators left out of their rubric—modesty. As young Pitt is modest too, one would hope some genuine English may revive!

Tuesday, June 5.

This is the season of opening my cake-house. I have chosen a bad spot, if I meant to retire; and calculated ill, when I made it a puppet show.

Last week we had two or three mastiff-days; for they were fiercer than our common dog-days. It is cooled again; but rain is as great a rarity as in Egypt; and Father Thames is so far from being a Nile, that he is dying for thirst himself.—But it would be prudent to reserve paragraphs of weather till people are gone out of town; for then I can have little to send you else from hence.

Berkeley Square, June 6.

As soon as I came to town today Le Texier called on me, and told me he has miscarried of *Pygmalion*.[21] The expense would have mounted to £150 and he could get but 60 subscribers at a guinea apiece. I am glad his experience and success have taught him thrift— I did not expect it. Sheridan[22] had a heavier miscarriage last night.[23] The two Vestris[24] had imagined a fête; and, concluding that whatever they designed would captivate the town and its purses,[25] were at the expense of £1200 and, distributing tickets at two guineas apiece,[26]

Bankes on the display of ability which he had made, and congratulated the House on the acquisition of a young gentleman, whose talents were likely to add a lustre to that assembly'; see also *London Chronicle* 31 May – 2 June, xlix. 526–7.

21. Jean-Jacques Rousseau, *Le Pygmalion*, first printed in the *Mercure de France*, Jan. 1771; see MASON i. 183, n. 10. For Le Texier's successful performance in Jan. 1777, see Mrs Philip Lybbe Powys, *Passages from the Diaries*, ed. Climenson, 1899, pp. 183–4.

22. Richard Brinsley Sheridan (1751–1816), dramatist and orator; proprietor of the King's Theatre in the Haymarket (OSSORY ii. 301, n. 18; *London Stage* Pt V, i. 370). Sheridan sold his interest in the King's Theatre after the season of 1780–1 (Walter Sichel, *Sheridan*, 1909, i. 47, 529, ii. 391).

23. The 'Grand Entertainment,' including the opera *L'Omaggio* (see n. 28 below), ballets, and a ball at the King's Theatre, Haymarket, advertised for 1 June and postponed to 5 June in the *Public Advertiser* 30, 31 May, 1, 5 June; see also *London Stage* Pt V, i. 436–7.

24. Gaetano Appolino Baldassare Vestris (1729–1808) and his natural son Marie-Jean-Augustin Vestris (1760–1842), called Vestr'Allard (MANN ix. 134, n. 19).

25. See ibid. ix. 134 and nn. 20, 24.

26. According to the advertisement, 'The performance under the direction of Vestris Sen., and to conclude with a ball. Tickets, at 2 guineas each, are ready to be delivered at the office in Union-court, where boxes may be taken. No masks will be admitted. The doors will be opened at 9:00, and the performance to begin at 10:00' (*London Stage* Pt V, i. 437; *Public Advertiser* 5 June).

disposed of not two hundred.[27] It ended in a bad opera,[28] that began three hours later than usual, and at quadruple the price. There were bushels of dead flowers,[29] lamps, country dances—and a cold supper[30] —yet they are not abused as poor Le Texier was last year.[31]

June 8.

I conclude my letter, and I hope our present correspondence, very agreeably; for your brother told me last night,[32] that you have written to Lord Hillsborough for leave to return.[33] If all our gov-

27. The *Morning Chronicle* 6 June reported: 'Notwithstanding the popularity of the *Vestris*, notwithstanding the avidity with which the public, of this great metropolis, generally runs after *dear* trifles, and notwithstanding the sort of weather, choice of the day, and a variety of other concurring circumstances, augured well to last night's exhibition at this place, there were not above 300 persons present. Most of them, it is true, were of the first fashion, but the elevated situation, of such as came, is no recompense to the managers for the solid expense they had put themselves to, in hopes of having a crowded company' (also in *Public Advertiser* 7 June).

28. *L'Omaggio*, author unknown, music by Giovanni Battista Bianchi (Pt I), Rauzzini (Pt II), and Giordani (Pt III); ballets composed by Vestris Sen. (*London Stage,* loc. cit.). The *Morning Chronicle* 6 June said, 'The theatrical entertainment called *L'Omaggio*, is, in plain English, an Italian drama, the main, and indeed the sole incident of which, is a representation of *the homage done to the lord of a manor by his tenants;* . . . it forms an elegant operatical pastoral, and affords good scope for the musician and the singers, the ballet-master and the dancers, to display their respective talents to great advantage.'

29. 'The theatre was fitted up in a manner equally novel and striking. From the end of the side boxes to the extreme of the stage, the whole was disposed after the manner of a French garden,— decorated with green lattice-work, and filled with evergreens, and pots full of the most seasonable flowers, and illuminated with a countless number of lamps

of variegated colours fancifully disposed' (ibid.).

30. 'After *L'Omaggio* was concluded, a cold collation was served in the adjoining apartments, in which plenty, variety, and excellence were eminently conspicuous. . . . After the company had supped, they danced cotillions, minuets, and country dances. We left them perfectly happy, footing it, in short time, to the harp, tabor and pipe, and violin, at three this morning' (ibid.).

31. The *Morning Herald* 7 June commented, 'It is somewhat remarkable . . . that of two foreigners who, within little more than a twelve-month, have produced *fêtes,* the one, with a most execrable puppet-show, should have undone himself; and the other, with the most pleasing entertainment of the kind, hurt his employers. The latter, indeed, have the prospect which, whatever is good generally presents, of improving on the public; and, as Texier's *fête,* from its innate demerit, was damned on the very face of it; by the contrary rule, Vestris's entertainment, if ever so often repeated, will still find new admirers.' See *ante* 16 June 1779 for HW's description of Le Texier's fête at the Pantheon that year.

32. Probably at the party at Marlborough House 7 June (see below).

33. Conway wrote Hillsborough 29 May (received 5 June), 'I shall hope that when this and some other points relative to the business of this island are settled, the fleet being returned and no immediate symptoms of alarm appearing, that I may be allowed to attend some private business which calls me to England, but I have no precise time final in my mind, and shall certainly see the affairs of this

ernors could leave their dominions in as good plight, it were lucky.[34] Your brother owned, what the *Gazette*[35] with all its circumstances cannot conceal, that Lord Cornwallis's triumphs have but increased our losses, without leaving any hopes.[36] I am told that his army, which when he parted from Clinton amounted to 17,000 men, does not now contain above as many hundred, except the detachments.[37] The *Gazette,* to my sorrow and your greater sorrow, speaks of Colonel O'Hara[38] having received two dangerous wounds.

Princess Amelia was at Marlborough House last night, and played at faro till twelve o'clock[39]—there ends the winter campaign!—I go to Strawberry Hill tomorrow; and I hope, *à l'irlandaise,* that the next letter I write to you—will be not to write to you any more.

island left on a proper footing before I should wish to leave it and particularly in respect to the command and government, though we have certainly many excellent military officers of rank here' (S.P. 47/9). Hillsborough answered 14 June, 'His Majesty is pleased to leave you at liberty to return whenever you shall be of opinion that his service admits of it' (ibid.). Conway finally returned in late Aug. (see CHUTE 361; *St James's Chronicle* 28–30 Aug.; *Daily Adv.* 30 Aug.).

34. The *London Packet* 6–8 June reported: 'Letters from Jersey mention, that great additions have been made there for the better defence of the place. The troops, with the militia, consist of 7060 men, and in every place where there is a possibility of the enemy's landing, strong batteries are erected.'

35. The *London Gazette* No. 12195, 2–5 June.

36. HW makes similar comments to Mann 8 June 1781; see MANN ix. 158–9 and n. 1.

37. In *Last Journals sub* 3 June (ii. 364), HW wrote of Cornwallis's victory 15 March over Gen. Greene, 'But though the Court had sounded the former as a decisive action, Broderick's account was most melancholy, and showed that it

had been so far from a final defeat, that Greene had been already in force again and ready to attack Lord Rawdon. . . . Cornwallis had not been able to get intelligence from a single person, nor could ever learn where the enemy was till he met them. He was equally in want of provisions and cloaks, and his army, which at his parting from Clinton had consisted of 17,000 men, was now reduced, excepting his detachments, to 1600.'

38. Now General O'Hara, Governor of Gibraltar (HW). Charles O'Hara (ca 1740–1802), natural son of James O'Hara, 2d Bn Tyrawley; Col., 1777, Maj.-Gen., 1781, Lt-Gen., 1793, Gen. 1798; Mary Berry's fiancé (see BERRY i. 119, n. 10). Cornwallis's letter of 17 March to Lord George Germain, in the *London Gazette* loc. cit., said, 'The zeal and spirit of Brigadier-General O'Hara merit my highest commendations, for, after receiving two dangerous wounds, he continued in the field whilst the action lasted.'

39. See *ante* 28 May 1781, n. 36. Lady Mary Coke wrote in her 'MS Journals,' 9 June, 'The assembly at Marlborough House was very brilliant but many of the company took the liberty to come in white aprons and one had a hat. The Princess Amelia stayed till twelve o'clock.'

From Conway, ca Friday 14 September 1781

Missing; implied *post* 16 Sept. 1781.

To Conway, Sunday 16 September 1781

Printed from *Works* v. 221–2.

Strawberry Hill, September 16, 1781.

I AM not surprised that such a mind as yours cannot help expressing gratitude:[1] it would not be your mind, if it could command that sensation as triumphantly as it does your passions. Only remember that the expression is unnecessary. I do know that you feel the entire friendship I have for you; nor should I love you so well if I was not persuaded of it. There never was a grain of anything romantic in my friendship for you. We loved one another from children, and as so near relations; but my friendship grew up with your virtues, which I admired though I did not imitate. We had scarce one in common but disinterestedness. Of the reverse we have both, I may say, been so absolutely clear, that there is nothing so natural and easy as the little moneyed transactions between us;[2] and therefore knowing how perfectly indifferent I am upon that head, and remembering the papers[3] I showed you, and what I said to you when I saw you last, I am sure you will have the complaisance never to mention thanks more.—Now to answer your questions.

As to coming to you, as that *feu grégeois*[4] Lord George Gordon has given up the election[5] to my great joy, I can come to you on

1. Apparently for financial assistance which HW had given Conway. In his letter to Hillsborough 29 May Conway mentioned 'some private business which calls me to England,' and again on 11 Aug. wrote, 'there are some matters to settle in England which will I apprehend make my presence there in some measure necessary' (S.P. 47/9).

2. See *ante* 21 April 1764, n. 3; Conway to Hertford 23 April, 11 May 1764 (MSS now WSL; *Works* ix. 117).

3. Not identified; possibly his will.

4. See Ossory ii. 358, n. 15.

5. To fill the vacancy created by the death on 30 Aug. of George Hayley, M.P. for the City of London (MANN ix. 183 and n. 7). In a letter 'to the Worthy Liverymen of the City of London,' printed in the *Public Advertiser* 17 Sept., Lord George Gordon says, 'I make no doubt but I might carry the election against all opponents' but for fear of provoking public disturbances 'I must beg leave to decline

Sunday next.[6] It is true, I had rather you visited your regiment[7] first, for this reason: I expect summons to Nuneham[8] every day; and besides, having never loved two journeys instead of one, I grow more covetous of my time, as I have little left, and therefore had rather take Park Place, going and coming, on my way to Lord Harcourt.

I don't know a word of news public or private. I am deep in my dear old friend's[9] papers. There are some very delectable; and though I believe, nay know, I have not quite all, there are many which I almost wonder, after the little delicacy they[10] have shown, ever arrived to my hands. I dare to say they will not be quite so just to the public; for though I consented that the correspondence with Voltaire[11] should be given to the editors of his works,[12] I am per-

the honour proposed to me at this time.' See also HW's comments in *Last Journals* ii. 373–4.

6. 23 Sept. HW went to Park Place 11 Oct. (Mason ii. 161; Ossory ii. 299).

7. The Royal Regiment of Horse Guards (Mann vii. 246, n. 8).

8. Nuneham, Oxon, seat of Lord Harcourt. Mason wrote HW 19 Sept. that Harcourt 'expects you at Nuneham and I hope you will not frustrate his expectation'; but HW wrote Mason 9 Oct., 'I shall not proceed to Nuneham. I have not heard from Lord Harcourt, but Mr Stonhewer . . . says the house is pulled to pieces, and consequently in great disorder, which I conclude is the reason of my not being summoned' (Mason ii. 154, 161).

9. Madame du Deffand, who died in September 1781 [1780], and left all her papers to Mr Walpole (HW). He wrote Lady Ossory 12 Sept. 1781, 'I have at last received all (I shall ever have) of Mad[ame] du Deffand's papers. *All* I know there are not, for I miss some' (Ossory ii. 235, 292; du Deffand i. pp. xliii–xlviii).

10. He means the executors of Madame du Deffand (HW): the Marquis d'Aulan, Mme du Deffand's nephew, executor and heir, and the Prince de Beauvau, who was entrusted with sending the legacy to HW (du Deffand i. pp. xliv–xlv; vi. 7–8). The Duchesse de Choiseul and the Abbé Barthélemy withdrew their letters from the collection without communicating with HW, and the Prince de Beauvau

apparently withdrew some other letters (ibid. i. pp. xliv–xlv). HW wrote Hon. Thomas Walpole 3 Jan. 1784, 'Indeed, the treatment I received from all concerned in her papers, has given me no high opinion of French honour or French friendship! I should blush if my conduct had not been the very reverse—and had they any delicacy, it would have taught them how to act' (Family 216).

11. Two folio MS volumes labelled *Lettres de Mons. de Voltaire à Madame du Deffand*, sold SH vi. 107 No. III, now in the Bibliothèque Nationale; other letters from Voltaire were included in miscellaneous MS volumes and papers sold SH vi. 107 Nos VI–XI, some of which are now WSL and some in the Bibliothèque Nationale (du Deffand i. pp. xlvi–xlvii; Voltaire, *Correspondence*, ed. Theodore Besterman, Geneva, 1953–65, xvii. 234, Appendix 54). Ten drafts of letters from Voltaire were among the papers of Decroix, one of the editors of the 1784–9 edition (ibid.).

12. Pierre-Augustin Caron de Beaumarchais (1732–99), Marie-Jean-Antoine-Nicolas de Caritat, Marquis de Condorcet (1743–94), and Jacques-Joseph-Marie Decroix (d. 1827); edited *Œuvres complètes de Voltaire avec des avertissements et des notes par Condorcet, imprimées aux frais de Beaumarchais, par les soins de M. Decroix, de l'imprimerie de la Société littéraire typographique*, [Kehl], 1784–9, 70 vols, 8vo. For Mme du Deffand's comments see du Deffand v. 59, 82, n. 3, 130.

suaded that there are many passages at least which they will suppress,[13] as very contemptuous to his chief votaries—I mean of the votaries to his sentiments—for, like other heresiarchs, he despised his tools. If I live to see the edition,[14] it will divert me to collate it with what I have in my hands.

You are the person in the world the fittest to encounter the meeting you mention for the choice of a bridge.[15] You have temper and patience enough to bear with fools and false taste. I, so unlike you, have learnt some patience with both sorts too, but by a more summary method than by waiting to instill reason into them. Mine is only by leaving them to their own vagaries, and by despairing that sense and taste should ever extend themselves. Adieu!

PS. In Voltaire's letters are some bitter traits on the King of Prussia,[16] which, as he is defender of their no-faith, I conclude will be *rayés* too.

To CONWAY, Sunday 18 November 1781

Printed from *Works* v. 223.

Berkeley Square, Sunday morning, November 18, 1781.

I HAVE been here again for three days, tending and nursing and waiting on Mr Jephson's play.[1] I have brought it into the world,

13. These have not been identified.
14. HW's copy is Hazen, *Cat. of HW's Lib.*, No. 3057. See HW's comments to Mary Berry 9 July 1789 (BERRY i. 28).
15. The bridge over the Thames at Henley, to whose singular beauty the good taste of Mr Conway materially contributed (HW). It was designed by William Hayward, architect of Henley-upon-Thames (d. Dec. 1781) (GM 1782, lii. 45), but was not completed until 1787. HW wrote Lady Ossory 10 Aug. 1785 that 'the bend of the arch was regulated by General Conway himself on three centres' (OSSORY ii. 484–5 and n. 1, 524).
16. For example, Voltaire wrote Mme du Deffand 21 Nov. 1766: 'Connaissez-vous, Madame, un petit abrégé de l'his-

toire de l'église orné d'une préface du Roi de Prusse? Il parle en homme qui est à la tête de cent quarante mille vainqueurs, et s'exprime avec plus de fierté et de mépris que l'Empéreur Julien. Quoi qu'il verse le sang humain dans les batailles il a été cruellement indigné de celui qu'on a répandu dans Abbéville' (Besterman, op. cit. lxiii. 115–16; see also xli. 95, 231; xliv. 93; lxii. 224).

1. *The Count of Narbonne*, which opened 17 Nov. at Covent Garden (*London Stage* Pt V, i. 476–80). For HW's part in producing the play see OSSORY ii. 300–2, 308–9, 311–12 and nn.; HW to Robert Jephson 7, 10, 13, 18, 21 Nov. 1781; J. M. Osborn, 'Horace Walpole and Edmond Malone' in *Horace Walpole:*

was well delivered of it, it can stand on its own legs²—and I am going back to my own quiet hill, never likely to have anything more to do with theatres. Indeed it has seemed strange to me, who for these three or four years have not been so many times in a playhouse, nor knew six of the actors by sight, to be at two rehearsals,³ behind the scenes, in the green-room,⁴ and acquainted with half the company. *The Count of Narbonne* was played last night with great applause,⁵ and without a single murmur of disapprobation. Miss Young⁶ has charmed me. She played with intelligence that was quite surprising. The applause to one of her speeches lasted a minute, and recommenced twice before the play could go on. I am sure you will be pleased with the conduct and the easy beautiful language⁷ of the play, and struck with her acting.

Writer, Politician, and Connoisseur, ed. W. H. Smith, New Haven, 1967, pp. 299–324.

2. The play ran for nine successive nights and for twelve further performances during the 1781–2 season (*London Stage* Pt V, i. 476–80, 483, 486, 487, 489, 491, 493, 518–19, 522; MASON ii. 167, n. 8).

3. On 10 and 16 Nov. (OSSORY ii. 302, n. 33).

4. HW wrote Lady Ossory 15 Nov., 'I have been tumbling into trap doors, seeing dresses tried on in the green room . . .' (ibid. ii. 310).

5. The *Public Advertiser* 19 Nov. said, 'The play was received throughout with applause, and in some parts of it with a vehemence of admiration we scarce ever remember.' The *London Courant* 19 Nov. wrote, 'The whole of this tragedy was received with the most unbounded applause, and if we may venture to exercise our judgment, is certainly the best that has been produced for many years past. The language is smooth and free, and in many parts beautifully poetic and descriptive.' See also HW to Jephson 18 Nov. 1781.

6. Elizabeth Younge (ca 1744–97), m. (1785) Alexander Pope (1763–1835), actor and painter. HW praises her in his letter to Jephson 18 Nov. 1781; the *Public Advertiser* 23 Nov. speaking of Act IV says, 'Miss Younge, in the performance of this beauteous sorrow, was never more excellent. She exceeds her acting in Queen Catharine [in *Henry VIII*], which was her *chef d'œuvre*.'

7. A detailed critique of the 'poetical diction' of the play appears in the *Public Advertiser* 20–3, 27, Nov.

From CONWAY, February 1782

Missing, except for a fragment of the cover, now WSL. Dated by HW's memoranda on the verso.

Address: To the Honourable Hor. <Walpole,> Strawberry <Hill, Twickenham, Middlesex.>

Memoranda (by HW): D. of Richmond. Ld Rawdon.[1]
Thurlow Bishop God damn.[2]
Thompson 26 49[3]
Fox's compl[iment] to Conway[4]
Auditors of Imprest omitted[5]
North's place[6]

1. Francis Rawdon (from 1790 Rawdon Hastings) (1754–1826), styled Lord Rawdon 1762–83, cr. (1783) Bn Rawdon; 2d E. of Moira 1793; cr. (1817) M. of Hastings; army officer. On 4 Feb. 1782 the Duke of Richmond moved in the Lords for information relating to the execution of Col. Isaac Hayne at Charleston, where Rawdon commanded; Rawdon considered this an imputation on his humanity and in a letter to Richmond of 21 Feb. demanded a public apology (Cobbett, *Parl. Hist.* xxii. 966–7); on 23 Feb. Conway 'signified to Lord Rawdon, on the part of the Duke of Richmond, his Grace's unqualified acquiescence, in making the excuse as required by Lord Rawdon' (memorandum printed ibid. xxii. 970; see also *Last Journals* ii. 397–8; Geo. III's *Corr.*, ed. Fortescue, v. 369).

2. HW wrote to Mason 28 Feb. 1782: 'The Chancellor [Edward, Bn Thurlow] went to Lord North and asked it [the vacant deanery of St Paul's]' for his younger brother, Thomas Thurlow (1737–91), Bp of Lincoln 1779–87 and Dean of St Paul's 1782–7; 'he replied, sorry, but it was promised. "God damn your promise, then I will get it somewhere else," and got it' (MASON ii. 192 and n. 9).

3. An error for 'Townson': John Townson (?1725–97), merchant, director of the East India Company, and M.P. Milborne Port 1780–7. HW wrote to Mason 28 Feb. 1782 that 'the profits of Thompson the contractor were to be but 26 out of 49' (ibid. ii. 191–2; see also n. 4).

4. See HW to Mann 1 March 1782 (MANN ix. 251–2).

5. From Burke's list of sinecure offices to be abolished in his Economical Reform Bill of 1782; see HW's memoranda on Richard Burke, Jr to HW 7 July 1782.

6. The North ministry was replaced by the second Rockingham administration in March (see MANN ix. 260–2; *post* 10 April 1782, n. 3).

From HERTFORD, Wednesday 10 April 1782

Printed for the first time from a photostat of BM Add. MSS 23219, f. 133.
Address: To the Honourable Hor. Walpole, Berkley Square.

Grosvenor Street, April 10th 1782.

Dear Horry,

THAT you may know what I know of your relation, I had a letter yesterday by the post from Lord Orford desiring me as Chamberlain to resign his place in the Bedchamber into the King's hands,[1] and adding that it was his lameness[2] which was the cause of it. I was as you know no longer entitled by virtue of that office to interfere,[3] but to prevent mistakes and explanations I sent the letter to the King, and gave his Lordship notice that as far as he had empowered me to act, his commands were obeyed, though I was myself dismissed.

I remain, dear Horry,

Always very sincerely yours,

HERTFORD

1. HW discusses Orford's resignation in the postscript 12 April of his letter to Mann 7 April 1782; see MANN ix. 266 and nn. 11–12.

2. This word, smudged by Hertford, was corrected above by HW. HW wrote Mann (loc. cit.) that Orford 'has long had a very swelled leg. . . . I must a little wonder, if he is angry, that he has palliated the cause of his resignation.'

3. In the changeover from the North ministry to the second Rockingham administration, Hertford was succeeded as lord chamberlain by the Duke of Manchester; the new cabinet and appointments were announced *sub* St James's 27 and 30 March in the *London Gazette* No. 12282, 26–30 March; *London Courant* 26 March; and *London Chronicle* 23–6 March, li. 296. Hertford resumed the post of lord chamberlain from April to December 1783.

To Conway, Tuesday 20 August 1782

Printed from the MS, now WSL; first printed Wright vi. 179. For the history of the MS see *ante* 29 June 1744 OS.
Endorsed: Mr Walpole 20 Aug. 1782.

Strawberry Hill, Aug. 20, 1782.

YOU know I am too reasonable to expect to hear from you when you are so overwhelmed in business,[1] or to write when I have nothing upon earth to say. I would come to town, but am to have company on Thursday and am engaged with Lady Cecilia[2] at Ditton on Friday, and on Monday I am to dine and pass the day at Sion Hill[3]—and as I am twenty years older than anybody of my age, I am forced to rest myself between my parties. I feel this particularly at this moment, as the allied Houses of Lucan and Althorpe[4] have just been breakfasting here, and I am sufficiently fatigued.

I have not been at Oatlands[5] for years, for consider I cannot walk, much less climb a precipice; and the Duke of Newcastle has none of the magnificence of petty princes in a romance or in Germany of furnishing calashes[6] to those who visit his domains. He is not undetermined about selling the place, but besides that nobody is determined to buy it, he must have Lord Lincoln's[7] consent.

I saw another proud prince yesterday, your cousin Seymour[8] from

---

1. Conway was appointed commander-in-chief in March 1782 (MANN ix. 262). HW wrote Lord Strafford 16 Aug. 1782, 'I have not been at Park Place, for Mr Conway is never there, at least only for a night or two. His regiment was reviewed yesterday at Ashford Common, but I did not go to see it' (CHUTE 365). The *Daily Adv.* 16 Aug. reported this review, and on 19 Aug. noted, 'Yesterday General Conway set off for Coxheath, to review the troops encamped there' (described ibid. 23 Aug.).

2. Johnston; see OSSORY ii. 347.

3. Syon Hill, Isleworth, Middlesex, Lord Holdernesse's house (OSSORY i. 160, n. 17). Lady Mary Coke attended this party and wrote in her 'MS Journals' 26 Aug., 'We had a great deal of company at dinner, Lord and Lady Hertford, Mr Walpole, Lady Margaret Compton. We played at cribbage which cost me three guineas and a half.'

4. Hon. Lavinia Bingham (1762–1831), dau. of Sir Charles Bingham, Bn and E. of Lucan, m. (1781) George John Spencer, styled Vct Althorp 1765–83, 2d E. Spencer, 1783.

5. Oatlands Park in Weybridge, Surrey, about nine miles from SH, seat of the 2d D. of Newcastle (OSSORY i. 250, n. 11; BERRY ii. 11–12, n. 9).

6. 'A kind of light carriage with low wheels, having a removable folding hood or top' (OED).

7. Thomas Pelham Clinton (1752–95), the D. of Newcastle's third son and heir, his elder brother having died in 1778 and his nephew in 1779; styled E. of Lincoln 1779–94; 3d D. of Newcastle-under-Lyme, 1794 (OSSORY i. 150, n. 37). Newcastle sold the place in July 1788 to the D. of York for £43,000; see ibid. iii. 7–8, nn. 13, 17.

8. Henry Seymour (*ante* 23 June 1752 OS), m. 1 (1753) Lady Caroline Cowper

Paris, and his daughter.[9] She was so dishevelled, that she looked like a pattern doll that had been tumbled at the custom-house.

I am mighty glad the war is gone to sleep like a *paroli* at faro,[10] and that the rain has cried itself to death, unless the first would dispose of all the highwaymen, footpads and house-breakers, or the latter drown them, for nobody hereabouts dare stir after dusk, nor be secure at home.[11] When you have any interval of your little campaigns, I shall hope to see you and Lady Ailesbury here.

From Conway, ca Saturday 14 September 1782

Missing; answered *post* 17 Sept. 1782.

To Conway, Monday 16 September 1782

Missing; implied *post* 17 Sept. 1782: 'I had not time yesterday to say what I had to say about your coming hither. . . .'

To Conway, Tuesday 17 September 1782

Printed from *Works* v. 223–4.

Strawberry Hill, September 17, 1782.

I HAD not time yesterday[1] to say what I had to say about your coming hither. I should certainly be happy to see you and Lady Ailesbury at any time; but it would be unconscionable to expect it

(d. 1773); m. 2 (1775) Anne-Louise-Thérèse de la Martellière de Chançay, widow of Guillaume de Panthou; they lived at Prunay between Versailles and St-Germain. He became a lover of Mme du Barry, separated from his wife, and stayed in France until 1792 (*ante* 25 Sept. 1775, n. 34; Namier and Brooke iii. 423; Ossory i. 119, nn. 13, 14).

9. He had two daughters by his first wife: Caroline (b. 1755), m. (1775) William Danby; and Georgiana (b. 1756), m. (1794) Comte Louis de Durfort (*ante* 25 Sept. 1775, n. 35); a daughter by his second

wife, mentioned Namier and Brooke iii. 423, not further identified; and, according to A. A. Locke, *The Seymour Family*, 1911, p. 346, also an illegitimate daughter born in France. The daughter in question here was probably Georgiana, who had returned to England the year before (Coke, op. cit. 22 June 1781).

10. See Ossory iii. 46, n. 33.

11. See ibid. ii. 353; Coke, op. cit. 11–23 Aug. 1782; Mann ix. 316–17.

———

1. Apparently in a missing letter.

when you have scarce a whole day in a month to pass at your own house, and to look after your own works.[2] Friends, I know, lay as great stress upon trifles as upon serious points; but as there never was a more sincere attachment than mine, so it is the most reasonable one too, for I always think for you more than myself. Do whatever you have to do, and be assured, that is what I like best that you should do. The present hurry cannot last always. Your present object is to show how much more fit you are for your post[3] than any other man, by which you will do infinite service too; and will throw a great many private acts of good-nature and justice into the account. Do you think I would stand in the way of any of these things? and that I am not aware of them? Do not think about me. If it suits you at any moment, come. Except Sunday next,[4] when I am engaged to dine abroad, I have nothing to do till the middle of October, when I shall go to Nuneham;[5] and, going or coming, may possibly catch you at Park Place.

If I am not quite credulous about your turning smoke into gold,[6] it is perhaps because I am very ignorant. I like Mr Mapleton[7] ex-

2. See *ante* 20 Aug. 1782, n. 1. Lady Mary Coke wrote in her 'MS Journals,' 12 Sept. 1782, 'I went to town this morning in hopes of seeing Lady Ailesbury . . . but she is still at Park Place. The General was in town but he has so much business that I thought it would be troublesome to interrupt him and therefore did not ask to see him.' Conway wrote Sir William Hamilton 15 Oct. 1782 of 'my farm, my garden, my little projects, of which amidst all my present Grand Occupations my head is still full and there indeed my heart leans, above all the attracts of ambition' (Percy Noble, *Park Place*, 1905, p. 121).

3. Mr Conway was now commander-in-chief (HW).

4. 22 Sept.

5. HW did not make this visit. Mason wrote HW 26 Sept. 1782 from Nuneham that the renovations there would not be finished in time for the October party (MASON ii. 274). Instead Mason visited HW at Strawberry Hill and wrote Harcourt 22 Oct., 'I have been at Strawberry. . . . I delivered all your messages . . . but he seems to be afraid of the gout at so late a season' (*Harcourt Papers*, ed. E. W. Harcourt, Oxford, [1880?–1905], vii. 75–6). HW

wrote Harcourt 23 Oct. 1782, 'Mr Mason . . . brought me your Lordship's most kind invitation. I am afraid . . . I dare not accept it so late in the season, and in such wet weather' (see CHUTE 524, 526).

6. Alluding to the coke-ovens, for which Mr Conway afterwards obtained a patent (HW). Conway obtained two patents: No. 1310, 1 Jan. 1782, 'Kiln and oven for burning lime, also for distilling and brewing purposes'; and No. 1689, 23 June 1789, 'Conveying the heat arising from the fires of coke-ovens, and adapting the same to the working of steam-engines, to cooking, also to calcining and fusing ores, and making brass and steel, and to heating buildings, or heating water for baths, also applicable to other purposes requiring fire or heat' (Bennet Woodcroft, *Alphabetical Index of Patentees of Inventions*, 1969, p. 122). OED *sub* 'coke, b' quotes 'H. H. [*sic*] Conway's Patent No. 1310.' For a description of Conway's distillery see Appendix 16.

7. Deleted in *Works* but restored by Wright. In the *World* No. 242, 23 Oct. 1787 (Appendix 16) 'Dr Mapleton, now at Odgeham' is described as Conway's 'chemical professor on a good establishment— a salary, a pretty house of four rooms on a

tremely; and though I have lived so long that I have little confidence, I think you could not have chosen one more likely to be faithful. I am sensible that my kind of distrust would prevent all great enterprises—and yet I cannot but fear, that unless one gives one's self up entirely to the pursuit of a new object, the risk must be doubled. But I will say no more; for I do not even wish to dissuade you, as I am sure I understand nothing of the matter, and therefore mean no more than to keep your discretion awake.

The tempest of Monday night alarmed me too for the fleet:[8] and as I have nothing to do but to care, I feel for individuals as well as for the public; and think of all those who may be lost, and of all those who may be made miserable by such loss. Indeed I care most for individuals—for as to the public, it seems to be totally insensible to everything!

I know nothing worth repeating; and having now answered all your letter,[9] shall bid you good night.

From CONWAY, ca Monday 30 September 1782

Missing, except for the following excerpt, included in HW to Lady Ossory 1 Oct. 1782, where HW wrote, 'I have this minute received a letter from Gen. Conway with these words . . .' (OSSORY ii. 358). On 16 Oct. HW wrote Mann that the news about Gibraltar 'had reached us on the 29th and even me, who live ten miles out of the world, on the 30th' (MANN ix. 327; see also ibid. ix. 326).

I HAVE a piece of good news[1] to tell you, which is the complete and entire defeat of the long meditated attack on Gibraltar, which began on the 13th at 3 P.M., and before midnight all the famous

floor, etc. etc.' at Park Place. He was presumably the medical adviser who treated Conway's illness in 1781 (ante 21 Jan. 1781).

8. The *Daily Adv.* 11 Sept. reported, 'An evening paper says, that Lord Howe, with the fleet under his command, sailed from Spithead on Monday night [9 Sept.], with all the transports, for the relief of Gibraltar'; he actually sailed 11 Sept. (ibid. 13 Sept.; *London Chronicle* 10–12 Sept., lii. 256). Because of contrary winds he did not arrive off Gibraltar Bay until 11 Oct. (MANN ix. 326, 330, n. 10).

9. Missing.

1. Reported in the *Daily Adv.* 2 Oct.: 'The grand attack upon Gibraltar, on the sea side, took place on the 13th ult. at three o'clock in the afternoon; and before midnight all the floating batteries and gun-boats were set on fire by the red-hot balls and shells from the garrison, and either blew up, or burnt to the water edge, and sunk. . . . Governor Elliot made every exertion which his humanity dictated to him to save as many of them as possible' (see ibid. 1 Oct. for a report received 'last night' on the land operation at Gibraltar, mentioned MANN ix. 327, n. 7). Lady Mary Coke heard this news 3

floating batteries were either burnt or sunk by our red-hot balls. They lost, it is said, 1500 men, but none of distinction named. They saved some in their own boats, and Gen. Elliot[2] some in those he sent out.

To HERTFORD, Wednesday 30 October 1782

Printed from a photostat of BM Add. MSS 23219, ff. 141–2, a draft in HW's hand, headed 'to Lord Hertford'; first printed Cunningham viii. 293–4.

Oct. 30, 1782.

My dear Lord,

I RETURN you Lord Beauchamp's pamphlet;[1] and since you ordered me and I promised to tell you my sincere opinion of it, I will; though I had rather not, as I do not love to take upon me to give advice.

It is certainly very well written for Lord Beauchamp's purpose and situation in Ireland[2]—but I confess I think the less it is seen by any one but those to whom it is addressed the better. There does not seem to me to be an argument in it in favour of the freedom and independence of *Ireland* that is not equally applicable to *America*. These principles are eternal and unalterable—and will it not

Oct.; 'This I had from one of the ministers who said though they had not received any official accounts they knew it was true. The Duke of Cumberland told me he did not think we should hear from Lord Howe in less than ten days' ('MS Journals,' 4 Oct. 1782). See also Conway to Sir William Hamilton, ca 15 Sept. 1782, in Percy Noble, *Anne Seymour Damer*, 1908, p. 151.

2. George Augustus Eliott (1717–90), K.B., 1783; cr. (1787) Bn Heathfield; army officer; Gov. of Gibraltar 1776–90.

———

1. *A Letter to the First Belfast Company of Volunteers, in the Province of Ulster*, Coxheath, 1782, and Dublin, 1782. HW's copy, London, 1783 (now WSL), is Hazen, *Cat. of HW's Lib.*, No. 1609:45:1.

2. On 17 May 1782, when Charles Fox moved in the House of Commons for the repeal of the Irish Declaratory Act (6 George I, c. 5), Beauchamp answered that 'unless the repeal of the declaratory act was attended by an express renunciation of the right to bind Ireland by British acts of Parliament, I knew that Ireland would not be satisfied' (*A Letter to the First Belfast Company of Volunteers*, Coxheath, 1782, p. 9; see also Cobbett, *Parl. Hist.* xxiii. 30–1). In his pamphlet Beauchamp reviews his arguments for securing Irish legislative independence and concludes, 'My ardent wish is to preserve for ever the connexion of the two kingdoms . . . but I know that the only connexion which can be lasting between them is a connexion of freedom, a connexion of common interest, a connexion of mutual benefits, and not a connexion of power' (*A Letter*, pp. 12–25, 36).

be asked how they are true with regard to Ireland and were not so towards America? Will it not be asked whether Ireland has not asserted its own independence on infinitely less provocation than America? I think both countries were in the right—but by what distinction can the cause of the one and the other be discriminated, except, as I said, by Ireland's cause being weaker than that of America?

I certainly am glad Lord Beauchamp declares so strongly in favour of liberty against prerogative.[3] He never can grow an advocate for the latter, or his own pamphlet will be a terrible witness against him.

There is one point in which I do not agree with him. He mumbles the case of the Revolution[4] too tenderly. Modern Tories want to make it an unique case; that is not true, for whenever oppression has driven a nation to vindicate their rights, the case has happened. And I trust it will not [be] an unique case in futurity more than it was in past times—that is, which I doubt will happen, when any country shall be tyrannized—and though the servility of lawyers may have kept the precedent out of their books, thank God! it will not be forgotten. America has shown it was not.

I have no scruple of speaking thus freely to your Lordship—you know I have never varied in my principles, and I have lived to have the satisfaction of seeing those principles triumphant. Ireland by having adopted them will become a great and flourishing country; and nothing but the revival of them here can restore this island to any part of the splendour which it had acquired by pursuing them. Lord Beauchamp will do himself and your Lordship's family honour by adhering to those principles now incorporated with the constitu-

3. Beauchamp cites the Magna Carta and states, 'that the limits of power ought to be permanently fixed; that subjects ought equally to know what they owe to the sovereign, and the sovereign what he owes to his subjects. The case of confederated nations under a common sovereign, calls equally for plain and immoveable landmarks of law' and he attributes the American war to 'the undefined and unexplained nature' of the laws binding Great Britain and the colonies (ibid. 15–16).

4. Beauchamp argues, 'I sometimes see in print congratulations to Ireland, on the revolution of 1782, and the phrase is not ill chosen, as to a people eager for liberty, and mindful of their great deliverer, it recalls the memorable revolution of 1688. That transaction was original in its nature, it remains on the page of history a lesson to all future times, to respect the rights of the people. It rests on its own merits, and appeals to no former passage of history for its justification, but as it was above all law, so no law has attempted to recognize the principles by which it was brought about, or to define the cases in which allegiance shall cease to be a duty, and resistance become justifiable in the subject' (ibid. 30–1).

tion of Ireland. England is disgraced, is sunk by having embraced the contrary despicable system. Allow me to add that, of all politicians, a politician-author is most bound to adhere to the principles he has professed in print, for even posterity in that case can call him to account, and his cotemporaries are not likely to wink at his contradictions.[5] I confess it was to give Lord Beauchamp this useful hint, that I have taken the liberty of saying so much; and I am sure I cannot show my regard for him so honourably, as by saying anything that may do credit to his character. Anybody can flatter; nobody should; a friend never. I am etc.

From Hertford, Wednesday 6 November 1782

Printed for the first time from a photostat of BM Add. MSS 23219, f. 140.

T[hames] Ditton, Wednesday morn.

Dear Horry,

I THANK you a thousand times for the sincerity and friendship with which you have given me your opinion.[1] I do not however in my own poor judgment agree with you (however general reasoning may apply) to a similarity of Ireland and America. They appear to me from their constitution and formation to be very different.

I agree with you that a political author of rank should be very cautious what he says and how he forgets it, and that character is and will be more essential to my son than all he can acquire by the least deviation which can affect it. The letter or pamphlet was wrote to Ireland[2] and of course will be made as public as possible.[3]

5. Lord Charlemont wrote, 'Party was undoubtedly the source of this publication, as it was difficult to believe that the son of the Earl of Hertford, who had also been his secretary during that administration when every claim of Ireland, either constitutional or commercial, was discountenanced and defeated, and who had, until now, uniformly espoused the usurped domination of England, should now have taken up the pen merely for the sake of this country. But his Lordship was a violent opponent of the present English ministry, and to foment disturbances in Ireland was a party measure by no means

unworthy of or foreign to the character of the noble publisher' (Hist. MSS Comm., 12th Report, App. pt x, *Charlemont MSS*, 1891, i. 82–3).

1. Of Lord Beauchamp's pamphlet, *A Letter to the First Belfast Company of Volunteers*, Dublin and Coxheath, 1782; see *ante* 30 Oct. 1782.

2. Beauchamp was replying to 'the address from the first Belfast company of volunteers to the other corps of the province of Ulster' (*A Letter*, p. [3]).

3. The *St James's Chronicle* 26–8 Nov.

The reasoning will suit their own, and of course, going from hence at such a moment as the present, will be employed with the name or at least a knowledge of the author.[4] I remain, dear Horry,

Very truly and affectionately yours,

HERTFORD

From HERTFORD, Sunday 10 November 1782

Printed from a photostat of BM Add. MSS 23219, f. 135; first printed Cunningham viii. 304, n. 1.
Address: To the Honourable Horatio Walpole.

London, November 10th 1782.

Dear Horry,

WITH a dagger in my heart which nothing in this world ever can extract, I am determined to exert all my feeble power to tell you, who loved my dearest and beloved Lady Hertford, that I am upon the point of losing her, the best woman, the best friend and best wife that ever existed.[1]

reported, 'Lord Beauchamp bids as fair to be as illustrious an oracle with the volunteers of Ireland as Lord Chatham was with the people of England. His estimable *Address to the Belfast First Company of Volunteers* is held in such high celebrity throughout the kingdom, that two gentlemen of the corps, to whom it is addressed, have got it engraved on a large plate, with an excellent likeness of his Lordship prefixed to it, and have already circulated above ten thousand impressions through the kingdom.'

4. Although the pamphlet was published anonymously, Beauchamp refers to himself in the first paragraph and quotes his speech in the House of Commons concerning the repeal of 6 George I, c. 5 (*ante* 30 Oct. 1782, n. 2). The second edition, London, 1783, has 'By a Member of the British Parliament' on the title-page. Lord Charlemont commented, 'A pamphlet now made its appearance, written by Lord Beauchamp, or by some one for him, as many thought the composition too good

for that cold-headed nobleman' (Hist. MSS Comm., 12th Report, App. pt x, *Charlemont MSS*, 1891, i. 82). A reply, *A Letter to Lord Viscount Beauchamp, upon the subject of his Letter to the First Belfast Company of Volunteers, in the Province of Ulster,* by Charles Coote, E. of Bellamont, was published in London, 1783.

———

1. She died Sunday 10 Nov. in her house in Lower Grosvenor Street, London (*St James's Chronicle* 9–12 Nov.; OSSORY ii. 370; MANN ix. 338). George Selwyn wrote Carlisle Monday 11 Nov., 'I was at her door on Friday, and although I believed her to be at home and indisposed, the servant gave me not the least reason to think that they had any apprehensions concerning her, nor had they till that night, when Dr Warren was sent for. . . . On Saturday she was in extreme danger, and yesterday in the evening, between 5 and 6, she expired' (Hist. MSS Comm., 15th Report, App. pt vi, *Carlisle MSS,* 1897, p. 568).

Do not make me any answer and pity me; I am not able to bear even the condolence of a friend.[2]

Yours, dear Horry,

HERTFORD

From HERTFORD, Monday 11 November 1782

Now first printed from a photostat of BM Add. MSS 23219, f. 138. This letter was apparently written 'past 12' midnight of Sunday night, i.e., early Monday morning; HW wrote Lady Ossory 16 Nov. 1782, 'It is justice to him to tell you that the very morning Lady Hertford expired, his first thought was to have this tribute [a character sketch of Lady Hertford] paid to her. I found a note from him on my table in town, which I could scarce read, to beg it . . .' (OSSORY ii. 373).

London, Monday past 12.

My dear Horry,

YOU will receive this from a most distressed friend, but it is in your power in the midst of my grief to give me comfort, and I shall esteem it an invaluable favour. I loved Lady Hertford and shall ever adore her memory with enthusiasm. She possessed every virtue, and her whole life exemplified and proved it. Her death corresponded perfectly.

From the time she was first affected[1] to the hour of her death she never uttered a complaint or an apprehension, and died with the composure of a philosopher without a feature of her countenance or her mind being disturbed. Her perfections do not lessen the weight I feel, but they require and shall find all the returns in my power.

Her character with a sketch of it drawn by you and inserted in a public print, will give me a satisfaction I cannot express.[2] I am, dear Horry,

Ever most faithfully yours,

HERTFORD

2. HW heard of Lady Hertford's death by express early Monday morning and immediately set out for London. 'The moment I arrived I sent to know if Lord Hertford would see me—he said he would in the evening,' but when HW arrived Hertford 'could not bear the interview' (HW to Lady Ossory 10 Nov. 1782, *sub* 12 Nov., OSSORY ii. 370–1).

1. HW wrote Lady Ossory 12 Nov., 'She had been seized on the preceding Sunday [3 Nov.] with a violent cough and spitting of blood, and left Ditton on the Tuesday for fear of being confined in that damp spot' (OSSORY ii. 370 and n. 34).

2. HW wrote a 'character' of Lady Hertford on Monday 11 Nov., which he describes to Lady Ossory 16 Nov.: 'They

From Hertford, Monday 11 November 1782 *bis*

Missing; received an hour after the preceding letter (Ossory ii. 373).

From Hertford, Monday 11 November 1782 *tres*

Now first printed from a photostat of BM Add. MSS 23219, f. 139. This letter was apparently written Monday evening after HW had delivered his 'character' of Lady Hertford.

Grosvenor Street, Monday.

Dear Horry,

I AM infinitely obliged to you for all you are so good to think, feel and say of my dearly beloved wife, now no more, and it is impossible for me ⟨with⟩[1] the affection, esteem and respect which are impressed so deeply on my mind not to admire what you have so elegantly and so justly expressed. I wish the whole world to see it in that or any other shape in which you think it can be best conveyed to their knowledge in a newspaper.[2] I shall receive you with a melancholy pleasure any morning that you come, but I am [so] torn by a grief which cannot be shown with composure when I see any friend of hers or my own, that you must make allowance for me. Indeed, dear Horry, the loss is as much as I can bear without yielding entirely to it, and I am almost afraid of viewing it in a full light. I remain, dear Horry,

Very truly and affectionately yours,

Hertford

I have returned it for the present, not knowing precisely how you meant I should employ it.[3] Pray tell me, for I have an anxiety about everything respectful and just to her memory that I cannot say.

were my immediate thoughts, and consequently the true . . . I set them down, transcribed and carried them at seven that evening, and gave them to his son Henry, when my Lord was not able to see me himself' (ibid. ii. 373). The article was printed in the *London Courant* 18 Nov.; see Appendix 12.

1. The MS has been smudged here.
2. HW's character of Lady Hertford was printed in the *London Courant* 18 Nov. (*ante* 11 Nov. 1782, n. 2).
3. HW apparently took charge of the publication of the character; see *post* 12 Nov. 1782.

From Hertford, Tuesday 12 November 1782

Now first printed from a photostat of BM Add. MSS 23219, f. 137.

Grosvenor Street, Tuesday.

Dear Horry,

I AM more obliged to you than I can ever express. You have drawn an elegant and a just picture of a friend whom I loved as myself and for whom I shall grieve as long as I live in this world of troubles.

Be so good, my dear Horry, upon the same principle that you have so kindly drawn it, to send it for publication. It may be better received in coming from a friend than one in immediate and the nearest connections with her. In any other point of view nothing could give me so much happiness as to send it with my own name to the bottom. I am, dear Horry,

Most truly and affectionately yours,

Hertford

I shall be happy to return you the personal and unbounded thanks of a distressed friend whenever you call in a morning.[1]

To Hertford, ca Monday 30 December 1782

Missing; answered *post* 5 Jan. 1783.

1. HW saw Hertford before 16 Nov. when he wrote Lady Ossory, 'Every word he utters is an encomium on her. Indeed his grief is as rational as it is deep: it is an uninterrupted funeral sermon on her' (Ossory ii. 372).

FROM HERTFORD, Sunday 5 January 1783

Printed for the first time from a photostat of BM Add. MSS 23219, f. 143.

Orford, January 5th 1783.

Dear Horry,

I AM assured of the sincerity of your good wishes,[1] and thank you cordially for the expression of them which I have just received. I hope my children in town did me justice in the part I felt upon your illness,[2] which I understood to be very severe, and I am very glad you are so much better. I propose returning in some short time to London, though I shall do it with a degree of fear and reluctance for many reasons. I am here in the most perfect and quiet retirement; and I have always lived alone when I have been at Orford,[3] which now gives the place double merit.

I am very glad that game or anything belonging to me could be acceptable to you, and I remain, dear Horry,

Very truly and affectionately yours,

HERTFORD

To CONWAY, Friday 30 May 1783

Missing. HW wrote Mason 31 May 1783, 'Yesterday . . . I wrote a line immediately to General Conway, desiring he would look over his memoranda for a recommendation of Lady Holderness [of a young relation of the Rev. Christopher Alderson's for an ensigncy] . . . and send me word whether anything was likely to be done for him soon. I expect to hear tomorrow before this goes away' (MASON ii. 303, 304). On 1 June 1783 HW wrote Alderson, 'On Friday . . . I did write immediately to Gen. Conway . . . to inquire if there was any possibility of his being served soon' (MS now WSL).

1. Apparently expressed in a missing letter in which HW thanked Hertford for a gift of 'game' (see last paragraph below).
2. An attack of fever and gout which began in late November and lasted until the end of December; see OSSORY ii. 373–5, 379; MANN ix. 343; MASON ii. 276, 279.

HW wrote Mann 7 Jan. 1783, 'For above three weeks I was too ill to see anybody but my most intimate friends' (MANN ix. 354).
3. The manor of Orford which Hertford had purchased in 1753; see *ante* 1 Sept. 1755, n. 6.

From CONWAY, Saturday 31 May 1783

Missing. HW wrote Mason 1 June, 'I have got a note from Mr Conway. He says he finds on his list a Mr Alderton [*sic*] recommended by Lady Holderness . . . as he bids me tell him if Mr Alderton is the person, as I shall tell him it is within a letter, I do not despair. I write a line to Mr Alderson to desire he will call on me in town on Friday' (MASON ii. 307).

To CONWAY, Sunday 1 June 1783

Missing. HW wrote Mason 1 June 1783, 'I have writ to Mr Conway again,' and 9 June 1783, 'I have seen Mr Alderson and told him what General Conway says, to whom I have spoken again, and who will serve his friend when he can' (MASON ii. 308).

To CONWAY, Sunday 27 July 1783

Printed from a photostat of the MS in the Pierpont Morgan Library; first printed (misdated 27 Aug. 1783) Wright vi. 197–9. For the history of the MS see *ante* 31 Oct. 1741 OS. The gaps in the MS were filled by Mrs Toynbee, whose readings we follow except for 'plan some way' which we read 'plan in the way.'

Address: To the Right Honourable General Conway in Little Warwick Street, London.
Postmark: ‹28› IY. ISLEWORTH. FREE.
Endorsed: Mr Walpole 27 July [written over 'Aug.'] 1783.

Strawberry Hill, Sunday.

THOUGH I begin my letter on and have dated it Sunday,[1] I recollect that it may miss you if you go to town on Tuesday,[2] and therefore I shall not send it to the post till tomorrow. I can give you but an indifferent account of myself. I went to Lord Dacre's,[3] but whether the heat and fatigue were too much for me, or whether

1. See Mrs Toynbee's article supporting the date 27 July 1783 in *Notes and Queries* 9 Feb. 1901, 9th ser. vii. 103–4.
2. Which he apparently did, according to the *London Chronicle* 29–31 July, liv. 109: 'Yesterday [Wednesday 30 July] at noon his Majesty came from Windsor to St James's . . . the Secretaries of State and General Conway had conferences with his Majesty till past four.'
3. Belhus, near Aveley, Essex (OSSORY i. 239, n. 5). HW wrote the Hon. Thomas Walpole 23 July 1783, 'Your son and I have been together at Lord Dacre's' (FAMILY 212). See also HW to Lord Dacre 31 Aug. 1783.

the thunder turned me sour, for I am at least as weak as small beer, I came back with the gout in my left hand and right foot.[4] The latter confined me for three days; but though my ankle is still swelled, I do not stay in my house—however I am frightened and shall venture no more expeditions yet, for my hands and feet are both so lame that I am neither comfortable to myself or anybody else, abroad, when I must confine *them,* stay by myself, or risk pain, which the least fatigue gives me.

At this moment I have a worse embargo even than lameness on me. The Prince d'Hessenstein[5] has written to offer me a visit—I don't know when. I have just answered his note,[6] and endeavoured to limit its meaning to the shortest sense I could, by proposing to give him a dinner *or a breakfast.*[7] I would keep my bed rather than crack our northern French together for twelve hours.

I know nothing upon earth but my own disasters. Another is, that all yesterday I thought all my gold-fish stolen. I am not sure that they are not; but they tell me they keep at the bottom of the water from the hot weather. It is all to be laded out tomorrow morning and then I shall know whether they are gone or boiled.

Whenever the weather cools to an English consistence, I will see you at Park Place or in town; but I think not at the former before the end of next month,[8] unless I recover more courage than I have at present, for if I was to get a real fit and be confined to my bed in such sultry days, I should not have strength to go through it. I have just fixed three new benches round my bowling green that I may make four journeys of the tour. Adieu!

Monday morning.

As I was rising this morning, I received an express[9] from your daughter that she will bring Madame de Cambis and Lady Mel-

---

4. HW describes his attack of gout in letters to Lady Ossory and to Lady Browne 23 July 1783; see Ossory ii. 408, More 204.

5. Fredrik Wilhelm (1735–1808), Furste von Hessenstein, natural son of Fredrik I of Sweden by Hedvig von Taube (Ossory ii. 413, n. 3). HW had met him at Mme du Deffand's 9 Sept. 1767 and again 22 July 1771 (du Deffand v. 319, 335–6).

6. Both Hessenstein's note and HW's answer are missing.

7. HW mentions Hessenstein's visit to

Lady Ossory 27 Aug. 1783; it presumably took place before 14 Aug., when Hessenstein took leave of George III 'previous to his returning home' (*London Chronicle* 14–16 Aug., liv. 162; Ossory ii. 413–14).

8. HW went on Tuesday 2 Sept., then visited Nuneham for 'two days and half' and stopped at Park Place again on his way home (Mann ix. 428, 432; Ossory ii. 415, 417; Chute 374–5).

9. Missing.

bourne[10] to dinner here tomorrow.[11] I shall be vastly pleased with the party—but it puts Philip and Margaret to their wit's end to get them a dinner—nothing is to be had here; we must send to Richmond and Kingston and Brentford; I must borrow Mr Ellis's[12] cook, and somebody's confectioner and beg somebody's fruit, for I have none of these of my own nor know anything of the matter—but that is Philip and Margaret's affair and not mine, and the worse the dinner is, the more Gothic Madame de Cambis will think it.

I have been emptying my pond, which was more in my head than the honour of my kitchen, and in the mud of the troubled water I have found all my gold, as Dunning and Barré did last year.[13] I have taken out fifteen young fish of a year and a half old for Lady Ailesbury, and reserved them as an offering worthy of Amphitrite, in The Vase, in the Cat's Vase, amidst 'the azure flowers that blow.'[14] They are too portly to be carried in a smelling bottle in your pocket. I wish you could plan ⟨in the⟩ way of a waterman's calling for them and transporting them to ⟨Park Place.⟩ They have not changed their colour, but will next year, at least so ⟨they say.⟩ How lucky it would be should you meet your daughter about Turnh⟨am Green⟩[15] and turn back with them!

---

10. Elizabeth Milbanke (d. 1818), m. (1769) Peniston Lamb, 2d Bt of Brocket Hall, Herts, cr. (1770) Bn and (1781) Vct Melbourne (I.) and (1815) Bn Melbourne (U.K.); mother of William IV's and Queen Victoria's prime minister.

11. HW wrote to Lord Harcourt 5 Aug. 1783, 'Madame de Cambis dined with me last week—and who do you think came with her? *Diane* de Poitiers of the next reign' (Chute 532).

12. HW's neighbour Welbore Ellis.

13. HW also alludes to Dunning and Barré in his letter to Lady Ossory 4 Aug. 1783 (Ossory ii. 412). Through Shelburne's influence Dunning had been created Bn Ashburton 8 April 1782 and had been made chancellor of the Duchy of Lancaster, a position worth some £4000 a year (ibid. ii. 412, n. 18), while in the same year the commissioners of the Treasury had approved an annual grant of £3200 for Barré which was to take effect when he ceased to hold office under the King (ibid. ii. 348, n. 20; 394, n. 8).

14. Line 3 of Gray's ode 'On the Death of a Favourite Cat, Drowned in a Tub of Gold Fishes'; see Gray ii. 23–4 and n. 3.

15. In Chiswick parish, Middlesex, between Hammersmith and Brentford.

To Conway, Friday 15 August 1783

Printed from *Works* v. 224–5.

Strawberry Hill, August 15, 1783.

THE address from the Volunteers[1] is curious indeed, and upon the first face a little Irish. What! would they throw off our Parliament, and yet amend it?[2] It is like correcting a question in the House of Commons, and then voting against it. But I suppose they rather mean to increase confusion here, that we may not be at leisure to impede their progress—at least this may be the intention of the leaders.[3] Large bodies are only led by being in earnest themselves,

1. On 1 July 1783 the Volunteer delegates from 45 companies of the province of Ulster resolved to hold a general meeting at Dungannon on 8 Sept., appointed a Committee of Correspondence, and voted to publish an address 'To the Volunteer Army of the Province of Ulster' (*The History of the Proceedings and Debates of the Volunteer Delegates of Ireland*, Dublin, 1784, pp. 1–4). On 18 July the Committee of Correspondence prepared another address stating that the reform movement had the support of 15,000 Volunteers as well as other freeholders, and asking all Ulster companies to send delegates to the Dungannon meeting with authority 'to declare approbation or disapprobation of the measures of a Parliamentary reform' (Patrick Rogers, *The Irish Volunteers and Catholic Emancipation*, 1934, p. 91). Charles Fox in a letter to Lord Northington 1 Nov. 1783 recommends 'a determination not to be swayed in any the slightest degree by the Volunteers, nor even to attend to any petition that may come from them' (Fox, *Memorials and Correspondence*, ed. Russell, 1853, ii. 164).

2. The Volunteers wanted the independence of the Irish parliament from the British, and also reforms in the Irish parliament, especially more popular representation. The address of 1 July states, 'Among the many glorious effects of which a more equal representation of the people in Parliament would be productive, the following are obvious:—The destruction of that party-spirit whose baneful influence has at all times been injurious to the public weal;—a revival of the native dignity of the Crown, by imparting to each branch of the legislature its distinct and proportional weight;—and the abolition of that train of courtly mercenaries who must ever continue to prey on the vitals of public virtue, till, the balance of the constitution being restored, the necessity for governing by regular systems of seduction, shall no longer exist' (*The History of the . . . Volunteer Delegates*, p. 3).

3. The Committee of Correspondence consisted of thirteen members, of whom the chairman was William Sharman of Moira, Lt-Col. in the Union regiment of Volunteers, M.P. Lisburn; the secretary was Henry Joy, Jr, printer of the *Belfast Newsletter* (ibid. 2, 4; Hist. MSS Comm., 12th Rep., App. pt x, *Charlemont MSS*, 1891, i. 112 and n. 1; DNB, *sub* William Sharman Crawford; H. R. Plomer *et al.*, *Dictionary of the Printers and Booksellers . . . 1726–1775*, Oxford, 1932, p. 392). The Committee sent a circular letter 19 July to prominent men in England and Ireland pointing out the need for reform in the Irish parliament and asking advice on specific measures. The Earl of Charlemont commented in his 'Memoirs of his Political Life,' 'The Volunteers, confiding in their strength, and flushed with success, were now determined to go deeply into all matters of internal reform. . . . The intention of the committee that not only the measure, but the plan also which was

when their leaders are not so:—but my head is not clear enough to apply it to different matters—nor could I do any good if it were. Our whole system is become a disjointed chaos—and time must digest it—or blow it up shortly.—I see no way into it—nor expect anything favourable but from chance, that often stops confusion on a sudden. To restore us by any system, it would require a single head furnished with wisdom, temper, address, fortitude, full and undivided power, and sincere patriotism divested of all personal views. Where is that prodigy to be found?—and how should it have the power, if it had all the rest? And if it had the power, how could it be divested of that power again? And if it were not, how long would it retain its virtues? Power and Wisdom would soon unite, like Antony and Augustus, to annihilate their colleague Virtue, for being a poor creature like Lepidus.⁴ In short, the mass of matter is too big for me: I am going out of the world, and cannot trouble myself about it. I do think of your part in it, and wish to preserve you where you are, for the bene-fits that you may contribute.⁵ I have a high opinion of Mr F[ox] and believe that by frankness you may become real friends;⁶ which would be greatly advantageous to the country. There is no competition in my mind where you are concerned: but F[ox] is the minister with whom I most wish you united—indeed, to all the rest I am indiffer-ent or adverse—but, besides his superior abilities, he has a liberality of acting that is to my taste. It is like my father's plainness, and has none of the paltry little finesses of a statesman.⁷

Your parties do not tempt me, because I am not well enough to join in them: nor yet will they stop me, though I had rather find only you and Lady A. and Mrs D.⁸ I am not seriously ill—nay, am

to be pursued, should be suggested and recommended to Parliament appeared to me exceptionable, imprudent, and danger-ous' (*Charlemont MSS*, i. 113). See also MANN ix. 438–9 and nn. 7, 8, 12.

4. HW uses this analogy also in a letter to Montagu 1 Dec. 1768 (MONTAGU ii. 272).

5. When the Coalition ministry was formed in March 1783 Conway agreed to continue as commander-in-chief without a seat in the Cabinet (HW's *Last Journals* ii. 509–10), but HW records, *sub* Aug. 1783, some friction between Conway and Fox: 'Expostulation of Charles Fox with General Conway on not obliging him with promotions in the army, nor acquainting

him and the Ministers with his measures. Conway justifies himself well' (ibid. ii. 531).

6. HW's mediation is indicated by Fox's letter to HW of 10 Sept. 1783: 'I am obliged to you for the conversation we had in Berkeley Square and I am very happy to say that I already find less cause of complaint than I did [against Con-way].'

7. See MANN ix. 275, 437, where HW also praises Fox and compares him to Sir Robert Walpole, and *Last Journals* ii. 519.

8. HW went to Park Place 2 Sept. (*ante* 27 July 1783, n. 8).

better upon the whole than I was last year: but I perceive decays enough in myself to be sensible that the scale may easily be inclined to the worst side. This observation makes me very indifferent to everything that is not much at my heart. Consequently what concerns you is, as it has always been for above forty years, a principal object. Adieu!

From Conway, ca Sunday 2 May 1784

Missing; answered *post* 5 May 1784.

To Conway, Wednesday 5 May 1784

Printed from *Works* v. 226–7.

Berkeley Square, Wednesday, May 5, 1784.

YOUR cherries, for aught I know, may, like Mr Pitt, be half ripe before others are in blossom; but at Twickenham, I am sure, I could find dates and pomegranates on the quickset hedges, as soon as a cherry in swaddling-clothes on my walls. The very leaves on the horse-chestnuts are little snotty-nosed things, that cry and are afraid of the north wind, and cling to the bough as if *old poker*[1] was coming to take them away. For my part, I have seen nothing like spring but a chimney-sweeper's garland; and yet I have been three days in the country[2]—and the consequence was, that I was glad to come back to town. I do not wonder that you feel differently. Anything is warmth and verdure when compared to poring over memorials. In truth, I think you will be much happier for being out of Parliament.[3] You

1. The devil; quoted by OED *sub* 'poker, sb2.'

2. HW wrote Mann 29 April 1784, 'I shall visit my Strawberry tomorrow' (MANN ix. 497).

3. Conway had sat in Parliament from Dec. 1741 to March 1784. On 19 Dec. 1783 he wrote Grafton, 'In regard to myself, I have only to say, that I have the most sincere sense of your Grace's goodness . . . in recommending me to the

borough of Bury, and that I hope you will consider your own convenience and inclination in your future disposal of it' (Augustus Henry, 3d D. of Grafton, *Autobiography*, ed. W. R. Anson, 1898, p. 386). Conway was replaced by Grafton's nephew, the Hon. George Ferdinand Fitzroy, who sat for Bury 2 April 1784 – Jan. 1787 (Namier and Brooke i. 379, ii. 246, 436). The King wrote Pitt 28 March 1784, 'Having heard this day that the

could do no good there; you have no views of ambition to satisfy:
—and when neither duty nor ambition calls (I do not condescend to
name avarice, which never is to be satisfied, nor deserves to be rea-
soned with, nor has any place in your breast) I cannot conceive what
satisfaction an elderly man can have in listening to the passions or
follies of others:[4] nor is eloquence such a banquet, when one knows
that, whoever the cooks are, whatever the sauces, one has eaten as
good beef or mutton before—and, perhaps, as well dressed. It is
surely time to live for one's self, when one has not a vast while to
live; and you, I am persuaded, will live the longer for leading a
country life. How much better to be planting, nay, making experiments on smoke[5] (if not too dear), than reading applications from
officers, a quarter of whom you could not serve, nor content three-
quarters! You had not time for necessary exercise; and, I believe,
would have blinded yourself. In short, if you will live in the air all
day, be totally idle, and not read or write a line by candle-light, and
retrench your suppers, I shall rejoice in your having nothing to do
but that dreadful punishment, pleasing yourself. Nobody has any
claims on you; you have satisfied every point of honour; you have
no cause for being particularly grateful to the Opposition;[6] and you
want no excuse for living for yourself. Your resolutions on economy
are not only prudent, but just—and, to say the truth, I believe that
if you had continued at the head of the army you would have ruined
yourself. You have too much generosity to have curbed yourself, and
would have had too little time to attend to doing so. I know by myself how pleasant it is to have laid up a little for those I love, for
those that depend on me, and for old servants. Moderate wishes may

Duke of Grafton has met with the repulse
of his candidate General Conway at St
Edmundsbury and that the Duke to prevent the introduction of a stranger has
been obliged to put up in his stead Captain George Fitzroy, I think it may be
agreeable to Mr Pitt to know of a certain
friend instead of a determined enemy'
(Chatham MSS, quoted Namier and
Brooke ii. 246).

4. Conway wrote Grafton 4 Jan. 1784,
'A system of Administration . . . forced
upon his Majesty, I much dislike; but a
system against the bent of the House of
Commons, and supported only by the
Crown, I take it to be impracticable. I
should be happy indeed, if with the aid of

your Grace, and such as are more able
than myself, I could contribute my mite
to soften the asperities of the times, or to
promote in the midst of them measures
essentially salutary to our poor, almost
sinking country: but I thoroughly feel my
want of weight and ability for such great
things, though I should never be dis-
couraged from the attempt should others
more able see the least opening for them'
(Grafton, op. cit. 388).

5. From coke-ovens; see *ante* 17 Sept.
1782, n. 6; *post* 30 June 1784, n. 15.

6. Under the Coalition administration
Conway had served as commander-in-chief
but was not a member of the Cabinet; see
ante 15 Aug. 1783, n. 5.

be satisfied—and, which is still better, are less liable to disappoint-ment. I am not preaching, nor giving advice—but congratulating you:—and it is certainly not being selfish, when I rejoice at your being thrown by circumstances into a retired life, though it will oc-casion my seeing less of you. But I have always preferred what was most for your own honour and happiness; and as you taste satisfac-tion already, it will not diminish, for they are the first moments of passing from a busy life to a quiet one that are the most irksome.[7] You have the felicity of being able to amuse yourself with what the grave world calls trifles—but as gravity does not happen to be wis-dom, trifles are full as important as what is respected as serious; and more amiable, as generally more innocent. Most men are bad or ridiculous, sometimes both:—at least my experience tells me, what my reading had told me before, that they are so in a great capital of a sinking country. If immortal fame is his object, a Cato[8] may die —but he will do no good. If only the preservation of his virtue had been his point, he might have lived comfortably at Athens, like Atticus[9]—who, by the way, happens to be as immortal; though I will give him credit for having had no such view. Indeed, I look on this country as so irrecoverably on the verge of ruin, from its enormous debt, from the loss of America, from the almost as certain prospect of losing India, that my pride would dislike to be an actor when the crash may happen.

You seem to think that I might send you more news. So I might, if I would talk of elections:[10] but those, you know, I hate; as, in

7. Conway wrote Hertford 21 July 1784, 'I am paid for my insignificance by a vast deal of ease and comfort; and I find it so much easier to manage a few hundred acres than to have any share in governing three kingdoms that I feel rather obliged than angry at all those who have anyhow contributed to shuffle me out of the most troublesome and danger-ous scene this country was ever engaged in. I don't desire to be an actor in the ruin of my country; and if the vessel must sink I had rather be a passenger than a pilot' (MS now WSL).

8. Marcus Porcius Cato (95–46 B.C.), 'the younger,' who committed suicide in preference to seeking pardon from Cæsar after being defeated.

9. Titus Pomponius Atticus (109–32

B.C.), friend and correspondent of Cicero.

10. The general election of 1784, after the dissolution of Parliament on 25 March, resulted in a victory for Pitt's administration (Namier and Brooke i. 87–9; MANN ix. 488, 502). The contest for the two seats for Westminster, be-tween Fox, Lord Hood, and Sir Cecil Wray, was 'the warmest ever known in this country, and . . . likewise extended to the greatest length [40 days]' (History of the Westminster Election, 1784, p. 270, of which HW's copy is Hazen, Cat. of HW's Lib., No. 557). HW describes the Westminster contest in a letter to Mann on 11 April (MANN ix. 489–90, 491) and in his 'Mem. 1783–91,' quoted ibid. 489, n. 20.

general, I do all details. How Mr Fox has recovered such a majority I do not guess;[11] still less do I comprehend how there could be so many that had not voted, after the poll had lasted so long.[12] Indeed, I should be sorry to understand such mysteries.—Of new peers, or new elevations, I hear every day, but am quite ignorant which are to be true.[13] Rumour always creates as many as the King, when he makes several. In fact, I do know nothing.

Adieu!

PS. The summer is come to town, but I hope is gone into the country too.

---

11. On the first day (1 April) the result of the poll was Fox 302, Hood 264, Wray 238 (list of the daily polling in *History of the Westminster Election, 1784*, p. 410 and *London Chronicle* 18–20 May, lv. 483). On the third day Fox dropped to third place, and on 7 April he wrote, 'Worse and worse, but I am afraid I must not give it up, though there is very little chance indeed' (Fox, *Memorials and Correspondence*, ed. Lord John Russell, 1853, ii. 267). Wray was ahead of Fox in total votes until 26 April, but on 27 April Fox jumped ahead of Wray: 'I gained forty-eight upon them today, and am now, as you see, twenty ahead' (ibid. ii. 268). He continued to gain a majority each day and on 5 May (when the total vote was Fox 6084 and Wray 5918) wrote, 'They polled only five today, and I thirty-five. One would think it must be soon over, but yet I do not think it will be this week' (ibid. ii. 269; *History*, p. 340). On 17 May the final result was Hood 6694, Fox 6233, Wray 5998 (*Journals of the House of Commons* xl. 588; *History*, p. 370). Fox's success was attributed partly to the campaigning of Georgiana, Duchess of Devonshire, and other ladies, and partly to public sympathy for a candidate who was combatting all the wealth and influence of the Court party (MANN ix. 489–90, n. 25; *History*, pp. 310, 313, 322, 329).

12. The poll was open from 1 April through 17 May. Once he had gained a firm majority Fox thought it might be closed by mutual agreement, but on 3 May he wrote, 'I gained twelve today upon very small numbers, but I see less prospect of finishing than I did. No proposal has been made from the other side; and as long as I continue gaining, it is our interest to go on, to prevent a scrutiny. I am quite sure of success; but I must own I heartily wish it over' (Fox, op. cit. ii. 269). Pitt wrote the King 27 April that Fox's majority would result in closing the polls early, but 'Mr Pitt still trusts the ground will be regained by a scrutiny' (George III, *Later Correspondence*, ed. A. Aspinall, Cambridge, 1962–7, i. 57).

13. According to the *London Chronicle* 6–8 May, lv. 442, 'Yesterday [6 May] there was a very numerous and splendid Court at St James's . . . the Duke of Chandos and Lord Galway kissed her Majesty's hand on their official promotions; as did Lord and Lady Sherborne, Lord and Lady Berwick, Lord and Lady Sommers, and Lord and Lady Burrington; as did also Pepper Arden, and Archibald Macdonald, Esqrs (the Attorney and Solicitor General), on their appointments . . . the Earl and Countess of Leicester . . . on their coming to that title . . . Lord Paget . . . on being created Earl of Uxbridge.' The same paper lists eight new Irish peers.

From Conway, ca Tuesday 18 May 1784

Missing; answered *post* 21 May 1784.

To Conway, Friday 21 May 1784

Printed from *Works* v. 228–9.

Strawberry Hill, May 21, 1784.

I AM perfectly satisfied with your epitaph,[1] and would not have a syllable altered. It tells exactly what it means to say, and, that truth being an encomium, wants no addition or amplification. Nor do I love late language for modern facts, nor will European tongues perish since printing has been discovered. I should approve French least of all. It would be a kind of insult to the vanquished: and besides, the example of a hero should be held out to his countrymen rather than to their enemies. You must take care to have the word *caused,* in the last line but one, spelled rightly, and not *caus'd.*

I know nothing of the Parliament but what you saw in the papers.[2] I came hither yesterday, and am transported, like you, with the beauty of the country; ay, and with its perfumed air too. The *lilactide* scents even the insides of the rooms.

I desired Lady A. to carry you Lord Melcombe's *Diary.*[3] It is curi-

1. An epitaph for the monument, erected by the States of Jersey, to the memory of Major Pearson, killed in the attack of that island by the French, in January 1781 (HW). Francis Peirson (1756–81), ensign 36th Foot, 1772, Maj. 95th Foot, 1779, was buried 10 Jan. 1781 under the tower of St Helier's Church. The monument, placed in the chancel, is inscribed: 'To the memory of Major Francis Peirson, who, when this island was invaded by the French, fell bravely fighting at the head of British and island troops. He died in the flower of youth and in the moment of victory the 6th day of January 1781, aged 24. The States of the island in grateful testimony of their deliverance caused this monument to be erected at the public expense'

(*Société jersiaise. Bulletins,* 1915–18, viii. 176; an account of his death and funeral is ibid. 1875–84, i. 318–23).

2. The new Parliament, with a majority for Pitt, assembled 18 May; in the debate on the election of a Speaker for the House of Commons Fox questioned the legality of the conduct of Thomas Corbett, high bailiff of Westminster, in granting a scrutiny and leaving the two seats for Westminster vacant (*London Chronicle* 18–20 May, lv. 481–2; *Daily Adv.* 19, 20 May; *Gazetteer and New Daily Advertiser* 19, 20 May). For the further progress of the scrutiny see MANN ix. 502 and nn. 7, 8.

3. *The Diary of the Late George Bubb Dodington . . . From March 8, 1748–9, to February 6, 1761,* ed. H. P. Wyndham,

ous indeed, not so much from the secrets it blabs, which are rather characteristic than novel, but from the wonderful folly of the author, who was so fond of talking of himself, that he tells all he knew of himself, though scarce an event that does not betray his profligacy; and (which is still more surprising that he should disclose) almost everyone exposes the contempt in which he was held, and his consequential disappointments and disgraces!—Was ever any man the better for another's experience?—What a lesson is here against versatility![4]

I, who have lived through all the scenes unfolded, am entertained—but I should think that to younger readers half the book must be unintelligible. He explains nothing but the circumstances of his own situation; and though he touches on many important periods, he leaves them undeveloped, and often undetermined. It is diverting to hear him rail at Lord Halifax[5] and others, for the very kind of double-dealing which he relates coolly of himself in the next page.[6] Had he gone backwards, he might have given half a dozen volumes of his own life with similar anecdotes and variations.[7]

I am most surprised, that when self-love is the whole groundwork of the performance, there should be little or no attempt at shining as an author, though he was one. As he had so much wit too, I am amazed that not a feature of it appears. The discussion in the Appendix, on the late Prince's question for increase of allowance,[8] is the only part in which there is sense or honesty.

Salisbury and London, 1784; HW's copies are Hazen, *Cat. of HW's Lib.*, Nos 429, 2837. In 'Mem. 1783–91,' HW notes 'Lord Melcombe's diary published' *sub* 18 May 1784.

4. HW makes similar comments to Mann 3 June 1784 (Mann ix. 503).

5. In describing the negotiations for a new administration in March–April 1757 (*Diary*, pp. 392–8), Dodington comments, 'During this while, Lord Hallifax (upon whose friendship and concurrence I depended from repeated assurances, and to whom I had communicated all this transaction, and, till now, without authority), privately saw and negotiated with the Duke of Newcastle, and took measures with him to defeat it. What makes this the more surprising is, that always before, at that very time, and ever since, he has spoken of the Duke of Newcastle

to me and others, as a knave and a fool, in the strongest terms' (ibid. 393). He continues, 'I went to Lord Hallifax, who had written to Fox, that he would accept, if Robinson took the Seals—*which he knew, at the same time, Robinson would not take*' (ibid. 395). Dodington says that Halifax 'acted shamefully in the affair' and blames his 'duplicity' for the failure of the arrangement.

6. Ibid. 396, with regard to Fox's becoming paymaster of the Army and Dodington treasurer of the Navy.

7. See HW's note on Dodington, Selwyn 292, n. 24.

8. 'A Narrative . . . upon the resolution of his Royal Highness [Frederick Louis, Prince of Wales] to bring a demand into Parliament, for an augmentation of his allowance to £100,000 *per ann.* and for a jointure upon the Princess,'

There is, in the imperfect account of Rochfort, a strong circum-stance or two that pleased me much.[9] There are many passages that will displease several others throughout.

Mr Coxe's[10] *Travels*[11] are very different: plain, clear, sensible, instructive, and entertaining. It is a noble work, and precious to me who delight in quartos: the two volumes contain twelve hundred pages—I have already devoured a quarter, though I have had them but three days.[12]

From Conway, ca June 1784

Missing; apparently several notes about Lady Ailesbury's illness, mentioned *post* 8 June 1784.

To Lady Ailesbury, Tuesday 8 June 1784

Printed from the MS now WSL. First printed, with omissions and misdated, *Works* v. 574–5; first printed in full and correctly dated Toynbee xiii. 158–9 and *Supp.* ii. 166. For the history of the MS see *ante* 23 Aug. 1760.

Strawberry Hill, Tuesday night, June 8th.

YOU frightened me for a minute, my dear Madam; but every letter since[1] has given me pleasure, by telling me how rapidly you recovered, and how perfectly well you are again.[2] Pray however

dated 5 March 1736–7; the motion was rejected by both Houses (*Diary*, pp. 439–69). After an estrangement of four and a half years from the King, the Prince's allowance was increased to £100,000 per annum 29 April 1742 (GRAY i. 249, n. 7).

9. The account (*Diary*, pp. 398–402) substantiates the decision of the leaders not to land at Rochefort, for it brings out the disagreements of the pilots in the council of war, the difficulties of land-ing at another location, and the later testimony of the Chevalier de Rohan that he had been waiting with seven to eight thousand men to attack a British

landing and that the sandbanks were strongly guarded. See *ante* 30 Sept. 1757.

10. Rev. William Coxe (1747–1828), his-torian, biographer, and traveller (OS-SORY ii. 257, nn. 7–9).

11. *Travels in Poland, Russia, Sweden, and Denmark*, London 1784–90, 3 vols, 4to. HW's copy is Hazen, *Cat. of HW's Lib.*, No. 31; see also MORE 215.

12. The rest of this letter is lost (Mary Berry).

1. Apparently from Conway (see below); missing.

2. Lady Mary Coke wrote in her 'MS Journals' 5 June 1784, 'I have the pleasure

do not give me any more such joys. I shall be quite content with your remaining immortal, without the foil of any alarm. You gave all your friends a panic, and may trust their attachment without renewing it. I received as many inquiries the next day as if an Archbishop was in danger, and all the Bench hoped he was going to heaven. I wish your Ladyship joy too of Miss Campbell's[3] recovery.

Mr Conway wonders I do not talk of Voltaire's Memoirs[4]—Lord bless me, I saw it two months ago; the Lucans[5] brought it from Paris and lent it to me: nay, and I have seen most of it before; and I believe this an imperfect copy, for it ends nohow at all.[6] Besides, it was quite out of my head. Lord Melcombe's Diary[7] put that and everything else out of my mind. I wonder much more at Mr Conway's not talking of this! It gossips about the living as familiarly as a modern newspaper. I long to hear what Princess A[melia] says about it. I wish the newspapers were as accurate! They have been circumstantial about Lady Walsingham's[8] Birthday clothes,[9] which to be sure one is glad to know, only unluckily there is no such person:[10] however, I

to assure you Lady Ailesbury is perfectly well and Sir William Fordyce does not think there is any danger of a return.'

3. Caroline Campbell (*ante* 5 Oct. 1777, n. 2), dau. of Lord William Campbell, Lady Ailesbury's brother, after her father's death in 1778 lived with Lady Ailesbury (Ossory ii. 50, 580, iii. 34; Mann ix. 613). See Appendix 17.

4. *Mémoires de M. de Voltaire, écrits par lui-même*, Geneva, 1784; HW's copy, London, 1784, is Hazen, *Cat. of HW's Lib.*, No. 3990. Although Voltaire burned his original manuscript, there were two copies made by his secretary, Wagnière. One of these was stolen in 1768 by La Harpe, who made a copy before returning the Wagnière transcript through Madame Denis. One of Wagnière's copies was sent to the Empress Catherine of Russia; the other was delivered to Beaumarchais before 1783 for the Kehl edition of Voltaire's works. The editors at first intended to include only excerpts from the *Mémoires*, but in 1784 several separate editions of the *Mémoires* appeared, determining the editors of the Kehl edition to include the *Mémoires* in their entirety in their last volume (Voltaire, *Œuvres complètes*, ed. Moland, 1877–85, i. 5–6, 70).

5. Sir Charles Bingham (1735–99), 7th Bt; cr. (1776) Bn and (1795) E. of Lucan; m. (1760) Margaret Smith (d. 1814), who was a favourite at the French Court because of her miniatures (Ossory i. 298, 312).

6. The London edition 1784, ends with an entry dated '1er janvier, 1760' about the King of Prussia. The Geneva edition, 1784, after this entry prints the 'Épître au Maréchal Keith. Sur les vaines terreurs de la mort et les frayeurs d'une autre vie' (pp. 157–74), by the King of Prussia. The *Mémoires* in the *Œuvres complètes*, ed. Moland, end with the same entry dated '12 fevrier 1760' without the 'Épître' (i. 64–5). See also More 215.

7. See *ante* 21 May 1784.

8. Augusta Georgina Elizabeth Irby (1747–1818), m. (1772) Thomas de Grey (1748–1818), 2d Bn Walsingham, 1781.

9. The *London Chronicle* 3–5 June, lv. 544, in a detailed description of the costumes at the Birthday drawing-room, reported, 'Lady Walsingham in a plain white lustring, trimmed in an elegant simplicity of style, with balloon *frivolity* and crape, which had an effect infinitely excelling the glare of colour.'

10. HW apparently forgot that the ti-

dare to say that her dress was very becoming, and that she looked charmingly.

The month of June according to custom immemorial is as cold as Christmas. I had a fire last night, and all my rosebuds, I believe, would have been very glad to sit by it. I have other grievances to boot, but as they are annuals too, *videlicet,* people to see my house,[11] I will not torment your Ladyship with them—yet I know nothing else. None of my neighbours are come into the country yet; one would think all the dowagers were elected into the new Parliament.

Adieu! my dear Madam; I hope your tongue runs like wildfire!

From Conway, ca Wednesday 23 June 1784

Missing; answered *post* 25 June 1784.

To Conway, Friday 25 June 1784

Printed from *Works* v. 229–30.

Strawberry Hill, June 25, 1784.

I CAN answer you very readily in your own tone, that is, about weather and country grievances, and without one word of news or politics; for I know neither, nor inquire of them. I am very well content to be a Strulbrug, and to *exist* after I had done *being:*[1] and I am still better pleased that you are in the same way of thinking, or of not thinking; for I am sure both your health and your mind will

tle of Bn Walsingham was revived in the de Grey family in 1780, when William de Grey was created Bn Walsingham. He was succeeded by his son, Thomas de Grey, in 1781. There were two Lady Walsinghams living at this time.

11. See Ossory ii. 435–6; Berry ii. 221.

———

1. 'When they came to fourscore years, which is reckoned the extremity of living in this country, they had not only all the follies and infirmities of other old men, but many more which arose from the dreadful prospect of never dying. They were not only opinionative, peevish, covetous, morose, vain, talkative; but uncapable of friendship, and dead to all natural affection, which never descended below their grandchildren. Envy and impotent desires, are their prevailing passions. But those objects against which their envy seems principally directed, are the vices of the younger sort, and the deaths of the old. . . . The least miserable among them, appear to be those who turn to dotage, and entirely lose their memories' (Jonathan Swift, *Gulliver's Travels,* Oxford, 1941, p. 196).

find the benefits of living for yourself and family only. It were not fit that the young should concentre themselves in so narrow a circle —nor do the young seem to have any such intention. Let them mend or mar the world as they please—the world takes its own way upon the whole; and though there may be an uncommon swarm of *animalculæ* for a season, things return into their own channel from their own bias, before any effectual nostrum of fumigation is discovered. In the meantime I am for giving all due weight to local grievances, though with no natural turn towards attending to them:—but they serve for conversation. We have no newly-invented grubs to eat our fruit—indeed I have no fruit to be eaten—but I should not lament if the worms would eat my gardener,[2] who, you know, is so bad an one, that I never have anything in my garden. I am now waiting for dry weather to cut my hay—though nature certainly never intended hay should be cut dry, as it always rains all June.—But here is a worse calamity: one is never safe by day or night: Mrs Walsingham,[3] who has bought your brother's late house at Ditton,[4] was robbed a few days ago in the high road, within a mile of home, at *seven* in the evening. The *dii minorum gentium* pilfer everything. Last night they stole a couple of yards of lead off the pediment of the door of my cottage. A gentleman[5] at Putney, who has three men servants, had his house broken open last week, and lost some fine miniatures, which he valued so much, that he would not hang them up. You may imagine what a pain this gives me in my baubles! I have been making the round of my fortifications this morning, and ordering new works.

I am concerned for the account you give me of your brother.[6] Life

2. John Cowie (d. 1795), of whom HW wrote Lady Ossory 28 June 1787, 'My gardener is so bad, that he does not restock me soon. I offered him an annuity some years ago, if he would leave me; but he desired to be excused, as it was not so good as his place, and he knew nobody else would take him—so I have been forced to keep him, because nobody else will' (Ossory ii. 567; Berry ii. 179, n. 7, 183). By 1791 HW had another gardener, Christopher Vickers, to whom he left a bequest in his will (ibid. i. 369, n. 3).

3. Charlotte Hanbury Williams (1738–90), m. (1759) Hon. Robert Boyle Walsingham.

4. At Thames Ditton, Surrey, which she

bought apparently in 1783, as Mary Hamilton wrote in her diary on 4 July 1783, 'she has 42 acres of land for which, house, offices, furniture, etc. she gave £5000'; and in a letter to Charlotte Gunning on 7 July, 'I accompanied Mrs Walsingham and her daughter from Mrs Garrick's to Thames Ditton. Mrs W. is very much pleased with this place . . . here she is sole mistress, and everything around her being her own property, it *interests* and amuses her' (Mary Hamilton, *Letters and Diaries*, ed. Elizabeth and Florence Anson, 1925, pp. 138, 140–1; More 251 and n. 4).

5. Not identified.

6. Deleted in *Works* but restored by Wright. He was apparently living at

does not appear to be such a jewel as to preserve it carefully for its own sake. I think the same of its *good things:* if they do not procure amusement or comfort, I doubt they only produce the contrary.—Yet it is silly to refine; for, probably, whatever any man does by choice, he knows will please him best, or at least will prevent greater uneasiness. I, therefore, rather retract my concern; for with a vast fortune Lord Hertford might certainly do what he would—and if, at his age, he can wish for more than that fortune will obtain, I may pity his taste or temper: but I shall think that you and I are much happier who can find enjoyments in an humbler sphere, nor envy those who have no time for trifling. I, who have never done anything else, am not at all weary of my occupation. Even three days of continued rain have not put me out of humour or spirits. *C'est beaucoup dire* for an *anglais.* Adieu!

To Conway, Wednesday 30 June 1784

Printed from *Works* v. 231–2.

Strawberry Hill, June 30, 1784.

INSTEAD of coming to you, I am thinking of packing up and going to town for winter, so desperate is the weather! I found a great fire at Mrs Clive's this evening, and Mr Raftor[1] hanging over it like a smoked ham. They tell me my hay will be all spoiled for want of cutting; but I had rather it should be destroyed by standing than by being mowed, as the former will cost me nothing but the crop, and 'tis very dear to make nothing but a water souchy of it.

You know I have lost a niece,[2] and found another nephew: he makes the fifty-fourth, reckoning both sexes.[3] We are certainly an affectionate family, for of late we do nothing but marry one another.[4]

Sudbourne Hall, Suffolk; see *post* 10 Oct. 1784.

———

1. Who lived with his sister at Little SH.

2. HW's grand-niece, Laura Keppel (1765–98), 2d dau. of Hon. Frederick Keppel, Bp of Exeter, and Laura, eldest dau. of Sir Edward Walpole; m. (28 June 1784) Hon. George Ferdinand Fitzroy (1761–1810), 2d Bn Southampton, 1797 (MANN ix. 508, nn. 15, 16).

3. See OSSORY ii. 452.

4. HW wrote Mann 8 July 1784, 'Both the bride and bridegroom are descendants of Charles II' (MANN ix. 508; OSSORY ii. 440, n. 1). Also, HW's grand-niece, Lady Elizabeth Laura Waldegrave, had mar-

Have not YOU felt a little twinge in a remote corner of your heart on Lady Harrington's death?[5] She dreaded death so extremely, that I am glad she had not a moment to be sensible of it. I have a great affection for sudden deaths—they save one's self and everybody else a deal of ceremony.

The Duke and Duchess of Marlborough breakfasted here on Monday,[6] and seemed much pleased, though it rained the whole time with an Egyptian darkness. I should have thought there had been deluges enough to destroy all Egypt's other plagues; but the newspapers talk of locusts—I suppose, relations of your beetles, though probably not so fond of green fruit; for the scene of their campaign is Queen Square, Westminster, where there certainly has not been an orchard since the reign of Canute.[7]

I have, at last, seen an air balloon[8]—just as I once did see a tiny review, by passing one accidentally on Hounslow Heath.[9] I was going last night to Lady Onslow at Richmond, and over Mr Cambridge's field[10] I saw a bundle in the air not bigger than the moon, and she

ried (1782) her cousin, George Waldegrave, styled Vct Chewton, 4th E. Waldegrave, 1784 (ibid. i. 304, n. 12, ii. 441). Another of HW's grand-nieces, Lady Charlotte Maria Waldegrave, m. (1784) George Henry Fitzroy.

5. She died 28 June at her house in Curzon Street, Mayfair (*London Chronicle* 26–9 June, lv. 624). Lady Mary Coke wrote in her 'MS Journals' 29 June 1784, 'The first news Lady Holdernesse told me was that the Dowager Lady Harrington died yesterday. She was poor woman in a great passion with one of her servants and in coming downstairs fell but was supported by a servant and never spoke; 'tis supposed to be an apoplectic fit.' Conway had almost become engaged to her in his youth (*ante* 18 July, 5 Aug. 1744 NS).

6. 28 June; they are listed in HW's 'Book of Visitors,' BERRY ii. 221. HW refers to this visit when the Marlboroughs came again on 2 July 1790 (ibid. i. 82).

7. The *Morning Chronicle* 29 June reports, 'A visitation of locusts has always been dreaded, as they devour the fruits of the earth and endanger famine. When anything of the kind impends us, it behoves every individual, to communicate what he knows advisable to be done to destroy the formation of such animalculæ, which may, when acquired a proper growth, be hurtful to the vegetable kingdom. At this present time, Queen's Square and its environs are pestered with an insect of the beetle kind; these seem to be of three sorts. One like the field black beetle without wings, another sort with wings, having legs like a chafer and a head like a locust, armed with a perforator and sucker; which enables them to pierce almost anything . . . there is another sort quite white . . . Our correspondent would be glad to be informed whether these beetles are engendered in the earth, or whether the soil about Queen Square nourishes them by any peculiar quality.'

8. For HW's comments on air-balloons see Mann ix. 449–50, nn. 7–10; OSSORY ii. 446–7; *post* 16 Oct. 1784.

9. HW wrote Lady Ossory 14 June 1774, 'I never go to reviews' (OSSORY i. 195; see also COLE i. 110; *ante* 20 Aug. 1782, n. 1).

10. Richard Owen Cambridge in 1751 bought a house in Twickenham Meadows near Richmond and across the Thames from Richmond Hill, and lived there until 1802 (BERRY i. 16, n. 20; 31, n. 12).

herself could not have descended with more composure if she had expected to find Endymion fast asleep. It seemed to 'light on Richmond Hill; but Mrs Hobart[11] was going by, and her coiffure prevented my seeing it alight. The papers say, that a balloon has been made at Paris, representing the Castle of Stockholm, in compliment to the King of Sweden,[12] but that they were afraid to let it off[13]—so, I suppose, it will be served up to him in a dessert. No great progress surely is made in these airy navigations, if they are still afraid of risking the necks of two or three subjects for the entertainment of a visiting sovereign. There is seldom a *feu de joie* for the birth of a dauphin that does not cost more lives. I thought royalty and science never haggled about the value of blood when experiments are in question.

I shall wait for summer before I make you a visit.[14] Though I dare to say that you have converted your smoke-kilns[15] into a manufacture of balloons, pray do not erect a Strawberry castle in the air for my reception, if it will cost a pismire a hair of its head. Good night!—I

11. Deleted in *Works,* but restored by Wright. There were two Mrs Hobarts in the neighbourhood: Albinia Bertie (ca 1738–1816), m. (1757) Hon. George Hobart, 3d E. of Buckinghamshire, 1793; she had a villa on Ham Common (OSSORY ii. 285, n. 2; BERRY i. 273, n. 9). Anne Margaret Bristow (d. 1788), m. (1761) Hon. Henry Hobart; her house was on Richmond Hill, directly across the Thames from Cambridge's (ibid. i. 63, nn. 8, 9).

12. Gustav III (1746–92), K. of Sweden 1771–92. His arrival in Paris 7 June and the entertainments planned for him are described in the *London Chronicle* 19–22 June, lv. 600, *sub* 'Extract of a Letter from Paris, June 11.' He left Paris suddenly 21 June because of threats of a war with Denmark (ibid. 29 June – 1 July, lvi. 4).

13. The *London Chronicle* 29 June – 1 July, lvi. 1–2, *sub* 'Extract of a Letter from Paris, June 24,' reported: 'Yesterday about three o'clock in the afternoon, an air balloon, 156 feet in circumference, was let off at Versailles for the entertainment of the King of Sweden. There was a large gallery fixed to it, in which were M. Charles, M. James, M. Montgolfier, and an officer of the army. It ascended very gradually till it was

totally out of sight, and remained so for some time; it then became visible, and passed over the Thuilleries at Paris, the gentlemen waving flags all the while they were in sight. About five o'clock the gentlemen were safely landed, after an aerial jaunt of more than 20 miles. A balloon was prepared, representing the Castle of Stockholm, which was intended to have been illuminated, and sent up at night; but the experiment was given up as too dangerous.'

14. HW visited Park Place 18–20 July; Conway wrote Hertford 21 July 1784: 'We have had lately a succession of friendly visits: the Harrowbys, Campbells, Richmonds; and just now the Churchills, Miss Hervey and Mr Walpole, who left us this morning' (MS now WSL). HW wrote Lady Ossory 19 Aug. 1784, 'Except three days at Park Place, I have not stirred hence' (OSSORY ii. 438).

15. For Conway's coke-ovens see *ante* 17 Sept. 1782, n. 6. Conway wrote Hertford 21 July 1784, 'I am . . . pursuing my little plans here with as much eagerness as if they would save the nation; though I doubt they will hardly save their author: if they don't quite ruin him it's something, and in the meantime they amuse infinitely.'

have ordered my bed to be heated as hot as an oven, and Tonton and I must go into it.

To Conway, Saturday 14 August 1784

Printed from *Works* v. 232–3.

Strawberry Hill, August 14, 1784.

AS Lady C[ecilia Johnston] offers to be postman, I cannot resist writing a line, though I have not a word to say. In good sooth, I know nothing, hear of nothing but robberies and house-breaking; consequently never think of ministers, India directors, and such honest men. Mrs Clive has been broken open, and Mr Raftor miscarried and died of the fright. Lady Browne[1] has lost all her liveries and her temper and Lady Margaret Compton[2] has cried her eyes out on losing a lurch[3] and almost her wig.[4]—In short, as I do not love exaggeration, I do not believe there have been above threescore highway robberies within this week, fifty-seven houses that have been broken open, and two hundred and thirty that are to be stripped on the first opportunity. We are in great hopes, however, that the King of Spain, now he has demolished Algiers, the metropolitan see of thieves,[5] will come and bombard Richmond, Twickenham, Hampton

1. Deleted in *Works*, but restored by Wright.

2. (ca 1703–86), dau. of the 4th E. of Northampton, one of HW's 'juvenile cotemporaries' with whom he played cards (Ossory i. 307–8, n. 10, ii. 285–6; More 406, 410). According to J. A. Home, the editor of Lady Mary Coke's *Journals*, she was 'an eccentric character; her oddities, her wig, her gambling, etc. etc., are frequently spoken of in this journal. In 1785, only a year before her death, she lost 150 guineas at cards in one night' (*Journals*, i. 29, n. 2). Her name was deleted in *Works*; see Mrs Toynbee's article in *Notes and Queries* 22 Dec. 1900, 9th ser. vi. 483, where she corrects the identification of Wright and Cunningham.

3. 'Used in various games to denote a certain concluding state of the score, in which one player is enormously ahead of the other; often, a "maiden set" or love-game . . . at cribbage, a game in which the winner scores 61 before the loser has scored 31; in whist, a treble' (OED, *sub* 'lurch, 2' which quotes HW's sentence). Lady Margaret Compton was noted for weeping when she was the loser; see Lady Mary Coke, op. cit. ii. 213, iii. 136, n. 1, iv. 441.

4. Lady Mary Coke wrote in 1774, 'Lady Margaret Compton was robbed three times last year. The Princess [Amelia] says she wishes she had pulled off her wig and dashed it in the highwayman's face; it indeed seems fitter for that purpose then any other, for it is worse then ever' (ibid. iv. 406).

5. The *London Chronicle* 10–12 Aug., lvi. 150, *sub* 'Extract of a Letter from Paris, Aug. 3,' reported 'the complete destruction of the city of Algiers, which was set on fire in six or seven different places, on the 16th of last month, and all

Court, and all the suffragan cities that swarm with pirates and banditti, as he has a better knack at destroying vagabonds than at recovering his own.

Ireland is in a blessed way;[6] and as if the climate infected everybody that sets foot there, the Viceroy's[7] aides-de-camp[8] have *blundered*
into a riot,[9] that will set all the humours afloat.[10]

the public buildings burnt to the ground';
the next paper 12–14 Aug., lvi. 159, stated,
'The Spaniards have at last carried their
long-concerted plan against Algiers into
execution, by bombarding that place,
where they are said to have destroyed
upwards of 3000 houses, 170 mosques,
and other public buildings, and burnt
effects to a very considerable amount.'
According to the *Gazette de Leyde* 20
Aug. the expedition, under the command
of Don Antonio Barcelo, 'lieutenant-
général des armées navales,' had only partial success. The Spaniards began the
bombardment 12 July without opposition, but on the following days were
hampered by contrary winds, high seas,
disunion among their leaders, and harass-
ment by the Algerian gun-boats, so that
'par-là il est arrivé que de 4000 bombes
il n'en est tombé, dit-on, pas plus de 50
dans la Place.' The bombardment was
stopped 21 July, and the squadron left
the Bay of Algiers 23 July.

6. Because of the violent meetings preliminary to a national congress of delegates to be held in Dublin in October
for the purpose of discussing Roman
Catholic suffrage and reform of representation in Parliament; see MANN ix.
528–9 and nn. 6–8. Rutland wrote Pitt
15 Aug. 1784, 'This city [Dublin] is, in
a great measure, under the dominion and
tyranny of the mob. Persons are daily
marked out for the operation of tarring
and feathering; the magistrates neglect
their duty, and none of the rioters . . .
have been taken, while the corps of
volunteers in the neighbourhood seem,
as it were, to countenance these out-
rages' (*Correspondence between . . . William Pitt and Charles, Duke of Rutland*,
1890, p. 37). He believed all the plots
were 'entirely French and Roman Catholic' in origin (ibid. 41).

7. Charles Manners (1754–87), styled M.
of Granby 1770–9, 4th D. of Rutland,

1779; lord lieutenant of Ireland 1784–7.

8. Listed in the *London Calendar*,
1784, p. 277; *Royal Kalendar*, 1785, p.
267. Col. Francis Dundas should be
added (Hist. MSS Comm., 14th Report [pt
i], *Rutland MSS*, 1888–1905, iii. 74, 137).

9. The *St James's Chronicle* 7–10 Aug.
reported *sub* Dublin, 5 Aug.; 'Last Monday night [2 Aug.], between the hours
of eleven and twelve, a number of officers in the army, most of them aides-de-
camp to his Grace the Duke of Rutland,
flushed it is thought with wine, entered
the shop of Mr Flattery, a publican, of
Ormond-Quay, near Essex-Bridge, after
assaulting a waiter that stood at the door,
under the pretense of calling for liquor;
here they had not been long before two
of them behaved with the utmost rudeness and indecency to Mrs Flattery, notwithstanding her earnest entreaties to
them to desist; she was at last overheard
by her husband, but on his appearance
one of those gentry, on observing a military stock upon him, cried—"What, you
are a Volunteer, a'nt you?" and tweaked
him by the nose: Flattery had too much
Irish blood to bear with this indignity,
in addition to the assaulting his wife,
and, therefore, knocked the person down;
the whole corps immediately attacked
him with their swords. . . .' A fight en-
sued; a mob assembled and pelted the
officers with stones; the disturbance ended
only after the arrival of the city guard
and Sheriff Smith. See also *Hibernian
Magazine* Aug. 1784, p. 485.

10. Pitt wrote Rutland 9 Aug. 1784
that 'there seems nothing to be so much
dreaded as any provocation or pretext for
the spirit of discontent' and advised
'quietly getting rid of the persons concerned in the riot' (*Correspondence*, pp.
34–5). Rutland answered 15 Aug. that
the riot, though exaggerated by the press,
'was, however, very unfortunately timed,
and an exceedingly foolish drunken busi-

I wish you joy of the summer being come now it is gone, which is better than not coming at all. I hope Lady C[ecilia] will return with an account of your all being perfectly well. Adieu!

To Hertford, ca Thursday 7 October 1784

Missing; answered *post* 10 Oct. 1784.

From Hertford, Sunday 10 October 1784

Printed for the first time from a photostat of BM Add. MSS 23219, f. 144.

Sudborne Hall, October 10th 1784.

Dear Horry,

YOU have made an abundant return by the letter[1] I have just received from you. My game scarce deserved any acknowledgment, much less that of form or what would be attended with any trouble; I will not therefore suppose you employed your pen ill for the first time, and I will thank you for giving me so exact an account of Lady Ailesbury, for whose recovery I must be anxious.[2] I hope by what you say there is no immediate danger at least, and that care, attention and remedies may yet prolong her life; but still constitutional complaints or weaknesses must have their end, and age as it advances grows less able to resist the attacks. I am sorry you are plagued with thieves and robbers;[3] somehow or other we have contrived to make England less an earthly paradise than we were taught to esteem it. At a greater distance from the metropolis we are free from such calamities, and have all the advantages which retired life brings with it; but we are too distant from the scenes of business and

ness. . . . At first I determined to dismiss those in my family who were concerned in it; but on reconsideration, as a suit at law was instituted, I thought it more just to forbid the delinquents from appearing in my presence till after their trial, when, if their culpability is strongly proved, I intend to remove them entirely' (ibid. 40).

1. Missing.

2. See *ante* 8 June 1784, n. 2; *post* 16 Oct. 1784. Lady Mary Coke wrote in her 'MS Journals' 20 Dec. 1784, 'Lady Ailesbury still at Park Place but better in health then she has been for some time.'

3. See HW to Lady Ossory 23 Oct. 1784, Ossory ii. 445.

HON. FRANCIS SEYMOUR CONWAY, MARQUESS OF
HERTFORD, BY SIR JOSHUA REYNOLDS

pleasure for events of either. You must therefore expect nothing to entertain you from hence.

Henry[4] and two of my daughters[5] are with me here, and my health, which you are so good to inquire after, is too good for me to mention without gratitude to the author and giver of it. I remain, dear Horry,

Your affectionate and faithful servant,

HERTFORD

To CONWAY, Saturday 16 October 1784

Printed from *Works* v. 233–4. HW dated this letter 15 October, but Mrs Toynbee correctly points out that the date should be 16 October, the day when Blanchard's balloon trip took place (see below, n. 4).

Strawberry Hill, October 15[16], 1784.

AS I have heard nothing from you, I flatter myself Lady A. mends, or I think you would have brought her again to the physicians:[1] you will, I conclude, next week, as towards the end of it the ten days they named will be expired. I must be in town myself about Thursday[2] on some little business of my own.

As I was writing this, my servants called me away to see a balloon— I suppose Blanchard's,[3] that was to be let off from Chelsea this morning.[4] I saw it from the common field before the window of my round

4. Hon. Henry Seymour-Conway, Hertford's 2d son, who was unmarried and had withdrawn from the by-election at Downton in July, 1784 in favour of his brother William (Namier and Brooke iii. 425, 426).

5. Hertford's two unmarried daughters were: Lady Elizabeth Seymour-Conway (1754–1825) and Lady Isabella Rachel Seymour-Conway, m. (1785) George Hatton (OSSORY i. 358, n. 18; *ante* 24 Aug. 1776, n. 3). They were living with their father at the time of Lady Hertford's death (Selwyn to Carlisle, 11 Nov. 1782, Hist. MSS Comm., 15th Report, App. pt vi, *Carlisle MSS*, 1897, p. 568).

1. One of her physicians was Sir William Fordyce (1724–92), Kt, surgeon to the 3d regiment of Foot Guards 1750–69; M.D. at Cambridge by royal mandate, 1770; licentiate of the Royal College of Physicians, 1786 (*ante* 8 June 1784, n. 2; BERRY i. 120, n. 23; *Army Lists*, 1755, p. 32, 1769, p. 53; *Royal Kalendar*, 1787, p. 217; GM 1792, lxii pt ii. 1156, 1218–19).

2. 21 Oct.; the 'business' is not explained.

3. Jean-Pierre Blanchard (1750–1809), French aeronaut; see MANN ix. 543, n. 6.

4. Saturday, 16 Oct. The *London Chronicle* 14–16 Oct., lvi. 376, reported, 'This being the day appointed for launching

tower. It appeared about a third of the size of the moon,[5] or less, when setting, something above the tops of the trees on the level horizon. It was then descending; and after rising and declining a little, it sunk slowly behind the trees, I should think about or beyond Sunbury, at five minutes after one.[6] But you know I am a very inexact guesser at measures and distances, and may be mistaken in many miles; and you know how little I have attended to those *airgonauts:* only t'other night I diverted myself with a sort of meditation on future *airgonation,* supposing that it will not only be perfected, but will depose navigation.[7] I did not finish it, because I am not skilled, like the gentleman that used to write political ship-news, in that style, which I wanted to perfect my essay: but in the prelude I observed how ignorant the ancients were in supposing Icarus melted the wax of his wings by too near access to the sun, whereas he would have been frozen to death before he made the first post on that road. Next, I discovered an alliance between Bishop Wilkins's[8] art of flying[9] and his plan of an universal language,[10] the latter of

Mr Blanchard's grand aerostatic machine from the Royal Military Academy, Little Chelsea, an amazing concourse of people were assembled.' The next issue 16–19 Oct., lvi. 377, described the ascension in detail: 'The balloon raised itself about ten feet, and was saluted with the acclamation of the spectators. After it had ascended to such an height as barely to clear the wall of the garden, it sunk again to the ground in the next garden, when both the gentlemen [Blanchard and John Sheldon] exerted themselves in throwing out ballast. . . . The balloon, freed from every kind of earthly danger, then moved rapidly into the air. . . . This was exactly at eight minutes past twelve o'clock. . . . it was out of sight . . . in less than twenty minutes' (see also *Daily Adv.* 19 Oct., *Gazetteer and New Daily Advertiser* 18 Oct.).

5. For an illustration see J. E. Hodgson, *History of Aeronautics in Great Britain,* Oxford, 1924, facing p. 165.

6. 'They passed over Hammersmith and Chiswick, then over Twickenham, where the balloon was discerned very clearly; after that it began gradually to descend, their joint weight being rather too great for the buoyancy of the inflammable air contained [in] it. Finding it impracticable

for them both to proceed any farther, Mr Sheldon agreed to alight, and to leave his companion to the prosecution of his journey. They accordingly, a little after one o'clock, descended to the earth, at Sunbury, near Hampton Court. . . . Here Mr Sheldon alighted in a field belonging to Mr Boehm, and having assisted Mr Blanchard in laying in a sufficient quantity of ballast . . . left him to mount once more into the clouds' (*London Chronicle* 16–19 Oct., lvi. 378).

7. HW expresses similar views to Lady Ossory 23 Oct. 1784 and to Mann 2 Dec. 1783 and 30 Sept. 1784 (OSSORY ii. 446–7; MANN ix. 449–50, 527–8).

8. John Wilkins, Bp of Chester, 1668 (*ante* 21 July 1758, n. 21).

9. HW is presumably referring to Wilkins's 'Discourse Concerning the Possibility of a Passage Thither' in the 3d edn, 1640, of his *Discovery of a World in the Moone,* and/or to chapters 6–8 of the second book of *Mathematicall Magick,* 1648, entitled 'Of the Volant Automata,' 'Concerning the Art of Flying,' and 'A Resolution of the two Chief Difficulties that seem to oppose the Possibility of a Flying Chariot.'

10. *An Essay towards a Real Character, and a Philosophical Language,* 1668; HW's

which he no doubt calculated to prevent the want of an interpreter when he should arrive at the moon.

But I chiefly amused myself with ideas of the change that would be made in the world by the substitution of balloons to ships. I supposed our seaports to become *deserted villages,* and Salisbury Plain, Newmarket Heath (another canvass for alteration of ideas), and all downs (but *the* Downs) arising into dockyards for aerial vessels. Such a field would be ample in furnishing new speculations—but to come to my ship-news:

'The good balloon *Dædalus,* Capt. Wing-ate, will fly in a few days for China; he will stop at the top of the Monument to take in passengers.

'Arrived on Brand Sands, the *Vulture,* Capt. Nabob; the *Tortoise* snow, from Lapland; the *Pet-en-l'air,* from Versailles; the *Dreadnought,* from Mount Etna, Sir W. Hamilton, commander; the *Tympany,* Mongolfier;[11] and the *Mine-A-in-a-bandbox,*[12] from the Cape of Good Hope. Foundered in a hurricane, the *Bird of Paradise,* from Mount Ararat. The *Bubble,* Sheldon,[13] took fire, and was burnt to her gallery;[14] and the *Phœnix* is to be cut down to a second-rate.'—In those days Old Sarum will again be a town and have houses in it. There will be fights in the air with wind-guns and bows and arrows; and there will be prodigious increase of land for tillage, especially in France, by breaking up all public roads as useless.—But enough of my fooleries, for which I am sorry you must pay double postage.

copy is Hazen, *Cat. of HW's Lib.,* No. 1136.

11. Joseph-Michel Montgolfier (1740–1810) and his brother, Jacques-Étienne Montgolfier (1745–99) invented the first hot-air balloon (*montgolfière*) which they launched at Annonay, France, on 5 June 1783 (NBG; MANN ix. 450, n. 8).

12. A slang expression, 'mine-arse-in-a-bandbox'; see Eric Partridge, *Dictionary of Slang and Unconventional English,* sub 'bandbox'; MASON i. 103, n. 27. Possibly an allusion to the character, Mine-all, in the farce, *Aerostation; or, The Templar's Stratagem,* by Frederick Pilon (1750–88), produced at Covent Garden 29 Oct., 5, 12, 17, 23 Nov. 1784, and published in Nov. 1784 (*London Stage* Pt V,

ii. 732, 748, 749, 751, 753, 754; *Public Advertiser* 11 Nov. 1784).

13. John Sheldon (1752–1808), anatomist; appointed professor of anatomy to the Royal Academy, 1783; F.R.S., 1784; surgeon to the Westminster Hospital, 1786 (GM 1808, lxxviii pt ii. 957; *Royal Kalendar,* 1785, p. 214; J. E. Hodgson and F. A. Eaton, *The Royal Academy and its Members 1768–1830,* 1905, p. 60).

14. An allusion to Sheldon's association with Allen Keegan in an attempt to launch a hot-air balloon from Lord Foley's garden in Portland Place in Sept. 1784. The ascent was postponed, and finally on 29 Sept. 'the balloon caught fire in the experiment, and was consumed' (*Daily Adv.* 28 Sept., 1 Oct.; Hodgson and Eaton, op. cit. 114–16).

To HERTFORD, ca Wednesday 10 November 1784

Missing. A letter of condolence on Lady Drogheda's death, answered *post* 16 Nov. 1784; HW wrote Lady Ossory 12 Nov. 1784, 'I never saw General Conway so much struck as when he brought me the news' (OSSORY ii. 449).

From HERTFORD, Tuesday 16 November 1784

Printed for the first time from a photostat of BM Add. MSS 23219, f. 145.

Sudborne Hall, November 16th 1784.

Dear Horry,

YOU know the loss I have sustained by the death of my dear daughter and friend Lady Drogheda;[1] her virtues must now be my best consolation, and your testimony of them, so kindly and so affectionately expressed,[2] is a great satisfaction to a father's mind. I thank you a thousand times for the regard you profess and the justice you do to her memory. She was as you say perfect;[3] it is therefore my own and her family's loss that I have to lament, not hers.

I remain, dear Horry, with perfect truth and gratitude for the friendship which you have so long showed me and my family,

Ever yours,

HERTFORD

1. She died 4 Nov. 1784 'at the Earl's seat at Moore Abbey' (*London Chronicle* 23–5 Nov., lvi. 509). Conway brought the news to HW, who wrote Lady Ossory 12 Nov., 'She has been carried off in six days by a bilious disorder' (OSSORY ii. 448, 449).

2. Presumably in a missing letter of condolence.

3. HW wrote a 'character' of Lady Drogheda to Lady Ossory 12 Nov. in which he said, 'She was really as perfect as a mortal could be' (ibid. ii. 448).

From HERTFORD, Saturday 20 November 1784

Printed for the first time from a photostat of BM Add. MSS 23219, f. 146.

Sudborne Hall, November 20th 1784.

Dear Horry,

YOU are entitled to every mark of attention from me, and if you feel interested in the union between your niece[1] and Lord Euston[2] I desire you to accept my compliments upon it.[3]

I know it only as common news; my communication with that part of the Fitzroys is, alas, much altered,[4] but I can never cease to feel an interest in the name when I reflect on the dear connection I had with the family.[5]

Lady Maria is a very pretty and a very sensible woman;[6] and he is, in appearance as well as in character, an amiable young man. It is their own fault if they are not happy.

I remain, dear Horry, always very truly and affectionately yours,

HERTFORD

1. HW's grand-niece, Lady Charlotte Maria Waldegrave.

2. George Henry Fitzroy (1760–1844), eldest son of Augustus Henry, 3d D. of Grafton; styled E. of Euston; 4th D. of Grafton, 1811.

3. The marriage took place 16 Nov. by special licence at Navestock, Essex, the seat of Lord and Lady Waldegrave (Ossory ii. 452 and n. 4). HW first heard of the engagement in August, and disapproved only because the D. of Grafton opposed it (ibid. ii. 441, 445, n. 4, 451–2).

4. For HW's account of the Duke of Grafton's rupture with Hertford see ibid. iii. 240–2, Appendix 3.

5. Lady Hertford was a Fitzroy and aunt of the 3d D. of Grafton.

6. HW wrote Lady Ossory 17 Nov. 1784, 'I will venture to foretell that if sense and sweetness of temper can constitute the chief felicity of a husband, Lord Euston will not be unhappy' (ibid. ii. 451; see also MANN ix. 411). For Lady Mary Coke's opinion see OSSORY ii. 441, n. 6.

To Conway, Sunday 28 November 1784

Printed from *Works* v. 234–6.

Sunday night, Nov. 28, 1784.

I HAVE received the parcel of papers[1] you sent me, which I conclude come from Lord Strafford, and will apply them as well as I possibly can, you may be sure—but with little of doing any good: humanity is no match for cruelty. There are now and then such angelic beings as Mr Hanway[2] and Mr Howard;[3] but our race in general is pestilently bad and malevolent. I have been these two years wishing to promote my excellent Mr Porter's[4] plan for alleviating the woes of chimney-sweepers, but never could make impression on three people; on the contrary, have generally caused a smile.[5]

George Conway's intelligence[6] of hostilities commenced between the Dutch and Imperialists[7] makes me suppose that France will support the former[8]—or could they resist? Yet I had heard that France

1. Against cruelty to dogs (HW); possibly sent to Conway to gain his support. Bentley had written an essay on this subject in 1760; see CHUTE, Appendix 2.

2. Jonas Hanway (1712–86), traveller and philanthropist; a founder of the Marine Society, 1756, and of the Magdalen Hospital, 1758. He wrote *A Sentimental History of Chimney Sweepers in London and Westminster*, 1785; see CHATTERTON 217 and n. 4.

3. John Howard (ca 1726–90), prison reformer and philanthropist (OSSORY ii. 566, n. 29; MORE 293).

4. David Porter (ca 1747–1819) of Little Welbeck Street, Marylebone; master chimney-sweeper, whom HW esteemed 'as one of the apostles of humanity' (to Lort 5 July 1789, CHATTERTON 217 and n. 2).

5. On 22 April 1788 Porter presented a petition for a bill for the better regulation of chimney-sweepers and their apprentices; the bill was passed by the Commons 30 May, by the Lords with amendments 13 June, and received the royal assent 25 June as 28 Geo. III, c. 48 (*Journals of the House of Commons* xliii. 406, 436–7, 519, 551, 637). HW may have solicited the younger Horace

Mann's support in Parliament for such a bill (MANN ix. 353).

6. Possibly from France; see MANN ix. 545, 546, n. 23.

7. In May Joseph II had demanded the right of free navigation on the Scheldt River for Belgian vessels, in opposition to previous treaties, and finally in October ordered a ship to sail from Antwerp down the Scheldt; the vessel was seized 8 Oct. by the Dutch (ibid. ix. 530, n. 12; 538–9, n. 6). When Imperial troops were ordered to march into Austrian Flanders, the Dutch responded by flooding the land around their forts Lillo, Frederick Henry, Liefkenshoeck, and Kruis-schans (ibid. ix. 541, n. 6; 543, n. 8; *London Chronicle* 23–5, 27–30 Nov., lvi. 512, 528; *Gazette de Leyde* 19 Nov., *sub* Leyde, 18 Nov.; 23 Nov., *sub* Brussels, 18 Nov.).

8. France under the Treaty of Versailles of 1756 was bound to assist Austria, but at this time was negotiating a treaty of defensive alliance with Holland, concluded on 10 Nov. 1785 (*Recueil de traités*, ed. G. F. de Martens, 2d edn, Göttingen, 1817–35, iv. 65–70; MANN ix. 544, n. 9). Dorset, the English ambassa-

would not. Some have thought, as I have done,[9] that a combination of partition would happen between Austria, France, and Prussia, the modern law of nations for avoiding wars. I know nothing: so my conjectures may all be erroneous; especially as one argues from reason; a very inadequate judge, as it leaves passions, caprices, and accidents, out of its calculation. It does not seem the interest of France, that the Emperor's power should increase in their neighbourhood and extend to the sea. Consequently it is France's interest to protect Holland in concert with Prussia.[10] This last is a transient power, and may determine on the death of the present King;[11] but the Imperial is a permanent force, and must be the enemy of France, however present connections[12] may incline the scale.

In any case, I hope we shall no way be hooked into the quarrel;[13] not only from the impotence of our circumstances, but as I think it would decide the loss of Ireland, which seems tranquillizing:[14] but

dor at Paris, wrote Carmarthen 25 Nov. 1784, 'It is at present very much my opinion that the French have no design of abandoning their new allies. Monsieur de Vergennes entertains great hopes that the Emperor will listen to terms of accommodation, but the steps his Imperial Majesty has taken do not seem to indicate a disposition to be easily soothed into a relinquishment of his original demands' (*Dispatches from Paris 1784–1790*, ed. Oscar Browning, Camden Third Series, Vol. XVI, i. 28). Louis XVI ordered two armies to the frontiers, one in Flanders and the other in Alsace, and declared that he would oppose hostile advances on Holland (*Gazette de Leyde* 26 Nov., *sub* Versailles, 15 Nov.; MANN ix. 545, n. 22; Noailles's instructions of 20 Nov. in Mercy-Argenteau, *Correspondance secrète*, ed. Arneth and Flammermont, 1889, i. 345–6, n. 1).

9. See MANN ix. 539.

10. The *Daily Adv.* 30 Nov., *sub* Utrecht, 19 Nov., reported, 'We are assured that France is to furnish 40,000 men, and Prussia 30,000, for the service of the Republic.' The crisis was averted when the Dutch agreed to grant free navigation to Austrian mercantile vessels but not to armed ships (ibid. 5 Jan. 1785, *sub* Vienna 18 Dec.; MANN ix. 554, 556).

11. Frederick II ('the Great').

12. I.e., the family connection, Marie-Antoinette being Joseph II's sister; for their letters on this crisis see *Marie Antoinette, Joseph II und Leopold II: Ihr Briefwechsel*, ed. Arneth, Leipzig, 1866, pp. 49–52.

13. Carmarthen wrote Dorset 6 Nov. 1784, 'It is undoubtedly the wish of this government to avoid taking any decided part at present in the disputes between the Emperor and Holland' (*British Diplomatic Instructions 1689–1789*, Vol. VII: France, Pt IV, ed. L. G. Wickham Legg, 1934, p. 253). But during the negotiations for preliminary articles of peace in 1785 Vergennes suspected the British of advising the Dutch to resist the Emperor 'pour les éloigner de la France et les amener à renouveler leurs anciennes liaisons avec la Grande-Bretagne' (Mercy-Argenteau, op. cit. i. 435, n. 1).

14. Rutland wrote Lord Sydney 15 Nov. 1784, 'Public tranquillity seems thoroughly established' (Hist. MSS Comm., 14th Report, App. pt i, *Rutland MSS*, 1894, iii. 149). Rutland recommended to Pitt 14 Nov. 1784 that a Protestant 'militia should be constituted and an act of Parliament passed rendering it high treason for bodies of men to assemble as volunteers, with arms, uniforms, accoutrements, etc., without a legal commission from Government' (ibid. 148;

should we have any bickering with France, she would renew the manœuvres she practised so fatally in America. These are my politics; I do not know with whose they coincide or disagree, nor does it signify a straw. Nothing will depend on my opinion; nor have I any opinion about them, but when I have nothing at all to do that amuses me more, or nothing else to fill a letter.

I can give you a sample of my idleness, which may divert Lady A. and your academy of arts and sciences for a minute in the evening. It came into my head yesterday to send a card to Lady Lyttelton,[15] to ask when she would be in town—here it is in an heroic epistle:

> From a castle as vast—as the castles on signs;
> From a hill that all Africa's—mole-hills outshines,
> This epistle is sent to a cottage so small,
> That the door cannot ope, if you stand in the hall,
> To a lady, who would be fifteen, if her knight
> And old swain were as young as Methusalem quite:
> It comes to inquire—not whether her eyes
> Are as radiant as ever—but how many sighs
> He must vent to the rocks and the echoes around,
> (Though nor echo nor rock in the parish is found)
> Before she obdurate his passion will meet—
> His passion to see her in Portugal Street.

As the sixth line goes rather too near the core, do not give a copy of it: however, I should be sorry if it displeased; though I do not believe it will, but be taken with good humour as it was meant.[16]

see also *Correspondence between . . . William Pitt and Charles, Duke of Rutland*, 1890, pp. 50–2).

15. HW apparently wrote these verses 27 Nov. 1784 but misdated his letter to Lady Lyttelton 28 Nov. (MS in Massachusetts Historical Society). A transcript by HW of the verses is headed: 'A card sent from Strawberry Hill to Elizabeth Rich, Baroness Dowager Lyttelton, to inquire when she will be in town, Nov. 27, 1784' (MS formerly in the Waller Collection, printed in Toynbee *Supp.* ii. 8n).

16. Mary Berry noted, 'It was taken in perfect good humour; and she returned the following answer, which Mr Walpole owned was better than his address' (*Works* v. 236, n. 1). Lady Lyttelton's reply of four verses, in her own hand, is written under HW's verses in the MS. HW's transcript of her reply is headed: 'Lady Lyttelton's answer the next day . . . Ripley Cottage, Nov. 28th' (Toynbee *Supp.* ii. 8n). HW wrote her 2 Dec. 1784 from Berkeley Square to commend her 'cleverness and good humour.'

From HERTFORD, Monday 27 June 1785

Printed for the first time from a photostat of BM Add. MSS 23219, ff. 147–8.

Sudborne Hall, June 27th 1785.

Dear Horry,

I RETURN you in the present parcel the books you was so good to lend me some years ago, and I accompany them with a thousand thanks and full as many excuses. I could not find them sooner, and I hope I have collected them all in the enclosed packet. If I have not, you will be so good to let me know it. Since the death of my dearest and lamented wife,[1] my thoughts, books, etc., etc. have been scattered about, and weak as it may seem, my mind is more distressed whenever I examine anything which was in her possession. You knew her mind, and can feel and excuse me if it is an error either of mind or nature.

You may perhaps expect me, as I am writing to a friend of so many years' date, to say that I enjoy very perfect health, thank God, in my retirement here. I have a companion with me in my son,[2] whom I love and esteem, that approves the tranquillity in which we live as much as myself, and we have a thousand little improvements and occupations which employ us. The life is a very different one from that in which my lot was cast for so many years; but everything changes in this world and has its season. The early years of it were passed in the country, and I can resume its amusements and employments without trouble or regret. We know little of what passes in the busy world. Mr Pitt, by the papers which are sent to us every day, seems to have lost a considerable share of the popularity which he derived from his name;[3] but as he has the King at his feet and the

1. See *ante* 10 Nov. 1782.
2. Probably the Hon. Henry Seymour-Conway; see *ante* 10 Oct. 1784. His obituary in GM notes, 'Lord Henry's disposition appears to have been always for retirement' (GM 1830, c pt i. 363), and HW described him as 'very indolent' and as having 'much humour' (MANN ix. 608). See also Appendix 13.
3. The *Daily Adv.* 16 June reported, 'On Tuesday [14 June] a considerable mob assembled at the end of Downing Street, to wait Mr Pitt's going to the House of Commons. At a quarter past three he went down amidst much rude behaviour from the populace all the way. His coach drove almost as fast as the horses could gallop; but the mob being stationed in rank on each side, they pressed hard upon him just as he stopped in Palace Yard, and crying out, "No Shop Tax! No Irish Bill!" attempted to lay hold of him as he alighted from his carriage; but he shot like lightning into the passage leading to the great stairs, and escaped without any other insult

Parliaments in his hands, I suppose he may still do almost everything he chooses with the people of this country in their present state of indifference and submission.[4]

I hope you enjoy your health without a return of gout, and that you will be always persuaded of the sincerity and regard with which I profess myself, dear Horry,

Yours etc.,

HERTFORD

From HERTFORD, Friday 9 September 1785

Printed for the first time from a photostat of BM Add. MSS 23219, f. 149.

Sudborne Hall, September 9th 1785.

Dear Horry,

I OWE to your friendship the earliest communication of any event in my family, however unimportant in every other respect, and in that light you will allow me to acquaint you that my daughter Bell[1] and her friends in Ireland have made a match for her there that I wish and think might have been a better in that marrying country. The gentleman of her choice is a Mr George Hatton,[2] a man of respectable family, character and conduct, but an younger brother

than that of being hissed' (see also *London Chronicle* 14–16 June, lvii. 570). The *St James's Chronicle* 14–16 June added, 'The bells in several parishes were muffled, and rang dumb peals the whole of the afternoon, and Mr Pitt was burnt in effigy at the Seven Dials, Charing Cross, and other places.' For the debate in the House of Commons on the taxes and Pitt's resolutions concerning trade between Great Britain and Ireland, see MANN ix. 564–5, n. 15; 578; 583, nn. 5–6; 589 and n. 6; 604, n. 13.

4. Pitt wrote confidently to Rutland 8 Aug. 1785 that 'the conclusion of our session has been in all respects triumphant. The zeal of our friends seems more confirmed than ever; and everything essential to the strength of our Government as satisfactory as possible. I find rumours are spread of a spirit of disunion in the Cabinet, especially on the subject of Ireland. I can assure you . . . that the reverse is the truth. Whatever room for discussion there may be in the modes to be adopted, in all substantial points, and in the common cause of Government, a more cordial cooperation never existed' (*Correspondence between . . . William Pitt and Charles, Duke of Rutland,* 1890, p. 111).

———

1. Lady Isabella Rachel Seymour-Conway.

2. (b. ca 1761), of Wexford, Ireland; M.P. Lisburn 1790–7, 1798–1800 (Parliament of Ireland) and 1801–2 (Parliament of the United Kingdom). He was the 3d son of John Hatton, Esq. of Clonard, co. Wexford, solicitor (Burke, *Landed Gentry,* 1868, p. 667).

with a very slender fortune.[3] He has in a manner lived with Lord Grandison for two or three years past, which will account for the connection,[4] and was known by my sons and daughters who were abroad with Lady Grandison.[5]

Could I have made my choice freely, I will acknowledge to you as a friend I should have waited some other offer, but when my daughter tells me she is unambitious and chooses retired life with a gentleman of Mr Hatton's temper and disposition, and that he has fortune enough to satisfy her views in life, I hope you will think I have done kindly as well as prudently in not withholding my consent.[6]

I hope you have enjoyed your health this summer and without gout. I am always, dear Horry,

Very truly and affectionately yours,

HERTFORD

From HERTFORD, Monday 12 September 1785

Printed for the first time from a photostat of BM Add. MSS 23219, f. 150.
Address: Woodbridge,[1] September twelfth 1785. To the Honourable Horatio Walpole, Strawberry Hill, Twickenham, Middlesex. Free Hertford.
Postmark: 13 SE. WOODBRIDGE FREE.

Sudborne Hall, September 12th 1785.

Dear Horry,

I HAVE lost my son Edward.[2] He died the end of last month at Lyons;[3] he has been, as you know, long in a decline, but we did not expect his death so soon, and at any period his death is an heavy

3. Lady Elizabeth Laura Waldegrave wrote Anne Clement 22 June 1794 that Lord Hertford gave each of his married daughters a dowry of £6000 (*ante* 4 Feb. 1766, n. 1).

4. Lady Mary Coke wrote in her 'MS Journals,' 2 Sept. 1785, 'Lady Bell Conway who has been some time in Ireland with her sister Lady Grandison is going to be married but I cannot learn to whom, but 'tis said to be a match agreeable to all her family.'

5. She and Lord Grandison (then Lord Villiers) were living in Switzerland in 1780 (ibid. 26 Nov. 1780; OSSORY i. 369, n. 14).

6. The wedding took place 9 or 19 Oct. 1785 'by special licence, at Dromana, the seat of the Earl of Grandison' (GM 1785, lv pt ii. 918; OSSORY ii. 500, n. 34).

———

1. 9 miles WSW of Sudbourne on the road to London.

2. See *ante* 3 June 1781, n. 9.

3. He died 29 Aug. 'at Lyons, in France, of a decline' (GM 1785, lv pt ii.

loss to his family who loved him for his virtues as much as for his natural connections with them.

I trust he is removed to greater happiness than he could have enjoyed in this world. My heart is open enough to melancholy impressions since the loss I have now bewailed near three years of the dear partner of my life, but I bow with resignation and reverence to every event under the superintendence of an all-wise and merciful God. Yours, dear Horry,

Very affectionately,

HERTFORD

From CONWAY, ca Tuesday 4 October 1785

Missing; answered *post* 6 Oct. 1785.

To CONWAY, Thursday 6 October 1785

Printed from *Works* v. 236–8.

Strawberry Hill, October 6, 1785.

I WONDERED I did not hear from you, as I concluded you returned. You have made me good amends by the entertaining story of your travels.[1] If I were not too disjointed for long journeys, I should like to see much of what you have seen; but if I had the agility of Vestris, I would not purchase all that pleasure for my eyes at the expense of my unsociability, which could not have borne the hospitality you experienced. It was always death to me, when I did travel England, to have lords and ladies receive me and show me their castles, instead of turning me over to their housekeeper: it hindered my seeing anything, and I was the whole time meditating

747, cited OSSORY ii. 500, n. 33); the *Political Magazine sub* 11 Sept. reported that 'An express arrived in town, with advice of the death of the Hon. and Rev. Edmund [*sic*] Seymour Conway, Dean [canon] of Christ Church, at Lyons in France' (ix. 240). He was buried 18 Sept. in the 'Ragley Old Vault,' Arrow Church, Warwickshire (*Miscellanea genealogica et heraldica,* 2d ser. iii [1890]. 2).

1. Apparently in a missing letter.

my escape: but Lady A. and you are not such sensitive plants, nor shrink and close up if a stranger holds out a hand.

I don't wonder you was disappointed with Jarvis's[2] windows at New College:[3] I had foretold their miscarriage:[4] the old[5] and the new are as mismatched as an orange and a lemon, and destroy each other; nor is there room enough to retire back and see half of the new; and Sir Joshua's washy Virtues make the Nativity a dark spot from the darkness of the Shepherds, which happened, as I knew it would, from most of Jarvis's colours not being transparent.

I have not seen the improvements at Blenheim. I used to think it one of the ugliest places in England;[6] a giant's castle who had laid waste all the country round him. Everybody now allows the merit of Brown's achievements there.[7]

Of all your survey I wish most to see Beau Desert.[8] Warwick Cas-

---

2. Thomas Jervais (or Jarvis) (d. 1799), glass-painter.

3. HW made similar comments to Lady Ossory 9 Sept. 1783, OSSORY ii. 417–18, after he had seen the west window at New College Chapel, Oxford, painted by Jervais from Reynolds's 'Nativity.' HW also had seen the portions of Jervais's window which were on exhibition in London (HW to Mason 11 May 1783, MASON ii. 301).

4. In a letter to Cole 12 July 1779 (COLE ii. 170), and in a MS note in HW's copy of *Anecdotes of Painting*, Vol. IV, 1780, quoted OSSORY ii. 417, n. 23. HW wrote Lady Ossory 9 Sept. 1783, 'I foresaw long ago that Jarvis's colours being many of them not transparent, could not have the effect of old painted glass' (ibid. ii. 417).

5. The original stained glass in New College Chapel was ordered by William of Wykeham and installed by 1386. In the ante-chapel this original glass remains in place (except for Jervais's west window), and repairs have been made with ancient glass (A. H. Smith, *New College, Oxford, and its Buildings*, 1952, pp. 31–2, 110–14; C. Woodforde, *The Stained Glass of New College, Oxford*, 1951, pp. 1–4, 38–9, 41–9).

6. After his visit in 1760 HW described Blenheim as 'execrable within, without, and almost all round' (*Country Seats* 26; see also MONTAGU i. 289).

7. 'Capability' Brown, commissioned in the 1760s by the 4th D. of Marlborough, created two large artificial lakes and re-designed the gardens and parks (Dorothy Stroud, *Capability Brown*, 1950, pp. 76–7); his 'plan for improving the grounds,' ca 1765, and two sketches are illustrated ibid. 85–7. Mrs Delany wrote 27 Dec. 1774, 'I passed through as much of Blenheim Park as showed me the *vast* superiority of taste in the days of George III from those of Anne the First. Blenheim is now as beautiful as it is magnificent, and the water . . . spreads, it adorns a country, and looks like the beauteous Thames' (Mary Granville, Mrs Delany, *Autobiography and Correspondence*, ed. Lady Llanover, 1861–2, v. 83); Mrs Philip Lybbe Powys 28 Aug. 1771 mentioned 'the famed Brown's so-much-talked-of improvements in the gardens' (*Passages from the Diaries*, ed. E. J. Climenson, 1899, p. 124). HW in his 'Book of Materials 1771' wrote, 'Brown's best works were at Blenheim, the approaches to Lord Cadogan's at Caversham, and to Lord Spencer's at Wimbledon' (Toynbee *Supp.* ii. 164; HW's *Anecdotes of Painting in England*, Vol. V, ed. Hilles and Daghlian, New Haven, 1937, p. 182).

8. Seat of the Earl of Uxbridge in Staffordshire; 'formerly the palace of the Bishops of Chester, . . . [it] is situated on the side of a lofty eminence, in an

tle,[9] and Stowe,[10] I know by heart:—the first I had rather possess than any seat upon earth—not that I think it the most beautiful of all, though charming, [but] because I am so intimate with all its proprietors for the last thousand years.[11]

I have often and often studied the new plan of Stowe:[12] it is pompous; but though the wings are altered, they are not lengthened. Though three parts of the edifices in the garden[13] are bad, they enrich that insipid country, and the vastness pleases me more than I can defend.

I rejoice that your jaunt has been serviceable to Lady A. The *charming-man*[14] is actually with me; but neither he nor I can keep our promise incontinently. He expects two sons[15] of his brother Sir

advanced part of the forest of Cannock, about a mile southwest from Longdon church. The mansion is a magnificent edifice of stone, built in the form of a half H; it is sheltered in the rear by rising grounds, adorned with a variety of trees, and enveloped in groves of the most perfect and luxuriant growth. The greatest part of it was re-built by Thomas Lord Paget, in the reign of Queen Elizabeth, and various additions have been since made by his successors. The principal entrance is under a light Gothic portico, which leads into a large and handsome hall, eighty feet by twenty-one, with a lofty arched ceiling, a large music gallery at the east end, and a beautiful Gothic window at the west end, and adorned with the arms of the first Sir William Paget, and Preston, whose daughter he married' (W. Pitt, *A Topographical History of Staffordshire*, Newcastle-under-Lyme, 1817, pp. 80–1).

9. Which HW had visited in 1751 and 1768 (MONTAGU i. 121–2; *Country Seats* 62–3).

10. The late Lord Temple's seat, inherited in 1779 by his nephew, 1st M. of Buckingham, 1784. HW had visited there in 1751, 1753, 1764, 1770 (MONTAGU i. 122, 151–2, ii. 313–16; CHUTE 75; *ante* 27 Aug. 1764, *sub* 9 Sept., and 12 July 1770). Conway had been there in 1753 (*ante* 24 June 1753).

11. For HW's research on the roll of the Earls of Warwick see COLE i. 133 and GRAY ii. 177; HW comments on the historical associations of Warwick Castle

in his letter to Lady Ossory 10 June 1777, OSSORY i. 352–3.

12. HW's copies of *Stowe: A Description of the Magnificent House and Gardens*, new edn, London 1768 (now WSL), and Buckingham, 1777, are Hazen, *Cat. of HW's Lib.*, Nos 2387: 4, 5; they contain 'A Plan of the Principal Floor . . . of Stowe House.' About 1770 Robert Adam made designs for the remodelling of Stowe which was completed in 1774, with emendations made probably by Jacques-François Blondel (Christopher Hussey, *English Gardens and Landscapes 1700–1750*, 1967, pp. 110–12 and plates 111, 112, 153A, 153B), and it is presumably to these HW refers. In the 1797 edition of *Stowe. A Description of the House and Gardens* the plan of the house shows a considerable extension of the wings.

13. The buildings in the gardens, spread over nearly 400 acres, were designed and remodelled by a succession of architects: Vanbrugh, Kent, Gibbs, Giovanni Battista Borra, Vincenzo Valdre, and Jacques-François Blondel (Hussey, op. cit. 96–112; MONTAGU ii. 44, n. 7).

14. Edward Jerningham, Esq. [1737–1812] (HW); HW's correspondent (see BERRY i. 67 and n. 39).

15. The two older sons were George William Stafford Jerningham (1771–1851), 7th Bt, 1809, 8th Bn Stafford, 1824; and William Charles Jerningham (1772–1820) (Burke, *Peerage*, 1928, pp. 1301, 2153).

William,[16] whom he is to pack up and send to the Pères de l'Oratoire[17] at Paris. I expect Lord and Lady W[aldegrave] tomorrow, who are to pass a few days with me: but both the *charming-man* and I will be with you soon.[18] I have no objection to a wintry visit: as I can neither ride nor walk, it is more comfortable when most of my time is passed within doors. If I continue perfectly well, as I am, I shall not settle in town till after Christmas: there will not be half a dozen persons there for whom I care a straw.

I know nothing at all. The peace between the Austrian harpy and the frogs is made.[19] They were stout, and preferred being gobbled to parting with their money.[20] At last, France offered to pay the money for them. The harpy blushed—for the first time—and would not take it, but signed the peace—and will plunder somebody else.

Have you got Boswell's most absurd enormous book?[21]—The best thing in it is a bon mot of Lord Pembroke.[22] The more one learns

16. Sir William Jerningham (1736–1809), of Cossey, Norfolk; 6th Bt, 1774.

17. The Congrégation des Prêtres de l'Oratoire, 'une société de prêtres séculiers,' on the Rue St-Honoré; see P.-T.-N. Hurtaut and — Magny, *Dictionnaire historique de la ville de Paris*, 1779, iii. 682–9. HW visited their chapel in 1765 (DU DEFFAND v. 280).

18. HW visited Park Place in early November; he wrote Lady Ossory 16 Nov. 1785 of receiving her letter 'at Park Place, where I have been for some days' (OSSORY ii. 504). HW and Jerningham had been there together in August (ibid. ii. 484).

19. The fifteen preliminary articles of peace between Austria and Holland, signed at Paris 20 Sept., are summarized in MANN ix. 607–8, n. 3; see also *London Chronicle* 1–4, 8–11 Oct., lviii. 327–8, 345. The definitive treaty was signed at Fontainebleau 8 Nov. 1785 (*Recueil de traités*, ed. G. F. de Martens, 2d edn, Göttingen, 1817–35, iv. 55–62).

20. The Emperor demanded indemnities of twelve million florins, but the Dutch ambassadors were empowered to offer only five million in August. On 2 Sept. Joseph II wrote the Comte de Mercy, 'Vous serez même autorisé de modifier la somme de douze millions jusqu'à six.' At the conference on 20 Sept. in Paris, as the Comte de Mercy wrote on 21 Sept., 'Le premier article fut très pénible; les ambassadeurs offrirent sept millions de leurs florins où le dédommagement des inondations devait être compris. Je rejetai vivement la proposition. . . . M. de Vergennes . . . employa les exhortations, les prières, les raisonnements d'égards pour la médiation du Roi, le tout pour me porter à une diminution de la somme de dix millions de florins courants de Hollande, que j'avais annoncée pour le dernier mot'; and Vergennes finally persuaded the Dutch to agree to the figure of ten million if it included the damages for the inundations (Mercy-Argenteau, *Correspondance secrète*, ed. Arneth and Flammermont, 1889, i. 444, n. 1, 445, 451–2, n. 1).

21. Boswell's *Journal of a Tour to the Hebrides, with Samuel Johnson, LL.D.*, 1785, published 'Oct. 1st,' according to HW's MS note on the title-page of his copy, now WSL (Hazen, op. cit., No. 3069; MANN ix. 634, n. 38).

22. 'Lord Pembroke said once to me at Wilton, with a happy pleasantry, and some truth, that "Dr Johnson's sayings would not appear so extraordinary were it not for his *bow-wow way*"' (Boswell's

of Johnson, the more preposterous assemblage he appears of strong sense, of the lowest bigotry and prejudices, of pride, brutality, fretfulness, and vanity—and Boswell is the ape of most of his faults, without a grain of his sense. It is the story of a mountebank and his zany.

I forgot to say, that I wonder how, with your turn and knowledge and enterprise in scientific exploits, you came not to visit the Duke of Bridgwater's operations[23]—or did you omit them, because I should not have understood a word you told me? Adieu!

From HERTFORD, Friday 12 May 1786

Printed for the first time from a photostat of BM Add. MSS 23219, f. 131. Dated by the contents.
Address: Honourable Hor. Walpole, Berkley Square.

Grosvenor Street, Friday morn.

Dear Horry,

I CAME home rather late last night from the City,[1] but I trust I am in time, with the disposition you have always to do right, to say that in every light it will become you to dine at my house with the Prince[2] and your family[3] tomorrow at half past four.[4]

Yours etc. ever,

HERTFORD

Journal of a Tour to the Hebrides, 1785, p. 8).

23. At his estate at Worsley, Lancs, where he had developed a system of underground canals in connection with his collieries, which visitors could see by 'subterraneous passage in a boat' (James Brindley, *The History of Inland Navigations. Particularly those of the Duke of Bridgwater*, 1769, pp. 49–50). Bridgwater began in 1759 his project of building a canal from the coal mines at Worsley to Manchester, which required an aqueduct at Barton over the river Irwell, finished in 1761. He then undertook a canal connecting Manchester with Liverpool, which after great opposition and financial difficulties was opened in

1772. He was acclaimed as the founder of inland navigation in England (Hugh Malet, *The Canal Duke. A Biography of Francis, 3rd Duke of Bridgewater*, 1961, pp. 57–9, 86–7, map between 88–9, 96–7; DNB).

———

1. According to the *Daily Adv.* 11 May, on Wednesday 10 May Hertford had presented his son 'Captain [Hugh] Conway . . . to his Majesty at St James's, on his marriage [2 April 1786] to the Hon. Miss [Lady Anna Horatia] Waldegrave,' HW's great-niece, who was presented the next day (see below, n. 4).

2. The Prince of Wales.

3. The Waldegraves; see next note.

4. On 2 April HW had declined the

From HERTFORD, Tuesday ?16 May 1786

Printed for the first time from a photostat of BM Add. MSS. 23219, f. 129. Dated tentatively by the contents; see below, n. 1.
Address: To the Honourable Hor. Walpole.

Grosvenor Street, Tuesday morn.

Dear Horry,

THE Prince of Wales has given me notice that he wishes to dine at my house on Thursday[1] next at five o'clock. Will you like to be of his party? If you do, you will give me great pleasure. I proposed it to my brother and he comes. We shall therefore not be all so young as to give alarm to the least presuming.

Yours, dear Horry,

Very truly,

HERTFORD

The French are I hear already nibbling to reduce the value of the Treaty[2] in favour of Irish linens.[3] If they succeed, Mr Eden[4]

Princess Amelia's invitation to dine with the Prince of Wales because he had not yet kissed the Prince's hand (MS in Royal Archives, Windsor Castle), but on 29 May 1786 HW wrote Mann, 'now by Princess Amelie I have been presented to the Prince of Wales at her house . . . I have dined at Lord Hertford's and since at his own palace' (MANN ix. 647; see also Lady Mary Coke, 'MS Journals' 28 May 1786). Lady Elizabeth Laura Waldegrave wrote to Anne Clement 16 May 1786, 'I went up to town for Lady Horatia's presentation last Thursday [11 May] . . . We returned here [Navestock] on Friday, went back to town on Saturday to dine at Lord Hertford's with all the family' (MS now WSL); the *Morning Herald* 15 May reported: 'On Saturday last [13 May], the Prince of Wales dined with Lord Hertford, and the Hon. Captain Conway and his new-married lady, at his Lordship's house, Grosvenor Street.'

1. ?18 May; possibly this dinner party was postponed from Thursday 18 May to Friday 19 May, for the *Daily Adv.* 20 May reported 'Yesterday . . . the Prince of Wales dined with the Earl of Hertford, at his house in Grosvenor Square,' while the same paper 19 May stated that 'Yesterday [Thursday 18 May] Prince Charles of Mecklenburgh dined with the Prince of Wales.'

2. Negotiations for a Treaty of Navigation and Commerce between Great Britain and France, begun in April 1786, continued until the treaty was signed by William Eden and J.-M. Gérard de Rayneval at Versailles 26 Sept.; see William, Lord Auckland, *Journal and Correspondence*, ed. 3d Bn Auckland, 1861–2, i. 96–162, 481–6. The complete text is in *Journals of the House of Commons* xlii. 266–73. The treaty was passed with amendments by the Irish House of Commons 5 March 1787, and by the Lords 12 March (*Journals of the House of Commons . . . Ireland* xxiv. 175–7, 196–7).

3. Pitt wrote Rutland 19 Aug. 1786 that the treaty would 'enumerate certain leading articles of manufacture which may be reciprocally imported at fixed duties . . . their linens at the same duty

will not add to his popularity or even to Mr Pitt's.[5]

To CONWAY, Sunday 18 June 1786

Printed from *Works* v. 238–40.

Sunday night, June 18, 1786.

I SUPPOSE you have been swearing at the east wind for parching your verdure, and are now weeping for the rain that drowns your hay. I have these calamities in common, and my constant and particular one, people that come to see my house, which unfortunately is more in request than ever. Already I have had twenty-eight sets,[1] have five more tickets given out, and yesterday before I had dined three German barons came.[2] My house is a torment, not a comfort!

as is now paid on other foreign linens (from which I am clear nothing can be feared, either to our manufactures or those of Ireland). . . . It may be easily settled, that the rate to be fixed for linens shall not extend to Ireland, if she wishes not to allow its importation; and, indeed, as all the duties in the tariff are only to take place *reciprocally,* Ireland may waive (if it is thought proper) the whole of the tariff, and rest only on the terms of the most favoured nation' (*Correspondence between . . . William Pitt and Charles Duke of Rutland,* 1890, p. 159). The eighth resolution of the Treaty, as passed by the Irish Parliament, was 'that the duty hereafter to be paid upon all linens made of flax or hemp, of the manufacture of the European dominions of the French King, imported into this kingdom, shall be no higher than the duty which linens the manufacture of Holland imported into this kingdom now pay [4d. per ell]' (*Journals of the House of Commons . . . Ireland,* xxiv. 176). Pitt discussed this duty in letters of 24 March and 14 April 1787, and wrote Rutland 29 April 1787, 'I have great satisfaction in telling you that, by a dispatch this instant received from Mr Eden, the French Government seem at length to have acquiesced entirely in the duties

on linens as settled by the Irish Parliament' (*Correspondence,* pp. 178–9, 180–3).

4. William Eden (1744–1814), cr. (1789) Bn Auckland; M.P.; deserted the Opposition to accept on 9 Dec. 1785 an appointment as envoy extraordinary and plenipotentiary to France for negotiating a commercial treaty, and as member of the Committee of Council relating to Trade and Plantations; for his unpopularity see MANN ix. 623–4, n. 4; OSSORY ii. 513–14, n. 3; Namier and Brooke ii. 378–9. Pitt wrote Eden 20 Aug. 1786, 'On the linens we could not concede farther, without risking a dissatisfaction that might seriously affect the success of the whole measure' (Lord Auckland, op. cit. i. 154).

5. Lord Sydney wrote Rutland 2 March 1787, 'The commercial treaty has been approved universally, with the exception of the Opposition members in both Houses. Mr Pitt distinguished himself as usual. . . . Upon the whole, his character never stood higher, and I really think that every day produces fresh instances of his superior ability to every other person' (Hist. MSS Comm., 14th Report, App. pt i, *Rutland MSS,* 1894, iii. 376–7).

———

1. Listed in HW's 'Book of Visitors,' BERRY ii. 224–5.

2. See ibid. ii. 225, *sub* 17 June.

I was sent for again to dine at Gunnersbury on Friday,[3] and was forced to send to town for a dress-coat and a sword. There were the Prince of Wales,[4] the Prince of Mecklenburg,[5] the Duke of Portland, Lord Clanbrassil, Lord and Lady Clermont,[6] Lord and Lady Southampton, Lord Pelham, and Mrs Howe. The Prince of Mecklenburg went back to Windsor after coffee; and the Prince and Lord and Lady Clermont to town after tea to hear some new French players at Lady William Gordon's.[7] The Princess, Lady Barrymore, and the rest of us, played three pools at commerce till ten. I am afraid I was tired and gaped. While we were at the dairy, the Princess insisted on my making some verses on Gunnersbury. I pleaded being superannuated. She would not excuse me. I promised she should have an ode on her next birthday; which diverted the Prince—but all would not do—so, as I came home, I made the following stanzas, and sent them to her breakfast next morning:

I.

In deathless odes for ever green
　　Augustus' laurels blow;
Nor e'er was grateful duty seen
　　In warmer strains to flow.

II.

Oh! why is Flaccus not alive
　　Your fav'rite scene to sing?
To Gunnersbury's charms could give
　　His lyre immortal spring.

3. 16 June. HW wrote Lady Ossory 5 July 1786 an account of this party and quoted his verses and Princess Amelia's letter (Ossory ii. 517–18).

4. Who wrote Ps Amelia 10 June 1786, 'I received another letter from you, appointing Friday as the day for our attending you in the country instead of Wednesday, which was the very thing I was going to entreat of you myself to do, as I had also a very particular engagement on Wednesday. Prince Charles of Mecklenburgh is now in London and dines with me on Monday. If therefore you choose it, my dear aunt, I will save you the trouble of sending to him and will ask him myself in your name' (George, Prince of Wales, *Correspondence*, ed. Aspinall, 1963–71, i. 228).

5. Karl Ludwig Friedrich (1741–1816), D. (1774) and Grand D. (1815) of Mecklenburg-Strelitz (as Karl II); the Queen's brother.

6. Frances Cairnes Murray (ca 1733–1820), m. (1752) William Henry Fortescue, cr. (1770) Bn, (1776) Vct, and (1777) E. of Clermont. Lady Mary Coke noted in her 'MS Journals' 15 June 1786, 'There is to be a great dinner at Gunnesbury tomorrow . . . Lady Clermont told me she should put Lord Clermont to bed at eight o'clock that he might not be too late tomorrow.'

7. Hon. Frances Ingram Shepheard (1761–1841), m. (1781) Lord William Gordon (Ossory ii. 213, n. 7). Her residence in London was Green Park Lodge (*Royal Kalendar*, 1786, p. 60).

III.

As warm as his my zeal for you,
Great Princess, could I show it:
But though you have a Horace too—
Ah, Madam, he's no poet.

If they are but poor verses, consider I am sixty-nine, was half asleep, and made them almost extempore—and by command! However, they succeeded, and I received this gracious answer:

'I wish I had a name that could answer your pretty verses. Your yawning yesterday opened your vein for pleasing me; and I return you my thanks, my good Mr Walpole, and remain sincerely your friend,

AMELIA.'[8]

I think this is very genteel at seventy-five.

Do you know that I have bought the Jupiter Serapis as well as the Julio Clovio![9] Mr Udny[10] assures me he has seen six of the hand, and not one of them so fine or so well preserved. I am glad Sir Joshua Reynolds saw no more excellence in the Jupiter than in the Clovio; or the Duke of Portland, I suppose, would have purchased it, as he has the vase for a thousand pounds.[11] I would not change. I told Sir W. Hamilton and the late Duchess, when I never thought

---

8. The original letter is in the Princeton University Library (OSSORY ii. 518, n. 5).

9. At the sale [24 April – 8 June 1786] of the Duchess Dowager of Portland (HW). Described in *A Catalogue of the Portland Museum, Lately the Property of the Duchess Dowager of Portland* (HW's copy, now WSL, is Hazen, *Cat. of HW's Lib.*, No. 3902), 37th day, lot 4154: 'The head of Jupiter Serapis, cut out of green basaltes,' £173.5.0. It was sold SH xiii. 82 to Hume, Berners Street, for £78. 15d.; illustrated in BERRY i. facing p. 29. The Clovis was sold in the Portland sale, 27th day, lot 2952: 'A most beautiful missal, illuminated . . . by the famous Don Julio Clovio,' £169.1.0. It was bought in at the SH sale xv. 90 by Earl Waldegrave for £441, and is now in the John Carter Brown Library, Providence, R.I.

10. In his letter to HW of 10 June 1786. John Udny (1727–1800), English con-sul at Venice ca 1761–76, at Leghorn 1776 – ca 1800; described in the *Genealogist*, 1878, ii. 89, as a 'dealer in pictures and antiquities' (MANN viii. 233, n. 10). HW noted in his copy of *A Catalogue of the Portland Museum*, 'Mr Udny assured Mr W. he had seen six more by the same hand, but none of them so fine or so well preserved.'

11. The Duke bought the vase for £1029; Reynolds wrote to the Duke of Rutland 23 June that Portland 'was resolved to have it at any price' (*Letters*, ed. F. W. Hilles, Cambridge, 1929, pp. 151–2). HW noted in his copy of *A Catalogue of the Portland Museum*, 'As the Duchess paid £2000 for the Vase, the Jupiter, the Augustus and the Hercules, and the Duke bought the Vase and the Augustus for £1265, and as the Jupiter and Hercules produced but £220, the Vase and Augustus really cost the family £3045' (p. 194). For the provenance of the Portland Vase, see OSSORY ii. 485–6, n. 6.

it would be mine, that I had rather have the head than the vase. I shall long for Mrs D. to make a bust to it, and then it will be still more valuable.[12] I have deposited both the Illumination and the Jupiter in Lady Di's cabinet,[13] which is worthy of them—and here my collection winds up—I will not purchase trumpery after such jewels. Besides, everything is much dearer in old age, as one has less time to enjoy. Good night!

To HERTFORD, ca Wednesday 18 October 1786

Missing; answered *post* 23 Oct. 1786.

From HERTFORD, Monday 23 October 1786

Printed for the first time from a photostat of BM Add. MSS 23219, f. 152.

Sudborne Hall, October 23d 1786.

Dear Horry,

I AM abundantly paid for my game by the return[1] you have made me for it.

Lady Horatia is charming; we are all in love with her in our way, and Hugh's passion is not abated.[2] I have no idea of an happier pair; they talk of leaving us next week for their own country retirement.[3]

12. HW noted in his copy of *A Catalogue of the Portland Museum*, 'It was a mere head; Mrs Damer has since added to it the bust in bronze.' He listed among Mrs Damer's works in 'Book of Visitors': '1787. She modelled a breast for Mr Walpole's Jupiter Serapis, and had it cast in bronze which she repaired and some of the curls' (BERRY ii. 272–3).

13. A cabinet at Strawberry Hill, ornamented with drawings by Lady Diana Beauclerc (HW); the so-called 'Beauclerk Closet.'

———

1. Apparently a missing letter.

2. Lady Anna Horatia Waldegrave and Capt. Hugh Conway had been married

2 April 1786 (*ante* 12 May 1786, n. 1). This visit is mentioned in Charlotte Augusta Keppel to Anne Clement 25 Oct. 1786: 'I had a letter from Horatia this morning. She is still at Lord Hertford's at Sudbourne. She talks of leaving that place next Sunday [29 Oct.]' (MS now WSL). Concerning the marriage settlement see HW to Joshua Sharpe 21 Aug. 1786.

3. Blissmore Hall, later called Clanville Lodge, 'situated in its park of some 60 acres' in Weyhill parish near Andover, Hants (*Vict. Co. Hist. Hants* iv. 394, 396; Violet Biddulph, *The Three Ladies Waldegrave*, 1938, p. 204). Charlotte Augusta Keppel wrote Anne Clement 25

I am sorry for the Princess Amelia, and as she suffers, I wish, with her other friends, to hear of her death.[4] I wrote to inquire after her, before it was too late, and received a very gracious answer through Lady Templetown.[5]

I am sorry for the loss of any friend of yours, and I see by the papers that Sir Horace Mann is dead.[6]

You are always good to my family; I therefore venture to acquaint you that I have now with me here a grandson[7] by my late daughter Sarah,[8] who is in every respect an uncommon and the most promising young man I ever saw.[9]

I remain, dear Horry,

Most sincerely yours,

HERTFORD

To CONWAY, Sunday 29 October 1786

Printed from *Works* v. 240–1.

Strawberry Hill, October 29, 1786.

I WAS sorry not to be apprised of your intention of going to town, where I would have met you; but I knew it too late, both as I was engaged, and as you was to return so soon. I mean to come to Park Place in a week or fortnight: but I should like to know what com-

Oct., 'I wish she was at home as I think she would be more comfortable at Blissimore not having had a home of her own since she has been married' (MS now WSL). Lady Horatia moved into Blissmore Hall in November (Lady Elizabeth Laura Waldegrave to Anne Clement 22 Nov., MS now WSL).

4. She died 31 Oct. HW recorded in his 'Mem. 1783–91,' *sub* Oct. 1786, '31st died Princess Amelie, aged 75. The last survivor of the children of George II.'

5. Elizabeth Boughton (d. 1823), m. (1769) Clotworthy Upton, cr. (1776) Bn Templetown; lady of the Bedchamber to Princess Amelia, April, 1786 (OSSORY ii. 534, n. 15). Lady Mary Coke in her 'MS Journals' Thursday 26 Oct. wrote of the Princess, 'She retains her senses perfect; on Tuesday when I was there Mrs How-

ard told me she had dictated two letters to Lady Templetown to be wrote by her to her relations in Germany.'

6. A premature report in the *London Chronicle* 17–19 Oct., lx. 384 and *Daily Adv.* 19 Oct. (see OSSORY ii. 533); he died 16 Nov. (MANN ix. 664).

7. Robert Stewart (1769–1822), son of Hertford's dau. Lady Sarah Stewart; styled Vct Castlereagh 1796–1821; 2d M. of Londonderry, 1821.

8. See *ante* 23 July 1770.

9. Chief secretary in Ireland 1798–1800, secretary for war and the colonies 1805–6 and 1807–9, and foreign secretary 1812–22, he played prominent rôles in effecting the Irish Union of 1800, in carrying on the war against Napoleon, and in settling European affairs at the Congress of Vienna, 1814.

pany you expect, or do not expect; for I had rather fill up your vacancies, than be a supernumerary.

Lady Ossory has sent me two charades made by Col. Fitzpatrick: the first she says is very easy, the second very difficult.[1] I have not come within sight of the easy one; and though I have a guess at the other, I do not believe I am right; and so I send them to you, who are master-general of the Œdipuses.

The first, that is so easy:

> In concert, song, or serenade,
> My first requires my second's aid.
> To those residing near the pole
> I would not recommend my whole.

The two last lines, I conclude, neither connect with the two first, nor will help one to deciphering them.

The difficult one:

> Charades of all things are the worst,
> But yet my best have been my first.
> Who with my second are concern'd
> Will to despise my whole have learn'd.

This sounds like a good one, and therefore I will not tell you my solution; for, if it is wrong, it might lead you astray; and if it is right, it would prove the charade is not a good one.

Had I anything better, I would not send you charades, unless for the name of the author.

I have had a letter[2] from your brother, who tells me that he has his grandson Stewart with him, who is a prodigy.—I say to myself,

> —Prodigies are grown so frequent,
> That they have lost their name—[3]

I have seen prodigies in plenty of late—ay, and formerly too—but, divine as they have all been, each has had a mortal heel, and has trodden back a vast deal of their celestial path! I beg to be excused from any more credulity.

I am sorry you have lost your factotum Stokes.[4] I suppose he

1. HW thanked her for the charades 4 Nov. 1786, but could not solve them. The solution to the first is probably 'lute-string'; HW's guess for the second was 'spelling-book.' See OSSORY ii. 533 and *post* Appendix 14.

2. *Ante* 23 Oct. 1786.

3. Dryden, *All for Love* I. i. 1–2; also quoted to Lady Ossory 14 Nov. 1774 (OSSORY i. 214).

4. Deleted in *Works* but restored by Wright; not further identified.

had discovered that he was too necessary to you. Every day cures one of reliance on others; and we acquire a prodigious stock of experience by the time that we shall cease to have occasion for any. Well! I am not clear, but making or solving charades is as wise as anything we can do. I should pardon professed philosophers, if they would allow that their wisdom is only trifling, instead of calling their trifling, wisdom. Adieu!

From HERTFORD, Thursday ?7 June 1787

Printed for the first time from a photostat of BM Add. MSS 23219, f. 52. The date is conjectural, based on the illness of the Prince of Wales in May 1787, when he was attended by Dr Robert Hallifax; see below, n. 1. This letter could also be dated 5 May 1791, when the Prince was recovering from another serious illness; see HW to Mary Berry 4–5 May 1791 (BERRY i. 257–8, 261); 'Mem. 1783–91,' *sub* May 1791; Adm. Rodney to Capt. J. W. Payne, *Correspondence of George, Prince of Wales 1770–1812*, ed. Aspinall, New York, 1963–71, ii. 149–50.

Address: To the Honourable Hor. Walpole.

G[rosvenor] Street, Thursday 8 o'clock.

Dear Horry,

I HAD a note last night from Dr Halifax[1] saying he was happy to acquaint me that all the symptoms attending the Prince's fever were become favourable.[2]

Yours ever,

HERTFORD

1. Robert Hallifax (1735–1810), apothecary to the King's household, and apothecary and physician (1788–1810) to the Prince of Wales; M.D. 1783 (BERRY i. 205, n. 32). Lady Mary Coke wrote in her 'MS Journals' 27 May: 'The Prince of Wales is very ill and attended by three physicians; Sir Richard Jebb came to the King last night and told him the Prince was ill of a fever and it was impossible at the beginning to say how it might end. This day the message at the door is that he had but an indifferent night but that he was rather better this morning—but the truth is difficult to be known; Doctor Halifax sat up with him last night.' See also her report *sub* Thurs. 31 May 1787.

2. According to HW's 'Mem. 1783–91,' *sub* May 1787, 'The very day after the Prince had been at the Drawing-Room on the reconciliation [with the King], he was taken most dangerously ill of an inflammatory fever. He had been ill for two days, but concealed it, and on 25th of May went to the races at Epsom, where being very hot, he drank large draughts of champagne, and returning to town, went to a ball at the Duchess of Gordon's, but found himself so ill, that he was forced to go home to bed; and on the 27 at night was in the utmost danger, having besides a great oppression on his

To Conway, Sunday 17 June 1787

Printed from *Works* v. 241–2.

Strawberry Hill, June 17, 1787.

I HAVE very little to tell you since we met but disappointments, and those of no great consequence.

On Friday night Lady Pembroke[1] wrote to me that Princess Lubomirski[2] was to dine with her the next day, and desired to come in the morning to see Strawberry.[3]—Well, my castle put on its robes, breakfast was prepared, and I shoved another company out of the house, who had a ticket for seeing it. The sun shone, my hay was cocked, we looked divinely—and at half an hour after two nobody came but a servant from Lady Pembroke, to say her Polish altitude had sent her word she had another engagement in town that would keep her too late:—so Lady Pembroke's dinner was addled; and we had nothing to do, but, like good Christians, if we chose it, to compel everybody on the road, whether they chose it or not, to come in and eat our soup and biscuits. Methinks this *liberum veto*[4] was rather impertinent, and I begin to think that the partition of Poland was very right.[5]

Your brother has sent me a card for a ball on Monday,[6] but I have excused myself. I have not yet compassed the whole circuit of my own garden, and I have had an inflammation in one of my eyes,[7] and don't think I look as well as my house and my verdure;

breast. He was blooded very frequently, but by [June] 7th the fever left him, and he was quite out of danger' (see also *St James's Chronicle* 24–6, 26–9 May; *London Chronicle* 26–9 May). Hertford was giving a ball in honour of the Prince on 18 June, which Lady Mary Coke thought 'very extraordinary and especially to the Prince of Wales in the state his health is in at present'; but he attended the ball and 'stayed till twelve o'clock but his health would not allow him to sup' ('MS Journals' 15, 19 June 1787).

———

1. Deleted in *Works* but restored by Wright; her letter is missing.

2. Isabella (Elizabeth) Helene Anne Czartoriska (1736–1816), m. 1 (1753) Stanislas (1722–83), Prince Lubomirski; m. 2

(Feb. 1786) Michael, Count Oginski (Ossory ii. 565, n. 27).

3. HW alludes to this request in his letter to Lady Ossory 14 June 1787, *sub* 15 June (ibid. ii. 565–6).

4. According to the Polish constitution, one deputy could dissolve a session of the Polish Diet and render invalid all its previous legislation (E. H. Lewinski-Corwin, *The Political History of Poland*, New York, 1917, p. 201).

5. However, Princess Lubomirska visited SH on 23 July, and breakfasted with HW on 25 July (Berry ii. 228; HW to Mrs Boyle Walsingham 26 July 1787).

6. 18 June, in honour of the P. of Wales; see Lady Mary Coke's comments quoted Ossory ii. 565, n. 26.

7. HW describes this affliction in his

and had rather see my haycocks, than the Duchess of Polignac[8] and Madame Lubomirski. *The Way to Keep Him*[9] had the way to get me, and I could crawl to it, because I had an inclination; but I have a great command of myself when I have no mind to do anything. Lady Constant[10] was worth an hundred *acs* and *irskis*.

Let me hear of you when you have nothing else to do; though I suppose you have as little to tell as you see I had.

To Conway, Sunday 24 June 1787

Printed for the first time from the MS now WSL; it was sold Sotheby's 5 Dec. 1921 (first Waller Sale, lot 12) to Ord for £2.18s.; resold by Christie's 15 Dec. 1947 (second Waller Sale, lot 40) to Maggs for WSL.

Endorsed: Mr Walpole 24 June 1787.

Memoranda (by Conway, of items in this letter):

  French ambassador gone suddenly
  money loaned P. of Orange
  Tarare
  Ld Montague dead.

Berkeley Square, Sunday morning.

I CAME to town yesterday and return tomorrow, but by leaving this here, you will receive it a day sooner than if from Twickenham.[1] This important exordium sounds as if I had something of

letter to Lady Ossory 14 June 1787 (ibid. ii. 561).

8. Gabrielle-Yolande-Claude-Martine de Polastron (ca 1749–93), m. (1767) Armand-Jules-François, Comte and (1780) Duc de Polignac; the favourite of Marie-Antoinette (ibid. ii. 309, n. 10).

9. The first comedy represented at the theatre in Richmond House (HW), by Arthur Murphy; performed there on 20, 30 April and 4, 17 May 1787. The cast included Lord Derby, Richard Edgcumbe, Major Arabin, Sir Harry Englefield, Mrs Damer, and Miss Caroline Campbell; for HW's opinion and newspaper accounts of the performance, see Ossory ii. 563–4 and nn. 13, 14. The prologue, written by Conway and spoken by Mrs Hobart, was printed in the *World* 21 May 1787 and *St James's*

Chronicle 17–19 May 1787 (see Appendix 15). The 'Prologue and Epilogue to the Play of the Way to Keep Him, Performed at Richmond House in April, 1787, in a Private Society,' printed separately, has been attributed to the SH Press but is rejected by Hazen, *SH Bibl.* 275.

10. The part played by Caroline Campbell; see Ossory ii. 563, n. 14. The *World* 21 April commented: 'Miss *Campbell* in Lady *Constant*—had not much room for effect—the best effect was her little air on the harp'; and again on 18 May: 'Miss Campbell played charmingly—we refer to the air with variations, of *God Save the King!* the compliment on the occasion.'

———

1. Where there was no postal service on Monday (Ossory ii. 196).

consequence to tell you—on the contrary, I want you to tell me that Lady Ailesbury is well again.[2]

Our letters met upon the road without even nodding to one another, I believe. I don't know whether the Acs and Iskis disappointed you as the latter did me[3] and the former your brother. He had invited them to his ball[4] ten days before, and then they chose to stay at Mrs North's[5] at Farnham.[6] The royalties were well served for receiving them on the terrace at Windsor, though they had never been presented.[7] The Duchess of Polignac was as dirty as if she had walked from Bath in the same dirty gown[8] that she had thought good enough for King Bladud.[9] They are gone away in a great hurry and their ambassador[10] too, without even taking leave

2. Possibly she had suffered a recurrence of 'her old complaint in her stomach' (Lady Mary Coke, 'MS Journals' 26 Aug. 1786). Lady Ailesbury was apparently in good health when she and Conway dined with Lady Mary Coke 6 June 1787 (ibid. 1, 7 June 1787).

3. See *ante* 17 June 1787.

4. 18 June (ibid., n. 6).

5. Henrietta Maria Bannister (1750–96), m. (1771) Brownlow North, Bp of Coventry and Lichfield 1771–4, of Worcester 1774–81, of Winchester 1781–1820 (MASON i. 391, nn. 1, 2).

6. Farnham Castle, W. Surrey, residence of the Bishop of Winchester. Lady Mary Coke wrote in her 'MS Journals' 21 June 1787, 'Madame de Polignac and the other ladies that were with her behaved with the utmost unpoliteness to Lord Hertford. He gave his ball to the Prince and to them, but they never came or sent an excuse till ten o'clock at night: so much for French politeness.'

7. Fanny Burney wrote, 'Sunday, June 17, I was tempted to go on the terrace, in order to see the celebrated Madame de Polignac, and her daughter, Madame de Guiche. They were to be presented, with the Duke de Polignac, to their Majesties, upon the terrace. Their rank entitled them to this distinction; and the Duchess of Ancaster, to whom they had been extremely courteous abroad, came to Windsor to introduce them. They were accompanied to the terrace by Mrs Harcourt and the General, with whom they were also well acquainted . . . Their Maj-

esties . . . stopped to converse with these noble travellers for more than an hour' (*Diary and Letters*, ed. A. Dobson, 1905, iii. 262–3). See also HW's 'Mem. 1783–91,' *sub* June 1787.

8. Fanny Burney commented about the French ladies: 'I was much amused by their dress, which they meant should be entirely *à l'anglaise;* for which purpose they had put on plain undress gowns, with close ordinary black silk bonnets! I am sure they must have been quite confused when they saw the Queen and Princesses, with their ladies, who were all dressed with uncommon care, and very splendidly' (op. cit. iii. 263).

9. A legendary king of Britain who, according to Geoffrey of Monmouth, was supposed to have founded Bath by his magic skill and to have been succeeded by his son, Lear. A later myth records that Bladud, heir of King Lud Hudibras, was miraculously cured of leprosy by the hot springs of Bath and founded the city there in gratitude (*The New Bath Guide*, new edn, Bath, 1787, pp. 3–6; *A Pictorial and Descriptive Guide to Bath*, 1905, pp. 4–7).

10. Jean-Balthazar d'Azémar de Montfalcon (1731–91), Comte d'Adhémar; ambassador to England 1783–7 (OSSORY ii. 403, n. 11). The *Daily Adv.* 21–3 June reported that on 20 June he 'took leave of the King at St James's,' on 21 June 'gave his farewell dinner to the ministers of state and foreign ambassadors,' and on 22 June 'took leave of Mr Pitt, at his house in Downing Street, and in

of the Queen. He had given out cards for a ball on Friday, but not only put it off, but sent cards of excuses to some that he had *not* invited[11]—a paltry trick that I wonder he practised, as he is *not* to return, the Duc de Liancour[12] being named to succeed him—yet with you I shall not be surprised if he does not come. *We* have certainly sent an hundred and thirty or forty thousand pounds to the Prince of Orange to enable him to open the war;[13] so the commercial treaty may die before it has cut its teeth! and I am sure the Archbishop of Toulouse[14] had rather scratch us than pick our

the evening set off to Paris.' According to Lady Mary Coke, the occasion of his and the ladies' return was the arrival of news 'that the King of France's second daughter is dying' ('MS Journals' 21 June 1787).

11. 'The French ambassador has put off his ball' (ibid.); the *London Chronicle* 23–6 June, lxi. 602, reported, 'His Excellency has, however, sent complimentary cards to all his acquaintance, apologizing for this accident [his unexpected departure], and promising hopes of his return before the middle of next month.'

12. François-Alexandre-Frédéric de La Rochefoucauld-Liancourt (1747–1827), Comte de Liancourt; cr. (1765) Duc de Liancourt; Duc de La Rochefoucauld, 1822 (A. Révérend, *Titres*, 1901–6, iv. 194–5). Adhémar was not succeeded by Liancourt, but by Anne-César de La Luzerne (1741–91), chevalier, cr. (1788) Marquis de la Luzerne, who arrived 13 Jan. 1788 and was ambassador until 1791; in the interim François Barthélemy (1747–1830), cr. (1800) Comte and (1815) Marquis de Barthélemy, remained as chargé d'affaires and (from 16 Sept. 1787) minister plenipotentiary (*Recueil des instructions données aux ambassadeurs et ministres de France . . . Angleterre*, ed. Paul Vaucher, 1965, iii. 535, 539, 554; Ossory ii. 510, n. 7, iii. 113, n. 4).

13. HW is referring to the struggle between the Patriot party and the Stadtholder (whose office had been hereditary in the House of Orange since the constitution adopted by the United Provinces in 1747). He wrote in 'Mem. 1783–91,' *sub* June 1787, 'The King of Prussia [Frederick William II] declaring he would

support the Prince of Orange with troops, but could not with money, our King insisted on sending and did send £130,000 to the Prince to enable him to put his troops in motion. Thus he quarrelled with Holland for supporting the Americans, because the Dutch [were] a republic, and now supported the Prince of Orange in the cause of royalty.' Although Pitt was reluctant to endanger British relations with France, Sir James Harris strongly recommended promising support to the Stadtholder, since France was supporting the Patriot party in Holland. The Cabinet on 26 May 1787 proposed to send £20,000; and on 10 June an additional sum of £70,000 was approved (Sir James Harris, Lord Malmesbury, *Diaries and Correspondence*, 1844, ii. 294–6, 304–7; J. H. Rose, *William Pitt and National Revival*, 1911, p. 360). The conflict between the Patriots and the Stadtholder reached a climax when the Princess of Orange, sister of the King of Prussia, on 28 June was stopped en route to The Hague by a body of Free Corps and was refused permission by the States of Holland to proceed; the King of Prussia demanded an apology for this insult (see Harris's letters to the M. of Carmarthen, op. cit. ii. 325–8, 330–1, 338–9; *London Chronicle* 30 June – 3 July, 3–5, 21–4 July, lxii. 7, 9–10, 76; *post* 20 July 1787, n. 12).

14. Étienne-Charles de Loménie de Brienne (1727–94), Abp of Toulouse, 1763, and of Sens, 1788; cardinal, 1789; comptroller-general of finances 1787–8; premier, 1788 (Ossory iii. 18, n. 22). He was Mme du Deffand's cousin. HW wrote Lady Ossory 6 Sept. 1788 that he 'is the most ambitious man alive, and in time of

pockets—where indeed another war will leave us nothing to steal. If we do not grow wiser, at least we begin to purge our bad humours; two of the worst of our wretches, Lord George Gordon[15] and Sir Elijah Impey[16] are said to be run away.

I send you *Tarare*,[17] which I read last night—it is a strange piece, and neither makes you laugh or cry. It borders both on indecency and liberty, the prologue on the former and the whole on the latter;[18] and the first a little resembles my hieroglyphic tale[19] of the amour between the princess that never was born and the prince that was dead, for there is a chorus of the *ghosts* of those that are not yet begotten.[20] The poetry is as indifferent as any poetry in their language; the best part is the art with which all the actors are made to echo *Tarare, Tarare*,[21] as in Hamilton.[22] One passage

less distress, would have been a thorn in our side, whom he hates supremely' (ibid. 19).

15. HW wrote in 'Mem. 1783–91,' *sub* 7 June 1787, 'Lord George was tried for two libels and found guilty on both. Before the day when sentence was to be pronounced on him, he absconded.' On 6 June he was convicted of libel for his pamphlet, *The Prisoners' Petition to the Right Honourable Lord George Gordon, to preserve their lives and liberties and prevent their banishment to Botany Bay*, published 22 Jan. 1787, and for statements published in the *Public Advertiser* 22, 24 Aug. 1786, accusing Marie-Antoinette of persecuting Cagliostro (T. B. Howell, *Complete Collection of State Trials*, 1816–26, xxii. 189–95, 224–5). On 14 June he did not appear in the Court of King's Bench to be sentenced, and his arrest was ordered (*London Chronicle* 12–14, 14–16 June, lxi. 568, 570, 576; *Morning Chronicle* 15 June). He fled to Holland, where he arrived 14 June (*London Chronicle* 16–19, 21–3 June, lxi. 578, 599). The Dutch magistrates ordered him to leave Amsterdam, and the States of Holland on 18 July 'sent their first officer express to Helvoetsluys . . . to command him, and see him leave Holland directly, or be taken into custody' (ibid. 24–6 July, lxii. 85).

16. (1732–1809), Kt, 1774; chief justice of Bengal 1774–89. The *London Chronicle* 12–14 June, lxi. 561, reported, 'About a week ago Sir Elijah Impey went to

Brighthelmstone, and from thence departed to the Continent.' For his trial in the House of Commons, see OSSORY iii. 3–4, n. 28.

17. *Tarare, opéra en cinq actes, avec un prologue*, by Pierre-Augustin Caron de Beaumarchais (1732–99), music by Antonio Salieri (1750–1825); first performed at the Opéra 8 June 1787; mentioned in HW to Hannah More 14 Oct. 1787 (MORE 255).

18. The philosophical theme of the opera is the struggle between tyranny, represented by the malevolent King Atar, and natural merit, represented by the virtuous soldier Tarare.

19. 'The King and his Three Daughters,' *Works* iv. 330–3.

20. In the prologue Nature calls forth the ghosts of the characters in the play for the Génie du Feu who assigns them a destiny on earth. Tarare is to be a happy soldier, Atar a king who is conquered by his subject.

21. E.g., in the choruses of Act V, scenes vi and ix.

22. In *Histoire de Fleur d'Épine*, a fairy tale by Anthony Hamilton (ca 1645–1720), Tarare says, ' "Je pris Tarare pour mon nom." "Tarare?" dit Fleur d'Epine. "Justement," poursuivit-il; "et ce qu'il y a de singulier à ce nom, c'est qu'il semble qu'on ne puisse l'entendre que l'envie de le répéter, comme vous venez de faire, ne prenne tout aussitôt" ' (Hamilton, *Œuvres*, 1825, ii. 151).

is quite sublime; the tyrannic sultan[23] cries, 'Qu'ai-je à craindre?' Tarare replies, 'De te voir toujours obéi.'[24]—May not this be applied to the American war and the £140,000 to Holland?

Poor Lord Beaulieu has lost his son Lord Montagu,[25] who is dead of drinking.

This is all I have learnt. Adieu!

From HERTFORD, Saturday 30 June 1787

Printed for the first time from a photostat of BM Add. MSS 23219, f. 153.

London, June 30th 1787.

Dear Horry,

YOU have been always so good and friendly to me and my family that it would be ingratitude rather than presumption not to think you interested in its events.

The last mails from Ireland have been accompanied by a letter[1] from Lord Drogheda acquainting me with the death of his eldest daughter.[2] The account he gives of this melancholy event is that she caught a cold in some part of the winter, which for the sake of Dublin amusements she had concealed too long from her friends. Her appearance was that of health and beauty, and the event of her death is the more extraordinary. She is gone at a very early period to join those respected and most beloved friends who preceded her,

23. 'Atar, Roi d'Ormus, homme féroce et sans frein' (*Tarare*, Paris, 1787, p. 18).

24. Act V, scene iii (ibid. 70).

25. Hon. John Hussey Montagu (1747–87), styled Lord Montagu 1784–7; M.P. Lady Mary Coke in her 'MS Journals' 24 June 1787 wrote, 'Lady Greenwich told me an express had arrived the day before [23 June] with the news of Lord Montagu's having died at Paris of a violent fever.—As he had good qualities and had every reason to wish for life I lament him and most sincerely pity his father—who having obtained great rank and in possession of a large fortune sees all his hopes baffled by the death of his only son who he adored; all his estates are now in his own disposal.' On 25

June she added, 'Lord Beaulieu . . . is distracted and tears his hair with extremity of grief but in all this agony of affliction he sent for Lord Brudenel and told him he should now consider the Duchess of Buccleugh as his daughter and settle upon her all the Montagu estate that he was in possession of' (ibid.). The *Daily Advertiser* 25 June reported the death 'in the south of France.'

1. Missing.

2. Lady Isabella Moore (1766 – 22 June 1787), 'at Moore Abbey, in Ireland, the seat of the Earl of Drogheda' (GM 1787, lvii pt ii. 639; John Debrett, *Peerage*, 1822, ii. 907; DNB, *sub* Moore, Charles, [1730–1822]).

in virtue and innocence. We shall mourn for her as early as possible, which will be tomorrow. I remain, dear Horry,

Always very truly and affectionately yours,

HERTFORD

To CONWAY, Friday 20 July 1787

Printed for the first time from the MS now WSL; it was sold Sotheby's 5 Dec. 1921 (first Waller Sale, lot 13) to Ord for £3.5s.; resold by Christie's 15 Dec. 1947 (second Waller Sale, lot 40) to Maggs for WSL.

Address: To the Right Honourable General Conway at Park Place near Henley.

Postmark: JY [illegible].

Endorsed: Mr Walpole 26th July 1787.

Strawberry Hill, July 20th 1787.

THE Cecilians[1] tell me they are going to you, and I am sorry I cannot be of the party which I should like. I have twenty embarrassments; on Monday[2] I must go to town on business of my own;[3] and I must return hither on business that is not quite my own, but that gives me ten times more trouble—in short, to talk to your nephew Hugh,[4] who is or is to be at Lady Lincoln's,[5] and the subject you may guess,[6] which is not quite his neither, and yet

1. Lady Cecilia and General Johnston.
2. 23 July.
3. However, HW in his 'Book of Visitors,' *sub* 23 July 1787, lists, 'Mr Beauchamp and 3. Princess Lubomirski, myself' (BERRY ii. 228; see also *ante* 17 June 1787, n. 5).
4. Capt. Hugh Seymour-Conway.
5. HW wrote the Ds of Gloucester 9 July 1787, 'Lady Lincoln has taken a house at Putney Common till October, and as her brother and Lady Horatia have promised her a visit there, I shall be so happy as to see them' (FAMILY 245–6). See BERRY i. 323, n. 28.
6. Possibly the P. of Wales's debts and his secret marriage to Mrs Fitzherbert, since Hugh Seymour-Conway was Master of the Robes and Privy Purse in the Prince's household (*Daily Adv.* 28 May

1787). In 'Mem. 1783–91' HW gives an account of the Prince's campaign during April and May 1787 to have his income increased, and *sub* July 1787 adds, 'I learnt that the Prince of Wales had owned to his intimates that Dundas [Henry Dundas (1742–1811), cr. (1802) Vct Melville] had had private connections with him for some time before the intended motion in Parliament and that Dundas himself when the motion had been first broached, had, when in liquor with some of the Cabinet who were reviling the Prince, blabbed that Mr Pitt had intended to be *liberal* to the Prince, and they two had certainly driven the King into the composition.' See also the Prince's letter to Hertford 22 April 1787 asking the support of his four sons in the House of Commons, and the Prince's

cannot be more pleasant to him than to me, or to any of us—but on that I cannot say more by the post. The Fitzroys[7] too are at Mrs Keppel's[8]—but I should not stay merely for them.

I know nothing in the world, but that last Wednesday, I and some others had a very great escape. I was with the Onslows at an old Mrs Crewe's[9] at Richmond. Lady Onslow went home in a chair, and I was to set Lord Onslow and his chaplain[10] down. Mrs Crewe's is in a narrow cul-de-sac; the night was very dark, or rather the lane, almost in the middle of which is a post, which the coachman[11] could not see and which he not only drove upon, but over. The first notice was an outrageous bang of the chaplain's skull against my teeth, which cut a deep gash in his forehead, and I thought had split my upper lip and knocked out two or three of my teeth, but the lip got only a small cut, and all my teeth I found on sounding had maintained their posts, and were mighty proud, as they are very near 70 years old, of being so firm—however they were so battered, that next day I could chew nothing solid. The coachman fared worse, for he was thrown on the head of the horses, and his underlip was much mangled. Lord Onslow had only a bruise on his knee. Whether the horses were sedate, or stunned, or confined by the wheel that remained locked to the post, I don't know, but they did not stir, or might have killed the coachman, or overturned us. Mrs Crewe's servants brought lights, and cried, 'Nothing is broken.' I said, 'Indeed but there is, for our heads are broken,' which made the parson laugh—and so ended our mishap—not but the pole was broken too, and the springs bent, and were forced to have a coach-surgeon. This is a long story about little or nothing, but I assure you is the present great topic of conversation at Richmond, Twickenham, Isleworth, and Hampton Court, and my teeth have had cards and visits of how d'ye's.

correspondence with Pitt and the King in May 1787 (George, Prince of Wales, *Correspondence*, ed. Aspinall, 1963–71, i. 280–1 and n. 3; 285, n. 1, 292–3, 302, 312).

7. Hon. George Ferdinand Fitzroy and his wife, Laura Keppel (*ante* 30 June 1784, n. 2), and their daughter Georgiana Maria; this visit is mentioned in HW to Ds of Gloucester 9 July 1787 (FAMILY 246; Burke, *Peerage*, 1928, p. 2141).

8. At her villa at Isleworth (OSSORY ii. 481; BERRY i. 320–1, n. 15).

9. Frances Anne Greville (d. 1818), m. (1766) John Crewe, cr. (1806) Bn Crewe. HW wrote Strafford 28 July 1787, 'Miss Crewe . . . has decorated a room for her mother's house at Richmond, which was Lady Margaret Compton's, in a very pretty manner' (CHUTE 390).

10. Not identified.

11. Presumably John Jenkins; see HW to Charles Bedford 18 June 1781.

I don't like the turmoils in Holland[12]—we have great alacrity at blundering into wars, besides little ingenuity in making peaces, which alone ought to be a reason against making war.

I am better pleased with the Emperor's bungling in Flanders.[13] Lord Onslow, who came from the levee,[14] says it is true that Belgiooso[15] made his escape in a tub,[16] a tale of one, to which I suppose

12. Since the States of Holland refused to give a satisfactory apology for the insult offered the Princess of Orange (see *ante* 24 June 1787, n. 13), the King of Prussia on 18 July ordered an army of 25,000 men to march to the frontiers of Holland (Harris and Ewart to Carmarthen, 17, 21 July 1787, in Sir James Harris, Lord Malmesbury, *Diaries and Correspondence*, 1844, ii. 338–41; *London Chronicle* 24–6 July, lxii. 88; GM 1787, lvii pt ii. 728–30). In view of the uprisings of the Dutch Free Corps in various cities, Sir James Harris wrote Ewart 13 July 1787, 'The Republic *can* only be saved by support from without. Matters are gone too far to be reconciled from within, and the ferment is at such a height that nothing short of compulsion can set it to rights' (Harris, op. cit. ii. 335). The French ambassador promised the assistance of an army stationed at Givet and a fleet at Brest against Prussian intervention, and the British promised military support to the King of Prussia (ibid. ii. 347, 351–2). See *post* 24 Sept. 1787.

13. Joseph II's reforms in the Austrian Netherlands led to a rebellion on 30 May in Brussels when the Archduchess and Duke of Saxe-Teschen were forced to promise to annul all innovations and restore the ancient form of government (*Gazette de Leyde* 8 June, *sub* Brussels 4 June; GM 1787, lvii pt i. 538–9). This action was ratified by the Prince de Kaunitz in the Emperor's absence. On 15 June 'A disturbance . . . happened at Antwerp, still more violent than that at Brussels; the people in that city being informed, that, notwithstanding the temporary suspension of the new laws, the officers who were appointed to carry them into execution, were assembled in a convent. They forced open the gates where they were sitting in Council; but found only the Sieur Van Delft and the

first Commissary Schorel, all the rest having the good fortune to escape. . . . The tumult now became general; near 20,000 persons were assembled; many houses were marked for destruction, and the whole city was in commotion' (ibid. lvii pt ii. 628–9; *London Chronicle* 26–8 June, lxii. 615). On 3 July Joseph II called an assembly in Vienna of the Archduchess, Duke Albert, and Belgioioso with the deputies from the different States of the Austrian Netherlands (ibid. 21–4 July, lxii. 73, 74; *Gazette de Leyde* 27 July, *sub* Brussels 23 July; Henri Pirenne, *Histoire de Belgique*, Brussels, 1921, v. 428–37). At the general assembly of the States on 18 July deputies were elected to be sent to Vienna, and meanwhile the Emperor had ordered an army of 40,000 to be ready to march; the *Daily Adv.* 31 July, *sub* Brussels 19 July, reported, 'The fermentation is absolutely at its height; all the citizens are in arms to support their Regencies . . . and nothing can equal the animosity which shows itself in Hainault and Flanders.'

14. On Wednesday 18 July, when 'Lord Onslow went into waiting as lord of the Bedchamber to the King' (ibid. 19 July).

15. Lodovico Carlo Maria (1728–1801), Conte di Barbiano di Belgioioso; Austrian minister to England 1770–82; minister plenipotentiary and vice-governor of the Austrian Netherlands 1783–7 (*Dizionario biografico degli Italiani*, 1960– , vi. 211–13; BERRY i. 195, n. 11; MORE 152).

16. This probably refers to the riots in Brussels 27–30 May, when the hostility of the people was great against Belgioioso who had tried to enforce the unpopular edicts of the Emperor. The people petitioned for Belgioioso's dismissal, and he offered his resignation, but the Emperor refused to accept it. Belgioioso set out from Brussels on 20 July and arrived in Vienna 28 July (*Lon-*

Peter[17] has contributed, for people seldom defend liberty and privileges, unless it is the interest of priests to be patriots.

The Princess de Lamballe[18] is arrived, *dont je me soucie aussi peu que de Madame la Duchesse de Polignac*[19]—unless she wants to come and see my house, and for that I shall *soucie* myself most unwillingly.[20]

I dine at Lady Cecilia's tomorrow with the Duchess of Bedford; the former tells me you are going *en famille* to Mount Edgcumbe, which surprised me, as you said you was too busy with your smoke to go to Jersey—however I should approve of the Mount more than the Island, though I would not take so long journey twice to see Mount Parnassus. Adieu!

don *Chronicle* 24–6 July, lxii. 81; *Daily Adv.* 28 Aug., *sub* Vienna 1 Aug.). After the meeting with the deputies from the Austrian States in August, Joseph II announced that Belgioioso would be replaced by Count Trautmansdorf (*Dizionario biografico degli Italiani*, vi. 212–13; Joseph II's letters to Kaunitz 25 May, 3, 16 June, 13 Aug. in *Joseph II, Leopold II, und Kaunitz: Ihr Briefwechsel*, ed. A. Beer, Vienna, 1873, pp. 262–3, 266–7, 276–7, 279; *Daily Adv.* 27 June, *sub* Brussels 17 June; 27 Aug., *sub* Vienna 8 Aug.).

17. I.e., the Pope. The *Gazette de Leyde* 5 June, *sub* Brussels 1 June, reported, 'Les changements, que l'Empereur a voulu faire au système politique et judiciaire de la Belgique, ont reveillé ceux que l'Ordre Ecclésiastique a déjà dû subir depuis quelque temps: et les plaintes sur ces derniers objets se sont jointes d'autant plus naturellement à des doléances plus prochaines de l'époque présente, que l'ancienne constitution de nos provinces a intimément lié les droits de cet Ordre aux privilèges de la nation, sanctionnés par la Joyeuse-Entrée. Ainsi les griefs du clergé sont entrés pour une grande partie dans les *Points*, sur lesquels l'Assemblée Générale des États de Brabant a demandé très hum-

blement la détermination favorable de L.A.R. sous l'agréation et ratification de Sa Majesté.' Joseph II's decrees between 1781 and 1786 against traditional Catholic institutions and forms of worship, and his edicts of 1 Jan. 1787 changing the judiciary and administrative system, caused the formation of a Patriotic Committee under the leadership of Hendrik van der Noot and François Vonck, which was mainly financed by the clergy (Emile Cammaerts, *Belgium*, 1921, pp. 260–3; Pirenne, op. cit. v. 403–10, 419–28, 440–1).

18. Marie-Thérèse-Louise de Savoie-Carignan (1749–92), m. (1767) Louis-Alexandre-Joseph-Stanislas de Bourbon, Prince de Lamballe. She arrived in London 10 July (GM 1787, lvii pt ii. 733; *London Chronicle* 24–6 July, lxii. 82). HW wrote Strafford 28 July 1787, 'I never saw her, not even in France'; but he mentions seeing her at Versailles in a letter to Lady Ossory 18 Aug. 1775 (CHUTE 389; Ossory i. 255).

19. See *ante* 17 June 1787.

20. She is not listed in HW's 'Book of Visitors,' and he wrote Lady Ossory 6 Sept. 1787, 'I have seen none of the French, Savoyard or Lorrain princes and princesses, sterling or pinchbeck' (Ossory ii. 567).

To HERTFORD, September 1787

Missing; answered *post* 24 Sept. 1787.

From HERTFORD, Monday 24 September 1787

Printed for the first time from a photostat of BM Add. MSS 23219, f. 157.

Sudborne Hall, September 24th 1787.

Dear Horry,

I TAKE an affectionate share in the satisfaction you express to me upon Lady Horatia's delivery,[1] and I will acknowledge I was, as well as yourself, not without some anxiety upon the accident which had happened to her.[2] I am sorry for Lord Dillon,[3] though from the state of his health and appearance for some time past, I did not expect him at so advanced an age to live long.

We hear even in our retirement of orange cockades, and accounts of military operations being arrived at Harwich.[4] Are we then to

1. Of a son, George Francis Seymour-Conway (17 Sept. 1787 – 1870), Kt, 1831; Admiral of the Fleet, 1866; K.C.B., 1852; G.C.B., 1860 (BERRY ii. 158, n. 23; DNB). Hugh Seymour-Conway wrote to the Duchess of Gloucester, 'The Prince of Wales having done us the honour to propose being godfather to our child, may we hope your R.H. will allow us to request that you will be the godmother; Lord Hertford is to be the other godfather' (Violet Biddulph, *The Three Ladies Waldegrave*, 1938, pp. 203–4).

2. What this 'accident' was has not been ascertained; Charlotte Augusta Keppel wrote Anne Clement 28 Sept. 1787 that Lady Horatia's health was good after the birth of her son (MS now WSL).

3. Henry Dillon (1705 – 15 Sept. 1787), 11th Vct Dillon, 1741 (GM 1787, lvii pt ii. 841; OSSORY i. 312, n. 4). Lady Mary Coke in 'MS Journals' 14 Sept. 1787 wrote, 'I sent to inquire after poor Lord Dillon and had a bad message'; and on 18 Sept.,

'Poor man, he died on Saturday and at the last very suddenly.'

4. See *ante* 20 July 1787, n. 12. On 13 Sept. Montmorin, French minister of foreign affairs, informed Eden in Paris and Barthélemy, the French chargé d'affaires in London, that France would offer Holland whatever assistance was necessary if the K. of Prussia marched into the Provinces (William, Lord Auckland, *Journal and Correspondence*, 1861–2, i. 193, 523). Carmarthen's letter of 13 Sept. to Eden states the King's decision 'that it is impossible for him to remain a quiet spectator of any armed interference on the part of France,' and summarizes the British principles for mediation (ibid. i. 524–30). Carmarthen wrote Eden 21 Sept., 'The French Court has notified its determination to give assistance to the party in Holland who resist the King of Prussia's just demand of satisfaction for the insult offered to the Princess of Orange. . . . His Majesty has, therefore, found himself under the necessity of taking immediate measures for equipping

have war notwithstanding the present circumstances of France[5] and the ingenuity of Mr Eden to make him useful to those in power?[6] I remain, dear Horry,

Very truly and faithfully yours,

HERTFORD

To CONWAY, ca Friday 26 October 1787

Missing; mentioned *post* 11 Nov. 1787: 'I sent you the good news on the very day before you wrote.' HW sent Lady Lyttelton the news of the end of the revolution in Holland on 28 Oct. 1787, and wrote, 'Mr Conway is gone to Jersey, but I tr⟨ust the paci⟩fication will bring him back incontinently, and that he will see ⟨no fir⟩e but those he kindles in his own lime-kilns.'

From CONWAY, ca Saturday 27 October 1787

Missing; answered *post* 11 Nov. 1787.

a considerable naval armament, and for augmenting his land forces, in order to be prepared for any circumstances which may arise' (ibid. i. 199–200, 202–5; see also *London Chronicle* 2–4 Oct., lxii. 328).

5. I.e., France's financial straits. Pitt wrote Eden 14 Sept. 1787, 'If the French Court will not adopt these principles [for mediation, above, n. 4], I believe the question must be decided by a war . . . I am far from feeling any wish in consequence of the present situation of France, to provoke extremities if they can be avoided. The advantage of a continued peace is more to this country than anything we might gain by taking the opportunity of going to war; but the actual mischief of suffering France to carry its point in Holland would more than counterbalance it' (Auckland, op. cit. i. 195). Pitt wrote Rutland 17 Sept., 'I

still think it possible from the infinite embarrassments of France, and the little preparation she has yet made, that things may stop short of actual extremity' (*Correspondence between . . . William Pitt and Charles Duke of Rutland*, 1890, p. 186).

6. In Paris Eden was negotiating with Montmorin for a peaceful mediation of the Dutch crisis by France, England and Prussia. Eden had negotiated the Commercial Treaty between France and England in 1786 (*ante* ?16 May 1786, n. 4), and the East India Convention in 1787 (Auckland, op. cit. i. 191; Cobbett, *Parl. Hist.* xxvi. 1255–7); he had recently been appointed ambassador to Spain (*London Chronicle* 17–19 July, lxii. 64; Auckland, op. cit. i. 186, 188). For the termination of the Dutch crisis, see *post* 11 Nov. 1787, n. 5.

To Conway, Sunday 11 November 1787

Printed from *Works* v. 242-3.

Berkeley Square, Nov. 11, 1787.

FROM violent contrary winds,[1] and by your letter[2] going to Strawberry Hill, whence I was come,[3] I have but just received it, and perhaps shall only be able to answer it by snatches, being up to the chin in nephews and nieces. . . .[4]

I find you knew nothing of the pacification[5] when you wrote. When I saw your letter, I hoped it would tell me you was coming back, as your island is as safe as if it was situated in the Pacific Ocean, or at least as islands there used to be, till Sir Joseph Banks[6] chose *to put them up.*[7] I sent you the good news on the very day before you wrote, though I imagined you would learn it by earlier intelligence. Well, I enjoy both your safety and your great success, which is enhanced by its being owing to your character and abilities.

1. Mr Conway was now in Jersey (HW); see HW to Lady Lyttelton 28 Oct. 1787.

2. Missing.

3. HW wrote Lady Lyttelton Sunday 28 Oct. 1787, 'At the end of the week . . . I shall remove to Londo⟨n to m⟩eet the court of Gloucester in London, the beginning ⟨of the mont⟩h.'

4. A passage has been omitted here in *Works,* indicated by asterisks; it probably concerned the return of the Duke and Duchess of Gloucester, who landed at Dover 10 Nov. and arrived at Gloucester House 11 Nov. after an absence of five and a half years (OSSORY ii. 581-2 and n. 2).

5. On 13 Sept. the Prussian troops entered the province of Guelderland and without meeting resistance occupied many towns. On the 16th the Prince of Orange re-possessed Utrecht and on the 20th arrived at The Hague. On 6 Oct. the deputies from Amsterdam to the States of Holland agreed to the restoration of the Prince of Orange, the disarming of the Free Corps, and the expulsion of the magistrates who represented the Patriot party; and on 10 Oct. Amsterdam capitulated to the Duke of Brunswick (Sir James Harris, Lord Malmesbury,

Diaries and Correspondence, 1844, ii. 371, 374, 378-9, 386-7, 394-6; *Daily Adv.* 13 Oct., *sub* 'Extract of a letter from Amsterdam' 7 Oct.; and 24 Oct., *sub* Hague 13 Oct.; *London Gazette* No. 12922, 18-22 Sept., *sub* Hague 18 Sept.). The news of the surrender of Amsterdam was announced in the *London Gazette* No. 12930, 16-20 Oct., *sub* Hague 12 Oct. A declaration and counter-declaration were signed 27 Oct. at Versailles by the Duke of Dorset, Eden, and Montmorin, in which it was agreed that 'armaments, and in general all warlike preparations' should be discontinued and the navies of both nations reduced to a peace-time establishment (*London Gazette* No. 12933, 27-30 Oct.; Cobbett, *Parl. Hist.* xxvi. 1264-5).

6. (1744-1820), cr. (1781) Bt.

7. A hunting expression meaning 'To cause (game) to rise from cover; to rouse, start' (OED). HW made a similar comment to Cole 15 June 1780: 'How I abominate Mr Banks and Dr Solander who routed the poor Otaheitians out of the centre of the ocean, and carried our abominable passions amongst them' (COLE ii. 225).

I hope the latter will be allowed to operate by those who have not quite so much of either.

I shall be wonderful glad to see little master Stonehenge[8] at Park Place: it will look in character there; but your own bridge[9] is so stupendous in comparison, that hereafter the latter will be thought to have been a work of the Romans. Dr Stukeley[10] will burst his cerements to offer mistletoe in your temple—and Mason, on the contrary, will die of vexation and spite that he cannot have *Caractacus* acted on the spot—[11]

> Peace to all such!—but were there one whose fires
> True Genius kindles, and fair Fame inspires,[12]

he would immortalize you, for all you have been carrying on in Jersey, and for all you shall carry off. Inigo Jones, or Charlton,[13] or somebody, I forget who, called Stonehenge *chorea gigantum*[14]—this will be the *chorea* of the pigmies—and as I forget too what is Latin for Lilliputians, I will make a bad pun, and say,

> ——*portantur avari*
> Pigmalionis *opes*——[15]

8. Mr Walpole thus calls the small druidic temple discovered in Jersey [12 Aug. 1785] which the states of that island had presented to their Governor General Conway to be transported to and erected at Park Place (Mary Berry). After seeing it in August 1788 HW wrote a description to Lady Ossory 6 Sept. 1788 (OSSORY iii. 14–15 and n. 3), and to Strafford 12 Sept. 1788 (CHUTE 396). For the inscription see OSSORY iii. 21 and n. 10. A model of the 'druidical temple' was in the Small Closet at SH ('Des. of SH,' *Works* ii. 494); see illustration.

9. See *ante* 25 Nov. 1764, n. 49.

10. Rev. William Stukeley (1687–1765), archæologist and antiquary. HW's copies of his *Palæographia sacra: or discourses on monuments of antiquity that relate to sacred history* (1736) and *Palæographia Britannica: or discourses on antiquities in Britain* (1743, 1746) are Hazen, *Cat. of HW's Lib.*, Nos 640, 668 (the latter now WSL).

11. HW in his letter to Lady Ossory 6 Sept. 1788 calls the druidic temple 'Caractacus's own summer residence' (OS-

SORY iii. 15), and wrote Strafford 2 Aug. 1788 that Conway's comedy *False Appearances* should be acted there (CHUTE 395).

12. Pope, 'Epistle to Dr Arbuthnot,' ll. 193–4.

13. Walter Charleton (1619–1707), M.D., physician to Charles II; F.R.S., 1662; Fellow and President of the College of Physicians.

14. Charleton's *Chorea Gigantum, or, The Most Famous Antiquity of Great Britan, Vulgarly Called Stone-Heng, Standing on Salisbury Plain, Restored to the Danes*, 1663, was a reply to *The Most Notable Antiquity of Great Britain, Vulgarly Called Stone Heng, on Salisbury Plain. Restored by Inigo Jones, Esquire*, ed. John Webb, 1655. Webb wrote *A Vindication of Stone-Heng Restored*, 1665, and in 1725 the three works were published together in the second edition of Inigo Jones's essay; HW's copy of it is Hazen, op. cit., No. 599.

15. 'The treasures of greedy Pygmalion are carried away' (Virgil, *Æneid*, Bk 1, ll. 363–4).

Drawn by the late Wm Alexander F.S.A. of the British Museum.

Engraved by George Cooke.

THE DRUID'S ALTAR AT PARK PLACE, HENLEY.

Seat of the Earl of Malmsbury.

London. Pub.^d by Wm Wood Junr 1819, by W. & G. Cooke, 12 York Place, Pentonville.

Pygmalion is as well-sounding a name for such a monarch as Oberon. —Pray do not disappoint me, but transport the cathedral[16] of your island to your domain on our *continent*. I figure unborn antiquaries making pilgrimages to visit your bridge, your daughter's bridge,[17] and the Druidic temple; and if I were not too old to have any imagination left, I would add a sequel to Mi Li.[18] Adieu!

From Beauchamp, ca July 1788

Missing; answered *post* 13 July 1788.

To Beauchamp, Sunday 13 July 1788

Printed from the MS now wsl; first printed Toynbee xiv. 59–60. The MS was sold Sotheby's 13 [14] March 1865 (Joseph Cottle Sale), lot 141 to Ellis for £1.5s.; Sotheby's 9 March 1870 (Autograph Letters Sale), lot 114 to Webster for £2.3s.; Sotheby's 5 May 1892 (Webster Sale), lot 216 to Heath for £4; offered J. Pearson and Co. Cat. 76, pt iii, 1894, p. 46, lot 394, for £6.15s.; it passed into the possession of Harry Stone, New York City, from whom wsl acquired it in 1940.

Strawberry Hill, July 13, 1788.

My dear Lord,

THOUGH I doubt, roving as you are,[1] whether this will light upon you, I must endeavour to thank you for the honour of your letter;[2] though it makes me not a little ashamed. When you asked for my simple volume,[3] I concluded it was for some Englishman; and as I have exposed myself too much to my countrymen by my

16. The druidic temple (HW).

17. The key-stones of the centre arch of the bridge at Henley are ornamented with heads of the Thames and Isis, designed by the Hon. Mrs Damer, and executed by her in Portland stone (Mary Berry); see Ossory ii. 484–5 and n. 2; *ante* 16 Sept. 1781, n. 15.

18. One of the *Hieroglyphic Tales*, containing a description of Park Place (HW); see HW's *Works*, iv. 342–7.

1. Anthony Storer wrote Eden 8 Aug. 1788, 'Lord and Lady Beauchamp are still at The Hague. Has his Lordship fallen in love with a Frau, or does he mean to be a Stadtholder?' (William, Lord Auckland, *Journal and Correspondence*, 1861–2, ii. 225).

2. Missing.

3. Possibly the French translation of HW's *Essay on Modern Gardening* by the Duc de Nivernais, SH, 1785 (Hazen, *SH Bibl.* 129–32).

trifling writings, it was in vain to excuse myself. I should have had more scruples, had I known it was intended for a learned foreigner[4] of a family distinguished by learning—indeed I had no notion of being known out of our own island, except at Paris where I have lived so much, and where by this time I must be pretty much forgotten—but I will say no more, because acting modesty always looks like asking for compliments, which at seventy-one would only prove that I am superannuated.

I live too much out of the world, and care too little about its affairs, to send you political news, of which I know nothing but the surface. This last week has produced some changes, chiefly in the Admiralty;[5] and from abroad we hear that a new war is tapped between Russia and Sweden.[6] If I am indifferent at home, I am totally so about their Northern Majesties, and if they will destroy

4. Not identified; for a list of recipients of presentation copies of the *Essay*, see HW's 'Book of Visitors,' Berry ii. 259–60.

5. Announced in the *London Gazette* No. 13006, 8–12 July, *sub* Whitehall 12 July; see also *Daily Adv.* 12, 14 July. HW in 'Mem. 1783–91' wrote, 'The day before the Parliament rose [11 July], a change in part of the Administration was declared. Lord Howe resigned his seat as first lord of the Admiralty, but to show that he was neither disgraced nor out of humour, he was to be created an earl, and a baron, with the reversion of the latter to his eldest daughter's husband (for he had no sons) Mr Curzon. His friends Leveson Gower and Brett were to resign their seats at the same board; and Lord Chatham was to be first lord and Lord Hood and Sir Peter Parker, commissioners. The fact was this; early in the preceding winter a great and extraordinary promotion of admirals had been made over several extremely meritorious seamen, who were omitted, to bring the list down to Leveson Gower, Lord Howe's great friend, and Sir Charles Middleton comptroller of the Navy, a favourite of the King, who was also unprecedently allowed to keep his post. This measure had given such extreme disgust to the Navy, that it was thought it would not be safe for Lord Howe to venture himself again at sea among the sailors. A complaint had been even made to the House of Commons on the injustice shown to so many meritorious officers and on the partiality to Sir Charles Middleton; and it was but by a very small majority that Lord Howe escaped a sentence of censure. . . . Pitt to secure and display his superiority in the Cabinet, insisted on setting his brother Lord Chatham at the head of the Admiralty.'

6. As a result of warlike preparations in June by Gustav III of Sweden, the Russian ambassador at Stockholm presented a rescript 18 June protesting the armaments, and the Empress published her declaration of war, dated 30 June (GM 1788, lviii pt ii. 644–5, 737–8; *London Chronicle* 12–15, 17–19 July, 2–5 Aug., lxiv. 55, 68, 124). On 17 June the Swedish fleet under the command of the Duke of Sudermania defeated a larger Russian fleet under Admiral Greig off Hoogland (GM 1788, lviii pt ii. 739–40). An 'Extract of a letter from Petersburgh' 7 July stated that 'The Court . . . has been put into the utmost astonishment on the reception of dispatches from Finland, informing her Imperial Majesty that the Swedish troops had entered her territories, and had pillaged and destroyed the cabinets of the custom houses; and that 5000 of these troops had attempted to take possession of Niestol' (*London Chronicle* 2–5 Aug., lxiv. 125; see also ibid. 5–7 Aug., lxiv. 130).

their subjects, I care not which has the disadvantage, for I cannot help thinking that the interests of thousands are of more consequence than those of one individual. War is a game, but unfortunately the cards, counters and fishes[7] suffer by an ill run, more than the gamesters.

I think your Lordship's son[8] fortunate in seeing Europe under your own eye and it will make it less necessary for him to travel, as is generally done, at an age when he should be studying his own country. I beg my respectful compliments to Lady Beauchamp and him, and have the honour to be with great regard, my dear Lord,

Your Lordship's most obed[ient] humble servant,

HOR. WALPOLE

To HERTFORD, ca Sunday 5 October 1788

Missing; answered *post* 13 Oct. 1788.

From HERTFORD, Monday 13 October 1788

Printed for the first time from a photostat of BM Add. MSS 23219, f. 158.

Sudborne Hall, October 13th 1788.

Dear Horry,

I THANK you for your letter[1] and inquiries; my health continues, thank God, extremely good, and if I had gout last spring, I have not had a symptom of it during this summer and autumn to disturb my ease or entertainment.

I hope you have been as free from it and from every other complaint.

Your niece, Lady Horatia, and her son[2] have been here some time,

---

7. 'A small flat piece of bone or ivory used instead of money or for keeping account in games of chance; sometimes made in the form of a fish' (OED, *sub* 'fish sb³').

8. Francis Charles Seymour-Conway (1777–1842), styled E. of Yarmouth 1794–1822; 3d M. of Hertford, 1822.

————

1. Missing.

2. George Francis (*ante* 24 Sept. 1787).

and I can assure you she can have contracted no sourness of temper from her last connection;³ her son is the finest boy to be seen. You will not expect news from this hermitage, and my retirement has not left me political connection of any sort to inform me what passes in public life. I remain in all situations, dear Horry,

Very truly and faithfully yours,

HERTFORD

From CONWAY, Tuesday 26 May 1789

Printed for the first time from the MS now WSL. For the history of the MS, see *ante* 9 Aug. 1767.
Address: To the Honourable Horatio Walpole.
Endorsed (by HW): May 26.
Memoranda (by HW, in pencil):

> Pr. of Wales desiring Q. to prevent the duel—took no notice.¹
> D of Clar[ence]² Mad. [illegible]
> Dd old B. if I had been D. of York³
> wd not you have curtsied?

3. Unexplained.

———

1. HW's 'separate account' of the duel between the Duke of York and Lt-Col. Charles Lennox, mentioned in 'Mem. 1783–91,' *sub* May 1789 has not been found; it may have described the Prince of Wales's intervention. The *London Chronicle* 21–3 May, lxv. 494, reported, 'The affair between the Duke of York and Mr Lenox is, we are happy to say, on the verge of being made up by the interference of a great personage.' After the duel Charles Fox wrote Mrs Armistead, 'When the King and Queen heard it, the first showed very little and the second *no* emotion at all, and both said coldly that they believed it was more Frederick's fault than Lennox's' (George, Prince of Wales, *Correspondence . . . 1770–1812*, ed. Aspinall, 1963–71, ii. 14, n. 2). The Prince of Wales in a letter to the King in June 1789 observed, 'The Queen did not utter a syllable either of alarm at the imminent danger which had threatened the life of my brother

but an hour before, of joy and satisfaction at his safety, or of general tenderness and affection towards him . . . the first word the Queen pronounced, and the whole tenor of the only conversation she afterwards held, was a defence of Mr Lenox's conduct, strongly implying a censure on that of my brother' (Charles James Fox, *Memorials and Correspondence*, ed. Russell, 1853, ii. 349).

2. Prince William Henry (1765–1837), D. of Clarence 1789–1830; King of England (as William IV) 1830–7.

3. Frederick, Bp of Osnabrück, George III's 2d son, cr. (1784) E. of Ulster and D. of York and Albany (*ante* 12 April 1764, n. 14). HW wrote in 'Mem. 1783–91,' loc. cit., 'D. of Clarence meeting Madam Schwellenberg in a passage at Kew, did not curtsie to him, but a page naming him, she turned, asked pardon, curtsied and said she had taken him for the D. of York. "Well, you damned old bitch," said he, "and if [it] had been the D. of York would not you have curtsied to him?" '

Pr. & D. of Clar. to K. <can feel with> Q. <she> they shd have continued4
Pr. dr. at Boodles5
29 Queen [illegible] Fr. Emb.6 Princes not <dance> nor stayed
June 1. Dr. of Clar. ball 3 <princes> Mad. Luzerne7
2. Span. Ambass.8 gilt plate to set 1000
4. Q. asked Princes9

4. The King wrote the Duke of Clarence 25 May objecting to his request for an increased allowance, mentioning 'the unkindness I met with during my illness from the ill-advised conduct of my sons,' and regretting the Duke of Clarence's 'being entirely a follower of those who are certainly not attentive to me' (George III, *Letters*, ed. B. Dobrée, 1935, pp. 203–4; the D. of Clarence's answer 1 June is in George III, *Later Correspondence*, ed. A. Aspinall, Cambridge, 1962–70, i. 419–21). The Prince of Wales wrote the King 14 Aug., 'Your Majesty's letter to my brother the Duke of Clarence in June last, was the first direct intimation I have ever received, that *my conduct, as well as that of my brother the Duke of York*, during your Majesty's late lamented illness, had brought on us the heavy misfortune of your Majesty's displeasure . . . I cannot omit this opportunity of lamenting those appearances of a less gracious disposition in the Queen towards my brother and myself than we were accustomed to experience' (ibid. i. 439–40).

5. HW wrote in 'Mem. 1783–91,' loc. cit., 'The neutral or mixed club at Boodles gave a most splendid ball at Ranelagh on the King's recovery. It cost very near £5000. The Prince of Wales got exceedingly drunk there, got on a table, talked irreligiously, indecently, and abused the Queen. Women got on tables to see and hear him, his friends made the music play louder to drown his voice, and at last he was carried out speechless'; see also Lady Susan Leveson Gower to her brother 4 June 1789, in Lord Granville Leveson Gower, *Private Correspondence 1781 to 1821*, ed. Cts Granville, 1916, i. 16; *London Chronicle* 26–8 May, lxv. 509.

6. Anne-César de la Luzerne. 'The French ambassador gave a great ball to the Queen at his house in Portman Square. At first she had wished to have

only peeresses and their daughters: then only her own set. Then pretended not to see the list, and several of the Opposition were invited—but to prove she interfered, the Duke of Queensberry, Lord Lothian and Lord Malmsbury were not invited, and the Chief Company were appointed at half an hour after eight, the rest at half after ten. The three Princes were there full dressed, but would neither dance nor stay supper, so offended were they with their mother, especially as she on Lenox's entrance made a familiar sign to him with her fan' ('Mem. 1783–91,' loc. cit.; see also Berry i. 38, n. 2; *London Chronicle* 28–30 May, lxv. 519).

7. Presumably Victoire-Marie-Françoise de Montmorin-Saint-Hérem, m. (1784) César-Guillaume (d. 1794), Comte de la Luzerne, nephew of the French ambassador (A. Révérend, *Titres*, 1901–6, iv. 153). 'The D. of Clarence gave a ball at Almack's, and took out first Madame de [la] Luzerne, the French ambassador's niece, to show no incivility had been meant to them' ('Mem. 1783–91,' *sub* 1 June 1789). Of this ball Lady Mary Coke wrote, 'None of the Queen's family are invited' ('MS Journals,' 31 May 1789). See also *London Chronicle* 30 May–2 June, lxv. 528.

8. Bernardo, Marquis del Campo, Spanish minister plenipotentiary and ambassador extraordinary ca 1783–95 (*London Calendar, Royal Calendar 1783–95 passim*). 'The Spanish ambassador Del Campo gave at Ranelagh the most magnificent of all the balls, to the Queen etc. She was served in a most beautiful service of gilt plate sent from Spain on purpose (and given afterwards to the ambassador). The Prince and D. of Clarence were there, but did not dance, the D. of York in his boots, only in the garden' ('Mem. 1783–91,' *sub* 2 June 1789; see also *London Chronicle* 2–4 June, lxv. 535).

I HAVE called at Brookes's where there were only one or two people, so I heard little more than a full confirmation[10]—Lord Rawdon was second to the Duke and Lord Winchelsea[11] to Lenox[12]—they had agreed to fire together—but the Duke did not fire.—[13]

Afterwards L[ennox] ask the Duke if he was satisfied that he had not deserved the epithets etc. The Duke said yes, in *this affair*—but *he would retract* nothing[14] etc.—

The Curl touched—much explanation *wanted*.[15]

9. 'The King's birthday was kept by the Queen at St James's, but he himself, though pretended to be so well, did not appear, which showed how ridiculous all the festivals and addresses on recovery were. The Queen too discovered how much she had been mortified by her sons not dancing and supping with her at the two ambassadors' [balls], for a message was sent to them in the King's name to desire they would dance on his birthnight' ('Mem. 1783–91,' *sub* 4 June 1789). HW continues with an account of the dance similar to that in GM 1789, lix pt i. 565–6.

10. Of the duel fought with pistols 26 May 1789 on Wimbledon Common by Lt-Col. Charles Lennox and his superior officer, the Duke of York, Col. in the Coldstream Foot Guards; see BERRY i. 25, n. 7; *London Chronicle* 23–6, 26–8 May, lxv. 504, 505.

11. George Finch (1752–1826), 9th E. of Winchilsea, 1769; a lord of the Bedchamber 1777–1812. A letter from the Prince of Wales to the King ca June 1789 contained the complaint, 'Lord Winchelsea has not been dismissed from your Majesty's service, nor has he received any reprimand or other expression of your Majesty's disapprobation' (Fox, op. cit. ii. 346).

12. Charles Lennox (1764–1819), 4th D. of Richmond, 1806; Lt-Col. in the Coldstream Foot Guards; Gen., 1814; lord lieutenant of Ireland 1807–13; Gov.-Gen. of Canada 1818–19 (BERRY i. 25, n. 7; George III, *Later Correspondence*, i. 418, 425; George, P. of Wales, op. cit. ii. 14 and n. 2).

13. According to the account given by the seconds, 'The signal being given,

Lieutenant-Colonel Lenox fired, and the ball grazed his Royal Highness's curl. The Duke of York did not fire' (*London Chronicle* 26–8 May, lxv. 505).

14. 'Lord Winchelsea then went up to the Duke of York, and expressed his hope, "That his Royal Highness could have no objection to say, he considered Lieut.-Col. Lenox as a man of honour and courage." His Royal Highness replied, "That he should say nothing; he had come out to give Lieut.-Col. Lenox satisfaction, and did not mean to fire at him; if Lieut.-Col. Lenox was not satisfied, he might fire again"' (ibid.).

15. On 30 May Gen. William Fawcett met with Lord Dover and Lord Amherst to deliver a message from the King: 'His Majesty had been pleased to express his concern at hearing that the dispute which had arisen with Lt-Col. Lenox of the Coldstream Regiment of Footguards, and which was of such public notoriety, was from recent report likely to be followed with further improper consequences, his Majesty thought it might be necessary for him to interfere'; but on 31 May Fawcett reported 'that the result of the meeting of the officers of the Coldstream Regiment of Guards seemed to be a quiet adjustment of the dispute with Lt-Colonel Lenox, so far as to remove any apprehension of any further bad consequence for the present' (George III, *Later Correspondence*, i. 418). The officers meeting 30 May concluded, 'It is the opinion of the regiment, that subsequent to the meeting at the Orderly Room the 15th of May, Lieutenant-Colonel Lenox had behaved with *courage*, but, from the peculiar difficulty of his situation, not with *judgment*' (*London Chronicle* 30 May–

To Conway, Wednesday 15 July 1789

Printed from *Works* v. 244–5.

Strawberry Hill, Wednesday night.

I WRITE a few lines only to confirm the truth of much of what you will read in the papers from Paris. Worse may already be come or is expected every hour.[1]

Mr Mackenzie and Lady Betty called on me before dinner, after the post was gone out;[1a] and he showed me a letter from Dutens,[2] who said two couriers arrived yesterday from the Duke of Dorset[3] and the Duchess of Devonshire, the latter of whom was leaving Paris directly.[4] Necker had been dismissed,[5] and was thought to be set out for Geneva. Breteuil,[6] who was at his country house, had been sent for to succeed him. Paris was in an uproar; and, after the couriers had left it, firing of cannon was heard for four hours together.[7]

2 June, lxv. 522). A pamphlet, 'A Short Review of the Recent Affair of Honour between His Royal Highness the Duke of York, and Lieutenant-Colonel Lenox . . . By the Captain of a Company in one of the Regiments of Guards,' 1789, presented a vindication of Lennox.

1. HW learned of the fall of the Bastille and other happenings of 14 July the evening of the 19th (BERRY i. 38–41).

1a. HW describes this visit to Mary Berry 15 July 1789, ibid. i. 35 and n. 40.

2. Louis Dutens (1730–1812), antiquary, clergyman, and close friend of Stuart Mackenzie; see ibid. i. 35, n. 41.

3. W. W. Grenville wrote the Marquess of Buckingham 14 July 1789, 'A messenger is arrived from the Duke of Dorset with an account of the dismission of Necker and Montmorin, and the appointment of Monsieur de Breteuil to be *chef du conseil des finances*, the Duc de la Vaugyon to be minister for the foreign department, and Monsieur de Broglio to be *ministre de guerre*' (Hist. MSS Comm., 13th Report, App. pt iii, *Fortescue MSS*, 1892, i. 483–4). Dorset left Paris on leave 8 Aug. and arrived in London 13 Aug. (*World* 14 Aug.; BERRY i. 36, n. 42).

4. The *World* 13 July reported that

'the Duchess of Devonshire, if Madame de Polignac's advice be followed, is to leave Paris—and for fear of the popular tumults, which every day look more and more alarming'; she arrived safely at Spa 17 July (ibid. 20 July; see BERRY i. 27, n. 23).

5. The King's letter of dismissal was brought to him 11 July, and he set out that evening for St-Ouen, then Brussels, and arrived at Basle 22 July (B. Huber to Eden 14, 16, 28 July 1789, in William, Lord Auckland, *Journal and Correspondence*, 1861–2, ii. 331, 335, 339; BERRY i. 36, n. 43).

6. Louis-Charles-Auguste le Tonnelier (1733–1807), Baron de Breteuil, succeeded Necker briefly as director-general of Finance, but later emigrated to Brussels, then to Soleure, Switzerland, and in 1794 to London (ibid. i. 36, n. 44).

7. According to W. W. Grenville's letter of 14 July to the Marquess of Buckingham, 'The accounts . . . of cannonades depend on the report of the messenger who brought this dispatch [from Dorset]. The violence of the mob at Paris has been hourly increasing for many days, and has proceeded to several acts of savage fury. Some of the French troops have openly declared their refusal to serve against their countrymen, but all

That must have been from the Bastille, as probably the Tiers État were not so provided. It is shocking to imagine what may have happened in such a thronged city!

One of the couriers was stopped twice or thrice, as supposed to pass from the King; but redeemed himself by pretending to be dispatched by the Tiers État. Madame de Calonne[8] told Dutens that the newly encamped troops desert by hundreds.

Here seems the egg to be hatched, and imagination runs away with the idea. I may fancy I shall hear of the King and Queen leaving Versailles, like Charles I—and then skips imagination six-and-forty years lower, and figures their fugitive majesties taking refuge in this country.[9]

I have besides another idea. If the Bastille conquers, still is it impossible, considering the general spirit in the country, and the numerous fortified places in France, but some may be seized by the *dissidents*,[10] and whole provinces be torn from the Crown?—On the other hand, if the King prevails, what heavy despotism will the États, by their want of temper and moderation, have drawn on their country! They might have obtained many capital points, and removed great oppression—no French monarch will ever summon États again, if this moment has been thrown away.

Though I have stocked myself with such a set of visions for the event either way, I do not pretend to foresee what will happen. Penetration argues from reasonable probabilities; but chance and folly are apt to contradict calculation, and hitherto they seem to have full scope for action. One hears of no genius on either side, nor do symptoms of any appear. There will perhaps: such times and tempests bring forth, at least bring out, great men. I do not take the Duke of Orléans or Mirabeau[11] to be built *du bois dont on les fait*—no; nor Monsieur Necker.[12] He may be a great traitor, if he

the Swiss and German troops, and the greater part of the national troops, are steady' (*Fortescue MSS*, i. 484).

8. Anne-Rose-Josèphe de Nettine (ca 1740–1813) m. 1 (1761) Joseph Micault d'Harvelay, 'Counsellor of State'; m. 2 (1788) at Bath, as his 2d wife, Charles-Alexandre de Calonne, director-general of Finance 1783–7 (see BERRY i. 36, n. 47). They had a house at Hyde Park Corner and a villa at Wimbledon (ibid.).

9. Charles I left London in 1642, and

forty-six years later (1688) James II fled to France where Queen Mary Beatrice and the Prince of Wales had already found refuge at St-Germain.

10. A reference to the Dissidents of Poland, the Protestants and Greek Orthodox who opposed the tyranny of Catholics; see MANN vi. 574 and n. 5, ix. 11.

11. Honoré-Gabriel Riquetti (1749–91), Comte de Mirabeau; see OSSORY iii. 186.

12. HW wrote Mary Berry 31 July

made the confusion designedly:—but it is a woeful evasion, if the promised financier slips into a black politician. I adore liberty, but I would bestow it as honestly as I could; and a civil war, besides being a game of chance, is paying a very dear price for it.

For us, we are in most danger of a deluge; though I wonder we so frequently complain of long rains. The saying about St Swithin is a proof of how often they recur; for proverbial sentences are the children of experience, not of prophecy.[13] Good night!—In a few days I shall send you a beautiful little poem[14] from the Strawberry Press.

From CONWAY, ca 1 September 1789

Missing; answered *post* 5 Sept. 1789.

To CONWAY, Saturday 5 September 1789

Printed from *Works* v. 245–7.

Strawberry Hill, September 5, 1789.

YOU speak so unperemptorily of your motions,[1] that I must direct to you at random: the most probable place where to hit you, I think, will be Goodwood;[2] and I do address this thither, because I

1789, 'I . . . do not hold him great and profound enough to quell the present anarchy' (BERRY i. 45). Necker was recalled 16 July, accepted 23 July, and returned to Paris 28 July (ibid. i. 45, n. 32).

13. According to legend, if it rains on St Swithin's Day (the 15th of July), there will be rain for the next forty days (ibid. i. 37 and n. 51).

14. This was Bonner's Ghost (HW). The impression of Hannah More's *Bishop Bonner's Ghost* was finished 18 July; see Hazen, *SH Bibl.* 137–40; MORE 313, 318.

1. Conway's letter is missing. According to Lady Mary Coke, 'Lady Ailesbury is to be in town on Sunday [6 Sept.] to take leave of them [the D. and Ds of

Argyll] . . . I could not accept of their invitation of passing the day with them tomorrow [6 Sept.] to meet Lady Ailesbury who comes from Park Place to take leave of them' ('MS Journals' 3, 5 Sept. 1789).

2. The *World* 8 Sept. reported that 'this day' Conway, Lady Ailesbury, and Mrs Damer 'set off from their house in Warwick Street, Pall Mall, on a visit to the Duke and Duchess of Richmond, at their seat at Goodwood near Chichester, Sussex.' HW wrote Mary Berry 27 Aug. 1789 that he sent his excuse 'to the Duchess of Richmond who wanted me to meet her mother, sister and General Conway at Goodwood next week' (BERRY i. 59 and n. 9).

am impatient to thank you for your tale,[3] which is very pretty and easy and genteel. It has made me make a reflection, and that reflection made six lines; which I send you, not as good, but as expressing my thoughts on your writing so well in various ways which you never practised when you was much younger.—Here they are:

> The muse most wont to fire a youthful heart,
> To gild *your* setting sun reserv'd her art;
> To crown a life in virtuous labours pass'd[4]
> Bestow'd her numbers, and her wit at last;
> And when your strength and eloquence retire,
> Your voice in notes harmonious shall expire.[5]

The *swan* was too common a thought to be directly specified—and, perhaps, even to be alluded to—no matter—such a trifle is below criticism.

I am still here, in no uncertainty, God knows, about poor Lady Dysart, of whom there are not the smallest hopes.[6] She grows weaker every day, and does actually still go out for the air, and may languish many days, though most probably will go off in a moment, as the water rises.[7] She retains her senses perfectly, and as perfectly her unalterable calmness and patience, though fully sensible of her situation. At your return from Goodwood, I shall like to come to you, if you are unengaged, and ready to receive me.[8] For the beauties of Park Place, I am too well acquainted with them, not, like all old persons about their cotemporaries, to think it preserves them long after they are faded; and I am so *unwalking*,[9] that prospects are more

---

3. Missing. Possibly Conway's verses on Miss Elizabeth Hervey's bow window (see Ossory iii. 86 and n. 3), mentioned by Lady Mary Coke in her 'MS Journals' 2 Oct. 1789: 'Miss Hervey is here [Park Place]. She is now building to her house in town a bow window upon which Mr Conway has wrote verses. . . . I've just seen Mr Conway's verses upon Miss Hervey's bow and hope to procure you a copy, but to understand them better it is necessary to tell you that Lady Morton and Lady Mary Bouldby whose houses are on each side of Miss Hervey's built bow windows some years ago without the latter having made the least objection or complaint, but the two former ladies have now wrote letters and got all their friends to try to persuade Miss Hervey from her intention, Lady Morton went

so far as to say it would shorten Lady Mary Bouldby's days as it would take away all her comfort.'

4. 'Past' in *Works* v. 246.

5. Printed in *Horace Walpole's Fugitive Verses*, ed. W. S. Lewis, 1931, pp. 183–4.

6. She died 5 Sept. at Ham House; see Berry i. 67–8 and n. 44; Ossory iii. 61, 63.

7. Her illness was diagnosed as 'water on her breast' or 'water in her chest' and she suffered from 'swelling of her legs and thighs' (Berry i. 56; Ossory iii. 61, n. 1).

8. HW visited Park Place from 21 to 24 Sept. (Berry i. 71–2).

9. As a result of a fall at Hampton Court, which brought on an attack of gout; see ibid. i. 70, 72; Ossory iii. 63–4.

agreeable to me when framed and glazed, and I look at them through a window. It is yourselves I want to visit, not your verdure. Indeed, except a parenthesis of scarce all August, there has been no temptation to walk abroad; and the Tempter himself would not have persuaded me, if I could, to have climbed that long lost mountain whence he could show one even the antipodes. It rained incessantly all June and all July; and now again we have torrents every day.

Jerningham's brother, the Chevalier,[10] is arrived from Paris, and does not diminish the horrors one hears every day. They are now in the capital dreading the sixteen thousand deserters[11] who hover about them. I conclude, that when in the character of banditti the whole disbanded army have plundered and destroyed what they can, they will congregate into separate armies under different leaders, who will hang out different principles, and the kingdom will be a theatre of civil wars; and, instead of liberty, the nation will get petty tyrants—perhaps petty kingdoms:—and when millions have suffered, or been sacrificed, the government will be no better than it was—all owing to the intemperance of the États, who might have obtained a good constitution, or at least one much meliorated, if they had set out with discretion and moderation. They have left too a sad lesson to despotic princes, who will quote this precedent of frantic États against assembling any more, and against all the ex-

10. Charles Jerningham (1742–1814), younger brother of Edward Jerningham, entered the French army, and in 1784 became maréchal de camp; he was Knight of Malta, and of St Louis (see BERRY i. 67, n. 41). HW saw both brothers at Richard Owen Cambridge's on 4 Sept. (ibid. i. 67).

11. Huber's letter to Eden from Paris 14 July 1789 noted that 'all the French guards joined (except those at Versailles), and the Swiss guards also joined the people, likewise a regiment of dragoons, two other regiments of foot, who came from St-Denis; the whole calling themselves *l'armée nationale*. The Swiss regiments who are here will certainly follow the guards, and there seems to be little doubt left of a general desertion. Meanwhile, the magistrates of Paris and every inhabitant, fearing the consequences of such an anarchy, have assembled in churches, and came to immediate resolutions of embodying themselves for the security of Paris, and march the *rondes*'

(William, Lord Auckland, *Journal and Correspondence*, 1861–2, ii. 330). On 17 Aug. Huber wrote, 'A regular militia of 26,000 men is now embodied; of these 6,000 are paid, of these 6,000 upwards of 3,000 are old Gardes Françaises' (ibid. ii. 348). The *Daily Adv.* 5 Sept., in 'Extract of a Letter from Paris' 31 Aug., reported, 'The banditti, hitherto unaccountable, that have been for some months past entertained in the environs of Paris, are not yet departed. As this is the last day *on which they are to be paid by the City*, it is feared they will spread themselves in different parts of the neighbourhood, and become a very dangerous body for the inhabitants and travellers.' Another letter from Paris 3 Sept. reported a threat to the President of the National Assembly that 'if the coalition of the aristocratic party continues to trouble the harmony of the Assembly, and allow the King the power of the negative, 15,000 men are ready to light up their houses' (ibid. 9 Sept.).

amples of senates and parliaments that have preserved rational freedom.

Let me know when it will be convenient to you to receive me. Adieu!

To Conway, Friday 25 June 1790

Printed from the MS now wsl; first printed Wright vi. 357–8. For the history of the MS see *ante* 29 June 1744 OS.
Endorsed: Mr Walpole 25 June 1790.

Strawberry Hill, June 25, 1790.

I AM glad at least that you was not fetched to town on last Tuesday,[1] which was as hot as if Phaeton had once more gotten into his papa's curricle and driven it along the lower road—but the old king has resumed the reins again, and does not allow us a handful more of beams than come to our northern share. I am glad too that I was not summoned also to the *Fitzroyal* arrangement[2]—it was better to be singed here, than exposed between two such fiery furnaces as Lady Southampton[3] and my niece Keppel. I pity Charles Fox to be kept on the Westminster gridiron.[4] Before I came out of town, I was diverted by a story from the hustings: one of the mob called to Fox, 'Well, Charley, are not you sick of your *coalition?*'

1. 22 June. 'The heat of the 21st and 22d days of this month, in London, was as great as anything ever remembered. The thermometer was at 86 degrees' (*World* 24 June).

2. Presumably a party of the Fitzroy families to celebrate the marriage in Dublin in June 1790 of Anna Maria Keppel to William Stapleton (BERRY i. 119 and n. 11; OSSORY i. 382, n. 2; GM 1790, lx pt ii. 667). The *Gazetteer and New Daily Advertiser* 23 June reported, 'Miss Keppel who accompanied the Countess of Westmorland to Ireland, has sacrificed at the altar of Hymen; Captain Stapleton is the happy man.'

3. Lady Southampton's son, George Ferdinand Fitzroy, was married to Mrs Keppel's daughter, Laura; both mothers were obese.

4. HW wrote, 'Horne Tooke stood for Westminster against the coalition of Lord Hood and Mr Fox, but lost it by a great majority, especially for Fox' ('Mem. 1783–91,' *sub* June 1790; BERRY i. 78, n. 8). Because of the enormous expense of the Westminster elections since 1780, Lord Lauderdale and Pitt had agreed on 15 March 1790 'that each party should propose and support only one candidate respectively at the first general election, and during the whole of next Parliament' (Namier and Brooke i. 337; Lord Stanhope, *Life of . . . William Pitt*, 1861, ii. 52–3). But Horne Tooke's supporters railed against this 'degrading contract formed between Ministry and Opposition' (*World* 18 June); and the *World* 23 June reported, 'In consequence of the increasing success of Mr Tooke's poll, the friends of Charles Fox were busy, in defiance of the heat of yesterday, in every

'Poor gentleman!' cried an old woman in the crowd, 'why should not he like a *collation?*'[5]

I am very sorry Mrs Damer is so tormented, but I hope the new inflammation will relieve her[6]—as I was writing that sentence this morning, Mesdames de Boufflers[7] came to see me from Richmond, and brought a Comte de Moranville[8] to see my house.[9] The puerile pedants of their États are going to pull down the statues of Louis Quatorze,[10] like their silly ancestors who proposed to demolish the tomb of John Duke of Bedford.[11] The Vicomte de Mirabeau[12] is

hole and corner of Westminster; and it is but truth to say, they found every place —*hissing hot* . . . The most unpopular man in England now, is Charles Fox!' When the polls closed 2 July, the final vote was Fox 3,516, Hood 3,217, and Tooke 1,697 (GM 1790, lx pt ii. 659; *London Chronicle* 1–3 July, lxviii. 13).

5. 'When the word *Coalition* was hooted on Wednesday [16 June] about the hustings in the face of Charles Fox—a pleasant apple-woman called out "Bless his black face! and what then? Where be the harm of being fond of a—*Collation?*" ' (*World* 18 June).

6. She wrote Mary Berry 11 Oct. 1790, 'Till my leg is healed I can answer for nothing as to time. This [Dr George] Fordyce told me this morning, though he believes, from the present appearance, that it will be soon well' (*Berry Papers*, ed. Lewis Melville, 1914, p. 26). Conway wrote Sir William Hamilton 28 Nov. 1790 concerning Mrs Damer's trip to Lisbon, 'She was not ill, but only not quite well; the harsh winters here generally affect her, and in point of climate I believe that is among the first' (Percy Noble, *Anne Seymour Damer*, 1908, p. 119).

7. The Comtesse de Boufflers-Rouverel and her daughter-in-law the Comtesse Amélie-Constance de Boufflers, who had emigrated to England in September 1789, lived at Richmond in a house lent by Vorontsov, the Russian ambassador (see BERRY i. 76, n. 19; OSSORY iii. 68).

8. Not identified.

9. HW lists this party in 'Book of Visitors' on 24 June (BERRY ii. 236).

10. In the National Assembly 19 June M. Alexandre Lameth declared, 'Lorsque de toutes les parties du royaume, les français vont se rassembler dans la capi-

tale pour resserrer plus étroitement encore le nouveau pacte social, et en faire un pacte de famille, souffrirons-nous que les regards des braves Francs-Comtois soient exposés à tomber, dans la Place des Victoires, sur ce monument élevé, par la flatterie d'un courtisan, à l'orgueil d'un despote, et dans lequel la Franche-Comté est figurée parmi les esclaves qui sont enchaînés aux pieds de la statue de Louis XIV?' The Assembly 'décrète que les symboles de la servitude qu'on voit au pieds des statues des Rois dans la capitale seront détruits incessamment' (*Journal de Paris* 21 June; *London Chronicle* 24–6 June, lxvii. 606; *Procès-verbal de l'Assemblée nationale*, No. 324, xxii. 23).

11. Regent of France, 1422 (*ante* 29 Oct. 1774, n. 12), who was buried at Rouen. HW probably read this passage in *A Collection of all the Wills . . . of the Kings and Queens of England*, printed by John Nichols, 1780: 'He was buried in the cathedral at Rouen, where his monument was defaced by the Hugonots in 1462 [1562]; but a brass plate with his epitaph under his arms (torn away) between two ostrich feathers still remains affixt to a pillar. Lewis XI, when solicited to deface the monument of this illustrious hero, magnanimously refused' (p. 277). HW's copy is Hazen, *Cat. of HW's Lib.*, No. 3350; he also owned Richard Gough's *Account of a Rich Illuminated Missal, Executed for John Duke of Bedford*, 1794 (ibid. No. 3812, now WSL), which describes the portrait of Bedford in the missal. See T. A. Cook, *The Story of Rouen*, 1899, pp. 197–9, 316; A. Chéruel, *Histoire de Rouen*, Rouen, 1840, pp. 117, 192–4.

12. André - Boniface - Louis Riquetti (1754–92), Vicomte de Mirabeau, brother

arrested somewhere for something[13]—perhaps for one of his least crimes—in short, I am angry that the cause of liberty is profaned by such fools and rascals. If the two German kings make peace as you hear and as I expected,[14] the Brabanters, who seem not to have known much better what to do with their revolution, will be the first sacrifice on the altar of peace.[15]

I stick fast at the beginning of the first volume of Bruce,[16] though I am told it is the most entertaining—but I am sick of his vanity, and (I believe) of his want of veracity,—I am sure of his want of method, and of his obscurity.

I hope my wives[17] were not at Park Place in your absence[18]—the

of the Comte de Mirabeau; colonel of the régiment de Touraine (NBG).

13. In the National Assembly 18 June a letter from the municipality of Perpignan was read, giving an account of the Vicomte de Mirabeau's arrest at Castelnaudari. According to the *Journal de Paris* No. 171, 20 June, 'Après des querelles qui étaient allées jusqu'à des menaces entre lui et une partie de ses soldats, M. le Vicomte de Mirabeau ayant trouvé un asile chez le Maire de Perpignan, M. d'Aguilar, chez que le régiment avait mis la caisse et ses drapeaux en dépôt, M. le Vicomte de Mirabeau en quittant Perpignan a emporté avec lui les *cravates* des drapeaux déposés chez le Maire, qui lui avait donné l'hospitalité; c'est que le régiment ayant allé redemander ses drapeaux, et les trouvant sans *cravates*, a voulu que le Maire lui répondit d'un enlèvement qui s'était fait chez lui, et s'emparant de sa personne, l'a conduit dans un fort où il la tient sous forte garde. . . . Les officiers municipaux de Perpignan ayant écrit . . . aux municipalités de la route pour les inviter à arrêter M. le Vicomte de Mirabeau, le courrier extraordinaire l'atteint à Castelnaudari, dont la municipalité l'a fait arrêter sur le champ, et visitant ses malles, y a trouvé les *cravates* enlevées.' The Assembly passed decrees to order the Mayor's release and to provide for Mirabeau's safety; on 27 June Mirabeau appeared before the Assembly to justify himself (ibid. 29 June). HW probably read the account in the *London Chronicle* 22–4, 24–6 June, lxvii. 599, 606–7.

14. The representatives of Leopold II,

King of Hungary, and Frederick William II, King of Prussia, met at Reichenbach 27 June; the English and Dutch ministers joined the discussions as mediators 29 June; the declarations and counter-declarations were signed 27 July (*London Gazette* No. 13228, 14–17 Aug.; *London Chronicle* 17–19 Aug., lxviii. 169–70; *Cambridge History of British Foreign Policy 1783–1919*, ed. Sir A. W. Ward and G. P. Gooch, New York, 1970, i. 195–7).

15. The Convention of Reichenbach restored the Belgian provinces to Leopold II, but guaranteed complete amnesty to the Belgians and the restoration of their ancient constitution. According to Article V, 'Austria shall have full liberty to enforce obedience from its revolted subjects in the Netherlands, under condition that the King of Hungary restore to them all the privileges they enjoyed under the government of Maria Theresa' (GM 1790, lx pt ii. 754). HW wrote in 'Mem. 1783–91,' *sub* Aug. 1790, 'Peace made between Prussia and Hungary, the former abandoning the Brabanters.'

16. James Bruce (1730–94), *Travels to Discover the Source of the Nile in the Years 1768[–73]*, 5 vols 4to, Edinburgh, 1790; see OSSORY iii. 93, n. 5; John Pinkerton, *Walpoliana*, [1799], ii. 2–3; *post* 7 July 1790.

17. Mary and Agnes Berry.

18. They apparently were not; Conway and Lady Ailesbury 'settled at Park Place' on 14 June, after Conway 'had been kept the last fortnight by being of a board of General Officers for some purpose' (Lady Mary Coke, 'MS Journals,' 17 June 1790), and HW wrote

loss of them is irreparable to me, and I tremble to think how much more I shall feel it in three months, when I am to part with them for—who can tell how long![19] Adieu!

From Conway, ca Monday 5 July 1790

Missing; apparently answered *post* 7 July 1790. HW wrote Mary Berry 10 July 1790, 'General Conway in his last letter asked me if it was not a theme to moralize on, this earthquake that has swallowed up all Montmorencis, Guises, Birons, and great names?' (see Berry i. 86).

To Conway, Wednesday 7 July 1790

Printed from *Works* v. 247–8.

Strawberry Hill, Wednesday night, July 1790.

IT is certainly not from having anything to tell you, that I reply so soon,[1] but as the most agreeable thing I can do in my confinement. The gout came into my heel the night before last, perhaps from the deluge and damp. I increased it yesterday by limping about the house with a party[2] I had to breakfast. Today I am lying on the settee, unable to walk alone, or even to put on a slipper. However, as I am much easier this evening, I trust it will go off.[3]

I do not love disputes, and shall not argue with you about Bruce;[4] but if you like him, you shall not choose an author for me. It is the most absurd, obscure, and tiresome book I know. I shall admire if you have a clear conception about most of the persons and matters

Mary Berry 2 July 1790, 'I am glad you stayed long enough at Park Place to see all its beauties,' and 3 July 1790, 'Mrs Damer tells me in a letter today, that Lady Ailesbury was charmed with you both' (Berry i. 74, 79).

19. The Berrys left London for the Continent 10 Oct. 1790 and returned 11 Nov. 1791 (ibid. i. 110, 374).

———

1. Conway's letter is missing.
2. 'Lady Herries and Footes, *myself*,'

listed in HW's 'Book of Visitors,' *sub* 6 July 1790 (Berry ii. 236). Probably Sir Horace Mann's niece, Lady Herries, her two older brothers, John and Robert Foote, and their wives; see ibid. i. 81 and nn. 31, 32.

3. HW wrote Mary Berry 10 July 1790, 'I laid on my couch for three days, but as never was so tractable a gout as mine, I have walked all over the house today without assistance' (ibid. i. 83).

4. See *ante* 25 June 1790, n. 16.

in his work—but, in fact, I do not believe you have. Pray, can you distinguish between his *cock* and *hen* Heghes,[5] and between all Yasouses[6] and Ozoros?[7]—and do you firmly believe that an old man and his son were sent for and put to death, because the King had run into a thorn-bush, and was forced to leave his clothes behind him?[8] Is it your faith, that one of their Abyssinian majesties pleaded not being able to contribute towards sending for a new Abuna,[9] because he had spent all his money at Venice in looking-glasses?[10] And do you really think that Peter Paez[11] was a jack-of-all-trades, and built palaces and convents without assistance, and furnished them

5. Apparently a misprint for 'Iteghè,' meaning queen or regent; among the king's many wives 'there was one who was considered particularly as queen, and upon her head was placed the crown, and she was called Iteghè' (James Bruce, *Travels to Discover the Source of the Nile*, Edinburgh, 1790, iii. 281). The Iteghè at the time of Bruce's visit in Gondar was the Dowager Empress, Welleta Georgis, mother of King Yasous II (ibid. ii. 601, 611, iii. 207–9). The 'Itcheguè' was the chief or general of the monks of Debra Libanos, one of the two religious faiths in Abyssinia (ibid. ii. 586–9, iii. 319).

6. Bruce wrote, 'The family of King Yasous was very numerous on the mountain. It was the favourite store whence both the soldiery and the citizens chose to bring their princes' (ibid. ii. 539). The reign of Yasous I (the Great), 1680–1704, is described ibid. ii. 425–517. His grandson Yasous II was King 1729–53, with his mother as Queen-Regent (ibid. ii. 608–59). 'The crown of Abyssinia is hereditary, and has always been so, in one particular family, supposed to be that of Salomon by the Queen of Saba, Negesta Azab' (ibid. iii. 262).

7. A title, meaning princess; e.g., the daughters of the Iteghè were Ozoro Esther, Ozoro Welleta Israel, and Ozoro Altash (ibid. ii. 612–13, iii. 241). King Yasous I's first wife was Ozoro Malacotawit, his mistress Ozoro Kedustè (ibid. ii. 511).

8. Tecla Haimanout II in December 1770 was riding across a brook under a 'branch of kantuffa'; 'it took first hold of his hair, and the fold of the cloak that covered his head, then spread itself over his whole shoulder in such a manner, that . . . no remedy remained but he must throw off the upper garment, and appear in the under one, or waistcoat, with his head and face bare before all the spectators' (ibid. ii. 709, iv. 66–7, v. 50). The 'shum' of the district was summoned, and he and his son were hanged. HW wrote another version of this incident to Mason 29 Feb. 1776; see MASON i. 249 and n. 8.

9. 'The Abuna is the head of the Abyssinian church'; he was brought from Cairo and upon arrival had to state 'which of the two opinions [that of Eustathius or of Debra Libanos] he adopts. If he has been properly advised, he declares for the ruling and strongest party' (Bruce, op. cit. ii. 587).

10. 'At this time died Abuna Christodulus; and it was customary for the king to advance the money to defray the expense of bringing a successor. But Yasous [II]'s money was all gone to Venice for mirrors; and, to defray the expense of bringing a new Abuna, as well as of redeeming of the sacred reliques, he laid a small tax upon the churches' (ibid. ii. 642).

11. Pedro Páez (1564–1622), Spanish Jesuit missionary, who converted King Socinios, and dedicated the church of Gorgora 16 Jan. 1621 (ibid. ii. 268, 342). Bruce wrote, 'Besides possessing universal knowledge in scholastic divinity, and the books belonging to his profession, he understood Greek, Latin, and Arabic well, was a good mathematician, an excellent mechanic, wrought always with his own hands, and in building was at once a careful, active labourer, and an architect of refined taste and

with his own hands? You, who are a little apt to contest most assertions, must have strangely let out your credulity![12] I could put forty
questions to you as wonderful, and, for my part, could as soon
credit . . .[13]

I am tired of railing at French barbarity and folly.[14] They are
more puerile now serious, than when in the long paroxysm of gay
levity. Legislators, a senate, to neglect laws, in order to annihilate
coats of arms and liveries![15] to pull down a king, and set up an
emperor![16] They are hastening to establish the tribunal of the
prætorian guards; for the sovereignty, it seems, is not to be hereditary. One view of their fête of the 14th[17] I suppose is to draw money
to Paris—and the consequence will be, that the deputies will return
to the provinces drunk with independence and self-importance, and
will commit fifty times more excesses, massacres, and devastations,
than last year. George Selwyn says, that *Monsieur,* the King's
brother,[18] is the only man of rank from whom they cannot take a
title.

judgment. He was, by his own study and industry, painter, mason, carver, carpenter, smith, farrier, quarrier, and was able to build convents and palaces, and furnish them without calling one workman to his assistance; and in this manner he is said to have furnished the convent at Collela, as also the palace and convent at Gorgora' (ibid. ii. 267, 345). Páez's claim to have penetrated to the source of the Nile is discussed ibid. iii. 616–24.

12. The authenticity of Bruce's account was challenged even before his book was published, and many inaccuracies, exaggerations, and misrepresentations have been pointed out; for a discussion of this see the edition of his *Travels* by C. F. Beckingham, Edinburgh, 1964, pp. 15–18.

13. A passage has been omitted here in *Works,* indicated by asterisks.

14. HW is answering some comments in Conway's missing letter; see BERRY i. 86.

15. 'L'Assemblée Nationale, considérant que la noblesse héréditaire ne peut subsister dans un État libre, décrète en conséquence, que les titres de Duc, Comte, Marquis, Baron, Excellence, Grandeur, Abbés et autres de toutes espèce, seront abolis; que tous les citoyens ne pourront prendre que leurs noms de famille et patronymiques; que personne ne pourra faire porter de livrée, ni parade d'armoiries' (*Journal de Paris,* No. 172, 21 June; see also *Procès-verbal de l'Assemblée Nationale,* Vol. XXII, No. 324, pp. 24–6; *London Chronicle* 24–6 June, lxvii. 606; BERRY i. 78–9 and n. 14).

16. On 10 Oct. 1789 the National Assembly had decreed that the King should be called 'Louis, par la grâce de Dieu, et la Loi constitutionnelle de l'État, Roi des Français,' which signified that his title was derived from the constitution (*Procès-verbal de l'Assemblée Nationale,* Vol. VI, No. 97, p. 2). The *London Chronicle* 24–6 June 1790, lxvii. 605, reported, 'In the Club des Jacobins, consisting of many of the leading members of the National Assembly . . . a member brought one [motion] forward for changing the name of the King to that of the Emperor of the French . . . upon the principle that he is the chief, and not the master of the nation.' See also BERRY i. 78.

17. Described in the *London Chronicle* 17–20 July, lxviii. 65–6, 71; see also MORE 343.

18. Louis-Stanislas-Xavier (1755–1824), Comte de Provence; King of France as Louis XVIII 1814–24 (BERRY i. 302–3 and nn. 37–8; 345).

How franticly have the French acted, and how rationally the Americans!—But Franklin and Washington were great men. None have appeared yet in France; and Necker has only returned to make a wretched figure! He is become as insignificant as his King; his name is never mentioned, but now and then as disapproving something that is done. Why then does he stay? Does he wait to strike some great stroke, when everything is demolished? His glory, which consisted in being minister though a Protestant, is vanished by the destruction of popery; the honour of which, I suppose, he will scarce assume to himself.

I have vented my budget, and now good night! I feel almost as if I could walk up to bed.

From CONWAY, ca Sunday 1 August 1790

Missing; answered *post* 9 Aug. 1790.

To CONWAY, Monday 9 August 1790

Printed from *Works* v. 248–9.

Strawberry Hill, August 9, at night.

MR Nicholls[1] has offered to be postman to you; *whereof,* though I have nothing, or as little as nothing, to say, I thought *as how* it would look kinder to send nothing in writing than by word of mouth.

Nothing the first. So the peace is made, and the stocks drank its health in a bumper;[2] but when they waked the next morning, they

1. Rev. Norton Nicholls (ca 1742–1809), rector of Lound and Bradwell, Suffolk; he was probably visiting his uncle at Richmond, William Turner, who died there at the age of 92 on 11 Nov. 1790 (Ossory ii. 26, n. 1; Daniel Lysons, *Environs of London*, Supplement, 1811, p. 429; GM 1790, lx pt ii. 1057). HW and Nicholls had been visiting Thomas Barrett in Kent in late July (MORE 342; BERRY i. 109).

2. HW wrote in 'Mem. 1783–91,' *sub* July 1790, 'Negotiation with and satisfaction from Spain announced, yet our armaments continued, but the stocks that had risen exceedingly, kept up'; see also *St James's Chronicle* 27–9 July. According to the declaration and counter-declaration signed at Madrid 24 July by the English and Spanish ministers Alleyne Fitzherbert and Count Floridablanca, Spain promised restitution of the British

found they had reckoned without their host, and that their Majesties the King of big Britain and the King of little Spain have agreed to make peace sometime or other, if they can agree upon it; and so the stocks drew in their horns: but having great trust in some-time or other, they only fell two pegs lower.[3] I, who never believed there would be war, keep my prophetic stocks up to par, and my consol-ation still higher; for when Spanish pride truckles, and English pride has had the honour of bullying, I dare to say we shall be content with the ostensible triumph, as Spain will be with some secret article that will leave her much where she was before.[4]— *Vide* Falkland's Island.[5]

Nothing the second. Miss Gunning's[6] match with Lord Bland-ford.[7] You asserted it so peremptorily, that though I doubted it, I quoted you.[8] Lo! it took its rise solely in poor old Bedford's dotage,[9] that still harps on conjunctions copulative—but now disavows it, as they say, on a remonstrance from her daughter.[10]

vessels captured in the port of Nootka, and indemnity for them, but deferred to continued negotiation all claims of the rights to settle and to trade on the northwest coast of America (*London Gazette Extraordinary* 5 Aug.; *London Chronicle* 7–10 Aug., lxviii. 140). See below, n. 4.

3. See the list of prices of stocks for August in GM 1790, lx pt ii. 772.

4. By the Convention signed 28 Oct. at the Escurial, Spain promised restora-tion of buildings and lands at Nootka captured from British subjects, and both powers agreed to reparation for any violence committed since April 1789; the British gained freedom of commerce and fishery in the Pacific ocean and the South Seas except for a prohibition from existing Spanish settlements and the coasts to the south of these settlements (*Lon-don Gazette Extraordinary* 4 Nov.; GM 1790, lx pt ii. 1046–7; *London Chronicle* 9–11 Nov., lxviii. 457; *Cambridge History of British Foreign Policy 1783–1919*, ed. A. W. Ward and G. P. Gooch, New York, 1970, pp. 200–1). Pitt wrote Bp Pretyman 4 Nov. 1790, 'The decisive answer ar-rived this morning and is perfectly sat-isfactory. . . . The terms will be found to secure all that we could demand in justice, or had any reason to desire'

(J. H. Rose, *William Pitt and National Revival*, 1911, p. 584). However, Anthony Storer wrote Lord Auckland 28 Nov., 'The convention itself, which, as it was said, was to put an end to all possible dis-pute and altercation, is very far from being precise' (William, Lord Auckland, *Journal and Correspondence*, 1861–2, ii. 377).

5. See MANN vii. 239–40, n. 1.

6. Elizabeth Gunning (1769–1823), only child of Maj.-Gen. John Gunning, m. (1803) Maj. James Plunkett of Kinnaird, co. Roscommon (BERRY i. 38, n. 3; 104).

7. George Spencer (after 1817, Spencer-Churchill) (1766–1840), styled M. of Bland-ford; 4th D. of Marlborough, 1817; m. (15 Sept. 1791) Susan Stewart (1767–1841), 2d dau. of the 7th E. of Galloway (ibid. i. 104, n. 16).

8. To Mary Berry 2 Aug. 1790: 'Gen-eral Conway wrote to me that it is all settled' (ibid. i. 108).

9. Gertrude, Duchess Dowager of Bed-ford, Blandford's grandmother, was 75 (Burke, *Peerage*, 1928, p. 2217).

10. The Duchess of Marlborough, Blandford's mother. HW wrote Mary Berry 2 Aug. 1790, 'My incredulity . . . hangs on the Duchess of Marlborough's wavering weathercockhood, which always rests at forbidding the banns' and 22

Nothing the third. Nothing will come of nothing, says King Lear, and

Your humble servant

Hor. Walpole

From Conway, Thursday 23 December 1790

Printed from the MS now wsl; first printed Toynbee, *Supp.* iii. 301–4. For the history of the MS see *ante* 11 Oct. 1759.

Park Place, 23 December, 1790.

THE day before yesterday we had the melancholy news of the poor Duchess's death;[1] I felt it very sensibly, having much regard and love for her; but more still on the Duke's and her family's account; his particularly, as from his constant attachment and perpetual habit of living with, and in appearance for her and his family alone; he must, I fear, suffer in every way all the affliction that the loss of such a friend and such domestic enjoyment can create. I hear however from Lord Lorne,[2] who, though excessively affected himself, had the attention and kindness to write to us both immediately, that the Duke bears the stroke with all the fortitude possible, and instead of yielding to it, makes every effort to comfort his family. —No hero could die with more firmness and tranquillity than the poor Duchess; she never uttered a groan, nor made a single complaint. She preserved her senses and speech to the very last.—Just before she expired she said, 'It's all over; send the Duke out of the room.' She then waved her hand for him to retire; immediately

---

Oct. 1790, 'the bridegroom's grandmother positively denies it—and she ought to know as first inventress' (Berry i. 108, 123). The Duchess of Bedford had denied the match to Lady Mary Coke 27 July ('MS Journals' 28 July).

1. The Ds of Argyll d. 20 Dec.; Lady Mary Coke wrote in 'MS Journals,' 21 Dec. 1790, 'I wrote you a few lines this day by the post to acquaint you of the death of the poor Duchess of Argyle which from the true accounts I have constantly given you of the miserable state of her health could not surprise you, yet I believe she did not give up hope herself till a very short time before she expired. It was but a few minutes that she said to the nurse, "I find it won't do, desire the Duke to leave the room," and then breathed her last. The Duke was present, some of the family coming into the room crying, he burst into tears which relieved him, since which he has been perfectly composed.'

2. George William Campbell (1768–1839), styled M. of Lorn; Bn Hamilton, 1799; 6th D. of Argyll, 1806.

after said to Dr Farquar[3] about a minute before her death: 'Now I am blind; I see nothing,' which was her last sign of life.

This is a melancholy subject to dwell upon, but in the moral and philosophical light, curious and instructive; a lesson by which brave and great men might learn from a weak woman how to die!

It is impossible not to reflect and moralize on such examples; with comfort too, to see how little death is to those who go, and only dreadful to those who stay behind.

But by this time I must have quite tired you upon this irksome subject and wish I could entertain you upon any more pleasing. For *that* I should not choose a most uncommon storm[4] we had last night, or this morning more properly, when it began between four and five, in such peals of thunder, lightning, wind, hail and rain as I think I never in my life heard, so combined, before. It was for some time one undistinguishable roar of thunder and wind with violent hail driving against our windows so violently, we thought they must all be broke, but all escaped; so does imagination, added perhaps to the gloom of the hour, readily heighten appearances, and what's better, no damage in our garden, or ground: I doubt we shall hear of more misfortunes at sea. We blessed ourselves that Mrs Damer was not there,[5] and Lady Ailesbury was not unmindful of Mrs Angustine[6] and her stack of chimneys, though both she and her tea-cups escaped.

3. Presumably Sir Walter Farquhar (1738–1819), physician in the army; M.D. Aberdeen, 1796; fellow of the College of Physicians, Edinburgh, and licentiate of the London College, 1796; cr. (1796) Bt; physician to the D. and Ds of Devonshire and later to the P. of Wales. Lady Mary Coke wrote in 'MS Journals,' 14 Dec. 1790, 'I've been in town at Argyll House. I did not see the Duchess. The Duke desires Mr Farquer to lie in the next room to her to be ready if any alarm happens in the night'; and again 16 Dec., 'I saw the doctors and Farquer told me she could last but a very short time.'

4. Described in the *Gazetteer and New Daily Advertiser* 24 Dec.; *London Chronicle* 23–5 Dec., lxviii. 616; HW to Robert Berry 23 Dec., BERRY i. 172–3.

5. She had sailed for Lisbon ca 8 Nov. and arrived there ca 15 Nov. (ibid. i. 142

and n. 22). Conway wrote Sir William Hamilton 28 Nov. 1790, 'The voyage to Lisbon is long, but she bears the sea tolerably well; the packet boats on that station are excellent; and she has met with the civilest captain and the best accommodations imaginable, this we heard from her at Falmouth; from Lisbon we have not yet heard, though we imagine she sailed on the 7th or 8th, and, as appeared to us, had fair winds for ten days or a fortnight afterwards' (Percy Noble, *Anne Seymour Damer*, 1908, p. 119). She stayed in Lisbon until 20 Feb. (ibid. 128).

6. Apparently the second wife of John Julius Angerstein (1735–1823), art collector and philanthropist; formerly Mrs Lucas (see DNB, *sub* 'Angerstein'; GM 1783, liii pt i. 543; William Jerdan, *National Portrait Gallery*, 1830, Vol. I, 'John Julius Angerstein, Esq.,' p. 3, n.;

I see Mr Pitt is got into some brangle about his taxes, though the plan has been generally and generously approved.[7]

The French hobble on still and more quietly than I thought they could; my *journaux* tell me there has lately been a great insurrection in a district called *Lot*,[8] which I am unacquainted with and something about *droits féodaux*[9] which I don't understand, but it seems to have been very violent.[10] The *droits féodaux* I thought more odious to the people and the Assembly have abolished them;

D. E. Williams, *Life and Correspondence of Sir Thomas Lawrence*, 1831, i. 356–7). A portrait of her and her husband is reproduced in R. S. Gower, *Sir Thomas Lawrence*, 1900, p. 122.

7. In the House of Commons on 20 Dec. there was considerable opposition to the additional malt tax; Sheridan proposed an amendment to postpone the second reading until 7 Feb., but this was defeated 126 to 91 (*Gazetteer* 21 Dec.; John Debrett, *Parliamentary Register*, 1780–96, xxviii. 293–304). The *Gazetteer*, 22 Dec., an Opposition paper, commented, 'Great exertions are expected to be made to produce a few more *speaking* gentlemen on behalf of the Malt Tax, and given to increase the number of *mutes*. If, indeed, the Minister's majority should not be greater than on Monday night, he will find it to be as *politic* as he must know it to be *just* to desist entirely from his plan.' On 22 Dec. on the motion for the third reading Thomas Powys summarized the objections, 'that it fell heavy on the poor and industrious class of people; . . . that it was partial, falling more heavily on some parts of the country than others, and upon all parts of the country more than the metropolis'; he moved that consideration of this tax be postponed to 12 Jan., but this was defeated 122 to 92 (*Gazetteer* 23 Dec.; Debrett, op. cit. xxviii. 319–22). The *Gazetteer* 24 Dec. reported, 'The Minister's majority, upon receiving the report of the new Malt Bill, declined by a seventh part, though it was known that very great exertions were made by the Treasury Bench, to make their numbers on Wednesday night a means of retorting the check they received in the debate of the former evening. We hope this circumstance will inspire Mr Pitt with a proper awe of the present Parliament, and induce him

to invent such taxes as may suffice for the national expenditure, without ruining those who are to pay them.' The tax was passed 23 Dec. in the Commons (*Journals of the House of Commons*, xlvi. 129, 135–6, 137).

8. A department in the SW part of France, formed of part of the old province of Quercy, the capital of which is Cahors.

9. Between 4 and 11 Aug. 1789 the National Assembly voted on articles of a decree which abolished all feudal privileges; it received the royal sanction on 3 Nov. 1789 (*Procès-verbal de l'Assemblée Nationale*, Vol. II, No. 40, pp. 6, 10–11, 40, 42–3, 47). Article I stated, 'L'Assemblée Nationale détruit entièrement le régime féodal' and provided that the feudal rights involving mortmain and personal servitude should be abolished without indemnity, and that all other feudal rights should be declared redeemable, the price and method of redemption to be decided by the Assembly. Article VI dealt with land rents and dues of produce, which were to be abolished eventually but were to be collected until the Assembly settled on the compensation. Further debate and legislation continued throughout 1789–90 on the question of compensation (Commission de recherche et de publication des documents, *Les Droits féodaux*, 1924, pp. 12–13, 19–22).

10. The *Journal de Paris* 15 Dec., No. 349, reported, 'De tous les mouvements qui ont obscurci de quelques ombres une si belle révolution, il n'y en a point eu d'un caractère plus effrayant que celui qui vient d'éclater dans le Département du Lot, et dont on a rendu compte ce matin à l'Assemblée Nationale. Dans les troubles qui avaient déjà eu lieu dans le même Département, les paysans,

so I don't readily comprehend the cause of [the] quarrel. I see in our papers today that Cardinal Bernis has stoutly refused the municipal oath; and is to have his goods confiscated.[11] What will Luzerne[12] do? His brother the late Ministre de la Marine[13] is I think a great *aristocrate*.[14]

trompés sur le vrai sens des décrets relatifs aux droits féodaux, avaient planté des *Mai* pour épouvanter ceux qui voudraient percevoir ces droits, quels qu'ils fussent. Un régiment a reçu l'ordre d'arracher ces *Mai;* les paysans ont cru qu'on leur arrachait la liberté elle-même. Un de ces hommes qui épient les passions du peuple pour en faire des instruments de leur ambition et de leurs crimes, un nommé Linard, a appellé ces malheureux paysans autour de lui; il les a armés de haches, de faux; il a nourri et irrité les fureurs qu'il leur inspirait par les sons d'une musique sauvage et sanguinaire. Bientôt ils ont été au nombre de quatre à cinq mille; pour faire plus de mal, pour exercer plus de ravages, il leur a donné une sorte de tactique; il les a fait combattre avec ordre; des troupes de ligne, des Gardes Nationales ont été par eux repoussées; ils se sont présentés devant une ville (Gourdon), ils l'ont prise et pillée.' See also *Mercure de France* 18 Dec., No. 51, and 25 Dec., No. 52, which states that the source of the news was a letter dated Cahors, 7 Dec., brought by special courier from the Department of Lot (pp. 226–7, 254).

11. The *Gazetteer*, Wednesday 22 Dec., reported, 'A letter was lately wrote by the French Assembly to Cardinal Bernis, the French ambassador at Rome, requesting to know if he was disposed to take the civic oath, and fixing a term for his answer, with an alternative in case of his refusal or silence, that his bishopric, and its appendages, would be sequestrated.—His Eminence, in the true clerical and aristocratic spirit, returned an answer, in which he mentioned, that having taken an oath to God and the King, he did not think himself bound to take any other, and that as to *threats,* having but a short time to live, he was content to die a poor Cardinal and Bishop, and faithful to God, the Holy See, and the King.' See also *Daily Adv.* 28 Dec.; *London Chronicle* 28–30 Dec., lxviii.

625. The National Assembly had passed a decree of 17 Nov. requiring an oath of allegiance to the Constitution from all ambassadors and ministers of France at foreign courts within a month, and a decree of 27 Nov. requiring an oath from all bishops and priests within 8 days. Actually, Bernis wrote 24 Dec. a declaration of loyalty, but with a reservation 'à ce que je dois à Dieu et à la religion' (Fréderic Masson, *Le Cardinal de Bernis*, 1884, pp. 491–2). It was presented to the National Assembly 30 Jan. 1791, and referred to Montmorin, who wrote Bernis 1 Feb. 1791 that the oath had to be without modification or restriction. Bernis answered officially 23 Feb. 1791, 'Je ne puis me dispenser de professer dans un acte authentique et public la Religion Catholique, Apostolique et Romaine,' and was recalled 22 March 1791 (ibid. 494–5; *Recueil des instructions données aux ambassadeurs et ministres de France . . . Rome*, ed. G. Hanotaux, 1913, iii. 475, 507).

12. Probably Anne-César de la Luzerne, the French ambassador to England, who stayed in England until his death 14 Sept. 1791 (*Daily Adv.* 31 Dec. 1790; GM 1791, lxi pt ii. 877). His brother César-Guillaume, Duc de la Luzerne (1738–1821), Bishop and Duc de Langres, 1770, deputy to the États Généraux in 1789, opposed the civil constitution of the clergy and left France in 1791 (NBG; A. Révérend, *Titres*, 1901–6, iv. 153).

13. César-Henri, Comte de la Luzerne (1737–99), Lt-Gen., 1784; ministre de la marine Oct. 1787 – July 1789; he was recalled in Aug. 1789 by the King but was forced to resign 20 Oct. 1790 by the National Assembly (ibid.; William, Lord Auckland, *Journal and Correspondence*, 1861–2, ii. 346; *Gazetteer* 25 Oct.). He came to England in 1791 to visit his brother the French ambassador and later retired to Austria (NBG; *London Chronicle* 15–17 Sept. 1791, lxx. 266).

14. That is, a member of the aristocratic party, of which the *London Chron-*

I had a letter from Holland yesterday which says that all the Belgian provinces have accepted the Emperor's terms, and taken the oaths of allegiance,[15] so the Emperor is at liberty, should he be disposed to disquiet the Assemblée and their system.[16]—Adieu.

H. S. C.

From CONWAY, ca Sunday 25 September 1791

Missing; answered *post* 27 Sept. 1791.

icle 28–30 Dec., lxviii. 626, reported: 'Numbers of the Aristocrates have stolen away from Paris since the plot of Lyons has been discovered, but now it is almost physically impossible to obtain a passport.' The *Mercure de France* 26 June, No. 26, wrote, 'On apprend que, de sept Compagnies de Garde Nationale [at Avignon], quatre étaient ce qu'ils appellent *Aristocrates; mot que tout homme qui a une conscience ou un cœur devrait s'abstenir de prononcer, depuis qu'il est gravé sur le fer de tous les assassins, et devenu le prétexte de tous les attentats' (p. 317).

15. The Emperor's declaration of 14 Oct. required recognition of his legitimate authority and promised general amnesty to those who laid down their arms by 21 Nov.; the Belgian Congress refused to accept the manifesto at a meeting at Namur 5 Nov., and on 21 Nov. declared the Emperor's third son 'grand-duc héréditaire de Belgique' (Henri Pirenne, *Histoire de Belgique*, Brussels, 1902–32, v. 542–3; GM 1790, lx pt ii. 1135–6). The Austrian troops under Field Marshal Bender marched 24 Nov. towards Brussels and forced the surrender of the city on 2 Dec. (Pirenne, op. cit. v. 544). On 10 Dec. a convention was

signed between the ministers of the Emperor, Britain, Prussia, and Holland 'for the confirmation of his Imperial Majesty's authority over the said provinces, for the security of those provinces, and for the mutual interest of the mediating powers, that the bonds of friendship should be reciprocally more closely drawn between them'; in this convention the Emperor promised restoration of the Belgian constitutional privileges, general amnesty, and certain concessions agreed upon at The Hague 29 Oct. (ibid. v. 545; GM 1790, lx pt ii. 1136–7; *Daily Adv.* 24 Dec.).

16. The *Gazetteer* 24 Dec. reported, 'All accounts of plans said to be in agitation, for effecting a counter-revolution in France, are to be offered to the public with great caution. . . . Reports, however, now go so far as to state, that two large armies will very shortly enter France, one by the eastern, the other by the southern provinces; and that the Emperor of Germany, being now in quiet possession of his hereditary dominions and elective title, will interfere for his sister, while the French princes, assisted by the King of Sardinia, lead an army for their brother.'

To Conway, Tuesday 27 September 1791

Printed from *Works* v. 249–51.

Strawberry Hill, September 27, 1791.

YOUR letter[1] was most welcome, as yours always are, and I answer it immediately, though our post comes in so late[2] that this will not go away till tomorrow.—Nay, I write, though I shall see you on Sunday,[3] and have not a tittle to tell you. I lead so insipid a life, that, though I am content with it, it can furnish me with nothing but repetitions. I scarce ever stir from home in a morning, and most evenings go and play at *loto* with the French at Richmond,[4] where I am heartily tired of hearing of nothing but their absurd countrymen, absurd both *democrates* and *aristocrates*. Calonne sends them gross lies, that raise their hopes to the skies:[5] and in two days they hear of nothing but new horrors and disappointments; and then, poor souls! they are in despair. I can say nothing to comfort them, but what I firmly believe, which is, that total anarchy must come on rapidly.[6]—Nobody pays the taxes that are laid, and which, intended to produce eighty millions a month, do not bring in six. The new Assembly will fall on the old,[7] probably

1. Missing.

2. It arrived about 12:30 and left at 1 P.M. (Berry i. 89; Ossory iii. 112).

3. HW stayed at Park Place 2–5 Oct. (Berry i. 357, 360, 362).

4. See ibid. i. 247.

5. Calonne had attended the conference 26–8 Aug. 1791 at Pillnitz at which the Comte d'Artois tried to persuade the Emperor and the King of Prussia to support a counter-revolution (*Mercure de France* 24 Sept., No. 39, pp. 259–61; GM 1791, lxi pt ii. 861–2, 956–7); he was at this time at the Comte d'Artois' headquarters at Schönbornlust, near Coblentz, and his letter of 24 Sept. 1791 to Bn de Waechter expresses his confidence in the military and financial aid of the European powers (Christian de Parrell, *Les Papiers de Calonne*, Cavaillon, 1932, pp. 72, n. 1, 99–102; see also Berry i. 310 and n. 10, 355, n. 17). Lord Malmesbury wrote Portland from Coblentz 20 Oct., 'Calonne is the active and leading man, and all their schemes are strongly marked with the impression of his own imagination and sanguine character. Their object goes to interest all the different sovereigns of Europe in their cause, to obtain according to the position or faculty of each Court, pecuniary or military assistance, and to enter France at the head of an army, preceded by a new project of constitution in the form of a manifesto . . . but they seem to have forgot, that, as yet, they have obtained nothing but professions' (Sir James Harris, Lord Malmesbury, *Diaries and Correspondence*, 1844, ii. 442–3).

6. HW had expressed this view to Lady Ossory 25 April 1791 (Ossory iii. 109).

7. The 'new' Legislative Assembly convened 1 Oct. (*Journal de Paris* 2 Oct., No. 275; GM 1791, lxi pt ii. 1049); the National Assembly had dissolved itself 30 Sept. 1791, having voted that no member could be elected to the Legislative Assembly (ibid. 955–6; *Journal de Paris* 1 Oct., No. 274).

plunder the richest, and certainly disapprove of much they have done; for can eight hundred new ignorants approve of what has been done by twelve hundred almost as ignorant, and who were far from half agreeing?—And then their immortal constitution[8] (which, besides, is to be mightily mended nine years hence)[9] will die before it has cut any of its teeth but its grinders. The exiles are enraged at their poor King for saving his own life by a forced acceptance;[10] and yet I know no obligation he has to his *noblesse,* who all ran away to save their own lives; not a gentleman, but the two poor gendarmes at Versailles, having lost their lives in his defence.[11] I suppose La Fayette,[12] Barnave,[13] the Lameths,[14] etc. will

8. 'La Constitution française, présentée au Roi par l'Assemblée Nationale le 3 septembre 1791, et acceptée par Sa Majesté le 14 du même mois, 1791' (in *Procès-verbal de l'Assemblée Nationale,* Vol. LXVIII, following the minutes of 3 Sept. 1791, No. 755; translated in GM 1791, lxi pt ii. 1197–1206; see also OSSORY iii. 124 and n. 17).

9. The National Assembly on 29 and 30 Aug. debated the necessity of a decree providing for periodic national conventions for the purpose of revising the constitution; a committee recommended that an Assemblée de Révision be called 1 June 1800, but the Assembly voted in favour of suspending the right of revising the constitution for 30 years (*Procès-verbal de l'Assemblée Nationale,* Vol. LXVIII, Nos 750–751; the Projet de Décret is printed after No. 750). A new version of the decree was presented 2 Sept., stating that an Assemblée de Révision should be ordered after having been recommended by three successive legislatures, and on 3 Sept. a final version of Art. VII was passed (ibid. Nos 754, 755; *Journal de Paris* 31 Aug., No. 243, 3, 4 Sept., Nos 246, 247). See also *Gazetteer and New Daily Advertiser* 3 Sept.; *London Chronicle* 6–8, 8–10 Sept., lxx. 236, 246.

10. The constitution was presented to Louis XVI 3 Sept. and his letter accepting it was read before the Assembly 13 Sept.; on 14 Sept. the King appeared before the Assembly and swore fidelity to the constitution (*Procès-verbal,* Vol. LXXI, No. 766; *Journal de Paris* 4, 14, 15 Sept., Nos 247, 257, 258; *London*

Chronicle 17–20 Sept., lxx. 278–9, 280). The King's brothers, the Comte de Provence and Comte d'Artois, published a letter dated 10 Sept. protesting the King's agreement to the constitution: 'Votre voix étant étouffée par l'oppression, nous en serions les organes nécessaires, et nous exprimerions vos vrais sentiments. . . . Comment pourriez-vous, Sire, donner une approbation sincère et valide à la prétendue constitution' (*Mercure de France* 24 Sept., No. 39, pp. 322–36; translated in *London Chronicle* 27–9 Sept., lxx. 306).

11. On 6 Oct. 1789 two guards at one entrance to the palace at Versailles were killed by the mob of women and other revolutionaries who had marched from Paris the day before; the guards' heads were impaled on pikes and carried through the streets of Paris (*London Chronicle* 10–13 Oct. 1789, lxvi. 358–9; William, Lord Auckland, *Journal and Correspondence,* 1861–2, ii. 362; OSSORY iii. 72).

12. Marie-Joseph-Paul-Yves-Roch-Gilbert du Motier (1757–1834), Marquis de la Fayette; appointed Gen. of the Army of the Centre, Dec. 1791. Exiled for conspiracy, he left France 19 Aug. 1792 accompanied by Alexandre Lameth and others; they were taken as prisoners of war to Namur by the Austrian army. Lafayette was imprisoned at Wesel in Westphalia, then at Magdeburg for a year; in 1794 he was moved to Neisse, near the Austrian border, and then to Olmütz until Sept. 1797.

13. Antoine-Pierre-Joseph-Marie Barnave (1761–93), after the flight of Louis

run away too, when the new tinkers and cobblers,[15] of whom the present elect are and will be composed, proceed on the levelling system taught them by their predecessors, who, like other levellers, have taken good care of themselves. Good Dr Priestley's[16] friend, good Monsieur Condorcet,[17] has got a place in the Treasury of £1,000 a year:[18]—*ex uno disce omnes!*[19]—And thus a set of rascals, who might, with temper and discretion, have obtained a very wholesome constitution, witness Poland![20] have committed infinite mischief, infinite cruelty, infinite injustice, and left a shocking precedent against liberty, unless the Poles are as much admired and imitated as the French ought to be detested.

I do not believe the Emperor will stir—yet.[21] He, or his ministers, must see that it is the interest of Germany to let France destroy

XVI became a strong royalist; was denounced in the Legislative Assembly 15 Aug. 1792 and arrested 19 Aug.; imprisoned for ten months at Grenoble, then at Fort Barraux, and in Nov. 1793 at Paris; he was tried and guillotined (Ossory iii. 159, n. 18).

14. Alexandre-Théodore-Victor Lameth (1760–1829), deputy to the States-General, 1789; in the National Assembly formed with Barnave and Adrien Duport the 'Triumvirate' who led the extreme left party; became a royalist, fled with Lafayette in 1792, was arrested with him on 19 Aug. and imprisoned by the Austrians for three years; took refuge in London and then in Hamburg; returned to France after the Revolution. Charles-Malo-François, Comte de Lameth (1757–1832), army officer; deputy to the States-General, 1789; elected president of the National Assembly 5 July 1791, where he strongly supported the King; denounced by the Legislative Assembly with his brother Alexandre and others 15 Aug. 1792 for treason; fled to Hamburg. Théodore, Comte de Lameth (1756–1854), army officer; deputy to the Legislative Assembly 1790–2, where he courageously defended the King; took refuge in Bern, Switzerland until 1798. See ibid. iii. 159 and n. 19.

15. I.e., the Legislative Assembly; see ibid. iii. 124; *London Chronicle* 20–2 Sept., lxx. 288.

16. Joseph Priestley (1733–1804), theologian and scientist, whose house Fair-

hill, near Birmingham, containing books, papers, and apparatus, was destroyed on 14 July by rioters who opposed the Revolution Club (see Berry i. 315 and n. 14; Ossory iii. 116–17 and n. 14).

17. Marie-Jean-Antoine-Nicolas de Caritat (1743–94), Marquis de Condorcet, member of the Legislative Assembly, 1791, and of the National Convention, 1792. As secretary of the French Academy of Sciences he wrote Priestley 30 July 1791 to express the sympathy of that group for the loss of his house and other property (ibid. iii. 125, n. 20).

18. As one of six commissioners of the National Treasury (ibid. iii. 125, n. 21).

19. 'From one learn to know all'; a variation on 'Accipe nunc Danaum insidias et crimine ab uno disce omnis' (Virgil, *Æneid*, Bk II, l. 66).

20. The new constitution of Poland, approved 3 May 1791, was obtained without bloodshed through the moderate measures of the Reform Party (see Berry i. 286, n. 21; Ossory iii. 120, n. 11; 157).

21. When Leopold received the news 25 Sept. of Louis XVI's acceptance of the constitution, he withdrew from further negotiations on the question of military interference in France, recognized the French constitution, and renewed diplomatic relations by receiving the French ambassador, Noailles (Albert Sorel, *L'Europe et la Révolution Française*, 1885–1904, Vol. II, bk iii, pp. 277–9; *London Chronicle* 22–4 Sept., 13–15, 15–18 Oct., lxx. 295, 361, 374, 375).

itself. His interference yet might unite and consolidate—at least check farther confusion:—and though I rather think that twenty thousand men might march from one end of France to the other, as, though the officers often rallied, French soldiers never were stout; yet having no officers, no discipline, no subordination, little resistance might be expected. Yet the enthusiasm that has been spread might turn into courage. Still it were better for Cæsar to wait. Quarrels amongst themselves will dissipate enthusiasm; and if they have no foreign enemy, they will soon have spirit enough to turn their swords against one another, and what enthusiasm remains will soon be converted into the inveteracy of faction. This is speculation, not prophecy:—I do not pretend to guess what will happen:—I do think I know what will not: I mean, the system of experiments that they call a constitution, cannot last. Marvellous indeed would it be, if a set of military noble lads, pedantic academicians, curates of villages, and country advocates, could in two years, amidst the utmost confusion and altercation amongst themselves, dictated to or thwarted by obstinate clubs of various factions, have achieved what the wisdom of all ages and all nations has never been able to compose—a system of government that would set four-and-twenty millions of people free, and contain them within any bounds! This too without one great man amongst them.—If they had had, as Mirabeau seemed to promise to be—but as we know that he was too—a consummate villain,[22] there would soon have been an end of their vision of liberty. And so there will be still, unless, after a civil war, they split into small kingdoms or commonwealths.—A little nation may be free; for it can be upon its guard. Millions cannot be so; because, the greater the number of men that are one people, the more vices, the more abuses there are, that will either require or furnish pretexts for restraints; and if vices are the mother of laws, the execution of laws is the father of power:—and of such parents one knows the progeny.

I did not think of writing such a rhapsody when I began—it shows how idle I am—I hope you will be so when you receive it. Adieu! I have tired my hand.

Yours ever,

HOR. WALPOLE

22. See Ossory iii. 111.

PS. The King of the French has written to the King of France and Great Britain, to notify his accession to the throne of Fontainebleau, where he is determined to reign as long as he is permitted, and obey all the laws that have been made to dethrone him.[23]

N.B. The Cardinal de Loménie, whom they call the Cardinal de *l'Ignominie* with much reason, is the only gentleman elected for the new chaos, and he has declined.[24]

To Hon. Hugh Seymour-Conway (later Lord Hugh Seymour), Friday 13 January 1792

Printed from a photostat of the MS in the possession of Earl Bathurst, of Cirencester Park, Cirencester; first printed Hist. MSS Comm., *Bathurst MSS*, 1923, p. 702.

Address: To the Honourable Captain Hugh Conway, at Hambledon near Hornedeane, Hampshire.

Postmark: 13 JA 92. FREE.

Berkeley Square, Jan. 13th 1792.

Dear Sir,

I AM in great distress, for after all possible inquiries, I can learn no tidings of *Catchem*. No such dog was known at Houghton, where my agent[1] has been a whole week, and both coming and going

---

23. Louis XVI's proclamation of 28 Sept. stating his submission to the constitution and urging the end of revolution and the reestablishment of order is printed in *Journal de Paris* 30 Sept., No. 273; translated in *London Chronicle* 1–4 Oct., lxx. 327; *Daily Adv.* 5 Oct. Louis XVI notified Leopold 18 Sept. of his acceptance of the constitution (*Marie Antoinette, Joseph II und Leopold II, Ihr Briefwechsel*, ed. Alfred Ritter von Arneth, Leipzig, 1866, p. 212), and Montmorin officially informed the other European Courts (*London Chronicle* 27–9 Sept., 29 Sept.–1 Oct., lxx. 307, 312; *Daily Adv.* 30 Sept.). The King in his speech to the National Assembly 30 Sept. declared, 'J'ai notifié aux puissances étrangères mon acceptation de cette Constitution' (*Journal de Paris* 1 Oct., No. 274).

24. HW called him 'atheist and lover of his niece' (du Deffand v. 375). His 'ignominy' stemmed from his taking the oath to the civil constitution of the Church, which led to his name being formally expunged from the list of Cardinals 'in the secret consistory held at Rome on the 26th of September' (*London Chronicle* 18–20 Oct., lxx. 383; see also Ludwig, Freiherr von Pastor, *History of the Popes*, trans. E. F. Peeler, Vol. XL, 1953, p. 177 and n. 6; *Select Documents Illustrative of the History of the French Revolution*, ed. L. G. Wickham Legg, Oxford, 1905, ii. 201–2).

---

1. Charles Bedford (ca 1742–1814), HW's deputy in the Exchequer.

he stopped at Eriswell[2] and was not more successful. Whether the dog is dead, or has been stolen during the confusion of the late Lord's illness, or since his death,[3] I cannot learn[4]—and it makes me very unhappy, as I would not for an hundred times the dog's value have neglected a commission of dear Lady Louisa and Lord George[5] after all their goodness to you—and to me too.[6] All I can do now, is to acquaint you that Lord Orford's dogs will be sold at Tattershall's[7] next Thursday; and you will consult Lord George about the marks of the dog, and employ a proper person to examine all the dogs and search for the one that Lord George wants and secure him, which I have nobody belonging to me capable of doing. If he could have been found, he would have been brought directly to me, and not have been sent to the sale—I had set my heart on getting him for Lord George, but suspect there [has] been some roguery, as my poor nephew was surrounded by a shocking crew, as I find from every step I take.

Yours most sincerely, dear Sir,

O.

2. In Suffolk, near Barton Mills, where the late Lord Orford had lived in the parsonage house (see Ossory iii. 145 and n. 12).

3. George, 3d Earl of Orford died 5 Dec. 1791, at which time HW succeeded him as the 4th Earl.

4. HW wrote to Lady Louisa Lennox 17 Jan. 1792: 'I have discovered that Mr Catchem was Mrs Catchup—and she is certainly dead, but they think left puppies, and they will be inquired after' (More 366).

5. Lennox.

6. The Lennoxes, friends and neighbours of Hugh Seymour-Conway and his wife, had looked after Hugh in 1790 following an accident in which he had been struck a severe blow on the head while on shipboard; they had also kept HW informed of his condition (see Berry i. 262 and nn. 3, 4; More 351–7).

7. —— Tattersal (d. 1795), 'an eminent horse-dealer' in Hyde Park Corner (GM 1795, lxv pt i. 348).

To Conway, Tuesday 7 August 1792

Missing, except for the cover, now WSL; it was sold by Sotheby's 5 Dec. 1921 (first Waller Sale, lot 15) along with HW to Conway 22 Sept. 1793 to Ord for £2.15s.; resold by Christie's 15 Dec. 1947 (second Waller Sale, lot 40) to Maggs for WSL.

Address: To the Right Honourable General Conway at Park Place near Henley.

Postmark: FREE AU 7 92 C.

Frank: Isleworth August the seventh 1792. Free Orford.

From Conway, ca Wednesday 15 August 1792

Missing; answered *post* 31 Aug. 1792.

To Conway, ca Thursday 16 August 1792

Missing; mentioned *post* 31 Aug. 1792.

To Conway, Friday 31 August 1792

Printed from *Works* v. 251–3.

Strawberry Hill, August 31, 1792.

YOUR long letter and my short one[1] crossed one another upon the road. I knew I was in your debt: but I had nothing to say but what you know better than I; for you read all the French papers,[2] and I read none, as they have long put me out of all patience: and besides, I hear so much of their horrific proceedings, that they quite disturb me, and have given me what I call *the French disease;* that is, a barbarity that I abhor, for I cannot help wishing destruction to thousands of human creatures whom I never saw.—But when men have worked themselves up into tigers and hyenas, and labour

---

1. Both missing.   2. See *ante* 23 Dec. 1790.

to communicate their appetite for blood, what signifies whether they walk on two legs or four, or whether they dwell in cities, or in forests and dens?—Nay, the latter are the more harmless wild beasts; for they only cranch³ a poor traveller now and then, and when they are famished with hunger:—the others, though they have dined, cut the throats of some hundreds of poor Swiss for an afternoon's luncheon.⁴ Oh! the execrable nation!

I cannot tell you any new particulars, for Mesdames de Cambis and d'Hénnin,⁵ my chief informers, are gone to Goodwood to the poor Duchesse de Biron, of whose recovery I am impatient to hear— and so I am of the cause of her very precipitate flight and panic.⁶ She must, I think, have had strong motives; for two years ago I feared

3. Crunch (OED, sub 'craunch').

4. On 10 Aug. while the King, Queen, and Dauphin were confined for safety in the President's room adjoining the Legislative Assembly, the mob at the Tuileries attacked the Swiss Guards, numbering about 950, who had been ordered to hold their fire, and massacred about 700 of them. Other Swiss Guards from the garrison at Courbevoie, receiving an order signed by the King and president of the Assembly, laid down their arms and were killed or taken prisoner (*Mercure de France* 18 Aug., Nos 32, 33, pp. 101–3; *London Chronicle* 14–16 Aug., lxxii. 158–9; Ossory iii. 152 and n. 4; More 372–3).

5. Étiennette Guignot de Monconseil (ca 1750–1824), m. (1766) Charles-Alexandre-Marc-Marcellin d'Alsace-Hénin-Liétard, Prince d'Hénin; she visited SH 13 June 1792 (BERRY ii. 14, n. 6; 240). When she was at Goodwood in Aug. 1791, Mrs Damer described her to Mary Berry 28 Aug.: 'I am sure she was the only one of us all, who had *no* interest in what was going on. . . . She has an unsurmountable crossness. So much *acid* is diffused in her composition that it eternally starts forth and often when one least expects it' (*Berry Papers,* ed. Lewis Melville, 1914, p. 71).

6. After the massacres of 10 Aug. the Duchess fled from Paris, whence she had returned earlier in the year for fear her property would be confiscated (see Gaston Maugras, *Le Duc de Lauzun et la cour de Marie-Antoinette,* 1895, pp. 461–2).

Mrs Elizabeth Montagu wrote her sister, Mrs Sarah Scott, 'The Duchess of Biron finding her servants intended to betray her, was obliged to take her flight without an attendant. She got the master of a smuggling vessel to land her near Portsmouth, but from the apprehensions she had suffered was incapable of taking any care of herself; happily one of the Conways saw her on the shore; he gave great attention and informed the Duke of Richmond of her situation; his Grace carried [her] to Goodwood and sent for Madame de Cambise, her intimate friend to come to her,—which she did immediately; but the Duchess still remained in a state of almost insensibility. I am grieved for her, she is a woman of unblemished character, and pleasing manners, of the highest birth, and vast fortune; after a most generous present to her unworthy husband an income of £9000 a year remained to her, when she was in England two years ago, and out of which she was very bountiful to her distressed countrywomen. I suppose the intention of her servants was to accuse her of sending money to the Emigrant Princes, which would have served for a pretence to murder her, and plunder her fine hotel' (*Mrs Montagu, 'Queen of the Blues,'* ed. Reginald Blunt, 1923, ii. 285). The Prince of Wales wrote the Queen 29 Aug. that the Duchesse 'managed to scramble over somehow or other and . . . is now at Goodwood' (*Correspondence . . . 1770–1812,* ed. A. Aspinall, New York, 1963–71, ii. 271).

she was much too courageous, and displayed her intrepidity too publicly.[7] If I did not always condemn the calling *bad* people *mad* people, I should say all Paris is gone distracted: they furnish provocation to every species of retaliation, by publishing rewards for assassination of kings and generals, and cannot rest without incensing all Europe against them.[8]

The Duchess of York[9] gave a great entertainment at Oatlands[10] on her Duke's birthday, sent to his tradesmen in town to come to it, and allowed two guineas apiece to each for their carriage[11]—gave them a dance, and opened the ball herself with the Prince of Wales.[12] A company of strollers came to Weybridge to act in a barn: she was solicited to go to it, and did out of charity, and carried all her servants. Next day a Methodist teacher came to preach a charity sermon in the same theatre, and she consented to hear it on the same motive—but her servants desired to be excused, on not understanding English.—'Oh!' said the Duchess, 'but you went to the comedy, which you understood less, and you shall go to the sermon'; to which she gave handsomely, and for them. I like this.

Tack this to my other fragment, and then, I trust, I shall not be a defaulter in correspondence. I own I am become an indolent poor creature:—but is that strange? With seventy-five years over my head, or on the point of being so; with a chalk-stone in every finger; with feet so limping, that I have been but twice this whole summer round

7. Presumably HW refers to an incident at the Paris opera in Dec. 1790, when apples and a penknife were thrown at the Duchesse de Biron because she applauded a song which was considered a compliment to the Queen; see BERRY i. 175–6 and n. 8.

8. In the Legislative Assembly 26 Aug. M. Jean Debry proposed raising a corps of 1200 volunteers, to be called the *Douze-cents*, whose mission would be 'de s'attacher corps-à-corps aux chefs des armées ennemies, des rois qui les dirigent, et de les poignarder'; M. Vergniaux objected that 'lorsque vous aurez décrété la formation d'un corps de Tyrannicides, sans doute les rois qui vous attaquent formeront aussi des corps de Generalicides' (*Journal de Paris* 1 Oct. covering Aug.–Sept. 1792, bound with Vol. I, 1793; *London Chronicle* 30 Aug. – 1 Sept., lxxii. 213–14; CHUTE 446–7, n. 25).

9. Frederica Charlotte Ulrica Catherina (1767–1820), Princess Royal of Prussia, m. (1791) Frederick, D. of York and Albany, 1784 (OSSORY iii. 132 and n. 19).

10. In Weybridge, Surrey, about nine miles from SH; purchased from the D. of Newcastle in July 1788 (*ante* 20 Aug. 1782; OSSORY iii. 7, nn. 13, 17).

11. 'Yesterday [16 Aug.] his Royal Highness the Duke of York entered into the thirtieth year of his age . . . their Royal Highnesses the Duke and Duchess of York gave a grand fête at Oatlands' (*Daily Adv.* 17 Aug.; *London Chronicle* 16–18 Aug., lxxii. 161). The *World* 17 Aug. reported that 'the different tradesmen of his Royal Highness observed the same by illuminations' and listed the 'most distinguished.'

12. He is mentioned as being present by the *World* 17 Aug.

my own small garden, and so much weaker than I was, can I be very comfortable, but when sitting quiet and doing nothing?[13] All my strength consists in my sleep, which is as vigorous as at twenty:—but with regard to letter-writing, I have so many to write on business which I do not understand, since the unfortunate death of my nephew,[14] that, though I make them as brief as possible, half-a-dozen short ones tire me as much as a long one to an old friend; and as the busy ones must be executed, I trespass on the others, and remit them to another day. Norfolk has come very *mal-à-propos* into the end of my life, and certainly never entered into my views and plans; and I, who could never learn the multiplication table, was not intended to transact leases, direct repairs of farm-houses, settle fines for church lands, negotiate for lowering interest on mortgages, etc.[15] In short, as I was told formerly, though I know several things, I never understood anything useful. Apropos, the letter[16] of which Lady Cecilia[17] told you is not at all worth your seeing. It was an angry one to a parson[18] who oppresses my tenants, and will go to law with them about tithes. She came in as I was writing it; and as I took up the character of parson myself, and preached to him as pastor of a flock, which it did not become him to lead into the paths of law, instead of those of peace, I thought it would divert, and showed it to her.

Adieu! I have been writing to you till midnight, and my poor fingers ache.

Yours ever,

ORFORD

On 21 Jan. 1793 Louis XVI was guillotined at Paris; his Queen Marie-Antoinette was to share his fate the following October (see *post* 17 July 1793, n. 4).

---

13. HW writes a similar estimate of his health to Hannah More 21 Aug. 1792 (MORE 374).

14. Lord Orford, whom HW succeeded as 4th Earl.

15. See OSSORY iii. 134, n. 3; 136, n. 2; 145.

16. Missing.

17. Johnston; deleted in *Works*, but restored by Wright.

18. Not identified.

From CONWAY, ca Thursday 6 June 1793

Missing; answered *post* 13 June 1793.

To CONWAY, Thursday 13 June 1793

Printed from *Works* v. 253–4.

Strawberry Hill, June 13, 1793.

I THANK you much for all your information[1]—some parts made me smile:—yet, if what you heard of your brother[2] proves true, I rather think it deplorable![3] How can love of money, or the still vainer of all vanities, ambition of wearing a high but most insignificant office, which even poor Lord Salisbury[4] could execute, tempt a very old man, who loves his ease and his own way, to stoop to wait like a footman behind a chair, for hours, and in a Court whence he had been cast ignominiously?[5] I believe I have more pride than most men alive: I could be flattered by honours acquired by merit, or by some singular action of éclat—but for titles, ribbands, offices of no business, which anybody can fill, and must be given to many, I should just as soon be proud of being the top squire in a country

1. Conway's letter is missing.
2. Deleted in *Works;* restored by Wright.
3. Lord Hertford was created E. of Yarmouth and M. of Hertford 5 July 1793; he kissed hands 26 June (*Daily Adv.* 27 June). Apparently there was a rumour that he would become lord chamberlain of the Household again, which office he had held from Nov. 1766 to April 1782 and April to Dec. 1783 (*ante* 10 April 1782, n. 3). See Capt. Hugh Conway's letters to Lady Horatia in Aug. 1793 for his comments on his father's marquisate (Violet Biddulph, *The Three Ladies Waldegrave*, 1938, pp. 209–10, 212).
4. Deleted in *Works;* restored by Wright. James Cecil (1748–1823), 7th E. of Salisbury, 1780; cr. (1789) M. of Salisbury; lord chamberlain of the Household 1783–1804; on this appointment

HW commented in 'Mem. 1783–91,' *sub* Dec. 1783, 'The office therefore from mere want of a proper subject, was given to the Earl of Salisbury, a stately simpleton.'
5. Hertford, who was a faithful adherent of Lord North, had resigned in Dec. 1783 on the fall of the coalition government of Fox and North. HW wrote in ibid., 'Resignations poured in upon King. Lord Hertford resigned. King struck, as he had hints he might stay. . . . King said sorry, and complained he was surprised at Lord Hertford.' According to the *London Chronicle* 23–5 Dec. 1783, liv. 609, 'When the Earl of Hertford came up to his Majesty on Friday [19 Dec.] to resign, the King, who had been surprised at the quantity of the resignations, could no longer refrain from expressing his astonishment, but exclaimed, "What you, my Lord Hertford!" '

village. It is only worse to have waded to distinction through dirt, like Lord Auckland.[6]

All this shifting of scenes may, as you say, be food to the Fronde[7]— *Sed defendit numerus*.[8] It is perfectly ridiculous to use any distinction of parties but the *ins* and the *outs*. Many years ago I thought that the wisest appellations for contending factions ever assumed, were those in the Roman Empire, who called themselves *the greens and the blues*:[9] it was so easy, when they changed sides, to slide from one colour to the other—and then a blue might plead that he had never been *true blue*, but always a *greenish blue*; and vice versa.

I allow that the steadiest party man may be staggered by novel and unforeseen circumstances. The outrageous proceedings of the French republicans have wounded the cause of liberty, and will, I fear, have shaken it for centuries; for Condorcet[10] and such fiends are worse than the imperial and royal dividers of Poland.[11]—But I

6. Deleted in *Works*; restored by Wright. William Eden had been created Baron Auckland (G.B.) 22 May 1793 (William, Lord Auckland, *Journal and Correspondence*, 1861-2, ii. 509; *Daily Adv.* 8 June). Originally a Tory, he supported the coalition government in 1783, then deserted the Whigs to become under Pitt envoy to France to negotiate a commercial treaty 1785-8, ambassador to Spain 1788-9 and to the United Provinces 1789-93 (Namier and Brooke ii. 378-9).

7. The conflict between the Girondins and the Montagnards, or Jacobins, came to a crisis on 31 May and 2 June, when the National Convention, forced by the demands of the Conseil Révolutionnaire, voted the arrest of 22 leading Girondins, the Committee of Twelve, and two ministers, Clavière and Lebrun (five exceptions were made later). The expulsion of the Gironde threw the political power of the National Convention into the hands of the Montagne (see *Journal de Paris* 1, 3 June, Nos 152, 154, pp. 610, 615, 618; *Mercure de France* 8 June, No. 97, pp. 267, 272-5; GM 1793, lxiii pt ii. 753). By 'Fronde,' HW means the English Opposition; but he may also be alluding to the above shift in France.

8. 'Sed illos/Defendit numerus,' (Juvenal II. 45-6); 'but the number protects them.'

9. HW expressed this opinion in his

'Anecdotes 1784-96'; see BERRY ii. 253. The colours, *prasini* and *veneti*, which had been used by the contestants and their supporters in chariot races, were adopted by political factions in the reign of Justinian. 'A secret attachment to the family or sect of Anastasius, was imputed to the greens; the blues were zealously devoted to the cause of orthodoxy and Justinian, and their grateful patron, protected, above five years, the disorders of a faction, whose seasonable tumults overawed the palace, the senate, and the capitals of the East' (Edward Gibbon, *History of the Decline and Fall of the Roman Empire*, 1st edn, 1776-88, iv. 60, n. 42, 62, 64-6).

10. Although not one of the Girondins proscribed on 2 June, Condorcet was denounced in the National Convention 8 July for his letter *Aux Citoyens français sur la nouvelle constitution*, and his arrest was decreed; on 2 Oct. the revolutionary tribunal convicted him of conspiracy. He lived in hiding until he was arrested 7 April 1794 and was found dead in his cell two days later (*Mercure de France* 13 July, No. 102, p. 90; Janine Bouissounouse, *Condorcet*, 1962, pp. 272, 283, 308-9).

11. After the treaty for the second partition of Poland was signed by Russia, Prussia, and Austria 23 Jan. 1793, the last Diet was assembled to ratify the cession of territory already occupied by

do not see why detestation of anarchy and assassination must immediately make one fall in love with Garters and Seals.

I am sitting by the fire, as I have done ever since I came hither; and since I do not expect warm weather in June, I am wishing for rain, or I shall not have a mouthful of hay, nor a noseful of roses.— Indeed, as I have seen several fields of hay cut, I wonder it has not brought rain, as usual. My creed is, that rain is good for hay, as I conclude every climate and its productions are suited to each other. Providence did not trouble itself about its being more expensive to us to make our hay over and over; it only took care it should not want water enough. Adieu!

To Conway, Wednesday 17 July 1793

Printed from *Works* v. 255–6.

Strawberry Hill, Wednesday night, late, July 17, 1793.

I AM just come from dining with the Bishop of London[1] at Fulham, where I found Lord and Lady F[rederick] C[ampbell] who told me of the alarm you had from hearing some screams that you thought Lady A.'s, and the disorder brought upon you by flying to assist her.[2] I do not at all wonder at your panic, and rejoice it was not

Russian and Prussian troops. The Polish King and deputies were forced to accept a treaty of cession with Russia 23 July, and with Prussia 2–3 Sept. (see GM 1793, lxiii pt ii. 658, 755, 947; *London Chronicle* 24–6 Sept., lxxiv. 300). The *Times* 17 July reported: 'The progress of the Polish revolution is more and more strongly marked with infamy and injustice, the nearer it draws to its conclusion. The King and the Diet of Poland stand nobly firm in opposing their acquiescence to the partition; the Empress and the King of Prussia are, therefore, going to substitute a delegation of their own creatures in lieu of the national representation, which is to congratulate these two sovereigns on the happiness which Poland is to enjoy under their *equitable* and *benignant* reigns; and thus, is this farce of a representation to be made the ground of the general acquiescence of the people to the partition of their country.'

————

1. Beilby Porteus (1731–1809), Bp of Chester 1776–87, of London 1787–1809. He wrote Hannah More 12 Aug. 1793, 'Your friend Lord Orford and myself are, I believe, the only persons in the kingdom who are worthy of the hot weather . . . we both agreed that it was perfectly celestial' (William Roberts, *Memoirs of the Life and Correspondence of Mrs Hannah More*, 1834, ii. 368; More 387).

2. Not otherwise explained; two years later Conway died of a 'cramp in the stomach' (see *post* 7 July 1795, n. 12). In his later years Conway's eyesight and hearing were failing; see BERRY ii. 44 and n. 8.

founded, and that you recovered so soon. I am not going to preach against your acting so naturally:—but as you have some complaint on your breast, I must hope you will remember this accident, and be upon your guard against both sudden and rapid exertions, when you have not a tantamount call. I conclude the excessive heat we have had for twelve complete days contributed to overpower you.

It is much cooler today, yet still delicious; for be it known to you that I have enjoyed weather worthy of Africa, and yet without swallowing mouthfuls of mosquitoes, nor expecting to hear hyenas howl in the village, nor to find scorpions in my bed. Indeed, all the way I came home, I could but gaze at the felicity of my countrymen. The road was one string of stage-coaches loaded within and without with noisy jolly folks, and chaises and gigs that had been pleasuring in clouds of dust; every door and every window of every house was open, lights in every shop, every door with women sitting in the street, every inn crowded with jaded horses, and every ale-house full of drunken topers; for you know the English always announce their sense of heat or cold by drinking.—Well! it was impossible not to enjoy such a scene of happiness and affluence in every village, and amongst the lowest of the people—and who are told by villainous scribblers that they are oppressed and miserable.—New streets, new towns are rising every day and everywhere; the earth is covered with gardens and crops of grain.

How bitter to turn from this Elysium to the Temple at Paris! The fiends there have now torn her son[3] from the Queen! Can one believe that they are human beings, who 'midst all their confusions sit coolly meditating new tortures, new anguish for that poor, helpless, miserable woman, after four years of unexampled sufferings?[4] Oh! if such crimes are not made a dreadful lesson, this world might become a theatre of cannibals!

I hope the checks in Bretagne are legends coined by miscreants at

3. Louis-Charles (27 March 1785 – 8 June 1795), Dauphin 1789–93; titular K. of France 1793–5 as Louis XVII (Ossory iii. 80–1, n. 5; 185, n. 1). 'The National Convention having passed a decree, which directed that the Dauphin should be taken away from the Queen Mother, the Commissioners of the Guard about the Temple have reported, "that this order has been carried into execution, and that they have transferred the son of Marie-Antoinette to the lodging assigned him." When the Queen heard of the decree, she cried bitterly. The Dauphin was removed from the Temple on the 4th [actually the 3d], and is placed under the guard of Citizen [Antoine] Simon' (*Times* 16 July, *sub* Paris 8 July; *London Chronicle* 13–16, 16–18 July, lxxiv. 56, 62).

4. She was guillotined 16 Oct. (Ossory iii. 190, nn. 1–2).

Paris.[5] What can one believe? Well, I will go to bed, and try to dream of peace and plenty; and though my lawn is burnt, and my peas and beans, and roses and strawberries parched, I will bear it with patience till the harvest is got in. Saint Swithin can never hold his water for forty days, though he can do the contrary. Good night!

Yours ever,

O.

From Lady Ailesbury, Friday ?September 1793

Printed from the MS now wsl; first printed Toynbee *Supp.* iii. 307–8. The MS was sold Sotheby's 5 Dec. 1921 (Waller Sale, lot 1) with the MS of Lord Hardwicke to Lord Orford 27 Nov. 1743 (lot 2) to Philip Yorke for 18*s.*; resold Sotheby's 27 Feb. 1962 (Philip Yorke Sale, lot 483) to Maggs for wsl.

Dated after 5 Dec. 1791, when HW became Earl of Orford, and before 12 Oct. 1793, when Conway became field marshal. The reference to alterations at Park Place suggests a date between July and Sept. 1793 (see below, n. 4).

Park Place, Friday.

My dear Lord,

YOU will say there is no end of Park Place nonsense, yet who can be more partial to it than yourself?

Sent by General Conway[1] to Mrs Montagu[2] with two garden-swords to be used as scythes:

5. According to the *London Chronicle* 13–16 July, 'The report of the capture of Nantes is now contradicted beyond all doubt; and we learn by the French Gazettes of the 7th and 8th instant that the Republican army has gained some advantages in the Vendée country'; this was confirmed in the next issue 16–18 July (lxxiv. 56, 59–60). But the *Times* 19 July reported that 'the pretended *brilliant* successes of the Patriots against the Royalists of La Vendée and Brittany' were exaggerated and the Royalists 'are still sufficiently near to Nantes to cannonade that town with red hot balls.' See Ossory iii. 183 and n. 5.

1. He was appointed field marshal 12 Oct. 1793 and kissed hands 6 Nov. 1793

(Berry ii. 38, n. 4). Mrs Damer wrote Mary Berry 1 Nov., 'Another question I did not answer was about my father's new title. He *is* called Marshal, as he *was* called General, and that he used always to prefer (not being of the Duke of Argyle's opinion), in which he was right I think, for all *ought* to think their profession, be it what it may, their best title' (*Berry Papers*, ed. Lewis Melville, 1914, p. 110).

2. Elizabeth Robinson (1720–1800), m. (1742) Edward Montagu; bluestocking, 'Queen of the Blues.' Her country seat was Sandleford Priory, Berks (see More 321). After her first visit to Park Place, 4–6 Aug. 1791, she wrote to Mrs Carter, 9 Aug.: 'On Thursday last I went to Park Place on a visit to Lady Aylesbury. . . . I

Thro' neighb'ring regions while th' avenging steel
Marks the fell havoc of mistaken zeal,
These forms which in a suffering, fated land
Now arm with death the base assassin's hand:
Here may they harmless skim your peaceful mead,
And smooth the paths where virtue loves to tread,
Aid the gay imag'ry that lights the scene
And paint with livelier tints the velvet green.

You will pity me when I tell you I am in expectation tomorrow of a visit from the Margrave and Margravine of Anspach;[3] they come upon us by force, and are to stay two nights; I cannot say how particularly troublesome this is at present, being full of dirt and litter, not to mention the noise;[4] if it had been possible to refuse I would. Mrs Hervey[5] (who desires her compliments) is here, and will be of great use in helping to entertain these great personages.

Affectionately yours,

C. AILESBURY

can only say of it, as the amorous admirer did of Cleopatra, *enjoyment cannot wither nor custom stale its infinite variety*. It presents you with scenes of every character in their utmost perfection. Nature had lavished her most precious stores, and use has exerted her most judicious assistance upon it. I had for some summers received kind invitations from Lady Aylesbury and General Conway to spend a few days with them . . .' (Huntington Library MS MO 3689).

3. Conway in a letter to Prince Ferdinand of Austria 14 March 1792 (now WSL) wrote, 'Le Margrave et Margravine d'Anspach paraissent dans le décision de s'établir dans notre pays et a déjà acheté une maison, ou villa, sur la Thamise, et cherche à trouver une dans Londres: on entend ici, que ses possessions en Allemagne sont aliénées et vendues au Roi de Prusse, de sorte qu'il parait entièrement détaché de son pays; et fait au nôtre l'honneur de la préférence pour sa retraite.' The Margrave and Margravine, who had come to England in Dec. 1791 (OSSORY iii. 133, n. 28), bought Brandenburgh House in Hammersmith and Benham, Berks, the latter from Lord Craven (BERRY ii. 88;

The Beautiful Lady Craven, ed. A. M. Broadley and Lewis Melville, 1914, i. pp. lxxviii–ix; ii. 99–103).

4. Conway's alterations to Park Place covered several years. His neighbour, Mrs Philip Lybbe Powys, noted in her Diary, 'In July 1793 General Conway altered the house, and whitened it'; and under 9 July 1795 mentioned the alterations 'which were now nearly completed, having made the house equal to the spot it stands upon'; and under 3 Jan. 1799 referred to 'the noble library the Marshal had just completed' before his death (*Passages from the Diaries*, ed. E. J. Climenson, 1899, pp. 111, 284, 323). Both HW and Mrs Damer mention the singing plasterers who were working in late Sept. – early Oct. 1793, and HW on 19 Oct. calls the house 'unroofed and unceiled' (see *post* 22 Sept. 1793, n. 30).

5. Elizabeth March (b. between 1748 and 1756, d. ?1820), m. (1774) Col. William Thomas Hervey; William Beckford's half-sister; novelist; she was at Park Place with HW in Nov. 1790 and visited SH 30 May and 11 July 1791 (BERRY i. 132 and n. 18; 280; 310; OSSORY iii. 89, n. 8).

From CONWAY, ca Friday 20 September 1793

Missing; answered *post* 22 Sept. 1793.

To CONWAY, Sunday 22 September 1793

Printed from the MS now WSL; first printed Toynbee *Supp.* ii. 64–8. For the history of the MS see *ante* 7 Aug. 1792.
Endorsed: Lord Orford 22 Sept. 1793.

Sunday morning, ten o'clock, Sept. 22d 1793.

I THIS moment receive your letter[1] for which I give a thousand thanks, and begin to answer it incontinently, though I fear I shall not be able to finish before our early post today, as I am expecting early people.[2] I will first reply to your first article, the only one to which I can speak with any knowledge at all.

I am as much recovered, as indeed I ever am or shall be.[3] My finger is perfectly healed, and the gout gone out of all the other joints—weakness and lameness remain—but they are now *me,* and there is no more to be said.

Of the Duchess of York I know nothing:[4] Mrs Anderson[5] brought me a sort of message t'other day, that it will probably be the day after tomorrow: but it was not positive, nor do I put entire trust in the messenger. The suspense is very inconvenient, for I want much to go [to] town for a day or two.[6]

1. Missing.
2. Not identified.
3. HW wrote Lady OSSORY 6 Sept., 'I have been very ill with the gout for above a month' (OSSORY iii. 188; BERRY ii. 4).
4. She visited SH 25 Sept.; see ibid. ii. 11, 245. Gen. Budé notified HW 24 Sept. of her coming (ibid. ii. 9).
5. Caroline Georgina Johnston (ca 1764–1823), only surviving dau. of Gen. James and Lady Cecilia Johnston; m. (1780) Francis Evelyn Anderson, cr. (1794) Bn Yarborough (ibid. i. 23, n. 38). HW repeated this complaint to Mary Berry 24 Sept. 1793; 'As the busybody had

told me that the Duchess of York talked of coming hither today, I could not help being prepared, though I did not trust to such authority' (see ibid. ii. 6–7). Mrs Anderson did not accompany the Duchess to SH (ibid. ii. 11, 13).
6. HW wrote Mary Berry 29 Sept. 1793, 'I went to town on Friday [27 Sept.] to give orders about new-papering and distempering my dining room . . . In half an hour after my landing, walked into my room General Conway, come only for a single day'; HW returned to SH the following Sunday (ibid. ii. 17).

I am as much in the dark about defeats and successes. Our nephew Lord Hugh[7] called here for a moment on Friday in his way to the Pavilions,[8] and thinks he shall return to Lord Hood in a week.[9] I was too ignorant to ask any questions that could convey information to you. He was in high spirits, as all soldiers are *par etiquette*. He said Lord Hood would be able to keep the town or would burn the French ships.[10] For their fleet in the Channel,[11] he scoffed it, and has no idea of their venturing out.

Last night at Richmond (for I have no sounder intelligence) Madame de Cambis told me she *had just* received a note from one,[12] who had *just seen* the Duchess of Devonshire, who *was just* come,[13] and who says the victory at Menin is true[14]—*j'en doute*—for the next moment I heard that Sir James Murray is come,[15] but nobody knew what he had brought—now victories are mighty apt to steal out of a

7. According to the *London Gazette Extraordinary* 16 Sept., *sub* Admiralty Office 15 Sept., 'Lord Hugh Conway, Captain of his Majesty's ship the *Leviathan*, arrived here this day with a dispatch from Vice-Admiral Lord Hood' dated 29 Aug. giving his account of the capture of Toulon. Lord Hugh also brought from Bruges a letter to the Prince of Wales about the defeat of the Dutch troops at Menin (see George, P. of Wales, *Correspondence . . . 1770–1812*, ed. A. Aspinall, 1963–71, ii. 385–6).

8. The Duke of Gloucester's lodge at Hampton Court Palace (BERRY ii. 13, n. 4).

9. He spent four days in London and a week at Hambledon with Lady Horatia, and left on 2 Oct. (Violet Biddulph, *The Three Ladies Waldegrave*, 1938, pp. 213–14; *World* 2 Oct.).

10. For Elphinstone's successful defence of Toulon, see below n. 35, and BERRY ii. 8, n. 12. On his return to Toulon Lord Hugh wrote Lady Horatia in Nov. 1793, 'Lord Hood is however at ease on the subject if I may guess from his not having yet taken any steps towards burning the French ships . . . which I own myself I have been anxious for from our first arrival here, as it is the only way in which I can conceive England may be benefited by our having taken possession of this place' (Biddulph, op. cit. 215).

11. 'It appears, by accounts received at Lloyd's coffee-house, that the fleet in the Channel which was supposed to be French, turns out to be a Dutch fleet of merchantmen' (*London Chronicle* 17–19 Sept., lxxiv. 280).

12. Not identified.

13. 'Thursday evening [19 Sept.], at seven o'clock, the Duchess of Devonshire, and her suite, arrived at Devonshire House, Piccadilly' (*World* 21 Sept.; *Daily Adv.* 21 Sept.). She had left for Basle, Switzerland 24 June (*Morning Herald* 24 June); she travelled in Italy, left there in late August, and returned through Switzerland and Brussels (Hugh Stokes, *The Devonshire House Circle*, 1917, p. 275).

14. See below, n. 33.

15. (after 1794, Murray-Pulteney) (ca 1755–1811), 7th Bt, 1771; army officer. 'On Saturday last [21 Sept.] Colonel Sir James Murray, Adjutant-General of the British Army under his Royal Highness the Duke of York, arrived in town, and alighted from the carriage in which he came, at the Secretary of State's office. Immediately . . . the ministers were summoned to a council, which was held at Lord Grenville's office. A number of papers were laid before the Cabinet by Sir James, who also gave the most favourable account of the state of our army, and assurances of the late victories being followed up by fresh successes' (*World* 23 Sept.).

packet, whether the bearer will or not—but all was to be in the *Gazette* of last night[16]—and that I have not seen—but I have no great curiosity for a victory that stays to make its toilet before it appears in public.

The French here call Lord Hood's acceptance of the Constitution of 1789 and promise of restoring everything to France very generous —but I doubt if anybody is content.[17] If our ministers are *not*, who is to blame? Did they send a tar to sea without instructions? Is the largest whale in the ocean a civilian, and capable of judging of such nice questions as constitutions, and of such constitutions, as nobody has been able to remake in a practicable manner, though all France has been hammering them for these four years!—Well! I see endless matter for altercation and the cards more confounded than ever!

As to resignations[18]—I always conclude, they will be patched up— everybody is more angry the first minute than the second—they are begged to stay and perhaps take a third minute to consider. When opponents assert what will happen, but do not know has happened, they only tell what they wish.

Prince Augustus is arrived, but so ill that he is to be sent directly to Lisbon.[19] He is not only six feet four, but they say, broad

16. See below, n. 33.

17. Lord Hood issued a proclamation 28 Aug., off Toulon: 'Whereas the Sections of Toulon have, by their commissioners to me, made a solemn declaration in favour of monarchy, have proclaimed Louis XVII son of the late Louis XVI their lawful king, and have sworn to acknowledge him, and no longer suffer the despotism of the tyrants, which at this time govern France, but will do their utmost to establish monarchy, as accepted by their late Sovereign in 1789, and restore peace to their distracted and calamitous country, I do hereby repeat, what I have already declared to the people of the south of France, that I take possession of Toulon, and hold it in trust only for Louis XVII until peace shall be re-established in France, which I hope and trust will be soon' (*London Gazette Extraordinary* 16 Sept.). The *Morning Post* 20 Sept. commented, 'Lord Hood certainly meant well, but his conduct, we conceive, will not render him very popular with either party.'

18. The newspapers reported and denied various resignations; for example, 'The report of the Earl of Camden's being about to quit his situation as president of the Council, owing to his infirm state of health, appears to be wholly unfounded. . . . The Duke of Richmond *certainly has not* resigned his situation as master-general of the Ordnance, as was reported in most of the prints of yesterday' (*World* 19 Sept.).

19. He landed at Portsmouth 21 Sept., and left about 1 o'clock for Windsor (*London Chronicle* 21–4 Sept., lxxiv. 296). The Prince of Wales wrote the Queen 15 Sept., 'I inquired of Lord Hugh Conway after my brother Augustus, who assures me that he quitted the Fleet on board the *Aquilon* the eighth of August in perfect health, and that he attributes the delay in his arrival to his having been tempted to stop at Gibraltar, Cadiz, or Lisbon' (George, P. of Wales, op. cit. ii. 387; Biddulph, op. cit. 210). The *World* 23 Sept. reported, 'Prince Augustus Frederick was stated in

in proportion—ay, as large as *your* Duke of Cumberland.[20]

I will not pretend now to answer the rest of your letter—nay, now I recollect, it will not reach you a moment the sooner for being put into our post *today,* which would only go to London, and not depart thence till tomorrow night.

Of the changes you have heard I know nothing,[21] nor do I see any more reason for them than if the persons in question were to change their coats for the waistcoats of each other. Could the Speaker[22] take Dunkirk,[23] or Sir Gilbert Elliot[24] stop Carteau[25] with the Mace? or would Dundas[26] giving up the Seals put motion into the King of Prussia? For what Lord Lauderdale[27] says, I believe it no

some of the prints to be so *alarmingly ill* as to render his removal from on board the *Aquilon* frigate, in which he arrived at Portsmouth from Leghorn, dangerous. His Royal Highness is, however, now at Windsor, and though *slightly* indisposed, we are happy to say, not *dangerously ill.*' HW is alluding to the King's aversion to the Prince's returning home, which would entail his setting up a household for him.

20. William Augustus, whom Conway served as aide-de-camp at Fontenoy and Culloden and during the Seven Years' War, was supposed to have weighed 18 stone in 1750 (MANN iv. 208–9).

21. 'The rumours of a change in the Cabinet prevail so much in the best-informed circles, that it is universally believed some new dispositions will take place previously to the meeting of Parliament' (*Daily Adv.* 20 Sept.; see also BERRY ii. 19 and n. 11). The only appointment at this time was that of Sir Gilbert Elliot to the Privy Council on 25 Sept. (*London Gazette* No. 13576, 24–8 Sept.; BERRY ii. 19, n. 12).

22. Henry Addington (1757–1844), cr. (1805) Vct Sidmouth; Speaker of the House of Commons June 1789 – Feb. 1801; prime minister March 1801 – May 1804 (see Namier and Brooke ii. 12). According to the *London Chronicle* 17–19 Sept., lxxiv. 280, Sir Gilbert Elliot was rumoured to be the new Speaker.

23. Which had been lost to the French 8 Sept. (*London Chronicle* 10–12 Sept., lxxiv. 255–6); the *Daily Adv.* 24 Sept. reported, 'A letter was read in the Convention on the 12th from General Houchard, dated the 10th, mentioning the suc-

cess of his attack upon the combined armies at Hondschoote, and the raising of the siege of Dunkirk. The municipality of that city sent a list of what the English army left behind them . . . General Landrin entered Dunkirk on the 9th at five o'clock in the morning (shortly after the English retired) with 10,000 men.'

24. Who was appointed civil commissioner of Toulon 26 Sept. (*Daily Adv.* 27 Sept.; *World* 27 Sept.; see also BERRY ii. 19, n. 12).

25. Jean-François Carteaux (1751–1813), painter and general, who was in command of the French troops marching to the relief of Toulon; he was defeated by Elphinstone 30 Aug. The latter wrote Lord Hood 31 Aug., 'We found that we had beaten the *élite* of Carteaux's army, consisting of between seven and eight hundred men and some cavalry, which had been sent from Marseilles for the purpose of overawing Toulon' (*London Gazette* No. 13574, 17–21 Sept.; BERRY ii. 8, nn. 10–12).

26. Henry Dundas (1742–1811), cr. (1802) Vct Melville; Home secretary June 1791 – July 1794; president of the Board of Control June 1793 – May 1801; Privy Seal 1800–11; first lord of the Admiralty 1804–5. The *World* 25 Sept. reported, 'Lord Mansfield has been mentioned, among the idle rumours of the day, as the nominal successor of Mr Dundas, in the secretary of state's office.'

27. James Maitland (1759–1839), 8th E. of Lauderdale, 1789; M.P.; representative peer 1790–6; called 'Citizen Maitland' because of his enthusiasm for the French revolution.

more than his thirty thousand signatures from Glasgow.[28] At the same time I see much cause for fearing disturbance, and as I have long said, I have more hopes from *General* Famine in France[29] than from anything done against them, and that *General* they cannot cut off by the guillotine.

I am glad your stucco is raised by a nightingale,[30] as the walls of Thebes were by the bricklayer Amphion's[31] lyre. I am more **glad** Lady Ailesbury has vented her disorder.[32]

Sunday night late.

I am glad I did not send away my letter this morning, for I have been at Richmond this evening and have brought home a cargo of good news. The *Gazette* you will see with the recapture of Menin[33] and Elphinstone's[34] gallant defence of Toulon.[35] Kalcreuth[36] has cut

28. The Glasgow Petition against the war 'signed by forty thousand respectable inhabitants of Glasgow, has been presented [11 Sept.] to his Majesty' (*Morning Post* 19 Sept.; the petition is printed ibid.). See also *London Chronicle* 10–12 Sept., lxxiv. 251.

29. 'The dreadful scarcity that exists at the present moment of bread in Paris, will probably be the cause of some fresh commotions and massacres in that city' (*World* 19 Sept.). Since 4 May, when the National Convention passed a decree to establish a maximum price for wheat, several laws had been passed to regulate the prices and distribution of grains, but the failure of enforcement caused a greater scarcity of bread in some regions (*Journal de Paris* 4, 5 May, Nos 124, 125, pp. 496–7, 499).

30. Mrs Damer wrote Mary Berry 8 Oct. 1793, 'I was prevented this whole morning, yesterday and today by the plasterers who were by dozens about my windows, singing, and splattering and making such a noise, that as I never could settle which was *worst*, their looking in at the window or the room nearly dark, I gave up writing to you. I trust they have nearly done here, but no one can have an idea of the house, you think it my fancy, would you could see it' (*Berry Papers*, ed. Lewis Melville, 1914, p. 106). HW wrote Mary Berry 19 Oct. 1793 that Park Place was 'now unroofed and unceiled' (BERRY ii. 37).

31. Amphion, a Theban prince, son of Jupiter and Antiope who married Epopeus, King of Sicyon; he and his twin brother seized Thebes to avenge the cruel treatment of their mother. As a youth Amphion received from Mercury a lyre of gold, with which he later built the wall of Thebes by causing the stones to take their places in response to the music.

32. See *ante* 17 July 1793.

33. The *London Gazette* No. 13574, 17–21 Sept., printed a dispatch of 17 Sept. from Sir James Murray, adjutant-general to the forces under the Duke of York, and another of 16 Sept. from Lord Elgin, envoy extraordinary at Brussels, announcing the recapture of Menin on 15 Sept.

34. Hon. George Keith Elphinstone (1746–1823), Capt. R.N., 1775; Rear-Adm., 1794; Vice-Adm., 1795; Adm., 1801; cr. (1797) Bn Keith and (1814) Vct Keith.

35. The *London Gazette* loc. cit. printed Elphinstone's letter of 31 Aug. (quoted above, n. 25) and Lord Hood's report: 'Yesterday afternoon [30 Aug.] a part of Carteaux's army, consisting of 750 men, approached near Toulon. Captain Elphinstone, whom I had appointed Governor of the Great Fort of Malgué and its dependencies, marched out, at the head of 600 troops, and put it to the rout, took four pieces of cannon, their ammunition, etc.'

36. Friedrich Adolf, Graf von Kalkreuth

to pieces a regiment of *sans culottes* and part of another. Mr Mac-kinsy[37] showed me a *positive* letter he had just received, that the Duke of Brunswic having been attacked, had defeated the enemy and taken 3,000 prisoners and 27 pieces of cannon.[38] It is thought too that the Prince of Cobourg[38a] has joined the Duke of York,[39] but I am not certain of it, though I had heard for these two days that he had said he would—I am glad his very *Serene* Highness of Brunswic has waked at last—but here is better than all, if it proves true—Lady Mt Edgcumbe[40] has received a letter today from Lady Camelford,[41] —mind, she is Lady Grenville's[42] mother, telling her that she hears and *believes,* though not confident of the truth, that a flag has been sent from *Brest* to Lord Howe,[43] offering itself to him, and that he had called a council of war, and that she is told a messenger is ar-rived at the Admiralty, but is not sure of it—however, as Lady

(1737–1818), Prussian army officer. The *London Gazette* No. 13575, 21–4 Sept. in an extract from a letter of Lord Yarmouth to Lord Grenville of 15 Sept., re-ported, 'While the Duke [of Brunswick] was so well employed on one side, Gen-eral Kalcreuth was attacked in another quarter, but very faintly; and the action concluded by his cutting to pieces the regiment emphatically called les Sans Culottes, and taking 62 men of another corps'; see also *London Chronicle* 24–6 Sept., 28 Sept.–1 Oct., lxxiv. 297, 318; *Morning Post* 1 Oct., *sub* Frankfort 17 Sept.

37. Hon. James Stuart Mackenzie (*ante* 14 Aug. 1759, n. 33); he dined at SH ca 15 Sept. (see BERRY ii. 5).

38. The *London Gazette* loc. cit. printed an extract of a letter 15 Sept. from the Earl of Yarmouth, 'that the Duke of Brunswick was yesterday attacked by the French near Pirmazens, but that, by a very judicious manœuvre, he turned their flank so completely as to surround them, when they threw down their arms and surrendered themselves prisoners of war, to the amount of 3000. He took 27 pieces of cannon and two howitzers.' See also BERRY ii. 7.

38a. Friedrich Josias (1737–1815), P. of Saxe-Coburg (BERRY ii. 12, n. 15).

39. The *London Chronicle* 17–19 Sept. reported that the Prince of Saxe-Coburg was on the march to make a junction

with the Duke of York, and the issue of 21–4 Sept. confirmed this: 'Yesterday [23 Sept.] Mr Mason, one of his Majesty's messengers, arrived at Whitehall, with dis-patches from the army of his Royal High-ness the Duke of York.—These were dated the 20th instant at Menin, and mention that the army of the Prince of Saxe-Co-bourg was within a day's march of his Royal Highness—that of General Beau-lieu was close at hand. . . . The Duke of York's headquarters are now at Menin; the Prince de Saxe-Cobourg's, at St-Am-and' (lxxiv. 279, 296).

40. See *ante* 17 June 1771, n. 7.

41. Anne Wilkinson (1738–1803), m. (1771) Thomas Pitt, cr. (1784) Bn Cam-elford, who had died in Florence 19 Jan. 1793.

42. Anne Pitt (1772–1864), dau. of Thomas Pitt, 1st Bn Camelford, m. (1792) William Wyndham Grenville, cr. (1790) Bn Grenville.

43. Richard Howe, cr. (1788) E. Howe (*ante* 26 Sept. 1757, n. 5); vice-admiral of Great Britain 1792–6; commander-in-chief in the Channel 1793–7. The *London Chronicle* 19–21 Sept., lxxiv. 288, re-ported a rumour 'that a flag of truce had been sent to Lord Howe from the citi-zens of Brest, with an offer to deliver up that port to him upon the same terms that Toulon had been ceded to Lord Hood' (see also BERRY ii. 18, nn. 9, 10).

Camelford is no fool, it would be extraordinary if the mother-in-law of a Secretary of State[44] should write all this voluntarily, if she had no authority but common report—Lord Lauderdale might romance so—well, I am inclined to believe it, and will go to bed in a more comfortable humour. Good night!

To Lady Ailesbury, Monday 30 September or Tuesday 1 October 1793

Missing. Mrs Damer wrote Mary Berry 8 Oct. 1793, 'I find by a letter of Lord Orford to my mother, that he has had a bilious attack, and been quite ill for some days, of which according to his *comfortable, satisfactory* custom he says not a word to me, only at the end of his letter to her desires, if I write to Yorkshire, that I will not mention this "to his wives," as he means either to keep it a secret, or tell you when he is well (I forget which). This needs no comments. He was taken ill, I understand, last Sunday sennight [29 Sept.], but on Monday or Tuesday last, when he wrote, was sufficiently recovered to be going to take the air' (*Berry Papers,* ed. Lewis Melville, 1914, p. 106).

To Conway, ca Sunday 6 October 1793

Missing. Mrs Damer wrote Mary Berry 8 Oct. 1793, 'I think too you should know about Lord Orford. . . . My father had a letter from him today, but he did not show it me, but said that he wrote out of spirits, had felt some return of the complaint, that however he thought himself mending' (*Berry Papers,* ed. Lewis Melville, 1914, pp. 107–8).

From Conway, January 1794

Missing; implied *post* 10 Jan. 1794.

44. William Wyndham Grenville (1759–1834), younger brother of George, 1st M. of Buckingham; cr. (1790) Bn Grenville; home secretary 1789–91; foreign secretary 1791–1801; prime minister 1806–7.

To Conway, Friday 10 January 1794

Printed from *Works* v. 256–7. The MS of the cover is now WSL; for its history see *ante* 7 Aug. 1792.
Address: To the Right Honourable Marshal Conway at Park Place near Henley.
Postmark: FREE JA 10 94 P.
Frank: London January the tenth 1794. Free Orford.

Berkeley Square, January 10, 1794.

I CERTAINLY sympathize with you on the reversed and gloomy prospect of affairs,[1] too extensive to detail in a letter; nor indeed do I know anything more than I collect from newspapers and public reports; and those are so overcharged with falsehoods on all sides, that, if one waits for truth to emerge, one finds new subjects to draw one's attention before firm belief can settle its trust on any. That the mass and result are bad, is certain; and though I have great alacrity in searching for comforts and grounds of new hopes, I am puzzled as much in seeking resources, as in giving present credit. Reasoning is out of the question: all calculation is baffled: nothing happens that sense or experience said was probable. I wait to see what will happen, without a guess at what is to be expected. A storm, when the Parliament meets, will no doubt be attempted.[2] How the ministers are pre-

1. The *London Chronicle* 7–9 Jan. printed contradictory reports on the successful raising of the siege of Landau by the French Republicans and the retreat of the Allied armies towards the Rhine (lxxv. 30, 31). The next issue 9–11 Jan., *sub* Mannheim, 28 Dec., gave further bad news: 'Yesterday . . . we received the disagreeable intelligence . . . that General Wurmser had been forced, by the excessive superiority of the French, to retire entirely from Alsace'; and *sub* 31 Dec., 'The Austrians have retired beyond the Rhine. The Duke of Brunswick covered their retreat. . . . The army of Wurmser extends from our city [Mannheim] into the Brisgau. The Prussians are posted on the other side of the Rhine' (lxxv. 34, 39; see also *Daily Adv.* 12, 14 Jan.). News of the French attack on Toulon 16–17 Dec. and the evacuation of the British and Spanish troops 18–19 Dec. reached London 15 Jan. in the dispatches of Lord Hood and Lt-Gen. David Dundas (*London Gazette Extraordinary* 17 Jan.; *Daily Adv.* 17 Jan.; *London Chronicle* 16–18 Jan., lxxv. 57–8). However, Grenville had received the news of Toulon and of the reverses in Flanders before 6 Jan.; see Elgin's letter of 29 Dec. 1793 and Buckingham's of 6 Jan. 1794, Hist. MSS Comm., 14th Report, App. pt v, *Fortescue MSS*, 1894, ii. 488, 491.

2. On 21 Jan. in the House of Commons Lord Wycombe stated the Opposition view against continuing the war, condemned the mismanagement of the military campaigns, and moved an amendment in favour of peace negotiations; he was supported by Col. Banastre Tarleton and John Courtenay. The principal speech was delivered by Sheridan, who analysed the ministerial arguments for pursuing the war and against negotiating with the revolutionary rulers of France; he pointed out the weakness of

pared to combat it, I don't know—but I hope sufficiently—if it spreads no farther:—at least I think they have no cause to fear the new leader[3] who is to make the attack. . . .[4]

I have neither seen Mr Wilson's[5] book nor his answerers.[6] So far from reading political pamphlets, I hunt for any books, except modern novels, that will not bring France to my mind, or that at least will put it out for a time. But every fresh person one sees, revives the conversation: and excepting a long succession of fogs, nobody talks of anything else; nor of private news do I know a tittle. Adieu!

Yours ever,

O.[7]

the Allies and the failures of the campaigns in all quarters: 'Defeat has thinned their ranks, and disgrace has broken their spirits'; and he deplored the corruption and inefficiency of the Administration. Finally, Fox declared that if England would not treat with the Jacobin party, the war would last 'till we have exterminated French Jacobinism, or in other words, till we have conquered France'; and moved an amendment, 'To recommend to his Majesty to treat . . . for a peace with France . . . without any reference to the nature or form of the government that might exist in that country' (John Debrett, *Parliamentary Register*, 1780–96, xxxvii. 10–23, 131, 153, 174; R. B. Sheridan, *Speeches*, 1842, ii. 245–76). Pitt answered that there would be no permanence or security in coming to terms with the existing leaders of France; the House supported the Administration 277 to 59 (Debrett, op. cit. xxxvii. 176, 182; *London Chronicle* 23–5 Jan., lxxv. 84–5).

3. HW may be referring to John Henry Petty (1765–1809), styled Vct Fitzmaurice 1765–84 and Earl Wycombe 1784–1805; 2d Marquess of Lansdowne, 1805; he opened the debate against the war. But it was Sheridan who according to plan made the chief attack. He wrote the Duchess of Devonshire 17 Jan., 'I shan't go to town 'till Monday [20 Jan.] unless I find the meeting is tomorrow of our numerous and uncombined Army to settle the *moderation* of Tuesday next [the opening of Parliament]. As *Friends of the People* we are going to do as rash

and ill-timed a thing as possible . . . I believe the Government will avow the strongest determination of persevering in the war. The prospect of success is certainly less than ever . . . I have talk'd an hour with Sir Sidney Smith [just arrived from Toulon], and have seen many private letters' (*Letters*, ed. Cecil Price, Oxford, 1966, ii. 2–3). This and other letters indicate that Sheridan was provided with the most recent reports on the war fronts (ibid. ii. 4; *Fortescue MSS*, ii. 458).

4. A passage has been omitted here, indicated by asterisks in *Works* v. 256.

5. James Currie (1756–1805), M.D., under the pseudonym of Jasper Wilson, wrote 'A Letter, Commercial and Political, Addressed to the Rt Honble William Pitt, in which the Real Interests of Britain, in the Present Crisis, Are Considered, and some Observations are Offered on the General State of Europe,' 1793; not listed in HW's library.

6. For example, 'Observations and Reflections on the Origin of Jacobin Principles . . . and on a Letter addressed to the Right Honourable William Pitt, by Jasper Wilson,' etc., 1794 (BM Cat.).

7. Five months after this letter was written, on 14 June, Lord Hertford died, aged 75, at the house of his daughter Lady Lincoln at Putney, Surrey, 'of a mortification, in consequence of a slight hurt he received in riding' (GM 1794, lxiv pt i. 581; GEC; OSSORY iii. 197). He was buried 23 June beside his wife at Arrow, Warwickshire.

To Conway, Thursday 2 July 1795

Printed from *Works* v. 257.

Strawb[erry Hill], July 2, 1795.

I *will* write a word to you, though scarce time to write one, to thank you for your great kindness about the soldier,[1] who shall get a substitute if he can.

As you are, or have been in town, your daughter[2] will have told you in what a bustle I am, preparing—not to resist, but to receive an invasion of Royalties tomorrow—[3] and cannot even escape them like Admiral Cornwallis,[4] though seeming to make a semblance; for I am to wear a sword,[5] and have appointed two aides-de-camp, my nephews, George and Horace Churchill.[6] If I *fall,* as ten to one but I do, to be sure it will be a superb tumble, at the feet of a queen and eight daughters of kings; for, besides the six Princesses,[7] I am to have the

1. Not identified. This sentence may imply two missing letters, to and from Conway.

2. Mrs Damer, who lived at No. 8, Grosvenor Square (BERRY ii. 106, n. 3); she assisted HW in receiving the Queen and Princesses on 3 July (*post* 7 July 1795).

3. HW describes this visit *post* 7 July 1795; for the Queen's account, see *Harcourt Papers,* ed. E. W. Harcourt, Oxford, [1880?–1905], vi. 46–7; for Princess Elizabeth's, see her *Letters,* ed. Philip C. Yorke, 1898, pp. 35–6.

4. Vice-Adm. William Cornwallis (1744–1819), when in command of a squadron in the Channel, on 16 June 'fell in with the Grand Fleet of France, consisting of 13 sail of the line, 14 frigates, two brigs, and a cutter, who chased his squadron, consisting only of five line of battle ships and two frigates. . . . The chase continued upwards of 30 hours; and at length the French got so near our ships, off Belleisle, as to begin a cannonade. A running fight continued for 11 hours. . . . The French finding they could do nothing, at length gave over the chase'; the British squadron returned to Plymouth 24 June (*London Chronicle* 25–7 June, lxxvii. 616). Corn-

wallis's report of 19 June is printed in the *London Gazette* No. 13790, 23–7 June; see also *Daily Adv.* 27, 29 June. The Marquis Cornwallis's comment to Maj.-Gen. Ross 28 June was, 'I . . . am glad to find that people see the Admiral's conduct in the light it deserves. To make a handsome retreat before a very superior force must ever, either by sea or land, be a most difficult operation, and put the firmness and capacity of the Admiral or General to the severest trial' (*Correspondence,* ed. Charles Ross, 1859, ii. 291).

5. Lord Harcourt wrote HW in late June 1795, 'I moreover added, that though your Lordship wished to show her Majesty every possible mark of respect, it would be highly inconvenient, not to say dangerous, to you to wear a sword' (CHUTE 545).

6. Sons of Charles and Lady Mary Churchill, both army officers; see *ante* 17 July 1764. The Queen wrote Lord Harcourt 8 July, 'Leur goût ne s'accorde pas avec celui de leur oncle, mais hélas ils sont fait pour la guerre . . . d'ailleurs ils ont des bonnes manières' (*Harcourt Papers* vi. 47).

7. Only three came, according to HW's 'Book of Visitors' (BERRY ii. 248).

Duchess of York and the Princess of Orange![8] Woe is me, at 78, and with scarce a hand and foot to my back! Adieu!

Yours, etc.,

A POOR OLD REMNANT

To CONWAY, Tuesday 7 July 1795

Printed from *Works* v. 257–8. The MS of the cover is now WSL; for its history see *ante* 7 Aug. 1792.
Address: To the Right Honourable Marshal Conway at Park Place near Henley.
Postmark: FREE JY 7 9<5>
Frank: Isleworth July the seventh 1795. Free Orford.

Strawberry Hill, July 7, 1795.

I AM not dead of fatigue with my royal visitors,[1] as I expected to be, though I was on my poor lame feet three whole hours. Your daughter, who kindly assisted me in doing the honours,[2] will tell you the particulars, and how prosperously I succeeded. The Queen was uncommonly condescending and gracious, and deigned to drink my health when I presented her with the last glass, and to thank me for all my attentions.—Indeed my memory *de vieille cour* was but once in default. As I had been assured that her Majesty would be attended by her Chamberlain,[3] yet was not, I had no glove ready when I re-

---

8. Frederika Sofia Wilhelmina (1751–1820) of Prussia, m. (1767) William V, P. of Nassau-Orange, Stadtholder; at this time she lived in Hampton Court Palace (ibid. ii. 140, n. 7).

---

1. See *ante* 2 July 1795. The Queen wrote Lord Harcourt 8 July, 'The company of the host is what we one and all were the most pleased with; and I should myself have enjoyed his presence still more, had I not continually been thinking of the fatigue our visit made him suffer' (*Harcourt Papers*, ed. E. W. Harcourt, Oxford, [1880?–1905], vi. 46). Princess Elizabeth was enthusiastic about SH: 'I could run on in raptures about every-

thing . . . If he [HW] could know how much his attentions were felt, I am sure he would be pleased' (to Ld Harcourt 5 July 1795, *Letters*, ed. Philip C. Yorke, 1898, pp. 35–6).

2. The Queen wrote Lord Harcourt 8 July that Mrs Damer 'did all possible honour to his choice by her attention, as well as by her manner in showing my Lord's collection' (*Harcourt Papers*, vi. 46–7).

3. George Douglas (1761–1827), styled Lord Aberdour 1768–74; representative peer 1784–90; 16th E. of Morton, 1774; cr. (1791) Bn Douglas of Lochleven; chamberlain of the Queen's Household 1792–1818 (*Royal Kalendar*, 1795, p. 100).

ceived her at the step of her coach: yet she honoured me with her hand to lead her upstairs; nor did I recollect my omission when I led her down again. Still, though gloveless, I did not squeeze the royal hand, as Vice-Chamberlain Smith[4] did to Queen Mary.[5]

You will have stared, as I did, at the Elector of Hanover deserting his ally the King of Great Britain, and making peace with the monsters.[6] But Mr Fawkener,[7] whom I saw at my sister's[8] on Sunday, laughs at the article in the newspapers,[9] and says it is not an unknown practice for stock-jobbers to hire an emissary at the rate of five hundred pounds, and dispatch to Franckfort, whence he brings forged attestations of some marvellous political event, and spreads it on 'Change; which produces such a fluctuation in the stocks, as amply overpays the expense of his mission.[10]

This was all I learnt in the single night I was in town. I have not read the new French constitution,[11] which seems longer than prob-

4. A slip for John Grubham Howe (1657–1721), known as 'Jack How'; M.P.; vice-chamberlain to Queen Mary 1689–92; privy-councillor, 1702; paymaster-general, 1703 (Collins, *Peerage*, 1812, viii. 140–1). 'If rumour could be trusted, he had fancied that Mary was in love with him, and had availed himself of an opportunity which offered itself while he was in attendance on her as vice-chamberlain to make some advances which had justly moved her indignation' (T. B. Macaulay, *History of England*, 1856–61, iv. 358; see also Gilbert Burnet, *History of his own Time*, 1724–34, ii. 334).

5. Mary II (1662–94), m. (1677) William, P. of Orange; Q. of England 1689–94. 'It is said that Queen Mary asked some of her attendant ladies, what a squeeze of the hand was supposed to intimate?— They said, "Love."—"Then," said the Queen, "my Vice-Chamberlain must be violently in love with me, for he always squeezes my hand"' (Mary Berry).

6. According to the *Morning Herald* 4 July, 'Yesterday Mr Sylvester, one of the King's messengers, arrived at Mr Secretary Dundas's office, with dispatches from the commander-in-chief of the British forces on the Continent, dated Head-quarters, at Delmenhorst, June 26. They bring the important intelligence, that a peace is on the eve of being concluded between the Electorate of Hanover and

the French Republic;— an event that will speedily be followed by all the other States of the Empire' (see also *Daily Adv.* 4 July; *London Chronicle* 2–4 July, lxxviii. 16). The King of Great Britain was the Elector of Hanover, but England and Austria were still at war with France; of the Allies of 1793, Prussia made a separate peace with France on 5 April 1795, the United Provinces on 16 May, and Spain on 11 July (*Cambridge History of British Foreign Policy 1783–1919*, ed. A. W. Ward and G. P. Gooch, New York, 1970, pp. 254–8).

7. Deleted in *Works* but restored by Wright. Charles Churchill's nephew, William Augustus Fawkener (1747–1811), clerk in ordinary to the Privy Council 1778–1811; envoy to Portugal 1786–7; envoy to Russia, 1791 (BERRY i. 95, n. 24).

8. Lady Mary Churchill's, in Lower Grosvenor Street.

9. See above, n. 6.

10. According to the *Morning Herald* loc. cit., 'The peace accounts from the Continent operated to the elevation of the Funds yesterday [3 July]'; see also GM 1795, lxv pt ii. 624.

11. Presented to the National Convention 23 June by M. Boissy d'Anglas speaking for the Commission of Eleven (*Journal de Paris* 24 June, No. 276); printed in translation in the *Morning Herald* 6, 7, 9, 10 July.

ably its reign will be. The five sovereigns will, I suppose, be the first guillotined. Adieu!

Yours ever,

O.[12]

12. Two days later on 9 July Conway died suddenly at Park Place of a 'cramp in the stomach' (GM 1795, lxv pt ii. 620); Mrs Damer wrote Mary Berry, 'He had been remarkably well and cheerful at supper' on the evening of 8 July and died between four and five o'clock the following morning, owing in great measure 'to his imprudence in exposing himself to cold and damp' (Mary Berry, *Extracts from the Journals and Correspondence,* ed. Lady Theresa Lewis, 1866, i. 462; see also Mrs Philip Lybbe Powys, *Passages from the Diaries,* ed. E. J. Climenson, 1899, p. 284). He was buried 20 July in the 'Ragley Old Vault,' Arrow Church, Warwickshire, with the following inscription:

The Right Honble
Henry Seymour Conway
Field Marshal of his Majesty's
Forces
Colonel of the Royal Regiment
of Horse Guards Blue
Governor of the Island of Jersey
& one of the Lords of his
Majesty's most Honble
Privy Council
Obiit 9 July 1795
Ætatis Suæ 75

(*Miscellanea genealogica et heraldica,* 2d ser. iii [1890]. 2). HW went to stay at Park Place until 1 Aug.; see Mrs Damer to Mary Berry 1 Aug. in *Berry Papers,* ed. Lewis Melville, 1914, pp. 127–8.

APPENDICES

APPENDIX 1

LORD HERTFORD'S LETTER OF 29 APRIL 1723 TO WALPOLE'S MOTHER

Printed for the first time from a photostat of BM Add. MSS 23218, f. 2. Since Hertford was less than five years old when it was written, it was doubtless dictated, perhaps to his half-sister Jane.

Address: For Mrs Warpoolle in Stable yard in Chellcy near London These [?].

Postmark: 1 MA.

Memoranda (by HW, made much later):

       Fa[illegible]

       Mr Garrick

        affair

       Archbp.

Ragly: Aprill:29: 1723

Dear Auntt

this comes to return you my humble thanks for all the pretty play things you was soe kind to send us i had a letter very lattly from my dear Mama:[1] and i thank God she is ye[t] very well and my Mama write me now she hoped to come home very soon[2] which is noe small joy to my dear sisters[3] ane my self. my sisters give their humble sarvies to you and my brother[4] joyns with me in our humble duty to you and to my unkell Warpoolle. i beg when you see my Granmama[5] you will give my humble duty to her and lett her know that wee are all very well: Conclude att this time from your dutyfull nephew

FRANCIS CONWAY

---

1. Charlotte Shorter (d. 1734), m. (1716) as his third wife Francis Seymour Conway (1679–1732), cr. (1703) Bn Conway of Ragley.

2. She was probably at Lisburn, Ireland, where in August she gave birth to a third son, George Augustus (d. Sept. 1723) and where a stepdaughter, Letitia, died that year (Collins, *Peerage*, 1812, ii. 561, 563).

3. Certainly living at this time were his half-sisters Henrietta (d. 1771), Catharine (1707–37), and Jane (1714–49) (*ante* 1 Feb. 1737 OS, n. 3; 11 June 1737 OS, n. 1; 29 Aug. 1746 OS, n. 3).

4. Henry Seymour Conway.

5. Elizabeth Philipps (d. 1728), m. John Shorter (b. ca 1660) (MASON i. 24, n. 5; *Historical Register . . . Chronological Diary*, 1728, xiii. 41; *Political State of Great Britain*, 1728, xxxvi. 93).

APPENDIX 2

WALPOLE'S 'TO ZELINDA, FROM FLORENCE'

Printed for the first time from the copy in HW's *MS Poems,* formerly Walde-grave, now WSL, pp. 30–2. See Conway to HW ca 30 Nov. 1740 OS.

La foule des beaux arts, dont je veux tour à tour
Remplir le vide de moi-même,
N'est point encore assez pour remplacer l'amour.

Voltaire[1]

Hear, thou inconstant, how each various art
I tried, to blot thy image from my heart:
Hear too, how ineffectual all have prov'd
To touch the object that so well I lov'd.
How thro' the paths of beauty I have stray'd,
Courted each fair one, ev'ry blooming maid,
Need I repeat?—my coquetry you knew,
And smil'd, as knowing I could love but you.
I fled you; seas I cross'd, o'er mountains rang'd,
But found my country, not my heart was chang'd.
I dress'd; the livery of Courts I wore,
And learn'd a language I had scorn'd before:
I tried to be ambitious, sought to please,
And flatter'd princes, as I thought, with ease—
But oh! mistaken! when my soothing tongue
Their prowess or their vices should have sung;
I prais'd their lips, their eyes, their easy move,
And found 'twas not my court I made—but love.
Or if the blind ones with such praise were caught,
If I attain'd the favour I had sought;
How little was I pleas'd with my success!
How did each honour, how each grace oppress!
Where was Zelinda, at whose shrine her slave
Might offer ev'ry honour monarchs gave?
Had they bestow'd their crowns, e'en crowns were vain,
Unless to bind her brow, and bid Zelinda reign.

1. 'À Une Dame, ou soi-disant telle,' ll. 59–61; printed *Mercure de France,* Sept. 1732, p. 1891; Voltaire's *Œuvres complètes,* ed. Moland, 1877–85, x. 276.

Nor found I hence the carelessness I sought;
Each glitt'ring object but increas'd my thought:
Each gay alcove, voluptuous recess
Where glowing dames their gaudy knights caress,
Now these, now new ones to my sick'ning eye
Presented scenes of foul inconstancy;
Such as—Oh Heav'n! that that pure breast should prove
The wanton harbour of promiscuous love.

    With Courts disgusted, to the silent mead
Again a fugitive I bent my speed.—
But there a worse chagrin I felt, to find
A lot that ne'er must calm my troubled mind;
There swains and nymphs the God of Love invoke,
And add new vows to those they never broke.

    If languages I learnt; as I improv'd
'Twas but to tell in other words I lov'd:
To sound Zelinda's praise in ev'ry clime,
To modulate her name to softer rhyme;
My fond description tunefully to deck,
To sing that shape and flexile grace of neck;
Those eyes where cupids azure-wing'd disport;
Those melting lips I us'd so oft to court,
Where soften'd sounds of liquid language hung,
And lov'd to melt on that harmonious tongue;
Oh! how did wit around those soft lips shine!
—And yet I lov'd to silence them with mine.

    Oft as the gallant Gaul in mirthful mood,
Or Roman, more deliberately lewd,
Ask'd—are the maidens of your island fair?
As angels, said I—for Zelinda's there.

    The present world explor'd, my restless mind
To books and graver history inclin'd:
In vain: alone could my attention move
Heroes that fought, or kings that died for love.

    I took my lute; but that too long had known
The am'rous touch, and breath'd to love alone.

    My pallet next and colours I essay'd;
Dabbled in painting, with my pencil play'd:
But that against its master too combin'd,

And shadow'd out th' idea of his mind;
Its little mimickry it needs would show;
There were the features; the complexion—no!
I chid it, and to graver subjects said
Be bent thy art—behold how it obey'd!
In solemn azures, holy crimsons dyed
Its point, to draw a chaste Madonna tried:
In heav'nly beauty see Maria rise;
Demure the looks were—wanton were the eyes.

APPENDIX 3

WALPOLE'S 'STREPHON'S COMPLAINT'

Printed for the first time from the MS formerly Rutnam, now WSL. See Conway to HW 6 Aug. 1741 OS and n. 11.

To the tune of *Il est dans le voisinage*

1.

There lives not far on yonder plain
    the brightest of the female train;
Ye shepherds of your hearts beware
    for oh! she's false as she is fair!
A thousand times I've heard her own
    her heart was mine and mine alone,
She'll swear the very same to you;
    fool that I was to think her true!

2.

Last night beneath yon beech's shade
    you, Venus, heard the vows she made,
That light and day should sooner part
    than Strephon from his Cloe's heart;
And yet this very morn was seen
    when Damon came upon the green
Which way her am'rous glances flew
    fool that I was to think her true!

3.

E'en Celadon that piping swain
    the dullest lout upon the plain,
She heard, and with his sing-song art
    he dearly bought her fickle heart;
I heard him curse the perjur'd grove
    and rave at disappointed love;
Too well the swain's distress I knew:
    fool that I was to think her true!

4.

For ev'ry youth alas! by turns
    her easy wanton bosom burns,
And Damon whom she loves today
    tomorrow Damon she'll betray;
Thus with too successful art
    trifling with each shepherd's heart,
She only favours to undo;
    fool that I was to think her true!

[5.]

Yet banished from the charming fair,
    shall I the shameful truth declare?
Such agonies my bosom rack
    I fear my foolish heart will break;
And hov'ring fondly round the snare
    still wish the same false vows to hear,
Again the dear deceit renew,
    and yet forget she was untrue!

Answer.

Cease, lovely shepherd, cease to chide
    thy anger how can I abide?
Yet how that anger disapprove
    that seems to witness Strephon's love?
For had I twenty hearts to give,
    my Strephon's I would only live,
And leaving all the world for you
    show that your Cloe's not untrue.

APPENDIX 4

LORD LYTTELTON'S VERSES ON THE MARRIAGE OF CONWAY AND LADY AILESBURY

Printed for the first time from the copy in the Commonplace Book of Elizabeth Rich, the second wife of Lyttelton, formerly in the possession of the late Dr Frank L. Pleadwell, U.S.N. This commonplace book was item No. 3064 in the sale of the Stainforth Collection in 1867; it was bought from G. H. Last of Bromley in April 1929 by Dr Pleadwell.

Written by my Lord, on the Marriage of General H. S. Conway, with the Countess of Ailesbury

1.

Debate and Discord lately rose
Among the powers above
Of beauteous Ailesbury to dispose
Mars, Venus, Pallas strove;

2.

'Tis mine exclaimed the Cyprian Queen
Her second choice to guide;
And to the loveliest youth I mean
To give this fairest bride.

3.

Her to bestow, stern Mars replies
To me belongs, not you;
The brightest fair one is a prize
To highest valour due;

4.

To wit and wisdom, Pallas swore
She had her heart decreed,
She who alone could boast the power
This lady's heart to lead.

5.

From angry words to blows they fall,
As once on Ilion's strand;
When Love to reconcile them all,
To Conway gave her hand.

APPENDIX 5

THE *FRASER'S MAGAZINE* VERSION OF CONWAY'S LETTER TO WALPOLE 4 JULY 1758

Printed in *Fraser's Magazine,* 1850, xli. 430–1. This seems to be based on a later draft than the one now WSL we have printed *ante* i. 539–43. Although it omits the final paragraph in the earlier draft, several other passages have been added to it.

Park Place, 4th July, 1758.

Dear Horry,

You'll be surprised you have not heard from me before,—at least you have a good right to be so. You don't expect a regular answer to all your gazettes extraordinary, but your last packet was such an one as did certainly deserve a little more than ordinary notice. The truth is, I had a little feverish feel, for which, between Lady Ailesbury's prudence and mine, I was blooded, which disabled me. Nothing less than disability should have prevented my taking the very first moment to thank you; for you can't imagine how very much in haste I was to let you know how very kindly I take your intention of dedicating to me, as well as the manner in which you do it. I can't help reflecting how most authors would think a dedication thrown away upon an insignificant cousin like myself, and being still the more obliged to you for the reflection, and esteeming yours as much above common dedications as disinterested friendship is superior to mercenary adulation.

But, having done this justice to you and myself, I must now, since you desire it, proceed to tell you an objection I have to a very little part of it, by which you will find that you have not guessed at all right at the sort of objections I have to make; and that for *modest reasons,* which you seem to expect, I doubt you must read *vain ones.*

I must own, then, that I do rather apprehend that *the censure of a world governed by prejudice* does convey an idea that it is the censure of the *whole world,* or the *greatest part of it,* that I lie under; which, though ever so true (and I should hope it is not quite so), I should not like to see settled and going down to posterity with your works: for though you say that *that world is governed by prejudice,* yet I doubt if that expression *from a friend* would countervail the establishing the fact of that *general censure upon a friend's authority.*

And as you say your esteem is *not to be shaken by that censure,* I own it does seem to me to imply that there was something in the nature of such a censure which *might shake friendships,* and that it required a sort of effort not to be shaken by it.

Perhaps I am ridiculously scrupulous, but the subject is a tender one, and, at least, I hope you will think my scruples pardonable. All this lies in the compass of one single line, the alteration of which would, I think, certainly leave it unexceptionable to any but 'modest objections,' and those I am at present well enough disposed to waive. I leave it, however, entirely to your much better judgment, and shall think myself safer in your hands than in my own. I have also a mind (if you leave that out in the first part especially) to put *malice or prejudice* in where it is marked with a cross afterwards; but this, also, I leave entirely to you.

Excuse my tampering at all with a work I am, probably, only capable of spoiling, and my vanity that is not content with more praise than I deserve. I will say no more upon the subject, but that I shall think myself happy, and, though it sounds formal, honoured too, in this public, and I dare say permanent, mark of your friendship. I forgot to say that I think *proposed to attack* is less exceptionable than *would have undertaken to attack,* as they did all consent in one council of war, etc.

The Duchess of Richmond left us yesterday morning to go to Goodwood, where the Duke was just arrived when his express came away. You'll have heard, to be sure, all that relates to the expedition subsequent to St Maloes and Cancale Bay. Lord Downe, who was expeditious in his return as Mr Delaval was in his descent, was in town on Sunday morning, as I hear, so that I am surprised we have yet heard no more of them from town. Their return was not even mentioned in the newspapers of yesterday, where there are only some *natural* accounts from Paris of their having destroyed to the amount of many millions at St Maloes, landed somewhere else—I don't know where, kept all their troops employed in continual marches, and harassed them to death; whereas my intelligence says they have landed nowhere—not even drunk tea under the cannon of Cherbourg, as you suppose; but having peeped at Havre and Cherbourg, and ordered two debarkations, are returned half-starved and sickly, having found that greater heroes than we may be prevented by *high winds* and *open bays*.

I hear none were allowed to come on shore, at least very few; and that they expected to go out again. I scarce think it will be to the coast of France if they do, though they pretend that the army for Flanders is all named.

I wrote to Lord Ligonier, the moment I heard of the troops destined to Flanders, to beg he would name me to his Majesty; but had for answer that all the generals were already fixed *by his Majesty himself*. He added, that he thought we were left very weak at home, and that, in case of any accident here, he should not desire *a better second than myself,* if I chose to share my fate with him. You see how like this looks to a condemnation to home service and the yellow list, and you know my thoughts on that subject.

Adieu, and believe me most sincerely yours,

H.S.C.

APPENDIX 6

WALPOLE'S ADDRESS 'FROM THE CORPORATION OF THETFORD' TO CONWAY

This address, transmitted to Conway by the Corporation of Thetford but actually drafted by HW, was through HW's efforts circulated in the London newspapers in early May 1764 (see HW to Conway 5 June 1764, n. 1) after Conway's dismissal from his civil office and regiment because of his votes against general warrants. The version given here is printed from the copy in the *London Chronicle* 3–5 May 1764, xv. 427.

We the Mayor, Aldermen, and Corporation of Thetford, desire to return you our most unfeigned and grateful thanks for your late spirited, conscientious and unbiased conduct in Parliament, particularly on that most important question to the liberties of us all, the seizure of private papers by the warrant of a secretary of state; a question, which remaining undecided, must make every Englishman tremble, and which, till declared to be illegal, leaves the Glorious Revolution imperfect.

Your behaviour, Sir, on that occasion, was worthy the unblemished integrity which you have always manifested. Superior to bribes or menaces, you have demonstrated your civil courage to be equal to your military. You have fought the battles of your country against *domestic* and foreign enemies. We know your services; and we have heard that they were particularly recommended to favour by that great judge of martial merit, Prince Ferdinand. *These honours*, Sir, cannot be taken from you. Some sort of rewards may be envied you by selfish and designing ministers, who may know that you scorn to support unconstitutional measures; but your country (and may it continue this free country) in whose cause you have fought from the noblest and most disinterested motives, will join in conferring the best of rewards—*its applause*. There are seasons when it would be a disgrace not to be disgraced. Continue to act as you have done, and may every borough in the kingdom be as worthily represented as the Corporation of Thetford.

Dated at our Guildhall, the 28th of April, 1764.

APPENDIX 7

CONWAY'S NEGLECT OF WALPOLE IN THE FORMATION OF THE FIRST ROCKINGHAM ADMINISTRATION

Walpole, who had fervently risen to Conway's defense upon the latter's dismissal from his civil and military posts in 1764 (see the preceding appendix), was hurt extremely by his cousin's failure to make at least the gesture of offering him a place in the new Rockingham administration, formed in July 1765, in which Conway was secretary of state for the south. Some three-and-a-half to four years later Walpole wrote the following passage in his memoirs, in which he describes his resentment and attributes Conway's neglect of him to the coldness and 'insensibility' of Conway's personality. The text printed here is taken from Walpole's original draft, pages 236–8, (now WSL) on which he made numerous corrections and one significant addition (n. 1 below); there are further changes of words and punctuation in the version printed in *Mem. Geo. III*, ii. 148–52.

The dissolution of our Opposition now afforded me that opportunity of retreating from those who had composed it, for which I had so eagerly longed: nor was I dilatory in executing my resolution. Many new reasons concurred to make me adhere to the plan I had formed. It was against my opinion that my friends had accepted the Administration; and though I would not peremptorily advise Mr Conway to decline taking part, when he told me he thought himself obliged in honour to obey the King's and Duke's commands, still I saw so much weakness both in the leaders and in the numbers, that I entertained no hopes of the permanence of their power. Chiefs who could not conduct a party with sense, seemed little qualified to govern a nation. I had given notice, that if they ever attained power, I would have nothing farther to do with them. They had attained it now, but with so little prospect of maintaining their ground, that nothing was so probable as their being soon driven to opposition again. In that I was determined to engage with them no more. If I quitted them while triumphant, they would have no right to call upon me, should they again be defeated by their own want of skill. I had fully satisfied my honour and engagements, and had anybody cause to complain, it was myself—but I chose to part with them on good terms: nor would I, where I was really hurt, condescend to utter a reproach. This topic truth demands that I should explain. I had entered into opposition on the view of the violent measures, and still more dangerous designs, of the Court. Personal dislike to the Bedford faction had inflamed my natural warmth, and the oppression exercised on Mr Conway had fixed me in an unalterable desire of overturning that Administration. Not the smallest view of self-interest had entered into my imagination. On the contrary I risked an easy ample fortune with which I was thoroughly contented. When I found unjust power exerted to wrong me, I am not ashamed to say that I flattered myself that, if ever our party was successful, I should obtain to have the payments of my place settled on some foundation that should not expose me to the caprice or wanton tyranny of every succeeding Minister, for court I was resolved to make to none whether friend or foe; a haughtiness I maintained throughout my life, never once condescending to go to the levee of any first Minister. My wish of making this independence perfectly easy, I had hinted to Mr Conway during our opposition. He received it with silence. It was not in my nature to repeat such a hint. As disinterestedness was my ruling passion, I did hope that on the change some considerable employment would be offered to me, which my vanity would have been gratified in refusing. It was mortifying enough to me, when Mr Conway (for I have said that during the last negotiation I was confined in bed with the gout) reported to me the proposed arrangement of places, to find that my name had not been so much as mentioned. That I would take no place was well known; I had frequently declared it. From the Duke of Cumberland, to whom I had never paid court, from the Duke of Newcastle, whom I had constantly ridiculed, from Lord Rockingham and the Cavendishes, whom I had treated with a very moderate share of regard, I had no reason to expect much attention; and though some notice is due to all men who are respected in a party, *they* were excusable in proposing nothing for me, when they found nothing asked for me by my own intimate friend and relation. He must be supposed to know my mind best: if he was silent, what called on them to be more solicitous for my interest? But what could excuse this neglect in Mr Conway? For him I had sacrificed everything; for him I had been oppressed, injured, calumniated. The foundation of his own fortune, and almost every step of his fortune, he owed solely to me. How thoroughly soever he knew my sentiments, was a compliment at least not due to me? Whatever was due to me, much or little, he totally forgot it—and so far from once endeavouring to secure my independence, in his whole life after he never once mentioned it. I had too much spirit to remind him of it, though he has since frequently vaunted to me his own independence. Such failure of friendship, or to call it by its truer name, such insensibility, could not but shock a heart at once so tender and so proud as mine: his ensuing conduct completely opened my eyes. When I saw him eager and anxious to exalt his brother Hertford to the Vice-royalty of Ireland, and his brother-in-law Lorn to a regiment, and when he omitted no occasion of serving them and the Duke of Argyle and Lord Frederic Campbell, all four, men who had abandoned him to persecution without a pang, I saw clearly into his nature. He thought it noble, he thought it would be fame to pardon the neglect he had met with, and that the world would applaud his generous return of their ungenerous and interested behaviour. No glory would have accrued from his serving me, as it would have been natural and no more than the world expected. His heart was so cold that it wanted all the beams of popular applause to kindle it into action. I had command enough of myself not to drop a syllable of reproach on a friendship so frozen; but without a murmur, and with my wonted cheerfulness, as soon as my strength was tolerably recruited, I declared my intention of making a visit to Lord Hertford at Paris, before he quitted his embassy. I acted with the same unconcern to the whole party, for I would neither suffer them nor my enemies to know that I had any cause to be dissatisfied with Mr Conway. When I scorned to open myself even to him, it was not likely I should be more communicative to others. As disgust with my friends did not, as most commonly happens, reconcile me to my enemies, I foresaw that I might still have occasion to make use of my power with Mr Conway to the annoyance of the latter, for though Mr Conway had none of the warmth of friendship, yet he had more confidence in me, and knew he might have, than in any man living; and notwithstanding the indifference I have described, he frequently trusted me afterwards with secrets that he reserved from his wife and his brother.

He no sooner discovered that my intention was to remain in France much longer than he at first suspected, than he broke out into complaints, entreaties and reproaches; and, as if he had satisfied all the duties of friendship, and I had violated them, he tried with angry words to divert me from my purpose, urged the occasion he should have for my advice, and called my retreat, desertion of my friends. Satisfied with making him feel the want of me, and now hardened against the calls of friendship, I treated the matter lightly, civilly and desultorily. I reminded him of the declaration I had often made of quitting the party as soon as they should be successful, which he could not deny; and with a little mixture of scorn, I said, I knew the obligations the party had had to me, I knew none I had to them. Vexed and his pride hurt, he employed Lady Ailesbury to tell me in his presence that he looked upon my behaviour as deserting him, and himself dropped many peevish accents. Fixed in the plan I had laid down to myself, nothing could provoke me to be serious. I carried off all with good humour, and above owing to a retort of reproaches what I ought to have owed to his sentiments, I parted with him with such inflexible and consequently mysterious, cheerfulness, that he knew not what interpretation to put on my behaviour—if he did guess, he was more blameable than I suspected. His insensibility had made me insensible; his ingratitude would have given me stronger sensations. But it is justice due to him to say that I think he was incapable of ingratitude: his soul was good, virtuous, sincere; but his temper was chill, his mind absent, and he friendly was so accustomed to my suggesting to him whatever I thought it right for him to do, that he had no notion of my concealing a thought from him; and as I had too much delicacy to mention even my own security, I am persuaded it never came into his thought. His temper hurt me, but I forgave his virtue, of which I am confident, and know superior to my own.

We have continued to this day on an easy and even confidential footing; but conscious that I would not again devote myself for him, I have taken strict care never to give him decisive advice when it might lead him to a precipice.[1]

---

1. The passage 'But it is justice . . . superior to my own' was inserted later between two paragraphs in the MS.

APPENDIX 8

POWYS'S VERSES WRITTEN IN THE COTTAGE AT PARK PLACE

Printed from HW's cutting pasted in his 'Book of Materials,' 1759, p. 240. Previously printed in HW's *Anecdotes of Painting*, Vol. V, ed. Hilles and Daghlian, New Haven, 1937, pp. 167–71; identified by HW as 'by the Reverend Mr Powis,' i.e., the Rev. Thomas Powys (1736–1809), a neighbour of Conway (OSSORY ii. 446, n. 11).

For the Public Advertiser.

Verses writ in a cottage belonging to General Conway, at **Park Place**, near Henley in Berkshire.

> The works of art let others praise
> Where Pride her waste of wealth betrays,
> And Fashion, independent grown,
> Usurps her parent Nature's throne;
> Lays all her fair dominions waste,
> And calls the depredations—taste.
> But I, who ne'er, with servile awe,
> Give Fashion's whims the force of law,
> Scorn all the glitter of expense,
> When destitute of use and sense;
> More pleas'd to see the wanton rill,
> Which trickles from some craggy hill,
> Free thro' the valley wind its way,
> Than when immur'd in walls of clay,
> It strives in vain its bonds to break,
> And stagnates in a crooked lake.
> With sighs I see the native oak
> Bow to th' inexorable stroke,
> Whilst an exotic puny race
> Of upstart shrubs usurps its place;
> Which, born beneath a milder sky,
> Shrink at a wint'ry blast, and die.
> I can't behold without a smile
> The venerable Gothic pile
> (Which in our father's wiser age

Was shelter'd from the tempest's rage)
Stand to the dreary north expos'd,
Within a Chinese fence enclos'd.
For me, each leaden god may reign
In quiet o'er his old domain;
(Their claim is good by poets' laws,
And poets must support their cause.)
Let Pan be plac'd in pastures fair,
And seem to watch his fleecy care;
Amidst her flow'rs let Flora stand
Let Ceres guard her cultur'd land;
Their oaks let dryads still defend;
Let naiads still their springs attend:
But when old Neptune's fish-tail'd train
Of tritons haunts an upland plain,
And Dian seems to urge the chase
In a snug garden's narrow space;
When Mars, with insult rude, invades
The virgin muses' peaceful shades;
With light'ning arm'd, when angry Jove
Scares the poor tenants of the grove,
I cannot blindly league with those
Who thus the poets' creed oppose.
   To Nature, in my earliest youth,
I vow'd my constancy and truth,
When in her *Hardwick's* much-lov'd shade,
Enamour'd of her charms, I stray'd;
And, as I rov'd the woods among,
Her praise in lisping numbers sung:
Nor will I now resign my heart
A captive to her rival art.—
Far from the pageant scenes of pride,
She still my careless steps shall guide;
Whether, by contemplation led,
The rich romantic wild I tread,
Where Nature, for her pupil man,
Has struck out many a noble plan;
Or whether, from yon wood-crown'd brow,
I view the lovely vale below;

For when, with more than common care,
Nature had stretch'd the landscape there,
Her Conway caught the fair design,
And soften'd ev'ry harsher line;
In pleasing lights each object plac'd,
And heighten'd all the piece with taste.
    O, Conway! while the public voice
Applauds our sov'reign's well-weigh'd choice,
And Albion's friends, exulting, see
Her fame, her int'rest, rise with thee;
Fain would my patriot muse proclaim
The statesman's and the soldier's fame,
And bind immortal on thy brow
The civic crown, and laurel bough.
But, tho' unskilled to join the choir,
Who aptly tune the courtly lyre;
Tho', with the vassals of thy state,
I never at thy levee wait;
Yet be it oft my happy lot
To meet thee in this rural cot;
To see thee here, thy mind unbend,
And quit the statesman for the friend;
While smiles unbought, and void of art,
Spring genuine from the social heart.
    Happy the muse, which, here retir'd,
By gratitude like mine inspir'd,
Dupe to no party, loves to pay
To worth like thine her grateful lay;
And, in no venal verse, commend
The man of taste, and nature's friend.

Cottage, July, 1766.

APPENDIX 9

ITINERARY OF CONWAY'S MILITARY TOUR OF THE CONTINENT IN 1774

This itinerary (for a map of which see the endpapers to Vol. 39) is based upon the MS 'Journal of a Military Tour of the Continent with Gen. Conway' (Bodl. MS Eng. Hist. C 282), kept by Capt. David Scott of the Royal Artillery, who accompanied Conway and presumably served as his aide; the journal fills 216 MS pages.

Conway's tour was made primarily for pleasure, though there were the inevitable rumours of his carrying on secret negotiations with the crowned heads of Europe (see HW to Conway 7 Sept. 1774, n. 2). In the course of his trip (which took him through France, the Austrian Netherlands, Germany, Bohemia, Moravia, Austria, Hungary, and Silesia) he visited numerous battlefields, garrisons, and fortifications, meeting on the way a great many high-ranking army officers, government officials, and members of the ruling aristocracy, as well as a fair number of itinerant Englishmen, some of whom are mentioned below. On the whole (excepting in France) he was received cordially; the high points of his trip were his gracious receptions by Joseph II of Austria and Frederick II of Prussia, both of whom invited him to visit their military camps at Prague, at Pest, and in Silesia.

The itinerary below attempts merely to indicate the broad outlines of Conway's trip; we have omitted numerous small towns through which he passed and small-town dignitaries whom he met, as well as Scott's copious notes on historical battles and other military matters. At times the dates of arrival at various places are unclear, since Scott did not always take care to mark one day from another.

June   8. Leaves London, 9 A.M. Reaches Dover.

9. Leaves Dover, lands at Calais. Reaches Dunkirk.

10. Berg. Cassel.

?11. St-Omer.

?12. Aire. Béthune. Arras.

13–14. Douai.

?15–16. Lille.

17. Tournai. Visits site of Battle of Fontenoy.

18. Oudenarde. Grammont.

19. Visits Steenkerke Battlefield (1692). Halle. Brussels; sees Grand Duke Peter Leopold of Tuscany, who is on a tour of the Low Country.

20. Mons.

21. Charleroi.

22. Namur.
23. Tongres.
24. Maestricht. Conway well-treated by Dutch, though French were inhospitable. Aix-la-Chapelle.
25. Takes ferry across Rhine. Düsseldorf. Sees art collection of Elector Palatine, including Van Dykes, Rubens, Poussins.
?26. Duisburg.
27. Hamm.
28. Paderborn.
29. Detmold. Pyrmont.
30. Hameln. Hanover.

July
1–3. Hanover. Meets Marshal Spörcken.
4. Brunswick.
5. Visited by Hereditary Prince of Brunswick (Karl Wilhelm Ferdinand). Has private audience of Prince Ferdinand.
6. Dines with Hereditary Prince and Princess.
9. Leaves Brunswick. Reaches Zell (Celle).
11. Leaves Zell. Reaches Helmstedt.
12. Magdeburg.
13. Brandenburg.
14. Potsdam. Tour of Sans Souci.
15. Received by King of Prussia.
17. Leaves Potsdam. Reaches Berlin.
18. Witnesses war games at Berlin.
19. Leaves Berlin. Reaches Luckau in Saxony.
20. Grossenhain.
21. Dresden.
24. Presented to Elector and Electress of Saxony.
26. Leaves Dresden. Enters Bohemia.
27. Prague.
28. Sets out for Vienna.
29. Reaches Iglau in Moravia.
30. Enters Austria.
31. Reaches Vienna. Greeted by Sir Robert Murray Keith, English envoy and plenipotentiary. Sees Prince Kaunitz, the first minister.

August
1. Sees Prince Colloredo, the Chancellor Imperial.

2. Dines at Keith's with 14 other Englishmen, including Lord George Cavendish, Lord Monson, Sir Thomas Clarges, and Sir William Forbes.

3. Conway presented to Emperor Joseph.

4. Conway presented to Empress Maria Theresa.

14. Leaves Vienna. Reaches Pressburg, residence of Viceroy of Hungary, Prince Albert of Saxony.

15. Arrives at Schemnitz.

16. Grand tour of mines of Schemnitz. Arrives at Kremnitz.

17. Visits furnaces at Kremnitz.

18. Turócz.

19. Pest and Buda. Visits Imperial camp at Pest.

20. Rainy day, 'nothing done.'

21. Views inspection of troops by Emperor.

25. Manœuvres end. Departs from Pest.

26. Reaches Pressburg again. Reaches Vienna.

27. Leaves Vienna.

29. Olmütz, former capital of Moravia.

30. Breslau, capital of Silesia. Visits encampment of King of Prussia at Schmelwitz.

Sept.   3. Camp breaks up. King leaves for Potsdam, Conway departs for Breslau.

4. Liegnitz.

5. Lanshut.

6. Schweidnitz.

8. Leaves Schweidnitz. Reaches Glatz.

9. Leaves Glatz.

10. Prague.

12. Visits encampment of Emperor at Prague.

13. Sees Emperor.

14–20. Troop manœuvres.

21. Conway has farewell audience with Emperor, leaves Prague.

23. Crosses from Bohemia to Bavaria.

24. Nuremberg.

26. Leaves Nuremberg for Strasbourg.

27. Passes through Blenheim, site of 1704 battle. Reaches Ulm.

Oct.

28. Leaves Ulm.

30. Crosses Rhine, reaches Strasbourg.

8. Leaves Strasbourg for Metz. Reaches Lunéville, sees palace of late King Stanislas.

9. Nancy.

13. Leaves Nancy, reaches Metz.

15. Side-trip to Luxembourg.

16. Returns to Metz.

17. Leaves Metz for Paris.

19. Arrives at Paris, stays at Hôtel de Danemark, meets Lady Ailesbury, Mrs Damer, and Lady Henrietta Stanhope, who had arrived ten days before to greet him.

APPENDIX 10

WALPOLE'S UNSENT LETTER TO HERTFORD OF 2 OCTOBER 1774

See *ante* iii. 682. The night before he wrote the letter, HW had called on Hertford to urge him to seek a seat for Conway in Parliament in case the Duke of Grafton, who had sponsored him for Thetford, failed to bring him in again. HW's account of what followed is in *Last Journals* i. 390–1.

At eight that night Lord Hertford arrived, and an hour after I went to him, but was struck by his porter telling me his Lord was busy and could not possibly see me, but carried me up to Lady Hertford. Lady Ailesbury and another lady were playing at cribbage in her room. She said her Lord was writing to Coventry, which he should lose, and had Lady Powis's agent with him. I thought his brother's impending danger as important as a borough lost, or as Lady Powis's boroughs. My suspicions redoubled. After some time Lady Hertford said she would go and ask my Lord if he would see me. She returned, and said not a word. I carried her into another room, and said, 'Good God, Madam! what is my Lord afraid of that he will not see me? I have told your Ladyship I would say nothing that can be disagreeable to him till the answer comes from Euston.' She protested he was so busy writing, that on looking into his room he had scolded her, and that he would soon come upstairs. A little after, Colonel Keene came up, and she asked him if her Lord was still writing? he said Yes. This offended me still more, that Colonel Keene was admitted when I was not, though wanting to speak on his brother. Soon after their son Henry came and asked for more pens; his father had used all below. This seemed a shallow art to impose upon and delay me. I grew very much out of humour, and showed it on purpose, that I might force my way to my Lord. Twelve o'clock came, and my Lord sent word he had not time to sup. This struck even Lady Ailesbury, and by signs I made her understand my anger. After supper, at which I had not spoken a word, Lady Ailesbury called for her chair, and I asked for one. Lady Hertford saw my uneasiness and sent her son to ask my Lord if he would see me: I said dryly, 'Madam, I will not trouble my Lord; I have nothing to say'; and walked out of the room with Lady Ailesbury. On the stairs I trembled so with passion that I had like to have fallen from the top to the bottom, and I said to Lady Ailesbury, 'I will never set my foot in this house again.' This frightened her, and she said, 'Pray don't say so.' Mr Conway (the second son) met us on the stairs, and said his father would see me; but I thought without showing great resentment I should not force him to bring in his brother, and therefore would not go to him, but repeated 'I will not trouble him; I have nothing to say.' When we were in our chairs and a little way from the door, I stopped Lady Ailesbury and told her my sentiments. The porter came out and said his Lord desired to see me, but I persisted, only repeating the same words. I carried Lady Ailesbury to my own house; she was in tears and as angry then as I, and said it was shocking in Lord Hertford not to see her, when she was going to Paris in two days. I said, 'Madam, he wants you gone, and me out of town, till it is too late to find a borough for your husband, and then he will plead the lapse of time as an excuse': and I added a great deal of very intemperate invective on him. I told her, however, what was true, that, angry as I was, it was a right measure to be so, and necessary to make it impossible for Lord Hertford to desert his brother.

I slept very ill, and early in the morning wrote a very passionate letter to Lord Hertford, telling him of the indignity he had shown to his brother, his brother's wife, and me, and breaking off all intercourse with him; which, however, I did not intend to execute, but to make a seat for his brother the terms of reconciliation. I had the patience, however, to wait and see, before I sent my letter, whether my Lord or Lady would not come or write to me.

APPENDIX 11

LORD HERTFORD'S LETTER TO GEORGE III OF 30 MARCH 1778

See *ante* ca 27 March 1778. Printed from a photostat of the MS in the Royal Archives, Windsor Castle; previously printed in George III's *Corr.*, ed. Fortescue, iv. 88–9.

Grosvenor Street, March 30th 1778.

Sire,

After desiring your Majesty to give yourself no further trouble with or about the letter I put into your hands of Mr Walpole's than to throw it into the fire, I am ashamed to mention the subject again to your Majesty, but I find myself so anxiously pressed by Mr Walpole to return it that he may preserve a copy of that as well as of every other paper he has ever wrote upon the subject of his nephew, that I presume upon your Majesty's indulgence to ask it if it is not destroyed, which it most probably is.

Mr Walpole grounds his anxiety upon a persuasion that he shall sooner or later be called upon to make every part of his conduct in regard to his nephew public, thinking that he has been privately and obscurely injured in his reputation for his behaviour with respect to his nephew, though he has acted therein solely upon a principle of duty to his nephew and the Walpole family, and adding that at his time of life he cares for nothing so much as leaving a fair character behind him, which he has thoughts of preserving in this instance, by showing when it is necessary every word he has ever wrote upon the subject.

His treating it so seriously will I hope excuse me for taking this liberty and of dwelling so long upon such a trifle and if I do not receive the letter from your Majesty I will make my excuses to him in the best manner I can by not having been able to foresee that I should be called upon for a copy of it.

Enclosed I have the honour of sending your Majesty an account[1] I have just received of Lord Orford's continuing well.

I remain, Sire, with the greatest duty and respect, your Majesty's

Most faithful and devoted humble servant,

HERTFORD

1. Lord Orford to Lord Hertford 31 March 1778, printed Fortescue, op. cit. iv. 89.

APPENDIX 12

WALPOLE'S CHARACTER OF
LADY HERTFORD

See *ante* 11 Nov. 1782, n. 2. Printed from the copy in the *London Courant and Daily Advertiser* 18 Nov. 1782.

The late Countess of Hertford, whose death cannot be too much lamented, was possessed of so many virtues, and was so incapable of any ostentation, that it is but justice to so dear a memory to expatiate on the merits that she would rather have concealed than displayed, if she had not scorned any extreme of affectation. To say that she was a blameless wife and a careful mother, are cold encomiums in comparison of what she deserved. Her indefatigable performance of every duty was so exemplary, that no attention to herself entered into her composition. Though alarmed at whatever threatened her family, her personal intrepidity was heroic; of which she gave numerous instances. Yet while she was a model of domestic virtue, she was no less an ornament to society. Her good humour and good breeding were constant in private life, as her easy dignity became the public stations which fell to her lot; and it was a proof of her good sense, that though her natural bashfulness was extreme, no woman represented Majesty with more grace, nor tempered it with more condescension.—All these feminine excellencies were ennobled by a spirit worthy of her great descent; yet her character was affability, not pride. Her consciousness of what she was, reminded her of what was due to others; and the native cheerfulness of her disposition, and the innocence of her mind, gave the colour of simplicity to all her actions.—Tender to anxiety in her affections, her own tranquillity alone was disturbed by them: No duty was neglected, no business interrupted. The sacrifice of her amusements supplied the time she gave to her cares. A life passed in such constant occupation was rapidly terminated, yet without occasioning the smallest discomposure to a mind that had existed only for others. A philosopher despising the world, or a Christian longing for a better, never met death with more unaffected fortitude, than a woman torn from so many sentiments. Her departing countenance was placid as her conscience, her possession of herself entire; and she died without a groan, resigning all sublunary blessings with the same piety with which she had enjoyed them.

APPENDIX 13

WALPOLE'S CHARACTER OF HON. HENRY SEYMOUR-CONWAY (LATER LORD HENRY SEYMOUR)

This character, printed here for the first time, is excerpted from HW's characters of Seymour-Conway, the 5th Duke of Devonshire, and Charles James Fox, bound into HW's MS of *Last Journals* (*penes* Lord Waldegrave, Chewton Mendip), before the entry for Jan. 1783. See *ante* ii. 179–80.

He had a most superior, quick and at the same time, exact understanding; infinite wit, and as much humour as he pleased, with the highest sense of all his duties, and strict honour and integrity: but all his virtues and abilities were drowned in the most invincible indolence, if that can be invincible, with which no one passion contended. He despised fortune, ambition, applause and pleasure, was void of every vice, was amused with knowledge rather [than] sought it; and as he had a handsome face and fine person, was more properly a statue of virtue, than what Nature had made him, a most sensible and most virtuous man.

SOLUTIONS TO FITZPATRICK'S CHARADES IN WALPOLE'S LETTER TO CONWAY OF 29 OCTOBER 1786

The editors wish to thank the individuals who responded to their appeal in *Country Life* 21 Oct. 1971 for solutions to these charades. What appears to be the correct solution to the first one ('lutestring') was supplied by Mrs P. A. Hodges of Teddington, Middlesex; later correspondents offering the same answer were Miss J. E. Payne of Thornton Heath, Surrey, and Messrs Ralph Catterell of Richmond, Virginia, and Warren Derry of Bath.

No completely convincing solution has yet been offered for the second charade; 'plain-song,' the best response, was suggested by Dr L. J. A. Loewenthal of Barcelona, Spain, and Mr Bruce Simonds of Hamden, Connecticut.

Other solutions to the two charades were offered by Messrs H. P. Finn of Laughton near Rugby; Terry Palmer of Gordon, Berwick-shire; Robert G. J. Wood of Sutton Abinger, Surrey; H. D. Poole of Sevenoaks, Kent; and Miss Jane Leake of Villanova, Pennsylvania.

APPENDIX 15

CONWAY'S PROLOGUE TO *THE WAY TO KEEP HIM*

See *ante* 17 June 1787, n. 9; printed from the copy in the *World* 21 May 1787. The *World* 20 April 1787 commented: 'The Prologue . . . does not any discredit to its author. The writing is poetic, and effectual as to every sensation it means to excite.'

Spoken at Richmond House, by the Hon. Mrs Hobart, Written by the Right Hon. General Conway.

> Since I was doom'd to tread the awful stage,
> Thank Heaven, that plac'd me in this polish'd age!
> There was a time, we're told, when in a cart
> I might have play'd our lovely widow's part;
> Or travell'd, like a pedlar with a pack,
> And my whole homely wardrobe at my back;
> But, troth, I feel no fancy for such mumming;
> And sure one's dress should be at least becoming!
> No rainbow silk then flaunted in the wind;
> No gauzes swell'd before, nor cork behind;
> No diamonds then, with all their sparkling train,
> Nor rouge, nor powder, e'en a single grain.
> But these were simple times, the learn'd agree—
> Simple, indeed!—too simple much for me!
>
> Another age produc'd a diff'rent scene;
> All grand and stately, as the first was mean;
> The change indeed was total, *à la lettre;*
> Yet I can hardly say 'twas for the better.
> For was't not strange, to see a well-drest play'r
> Strut on high buskins in the open air;
> Then bawl to gall'ries high as any steeple;
> Or squeak thro' pipes to forty thousand people?
>
> Good Heavens, how horrid! what a monstrous notion!
> 'Twould quite deprive one of all speech and motion.
> And then to wear one settled, strange grimace,
> Or endless simpers on a pasteboard face;

To hide the beauties bounteous Nature made,
Beneath a stifling vizard's filthy shade;
To lose of Siddons' glance the proud control,
Of swimming eye that paints the melting soul;
Th' obedient brow that can be stern, or meek;
The dimpling blush that dwells on Farren's cheek;
The well-tun'd airs that suit each varying part;
And looks that talk the language of the heart!

These ancients, we're assur'd, were wond'rous wits;
In taste I'd rather trust our honest cits:
They might be learned, with their musty rules,
For me, I set them down as arrant fools;
And must conclude, 'midst all those boasted arts,
Their audiences had neither eyes nor hearts.

To modern stages too, in my conception,
One fairly might produce some just objection;
'Tis such a concourse, such a staring show,
Mobs shout above, and critics snarl below;
But when their battle, in its dire array,
Vents its full rage on players or on play,
You'd think yourself a hundred leagues from shore;
The boatswain whistles, and the monsters roar.
True; for ambition, 'tis an ample field;
Vast crops of praise its fertile regions yield;
But rankling thorns infest the genial soil,
And keenest tempests blast the planter's toil.

While here, in this fair garden's calm retreat,
At once the Virtues, and the Muses' seat;
Where friendly suns their kindliest influence shed,
Each tender plant may dauntless rear its head.
Tho' no tall pine erect its stately charms,
Or cedar spread around its Tragic arms;
Venus' myrtle may its sweets disclose,
While virgin blushes tinge the new-blown rose;
And sister arts their friendly aid may join,
For some fair brow a mingl'd wreathe to twine.

But quitting metaphor;—this bumble band,
Who own *your* pow'r, and bow to *your* command;
Shall scorn the noisy plaudits of the crowd,
The vain, the great, the fickle and the loud;
Blest in the candour of a chosen few,
Whose hearts are partial to their judgments true;—
You to their faults will be a little blind;
You to their talents will be very kind.
And such th' applause we covet for our play;
Where the heart dictates and the hands obey.

THE LESSER ARCH AT PARK PLACE, BY PAUL SANDBY

APPENDIX 16

THE DESCRIPTION OF PARK PLACE IN THE *WORLD* 23 OCTOBER 1787

HW's cutting of this article is pasted with his MS notes in his 'Book of Materials,' 1775, pp. 128–9; previously printed in his *Anecdotes of Painting in England*, Vol. V, ed. Hilles and Daghlian, New Haven, 1937, pp. 171–6. Another article apparently cribbed from this one is in the *Times* for 7 Aug. 1789 (quoted BERRY i. 74–5, nn. 9–11).

This is by far the finest place upon the Thames. Nature and Art have both worked well on it, and with a boldness, not elsewhere to be found in this neighbourhood of London. The hills indeed rise as steep, though they do not swell as high as in landscape ground of the first character. On the top of them stands the house, at the bottom runs the river, here and there broken into aytes, and so receiving a pastoral character. The bridge at Henley, the prettiest on the river, offers not only a point of view, but an idea which is gratifying. The two faces on the center arch are the sculpture of Mrs Damer! The planting, and all the arrangements of the ground, have been well done by General Conway.

The ornamented ground is 275 acres.

The Park contains 130 acres.

The farms in the demesne are 500 acres.

The ornamented ground, heretofore, was comparatively insignificant. It ended with the wood. All the shrubberies, the subterranean passage, the noble valley from it, the arch at the end of it, the cottage, and yet, better than all, the terrace, through its whole length, three-quarters of a mile, all were done by the General.

The subterraneous passage, 275 yards long, is marked with much good sense. On the entrance and conclusion of it, there is no silly waste of money, no grotto work, nor other childish bauble. Nothing but what is merely necessary in arching, with a little masonry, where the rude flint could not be depended on.

The arch measures 43 feet across. The enormous stones facing it, and with such a noble effect, were brought from fourteen different counties. The iron cramping them together weighs two tons. The expense was £2000.

The cottage has a pretty room in it, and exquisite scenery from the three sides. On one side Henley Church, on a second the meanders of the river, and in front the river again, glittering through the foliage of a steep woody glen, almost equals Wales in its sweetest manner.

In the cottage the prints should be changed—coloured daubings of the King and Queen, Lady Coventry, Duchess of Ancaster—a bad medley, with [Paul] Hiffernan's horrid nonsense of the Heroine in the Cave, for Reddish's benefit in 1774—all these should give place to better prints, or none at all.

The bird's-eye view of Henley is rather too red. The hills, which are Mr Freeman's and Mr Hall's, are beautifully planted, and complete the requisites of landscape inequality, wood and water.

The offskip is most extensive over Berkshire, the New Forest in Hampshire, nay, at the opening, the South Downs in Sussex. Of course, Lord Portchester's place, the Duke of Bolton's, Sir Charles Hardy's, Mr Crew's, the house of Price, Mrs Morton's, Mr Martin's, Whiteknight's, which is well improved; Caversham's, with the massacres upon Marsac's trees, etc. etc. etc. all are in the view.

The house, indifferent as it is, held Lord Arch. Hamilton, and afterwards the Prince of Wales. The bow-window room, the best in the house,[1] was added since their time. The charms of the place require a new house, and it is in contemplation. There are on the ground 100,000 bricks for the purpose. That the present owner may have the putting them together, must be the wish of everyone who thinks of his taste, his liberality, and what his genius may do working with the genius of this delightful ground.

Ornament in all its forms is apparently well consulted, but use also seems never overlooked. The kitchen garden is complete. The trees are well trained. There are hot walls, a greenhouse, a poultry place and pheasantry in perfect order.

The flower garden, a rood or two, with the exact agreement of plats, and fraternity of alley walks, the little basin with gold and silver fish, the small statues and vases, with foliage wreathing in arbour-like festoons, all a little model of the French style, all are well enough—as flowers must be had, and could not be had in greater quantities and in better order than thus by themselves.

1. In that room are the beautiful pictures worked in worsteds by Lady Ailesbury, wife of General Conway (HW).

The yet better show of use is in the experimental husbandry and the chemical experiments of the place.

Six acres of cabbages for seed were sold last year in the London market.

Two acres of caraways were last year sold in seed, two distilled and sold in oil.

Eight acres of lavender were distilled. The essential oil sold for £170.

Of potatoes there were 23 acres, distilled into vinous spirit, or whisky. After the distillation the potatoes are excellent food for hogs.

The distillery is an attempt which cost £4000 to economize on fire. The primary object is to coke pit coal for the maltsters.

Coal, it is well known, after cokeing gets in bulk more than it loses in weight, in the great proportion of one or two in four. Twelve sacks of coal, after burning, yield 16 or 18 sacks in coke. The fire, thus used in this operation, effects at the same time the distillation on one side, while on the other, it has been applied experimentally merely to the fluxing copper and iron. The latter has not always prospered, the former never failed, to the great amount of 400 weight of metal having been run off, while a chaldron of coals was cokeing, and while large distillations were working at the same time!

A chaldron of coals can be coked in a day.

The dimensions of the still are these: the copper holds 400 gallons, the worm tub or refrigeratory 800.

There is a chemical professor on a good establishment—a salary, a pretty house of four rooms on a floor, etc. etc. Dr Napleton [Mapleton], now at Odgeham was, Mr Blair is, in this situation.

The lavender oil is the purest and most strong ever in the market. Smith of Bond Street bought it all: it sold last year for £170, which is above £20 per acre, and this on ground hitherto fruitless which was tried with oats and failed.

The soil is a chalk which the lavender loves.

Whether the scheme may answer on a money estimate is not certain. The vent of the coke is doubted. If it could be sold, and in as large quantities as the distillery would allow it to be made, the balance in favour of the undertaking would be obvious and certain.

The coke sells for a shilling or two more than the coals by the chaldron. The increase of bulk makes the profit ten shillings more. This would more than pay the charges of management in the distillery. There is another contingent improvement on the side of metallurgy. Yet metallurgy, so far from the mine and any colliery, can scarcely be practised. What purposes can supply its place, whether any enlargement of the distillery, any malting, or what other elaboration, yet remains to be determined. Yet whatever be the event, whether the undertaking succeed or fail in point of profit—as a point, on which praise must fasten, there can be but one opinion. It may lead to consequences conspicuous to the place itself. It may excite similar undertakings in more favourable situations—more favourable for fuel and the metals! But end where it will, the merit of the beginning is with General Conway, who thus can direct expense, and apply science to purposes in life, rather repulsive on every side but in regard to their use.

How far the scheme may be big with promise to the coal countries, is well worth the best care of our chemists and machinists. As such, the appeal is to Bolton and Westwood, of Birmingham, Dr Higgins and Bishop Watson.

So much for the place of General Conway, which is rich in everything from nature and art, from the rare combination of opposite qualities, the love of projection with sufficient property, philosophic addiction, and the elegant arts; the decent estimate of bullion and the exact knowledge of each fairer object to which it is convertible!

Yet more to soothe and decorate his happy allotment in this good ground, he has the charm of character, the *mens sibi conscia*—all that fine taste can administer with letters and temper, all the brightest lustres of a politician and a soldier; and that he is esteemed for private goodness by all who in their own privacy are good men.

Literary history must remember what it were baseness to forget that David Hume had his first substantial patronage from General Conway![2]

---

2. Not true; Hume was first secretary to Lord Hertford, ambassador to France (HW).

APPENDIX 17

CONWAY'S 'ELEGY ON THE DEATH OF MISS CAROLINE CAMPBELL'

Caroline Campbell, Lady Ailesbury's niece, died 12 Jan. 1789 at Conway's town house; Conway's 'Elegy' was printed in the *World* 20 Feb., the *London Chronicle* 21–4 Feb., lxv. 187, and separately as a six-page pamphlet. HW wrote on his copy of the pamphlet, now WSL, 'By General Conway, 1789'; it is often offered as a SH Press piece, but is rejected by Hazen, *SH Bibl.* 145 (see also OSSORY iii. 34, n. 1; Hazen, *Cat. of HW's Lib.*, No. 3222:22:2).

Since 'tis the will of all-disposing heaven,
To seize the boon its kinder hand had given;
Whether on earth thy friendly spirit rove,
Midst the once happy partners of thy love;
(Scenes where virtues reign'd, thy talents shone,
And fond affection made each heart thy own;)
Or, bounding swift, has wing'd its airy flight
To the pure regions of eternal light;
   Look down, fair Saint, and O, with pity see,
Where sad remembrance lifts each thought to thee.
Accept the heaving sigh, the trickling tear;
The last, best offerings of a heart sincere.
What tho' no costly hecatombs should bleed,
Nor lengthen'd train in sable pomp succeed;
Yet shall the sweetest flowers thy grave adorn,
Wash'd by the kindliest tears of dewy morn.
There shall each friend, thy heav'nly virtues made;
With pious dirge invoke thy gentle shade;
Like fragrant incense the soft breath shall rise
And smooth thy passage to thy kindred skies.
   Severely kind, O why did adverse fate
Grant such vast bounties with so scant a date?
Give such sweet fragrance to this short-liv'd flower;
The virtues of an age, to last an hour!
It gave her wit might grace a muse's tongue,
The charm of numbers, and the power of song;
The angelic touch to strike the trembling string,
And tune such notes as its own seraphs sing.

But O! o'er-bounteous, with that sacred art,
It gave each nicer movement to the heart;
And her soft breast, with strong sensation fir'd,
Felt the keen impulse which those arts inspir'd.
Too great a portion of celestial flame
Strain'd the frail texture of her weaker frame;
The subtle fire too pow'rful forc'd its way
Thro' the soft yielding mould of mortal clay:
As the clear air in crystal prison pent,
Oft bursts its fair but brittle tenement;
While in the dust the glittering fragments lie,
The purer æther gains its native sky.

Ere the Stern Sisters cut the vital thread,
I saw, and kiss'd her on the fatal bed,
Just as her gentle spirit took its flight,
And her faint eyelids clos'd in endless night;
No strong convulsions shook her parting breath;
No tremors mark'd the cold approach of death:
Her heart still heav'd, with vital spirit warm,
And each soft feature wore its wonted charm.

Oh me! In this perplexing maze of fate;
This doubtful, erring, varying restless state;
Tho' guilt with swelling sail elate shall steer,
With pomp and pleasure crown'd, its full career;
Tho' worth like thine no pitying power shall save,
From sickness, pain, and [an] untimely grave:
Yet stay, rash mortal, nor presume to scan,
By thy imperfect rule th' Almighty's plan,
O censure not his sovereign, high behest,
But prostrate own, whatever is, is best:
Judgment's the part of heaven; submission, thine:
We may lament; but we must not repine.
Each has his lot (for so does heaven ordain)
His stated share of happiness and pain:
And mortals, best its just commands fulfil,
When they enjoy the good, the patient bear the ill.

APPENDIX 18

WALPOLE'S 'BIOGRAPHICAL SKETCH OF MARSHAL CONWAY'

Printed from Mary Berry, *Extracts from the Journals and Correspondence*, ed. Lady Theresa Lewis, 1866, i. 464–5.

Henry Seymour Conway, born in July 1719, at Beaufort House, Chelsea, was second son of S. C. Lord Conway by his third wife, Charlotte, second daughter of John Shorter, Esq., of Bybrook, in Kent, and youngest sister of Catherine Lady Walpole. Henry was bred at Eton School, and from thence removed to Geneva.

In 1742 [1741] he was chosen into Parliament, and in 1744 [1745] was appointed aide-de-camp to his R. H. William Duke of Cumberland. He was present in the actions of Dettingen, Loffelt [Laffeldt], and Fontenoy, at the latter of which [actually Laffeldt] he was taken prisoner; in 1748 [1757] he was second in command in the attempt on Rochefort, when he, as before, gave remarkable instances of his valour, as he did of his talents as an author in a noble defence of General Mordaunt and himself, on the miscarriage of that expedition, as he had in various instances as an orator in England and Ireland, in which last kingdom he had been secretary of state to William fourth Duke of Devonshire.

In the reign of George the Third he continued groom of the Bedchamber to his Majesty, as he had been to George the Second, and colonel of a regiment till 1765 [1764] when he was dismissed from both those preferments for his constitutional resistance of war, and for his still more constitutional rejection of all offers of corruption and threats from the minister, G. Grenville. On the change of the ministry he was appointed secretary of state, in which post he was entreated by Mr. P[itt] to remain, but resigned it after all manner of persuasion had been employed to retain him in it, when he was made lieut.-general of the Ordnance, and afterwards governor of Jersey, where— etc.

APPENDIX 19

WALPOLE'S 'CHARACTER OF MARSHAL CONWAY'

Printed from Mary Berry, *Extracts from the Journals and Correspondence,* ed. Lady Theresa Lewis, 1866, i. 463–4.

An assemblage of dauntless and even of thoughtless intrepidity
   clothed in mildness, patience, and unaffected temper;
Of benevolence and generous charity, founded on good nature
      and extended beyond considerate economy;
Of most graceful eloquence sometimes too refining from his
   tenderness of conscience, but capable, tho' rarely, of being
         ruffled by injustice into pointed spirit;
Of disinterestedness, superior to all temptations of fortune or
   ambition, which he trampled under foot, when in
         competition with his honour.
Indefatigable in whatever he undertook, and fonder of employ-
   ments that fed his love of science in his profession, than of
   greater offices that opened the secrets of politics;
Of greater and more useful knowledge in military architecture
      than perhaps was possessed by any man of his time;
Of deep insight into chemistry and natural philosophy, which
      he displayed by useful experiments and successful
            discoveries;
Of original taste in architecture, particularly in the construction
   of bridges, and in ornamenting grounds in a style equally
         unborrowed and admired;
Of felicity in writing verse, a talent which he exercised but late
      in his life, and possessed of wit which appeared only
            occasionally and unsought.
All these endowments formed the singular and most amiable
         character of Marshal Conway,
And the whole assemblage was united to a soul of untainted
            virtue,
And was venerated to his last hours as it had been through his
            whole life
By the esteem of all who knew, or had examined the composition
         of so excellent a man.

Such a character was slightly shaded, not clouded, by trifling
imperfections.

He was subject to absence of mind, either natural or from the
plenitude of its occupations, as acute logic led him to
dispute. . . .